THE **PFIN** SOLUTION

Print
+
Online

PFIN⁶ delivers all the key terms and core concepts for the **Personal Finance** course.

PFIN Online provides the complete narrative from the printed text with additional interactive media and the unique functionality of **StudyBits**—all available on nearly any device!

What is a StudyBit™? Created through a deep investigation of students' challenges and workflows, the StudyBit™ functionality of **PFIN Online** enables students of different generations and learning styles to study more effectively by allowing them to learn their way. Here's how they work:

COLLECT WHAT'S IMPORTANT
Create StudyBits as you highlight text, images or take notes!

WEAK

FAIR

STRONG

UNASSIGNED

RATE AND ORGANIZE STUDYBITS
Rate your understanding and use the color-coding to quickly organize your study time and personalize your flashcards and quizzes.

StudyBit™

TRACK/MONITOR PROGRESS
Use Concept Tracker to decide how you'll spend study time and study YOUR way!

85%

PERSONALIZE QUIZZES
Filter by your StudyBits to personalize quizzes or just take chapter quizzes off-the-shelf.

CORRECT

INCORRECT

INCORRECT

INCORRECT

PFIN6
Randall S. Billingsley, Lawrence J. Gitman, and Michael D. Joehnk

SVP, GM, Science, Technology & Math:
  Balraj Kalsi

Product Manager: Laura Redden

Content/Media Developer: Patricia Hempel

Product Assistant: Eli Lewis

Marketing Manager: Emily McLellan

Content Project Manager: Nadia Saloom

Manufacturing Planner: Ron Montgomery

Production Service: MPS Limited

Sr. Art Director: Bethany Casey

Interior Designer: Chris Miller/Cmiller Design

Interior Images: iStockphoto.com/
  mihailomilovanovic; iStockphoto.com/
  penfold; iStockphoto.com/simon2579;
  iStockphoto.com/tonefotografia;
  isak55/Shutterstock.com; iStockphoto
  .com/77studio

Cover Designer: Lisa Kuhn: Curio Press/Trish &
  Ted Knapke: Ke Design

Cover Image: adventtr/E+/ Getty Images

Special Page Images: Computer and tablet
  illustration: ©iStockphoto.com/furtaev;
  Smart Phone illustration: © iStockphoto
  .com/dashadima; Feedback image: Rawpixel
  .com/Shutterstock.com

Intellectual Property
  Analyst: Diane Garrity
  Project Manager: Carly Belcher

For product information and technology assistance, contact us at
Cengage Learning Customer & Sales Support, 1-800-354-9706

For permission to use material from this text or product,
submit all requests online at **www.cengage.com/permissions**
Further permissions questions can be emailed to
permissionrequest@cengage.com

Library of Congress Control Number: 2016957209

Student Edition ISBN: 978-1-337-11702-9

Student Edition with Online Printed Access Card ISBN: 978-1-337-11700-5

Cengage Learning
20 Channel Center Street
Boston, MA 02210
USA

Cengage Learning is a leading provider of customized learning solutions with employees residing in nearly 40 different countries and sales in more than 125 countries around the world. Find your local representative at **www.cengage.com**

Cengage Learning products are represented in Canada by Nelson Education, Ltd.

To learn more about Cengage Learning Solutions, visit **www.cengage.com**

Purchase any of our products at your local college store or at our preferred online store **www.cengagebrain.com**

Printed in the United States of America
Print Number: 03   Print Year: 2018

Part 3
MANAGING CREDIT

Mark Viker/Getty Images

6 Using Credit 144

7 Using Consumer Loans 170

Part 4
MANAGING INSURANCE NEEDS

Rawpixel.com/Shutterstock.com

8 Insuring Your Life 196

9 Insuring Your Health 224

Part 5
MANAGING INVESTMENTS

Jan Stromme/Getty Images

Part 6
RETIREMENT AND ESTATE PLANNING

Cathy Yeulet/123RF

ABOUT THE AUTHORS

RANDALL S. BILLINGSLEY is a finance professor at Virginia Tech. He received his bachelor's degree in economics from Texas Tech University and received both an M.S. in economics and a Ph.D. in finance from Texas A&M University. Professor Billingsley holds the Chartered Financial Analyst (CFA), Financial Risk Manager (FRM), and Certified Rate of Return Analyst (CRRA) professional designations. An award-winning teacher at the undergraduate and graduate levels, his research, consulting, and teaching focus on investment analysis and issues relevant to practicing financial advisors. Formerly a vice-president at the Association for Investment Management and Research (now the CFA Institute), Professor Billingsley's published equity valuation case study of Merck & Company was assigned reading in the CFA curriculum for several years. In 2006, the Wharton School published his book, *Understanding Arbitrage: An Intuitive Approach to Financial Analysis*. In addition, his research has been published in refereed journals that include the *Journal of Portfolio Management*, the *Journal of Banking and Finance*, *Financial Management*, the *Journal of Financial Research*, and the *Journal of Futures Markets*. Professor Billingsley advises the Student-Managed Endowment for Educational Development (SEED) at Virginia Tech, which manages an equity portfolio of about $5 million on behalf of the Virginia Tech Foundation.

Professor Billingsley's consulting to date has focused on two areas of expertise. First, he has acted extensively as an expert witness on financial issues. Second, he has taught seminars and published materials that prepare investment professionals for the CFA examinations. This has afforded him the opportunity to explore and discuss the relationships among diverse areas of investment analysis. His consulting endeavors have taken him across the United States and to Canada, Europe, and Asia. A primary goal of Professor Billingsley's consulting is to apply the findings of academic financial research to practical investment decision making and personal financial planning.

LAWRENCE J. GITMAN is an emeritus professor of finance at San Diego State University. He received his bachelor's degree from Purdue University, his M.B.A. from the University of Dayton, and his Ph.D. from the University of Cincinnati. Professor Gitman is a prolific textbook author and has more than 50 articles appearing in *Financial Management*, *The Financial Review*, the *Journal of Financial Planning*, the *Journal of Risk and Insurance*, the *Financial Services Review*, the *Journal of Financial Research*, *Financial Practice and Education*, the *Journal of Financial Education*, and other scholarly publications.

His major textbooks include *The Future of Business*, Sixth Edition, and *The Future of Business: The Essentials*, Fourth Edition, both of which are co-authored with Carl McDaniel; and *Fundamentals of Investing*, Twelfth Edition, which is co-authored with Michael D. Joehnk and Scott B. Smart. Gitman and Joehnk also wrote *Investment Fundamentals: A Guide to Becoming a Knowledgeable Investor*, which was selected as one of 1988's 10 best personal finance books by *Money* magazine; *Principles of Managerial Finance*, Sixth Brief Edition, and *Principles of Managerial Finance*, Thirteenth Edition, both co-authored with Chad J. Zutter; *Foundations of Managerial Finance*, Fourth Edition; and *Introduction to Finance*, co-authored with Jeff Madura.

An active member of numerous professional organizations, Professor Gitman is past president of the Academy of Financial Services, the San Diego Chapter of the Financial Executives Institute, the Midwest Finance Association, and the FMA National Honor Society. In addition, he is a Certified Financial Planner® (CFP®). Gitman formerly served as a director on the CFP® Board of Governors, as vice-president–financial education for the Financial Management Association, and as director of the San Diego MIT Enterprise Forum. Gitman has two grown children and lives with his wife in La Jolla, California, where he is an avid bicyclist.

MICHAEL D. JOEHNK is an emeritus professor of finance at Arizona State University. In addition to his academic appointments at ASU, Professor Joehnk spent a year (1999) as a visiting professor of finance at the University of Otago in New Zealand. He received his bachelor's and Ph.D. degrees from the University of Arizona and his M.B.A. from Arizona State University. A Chartered Financial Analyst (CFA), he has served as a member of the Candidate Curriculum Committee and of the Council of Examiners of the Institute of Chartered Financial Analysts. He has also served as a director of the Phoenix Society of Financial Analysts and as secretary/treasurer of the Western Finance Association, and he was elected to two terms as a vice-president of the Financial Management Association. Professor Joehnk is the author or co-author of some 50 articles, five books, and numerous monographs. His articles have appeared in *Financial Management,* the *Journal of Finance,* the *Journal of Bank Research,* the *Journal of Portfolio Management,* the *Journal of Consumer Affairs,* the *Journal of Financial and Quantitative Analysis,* the *AAII Journal,* the *Journal of Financial Research,* the *Bell Journal of Economics,* the *Daily Bond Buyer, Financial Planner,* and other publications.

In addition to co-authoring several books with Lawrence J. Gitman, Professor Joehnk was the author of a highly successful paperback trade book, *Investing for Safety's Sake.* Dr. Joehnk was also the editor of *Institutional Asset Allocation,* which was sponsored by the Institute of Chartered Financial Analysts and published by Dow Jones-Irwin. He was a contributor to the *Handbook for Fixed Income Securities* and to *Investing and Risk Management,* Volume 1 of the Library of Investment Banking. In addition, he served a six-year term as executive co-editor of the *Journal of Financial Research.* He and his wife live in Flagstaff, Arizona, where they enjoy hiking and other activities in the nearby mountains and canyons.

ACKNOWLEDGEMENTS

In addition to the many individuals who made significant contributions to the book by their expertise, classroom experience, guidance, general advice, and reassurance, we also appreciate the students and faculty who used the book and provided valuable feedback, confirming our conviction that a truly teachable personal financial planning text could be developed.

We are indebted to the academicians and practitioners who have created the body of knowledge contained in this text. We particularly wish to thank several people who gave the most significant help in developing and revising it. They include Eric Johnson, ChFC, CLU, LTCP, of StateFarm for his helpful insights on insurance products and planning; Professor Sam Hicks, CPA, of Virginia Tech, for his thorough review of the entire book; Professor Hongbok Lee, of Western Illinois University, for helpful observations, and Thomas C. Via Jr., CLU, of Leonard L. Brown Agency for his help on life and property insurance issues.

The editorial staff at Cengage Learning has been most helpful in our endeavors. We particularly wish to thank Steven E. Joos, the former Product Director, 4LTR Press; Laura Redden, Product Manager; Tricia Hempel, Content/Media Developer; Lauren Dame, Product Assistant, and Nadia Saloom, Content Project Manager.

Finally, our wives – Bonnie, Robin, and Charlene – have provided needed support during the writing of this book. We are forever grateful to them.

Randall S. Billingsley, FRM, CFA
Virginia Tech

Lawrence J. Gitman, CFP®
San Diego State University

Michael D. Joehnk, CFA
Arizona State University

1 | Understanding the Financial Planning Process

LEARNING OBJECTIVES

After studying this chapter, you will be able to...

LO1 Identify the benefits of using personal financial planning techniques to manage your finances.

LO2 Describe the personal financial planning process and define your goals.

LO3 Explain the life cycle of financial plans, their role in achieving your financial goals, how to deal with special planning concerns, and the use of professional financial planners.

LO4 Examine the economic environment's influence on personal financial planning.

LO5 Evaluate the impact of age, education, and geographic location on personal income.

LO6 Understand the importance of career choices and their relationship to personal financial planning.

After finishing this chapter go to **PAGE 26** for **STUDY TOOLS**

JGI/Jamie Grill/Getty Images

How Will This Affect Me? The heart of financial planning is making sure your values line up with how you spend and save. That means knowing where you are financially and planning on how to get where you want to be in the future no matter what life throws at you. For example, how should your plan handle the projection that Social Security costs may exceed revenues by 2037? And what if the government decides to raise marginal tax rates to help cover the federal deficit? An informed financial plan should reflect such uncertainties and more.

This chapter describes the financial planning process and explains its context. Topics include how financial plans change to accommodate your current stage in life and the role that financial planners can play in helping you achieve your objectives. After reading this chapter you will have a good perspective on how to organize your overall personal financial plan.

1-1 THE REWARDS OF SOUND FINANCIAL PLANNING

LO1 What does living "the good life" mean to you? Does it mean having the flexibility to pursue your dreams and goals in life? Is it owning a home in a certain part of town, starting a company, being debt free, driving a particular type of car, taking luxury vacations, or having a large investment portfolio? Today's complex, fast-paced world offers a bewildering array of choices. Rapidly changing economic, political, technological, and social environments make it increasingly difficult to develop solid financial strategies that will improve your lifestyle consistently. Moreover, the financial crisis of 2008–2009 dramatizes the need to plan for financial contingencies. No matter how you define it, the good life requires sound planning to turn financial goals into reality.

The best way to achieve financial objectives is through *personal financial planning*, which helps define your financial goals and develop appropriate strategies to reach them. And being financially self-aware provides more insight into the range of available financial choices and their trade-offs. Your comfortable retirement should not depend solely on employee or government benefits—such as steady salary increases or adequate funding from employer-paid pensions or Social Security. Creating flexible plans and regularly revising them is the key to building a sound financial future.

Successful financial planning also brings rewards that include greater flexibility, an improved standard of living, wiser spending habits, and increased wealth. Of course, planning alone does not guarantee success; but having an effective, consistent plan can help you use your resources wisely. Careful financial planning

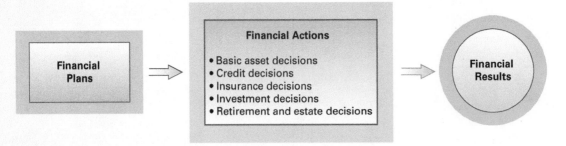
increases the chance that your financial goals will be achieved and that you will have sufficient flexibility to handle such contingencies as illness, job loss, and even financial crises.

The goal of this book is to remove the mystery from the personal financial planning process and replace it with the tools you need to take charge of your personal finances. To organize this process, the text is divided into six parts, as follows:

▶ **Part 1:** Foundations of Financial Planning
▶ **Part 2:** Managing Basic Assets
▶ **Part 3:** Managing Credit
▶ **Part 4:** Managing Insurance Needs
▶ **Part 5:** Managing Investments
▶ **Part 6:** Retirement and Estate Planning

Each part explains a different aspect of personal financial planning, as shown in Exhibit 1.1. This organizational scheme revolves around financial decision making that's firmly based on an operational set of financial plans. We believe that sound financial planning enables individuals to make decisions that will yield their desired results.

1-1a Improving Your Standard of Living

With personal financial planning we learn to acquire, use, and control our financial resources more efficiently. It allows us to gain more enjoyment from our

standard of living the necessities, comforts, and luxuries enjoyed or desired by an individual or family

income and thus to improve our **standard of living**—the necessities, comforts, and luxuries we have or desire.

Our quality of life is closely tied to our standard of living. Although other factors—geographic location, public facilities, local cost of living, pollution, traffic, and population density—also affect quality of life, wealth is commonly viewed as a key determinant. Material items such as a house, car, and clothing as well as money available for health care, education, art, music, travel, and entertainment all contribute to our quality of life. Of course, many so-called wealthy people live "plain" lives, choosing to save, invest, or support philanthropic organizations with their money rather than indulge in luxuries.

One trend profoundly affecting our standard of living is the *two-income family*. What was relatively rare in the early 1970s has become commonplace today, and the incomes of millions of families have risen sharply as a result. About 75 percent of married adults say that they and their mate share all their money. Two incomes not only buy more, but they also require greater responsibility to manage the money wisely.

1-1b Spending Money Wisely

Using money wisely is a major benefit of financial planning. Whatever your income, you can either spend it now or save some of it for the future. Determining your current and future spending patterns is an important part of personal money management. The goal, of course, is to spend your money so that you get the most satisfaction from each dollar.

Current Needs Your current spending level is based on the necessities of life and your **average propensity to consume**, which is the percentage of each dollar of income, on average, that is spent for current needs rather than savings. A minimum level of spending would allow you to obtain only the necessities of life: food, clothing, and shelter. Although the quantity and type of food, clothing, and shelter purchased may differ among individuals depending on their wealth, we all need these items to survive.

Some people with high average propensities to consume earn low incomes and spend a large portion of it on basic necessities. On the other hand, individuals earning large amounts quite often have low average propensities to consume, in part because the cost of necessities represents only a small portion of their income.

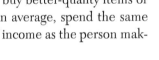

Still, two people with significantly different incomes could have the same average propensity to consume because of differences in their standard of living. The person making more money may believe it is essential to buy better-quality items or more items and will thus, on average, spend the same percentage of each dollar of income as the person making far less.

Future Needs A carefully developed financial plan should set aside a portion of current income for future spending. Placing these funds in various savings and investment vehicles allows you to earn a return on your funds until you need them. For example, you may want to build up a retirement fund to maintain a desirable standard of living in your later years. Instead of spending the money now, you defer actual spending until the future when you retire. Nearly 35 percent of Americans say retirement planning is their most pressing financial concern. Other examples of deferred spending include saving for a child's education, a primary residence or vacation home, a major acquisition (such as a car or home entertainment center), or even a vacation.

The portion of current income we commit to future needs depends on how much we earn and also on our average propensity to consume. Many affluent Americans say they need at least $5 million to feel rich. And more generally, most people say that it would take about twice their current net worth to feel wealthy. The more we earn and the less we devote to current spending, the more we can commit to meeting future needs. Regardless of income or wealth, some portion of current income should be set aside regularly for future use. Doing so creates good saving habits and provides for your future needs.

1-1c Accumulating Wealth

In addition to using current income to pay for everyday living expenses, we often spend it to acquire assets such as cars, a home, or stocks and bonds. Our assets largely determine how wealthy we are. Personal financial planning plays a critical role in the accumulation of wealth by directing our financial resources to the most productive areas.

One's **wealth** is the net total value of all the items that the individual owns. Wealth consists of financial and tangible assets. **Financial assets** are intangible, paper assets such as savings accounts and securities (stocks, bonds, mutual funds, and so forth). They are *earning assets* that are

---

Financial Planning Tips

BE SMART IN PLANNING YOUR FINANCIAL GOALS

Success is most likely if your goals are:

Specific: What do I want to achieve? What is required of me, and what are my constraints?

Measurable: How much money is needed? How will I know if I am succeeding?

Attainable: How can I do this? Is this consistent with my other financial goals?

Realistic: Am I willing and able to do this?

Timely: What is my target date? What short-term goals must be achieved along the way to achieve my longer-term goals?

Inspired by Paul J. Meyers, *Attitude Is Everything*, The Meyer Resource Group, 2003.

---

average propensity to consume the percentage of each dollar of income, on average, that a person spends for current needs rather than savings

wealth the total value of all items owned by an individual, such as savings accounts, stocks, bonds, home, and automobiles

financial assets intangible assets, such as savings accounts and securities, that are acquired for some promised future return

Exhibit 1.2

The Average American, Financially Speaking

This financial snapshot of the "average American" gives you an idea of where you stand in terms of income, net worth, and other measures. It should help you set some goals for the future.

	Income and Assets
What Do We Earn? (*median*)	
All families	$46,700
What Are We Worth? (*median*)	
All families	$81,200
Home Ownership (*median*)	
Value of primary residence	$170,000
Mortgage on primary residence	115,000
How Much Savings Do We Have? (*median*)	
Pooled investment funds (excluding money market)	$80,000
Stocks	27,000
Bonds	94,500
Bank accounts/CDs	20,100
Retirement accounts	59,000

Source: Adapted from Jesse Bricker, Lisa J. Dettling, Alice Henriques, Joanne W. Hsu, Kevin B. Moore, John Sabelhaus, Jeffrey Thompson, and Richard A. Windle, "Changes in U.S. Family Finances from 2010 to 2013: Evidence from the Survey of Consumer Finances," Board of Governors of the Federal Reserve System, Washington, D.C., October 24, 2014. Data is for 2013. http://www.federalreserve.gov/pubs/bulletin/2014/pdf/scf14.pdf, Tables 1–4, accessed September 2016.

held for their expected future returns. **Tangible assets**, in contrast, are physical assets such as real estate and automobiles. These assets can be held for either consumption (e.g., your home, car, artwork, or jewelry) or investment purposes (e.g., a duplex purchased for rental income). The goal of most people is to accumulate as much wealth as possible while maintaining current consumption at a level that provides the desired standard of living. To see how you compare with the typical American in financial terms, check out the statistics in Exhibit 1.2.

> Everyone—including recent college graduates, young married couples, and others—needs to develop a personal financial plan.

enough, you need personal financial planning. If you have enough money, planning can help you spend and invest it wisely. If your income seems inadequate, taking steps to plan your financial activities will lead to an improved lifestyle. **Personal financial planning** is a systematic process that considers the important elements of an individual's financial affairs and is aimed at fulfilling his or her financial goals.

Everyone—including recent college graduates, young married couples, and others—needs to develop a personal financial plan. Knowing what you need to accomplish financially, and how you intend to do it, gives you an edge over someone who merely reacts to financial events as they unfold. Just think of the example provided by the financial crisis of 2008–2009. Do you think that a financial plan would have helped in weathering the financial storm?

1-2a Steps in the Financial Planning Process

The financial planning process translates personal financial goals into specific financial plans, which then

1-2 THE PERSONAL FINANCIAL PLANNING PROCESS

tangible assets physical assets, such as real estate and automobiles, that can be held for either consumption or investment purposes

personal financial planning a systematic process that considers important elements of an individual's financial affairs in order to fulfill financial goals

LO2 Many people mistakenly assume that personal financial planning is only for the wealthy. However, nothing could be further from the truth. Whether you have a lot of money or not

Exhibit 1.3

The Six-Step Financial Planning Process

The financial planning process translates personal financial goals into specific financial plans and strategies, implements them, and then uses budgets and financial statements to monitor, evaluate, and revise plans and strategies as needed. This process typically involves the six steps shown in sequence here.

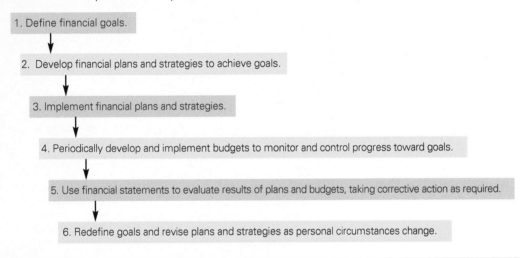

1. Define financial goals.

2. Develop financial plans and strategies to achieve goals.

3. Implement financial plans and strategies.

4. Periodically develop and implement budgets to monitor and control progress toward goals.

5. Use financial statements to evaluate results of plans and budgets, taking corrective action as required.

6. Redefine goals and revise plans and strategies as personal circumstances change.

help you implement those goals through financial strategies. The financial planning process involves the six steps shown in Exhibit 1.3.

You start with financial goals, formulate and implement financial plans and strategies to reach them, monitor and control progress toward goals through budgets, and use financial statements to evaluate the plan and budget results. This leads you back to redefining your goals so that they better meet your current needs, and to revising your financial plans and strategies accordingly.

Let's now look at how goal setting fits into the planning process. In Chapters 2 and 3, we'll consider other information essential to creating your financial plans: personal financial statements, budgets, and taxes.

Patpitchaya/Shutterstock.com

1-2b Defining Your Financial Goals

Financial goals are the results that an individual wants to attain. Examples include buying a home, building a college fund, and achieving financial independence. What are your financial goals? Have you spelled them out? It's impossible to effectively manage your financial resources without financial goals. We need to know where we are going, in a financial sense, to effectively meet the major financial events in our lives. Your financial goals or preferences must be stated in monetary terms because money and the satisfaction it can bring are an integral part of financial planning.

> **financial goals** results that an individual wants to attain, such as buying a home, building a college fund, or achieving financial independence

Practicing Financial Self-Awareness

Are you aware of your financial behavior, its causes, and its consequences? For example, are you routinely relying too heavily on your credit card? Are you saving enough to buy a new car or to fund your retirement? And the bottom line: Are you continuing the same financial behavior you have in the past and yet expecting different results?

The first decisive step in taking control of your life is to be aware of what you're thinking, feeling, and doing. Be financially self-aware: observe your own thoughts, feelings, and behavior concerning your finances. Take notes on things that affect how you feel, and what you do about financial decisions. Watch yourself, and be honest about your feelings concerning money and your future.

Then ask yourself two critically important questions:

- **Is the way I spend money consistent with what I believe?** Financial planning that works taking the time to develop a plan that purposely lines up your values and your use of money.

- **Have I clearly stated the financial goals that are important to me and, if so, what am I doing today to make sure I achieve them?** The heart of financial planning is determining where you are today and where you want to be in the future. This implies the need for a financial plan: limited resources sometimes bring painful trade-offs.

Source: Adapted from Carl Richards, "Practicing Radical Self-Awareness," Behaviorgap.com, http://us2.campaign-archive1.com/?u=23ce2ac179e81 58f7583c4e3f&id=86f42577bc&e=b50e826a9e, accessed September 2016.

The Role of Money About 75 percent of Americans believe that money is freedom. **Money** is the medium of exchange used to measure value in financial transactions. It would be difficult to set specific personal financial goals and to measure progress toward achieving them without the standard unit of exchange provided by the dollar. Money, as we know it today, is the key consideration in establishing financial goals. Yet it's not money, as such, that most people want. Rather, we want the **utility**, which is the amount of satisfaction received from buying quantities of goods and services of a given quality, that money makes possible.

People may choose one item over another because of a special feature that provides additional utility. For example, some people will pay more for a car with satellite radio than one with only an audio player. The added utility may result from the actual usefulness of the special feature, from the "status" it's expected to provide, or from both. Regardless, people receive varying levels of satisfaction from similar items, and their satisfaction isn't necessarily directly related to the cost of the items. We, therefore, need to consider utility along with

money the medium of exchange used as a measure of value in financial transactions

utility the amount of satisfaction received from purchasing certain types or quantities of goods and services

cost when evaluating alternative qualities of life, spending patterns, and forms of wealth accumulation.

Go to Smart Sites

Is getting the lowest price important to you? Where can you search for the best prices? A highlight box in each chapter of PFIN Online includes "Smart Sites," a list of resources and sites that offer additional information on topics in the PFIN text. Log in at www.cengagebrain.com.

Investment Planning
11
11-CI Chapter Introduction
11-1 The Objectives and Rewards of Investing
11-2 Securities Markets
11-3 Making Transactions in the Securities Markets
11-4 Becoming an Informed Investor
11-5 Online Investing
11-6 Managing Your Investment Holdings
11-CR Chapter Review

The Psychology of Money Money and its utility are not only economic concepts; they're also closely linked to the psychological concepts of values, emotion, and personality. Your personal value system—the important ideals and beliefs that guide your life—will also shape your attitude toward money and wealth accumulation. If you place a high value on family life, you may choose a career that offers regular hours and less stress or choose an employer who offers flextime rather than a higher-paying position that requires travel and lots of overtime.

You may have plenty of money but choose to live frugally and do things yourself rather than hire someone to do them for you. Or you may spend a high proportion of your current income on acquiring luxuries. Financial goals and decisions should be consistent with your personal values. You can formulate financial plans that provide the greatest personal satisfaction and quality of life by identifying your values.

Money is an important motivator of personal behavior because it has a strong effect on self-image. Each person's unique personality and emotional makeup determine the importance and role of money in his or her life. You should become aware of your own attitudes toward money because they are the basis of your "money personality" and money management style.

Some questions to ask yourself include: How important is money to me? Why? What types of spending give me satisfaction? Am I a risk taker? Do I need large financial reserves to feel secure? Knowing the answers to these questions is a prerequisite for developing realistic and effective financial goals and plans. Trade-offs between current and future benefits are strongly affected by values, emotions, and personality. Effective financial plans are both economically and psychologically sound. They must not only consider your wants, needs, and financial resources but must also realistically reflect your personality and emotional reactions to money.

1-2c Money and Relationships

The average couple spends between 250 and 700 hours planning their wedding. While most couples spend less than $10,000 on the big day, the average cost has risen to more than $32,000, depending on where they live. But with all the hoopla surrounding the wedding day, many couples overlook one of the most important aspects of marriage: financial compatibility. Money can be one of the most emotional issues

in any relationship, including that with a partner, parents, or children. Most people are uncomfortable talking about money matters and avoid such discussions, even with their partners. However, differing opinions on how to spend money may threaten the stability of a marriage or cause arguments between parents and children. Learning to communicate with your partner about money is a critical step in developing effective financial plans.

The best way to resolve money disputes is to be aware of your partner's financial style, consistently communicate openly, and be willing to compromise. It's highly unlikely that you can change your partner's style, but you can work out your differences. Financial planning is an especially important part of the conflict resolution process. You need to work together to develop your financial goals.

1-2d Types of Financial Goals

Financial goals cover a wide range of financial aspirations: controlling living expenses, meeting retirement needs, setting up a savings and investment program, and minimizing your taxes. Other important financial goals include having enough money to live as well as possible, being financially independent, sending children to college, and providing for retirement.

Financial goals should be defined as specifically as possible. Saying that you want to save money next year is not a specific goal. How much do you want to save, and for what purpose? A goal such as "save

10 percent of my take-home pay each month to start an investment program" states clearly what you want to do and why.

Because they are the basis of your financial plans, your goals should be realistic and attainable. If you set a savings goal too high—for example, 25 percent of your take-home pay when your basic living expenses already account for 85 percent of it—then your goal is unattainable and there's no way to meet it. But if savings goals are set too low, you may not accumulate enough for a meaningful investment program. If your goals are unrealistic, they'll put the integrity of your financial plan at risk and be a source of ongoing financial frustration.

It's important to involve your immediate family in the goal-setting process. When family members "buy into" the goals, it reduces the likelihood of future conflicts and improves the family's chances for financial success. After defining and approving your goals, you can prepare appropriate cash budgets. Finally, you should assign priorities and a time frame to financial goals. Are they short-term goals for the next year, or are they intermediate or long-term goals that will not be achieved for many more years? For example, saving for a vacation might be a medium-priority, short-term goal, whereas buying a larger home may be a high-priority, intermediate goal and purchasing a vacation home a low-priority, long-term goal. Normally, long-term financial goals are set first, followed by a series of corresponding short-term and intermediate goals.

goal dates target dates in the future when certain financial objectives are expected to be completed

1-2e Putting Target Dates on Financial Goals

Financial goals are most effective when they are set with goal dates. **Goal dates** are target points in the future when you expect to have achieved or completed certain financial objectives. They may serve as progress checkpoints toward some longer-term financial goals and/or as deadlines for others.

Shutter_M/Shutterstock.com

financial risk and protect both income (life, health, and disability insurance) and assets (property and liability insurance). Most consumers regard insurance as absolutely essential—and for good reason. One serious illness or accident can wipe out everything you have accumulated over many years of hard work. But having more insurance than necessary can be costly too. We'll examine how to manage your insurance needs in Chapters 8, 9, and 10.

Savings and Investment Planning As your income begins to increase, so does the importance of saving and

investment planning. Initially, people save to establish an emergency fund for meeting unexpected expenses. Eventually, however, they devote greater attention to investing excess income as a means of accumulating wealth, either for major expenditures, such as a child's college education, or for retirement. Individuals build wealth through savings and subsequently making various investments: common or preferred stocks, government or corporate bonds, mutual funds, real estate, and so on. The higher the returns on the investment of excess funds, the greater the wealth they accumulate.

Exhibit 1.5 shows the impact of two different rates of return on accumulated wealth. The graph shows that if you had $1,000 today and could keep it invested at 4 percent, then you would accumulate a considerable sum of money over time. For example, at the end of 40 years, you'd have $4,801 from your original $1,000. Earning a higher rate of return provides even greater rewards. Some might assume that earning, say, only 2 percentage points more (e.g., 6 percent rather than 4 percent) would not matter much. But it certainly would! Observe that if you could earn 6 percent over the 40 years, then you'd accumulate $10,286, which is more than twice as much as you'd accumulate at 4 percent. This powerful observation is important to

Exhibit 1.5

How a $1,000 Investment Grows over Time

Four or 6 percent: How big a deal is a 2-percent difference? The deal is more than twice the money over a 40-year period! Through the power of compound interest, a higher return means dramatically more money as time goes on.

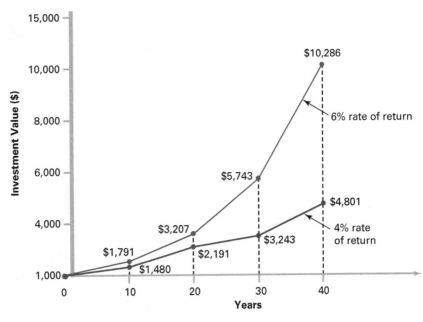

keep in mind when comparing competing investment and savings alternatives.

As we'll explore in Part 5 on managing investments, seemingly small differences in various investment management fees can also translate into significant differences in net investment returns over long periods of time. The length of time you keep your money invested is just as important as the rate of return you earn on your investments. You can accumulate more than twice as much capital by investing for 40 rather than 30 years with either rate of return (4 percent or 6 percent). This is the magic of compound interest, which explains why it's so important to create strong savings and investment habits early in life. We'll examine compounding more fully in Chapter 2, savings in Chapter 4, and investments in Chapters 11, 12, and 13.

Employee Benefit Planning Your employer may offer a wide variety of employee benefit plans, especially if you work for a large firm. These could include life, health, and disability insurance; tuition reimbursement programs for continuing education; pension, profit-sharing, and 401(k) retirement plans; flexible spending accounts for child care and health care expenses; sick leave, personal time, and vacation days; and other miscellaneous benefits such as employee discounts and subsidized cafeterias or parking.

Managing your employee benefit plans and coordinating them with your other plans is an important part of the overall financial planning process. Especially in today's volatile labor market, you can no longer assume that you'll be working at the same company for many years. If you change jobs, your new company may not offer the same benefits. So your personal financial plans should include contingency plans to replace employer-provided benefits as required. We'll discuss employee benefits in greater detail in this chapter under Special Planning Concerns and in Chapters 2 (planning); 3 (taxes); 8, 9, and 10 (insurance); and 14 (retirement).

Tax Planning Despite all the talk about tax reform, our tax code remains highly complex. Income can be taxed as active (ordinary), portfolio (investment), passive, tax-free, or tax-deferred. Then there are tax shelters, which use various aspects of the tax code (such as depreciation expenses) to legitimately reduce an investor's tax liability. Tax planning considers all these factors and more. It involves looking at your current and projected earnings and then developing strategies that will defer and minimize taxes. Tax plans are closely tied to investment plans and will often specify certain investment strategies. Although tax planning is most common among individuals with high incomes, people with lower incomes can also obtain sizable savings. We'll examine taxes and tax planning in Chapter 3.

Retirement and Estate Planning While you're still working, you should be managing your finances to attain those goals you feel are important after you retire. These might include maintaining your standard of living, extensive travel, visiting children, frequent dining at better restaurants, and perhaps a vacation home or boat. Retirement planning should begin long before you retire.

Most people don't start thinking about retirement until well into their 40s or 50s. This is unfortunate, because it usually results in a substantially reduced level of retirement income. The sooner you start, the better off you'll be. Take, for instance, the traditional IRA (individual retirement account), whereby certain wage earners were allowed to invest up to $6,500 per year in 2016. We'll look at IRAs and other aspects of retirement planning in Chapter 14.

> **EXAMPLE:** The Sooner You Start an IRA, the Better If you start investing for retirement at age 40, put only $2,000 a year in an IRA earning 5 percent for 25 years, you will have $95,454 at age 65. However, if you start the same retirement plan 10 years earlier at age 30, you'll have $180,641 at age 65!

Accumulating assets to enjoy in retirement is only part of the long-term financial planning process. As people grow older, they must also consider how they can most effectively pass their wealth on to their heirs, an activity known as *estate planning*. We'll examine this complex subject—which includes such topics as wills, trusts, and the effects of gift and estate taxes—in Chapter 15.

Angela Waye/Shutterstock.com

1-3c Special Planning Concerns

Students may not think that they need to spend much time on financial planning—not yet, anyway. However, the sooner you start, the better prepared you'll be to adapt your plans to changing personal circumstances. Such changes include changing or losing a job, relocating to a new state, getting married, having children, being in a serious accident, getting a chronic illness, losing a spouse through divorce or death, retiring, or taking responsibility for dependent parents. These and other stressful events are "financial shocks" that require re-evaluation of your financial goals and plans.

Go to Smart Sites

Would you like to know about free educational programs and tutorials on financial planning? The Federal Reserve Bank of Chicago has put together a number of resources for self-help on many topics.

Managing Two Incomes Did you know that the earnings of the average dual-income family will add up to more than $1 million over the wage earners' lives? Today, two-income couples account for the majority of U.S. households, and many depend on the second income to make ends meet. Often, however, a second income doesn't add as much as expected to the bottom line. Higher expenses such as child care, taxes, clothing, dry cleaning, transportation, and lunches may consume a large part of the second paycheck. And two-income families tend to spend what they earn rather than save it.

Spouses should decide together how to allocate income to household expenses, family financial goals, and personal spending goals. Will you use a second income to meet basic expenses, afford a more luxurious lifestyle, save for a special vacation, or invest in retirement accounts? Some couples place all income into a single, joint account. Others each contribute *equal* amounts into a joint account to pay bills but retain individual discretion over remaining income. Still others contribute a *proportional* share to finance joint expenses and goals. In any case, both spouses should have money of their own to spend without accountability. For examples of managing two incomes, see the worksheets in Chapter 2.

Managing Employee Benefits If you hold a full-time job, then your employer probably provides various employee benefits, ranging from health and life insurance to pension plans. These valuable benefits can have a

major financial impact on family income. Most American families depend solely on employer-sponsored group plans for their health insurance coverage and also for a big piece of their life insurance coverage and retirement needs.

Today's employee benefits packages cover a full spectrum that may include:

- ▶ Health and life insurance
- ▶ Disability insurance
- ▶ Long-term care insurance
- ▶ Pension and profit-sharing plans
- ▶ Supplemental retirement programs such as 401(k) plans
- ▶ Dental and vision care
- ▶ Child care, elder care, and educational assistance programs
- ▶ Subsidized employee food services

Some companies and industries are known for generous benefit plans; others offer far less attractive packages. In general, large firms can afford more benefits than small ones can. Because employee benefits can increase your total compensation by 30 percent or more, you should thoroughly investigate your employee benefits to choose those appropriate for your personal situation. Be sure to coordinate your benefits with your partner's to avoid paying for duplicate coverage. Companies change their benefit packages and many are shifting more costs to employees. Although an employer may pay for some benefits in full, typically employees pay for part of the cost of group health insurance, supplemental life insurance, long-term care insurance, and participation in voluntary retirement programs.

Due to the prevalence of two-income families and an increasingly diverse workforce, many employers are replacing traditional programs, where the company sets

Financial Planning Tips

Just like you, financial plans go through stages and must adapt to changes over your lifetime. Here are some of the critical life events that may make you reconsider and possibly revise an existing financial plan.

- **Marriage.** Finances must be merged, and there may be a need for life insurance.

- **Children.** It's time to start a college saving plan and revise your budget accordingly. A will is needed that makes provisions for guardianship if both parents die while the children are minors.

- **Divorce.** Financial plans based on two incomes are no longer applicable. Revised plans must reflect any property settlements, alimony, and/or child support.

- **Moving into middle age.** Although having started a savings and investing plan early in life should be paying off, the number of working years is declining, along with future earning ability. The shorter time horizon implies that you may want to take less risk by keeping less money in the stock market. While the greater safety is appealing, the reduced expected returns are also sobering. In addition, this could be the time to consider long-term care insurance for possible use in retirement.

- **Death of a parent.** The estate must be settled, and help may be needed in managing a possible inheritance.

- **Retirement.** Hopefully, your financial plan provided the amount needed to fund retirement. During retirement, you will try to preserve your capital and will rely on the income generated by your investments to fund your living expenses. Although investment risk should be reduced greatly, it cannot be eliminated because inflation risk must be managed. Money will be withdrawn from tax-deferred retirement accounts but taxes will be due. The risk of increases in future tax rates can be managed, in part, with Roth IRAs, which are retirement accounts where your *original* contributions are not tax-deductible but your *earnings* on the account are not taxed. Estate planning and long-term care issues should also be addressed.

---

the type and amount of benefits, with **flexible-benefit (cafeteria) plans**. In flexible-benefit programs, the employer allocates a certain amount of money to each employee and then lets the employee "spend" that money for benefits that suit his or her age, marital status, number of dependent children, level of income, and so on. These plans usually cover everything from child care to retirement benefits, offer several levels of health and life insurance coverage, and have some limits on the minimum and maximum amounts of coverage. Within these constraints, you can select the benefits that do you the most good. In some plans, you can even take part of the benefits in the form of more take-home pay or extra vacation time!

flexible-benefit (cafeteria) plans the employer allocates a certain amount of money to each employee and then lets the employee "spend" that money on the benefits that suit his or her age, marital status, number of dependent children, and level of income

Managing Your Finances in Tough Economic Times Tough economic times can be due to broad macroeconomic trends like a recession, or they can be brought on by more personal, local developments. The effects of recessions and financial crises divide people into three groups: (1) those who are directly and severely hurt through job loss, (2) those who are marginally hurt by reduced income, and (3) those who are not directly hurt. If you are in either of the first two groups, then you must make significant lifestyle changes to reduce spending. Even if you are in the last group, a recession affects you indirectly. For example, retirement accounts typically drop in value, and financial plans must be revised. And everyone's expectations are at least temporarily affected, which causes most people to be more cautious about their expenditures during a recession or crisis.

The financial crisis of 2008 and 2009, and the subsequent long period of high employment, was a macroeconomic challenge of historic, global proportions. It drives home the benefits of having a sound financial plan—and dramatized the cost of not having one. The precipitous decline in stock and home prices, and the number of people laid off from their jobs, made everyone think a lot more about financial planning in general and how to survive a financial crisis in particular. Although we all hope that such broad crises will be rare, it is important to plan for a possible recurrence. All of the financial planning principles explained in this book remained valid during the global financial crisis of 2008–2009 and should continue to serve us well in any future similar situations.

So how do you best plan to survive a broad-based financial crisis? First, you remind yourself of the key principles of financial planning presented in this book:

▶ Spend less than you earn.

▶ Keep investing so your money continues to work toward your goals.

▶ Know where you are and plan for the unexpected. You cannot know where you are financially unless you carefully—and frequently—update your family's budget. And it is important to set aside money for an emergency fund. As discussed earlier in this chapter, you should set aside enough cash to last six months.

Second, don't panic when financial markets crash! This means that you shouldn't try to time the market by buying when the experts say it's at a low or by selling when they say it's at a high. Continue to invest for the long term but keep in mind how close you are to achieving your financial objectives. For example, if you pull all of your money out of the stock market when it has fallen, you will not be positioned to take advantage of its eventual recovery. Recessions and financial crises can be challenging. A financial plan that considers such contingencies will help you weather the storm. Part 5 of the book focuses on investment management.

DO IT NOW: Start Building an Emergency Fund
What would happen if you lost your job, got hurt, or had an unexpected big expense? Even if you're not making much money now, you could start building an emergency fund by putting aside even $10 a month. As this chapter points out, your goal is to eventually set aside enough to last at least 6 months. Considering the risk of not doing so, you can **do it now**.

1-3d Using Professional Financial Planners

Most financial planners fall into one of two categories based on how they are paid: by commissions or by fees. *Commission-based planners* earn commissions on the financial products they sell, whereas *fee-only planners* charge fees based on the complexity of the plan they prepare. Many financial planners take a hybrid approach and charge fees and collect commissions on products they sell, offering lower fees if you make product transactions through them.

1-4 THE PLANNING ENVIRONMENT

LO4 Financial planning takes place in a dynamic economic environment created by the actions of government, business, and consumers. Your purchase, saving, investment, and retirement plans and decisions are influenced by both the present and future states of the economy. Understanding the economic environment will allow you to make better financial decisions.

Consider that a strong economy can lead to high returns in the stock market, which in turn can positively affect your investment and retirement programs. The economy also affects the interest rates you pay on your mortgage and credit cards as well as those you earn on savings accounts and bonds. Periods of high inflation can lead to rapid price increases that make it difficult to make ends meet. Here we look at two important aspects of the planning environment: the major financial planning players and the economy.

1-4a The Players

The financial planning environment contains various interrelated groups of players, each attempting to fulfill certain goals. Although their objectives are not necessarily incompatible, they do impose some constraints on one another. There are three vital groups: government, business, and consumers. Exhibit 1.6 shows the relationships among these groups.

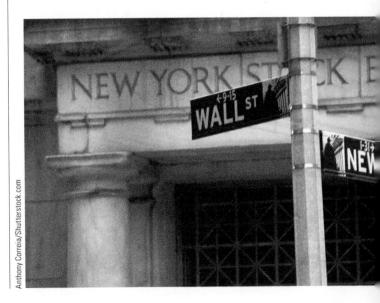

Anthony Correia/Shutterstock.com

Exhibit 1.6

The Financial Planning Environment

Government, business, and consumers are the major players in our economic system. They interact with one another to produce the environment in which we carry out our financial plans.

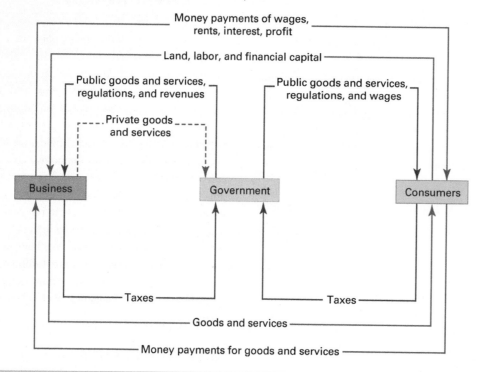

Government Federal, state, and local governments provide us with many essential public goods and services, such as police and fire protection, national defense, highways, public education, and health care. The federal government plays a major role in regulating economic activity. Government is also a customer of business and an employer of consumers, so it's a source of revenue for business and of wages for consumers. The two major constraints from the perspective of personal financial planning are taxation and regulation.

Business As Exhibit 1.6 shows, business provides consumers with goods and services and in return receives payment in the form of money. Firms must hire labor and use land and financial capital (economists call these *factors of production*) to produce those goods and services. In return, firms pay out wages, rents, interest, and profits to the various factors of production. Thus, businesses are an important part of the circular flow of income that sustains our free-enterprise system. In general, they create a competitive environment in which consumers may select from an array of goods and services. All businesses are limited in some way by federal, state, and local laws.

Consumers The consumer is the central player in the financial planning environment. Consumer choices ultimately determine the kinds of goods and services that businesses will provide. The consumer's choice of whether to spend or save also has a direct impact on present and future circular flows of money. Cutbacks in consumer spending are usually associated with a decline in economic activity, whereas increases in consumer spending help the economy to recover.

1-4b The Economy

Our economy is influenced by interactions among government, business, and consumers as well as by world economic conditions. Through specific policy decisions, the government's goal is to manage the economy to provide economic stability and a high level of employment. Government decisions have a major impact on the economic and financial planning environment.

The federal government's *monetary policy*—programs for controlling the amount of money in circulation (the money supply)—is used to stimulate or

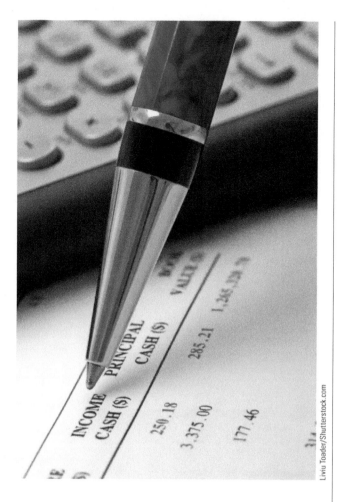
Liviu Toader/Shutterstock.com

moderate economic growth. For example, increases in the money supply tend to lower interest rates. This typically leads to a higher level of consumer and business borrowing and spending that increases overall economic activity. The reverse is also true. Reducing the money supply raises interest rates, which reduces consumer and business borrowing and spending and thus slows economic activity. The historically low interest rates in the wake of the financial crisis of 2008–2009 and beyond reflect the efforts of the Federal Reserve (Fed) to bolster the sagging economy and decrease unemployment.

The government's other principal tool for managing the economy is *fiscal policy*—its programs of spending and taxation. Increased spending for social services, education, defense, and other programs stimulates the economy, whereas decreased spending slows economic activity. Increasing taxes, on the other hand, gives businesses and individuals less to spend and, as a result, negatively affects economic activity. Conversely, decreasing taxes stimulate the economy. The importance of fiscal policy is illustrated by the government's massive spending to stimulate the U.S. economy in 2008 and 2009 as a way to address the greatest

financial crisis since the Great Depression of the 1930s in the United States.

Economic Cycles Although the government uses monetary and fiscal policy to manage the economy and provide economic stability, the level of economic activity changes constantly. The upward and downward movement creates *economic cycles* (also called *business cycles*), which vary in length and in extent. An economic cycle typically contains four stages: *expansion, peak, contraction,* and *trough.*

Exhibit 1.7 shows how each of these stages relates to real (inflation-adjusted) gross domestic product (GDP), which is an important indicator of economic activity. The stronger the economy, the higher the levels of real GDP and employment. During an **expansion**, real GDP increases until it hits a **peak**, which usually signals the end of the expansion and the beginning of a **contraction**. During a contraction (also known as a recession), real GDP falls into a **trough**, which is the end of a contraction and the beginning of an expansion. For about 75 years, the government has been successful in keeping the economy out of a depression, although we have experienced periods of rapid expansion and high inflation followed by periods of deep recession. And some would argue that the financial crisis of 2008–2009 came close to precipitating a depression.

Inflation, Prices, and Planning As we've discussed, our economy is based on the exchange of goods and services between businesses and their customers—consumers, government, and other businesses—for a medium of exchange called money. The mechanism that facilitates this exchange is a system of *prices*. The price of something is *the amount of money a seller is willing to accept in exchange for a given quantity of some good or service*—for example, $3 for a pound of meat or $10 for an hour of work.

The economy is said to be experiencing a period of **inflation** when the general level of prices *increases* over time. The most common measure of inflation, the **consumer price index (CPI)**, is based on changes in the cost

expansion the phase of the economic cycle when real GDP increases until it hits a peak

peak the phase of the economic cycle when an expansion ends and a contraction begins

contraction the phase of the economic cycle when real GDP falls

trough the phase of the economic cycle when a contraction ends and an expansion begins

inflation a state of the economy in which the general price level is increasing

consumer price index (CPI) a measure of inflation based on changes in the cost of consumer goods and services

Exhibit 1.7

The Business Cycle

The business cycle consists of four stages: expansion, peak, contraction, and trough.

Source: Adapted from William Boyes and Michael Melvin, *Economics*, 8th ed. (Cengage, 2011), p. 135.

of consumer goods and services. At times, the rate of inflation has been substantial. In 1980, for instance, prices went up by a whopping 13.6 percent. Fortunately, inflation has dropped dramatically in this country, and the annual rate of inflation has remained below 5 percent every year since 1983, except in 1990, when it was 5.4 percent. While there was mild deflation of −0.34 percent during the financial crisis in 2009, inflation moved up to about 3.2 percent in 2011, and has remained below 2 percent since then.

Inflation is of vital concern to financial planning. It affects not only what we pay for our goods and services but also what we earn in our jobs. Inflation tends to give an illusion of something that doesn't exist. That is, though we seem to be making more money, we really aren't. As prices rise, we need more income because our **purchasing power**—the amount of goods and services that each dollar buys at a given time—declines.

So be sure to look at what you earn in terms of its purchasing power, not simply in terms of absolute dollars.

> **EXAMPLE: Impact of Inflation on Financial Planning** Caroline earned $50,000 in 2017, and expected to receive annual raises that would bring her salary to $54,000 by 2020. While the annual growth rate in her salary is 2.6 percent, assume that inflation averaged 3 percent per year. Caroline's salary needs to grow to $54,636 just to keep pace with inflation. So, her *real* salary will decline.

> Sustained high rates of unexpected inflation can have devastating effects on retirement plans and other long-term financial goals.

Inflation also directly affects interest rates. High rates of inflation drive up the cost of borrowing money as lenders demand compensation for the eroding value of the loan payments they are to receive. Higher interest rates mean higher mortgage payments, higher monthly car payments, and so on. High inflation rates also have a detrimental effect on stock and bond prices. Finally, sustained high rates of unexpected inflation can have devastating effects on retirement plans and other long-term financial goals. Indeed, for many people, inflation can put such goals out of reach.

purchasing power the amount of goods and services that each dollar buys at a given time

1-5 WHAT DETERMINES YOUR PERSONAL INCOME?

LO5, LO6 An obvious and important factor in determining how well we live is the amount of income we earn. In the absence of any inheritance or similar financial windfall, your income will largely depend on such factors as your age, marital status, education, geographic location, and choice of career. A high level of income—whether derived from your job, your own business, or your investments—is within your reach if you have the dedication, commitment to hard work, and well-thought-out financial plans.

The data in Exhibit 1.8 show how income changes with age and education. For example, people with low incomes typically fall into the very young or very old age groups. Heads of households who have more formal education earn higher annual incomes than do those with less education.

Guru 3D/Shutterstock.com

1-5a Where You Live

Geographic factors can also affect your earning power. Salaries vary regionally, tending to be higher in the Northeast and West than in the South. Typically, your salary will also be higher if you live in a large metropolitan area rather than a small town or rural area. Such factors as economic conditions, labor supply, and industrial base also affect salary levels in different areas.

Living costs also vary considerably throughout the country. You'd likely earn more in Los Angeles than in

---

Exhibit 1.8

How Age and Education Affect Annual Income

The amount of money you earn is closely tied to your age and education. Generally, the closer you are to middle age (45–65) and the more education you have, the greater your income will be.

Annual Income (Head of Household)*	
Age	**Median Annual Income ($)***
25–34	57,366
35–44	71,417
45–54	73,857
55–64	62,802
65–74	47,432
75 and over	30,635
Education	**Median Annual Income ($)***
No formal educational credential	21,420
High school diploma or equivalent	36,210
Bachelor's degree	70,400
Master's degree	66,420
Doctoral or professional degree	100,490

*2015 data.

Source: Adapted from U.S. Census Bureau, Age of Head of Household by Median and Mean Income, Table H-10, http://www.census.gov/hhes/www/income/data/historical/household/index.html, accessed September 2016; and U.S. Bureau of Labor Statistics, data from Occupational Employment Statistics program, http://www.bls.gov/emp/ep_table_education_summary.htm, accessed September 2016.

Little Rock, Arkansas but your salary would probably not go as far owing to the much higher cost of living in Los Angeles.

1-5b Your Career

A critical determinant of your lifetime earnings is your career. The career you choose is closely related to your level of education and your particular skills, interests, lifestyle preferences, and personal values. Social, demographic, economic, and technological trends also influence your decision as to what fields offer the best opportunities for your future. Although not a prerequisite for many types of careers (e.g., sales, service, and certain types of manufacturing and clerical work), a formal education generally leads to greater decision-making responsibility—and consequently increased income potential—within a career. Exhibit 1.9 shows the differences in average compensation among selected college-educated majors over the course of their associated careers.

1-5c Planning Your Career

Career planning and personal financial planning are closely related activities, so the decisions you make in one area affect the other. Like financial planning, career planning is a lifelong process that includes short- and long-term goals. Since your career goals are likely to change several times, you should not expect to stay in one field, or to remain with one company, for your whole life.

 Go to Smart Sites

The U.S. News & World Report Career Center has material on a variety of career topics ranging from internships and résumés to the hottest careers and benefits.

The average American starting a career today can expect to have at least 10 jobs with five or more employers, and many of us will have three, four, or even more careers during our lifetimes. Some of these changes will be based on personal decisions; others may result from layoffs or corporate downsizing. For example, a branch manager for a regional bank who feels that bank mergers have reduced her job prospects in banking may buy a quick-print franchise and become her own boss. Job security is practically a

Median Annual Wages for College-Educated Majors (Ages 25–59)

Science, technology, engineering, and mathematics (STEM) majors typically have the highest income.

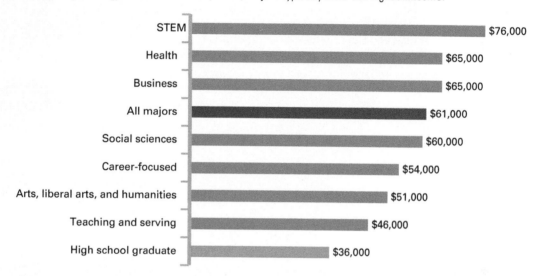

Major	Median Annual Wage
STEM	$76,000
Health	$65,000
Business	$65,000
All majors	$61,000
Social sciences	$60,000
Career-focused	$54,000
Arts, liberal arts, and humanities	$51,000
Teaching and serving	$46,000
High school graduate	$36,000

Source: Georgetown University Center on Education and the Workforce, analysis of U.S. Census Bureau, *American Community Survey* micro data, 2009-2013, "The Economic Value of College Majors, Figure 1.2, https://cew.georgetown.edu/wp-content/uploads/The-Economic-Value-of-College-Majors-Full-Report-web-FINAL.pdf, accessed September 2016.

thing of the past, and corporate loyalty has given way to a more self-directed career approach that requires new career strategies.

 Go to Smart Sites

One of the first steps in the job search process is to assess your personality. Link to the Keirsey Temperament Sorter®-11 as a starting point.

Careful career planning can improve your work situation and help you gain greater personal and professional satisfaction. Some of the steps are similar to the financial planning process described earlier:

▶ Identify your interests, skills, needs, and values.

▶ Set specific long- and short-term career goals.

▶ Develop and use an action plan to achieve those goals.

▶ Review and revise your career plans as your situation changes.

A personal portfolio of skills, both general and technical, will protect your earning power during economic downturns and advance it during prosperous times. It's important to keep your skills current with on-the-job training programs and continuing education. Adding proficiency in technology or languages puts you ahead of the pack in dealing with changing workplace requirements.

Good job hunting skills will serve you well throughout your career. Learn how to research new career opportunities and investigate potential jobs, taking advantage of online resources as well as traditional ones. Develop a broad base of career resources, starting with your college placement office, the public library, and personal contacts such as family and friends. Know how to market your qualifications to your advantage in your résumé and cover letters, on the phone, and in person during a job interview.

Ethan Cuts Back on Lunch Out and Lattes

Ethan buys lunch out most days and buys a latte every morning. He believes he could cut back a bit and save $5 a day, which is $35 a week and $140 a month. What is the impact of this seemingly modest cutback?

If Ethan invests his $35 savings a week every month at 5 percent, he will have the following in the future:

- 20 years: $57,545
- 30 years: $116,516
- 40 years: $213,643

The seemingly small act of investing only $5 a day would have a dramatic long-term effect on Ethan's future accumulated wealth.

NorGal/Shutterstock.com

STUDY TOOLS 1

LOCATED AT BACK OF THE TEXTBOOK
- ☐ Chapter Review Card

LOCATED AT WWW.CENGAGE.COM/LOGIN
- ☐ Review Key Term flashcards and create your own cards.
- ☐ Track your knowledge and understanding of key concepts in personal finance.

- ☐ Complete practice and graded quizzes to prepare for tests.
- ☐ Complete interactive content at PFIN6 Online.
- ☐ View the chapter highlight boxes at PFIN6 Online.

©viphotos/Shutterstock 140785408

Financial Planning Exercises

LO1 1. **Benefits of Personal Financial Planning.** How can using personal financial planning tools help you improve your financial situation? Describe changes you can make in at least three areas.

LO2, 3 2. **Personal Financial Goals and the Life Cycle. Use Worksheet 1.1.** Fill out Worksheet 1.1, "Summary of Personal Financial Goals," with goals reflecting your current situation and your expected life situation in 5 and 10 years. Discuss the reasons for the changes in your goals and how you'll need to adapt your financial plans as a result.

LO2 3. **Personal Financial Goals.** Recommend three financial goals and related activities for someone in each of the following circumstances:

    a. A junior in college

    b. A 30-year-old computer programmer who plans to earn an MBA degree

    c. A couple in their 30s with two children, ages 5 and 9

    d. A divorced, 52-year-old man with a 16-year-old child and a 78-year-old father who is ill

LO3 4. **Life Cycle of Financial Plans.** Explain the life cycle of financial plans and their role in achieving your financial goals.

LO4 5. **Impact of Economic Environment on Financial Planning.** Summarize current and projected trends in the economy with regard to GDP growth, unemployment, and inflation. How should you use this information to make personal financial and career planning decisions?

LO4 6. **Effects of Inflation.** How does inflation affect interest rates, security prices, and financial planning?

LO5 7. **Effect of Age and Geography on Income.** Evaluate the impact of age, and geographic location on personal income.

LO6 8. **Career Choices and Financial Planning.** Assume you graduated from college with a major in marketing and took a job with a large, consumer-products company. After three years, you are laid off when the company downsizes. Describe the steps you'd take to "repackage" yourself for another field.

LO5, 6 9. **Career Planning.** Tom Walker a 52-year-old retail store manager earning $90,000 a year, worked for the same company during his entire 25-year career. Tom was laid off and is still unemployed 10 months later, and his severance pay and unemployment compensation have run out. Because he adopted careful financial planning practices, he now has sufficient savings and investments to carry him through several months of unemployment. Tom is actively seeking work but finds that he is overqualified for available, lower-paying jobs and underqualified for higher-paying, more desirable positions. There are no openings for positions equivalent to the manager's job he lost. He lost his wife several years earlier and is very close to his two grown children, who live in the same city.

Tom has these options:

- Keep looking for a new job.

- Move to another area of the country where store manager positions are more plentiful.

- Accept a lower-paying job for two or three years and then go back to school evenings to finish his college degree and qualify for a better position.

- Consider other types of jobs that could benefit from his managerial skills.

    a. What important career factors should Tom consider when evaluating his options?

    b. What important personal factors should he consider when deciding among his career options?

    c. What recommendations would you give him in light of both the career and personal dimensions of his options noted above?

    d. What career strategies should today's workers use in order to avoid Tom's dilemma?

LO5, 6 10. **Income and Education.** Using Exhibit 1.8, discuss the relationship between annual income and the highest level of education completed. Provide specific examples of the difference between having no high school diploma and having a bachelor's degree, and between having a bachelor's degree and a professional degree.

2 | Using Financial Statements and Budgets

LEARNING OBJECTIVES

After studying this chapter, you will be able to...

LO1 Understand the relationship between financial plans and statements.

LO2 Prepare a personal balance sheet.

LO3 Generate a personal income and expense statement.

LO4 Develop a good record-keeping system and use ratios to evaluate personal financial statements.

LO5 Construct a cash budget and use it to monitor and control spending.

LO6 Apply time value of money concepts to put a monetary value on financial goals.

After you finish this chapter go to **PAGE 50** for **STUDY TOOLS**

JGI/Jamie Grill/Getty Images

How Will This Affect Me? A recent survey shows that only 38 percent of Americans could cover an unexpected $500 expense with money from their checking or saving accounts. The rest would have to cover it by reducing spending on other things, using a credit card, or borrowing money from family or friends.* These are scary numbers... and this chapter explains what you can do to avoid being part of that alarming statistic.

Everyone knows it's hard to get where you need to go if you don't know where you are. Financial goals describe your destination, and financial statements and budgets are the tools that help you determine exactly where you are in the journey. This chapter helps you define your financial goals and explains how to gauge your progress carefully over time.

---

*Claes Bell, "Budgets Can Crumble in Times of Trouble," http://www.bankrate.com/finance/smart-spending/money-pulse-0115.aspx, accessed September 2016.

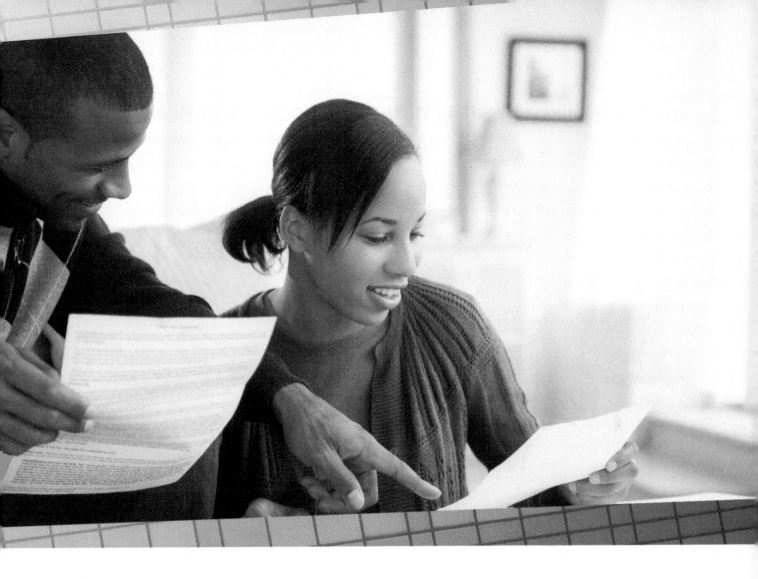

2-1 MAPPING OUT YOUR FINANCIAL FUTURE

LO1 On your journey to financial security, you need navigational tools to guide you to your destination: namely, the fulfillment of your financial goals. Operating without a financial plan is like traveling without a road map (or GPS). Financial plans, financial statements, and budgets provide direction by helping you work toward specific financial goals. *Financial plans* are the roadmaps that show you the way, whereas *personal financial statements* let you know where you stand financially. *Budgets*, detailed short-term financial forecasts that compare estimated income with estimated expenses, allow you to monitor and control expenses

> Before you can set realistic goals, develop your financial plans, or effectively manage your money, you must understand your current financial situation.

and purchases in a manner that is consistent with your financial plans. These tools provide control by bringing the various dimensions of your personal financial affairs into focus.

2-1a The Role of Financial Statements in Financial Planning

Before you can set realistic goals, develop your financial plans, or effectively manage your money, you must understand your current financial situation. You'll also need tools to monitor your progress. **Personal financial statements**

personal financial statements *balance sheets* and *income and expense statements* that serve as planning tools that are essential to developing and monitoring personal financial plans

Exhibit 2.1

The Interlocking Network of Financial Plans and Statements

Personal financial planning involves a network of financial reports that link future goals and plans with actual results. Such a network provides direction, control, and feedback.

are planning tools that provide an up-to-date evaluation of your financial well-being, help you identify potential financial problems, and help you make better-informed financial decisions. They measure your financial condition so you can establish realistic financial goals and evaluate your progress toward those goals. Knowing how to prepare and interpret personal financial statements is a cornerstone of personal financial planning.

The **balance sheet** describes your financial position—the assets you hold, less the debts you owe, equal your net worth (general level of wealth)—at a *given point in time*. In contrast, the **income and expense statement** measures financial performance *over* time. **Budgets** are *forward* looking; they allow you to monitor and control spending because they are based on expected income and expenses. Exhibit 2.1 summarizes

balance sheet a financial statement that describes a person's financial position at a *given point* in time

income and expense statement a financial statement that measures financial performance *over* time

budget a detailed financial report that looks *forward*, based on expected income and expenses

the various financial statements and reports and their relationship to each other in the personal financial planning process. *Financial plans* provide direction to annual budgets.

2-2 THE BALANCE SHEET: HOW MUCH ARE YOU WORTH TODAY?

LO2 Preparing a personal *balance sheet*, or *statement of financial position*, helps you get a handle on your financial well-being. Think of a balance sheet as a snapshot taken of your financial position on one day out of the year.

A balance sheet has three parts that, taken together, summarize your financial picture:

▶ **Assets:** What you own

▶ **Liabilities, or debts:** What you owe

▶ **Net worth:** The difference between your assets and liabilities

The accounting relationship among these three categories is called the *balance sheet equation* and is expressed as follows:

$$\text{Total assets} = \text{Total liabilities} + \text{Net worth}$$
and
$$\text{Net worth} = \text{Total assets} - \text{Total liabilities}$$

EXAMPLE: The Balance Sheet Identity Grace has total liabilities of $150,000 and a net worth of $75,000. This implies that she has total assets of $325,000 (total liabilities of $150,000 + net worth of $75,000 = $325,000 in total assets).

Let's now look at the components of each section of the balance sheet.

2-2a Assets: The Things You Own

Assets are the items you own. An item is classified as an asset whether it was purchased with cash or financed using debt. A useful way to group assets is on the basis of their underlying characteristics and uses. This results in four broad categories: liquid assets, investments, real property, and personal property.

▶ **Liquid assets**: Low-risk financial assets held in the form of cash or instruments that can be converted to cash readily and quickly, with little or no loss in value. Cash on hand or in a checking or savings account, money market deposit accounts, money market mutual funds, or certificates of deposit that mature within one year are all examples of liquid assets.

▶ **Investments**: Assets acquired to earn a return rather than provide a service. These assets are mostly intangible *financial assets* (stocks, bonds, mutual funds, and other types of securities), typically acquired to achieve long-term personal financial goals. Business ownership, the cash value of life insurance and pensions, retirement funds such as IRAs and 401(k) plans, and other investment vehicles such as commodities, financial futures, and options represent still other forms of investment assets.

▶ **Real and personal property**: Tangible assets that we use in our everyday lives. **Real property** refers to immovable property: land and anything fixed to

it, such as a house. Real property generally has a relatively long life and high cost, and it may *appreciate*, or increase in value. **Personal property** is movable property, such as automobiles, recreational equipment, household furnishings, and similar items. The left side of Worksheet 2.1 lists some of the typical assets you'd find on a personal balance sheet.

In personal financial analysis, it is important for all assets, regardless of category, to be recorded on the balance sheet at their current **fair market value**, which may differ considerably from their original purchase price. Fair market value is either the actual value of the asset (such as money in a checking account) or the price for which the asset can reasonably be expected to sell in the open market (as with a used car or a home). Under generally accepted accounting principles (GAAP), the accounting profession's guiding rules, assets appear on a company's balance sheet at *cost*, not *fair market value*.

2-2b Liabilities: The Money You Owe

Liabilities represent an individual's or a family's debts. They could result from department store charges, bank credit card charges, installment loans, or mortgages on housing and other real estate. A liability, regardless of its source, is something that you owe and must repay in the future.

Liabilities are generally classified according to maturity.

Pogonici/Shutterstock.com

▶ **Current, or short-term, liabilities**: Any debt currently owed and due within one year of the date

assets items that one owns

liquid assets assets that are held in the form of cash or can readily be converted to cash with little or no loss in value

investments assets such as stocks, bonds, mutual funds, and real estate that are acquired in order to earn a return rather than provide a service

real property tangible assets that are immovable: land and anything fixed to it, such as a house

personal property tangible assets that are movable and used in everyday life

fair market value the actual value of an asset, or the price for which it can reasonably be expected to sell in the open market

liabilities debts, such as credit card charges, loans, and mortgages

current (short-term) liabilities any debt due within one year of the date of the balance sheet

A balance sheet is set up to show what you own on one side (your assets) and how you paid for them on the other (your debt or net worth). As you can see, the Nelsons have more assets than liabilities.

BALANCE SHEET

Name(s) ___Silas and Emily Nelson___   Date ___December 31, 2017___

ASSETS			LIABILITIES		
Liquid Assets			**Current Liabilities**		
Cash on hand	$	150	Utilities	$	175
In checking		575	Rent		
Savings accounts		760	Insurance premiums		
Money market funds and deposits		800	Taxes		
			Medical/dental bills		125
Certificates of deposit			Repair bills		
Total Liquid Assets	$	2,285	Bank credit card balances		425
			Dept. store credit card balances		165
Investments					
Stocks		3,750	Travel and entertainment card balances		135
Bonds Corp.		1,000			
Certificates of deposit			Gas and other credit card balances		
Mutual funds		2,250			
Real estate			Bank line of credit balances		
Retirement funds, IRA		4,000			
Other			Other current liabilities		45
Total Investments	$	11,000	**Total Current Liabilities**	$	1,070
Real Property			**Long-Term Liabilities**		
Primary residence	$225,000		Primary residence mortgage	$160,000	
Second home			Second home mortgage		
Other			Real estate investment mortgage		
Total Real Property	$	225,000	Auto loans		4,350
			Appliance/furniture loans		800
Personal Property			Home improvement loans		
Auto(s): '13 Toyota Corolla	$	10,600	Single-payment loans		
Auto(s): '11 Ford Focus		6,700	Education loans		3,800
Recreational vehicles			Margin loans		
Household furnishings		3,700	Other long-term loans (from parents)		4,000
Jewelry and artwork		1,500			
Other			**Total Long-Term Liabilities**	$	172,950
Other					
Total Personal Property	$	22,500	**(II) Total Liabilities**	$	174,020
(I) Total Assets	$	260,785	**Net Worth [(I) – (II)]**	$	86,765
			Total Liabilities and Net Worth	$	260,785

of the balance sheet. Examples include charges for consumable goods, utility bills, rent, insurance premiums, taxes, medical bills, repair bills, and total **open account credit obligations**—the outstanding balances against established credit lines (usually through credit card purchases).

open account credit obligations current liabilities that represent the balances outstanding against established credit lines

long-term liabilities any debt due one year or more from the date of the balance sheet

▶ **Long-term liabilities:** Debt due one year or more from the date of the balance sheet. These liabilities typically include real estate mortgages, most consumer installment loans, education loans, and margin loans used to purchase securities.

Although most loans will fall into the category of long-term liabilities, *any loans, or any portion thereof, that come due within a year should be shown as current liabilities.* Examples of short-term loans include a six-month, single-payment bank loan, and a nine-month consumer installment loan for a refrigerator.

Regardless of the type of loan, *only the latest outstanding loan balance should be shown as a liability on the balance sheet*. This is because at any given time, it is the balance still due that matters, not the *initial* loan balance.

Another important and closely related point is that *only the outstanding principal portion of a loan or mortgage should be listed as a liability on the balance sheet*. You'll find the most common categories of liabilities on Worksheet 2.1.

2-2c Net Worth: A Measure of Your Financial Worth

Now that you've listed what you own and what you owe, you can calculate your **net worth**, the amount of actual wealth or **equity** that an individual or family has in its owned

assets. It represents the amount of money you'd have left after selling all your owned assets at their estimated fair market values and paying off all your liabilities (assuming there are no transaction costs). Rearranging this equation, we see that net worth equals total assets minus total liabilities. If net worth is less than zero, the family is *technically insolvent*. Although this form of **insolvency** doesn't necessarily mean that the family will end up in bankruptcy proceedings, it likely shows insufficient financial planning. Net worth typically increases over the life cycle of an individual or family, as Exhibit 2.2 illustrates.

> **EXAMPLE: Calculating Net Worth** A family has total assets of $225,000 and total liabilities of $175,000. Net worth is total assets of $225,000 less total liabilities of $175,000, which equals $50,000. This is effectively the amount of assets the family "owns" after paying off its liabilities. It is also referred to as the family's equity.

Assets − Liabilities = Equity

2-2d Balance Sheet Format and Preparation

You should prepare your personal balance sheet at least once a year, preferably every three to six months. Here's how to do it, using the categories in Worksheet 2.1 as a guide:

1. List your assets at their fair market value as of the date you are preparing the balance sheet. You'll find the fair market value of liquid and investment assets on checking and savings account records and investment account statements. Estimate the values of homes and cars

Arka38/Shutterstock.com

net worth an individual's or family's actual wealth; determined by subtracting total liabilities from total assets

equity the actual ownership interest in a specific asset or group of assets

insolvency the financial state in which net worth is less than zero

Exhibit 2.2

Median Net Worth by Age

Net worth starts to build in the younger-than-35 age bracket and continues to climb, peaking at the 65–74 age bracket. As indicated for the 74 and older age bracket, net worth declines after a person has been retired for a few years and has consequently used his or her assets to meet living expenses.

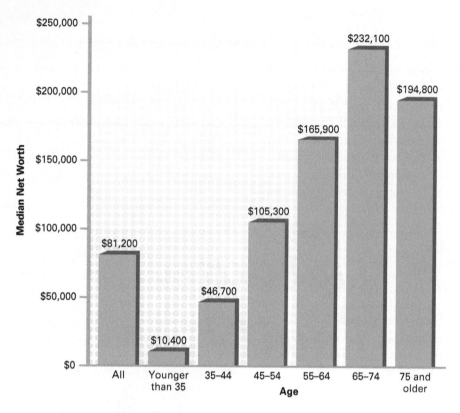

Source: Adapted from Jesse Bricker, Lisa J. Dettling, Alice Henriques, Joanne W. Hsu, Kevin B. Moore, John Sabelhaus, Jeffrey Thompson, and Richard A. Windle, "Changes in U.S. Family Finances from 2010 to 2013: Evidence from the Survey of Consumer Finances," Board of Governors of the Federal Reserve System, Washington, D.C. (October 24, 2014; data are for 2013), http://www.federalreserve.gov/pubs/bulletin/2014/pdf /scf14.pdf, Table 2, accessed September 2016.

using published sources of information, such as advertisements for comparable homes and the *Kelley Blue Book* for used car values (see **www.kbb.com**).

2. **List all current and long-term liabilities.** Show all outstanding charges, *even if you haven't received the bill,* as current liabilities on the balance sheet.

3. **Calculate net worth.** Subtract your total liabilities from your total assets. This is your net worth, which reflects the equity you have in your total assets.

2-2e A Balance Sheet for Silas and Emily Nelson

What can you learn from a balance sheet? Let's examine a hypothetical balance sheet as of December 31, 2017, prepared for Silas and Emily Nelson the young couple (ages 28 and 26) we met in Chapter 1 (see Worksheet 2.1). Here's what this financial statement tells us about the Nelsons' financial condition:

▶ **Assets:** Given their ages, the Nelsons' asset position looks quite good. The dominant asset is their house. They also have $11,000 in investments, which include retirement funds, and appear to have adequate liquid assets to meet their bill payments and cover small, unexpected expenses.

▶ **Liabilities:** The Nelsons' primary liability is the $160,000 mortgage on their townhouse. Their equity, or actual ownership interest, in the townhouse is $65,000 ($225,000 market value minus $160,000 outstanding mortgage loan). Their current liabilities are $1,070, with other debts of $12,950 representing auto, furniture, and education loans as well as a loan from their parents to help with the down payment on their home.

▶ **Net worth:** The Nelsons' net worth ($260,785 in total assets minus total liabilities of $174,020) is $86,765—especially considering their ages, an amount that is enviably above the median for their age group shown in Exhibit 2.2.

Comparing the Nelsons' total liabilities to their total assets gives a more realistic view of their current wealth position than looking at just assets or just liabilities in isolation.

2-3 THE INCOME AND EXPENSE STATEMENT: WHAT WE EARN AND WHERE IT GOES

LO3 When facing a lack of funds, the first question people ask themselves is, "Where does all the money go?" Preparing an *income and expense statement* answers this question. Think of this statement as a motion picture that not only shows actual results over time but also lets you compare them with budgeted financial goals.

The income and expense statement has three major parts: *income, expenses,* and *cash surplus* (or *deficit*). A cash surplus (or deficit) is merely the difference between income and expenses. The statement is prepared on a **cash basis**, which means that *only transactions involving actual cash inflows or actual cash outlays are recorded.* The term *cash* is used in this case to include not only coin and currency but also checks and debit card transactions drawn against checking and certain types of savings accounts. Income and expense patterns change over the individual's or family's life cycle.

2-3a Income: Cash In

Common sources of **income** include earnings received as wages, salaries, self-employment income, bonuses, and commissions; interest and dividends received from savings and investments; and proceeds from the sale of assets such as stocks and bonds or a car. Other income items include pension, annuity, and Social Security income; rent received from leased assets; alimony and child support; scholarships or grants; tax refunds; and miscellaneous types of income. Worksheet 2.2, Silas and Emily Nelson's Income and Expense Statement, has general categories for recording income. Note also that the proper figure to use is *gross* wages, salaries, and commissions, which constitute the amount of income you receive from your employer *before* taxes and other payroll deductions.

Go to Smart Sites

For current surveys and trends on consumer spending, check out the Consumer Expenditure Survey at the Department of Labor's Bureau of Labor Statistics.

2-3b Expenses: Cash Out

Expenses represent money used for outlays. Worksheet 2.2, Silas and Emily Nelson's Income and Expense Statement, categorizes them by the types of benefits they provide: (1) living expenses (such as housing, utilities, food, transportation, medical, clothing, and insurance), (2) tax payments, (3) asset purchases (such as autos, furniture, appliances, and loan payments on them), and (4) other payments for personal care, recreation and entertainment, and other expenses. Some are **fixed expenses**—usually contractual, predetermined, and involving equal payments each period (typically each month). Examples include mortgage and installment loan payments, insurance premiums, and cable TV fees. Others (such as food, clothing, utilities, entertainment, and medical expenses) are **variable expenses**, because their amounts change from one time period to the next.

Exhibit 2.3 shows the average annual expenses by major category as a percentage

cash basis a method of preparing financial statements in which only transactions involving actual cash receipts or actual cash outlays are recorded

income earnings received as wages, salaries, bonuses, commissions, interest and dividends, or proceeds from the sale of assets

expenses money spent on living expenses and to pay taxes, purchase assets, or repay debt

fixed expenses contractual, predetermined expenses involving equal payments each period

variable expenses expenses involving payment amounts that change from one time period to the next

The income and expense statement shows what you earned, how you spent your money, and how much you were left with (or, if you spent more than you took in, how much you went "in the hole").

INCOME AND EXPENSE STATEMENT

Name(s) _Silas and Emily Nelson_

For the _Year_ _____ Ended _December 31, 2017_

INCOME

Wages and salaries	Name: Silas Nelson	$	65,000
	Name: Emily Nelson		18,350
	Name:		
Self-employment income			
Bonuses and commissions	Silas-sales commissions		3,050
Investment income	Interest received		195
	Dividends received		120
	Rents received		
	Sale of securities		
	Other		
Pensions and annuities			
Other income			
	(I) Total Income	$	86,715

EXPENSES

Housing	Rent/mortgage payment (include insurance and taxes, if applicable)	$	11,820
	Repairs, maintenance, improvements		1,050
Utilities	Gas, electric, water		1,750
	Phone		480
	Cable TV and other		240
Food	Groceries		2,425
	Dining out		3,400
Transportation	Auto loan payments		2,520
	License plates, fees, etc.		250
	Gas, oil, repairs, tires, maintenance		2,015
Medical	Health, major medical, disability insurance (payroll deductions or not provided by employer)		2,250
	Doctor, dentist, hospital, medicines		305
Clothing	Clothes, shoes, and accessories		1,700
Insurance	Homeowner's (if not covered by mortgage payment)		1,200
	Life (not provided by employer)		1,865
	Auto		1,780
Taxes	Income and social security		18,319
	Property		2,100
Appliances, furniture, and other major purchases	Loan payments		800
	Purchases and repairs		450
Personal care	Laundry, cosmetics, hair care		700
Recreation and entertainment	Vacations		2,000
	Other recreation and entertainment		2,630
Other items	Tuition and books: Emily		1,400
	Gifts		215
	Loan payments: Education loans		900
	Loan payments: Parents		600
	(II) Total Expenses	$	65,164
	CASH SURPLUS (OR DEFICIT) [(I) – (II)]	$	21,551

Exhibit 2.3

How We Spend Our Income

Almost three-quarters of average annual expenditures fall into one of four categories: housing, transportation, food, and personal insurance and pensions.

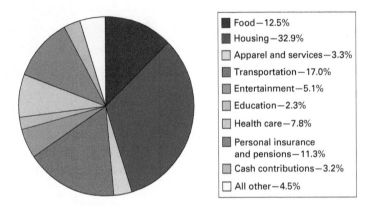

- ■ Food—12.5%
- ■ Housing—32.9%
- □ Apparel and services—3.3%
- ■ Transportation—17.0%
- ■ Entertainment—5.1%
- □ Education—2.3%
- □ Health care—7.8%
- ■ Personal insurance and pensions—11.3%
- □ Cash contributions—3.2%
- □ All other—4.5%

Source: "Consumer Expenditures—2015," Washington, D.C.: U.S. Department of Labor, Bureau of Labor Statistics, News Release, USDL-16-1768, based on Table A, August 30, 2016.

---

of after-tax income. It's a useful benchmark to see how you compare with national averages. However, your own expenses will vary according to your age, lifestyle, and where you live. For example, it costs considerably more to buy a home in San Diego than in St. Louis. Similarly, if you live in the suburbs, your commuting expenses will be higher than those of city dwellers.

2-3c Cash Surplus (or Deficit)

The third component of the income and expense statement shows the net result of the period's financial activities. Subtracting total expenses from total income gives you the cash surplus (or deficit) for the period. At a glance, you can see how you did financially over the period. A positive figure indicates that expenses were less than income, resulting in a **cash surplus**. A value of zero indicates that expenses were exactly equal to income for the period, while a negative value means that your expenses exceeded income and you have a **cash deficit**.

> **EXAMPLE:** Calculating a Cash Surplus or Deficit
> Oscar had cash income this year of $50,000 and cash expenses of $47,500. Consequently, his cash surplus is $2,500, which is income of $50,000 less expenses of $47,500. Had Oscar's expenses been $51,200 while earning the same income, he would have generated a cash deficit of $1,200, which is $50,000 minus $51,200.

2-3d Preparing the Income and Expense Statement

As shown in Worksheet 2.2, the income and expense statement is dated to define the period covered. To prepare the statement, follow these steps:

1. **Record your income from all sources for the period.**

2. **Establish meaningful expense categories.** Those shown on Worksheet 2.2 are a good starting point.

3. **Subtract total expenses from total income to get the cash surplus (a positive number) or deficit (a negative number).** This "bottom-line" summarizes the *net cash flow* resulting from your financial activities during the period.

Finally, when making your list of expenses for the year, remember to include the amount of income tax and Social Security taxes withheld from your paycheck as well as any other payroll deductions (health insurance, savings plans, retirement and pension contributions, and professional/union dues). These deductions (from gross wages, salaries, bonuses, and commissions) represent personal expenses, even if they don't involve a direct cash payment. You might be shocked when

> **cash surplus** an excess amount of income over expenses that results in *increased* net worth
>
> **cash deficit** an excess amount of expenses over income, resulting in insufficient funds as well as *decreased* net worth

listing what's taken out of your paycheck. Even if you're in a fairly low federal income tax bracket, your paycheck could easily be reduced by more than 25 percent for taxes alone.

BIGGEST BUDGETING MISTAKES

- **Failing to plan for inevitable expenses.** While some expenses are unexpected, most aren't. Plan for your car to need maintenance and put it in your budget. Include property, auto, health and life insurance, taxes, clothing, and gifts.

- **No emergency fund.** A real emergency—not just something unexpected—includes loss of income, severe illness, or death in the family.

- **Living above your means.** If you are making these budgeting mistakes, you may well spend more than you earn. A budget will help you prepare for the future without going deep into debt.

2-3e An Income and Expense Statement for Silas and Emily Nelson

Silas and Emily Nelson's balance sheet in Worksheet 2.1 shows us their financial condition as of December 31, 2017. Their income and expense statement for the year ending December 31, 2017, in Worksheet 2.2, was prepared using the background material presented earlier, along with the Nelsons' balance sheet. This statement shows how cash flowed into and out of their "pockets":

- ▶ **Income:** Total income for the year ending December 31, 2017, is $86,715. Silas' wages clearly represent the family's chief source of income, although Emily has finished her MBA and will now be making a major contribution. Other sources of income include $195 in interest on their savings accounts and bond investments, and $120 in dividends from their common stock holdings.

- ▶ **Expenses:** Total expenses for the year of $65,164 include their home mortgage, food, auto loan, clothing, and income and Social Security taxes. Other sizable expenses during the year include home repairs and improvements, gas and electricity, auto license and operating expenses, insurance, tuition, and education loan payments.

- ▶ **Cash surplus:** The Nelsons end the year with a cash surplus of $21,551 (total income of $86,715 minus total expenses of $65,164). The Nelsons can use their surplus to increase savings, make more investments,

bonds, or other vehicles, or make payments on some outstanding financial debts. If they had a cash deficit, the Nelsons would have to withdraw savings, liquidate investments, or borrow an amount equal to the deficit to meet their financial commitments (that is, to "make ends meet"). With their surplus of $21,551, the Nelsons have made a positive contribution to their net worth.

2-4 USING YOUR PERSONAL FINANCIAL STATEMENTS

LO4 Whether you're just starting out and have a minimal net worth or are further along the path toward achieving your goals, your balance sheet and income and expense statements provide insight into your current financial status. You now have the information you need to examine your financial position, monitor your financial activities, and track the progress you're making toward your financial goals. Let's now look at ways to help you create better personal financial statements and analyze them to better understand your financial situation.

2-4a Keeping Good Records

Although record keeping doesn't rank high on most "to do" lists, a good record-keeping system helps you manage your personal financial affairs effectively. It's best to prepare your personal financial statements at least once each year, ideally when drawing up your budget. Yet many people update their financial statements every three or six months. You may want to keep a *ledger*, or financial record book, to summarize all your financial transactions. The ledger has sections for assets, liabilities, sources of income, and expenses; these sections contain separate accounts for each item.

Managing Your Financial Records Your system doesn't have to be fancy to be effective. Start by taking an inventory. Make a list of everything you own and owe.

Exhibit 2.4

Ratios for Personal Financial Statement Analysis

Ratio	Formula	2017 Calculations for the Nelsons
Solvency ratio	$\dfrac{\text{Total net worth}}{\text{Total assets}}$	$\dfrac{\$86,765}{\$260,785} = 33.3\%$
Liquidity ratio	$\dfrac{\text{Total liquid assets}}{\text{Total current debts}}$	$\dfrac{\$2,285}{\$17,710^{(a)}} = 12.90\%$
Savings ratio	$\dfrac{\text{Cash surplus}}{\text{Income after taxes}}$	$\dfrac{\$21,551}{\$86,715 - \$20,419^{(b)}} = \dfrac{\$21,551}{\$66,296} = 32.5\%$
Debt service ratio	$\dfrac{\text{Total monthly loan payments}}{\text{Monthly gross (before-tax) income}}$	$\dfrac{\$1,387^{(c)}}{\$7,226^{(d)}} = 19.2\%$

(a) You'll find the Nelsons' total liquid assets ($2,285) and total current liabilities ($1,070) on Worksheet 2.1. The total current debt totals $17,710: current liabilities of $1,070 (from Worksheet 2.1) plus loan payments due within 1 year of $16,640 (from Worksheet 2.2). Note that loan payments due within 1 year consist of $11,820 in mortgage payments, $2,520 in auto loan payments, $800 in furniture loan payments, $900 in education loan payments, and $600 in loan payments to parents.

(b) Total taxes of $20,419 consist of the tax on income and social security ($18,319) and property tax ($2,100).

(c) On an annual basis, the Nelsons' debt obligations total $16,640 ($11,820 in mortgage payments, $2,520 in auto loan payments, $800 in furniture loan payments, $900 in education loan payments, and $600 in loan payments to parents; all from Worksheet 2.2). The Nelsons' total monthly loan payments are about $1,387 ($16,640 ÷ 12months).

(d) Dividing the Nelsons' annual gross income (also found in Worksheet 2.2) of $86,715 by 12 equals $7,226 per month.

Check it at least once a year to make sure it's up to date and to review your financial progress. Then, record transactions manually in your ledger or with financial planning software. You'll want to set up separate files for tax-planning records, with one for income (paycheck stubs, interest on savings accounts, and so on) and another for deductions, as well as for individual mutual fund and brokerage account records. You can develop a good record-keeping system using spreadsheet software like Excel.

2-4b Tracking Financial Progress: Ratio Analysis

Each time you prepare your financial statements, you should analyze them to see how well you're doing on your financial goals. For example, with an income and expense statement, you can compare actual financial results with budgeted figures to make sure that your spending is under control. Likewise, comparing a set of financial plans with a balance sheet will reveal whether you're meeting your savings and investment goals, reducing your debt, or building up a retirement reserve. You can compare current performance with historical performance to find out if your financial situation is improving or getting worse.

Calculating certain financial ratios can help you evaluate your financial performance over time. What's more, if you apply for a loan, the lender probably will look at these ratios to judge your ability to carry additional debt. Four important money management ratios are (1) solvency ratio, (2) liquidity ratio, (3) savings ratio, and (4) debt service ratio. The first two are associated primarily with the balance sheet; the last two relate primarily to the income and expense statement. Exhibit 2.4 defines these ratios and illustrates their calculation for Silas and Emily Nelson.

Balance Sheet Ratios When evaluating your balance sheet, you should be most concerned with your net worth at a given time. The **solvency ratio** shows, as a percentage, your degree of exposure to insolvency, or how much "cushion" you have as a protection against insolvency. Silas and Emily's solvency ratio is 33.3 percent, which means that they could withstand about a 33-percent decline in the market value of their assets before they would be insolvent. Consider that the stock market, as measured by the S&P 500 index, fell about 37 percent during the financial crisis of 2008. Also, the average home's value fell about 18 percent during that crisis year, as measured by the S&P/Case-Shiller U.S. National Home Price Index. The value of Silas and Emily's solvency ratio suggests that they are in good shape but may want to consider increasing it a bit in the future to manage a potential decline in the value of their assets even better.

Although the solvency ratio indicates the potential to withstand financial problems, it does not deal directly

solvency ratio total net worth divided by total assets; measures the degree of exposure to insolvency with the ability to pay current debts. This issue is addressed by the **liquidity ratio**, which shows your ability to pay current debts (any bills or charges that must be paid *within one year*) with existing liquid assets.

The calculated liquidity ratio indicates that the Nelsons can cover only about 13 percent of their existing one-year debt obligations with their current liquid assets. In other words, they have about 1.6 months of coverage (a month is one-twelfth, or 8.3 percent, of a year). If an unexpected event cut off their income, their liquid reserves would quickly be exhausted. Although there's no hard-and-fast rule for what this ratio should be, it seems too low for the Nelsons. They should consider strengthening it along with their solvency ratio. They should be able to add to their cash surpluses now that Emily is working full-time.

The amount of liquid reserves will vary with your personal circumstances and "comfort level." Another useful liquidity guideline is to have a reserve fund equal to at least six to nine months of after-tax income available to cover living expenses. The Nelsons' after-tax income for 2017 was $5,700 per month ([$86,715 total income − $18,319 income and Social Security taxes] ÷ 12). Therefore, this guideline suggests they should have at least $34,200 [6 × $5,700] in total liquid assets, which is much more than the $2,285 on their latest balance sheet. In troubled economic times, you may want to keep even more than six months of income in this fund as protection in case you lose your job.

Income and Expense Statement Ratios When evaluating your income and expense statement, you should ultimately focus on the bottom line, which shows the cash surplus (or deficit) resulting from the period's activities. You can relate the cash surplus (or deficit) to income by calculating a **savings ratio**, which is done most effectively with after-tax income.

Silas and Emily saved about a third of their after-tax income, which is excellent. (American families, on average, save about 5 percent to 8 percent). How much to save is an important personal choice.

Although maintaining an adequate level of savings is obviously important to personal financial planning, so is the ability to pay debts promptly. In fact, debt payments have a higher priority.

> **liquidity ratio** total liquid assets divided by total current debts; measures the ability to pay current debts
>
> **savings ratio** cash surplus divided by net income (after tax); indicates relative amount of cash surplus achieved during a given period
>
> **debt service ratio** total monthly loan payments divided by monthly gross (before-tax) income; provides a measure of the ability to pay debts promptly

The **debt service ratio** allows you to make sure you can comfortably meet your debt obligations. This ratio excludes current liabilities and considers only mortgage, installment, and personal loan obligations.

Monthly loan payments account for about 19 percent of Silas and Emily's monthly gross income. This relatively low debt service ratio indicates that the Nelsons should have little difficulty in meeting their monthly loan payments. In your financial planning, try to keep your debt service ratio under 35 percent or so, because that's generally viewed as a manageable level of debt. Of course, the lower the debt service ratio, the easier it is to meet loan payments as they come due.

2-5 CASH IN AND CASH OUT: PREPARING AND USING BUDGETS

> Just as your goals will change over your lifetime, so too will your budget as your financial situation becomes more complex.

LO5 Many of us avoid budgeting as if it were the plague. Yet preparing, analyzing, and monitoring your personal budget are essential steps for successful personal financial planning.

After defining your short-term financial goals, you can prepare a cash budget for the coming year. Recall that a *budget* is a short-term financial planning report that helps you achieve your short-term financial goals. You increase your ability to control your expenses by comparing actual with budgeted expenses. A cash budget is a valuable money management tool that helps you:

▶ Maintain the necessary information to monitor and control your finances

▶ Decide how to allocate your income to reach your financial goals

▶ Implement a system of disciplined spending—as opposed to just existing from one paycheck to the next

▶ Reduce needless spending so you can increase the funds allocated to savings and investments

▶ Achieve your long-term financial goals

Just as your goals will change over your lifetime, so too will your budget as your financial situation becomes more complex. Typically, the number of income and expense categories increases as you accumulate more assets and debts and have more family responsibilities. This process does not become simpler until retirement for most people.

2-5a The Budgeting Process

Like the income and expense statement, *a budget should be prepared on a cash basis*; thus, we call this document a **cash budget** because it deals with estimated cash income and cash expenses, including savings and investments, that are expected to occur in the coming year.

The cash budget preparation process has three stages: forecasting income (cash in), estimating expenses (cash out), and finalizing the cash budget. When you're estimating income and expenses, take into account any anticipated changes in the cost of living and their impact on your budget components. If your income is fixed—not expected to change over the budgetary period—then increases in various expense items will probably decrease the purchasing power of your income. Worksheet 2.3, the Nelsons' "Annual Cash Budget by Month," has separate sections to record income (cash receipts) and expenses (cash disbursements) and also lists the most common categories for each.

Forecasting Income The first step in preparing your cash budget is to forecast your income (cash in) for the coming year. Include all income expected for the year: the take-home pay of both spouses, expected bonuses or commissions, pension or annuity income, and investment income—interest, dividend, rental, and asset (particularly security) sale income. Unlike the income and expense statement, in the cash budget you should use *take-home pay* (rather than gross income). Your cash focuses on those areas that you can control—and most people have limited control over things like taxes withheld, contributions to company insurance and pension plans, and the like. Take-home pay is the amount of *disposable income* you receive from your employer.

Forecasting Expenses The second step in the cash budgeting process is by far the most difficult: preparing a schedule of estimated expenses for the coming year. This is commonly done using actual expenses (cash out) from previous years (as found on income and expense statements and in supporting information for those periods) along with predetermined short-term financial goals.

focal point/Shutterstock.com

Whether or not you have historical information, when preparing your budget, *be aware of your expenditure patterns and how you spend money.* After tracking your expenses over several months, study your spending habits to see if you are doing things that should be eliminated. For example, you may become aware that you are going to the ATM too often or using credit cards too freely. You'll probably find it easier to budget expenses if you group them into several general categories rather than trying to estimate each item. Worksheet 2.3 is an example of one such grouping scheme, patterned after the categories used in the income and expense statement.

Don't forget an allowance for "fun money," which family members can spend as they wish. This gives each person some financial independence and may help family members feel more comfortable with being on a budget.

Finalizing the Cash Budget After estimating income and expenses, finalize your budget by comparing projected income to projected expenses. Show the difference as a projected surplus or deficit. In a *balanced budget*, the total income for the year equals or exceeds total expenses. If you find that you have a deficit at projected year end, you'll have to *go back and adjust your expenses.* If you have several months of large surpluses, you should be able to cover any shortfall in a later month, as explained later. Budget preparation is complete once all projected monthly deficits are resolved and the total annual budget balances.

2-5b Dealing with Deficits

Even if the *annual* budget balances, in certain months expenses may exceed income, causing a monthly budget deficit. Likewise, a budget surplus occurs when income in some months exceeds expenses. Two remedies exist:

▶ Shift expenses from months with budget deficits to months with surpluses (or, alternatively, transfer income, if possible, from months with surpluses to those with deficits).

▶ Use savings, investments, or borrowing to cover temporary deficits.

Because the budget balances for the year, the need for funds to cover shortages is only temporary. In months with budget surpluses, you should return funds taken from savings or investments or repay loans. Either remedy is feasible for curing a monthly budget deficit in a balanced annual budget, although the second is probably more practical.

cash budget a budget that takes into account estimated monthly cash receipts and cash expenses for the coming year

The projected annual cash budget shows several months in which substantial cash deficits are expected to occur. The Nelsons can use this information to develop plans for covering those monthly shortfalls.

ANNUAL CASH BUDGET BY MONTH

Name(s) _Silas and Emily Nelson_

For the _Year_   Ended _December 31, 2018_

	Jan.	Feb.	Mar.	April	May	June	July	Aug.	Sep.	Oct.	Nov.	Dec.	Total for the Year
INCOME													
Take-home pay	$4,800	$4,800	$4,800	$4,800	$4,800	$5,200	$5,200	$5,200	$5,200	$5,200	$5,200	$5,200	$60,400
Bonuses and commissions						1,350						1,300	2,650
Pensions and annuities													
Investment income			50			50			50			50	200
Other income													
(I) Total Income	$4,800	$4,800	$4,850	$4,800	$4,800	$6,600	$5,200	$5,200	$5,250	$5,200	$5,200	$6,550	$63,250
EXPENSES													
Housing (rent/mtge, repairs)	$1,185	$1,485	$1,185	$1,185	$1,185	$1,185	$1,185	$1,185	$1,185	$1,185	$1,185	$1,185	$14,520
Utilities (phone, elec., gas, water)	245	245	245	175	180	205	230	245	205	195	230	250	2,650
Food (home and away)	696	696	1,200	696	696	696	696	696	696	696	696	696	8,856
Transportation (auto/public)	375	620	375	355	375	375	575	375	375	425	375	375	4,975
Medical/dental, incl. insurance	50	50	50	50	50	75	50	50	50	50	50	50	625
Clothing	150	150	670	200	200	200	300	600	200	300	300	300	3,570
Insurance (life, auto, home)				660	1,598					660	1,598		4,516
Taxes (property)		550						550					1,100
Appliances, furniture, and other (purchases/loans)	60	60	60	60	60	60	60	60	60	60	60	60	720
Personal care	100	100	100	100	100	100	100	100	100	100	100	100	1,200
Recreation and entertainment	250	300	3,200	200	200	400	300	200	200	200	200	2,050	7,700
Savings and investments	575	575	575	575	575	575	575	575	575	575	575	575	6,900
Other expenses	135	200	175	135	510	180	135	235	235	135	405	325	2,805
Fun money	200	200	230	130	200	200	200	200	200	200	200	230	2,390
(II) Total Expenses	$4,021	$5,231	$8,065	$4,521	$5,929	$4,251	$4,406	$5,071	$4,081	$4,781	$5,974	$6,196	$62,527
CASH SURPLUS (OR DEFICIT) [(I)-(II)]	$779	($431)	($3,215)	$279	($1,129)	$2,349	$794	$129	$1,169	$419	($774)	$354	$723
CUMULATIVE CASH SURPLUS (OR DEFICIT)	$779	$348	($2,867)	($2,588)	($3,717)	($1,368)	($574)	($445)	$724	$1,143	$369	$723	$723

What can you do if your budget shows an *annual budget deficit* even after you've made a few expense adjustments? Here you have three options, as follows:

▶ **Liquidate enough savings and investments or borrow enough to meet the total budget shortfall for the year.** Obviously, this option is not preferred because it violates the objective of budgeting: to set expenses at a level that allows you to enjoy a reasonable standard of living *and* progress toward achieving your long-term goals.

▶ **Cut low-priority expenses from the budget.** This option is clearly preferable to the first one. It balances the budget without using external funding sources by eliminating expenses associated with your least important short-term goals, such as flexible or discretionary expenses for nonessential items (e.g., recreation,

How to *Really* Spend Less

Spending less means changing your behavior:

- **Make a budget and use it to help set financial goals.** Decide how much less you want to spend and set a savings goal.

- **Use your savings account first and your checking account last.** Set up two bank accounts so that money can be transferred between them. Deposit your income into savings and transfer your budgeted amount into checking—not the other way around.

- **Spend cash—don't rely on credit cards.** It's harder to use cash for everything, so you'll spend less.

- **Have someone hold you accountable.** Let someone you trust—your spouse, friend, or parent, for instance—know your goals and have them follow your progress.

- **Before you buy, consider the alternatives.** Always wait at least two days before making a big purchase. Think about how it fits into your budget. Really think about your alternatives.

Source: Adapted from Brian Reed, "6 New Behavioral Strategies to Curb Your Spending in 2012," www.investinganswers.com/personal-finance/savings-budget/6-new-behavioral-strategies-curb-your-spending-2012-3963, accessed September 2016.

---

entertainment, and some types of clothing).

► **Increase income.** Finding a higher-paying job or perhaps a second, part-time job is the most difficult option. This takes more planning and may result in significant lifestyle changes. However, people who can't liquidate savings or investments or borrow funds to cover necessary expenses may ultimately have to choose this route to balance their budgets.

2-5c A Cash Budget for Silas and Emily Nelson

Using their short-term financial goals (Worksheet 1.1 in Chapter 1) and past financial statements (Worksheets 2.1 and 2.2), Silas and Emily Nelson have prepared their cash budget for the 2018 calendar year. Worksheet 2.3 shows the Nelsons' estimated total 2018 annual income and expenses by month as well as the monthly and annual cash surplus or deficit.

The Nelsons list their total 2018 take-home income of $63,250 by source for each month. By using take-home pay, they eliminate the need to show income-based taxes, Social Security payments, and other payroll deductions as expenses. The take-home pay reflects Silas and Emily's expected salary increases.

In estimating annual expenses for 2018, the Nelsons anticipate a small amount of inflation and have factored some price increases into their expense projections. They have also

allocated $6,900 to savings and investments, a wise budgeting strategy, and included an amount for fun money to be divided between them.

Alexandru Nika/Shutterstock.com

During their budgeting session, Silas and Emily discovered that their first estimate resulted in expenses of $63,877, compared with their estimated income of $63,250. To eliminate the $627 deficit in order to balance their budget and to allow for unexpected expenses, they made these decisions:

► Omit some low-priority goals: spend less on stereo components; take a shorter European vacation instead of the Colorado ski trip shown in Worksheet 1.1.

► Reschedule some of the loan repayment to their parents.

► Reduce their fun money slightly.

> **YOU CAN DO IT NOW: Save Automatically** We all know we should save regularly. One way to create a savings "habit" is to literally make it automatic.
>
> Open a savings account apart from your checking account. This will separate your savings from what you have available to spend. And then set up an *automatic* deposit from your checking to your savings account each month. This sets your "habit." You can **do it now.**

Don't Fool Yourself ... Pessimistic Budgeting Wins

People tend to be overly optimistic when budgeting for a few months than for longer time periods. They tend to underestimate short-term expenses, but they are more realistic with longer-term budgets. We are likely less confident about longer periods and adjust our expenses upward to be safe. So win by being *purposely pessimistic* in short-term budgeting.

These reductions lower Silas and Emily's total scheduled expenses to $62,527, giving them a surplus of $723 ($63,250 – $62,527) and balancing the budget on an annual basis with some money left over. Of course, the Nelsons can reduce other discretionary expenses to further increase the budget surplus and have a cushion for unexpected expenses.

The Nelsons' final step is to analyze monthly surpluses and deficits and determine whether to use savings, investments, or borrowing to cover monthly shortfalls. The bottom line of their annual cash budget lists the cumulative, or running, totals of monthly cash surpluses and deficits. Despite their $723 year-end cumulative cash surplus, they have cumulative deficits from March to August, primarily because of their March vacation and insurance payments. To help cover these deficits, Silas and Emily have arranged an interest-free loan from their parents. If they had dipped into savings to finance the deficits, they would have lost some interest earnings, which are included as income. They could also delay clothing and recreation and entertainment expenses until later in the year to reduce the deficits more quickly. If they weren't able to obtain funds to cover the deficits, they would have to reduce expenses further or increase income. At year end, they should use their surplus to increase savings or investments or to repay part of a loan.

budget control schedule a summary that shows how actual income and expenses compare with the various budget categories and where variances (surpluses or deficits) exist

budget variance the difference between the budgeted and actual amount paid out or received

2-5d Using Your Budgets

In the final analysis, a cash budget has value only if (1) you use it and (2) you keep careful records of actual income and expenses. These records show whether you are staying within your budget limits.

At the beginning of each month, record the budgeted amount for each category and enter income received and money spent on the appropriate pages. At month's end, total each account and calculate the surplus or deficit. Except for certain income accounts (such as salary) and fixed expense accounts (such as mortgage or loan payments), most categories will end the month with a positive or negative variance, indicating a cash surplus or deficit. You can then transfer your total spending by category to a **budget control schedule** that compares actual income and expenses with the various categories and shows the **budget variance**, which is the difference between the budgeted and actual amount paid out or received.

This monthly comparison makes it easy to identify major budget categories where income falls far short of—or spending far exceeds—desired levels (variances of 5 percent to 10 percent or more). After pinpointing these areas, you can take corrective action to keep your budget on course. Don't just look at the size of the variances. Analyze them, particularly the larger ones, to discover *why* they occurred. Only in exceptional situations should you finance budget adjustments by using savings and investments or by borrowing.

> **EXAMPLE: Calculating Budget Variance** Lila budgeted $125 last month for transportation but actually spent $150. She consequently had a variance that was a budget deficit of $25. Had Lila actually spent only $115, the variance would have been a $10 budget surplus.

Looking at the Nelsons' budget control schedule for a representative month in Worksheet 2.4, you can see that actual income and expense levels are reasonably close to their targets and have a positive budget variance for the month shown. The biggest variances were in medical/dental and recreation/entertainment, which presumably occurred because these expenses are paid unevenly over the months of the year.

2-6 THE TIME VALUE OF MONEY: PUTTING A DOLLAR VALUE ON FINANCIAL GOALS

LO6 Assume that one of your financial goals is to buy your first home in six years. Your first question is how much you want to spend on that home. Let's say you've done some "window shopping" and feel that,

The monthly budget provides important feedback on how the actual cash flow stacks up against the forecasted monthly cash budget. If the variances are significant enough and/or continue month after month, the Nelsons should consider altering either their spending habits or their cash budget.

MONTHLY BUDGET

Name(s) _Silas and Emily Nelson_

	Budgeted Amount (1)	Actual Amount (2)	Variance (3)*
INCOME			
Take-home pay	$4,800	$4,817	$17
Bonuses and commissions			0
Pensions and annuities			0
Investment income			0
Other income			0
(I) Total Income	$4,800	$4,817	$17
EXPENSES			
Housing (rent/mtge, repairs)	$1,185	1,185	0
Utilities (phone, elec., gas, water)	245	237	(8)
Food (home and away)	696	680	(16)
Transportation (auto/public)	375	385	10
Medical/dental, including insurance	50	0	(50)
Clothing	150	190	40
Insurance (life, auto, home)	0	0	0
Taxes (property)	0	0	0
Appliances, furniture, and other (purchases/loans)	60	60	0
Personal care	100	85	(15)
Recreation and entertainment	250	210	(40)
Savings and investments	575	575	0
Other expenses	135	118	(17)
Fun money	200	200	0
(II) Total Expenses	$4,021	$3,925	($96)
CASH SURPLUS (OR DEFICIT) [(1)-(2)]	$779	$892	$113

*Col. (3) = Col. (2) − Col. (1).

taking future inflation into consideration, you can buy a nice condominium for about $200,000 in six years. Of course, you won't need the full amount, but assuming that you'll make a 20 percent down payment of $40,000 (.20 × $200,000 = $40,000) and pay $5,000 in closing costs, you need $45,000. You now have a well-defined financial goal: _To accumulate $45,000 in six years to buy a home costing about $200,000._

The next question is how to get all that money. You can easily estimate how much to save or invest each year if you know your goal and what you expect to earn on your savings or investments. In this case, if you have to start from scratch (that is, if nothing has already been saved) and estimate that you can earn about 5 percent on your money, you'll have to save or invest about $6,616 per year for each of the next six years to accumulate $45,000 over that time. Now you have another vital piece of information: _You know what you must do over the next six years to reach your financial goal._

How did we arrive at the $6,616 figure? We relied on the **time value of money**, the idea that a dollar today is worth more than a dollar received in the future. With time value concepts, we can correctly compare dollar values occurring at different points in time. So as long as you can earn a positive rate of return (interest rate) on your investments (ignoring taxes and other behavioral factors), you should prefer to receive equal amounts of money sooner rather than later. The two key time value concepts, future value and present value, are discussed separately next. (_Note:_ The time value discussions and demonstrations initially rely on the use of financial tables.)

Appendix E explains how to use financial calculators, which determine the interest factors internally to conveniently make time value calculations. The calculator keystrokes for each calculation are shown in the text margin near the related discussion.) Also, all spreadsheet software, such as Excel, has "financial functions" that will run time-value calculations you can use to build your budgets.

2-6a Future Value

To calculate how much to save to buy the $200,000 condominium, we used **future value**, which is the value to which an amount today will

> **time value of money** the concept that a dollar today is worth more than a dollar received in the future

> **future value** the value to which an amount today will grow if it earns a specific rate of interest over a given period

grow if it earns a specific rate of interest over a given period. Assume, for example, that you make annual deposits of $2,000 into a savings account that pays 5 percent interest per year. At the end of 20 years, your deposits would total $40,000 (20 × $2,000). If you made no withdrawals, your account balance would have increased to $66,132! This growth in value occurs not only because of earning interest but also because of **compounding**—the interest earned each year is left in the account and becomes part of the balance (or principal) on which interest is earned in subsequent years.

Future Value of a Single Amount To demonstrate future value, let's return to the goal of accumulating $45,000 for a down payment to buy a home in six years. The correct way to approach this problem is to use the *future value* concept. For instance, if you can invest $100 today at 5 percent, you will have $105 in a year. You will earn $5 on your investment (.05 × $100 = $5) and get your original $100 back. Once you know the length of time and rate of return involved, you can find the future value of any investment by using the following simple formula:

$$\text{Future value} = \text{Amount invested} \times \text{Future value factor}$$

Tables of future value factors simplify the computations in this formula (see Appendix A). The table is easy to use; simply find the factor that corresponds to a given year and interest rate.

Returning to the problem at hand, let's say you already have accumulated $5,000 toward the purchase of a new home. Referring to Appendix A, you will find the future

value factor for a six year investment earning 5 percent is 1.340 (the factor that lies at the intersection of six years and 5 percent). To find the future value of that investment in six years earning 5 percent, you can use the preceding formula as follows:

$$\text{Future value} = \$5,000 \times 1.340$$
$$= \$6,700$$

In six years, then, you will have $6,700 if you invest the $5,000 at 5 percent. However, because you feel you are going to need $45,000, you are still $38,300 short of your goal.

Future Value of an Annuity How are you going to accumulate the additional $38,300? You'll again use the future value concept, but this time you'll use the *future value annuity factor*. An **annuity** is a fixed sum of money that occurs periodically; for example, a deposit of $1,000 per year for each of the next five years, with payment to be made at the end of each year. To find out how much you need to save each year in order to accumulate a given amount, use this equation:

$$\text{Yearly savings} = \frac{\text{Future amount of money desired}}{\text{Future value annuity factor}}$$

When dealing with an annuity you need to use a different table of factors, such as that in Appendix B. Note that it's very much like the table of future value factors and, in fact, is used in exactly the same way. The proper future value annuity factor corresponds to the given year *and* interest rate.

You'll need to save about $5,630.70 a year to reach your goal. Note in this example that you must add $5,630.70

TIMELINE

I = 5%

0 1 2 3 4 5

$5,000 $6,700
                                 6

End of Year

CALCULATOR

Inputs	Functions
5,000	PV
6	N
5	I
	CPT
	FV
Solution	
6,700.48	

See Appendix E for details.

compounding when interest earned each year is left in the account and becomes part of the balance (or principal) on which interest is earned in subsequent years

annuity a fixed sum of money that occurs annually

TIMELINE

End of Year

CALCULATOR

Inputs	Functions
38,300	FV
6	N
5	I
	CPT
	PMT
	Solution
	5,630.77

See Appendix E for details.

TIMELINE

End of Year

each year to the $5,000 you initially invested in order to build up a pool of $45,000 in six years. At a 5 percent rate of return, the $5,630.70 per year will grow to $38,300 and the $5,000 will grow to $6,700. So in six years, you'll have $38,300 + $6,700 = $45,000.

How much, you may ask, would you need to save each year if you didn't have the $5,000 to start with? In this case, your goal would still be the same (to accumulate $45,000 in six years), but because you'd be starting from scratch, the full $45,000 would need to come from yearly savings. Assuming you would still earn 5 percent over the six-year period, you can use the same future value annuity factor (6.802) to compute the amount of yearly savings as follows:

Yearly savings = $45,000/6.802 = $6,615.70

or approximately $6,616. Note that this amount corresponds to the $6,616 figure cited at the beginning of this section.

2-6b Present Value

Lucky you! You've just won $100,000 in your state lottery. You want to spend part of it now, but because you're 30 years old, you also want to use part of it for your retirement fund. Your goal is to accumulate $300,000 in the fund by the time you're age 55 (25 years from now). How much do you need to invest if you estimate that you can earn 5 percent annually on your investments during the next 25 years?

Using **present value**, the value today of an amount to be received in the future, you can calculate the answer. It represents the amount you'd have to invest today at a given interest rate over the

CALCULATOR

Inputs	Functions
45,000	FV
6	N
5	I
	CPT
	PMT
	Solution
	6,615.79

See Appendix E for details.

Sychugina/Shutterstock.com

specified time period to accumulate the future amount. The process of finding present value is called **discounting**, which is the inverse of *compounding* to find future value.

Present Value of a Single Amount

Assuming that you wish to create the retirement fund (future value) by

present value the value today of an amount to be received in the future; it's the amount that would have to be invested today at a given interest rate over a specified time period to accumulate the future amount

discounting the process of finding present value; the inverse of *compounding* to find future value

EXAMPLE: Calculating the Present Value of a Single Amount You want to have a retirement fund of $300,000 in 25 years by making a lump-sum deposit today that will earn 5 percent a year. Appendix C provides a present value factor of 0.295. Your deposit will be:

$$\text{Present value} = \$300,000 \times 0.295$$
$$= \$88,500$$

making a single, lump-sum deposit today, you can use this formula to find the amount that you need to deposit:

$$\text{Present value} = \text{Future value}$$
$$\times \text{Present value factor}$$

Tables of present value factors make this calculation easy (see Appendix C).

As shown in the calculator box, the $88,500 is the amount you'd have to deposit today into an account paying 5 percent annual interest in order to accumulate $300,000 at the end of 25 years.

Present Value of an Annuity You can also use present value techniques to determine how much you can withdraw from your retirement fund each year over a specified time horizon. This calls for the *present value annuity factor.* Assume that at age 55, you want to begin making equal annual withdrawals over the next 30 years from your $300,000 retirement fund. At first, you might think you could withdraw $10,000 per year ($300,000/30 years). However, the funds still on deposit would continue to earn 5 percent annual interest. To find the amount of the equal annual withdrawal, you again need to consider the time value of money. Specifically, you would use this formula:

$$\text{Annual withdrawal} = \frac{\text{Initial deposit}}{\text{Present value annuity factor}}$$

Therefore, you can withdraw $19,514.73 each year for 30 years. This value is clearly much larger than the $10,000 annual withdrawal mentioned earlier.

CALCULATOR

Inputs	Functions
300,000	FV
25	N
5	I
	CPT
	PV
	Solution
	88,590.83

See Appendix E for details.

TIMELINE

End of Year

Time value allows you to place monetary values on long-term financial goals.

TIMELINE

End of Year

EXAMPLE: Calculating the Present Value of an Annuity You've successfully accumulated $300,000 for retirement and want to make equal annual withdrawals over the next 30 years while earning 5 percent. Using the present value annuity factor of 15.373 in Appendix D, the equal annual withdrawal is:

$$\text{Annual withdrawal} = \$30,000/15.372$$
$$= \$19,514.73$$

Other Applications of Present Value
You can also use present value techniques to analyze investments. Suppose you have an opportunity to purchase an annuity investment that promises to pay $700 per year for five years. You know that you'll

CALCULATOR

Inputs	Functions
300,000	PV
30	N
5	I
	CPT
	PMT
	Solution
	19,515.43

See Appendix E for details.

receive a total of $3,500 ($700 × 5) over the five-year period. However, you wish to earn a minimum annual return of 5 percent on your investments. What's the most you should pay for this annuity today? You can answer this question by rearranging the terms in the formula to get:

Initial deposit = Annual withdrawal
　　　　　　　× Present value annuity factor

Adapting the equation to this situation, "initial deposit" represents the maximum price to pay for the annuity, and "annual withdrawal" represents the annual annuity payment of $700.

EXAMPLE: Determining the Value of an Investment What should you be willing to pay up front for an investment that will pay $700 a year for 5 years when you want to earn at least a 5 percent return?

This is calculated as the present value of an annuity, which Appendix D shows to have a factor of 4.329.

Initial deposit = $700 × 4.329 = $3,030.30

The most you should pay for the $700, five-year annuity, given your 5 percent annual return, is about $3,030. At this price, you'd earn 5 percent on the investment.

Using the present value concept, you can easily determine the present value of a sum to be received in the future, equal annual future withdrawals available from an initial deposit, and the initial deposit that would generate a given stream of equal annual withdrawals. These procedures, like future value concepts, allow you to place monetary values on long-term financial goals.

CALCULATOR

Inputs	Functions
700	PMT
5	N
5	I
	CPT
	PV
	Solution
	3,030.63

See Appendix E for details.

PLANNING OVER A LIFETIME

Budgeting

While budgeting is important across all stages of the life cycle, here are some key considerations in each stage.

PRE-FAMILY INDEPENDENCE: 20s

▸ Develop financial record-keeping system.

▸ Develop a budget and carefully track expenses.

▸ Budget savings each month and build up an emergency fund.

▸ Develop personal balance sheet, income statement, and calculate net worth at least annually.

▸ Develop short-, medium-, and long-term financial goals.

FAMILY FORMATION/CAREER DEVELOPMENT: 30–45

▸ Revise budget in light of family and career financial changes.

▸ Budget amount for children's education.

▸ Determine and set aside retirement contribution.

▸ Spend to meet previously determined short- and medium-term financial goals.

▸ Update personal balance sheet, income statement, and calculate net worth at least annually.

PRE-RETIREMENT: 45–65

▸ Revise budget to reflect typically higher income relative to expenses.

▸ Evaluate projected expenses and housing for retirement planning.

▸ More aggressively budget to increase retirement contributions.

▸ Spend to meet previously determined medium-term financial goals.

▸ Update personal balance sheet, income statement, and calculate net worth least annually.

RETIREMENT: 65 AND BEYOND

▸ Revise budget to adapt to retirement living expenses, health costs, insurance needs and income.

▸ Draw on retirement income sources and accumulated assets.

▸ Spend to meet previously determined long-term financial goals.

▸ Update personal balance sheet, income statement, and calculate net worth at least annually.

No Budget, No Plan: Jude Bought a Boat!

Jude, 28, has a good job as a sales rep. He's always found budgeting boring and has been intending to start a financial plan for years.

Recently, Jude went fishing with some friends on a rented boat and had a great time. He stopped at a boat sale on his way home. Before he knew it, a salesman had convinced Jude that the sale was just too good to pass up. So Jude bought a $10,000 boat and financed 80 percent of the cost for the next five years. He now finds himself relying on his credit card to get by each month.

What if Jude had kept track of his money, used a budget, and had a set of financial goals? Knowing where his money went and having a financial plan would have increased the chance that Jude would have made a more deliberate, informed financial decision.

Iakov Filimonov/Shutterstock.com

STUDY TOOLS 2

LOCATED AT BACK OF THE TEXTBOOK
☐ Chapter Review Card

LOCATED AT WWW.CENGAGE.COM/LOGIN
☐ Review Key Term flashcards and create your own cards.
☐ Track your knowledge and understanding of key concepts in personal finance.

☐ Complete practice and graded quizzes to prepare for tests.
☐ Complete interactive content at PFIN6 Online.
☐ View the chapter highlight boxes at PFIN6 Online.

©viphotos/Shutterstock140785408

LO2, 3 **1.** **Preparing financial statements.** Daniel Hernandez is preparing his balance sheet and income and expense statement for the year ending December 31, 2017. He is having difficulty classifying six items and asks for your help. Which, if any, of the following transactions are assets, liabilities, income, or expense items?

a. Daniel rents a house for $1,350 a month.

b. On June 21, 2017 Daniel bought diamond earrings for his wife and charged them using his MasterCard. The earrings cost $900, but he hasn't yet received the bill.

c. Daniel borrowed $3,500 from his parents last fall, but so far, he has made no payments to them.

d. Daniel makes monthly payments of $225 on an installment loan; about half of it is interest, and the balance is repayment of principal. He has 20 payments left, totaling $4,500.

e. Daniel paid $3,800 in taxes during the year and is due a tax refund of $650, which he hasn't yet received.

f. Daniel invested $2,300 in some common stock.

g. Daniel's Aunt Rose gave him a birthday gift of $300.

LO2, 4 **2.** **Preparing personal balance sheet. Use Worksheet 2.1.** Ella Campbell's banker has asked her to submit a personal balance sheet as of June 30, 2017, in support of an application for a $6,000 home improvement loan. She comes to you for help in preparing it. So far, she has made the following list of her assets and liabilities as of June 30, 2017:

	Asset/Liability	Sub-total
Cash on hand	$70	
Balance in checking account	180	
Balance in money market deposit account with Southwest Savings	650	900
Bills outstanding:		
Telephone	$20	
Electricity	70	
Charge account balance	190	
Visa	180	
MasterCard	220	
Taxes	400	
Insurance	220	$1,300
Condo and property		68,000
Condo mortgage loan		52,000
Automobile: 2013 Honda Civic		12,380
Installment loan balances:		
Auto loans	3,000	
Furniture loan	500	3,500

	Asset/Liability	Sub-total
Personal property:		
Furniture	1,050	
Clothing	900	1,950
Investments:		
U.S. government savings bonds	500	
Stock of Delta Corp.	3,000	3,500

From the data given, prepare Ella Campbell's balance sheet, dated June 30, 2017 (follow the balance sheet form shown in Worksheet 2.1). Then evaluate her balance sheet relative to the following factors: (a) solvency, (b) liquidity, and (c) equity in her dominant asset.

LO3 3. Preparing personal income and expense statement. *Use Worksheet 2.2.* Ivy and Jack Davis are about to construct their income and expense statement for the year ending December 31, 2017. Ivy works full time while Jack is finishing up graduate school. They have put together the following income and expense information for 2017:

Ivy's salary	$47,000
Reimbursement for travel expenses	1,950
Interest on:	
Savings account	110
Bonds of Gamma Corporation	70
Groceries	4,150
Rent	9,600
Utilities	960
Gas and auto expenses	650
Jack's tuition, books, and supplies	3,300
Books, magazines, and periodicals	280
Clothing and other miscellaneous expenses	2,700
Cost of photographic equipment purchased with charge card	2,200
Amount paid this year on photographic equipment	1,600
Ivy's travel expenses	1,950
Purchase of a used car (cost)	9,750
Outstanding loan balance on car	7,300
Purchase of bonds in Gamma Corporation	4,900

Using the information provided, prepare an income and expense statement for the Davis' for the year ending December 31, 2017 (follow the form shown in Worksheet 2.2).

LO5 4. Preparing cash budget. Lucas and Emma Mendoza are preparing their 2018 cash budget. Help the Mendozas reconcile the following differences, giving reasons to support your answers.

a.   Their only source of income is Lucas' salary, which amounts to $5,000 a month before taxes. Emma wants to show the $5,000 as their monthly income, whereas Emma argues that his take-home pay of $3,917 is the correct value to show.

b.   Emma wants to make a provision for *fun money*, an idea that Lucas doesn't understand. He asks, "Why do we need fun money when everything is provided for in the budget?"

LO6   5.   **Calculating present and future values.** Use future or present value techniques to solve the following problems.

a.   If you inherited $45,000 today and invested all of it in a security that paid a 7 percent rate of return, how much would you have in 25 years?

b.   If the average new home costs $275,000 today, how much will it cost in 10 years if the price increases by 5 percent each year?

c.   You think that in 15 years, it will cost $214,000 to provide your child with a 4-year college education. Will you have enough if you take $75,000 *today* and invest it for the next 15 years at 4 percent?

d.   If you can earn 4 percent, how much will you have to save *each year* if you want to retire in 35 years with $1 million?

LO6   6.   **Funding a retirement goal.** Owen Freeman wishes to have $800,000 in a retirement fund 20 years from now. He can create the retirement fund by making a single lump-sum deposit today.

a.   If upon retirement in 20 years, Owen plans to invest $800,000 in a fund that earns 4 percent, what is the maximum annual withdrawal he can make over the following 15 years?

b.   How much would Owen need to have on deposit at retirement in order to withdraw $35,000 annually over the 15 years if the retirement fund earns 4 percent?

c.   To achieve his annual withdrawal goal of $35,000 calculated in part b, how much more than the amount calculated in part a must Owen deposit today in an investment earning 4 percent annual interest?

3 | Preparing Your Taxes

LEARNING OBJECTIVES

After studying this chapter, you will be able to...

LO1 Discuss the basic principles of income taxes and determine your filing status.

LO2 Describe the sources of gross income and adjustments to income, differentiate between standard and itemized deductions and exemptions, and calculate taxable income.

LO3 Prepare a basic tax return using the appropriate tax forms and rate schedules.

LO4 Explain who needs to pay estimated taxes, when to file or amend your return, and how to handle an audit.

LO5 Know where to get help with your taxes and how software can make tax return preparation easier.

LO6 Implement an effective tax planning strategy.

After you finish this chapter go to **PAGE 80** for **STUDY TOOLS**

Eleanor Ivins/Getty Images

How Will This Affect Me? There's an old joke that people who complain about taxes can be divided into two groups: men and women. This chapter helps you pursue the tax-planning goal of maximizing the money that you get to keep by legally minimizing the taxes you have to pay. Income, various adjustments to income, deductions, and credits are considered in computing taxes. The chapter walks through the steps in completing representative tax returns. The impact of Social Security taxes and tax shelters are considered. And a framework for choosing a professional tax preparer or tax preparation software is provided. After reading this chapter you should be able to prepare your own taxes or to better understand and evaluate how your taxes are prepared by software or a tax professional.

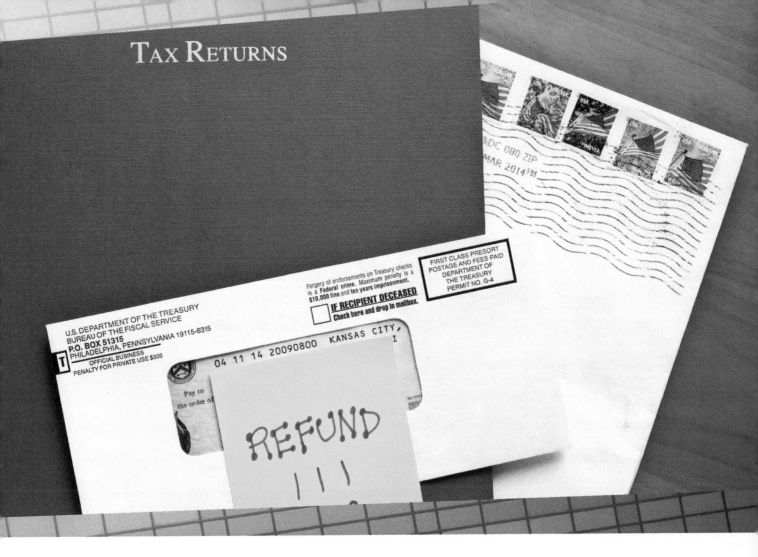

TAX RETURNS

3-1 UNDERSTANDING FEDERAL INCOME TAX PRINCIPLES

LO1 Taxes are dues that we pay for membership in our society; they're a cost of living in this country. Federal, state, and local tax receipts fund government activities and a wide variety of public services, from national defense to local libraries. Administering and enforcing federal tax laws is the responsibility of the Internal Revenue Service (IRS), a part of the U.S. Department of Treasury.

Because federal income tax is generally the largest tax you'll pay, you are wise to make tax planning an important part of personal financial planning. A typical American family currently pays *more than one-third of its gross income in taxes:* federal income and Social Security taxes as well as numerous state and local income,

> The overriding objective of tax planning is to maximize the amount of money you can keep by legally minimizing the amount of taxes you pay.

sales, and property taxes. You should make tax planning a year-round activity and always consider tax consequences when preparing and revising your financial plans and making major financial decisions.

The overriding objective of tax planning is *to maximize the amount of money you can keep by legally minimizing the amount of taxes you pay.* As long as it's done honestly and within the tax codes, there is nothing unethical or illegal about trying to minimize your tax bill. Here we concentrate on *income taxes paid by individuals*—particularly the federal income tax, the largest and most important tax for most taxpayers. To give you a good understanding of your future tax situation, we use a mid-career couple to demonstrate the key aspects of individual taxation.

taxes the dues paid for membership in our society; the cost of living in this country

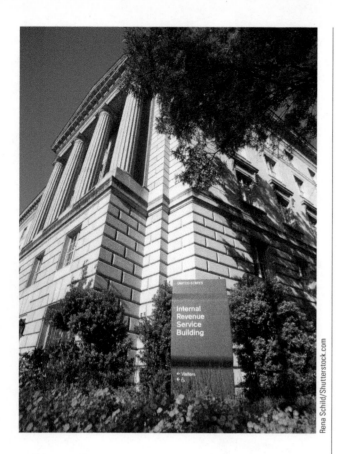

Rena Schild/Shutterstock.com

In addition to federal income tax, there are other forms of taxes to contend with—for example, federal self-employment taxes and state and local sales, income, property, and license taxes. Thus, a person saving to

purchase a new automobile costing $25,000 should realize that the state and local sales taxes, as well as the cost of license plates and registration, may add 10 percent or more to the total cost of the car.

Here we present key tax concepts and show how they apply to common situations. The tax tables, calculations, and sample tax returns presented in this chapter are based on the tax laws applicable to the calendar year 2015. *Although tax rates and other provisions will change, the basic procedures should remain the same.*

3-1a The Economics of Income Taxes

Income taxes are the major source of revenue for the federal government. Personal income taxes are scaled on progressive rates. To illustrate how this **progressive tax structure** works, consider the following data for *unmarried taxpayers* filing 2015 returns:

Taxable Income	Tax Rate (%)
$1 to $9,225	10
$9,226 to $37,450	15
$37,451 to $90,750	25
$90,751 to $189,300	28
$189,301 to $411,500	33
$411,501 to $413,200	35
Over $413,200	39.6

BEHAVIOR MATTERS

Do We Really Value Paying Taxes After All?

Surprisingly, your brain may like paying taxes! Recent research suggests that people can feel good about paying taxes that improve others' well-being. While most people would prefer to keep their money rather than pay taxes, paying taxes still is not the same thing as throwing the money away. Taxes can be viewed, even if only subconsciously, as a social good. And people don't like inequality and seek to preserve a positive self-image, which means that most are unlikely to cheat on their taxes. Interestingly, there is evidence that many people work harder when they realize that they will be taxed. In a recent experiment, participants worked harder when paid $100 and there was a $10 tax than when they were paid $90 with no taxes due.

So what could explain this? It's important for people to feel that their taxes actually do some good. When people clearly know what their taxes are used for—and if it appears to be for the common good—they can actually find paying taxes somewhat satisfying. This challenges governments everywhere to make their tax systems fully transparent and to explicitly show that the money is being spent in a positive way. Doing so makes sense in a democracy and creates the right incentives for taxpayers.

Source: Adapted from Patrick Temple-West, "Surprise, Your Brain Might Value Paying Taxes," http://blogs.reuters.com/unstructuredfinance /2012/04/02/surprise-your-brain-might-value-paying-taxes, accessed September 2016, based on a research article by Iwan Djanali and Damien Sheehan-Connor, "Tax affinity hypothesis: Do we really hate paying taxes"? *Journal of Economic Psychology*, August 2012.

Name	Taxable Income	Tax Calculation		Tax Liability
Jack	$50,000	= [($50,000 − $37,450) × 0.25]		
		+ [($37,450 − $9,225) × 0.15]		
		+ [$9,225 × 0.10]		
		= $3,137.50 + $4,233.75 + $922.50 =		$8,293.75
Dan	$100,000	= [($100,000 − $90,750) × 0.28]		
		+ [($90,750 − $37,450) × 0.25]		
		+ [($37,450 − $9,225) × 0.15]		
		+ $9,225 × 0.10]		
		= $2,590 + $13,325 + $4,233.75 + $922.50 =		$21,071.25

Of course, any nontaxable income can be viewed as being in the 0 percent tax bracket. As taxable income moves from a lower to a higher bracket, the higher rate applies *only to the additional taxable income in that bracket* and not to the entire taxable income. For example, consider two single brothers, Jack and Dan, whose taxable incomes are $50,000 and $100,000, respectively (see table above).

Note that Jack pays the 25 percent rate only on that portion of the $50,000 in taxable income that exceeds $37,450. Because this rate is progressive, the more money you make, the progressively higher is the marginal tax rate, although Dan's taxable income is twice that of Jack's, his income tax is two-and-a-half times higher than his brother's.

The tax rate for each bracket—10 percent, 15 percent, 25 percent, 28 percent, 33 percent, 35 percent, and 39.6 percent—is called the **marginal tax rate**, or the rate applied to the next dollar of taxable income. When you relate the tax liability to the level of taxable income earned, the tax rate, called the **average tax rate**, drops considerably. Jack's average tax rate, calculated by dividing the tax liability by taxable income, is about 16.6 percent

($8,293.75/$50,000.00). Dan's average tax rate is about 21.1 percent ($21,071.25/100,000). While tax rates are progressive, the *average* size of the bite is not as bad as the stated *marginal* tax rates might suggest.

3-1b Your Filing Status

The taxes you pay depend in part on your *filing status*, which is based on your marital status and family situation on the last day of your tax year (usually December 31). There are five different filing status categories:

▶ **Single taxpayers:** Unmarried or legally separated from their spouses by either a separation or final divorce decree.

▶ **Married filing jointly:** Married couples who combine their income and allowable deductions and file one tax return.

▶ **Married filing separately:** Each spouse files his or her own return, reporting only his or her income, deductions, and exemptions.

▶ **Head of household:** A taxpayer who is unmarried and pays more than half of the cost of keeping up a home for himself or herself and an eligible dependent child or relative.

▶ **Qualifying widow or widower with dependent child:** A person whose spouse died within

income taxes a type of tax levied on taxable income by the federal government and by many state and local governments

progressive tax structure a tax structure in which the larger the amount of taxable income, the higher the rate at which it is taxed

marginal tax rate the tax rate you pay on the next dollar of taxable income

average tax rate the rate at which each dollar of taxable income is taxed on average; calculated by dividing the tax liability by taxable income

Go to Smart Sites

How long does the average American have to work this year to pay federal, state, and local taxes? Find this year's date of "Tax Freedom Day" at the Tax Foundation Internet site. You'll also find information there about tax policy, tax rates, tax collections, and the economics of taxation. A highlight box in each chapter of PFIN Online includes "Smart Sites," a list of resources and sites that offer additional information on topics in the PFIN text.

two years of the tax year (e.g., in 2013 or 2014 for the 2015 tax year) and who supports a dependent child may use joint return tax rates and is eligible for the highest standard deduction.

Every individual or married couple who earns a specified level of income is required to file a tax return. For example, for those under 65, a single person who earned more than $10,300 and a married couple with a combined income of more than $20,600 must file a tax return (for 2015). (Note, the filing threshold is determined by adding the personal exemption to the standard deduction.) Like the personal tax rates, these minimums are adjusted annually based on the annual rate of inflation. Regardless, even if your income falls below the current minimum level, you must file a tax return in order to receive a refund of any income tax withheld during the year.

3-1c Your Take-Home Pay

Most of us actually pay taxes as we earn income throughout the year. Under this *pay-as-you-go* system, your employer withholds (deducts) a portion of your income every pay period and sends it to the IRS to be credited to your own tax account. Self-employed people must also prepay their taxes by forwarding part of their income to the IRS at four dates each year, which are referred to as quarterly estimated tax payments. After the close of the taxable year, you calculate the actual taxes you owe and file your tax return. When you file, you receive full credit for the amount of taxes withheld (including estimated tax payments) from your income during the year and either (1) receive a refund from the IRS (if too much tax was withheld from your paycheck and/ or prepaid in estimated taxes) or (2) have to pay additional taxes (if the amount withheld/prepaid didn't cover your tax liability).

Your employer normally withholds funds not only for federal income taxes but also for FICA (Social Security and Medicare) taxes and, if applicable, state and local income taxes (which may be deductible on federal returns). Other payroll deductions include life and health insurance, savings plans, retirement programs, professional or union dues, and charitable contributions—all of which lower your take-home pay. Your *take-home pay* is what you're left with after subtracting the amount withheld from your *gross earnings*.

> Your *take-home pay* is what you're left with after subtracting the amount withheld from your *gross earnings*.

Federal Withholding Taxes The amount of **federal withholding taxes** deducted from your gross earnings each pay period depends on both the level of your earnings and the number of withholding allowances you have claimed on a form called a *W-4*, which you must complete for your employer. Withholding allowances reduce the amount of taxes withheld from your income. A taxpayer is entitled to one allowance for himself or herself, one for a nonworking spouse (if filing jointly), and one for each dependent claimed (children or parents being supported mainly by the taxpayers). In addition, you may qualify for a *special allowance* or *additional withholding allowances* under certain circumstances. Taxpayers may have to change their withholding allowances during the tax year if their employment or marital status changes.

FICA and Other Withholding Taxes All employed workers (except certain federal employees) must pay a combined old-age, survivor's, disability, and hospital insurance tax under provisions of the **Federal Insurance Contributions Act (FICA)**. Known more commonly as the **Social Security tax**, it is paid equally by employer and

federal withholding taxes taxes based on the level of earnings and the number of withholding allowances claimed, which an employer deducts from the employee's gross earnings each pay period

Federal Insurance Contributions Act (FICA) or social Security tax the law establishing the combined old-age, survivor's, disability, and hospital insurance tax levied on both employer and employee

Earnings Information	Current	Year to Date
M /02		
...nal Gross	4,389.30	
...uctions	0.00	
...itions	0.00	
...rtime	0.00	
EARNINGS TOTAL	4,389.30	5,277.30
	351.14	418.18
-Taxable Gross	3,971.12	4,859.12
...able Gross		

Statutory & Other Deductions	Current	Year to Date
...eral Withholding	311.17	311.17
...itional Federal Withholding	0.00	*****
...ate Withholding	135.96	135.96
...itional State Withholding	0.00	*****
SDI	0.00	55.06
...icare	62.67	75.55
...icare Buyout	0.00	0.00
...ate Disability Insurance	0.00	0.00
RS	351.14	351.14
RS	0.00	0.00
...rnate Retirement	67.04	0.00

Josh randall/Shutterstock.com

employee. In 2015, the total Social Security tax rate was 15.3 percent, allocating 12.4 percent to Social Security and 2.9 percent to Medicare. The 12.4 percent applies only to the first $118,500 of an employee's earnings (this number rises with national average wages), whereas the Medicare component is paid on all wages. In 2015, self-employed people paid the full 15.3 percent tax but could deduct 50 percent of it on their tax returns.

Most states have their own income taxes, which differ from state to state. Some cities assess income taxes as well. These state and local income taxes will also be withheld from earnings. They are deductible on federal returns, but deductibility of federal taxes on the state or local return depends on state and local laws.

3-2 IT'S TAXABLE INCOME THAT MATTERS

LO2 Calculating your income taxes involves several steps and many computations. Exhibit 3.1 depicts the procedure to compute your **taxable income** and total tax liability. It looks simple enough—just subtract certain adjustments from your gross income to get your adjusted gross income; then subtract either the standard deduction or your itemized deductions and your total personal exemptions to get taxable income. And finally, compute your taxes, subtract any tax credits from that amount, and add any other taxes to it to get your total tax liability. This isn't as easy as it sounds, however! As we'll see, some problems can arise in determining what you may subtract.

3-2a Gross Income

Gross income essentially includes any and all income subject to federal taxes. Here are some common sources of gross income:

- Wages and salaries
- Bonuses, commissions, and tips
- Interest and dividends received
- Alimony received
- Business and farm income
- Gains from the sale of assets
- Income from pensions and annuities
- Income from rents and partnerships
- Prizes, lottery, and gambling winnings

In addition to these sources of income, others—such as child-support payments and municipal bond interest—are considered *tax exempt* and as such are excluded (totally or partially) from gross income.

Three Kinds of Income Individual income falls into one of three basic categories:

- **Active income:** Income *earned* on the job, such as wages and salaries, bonuses, and tips; also includes most other forms of *noninvestment* income, such as pension income and alimony
- **Portfolio income:** Earnings—interest, dividends, and capital gains (profits on the sale of investments)—generated from most types of investment holdings; includes savings accounts, stocks, bonds, mutual funds, options, and futures
- **Passive income:** A special category that includes income derived from real estate, limited partnerships, and other forms of tax shelters

These categories limit the amount of deductions and write-offs that taxpayers can take. Specifically, the amount of allowable, deductible expenses associated with portfolio and passive income *is limited to the amount of income derived from these two sources.* For deduction purposes, you cannot combine portfolio and passive income with each other or with active income. *Investment-related expenses can be used only with portfolio income*, and with a few exceptions, *passive investment expenses can be used only to offset the income from passive investments.* All the other allowances and deductions that we'll describe later are written off against the total amount of *active* income the taxpayer generates.

Capital Gains Technically, a *capital gain* occurs whenever a capital asset (such as a stock, a bond, or real estate) is sold for more than its original cost. So, if you purchased stock for $50 per share and sold it for $60, you'd have a capital gain of $10 per share.

Capital gains are taxed at different rates, depending on the holding period. Exhibit 3.2 shows the different holding periods and applicable tax rates based on the 2015 tax brackets.

The IRS imposes some restrictions on the amount of capital losses taxpayers can take in a given year. Specifically, a taxpayer can write off

taxable income the amount of income subject to taxes; it is calculated by subtracting adjustments, the larger of itemized or standard deductions, and exemptions from gross income

gross income the total of all of a taxpayer's income (before any adjustments, deductions, or exemptions) subject to federal taxes; it includes active, portfolio, and passive income

Exhibit 3.1

Calculating Your Taxable Income and Total Tax Liability Owed

To find taxable income, you must first subtract all adjustments to gross income and then subtract deductions and personal exemptions. Your total tax liability owed includes tax on this taxable income amount, less any tax credits, plus other taxes owed.

capital losses, dollar for dollar, against any capital gains. After that, he or she can write off a maximum of $3,000 in additional capital losses against active income. Thus, if a taxpayer had $10,000 in capital gains and $18,000 in capital losses in 2015 only $13,000 could be written off on 2015 taxes: $10,000 against the capital gains generated in 2015 and another $3,000 against active income. The remainder—$5,000 in this case—will have to be written off in later years, in the same order as just indicated: first against any capital gains and then up to $3,000 against ordinary (i.e., noncapital) income.

Selling Your Home: A Special Case Homeowners receive special tax treatment on the sale of a home. Single taxpayers can exclude from income the first $250,000 of gain ($500,000 for married taxpayers) on

Exhibit 3.2

Capital Gains Tax Categories as of 2015

Capital gains tax rates are as low as 0 percent for low-income levels or 20 percent for higher-income levels, as long as the holding period is over 12 months.

Holding Period	Tax Brackets/Assets Sold (2015)	Tax on Capital Gains
Less than 12 months	All (10%, 15%, 25%, 28%, 33%, 35%, and 39.6%) — any asset sold	Same as ordinary income
Over 12 months	10%, 15% — assets other than real estate and collectibles	0%
	25%, 28%, 33%, 35%, 39.6% — assets other than real estate and collectibles	15% or 20% (later rate only if in 39.6% tax bracket)
	Sale of depreciable real estate	25% on gain up to depreciation amount
	Collectibles	28% on all gains from collectibles

Go to Smart Sites

Fairmark Press offers a *Guide to Capital Gains and Losses* to help you understand the tax treatment of securities sales. It's just one of many tax guides you'll find at the site's *Tax Guide for Investors*.

the sale of a principal residence. To qualify, the taxpayer must own and occupy the residence as a principal residence for at least two of the five years prior to the sale. For example, the Jacksons (married taxpayers) just sold their principal residence for $475,000, which they purchased four years earlier for $325,000. They may exclude their $150,000 gain ($475,000 − $325,000) from their income because they occupied the residence for more than two years, and the gain is less than $500,000.

This exclusion is available on only one sale every two years. A loss on the sale of a principal residence is not deductible. Generally speaking, this law is quite favorable to homeowners.

3-2b Adjustments to (Gross) Income

Now that you've totaled your gross income, you can deduct your **adjustments to (gross) income**. These are allowable deductions from gross income, including certain employee, personal retirement, insurance, and support expenses. Most of these deductions relate to earning income. Here are some items that can be treated as adjustments to income:

- ▶ Educator expenses (limited)
- ▶ Higher education tuition costs (limited)
- ▶ IRA contributions (limited)
- ▶ Self-employment taxes paid (limited to 50 percent of the amount paid)
- ▶ Self-employed health insurance payments
- ▶ Penalty on early withdrawal of savings
- ▶ Alimony paid
- ▶ Reimbursed moving expenses (some limits)

[*Note:* The limitations on deductions for self-directed retirement plans, such as individual retirement accounts (IRAs) and Simplified Employee Pensions (SEPs), are discussed in Chapter 14.]

After subtracting the total of all allowable adjustments to income from your gross income, you're left with **adjusted gross income (AGI)**. AGI is an important value, because it's used to calculate limits for certain itemized deductions.

3-2c Deductions: Standard or Itemized?

As shown in Exhibit 3.1, the next step in calculating your taxes is to subtract allowable deductions from your AGI. This may be the most complex part of

adjustments to (gross) income allowable deductions from gross income, including certain employee, personal, retirement, insurance, and support expenses

adjusted gross income (AGI) the amount of income remaining after subtracting all allowable adjustments to income from gross income

Financial Planning Tips

It is all too common for some taxpayers to overlook tax deductions and credits that would decrease their tax bill. While there are qualifications and limitations on these tax deductions and credits, it's worth your time to be aware of these opportunities.

- **Medical travel expenses.** The costs of traveling to visit health care providers to receive medical care are deductible if the visits are recommended by a doctor. There is a standard mileage deduction (23 cents per mile in 2015) if you drive, and you can deduct direct expenses like taxis, parking fees, and tolls.

- **Health insurance and medical expenses.** Health insurance premiums are deductible—and that includes long-term-care insurance. Similarly, the cost of prescriptions and separate charges for medical coverage included in a dependent child's college fees are deductible. Medical bills that you pay for a person who is your dependent are also deductible.

- **Real estate taxes and home sale costs.** Real estate taxes paid are deductible, as are any "point" fees associated with a mortgage. Annual maintenance fees

for a condo also may be deducted because they are your share of the overall property's real estate taxes.

- **Volunteer and donation-related expenses.** When you donate to a charity or volunteer your time, the associated expenses are tax-deductible. For example, if you donate cookies to be sold by a charity, you can deduct the cost of making them. Transportation costs (14 cents per mile in 2015) can also be deducted.

- **Job search expenses.** The costs associated with looking for a new job are generally deductible. So you can write off employment placement agency fees, resume printing costs, and related travel expenses.

- **Tax and investment-related expenses.** The expenses paid for preparing your tax return are deductible. Further, any expenses associated with managing your investments are generally deductible. For example, you can write off financial advisors' fees and investment publication subscription costs.

- **College tuition tax credit.** You can get up to a $2,500 tax credit in college tuition for family members if your adjusted gross income falls within certain limits.

---

the tax preparation process. You have two options: take the *standard deduction*, a fixed amount that depends on your filing status, or list your *itemized deductions* (specified tax-deductible personal expenses). Obviously, you should use the method that results in larger allowable deductions.

Standard Deduction Instead of itemizing personal deductions, a taxpayer can take the standard deduction, which varies depending on the taxpayer's filing status (single, married filing jointly, and so on), age (65 or older), and vision (blind). The standard deduction is taken in place of itemizing deductions if it is larger than the itemized deductions. In 2015, the standard deduction for single filers was $6,300, and for married people filing jointly it was $12,600. Those over 65 and those who are blind are eligible for an

additional deduction for both age and blindness. For example, if a single taxpayer is over 65 and blind, the standard deduction is $9,400. The standard deduction amounts are usually adjusted annually to any changes in the cost of living.

Itemized Deductions Itemized deductions allow taxpayers to reduce their AGI by the amount of their allowable personal expenditures. Some of the more common ones allowed by the IRS include:

▶ Medical and dental expenses (*in excess* of 10 percent of AGI for those under the age of 65.)

▶ State, local, and foreign income (or state sales tax, if greater) and property taxes; state and local personal property taxes

▶ Residential mortgage interest and investment interest (limited)

▶ Charitable contributions (limited to 50 percent, 30 percent, or 20 percent of AGI depending on certain factors). Direct transfers from an IRA trustee to a charity

standard deduction a deduction that depends on the taxpayer's filing status, age, and vision and that can be taken by a taxpayer whose total itemized deductions are relatively small

itemized deductions personal expenditures that can be deducted from AGI when determining taxable income are not included in income and are not deductible as charitable contributions.

▶ Casualty and theft losses that are uninsured (in excess of 10 percent of AGI; reduced by $100 per loss)

▶ Job, investment, and other expenses (in excess of 2 percent of AGI)

▶ Moving expenses (some restrictions; also reimbursed expenses are deductible for those who don't itemize)

Choosing the Best Option Your decision to take the standard deduction or itemize deductions may change over time. Taxpayers who find they've chosen the wrong option and paid too much may recalculate their tax using the other method and file an *amended return (Form 1040X)* to claim a refund for the difference. For example, suppose you computed and paid your taxes, which amounted to $2,450, using the standard deduction. A few months later you discover that, had you itemized your deductions, your taxes would have been only $1,950. Using the appropriate forms, you can file for a $500 refund ($2,450 − $1,950). To avoid having to file an amended return, it is best to estimate your deductions using both the standard and itemized deduction amounts and then choose the one that results in lower taxes.

3-2d Exemptions

Deductions from AGI based on the number of persons supported by the taxpayer's income are called **exemptions**. A taxpayer can claim an exemption for himself or herself, his or her spouse, and any *dependents*. A dependent must be either a qualified child or a qualified relative. A major requirement for a qualified child is the age test—a child must be younger than 18 or, if a full-time student, 24. The major requirements to be considered a qualified relative are the support test, wherein the taxpayer must provide more than half of the relative's total support, and the gross income test—gross income must be less than the amount of the exemption.

All dependents must have a Social Security number, which can be a problem in the year of adoption for parents of adopted children. So a college student, for example, could be 20 years old and still be claimed as an exemption by her parents, so long as all other dependency requirements are met. In 2015, each exemption claimed was worth $4,000, an amount tied to the cost of living and adjusted annually.

A personal exemption can be claimed only once. If a child is *eligible* to be claimed as an exemption by her parents, then she doesn't have the choice of using a personal exemption on her own tax return regardless of whether the parents use her exemption.

In 2015, a family of four could take total exemptions of $16,000—that is, 4 × $4,000. Subtracting the amount claimed for itemized deductions (or the standard deduction) and exemptions from AGI results in the amount of *taxable income*, which is the basis on which taxes are calculated. A taxpayer who makes $50,000 a year may have only, say, $25,000 in taxable income after adjustments, deductions, and exemptions. It is the *lower*, taxable income figure that determines how much tax an individual must pay.

3-3 CALCULATING AND FILING YOUR TAXES

LO3 To calculate the amount of taxable income, we consider: (1) tax rates, (2) tax credits, (3) tax forms and schedules, and (4) the procedures for determining tax liability.

3-3a Tax Rates

The amount of *taxable income* is determined by subtracting itemized deductions (or the standard deduction for non-itemizers) *and* personal exemptions from AGI. *Both itemizers and nonitemizers* use this procedure, which is a key calculation in determining your tax liability. It is *reported taxable income* that determines the amount of income subject to federal income taxes. Once you know the amount of your taxable income, you can refer to *tax rate tables* (or to the *tax rate schedules* if taxable income is greater than $100,000) to find the amount of taxes you owe.

Tax rates vary not only with the amount of reported taxable income but also with filing status. Thus, different tax rate schedules apply to each filing category; four schedules are shown in Exhibit 3.3. The vast majority of taxpayers fall into the first three brackets and are subject to tax rates of either 10 percent, 15 percent, or 25 percent.

To see how the tax rates in Exhibit 3.3 work, consider two single taxpayers: one has taxable income of

exemptions deductions from AGI based on the number of persons supported by the taxpayer's income

Exhibit 3.3

Sample Tax Rate Schedules

Tax rates levied on personal income vary with the amount of reported taxable income and the taxpayer's filing status.

2015 Tax Rate Schedules

Schedule X—If your filing status is **Single**

If your taxable income is: Over—	But not over—	The tax is:	of the amount over—
$0	$9,225	- - - - - - . 10%	$0
9,225	37,450	$922.50 + 15%	9,225
37,450	90,750	5,156.25 + 25%	37,450
90,750	189,300	18,481.25 + 28%	90,750
189,300	411,500	46,075.25 + 33%	189,300
411,500	413,200	119,401.25 + 35%	411,500
413,200	- - - - - -	119,996.25 + 39.6%	413,200

Schedule Y-1—If your filing status is **Married filing jointly** or **Qualifying widow(er)**

If your taxable income is: Over—	But not over—	The tax is:	of the amount over—
$0	$18,450	- - - - - - . 10%	$0
18,450	74,900	$1,845.00 + 15%	18,450
74,900	151,200	10,312.50 + 25%	74,900
151,200	230,450	29,387.50 + 28%	151,200
230,450	411,500	51,577.50 + 33%	230,450
411,500	464,850	111,324.00 + 35%	411,500
464,850	- - - - - -	129,996.50 + 39.6%	464,850

Schedule Y-2—If your filing status is **Married filing separately**

If your taxable income is: Over—	But not over—	The tax is:	of the amount over—
$0	$9,255	- - - - - - . 10%	$0
9,225	37,450	$922.50 + 15%	9,225
37,450	75,600	5,156.25 + 25%	37,450
75,600	115,225	14,693.75 + 28%	75,600
115,225	205,750	25,788.75 + 33%	115,225
205,750	232,425	55,662.00 + 35%	205,750
232,425	- - - - - -	64,998.25 + 39.6%	232,425

Schedule Z—If your filing status is **Head of household**

If your taxable income is: Over—	But not over—	The tax is:	of the amount over—
$0	$13,150	- - - - - - . 10%	$0
13,150	50,200	$1,315.00 + 15%	13,150
50,200	129,600	6,872.50 + 25%	50,200
129.600	209,850	26,722.50 + 28%	129.600
209,850	411,500	49,192.50 + 33%	209,850
411,500	439,000	115,737.00 + 35%	411,500
439,000	- - - - - -	125,362.00 + 39.6%	439,000

Source: Internal Revenue Service.

$12,500; the other, $38,600. Here's how we would calculate their respective tax liabilities:

▶ For taxable income of $12,500: $922.50 + [($12,500 − $9,225) × 0.15] = $922.50 + $491.25 = $1,413.75.

▶ For taxable income of $38,600: $5,156.25 + [($38,600 − $37,450) × 0.25] = $5,156.25 + $287.50 = $5,443.75

The income of $12,500 is partially ($9,225) taxed at the 10 percent rate and partially ($3,275) taxed at the 15 percent rate. The first $9,225 of the $38,600 is taxed at 10 percent, the next $28,225 at 15 percent, and the remaining $1,150 at 25 percent. Keep in mind that taxpayers use the same procedures at this point whether they itemize or not. To show how the amount of tax liability will vary with the level of taxable income, Exhibit 3.4 lists the taxes due on a range of taxable incomes, from $1,500 to $460,000 for individual and joint returns.

Returning to our example involving the taxpayer with an income of $38,600 we see that this individual had an average tax rate of 14.1 percent ($5,443.75/$38,600), which

photastic/Shutterstock.com

is considerably less than the stated tax rate of 25 percent. Actually, the 25 percent represents the taxpayer's *marginal tax rate*—the rate at which the next dollar of taxable income is taxed. Notice that the marginal 25 percent tax rate applies only to that portion of the single person's income that exceeds $36,900, which is $1,150 in this example.

Some taxpayers are subject to the *alternative minimum tax (AMT)*, currently 26 percent of the first $185,400 and 28 percent of the excess. A taxpayer's tax liability is the higher of the AMT or the regular tax. The AMT is designed to ensure that high-income taxpayers with many deductions and tax shelter investments that provide attractive tax write-offs are paying their fair share of taxes.

The AMT includes in alternative minimum taxable income certain types of deductions otherwise allowed, such as the personal exemption, state and local income and property taxes, miscellaneous itemized deductions, unreimbursed medical expenses, and depreciation. Therefore, taxpayers with moderate levels of taxable income, including those living in states with high tax rates and self-employed persons with depreciation deductions, may be subject to the AMT calculation and additional tax.

Exhibit 3.4

Taxable Income and the Amount of Income Taxes Due (2015)

Given the progressive tax structure used in this country, it follows that the larger your income, the more you can expect to pay in taxes.

| Taxable Income | Single Filing Status | | Married Filing Jointly Status | |
	Tax Due	Tax Rate	Tax Due	Tax Rate
$ 1,500	$ 150	10%	$ 150	10.0%
8,000	800	10.0%	800	10.0%
15,000	1,789	15.0%	1,500	10.0%
30,000	4,039	15.0%	3,578	15.0%
60,000	10,794	25.0%	8,078	15.0%
100,000	21,071	28.0%	16,588	25.0%
200,000	49,606	33.0%	43,052	28.0%
412,000	119,576	35.0%	111,499	35.0%
460,000	138,529	39.6%	128,299	35.0%

3-3b Tax Credits

After determining the amount of taxes you owe, some taxpayers are allowed to reduce their tax using **tax credits**. A tax credit is much more valuable than a deduction or an exemption because it directly reduces, dollar for dollar, the amount of *taxes due*, whereas a deduction or an exemption merely reduces the amount of *taxable income*. An often-used tax credit is the *child tax credit*. This credit is currently $1,000 per child under 17. An *adoption tax credit* of up to $13,400 is available in 2015 for the qualifying costs of adopting a child under age 18. Other common tax credits include: credit for the care of elderly or the disabled, foreign tax credit, credit for prior year minimum tax, retirement savings contribution credit, and credit for a qualified electric vehicle. To receive any of these credits, the taxpayer must file a return along with a separate schedule in support of the tax credit claimed.

 Go to Smart Sites

Need a tax form or instructions on how to fill it out? At the IRS Internet site you can download tax forms, instructions, IRS publications, and regulations. Once there, you can also click on "More Online Tools" to access the IRS withholding calculator—you can use it to make sure you aren't having too much or too little withheld from your paycheck.

3-3c Tax Forms and Schedules

The IRS requires taxpayers to file their returns using specified tax forms. These forms and various instruction booklets on how to prepare them are available to taxpayers free of charge. Tax forms and instructions can be downloaded from **www.irs.gov**. Check out the Bonus Exhibits at PFIN6 Online for a list of commonly used tax forms and schedules.

Variations of Form 1040 All individuals use some variation of *Form 1040* to file their tax returns and *Form 1040* may be used by *all* taxpayers. *Form 1040EZ* is a simple, one-page form. You qualify to use this form if you are single or married filing a joint return; under age 65 (both if filing jointly); not blind; do not claim any dependents; have taxable income of less than $100,000 from only wages, salaries, tips, or

tax credits deductions from a taxpayer's tax liability that directly reduce his or her *taxes due* (rather than reducing *taxable income*)

taxable scholarships or grants; have interest income of less than $1,500; and do not claim any adjustments to income, itemize deductions, or claim any tax credits other than the earned income credit.

Worksheet 3.1 shows the *Form 1040EZ* filed in 2015 by Mateo Castillo, a full-time graduate student under the age of 25 at State University. Keep in mind that the tax form only shows dollar amounts and not cents, which is permissible in filing the form with the IRS. His sources of income include a $12,500 scholarship, of which $4,900 was used for room and board; $7,600 earned from part-time and summer jobs; and $50 interest earned on a savings account deposit. Because scholarships used for tuition and fees are not taxed, he should include as income only the portion used for room and board. He had a total of $495 withheld for federal income taxes during the year. Although Mateo would also complete a Salaries & Wages Report form, it is omitted for simplicity because it lists only the $4,900 of his scholarship that went toward his room and board, his part-time income of $7,600, and the details of his withholdings.

To use *Form 1040A*, a two-page form, your income must be less than $100,000 and be derived only from specified sources. Using this form, you may deduct certain IRA contributions and claim certain tax credits, but you cannot itemize your deductions. If your income is over $100,000 or you itemize deductions, you must use the standard *Form 1040* along with any applicable schedules.

Despite detailed instructions that accompany the tax forms, taxpayers still make a lot of mistakes when filling them out. Common errors include missing information and arithmetic errors. So check and recheck your forms *before submitting them to the IRS*. Tax software to assist with computations is available free of charge at **www.irs.gov**.

3-3d The 2015 Tax Return of Luke and Claire Burns

Let's now put all the pieces of the tax preparation puzzle together to see how Luke and Claire Burns calculate and file their income taxes. The Burns family owns their home and are both 35 years old. Married for 11 years, they have three children—Caleb (age 9), Charles (age 7), and Hazel (age 3). Luke is a manager for an insurance company headquartered in their hometown. Claire works part-time as a sales clerk in a retail store. During 2015, Luke's salary totaled $60,415, while Claire earned $9,750. Luke's employer withheld taxes of $6,260, and Claire's withheld $1,150. During the year, the Burns family earned $800 in interest on a joint account and realized $1,250 in capital gains on the sale of securities that

Form 1040EZ is easy to use, and most of the instructions are printed on the form itself. Mateo Castillo qualifies to use it because he is single, under age 65, not blind, and meets its income and deduction restrictions.

Department of the Treasury–Internal Revenue Service

Form 1040EZ

Income Tax Return for Single and Joint Filers With No Dependents (99) **2015**

OMB No. 1545-0074

Your first name and initial	Last name	Your social security number
Mateo R.	Castillo	123-45-6789
If a joint return, spouse's first name and initial	Last name	Spouse's social security number

Home address (number and street). If you have a P.O. box, see instructions. Apt. no.

1000 University Drive

▲ Make sure the SSN(s) above are correct.

City, town or post office, state, and ZIP code. If you have a foreign address, also complete spaces below (see instructions).

Anytown, CA 94620

Foreign country name   Foreign province/state/county   Foreign postal code

Presidential Election Campaign
Check here if you, or your spouse if filing jointly, want $3 to go to this fund. Checking a box below will not change your tax or refund. ☐ You ☐ Spouse

Income

Attach Form(s) W-2 here.

Enclose, but do not attach, any payment.

1	Wages, salaries, and tips. This should be shown in box 1 of your Form(s) W-2. Attach your Form(s) W-2.	1	12,500.
2	Taxable interest. If the total is over $1,500, you cannot use Form 1040EZ.	2	50.
3	Unemployment compensation and Alaska Permanent Fund dividends (see instructions).	3	
4	Add lines 1, 2, and 3. This is your **adjusted gross income.**	4	12,550.
5	If someone can claim you (or your spouse if a joint return) as a dependent, check the applicable box(es) below and enter the amount from the worksheet on Page 2. ☐ You ☐ Spouse If no one can claim you (or your spouse if a joint return), enter $10,300 if **single;** $20,600 if **married filing jointly.** See instructions for explanation.	5	10,300.
6	Subtract line 5 from line 4. If line 5 is larger than line 4, enter -0-. This is your **taxable income.** ▶	6	2,250.

Payments, Credits, and Tax

7	Federal income tax withheld from Form(s) W-2 and 1099.	7	495.
8a	**Earned income credit (EIC)** (see instructions) NO	8a	
b	Nontaxable combat pay election. 8b		
9	Add lines 7 and 8a. These are your **total payments and credits.** ▶	9	495.
10	**Tax.** Use the amount on **line 6 above** to find your tax in the tax table in the instructions. Then, enter the tax from the table on this line.	10	226.
11	Health care: individual responsibility (see instructions) Full-year coverage ☐	11	
12	Add lines 10 and 11. This is your **total tax.**	12	226.

Refund

Have it directly deposited! See instructions and fill in 13b, 13c, and 13d or Form 8888.

13a	If line 9 is larger than line 12, subtract line 12 from line 9. This is your **refund.** If Form 8888 is attached, check here ▶ ☐	13a	269.
▶ b	Routing number	▶ c Type: ☐ Checking ☐ Savings	
▶ d	Account number		

Amount You Owe

14	If line 12 is larger than line 9, subtract line 9 from line 12. This is the **amount you owe.** For details on how to pay, see instructions. ▶	14	0.

Third Party Designee

Do you want to allow another person to discuss this return with the IRS (see instructions)? ☐ **Yes.** Complete below. ☐ **No**

Designee's name ▶   Phone no. ▶   Personal identification number (PIN) ▶

Sign Here

Joint return? See instructions.

Keep a copy for your records.

Under penalties of perjury, I declare that I have examined this return and, to the best of my knowledge and belief, it is true, correct, and accurately lists all amounts and sources of income I received during the tax year. Declaration of preparer (other than the taxpayer) is based on all information of which the preparer has any knowledge.

Your signature	Date	Your occupation	Daytime phone number
Mateo R. Castillo	4/14/16	Student	
Spouse's signature. If a joint return, **both** must sign.	Date	Spouse's occupation	If the IRS sent you an Identity Protection PIN, enter it here (see inst.)

Paid Preparer Use Only

Print/Type preparer's name	Preparer's signature	Date	Check ☐ if self-employed	PTIN
Firm's name ▶			Firm's EIN ▶	
Firm's address ▶			Phone no.	

For Disclosure, Privacy Act, and Paperwork Reduction Act Notice, see instructions.
UYA

Form **1040EZ** (2015)

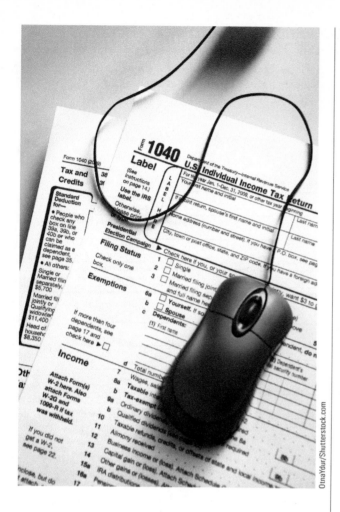
OtnaYdur/Shutterstock.com

Using this information, the Burns family intends to prepare their 2015 tax return so that their total tax liability is as low as possible. Like most married couples, the Burns family files a *joint return*.

Gross Income The Burns' gross income in 2015 amounted to $78,015—the amount shown as "total income" on line 22 of their tax return. They have both active income and portfolio income, as follows:

Active Income	
Luke's earnings	$60,415
Claire's earnings	9,750
Luke's business income (net)	5,800
Total active income	$75,965

Portfolio Income	
Interest from savings account	$ 800
Capital gains realized*	1,250
Total portfolio income	$ 2,050
Total income ($75,965 + $2,050)	$78,015

* Because this gain was realized on stock held for less than 12 months, the full amount is taxable as ordinary income.

They have no investment expenses to offset their portfolio income, so they'll be liable for taxes on the full amount of portfolio income. Although they have interest income, the Burns family doesn't have to file Schedule B (for interest and dividend income) with the Form 1040, because the interest is less than $1,500 and they earned no dividends. (If they receive dividends on stock in the future, they will have to complete a Qualified Dividends and Capital Gains Tax Worksheet, provided in the Form 1040 instruction booklet. Qualified dividends are taxed at the lower capital gains rates.) In addition, Luke will have to file Schedule C, detailing the income earned and expenses incurred in his bookkeeping business, and Schedule D to report capital gains income.

Adjustments to Gross Income The Burns family has only two adjustments to income: Claire's IRA contribution and 50 percent of the self-employment tax on Luke's net business income. Since Claire isn't covered by a retirement plan and because Luke's and her combined modified AGI is below $183,000 (in 2015) they can deduct her entire $4,000 contribution (the maximum contribution to an IRA was $5,500 or, depending on age, $6,500 in 2015) to an IRA account even though Luke's is already covered by a company-sponsored retirement program (see Chapter 14).

Self-employed taxpayers can deduct the employer's portion of the combined Social Security and

they had owned for 11 months. In addition, Luke kept the books for his brother's car dealership, from which he netted $5,800 during the year. Because no taxes were withheld from any of their outside income, during the year they made estimated tax payments totaling $1,000. The Burns' had $15,673 of potential itemized deductions during the year. Finally, the Burns family plans to contribute $4,000 to Claire's traditional IRA account. Beginning next year, the Burns family plans to switch Claire's account to a Roth IRA (see Chapter 14 for more information about that topic).

Finding the Burns' Tax Liability: Form 1040
Looking at the Burns' 2015 tax return (Worksheet 3.2), we can get a feel for the basic calculations required in the preparation of a *Form 1040*. Although we don't include the supporting schedules here, we illustrate the basic calculations that they require. In the above example, the tax form only shows dollar amounts and not cents, which is permissible in filing the form with the IRS. The Burns family has detailed records of their income and expenses, which they use not only for tax purposes but as an important input to their budgeting process.

Because they itemize deductions, the Burns family uses standard Form 1040 to file their tax return. When filed with the IRS, their return will include not only Form 1040 but also other schedules and forms detailing many of their expenses and deductions.

Form **1040**

Department of the Treasury–Internal Revenue Service   (99)

U.S. Individual Income Tax Return | **2015** | OMB No. 1545-0074 | IRS Use Only–Do not write or staple in this space.

For the year Jan. 1–Dec. 31, 2015, or other tax year beginning _____ , ending _____ | See separate instructions.

Your first name and initial: **Luke S.** | Last name: **Burns**

Your social security number: **123-45-6789**

If a joint return, spouse's first name and initial: **Claire B.** | Last name: **Burns**

Spouse's social security number: **987-65-4321**

Home address (number and street). If you have a P.O. box, see instructions. **1234 Success Circle** | Apt. no.

▲ Make sure the SSN(s) above and on line 6c are correct.

City, town or post office, state, and ZIP code. If you have a foreign address, also complete spaces below (see instructions). **Anytown, ME 04101**

Presidential Election Campaign
Check here if you, or your spouse if filing jointly, want $3 to go to this fund. Checking a box below will not change your tax or refund. ☐ You ☐ Spouse

Foreign country name | Foreign province/state/county | Foreign postal code

Filing Status
Check only one box.

1. ☐ Single
2. ☒ Married filing jointly (even if only one had income)
3. ☐ Married filing separately. Enter spouse's SSN above and full name here. ▶
4. ☐ Head of household (with qualifying person). (See instructions.) If the qualifying person is a child but not your dependent, enter this child's name here. ▶
5. ☐ Qualifying widow(er) with dependent child

Exemptions

6a ☒ **Yourself.** If someone can claim you as a dependent, **do not** check box 6a . . . . }
b ☒ **Spouse** . . . .

Boxes checked on 6a and 6b: **2**

c **Dependents:**

(1) First name Last name	(2) Dependent's social security number	(3) Dependent's relationship to you	(4) ✗ if child under age 17 qualifying for child tax credit (see instr.)
Caleb Burns	065-01-2347	Son	☒
Charles Burns	012-34-5678	Son	☒
Hazel Burns	034-56-1234	Daughter	☒

If more than four dependents, see instructions and check here ▶ ☐

No. of children on 6c who:
● lived with you **3**
● did not live with you due to divorce or separation (see instructions) **0**
Dependents on 6c not entered above **0**
Add numbers on lines above ▶ **5**

d Total number of exemptions claimed . . . .

Income

Attach Form(s) W-2 here. Also attach Forms W-2G and 1099-R if tax was withheld.

If you did not get a W-2, see instructions.

7	Wages, salaries, tips, etc. Attach Form(s) W-2	7	70,165.
8a	**Taxable** interest. Attach Schedule B if required	8a	800.
b	Tax-exempt interest. **Do not** include on line 8a	8b	
9a	Ordinary dividends. Attach Schedule B if required	9a	
b	Qualified dividends	9b	
10	Taxable refunds, credits, or offsets of state and local income taxes	10	
11	Alimony received	11	
12	Business income or (loss). Attach Schedule C or C-EZ	12	5,800.
13	Capital gain or (loss). Attach Schedule D if required. If not required, check here . . . ▶ ☐	13	1,250.
14	Other gains or (losses). Attach Form 4797	14	
15a	IRA distributions . . . . . 15a [ ] b Taxable amount	15b	
16a	Pensions and annuities . . 16a [ ] b Taxable amount	16b	
17	Rental real estate, royalties, partnerships, S corporations, trusts, etc. Attach Schedule E	17	
18	Farm income or (loss). Attach Schedule F	18	
19	Unemployment compensation	19	
20a	Social security benefits . . 20a [ ] b Taxable amount	20b	
21	Other income. List type and amount _____	21	
22	Combine the amounts in the far right column for lines 7 through 21. This is your **total income** ▶	22	78,015.

Adjusted Gross Income

23	Educator expenses	23	
24	Certain business expenses of reservists, performing artists, and fee-basis government officials. Attach Form 2106 or 2106-EZ .	24	
25	Health savings account deduction. Attach Form 8889	25	
26	Moving expenses. Attach Form 3903	26	
27	Deductible part of self-employment tax. Attach Schedule SE . .	27	410.
28	Self-employed SEP, SIMPLE, and qualified plans	28	
29	Self-employed health insurance deduction	29	
30	Penalty on early withdrawal of savings	30	
31a	Alimony paid b Recipient's SSN ▶	31a	
32	IRA deduction	32	4,000.
33	Student loan interest deduction	33	
34	Tuition and fees. Attach Form 8917	34	
35	Domestic production activities deduction. Attach Form 8903 . .	35	
36	Add lines 23 through 35	36	4,410.
37	Subtract line 36 from line 22. This is your **adjusted gross income** . . . . ▶	37	73,605.

For Disclosure, Privacy Act, and Paperwork Reduction Act Notice, see separate instructions.
UYA

Form **1040** (2015)

(continued)

Form 1040 (2015)   **Luke and Claire Burns**   123-45-6789   Page **2**

Tax and Credits	**38**	Amount from line 37 (adjusted gross income)	**38**	73,605.
	39a	Check if: ☐ **You** were born before January 2, 1951, ☐ Blind. ☐ **Spouse** was born before January 2, 1951, ☐ Blind. } Total boxes checked ▶ 39a	0	
	b	If your spouse itemizes on a separate return or you were a dual-status alien, check here▶ 39b ☐		
Standard Deduction for-	**40**	**Itemized deductions** (from Schedule A) **or** your **standard deduction** (see left margin) . . .	**40**	12,978.
• People who check any box on line 39a or 39b **or** who can be claimed as a dependent, see instructions.	**41**	Subtract line 40 from line 38	**41**	60,627.
	42	**Exemptions.** If line 38 is $154,950 or less, multiply $4,000 by the number on line 6d. Otherwise, see instructions .	**42**	20,000.
	43	**Taxable income.** Subtract line 42 from line 41. If line 42 is more than line 41, enter -0-	**43**	40,627.
	44	**Tax** (see instructions). Check if any from: **a** ☐ Form(s) 8814 **b** ☐ Form 4972 **c** ☐ _____	**44**	5,171.
• All others: Single or Married filing separately, $6,300	**45**	**Alternative minimum tax** (see instructions). Attach Form 6251	**45**	
Married filing jointly or Qualifying widow(er), $12,600	**46**	Excess advance premium tax credit repayment. Attach Form 8962	**46**	
	47	Add lines 44, 45, and 46 . . . . ▶	**47**	5,171.
Head of household, $9,250	**48**	Foreign tax credit. Attach Form 1116 if required	**48**	
	49	Credit for child and dependent care expenses. Attach Form 2441. .	**49**	
	50	Education credits from Form 8863, line 19	**50**	
	51	Retirement savings contributions credit. Attach Form 8880	**51**	
	52	Child tax credit. Attach Schedule 8812, if required	**52**	3,000.
	53	Residential energy credits. Attach Form 5695	**53**	
	54	Other credits from Form: **a** ☐ 3800 **b** ☐ 8801 **c** ☐ _____	**54**	
	55	Add lines 48 through 54. These are your **total credits**	**55**	3,000.
	56	Subtract line 55 from line 47. If line 55 is more than line 47, enter -0- . . . . ▶	**56**	2,171.
Other Taxes	**57**	Self-employment tax. Attach Schedule SE	**57**	819.
	58	Unreported social security and Medicare tax from Form: **a** ☐ 4137 **b** ☐ 8919	**58**	
	59	Additional tax on IRAs, other qualified retirement plans, etc. Attach Form 5329 if required . .	**59**	
	60a	Household employment taxes from Schedule H	**60a**	
	b	First-time homebuyer credit repayment. Attach Form 5405 if required	**60b**	
	61	Health care: individual responsibility (see instructions) Full-year coverage☐	**61**	
	62	Taxes from: **a** ☐ Form 8959 **b** ☐ Form 8960 **c** ☐ Instructions; enter code(s) _____	**62**	
	63	Add lines 56 through 62. This is your **total tax** . . . . ▶	**63**	2,990.
Payments	**64**	Federal income tax withheld from Forms W-2 and 1099	**64**	7,410.
	65	2015 estimated tax payments and amount applied from 2014 return	**65**	1,000.
If you have a qualifying child, attach Schedule EIC.	**66a**	**Earned income credit (EIC)** . . . . **NO.**	**66a**	
	b	Nontaxable combat pay election. . 66b		
	67	Additional child tax credit. Attach Schedule 8812	**67**	
	68	American opportunity credit from Form 8863, line 8	**68**	
	69	Net premium tax credit. Attach Form 8962	**69**	
	70	Amount paid with request for extension to file	**70**	
	71	Excess social security and tier 1 RRTA tax withheld	**71**	
	72	Credit for federal tax on fuels. Attach Form 4136	**72**	
	73	Credits from Form: **a** ☐ 2439 **b** ☐ Reserved **c** ☐ 8885 **d** ☐ _____	**73**	
	74	Add lines 64, 65, 66a, and 67 through 73. These are your **total payments** . . . . . . ▶	**74**	8,410.
Refund	**75**	If line 74 is more than line 63, subtract line 63 from line 74. This is the amount you **overpaid** . . .	**75**	5,420.
	76a	Amount of line 75 you want **refunded to you.** If Form 8888 is attached, check here . . . ▶ ☐	**76a**	5,420.
Direct deposit? See instructions.	▶ **b**	Routing number _____ ▶ **c** Type: ☐ Checking ☐ Savings		
	▶ **d**	Account number _____		
	77	Amount of line 75 you want **applied to your 2016 estimated tax** ▶ 77		
Amount You Owe	**78**	**Amount you owe.** Subtract line 74 from line 63. For details on how to pay, see instructions ▶	**78**	0.
	79	Estimated tax penalty (see instructions) 79		

Third Party Designee	Do you want to allow another person to discuss this return with the IRS (see instructions)? ☐ **Yes.** Complete below.		☐ **No**
	Designee's name ▶ Phone no. ▶	Personal identification number (PIN) ▶	

Sign Here
Joint return? See instr.
Keep a copy for your records.

Under penalties of perjury, I declare that I have examined this return and accompanying schedules and statements, and to the best of my knowledge and belief, they are true, correct, and complete. Declaration of preparer (other than taxpayer) is based on all information of which preparer has any knowledge.

Your signature	Date	Your occupation	Daytime phone number
Luke S. Burns.	4/10/16	**Manager**	
Spouse's signature. If a joint return, **both** must sign.	Date	Spouse's occupation	If the IRS sent you an Identity Protection PIN, enter it here (see inst.)
Claire B. Burns.	4/10/16	**Sales Clerk**	

Paid Preparer Use Only	Print/Type preparer's name	Preparer's signature	Date	Check ☐ if self-employed	PTIN
	Firm's name ▶			Firm's EIN ▶	
	Firm's address ▶			Phone no.	

www.irs.gov/form1040
UYA

Form **1040** (2015)

Medicare tax, which is a total of 7.65%. Thus, the self-employment tax is based on 92.35% (100% − 7.65%) of self-employment income. Using 2015 rates, Luke's self-employment tax will be 15.3 percent of 92.35% of his $5,800 net business income. Thus, he will be able to deduct one-half of the self-employment tax—$409.76 [(0.153 × 0.9235 × 5,800)/2]—on line 27.

Adjusted Gross Income After deducting the $409.76 self-employment tax and Luke's $4,000 IRA contribution from their gross income, the Burns family is left with a rounded AGI of $73,605, as reported on line 37.

Itemized Deductions or Standard Deduction?

The Burns family is filing a joint return, and no one is over age 65 or blind; so, as reported in the box on page 2 of *Form 1040*, they are entitled to a standard deduction of $12,600 in 2015. However, they want to evaluate their itemized deductions before deciding which type of deduction to take. Of course they'll take the higher deduction because it will result in the lower amount of taxable income and thus keep their tax liability to a minimum. Their preliminary paperwork resulted in the following deductions:

Medical and dental expenses	$ 1,223
State income and property taxes paid	2,560
Mortgage interest	8,893
Charitable contributions	475
Job and other expenses	2,522
Total	$15,673

The taxes, mortgage interest, and charitable contributions are deductible in full and so, at the minimum, the Burns family will have itemized deductions amounting

to $11,928 ($2,560 + $8,893 + $475). However, to be deductible, the medical and dental expenses and the job and other expenses must exceed stipulated minimum levels of AGI—only that portion exceeding the specified minimum levels of AGI can be included as part of their itemized deductions. For medical and dental expenses the minimum is 10 percent of AGI, and for job and other expenses it is 2 percent of AGI. Because 10 percent of the Burns' AGI is $7,360 (0.1 × $73,605), they fall short of the minimum and cannot deduct any medical and dental expenses. In contrast, because 2 percent of their AGI is $1,472 (0.02 × $73,605), they can deduct any job and other expenses exceeding that amount, or $2,522 − $1,472 = $1,050. Adding that amount to their other allowable deductions ($11,928) results in total itemized deductions of $12,978. This amount exceeds the standard deduction of $12,600 so the Burns family would reduce their tax bill by itemizing their deductions. They would enter the details of these deductions on Schedule A and attach it to their *Form 1040*. (The total amount of the Burns' itemized deductions is listed on line 40 of *Form 1040*.)

The Burns family is entitled to claim two exemptions for themselves, and another three for their three dependent children, for a total of five (see line 6d). Because each exemption is worth $4,000 they receive a total personal exemption of $20,000 (5 × $4,000). This amount is listed on line 42 of their *Form 1040*.

The Burns' Taxable Income and Tax Liability

Taxable income is found by subtracting itemized deductions and personal exemptions from AGI. In the Burns' case, (rounded) taxable income totals $73,605 − $12,978 − $20,000 = $40,627, as shown on line 43. Given this information, the Burns family can now refer to the tax rate schedule (like the one in Exhibit 3.3) to find their appropriate tax rate and, ultimately, the amount of taxes they'll have to pay. As we can see, the Burns' $40,627 in taxable income places them in the 15 percent marginal tax bracket. Using the schedule in Exhibit 3.3, they calculate their tax as follows: $1,845 + [0.15 × ($40,627 − $18,450)] = $5,172. They enter this amount on line 44.

The Burns family also qualifies for the child tax credit: $1,000 for each child under age 17. They enter $3,000 on lines 52 and 55 and subtract that amount from the tax on line 47, entering $2,172 on line 56. In addition, the Burns family owe self-employment (Social Security) tax on

Luke's $5,800 net business income. As previously discussed, will increase their tax liability by $819 (0.153 × 0.9235 × $5,800) and would be reported on Schedule SE and entered on line 57 of *Form 1040*. (Recall that the Burns family deducted 50 percent of this amount, or $410, on line 27 as an adjustment to income.) The Burns family enters their total tax liability on line 63: $2,991 ($2,172 + 819).

Do They Get a Tax Refund? The total amount of taxes withheld is $7,410 ($6,260 from Luke's salary and $1,150 from Claire's wages, combined on line 64). They also made estimated tax payments of $1,000 (shown on line 65) for a total on line 74 of $8,410, which exceeds their tax liability. As a result, they are entitled to a refund of $5,419: the $8,410 withholding less their $2,991 tax liability. (About 65 percent of all taxpayers receive refunds each year.) Instead of paying the IRS, they'll be getting money back. (Generally, it takes one to two months after a tax return has been filed for a refund check to be mailed. If filed electronically, it usually takes about three weeks to get a refund.)

All the Burns family has to do at this point is to sign and date their completed Form 1040 and send it, along with any supporting forms and schedules, to the IRS Center that serves their state on or before April 15, 2016.

One reason for the Burns' large refund was the child tax credit. With such a sizable refund, the Burns family may want to stop making estimated tax payments because their combined withholding more than covers the amount of taxes they owe. Another option is to change their withholding to reduce the amount withheld.

Note that if total tax payments had been less than the Burns' tax liability, they would have owed the IRS money—the amount owed is found by subtracting total tax payments made from the tax liability. If they owed money, they would include a check for the amount due with Form 1040 when filing their tax return.

3-3e Issues for High Income Taxpayers

The U.S. Congress has added provisions to the tax law that results in high income taxpayers either losing deductions available to lower income taxpayers or adding taxes that apply only to high income taxpayers. The major provisions are the reduction of personal exemptions and itemized deductions, child care credits, and additional taxes on salaries and net investment income. The reductions typically apply when the adjusted gross income reaches a threshold amount. Once that level is reached, the actual computation of the phase-out varies a great deal—one of the many reasons to use tax preparation software or a tax preparer for completing a return. Yet even with these provisions to increase tax, the top 1 percent of taxpayers have a lower average tax rate than the next lower group, primarily because of the lower tax rate on capital gains and dividends.

The reductions of personal exemptions and itemized deductions begins when a single taxpayer's AGI is $258,250 ($309,900 for joint taxpayers). The reduction of the Child Tax Credit begins when the single taxpayer's modified adjusted gross income is $75,000 ($110,000 for joint taxpayers). The additional tax on salaries and the tax on net investment income applies to single taxpayers with modified AGI over $200,000 ($250,000 for joint taxpayers). The additional tax on salaries is for the Medicare portion of the FICA tax.

3-4 OTHER FILING CONSIDERATIONS

LO4, LO5 Other considerations related to tax filing include the need to pay estimated taxes, file for extensions, or amend the return; the possibility of a tax audit; and whether to use a tax preparation service or computer software to assist you in preparing your return.

3-4a Estimates, Extensions, and Amendments

Like Luke Burns who provided accounting services to his brother's business, you may have income that's not subject to withholding. You may need to file a declaration of estimated taxes with your return and to pay quarterly taxes. Or perhaps you are unable to meet the normal April 15 filing deadline or need to correct a previously filed return. Let's look at the procedures for handling these situations.

Estimated Taxes Because federal withholding taxes are regularly taken only from employment income, such as that paid in the form of wages or salaries, the IRS requires certain people to pay **estimated taxes** on income earned from other sources. Estimated tax payments are most commonly required of investors, consultants, lawyers, business owners, and various other professionals who are likely to receive income that is not subject to withholding.

The declaration of estimated taxes (*Form 1040-ES*) is not filed with the tax return. Estimated taxes must be paid in four installments, which are usually on April 15, June 15, and September 15 of the current year, and January 15 of the following year. Failure to estimate and pay these taxes in accordance with IRS guidelines can result in a penalty levied by the IRS.

April 15: Usual Filing Deadline As we've seen from the Burns family example, at the end of each tax year, those taxpayers required to file a return must determine

Go to Smart Sites

Looking for a tax preparer who is also an authorized e-file provider in your area? Many tax professionals are also authorized to file your return electronically—the IRS has a authorized e-file provider locator on its Internet site (www.irs.gov).

the amount of their *tax liability*—the amount of taxes they owe due to the past year's activities. The tax year corresponds to the calendar year and covers the period January 1 through December 31. Taxpayers may file their returns any time after the end of the tax year and *must* file no later than April 15 of the year immediately following the tax year (or by the first business day after that date if it falls on a weekend or federal holiday).

If you have a computer, an Internet connection, and tax preparation software, you can probably use the IRS's *e-file* and *e-pay* to file your return and pay your taxes electronically either by using a credit card or by authorizing an electronic withdrawal from your checking or savings account. You can use an "Authorized *e-file* Provider," who may charge a fee to file for you, or do it yourself using commercial tax preparation software.

Depending on whether the total of taxes withheld and any estimated tax payments is greater or less than the computed tax liability, the taxpayer either receives a refund or has a balance due. Taxpayers can pay their taxes using a credit card. However, because the IRS cannot pay credit card companies a fee, taxpayers must call a special provider and pay a service charge to arrange for the payment.

> **EXAMPLE: Determining the Amount Owed or Refunded** Mia had $2,000 withheld and paid estimated taxes of $1,200 during the year. After filling out the appropriate tax forms, she had a tax liability of only $2,800. Consequently, Mia overpaid his taxes by $400 ($2,000 + $1,200 − $2,800) and will receive a $400 refund from the IRS. On the other hand, if Mia's tax liability had been $4,000, then she would owe the IRS an additional $800 ($4,000 − $2,000 − $1,200).

Filing Extensions and Amended Returns It's possible to receive an extension of time for filing your federal tax return. You can

estimated taxes tax payments required on income not subject to withholding that are paid in four installments

Financial Planning Tips

While it's true that the IRS typically only audits about 1 percent of tax returns, some practices significantly increase your chance of being audited. It's wise to be aware of the following possible triggers:

- **High income.** The more income you make, the more likely you are to experience an audit. For example, if you make more than $200,000, your chance is about 2.61 percent, and if you make $1 million or more, your chance rises to about 10 percent.

- **Unreported taxable income.** If your 1099s and W-2s add up to more than the income reported on your tax return, expect a bill from the IRS—and a possible audit.

- **Higher-than-average deductions.** If your deductions are large relative to your income, the IRS can flag your return for a potential audit. Make sure that you know the IRS regulations for deductions and donations, and keep all supporting documents and receipts.

- **Home office deductions.** A home office is supposed to be used exclusively for business. The IRS has found that this requirement is frequently not met, and the deduction is consequently denied. Thus, this is a red flag for an audit. If you take this deduction, be ready to prove it.

- **Business meals, travel, and entertainment.** IRS experience shows that the self-employed are responsible for most of the underreporting of income and overstating of deductions. Large deductions for meals, travel, and entertainment are an audit flag. Make sure to keep good records if you plan to take these kinds of deductions.

- **Making Large Charitable Deductions.** The IRS knows the average charitable contribution for a given taxpayer's income level. And making non-cash donations over $500 without filing a Form 8283 increases the chance of an audit. Be sure to keep all supporting documents.

- **Business use of a vehicle.** Claiming 100 percent business use of a car is a red flag to the IRS because it's rare for an individual to really use a car exclusively for business. Make sure that you keep detailed mileage logs.

- **Unreported foreign bank account.** You are required to disclose offshore accounts. If the IRS finds an unreported account, it's an audit flag.

Source: Adapted from "15 IRS Audit Flags," http://www.kiplinger.com/slideshow/taxes/T056-S011-irs-tax-audit-red-flags/index.html, accessed September 2016.

---

apply for an automatic six-month **filing extension**, which makes the due date October 15, simply by submitting *Form 4868*. In filing for an extension, however, the taxpayer must estimate the taxes due and remit that amount with the application. The extension does *not* give taxpayers more time to pay their taxes.

After filing a return, you may discover that you overlooked some income or a major deduction or made a mistake, so that you paid too little or too much in taxes. You can easily correct this by filing an **amended return** (*Form 1040X*) showing the corrected amount of income or deductions and the amount of taxes you should have paid, along with the amount of any tax refund or additional taxes owed. You generally have three years from the date you file your original return or two years from the date you paid the taxes, whichever is later, to file an amended return.

3-4b Audited Returns

Because taxpayers themselves provide the key information and fill out the necessary tax forms, the IRS has no proof that taxes have been correctly calculated. In addition to returns that stand out in some way and warrant further investigation, the IRS also randomly selects some returns for a **tax audit**—an examination to validate the return's accuracy. The odds of being audited are actually quite low; the IRS audits less than 1 percent of returns. Despite the traditionally scary aura that surrounds the audit concept, the outcome of an audit is not always additional tax owed to the IRS. Yet the IRS indicates that for every $1 it spends on audits, it brings in $4.

filing extension an extension of time beyond the usual April 15 deadline during which taxpayers, with the approval of the IRS, can file their returns without incurring penalties

amended return a tax return filed to adjust for information received after the filing date of the taxpayer's original return or to correct errors

tax audit an examination by the IRS to validate the accuracy of a given tax return

Typically, audits question (1) whether all income received has been properly reported and (2) whether the deductions claimed are legitimate and for the correct amount. The IRS can take as many as three years—and in some cases, six years—from the date of filing to audit your return, so you should retain records and receipts used in preparing returns for about seven years. Severe financial penalties, even prison sentences, can result from violating tax laws.

In sum, you should take advantage of all legitimate deductions to minimize your tax liability, but you must also be sure to properly report all items of income and expense as required by the Internal Revenue Code.

karen roach/Shutterstock.com

3-4c Tax Preparation Services: Getting Help on Your Returns

Many people with simple tax situations prepare their own tax returns. Some taxpayers with quite complicated financial affairs may also invest their time in preparing their own returns. The IRS offers many publications with step-by-step instructions to help you prepare your tax return. You can order them directly from the IRS by mail or download them from the IRS Internet site (**www.irs.gov**). An excellent (and free) comprehensive tax preparation reference is IRS *Publication 17, Your Federal Income Tax—for Individuals*. The online Interactive Tax Assistant is also useful (**www.irs.gov/uac /Interactive-Tax-Assistant-(ITA)-1**).

Help from the IRS The IRS, in addition to issuing various publications for use in preparing tax returns, also provides direct assistance to taxpayers. The IRS will compute taxes for those whose taxable income is less than $100,000 and who do not itemize deductions. Persons who use this IRS service must fill in certain data, sign and date the return, and send it to the IRS on or before April 15 of the year immediately following the tax year.

The IRS attempts to calculate taxes that result in the "smallest" tax bite. It then sends taxpayers a refund (if their withholding exceeds their tax liability) or a bill (if their tax liability is greater than the amount of withholding). People who either fail to qualify for or do not want to use this total tax preparation service can still obtain IRS assistance in preparing their returns from a toll-free service. Consult your telephone directory for the toll-free number of the IRS office closest to you.

Private Tax Preparers More than half of taxpayers use professional *tax preparation services* to improve accuracy and minimize their tax liability. The fees charged by professional tax preparers can range from at least $100 for simple returns to $1,000 or more for complicated returns. You can select from the following types of tax preparation services:

▶ **National and local tax services:** These include national services such as H&R Block and independent local firms. These services are best for taxpayers with relatively common types of income and expenditures.

▶ **Certified public accountants (CPAs):** Tax professionals who prepare returns and can advise taxpayers on planning.

▶ **Enrolled agents (EAs):** Federally licensed individual tax practitioners who have passed a difficult, two-day, IRS-administered exam. They are fully qualified to handle tax preparation at various levels of complexity.

▶ **Tax attorneys:** Lawyers who specialize in tax planning.

Always check your own completed tax returns carefully before signing them. Remember that *taxpayers themselves must accept primary responsibility for the accuracy of their returns.* The IRS requires professional tax preparers to sign each return as the preparer, enter their Preparers Tax Identification Number (PTIN), the firm's Employer Identification number (EIN), and address, and give the taxpayer a copy of the return being filed. Tax preparers with the necessary hardware and software can electronically file their clients' tax returns so that eligible taxpayers can receive refunds more quickly.

There's no guarantee that your professional tax preparer will determine your tax liability correctly. To reduce the chance of error, you should become familiar with the basic tax principles and regulations, check all documents (such as *W-2s* and *1099s*) for accuracy, maintain good communication with your tax preparer, and request an explanation of any entries on your tax return that you don't understand.

3-4d Computer-Based Tax Returns

Many people use their personal computers to help with tax planning and preparing tax returns. Several good tax software packages will save hours when you're filling out

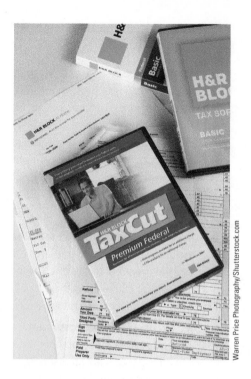

Warren Price Photography/Shutterstock.com

the forms and schedules involved in filing tax returns. The programs often identify tax-saving opportunities you might otherwise miss. These computer programs aren't for everyone, however. Simple returns, like the *Form 1040EZ*, don't require them. And for complex returns, there's no substitute for the skill and expertise of a tax accountant or attorney. Tax preparation software will be most helpful for taxpayers who itemize deductions but don't need tax advice.

There are two general kinds of software: tax planning and tax preparation. Planning programs such as Quicken let you experiment with different strategies to see their effects on the amount of taxes you must pay. The other category of tax software focuses on helping you complete and file your tax return. These programs take much of the tedium out of tax preparation, reducing the time you spend from days to hours. If you file the *Form 1040* and some supporting forms, invest in the stock market, own real estate, or have foreign income or a home-based

Financial Planning Tips

WORKING WITH THE BEST TAX PREPARER

Because you are legally responsible for your tax returns, even if someone else prepared them, it's important to choose the right person or firm to prepare them for you. Keep in mind the following tips in making this major decision and working with your preparer:

- **Qualifications.** All paid tax return preparers are required to have a Preparer Tax Identification Number (PTIN). Make sure that a prospective preparer has a PTIN.

- **Preparer's history.** Check with the Better Business Bureau for the preparer's history of problems. Make sure that there have been no disciplinary actions, and check the status of any CPA's license through the state boards of accountancy. The same check should be made for state bar associations for attorneys and with the IRS Office of Enrollment for Enrolled Agents (EAs).

- **Understand the fees that the preparer will charge you.** Make sure that you understand and accept the fee for services rendered and compare preparers' fees. It does not make sense to use preparers who ask for a percentage of your refund.

- **Electronic filing.** Be certain that the prospective preparer offers IRS e-file. You can opt to file a paper return instead, but it is typically easiest to file electronically—and if you're getting a refund, you'll get it faster that way.

- **Accessibility.** Make sure that you can get hold of the tax preparer easily in case you have questions *before* or *after* the return is filed.

- **Requests for records and receipts.** Good preparers will ask to see your records and receipts. They will also ask questions about your total income, tax-deductible expenses, and more. It's best to avoid preparers who are willing to file your return electronically without seeing your W-2 form and other records.

- **Return signature.** Never use a preparer who asks you to sign a blank tax form. Similarly, review the entire return, verify its accuracy, and make sure that the preparer has supplied his or her PTIN before you sign it.

Source: Adapted from Internal Revenue Publication, "Tips for Choosing a Tax Return Preparer," www.irs.gov/uac/Tips-for -Choosing-a-Tax-Return-Preparer, accessed September 2016.

business, you'll probably benefit from using tax preparation programs.

The two major software players are Intuit's TurboTax and H&R Block, both of which are available for either Windows or Macintosh. TurboTax also has a Web-based version that lets you work on your returns from any computer. Both companies also offer an add-on program that accurately assigns fair market value to the household items most commonly donated to charity. Both programs feature a clean interface and guide you through the steps in preparing your return by asking you the questions that apply to your situation. In addition to the primary tax-form preparation section, they include extensive resources and links to additional Internet references, video clips to make tricky concepts easier to understand, tax planning questionnaires, deduction finders, and more. State tax return packages are available for an additional cost. All major software providers have free, online versions for preparing federal taxes for people who meet specific requirements, which vary by provider. See **www.irs.gov/uac/Free-File%3A-Do-Your-Federal-Taxes-for-Free** for a list of free federal software providers with their individual restrictions.

The IRS has "fill-in forms," which allow you to enter information while the form is displayed on your computer by Adobe Acrobat Reader. After entering the requested information, you can print out the completed form. Fill-in forms give you a cleaner, crisper printout for your records and for filing with the IRS. Unlike tax preparation software, these fill-in forms have no computational capabilities, so you must do all your calculations before starting. These forms are labeled "Fill-in forms" at the IRS Internet site.

3-5 EFFECTIVE TAX PLANNING

LO6 *Tax planning* is a key ingredient of your overall personal financial planning. The overriding objective of effective tax planning is to maximize total after-tax income by reducing, shifting, and deferring taxes to as low a level as legally possible. By all means, don't confuse tax avoidance with tax evasion, which includes such illegal activities as omitting income or overstating deductions. **Tax evasion**, in effect, involves a failure to accurately report income or deductions and,

in extreme cases, a failure to pay taxes altogether. Persons found guilty of tax evasion are subject to severe financial penalties and even prison terms. **Tax avoidance**, in contrast, focuses on reducing taxes in ways that are legal and compatible with the intent of Congress.

3-5a Fundamentals of Tax Planning

Tax planning can involve the use of various investments, retirement programs, and estate distribution procedures to (1) reduce, (2) shift, or (3) defer taxes. You can *reduce* taxes, for instance, by using techniques that create tax deductions or credits or that receive preferential tax treatment—such as investments that produce depreciation (such as real estate) or generate tax-free income (such as municipal bonds). You can *shift* taxes by using gifts or trusts to transfer some of your income to other family members who are in lower tax brackets and to whom you intend to provide some level of support anyway, such as a retired, elderly parent.

> Tax planning is closely interrelated with many financial planning activities, including investment, retirement, and estate planning.

The idea behind *deferring* taxes is to reduce or eliminate your taxes today by postponing them to the future when you may be in a lower tax bracket. Perhaps more important, *deferring taxes gives you use of the money that would otherwise go to taxes*—thereby allowing you to invest it to make even more money. Deferring taxes is usually done using retirement plans, such as IRAs, or by investing in certain types of annuities, variable life insurance policies, or even Series EE bonds (U.S. savings bonds).

The fundamentals of tax planning include making sure you take all the deductions to which you're entitled and also take full advantage of the various tax provisions that will minimize your tax liability. Thus, comprehensive tax planning is an ongoing activity with both an immediate and a long-term perspective. In fact, a major component of a comprehensive personal financial plan is a summary of the potential tax impacts of various recommended financial strategies. Tax planning is closely interrelated with many financial planning activities, including investment, retirement, and estate planning.

tax evasion the illegal act of failing to accurately report income or deductions and, in extreme cases, failing to pay taxes altogether

tax avoidance the act of reducing taxes in ways that are legal and compatible with the intent of Congress

3-5b Some Popular Tax Strategies

Many tax strategies are fairly simple and straightforward and can be used by the average, middle-income taxpayer. You certainly don't have to be in the top income bracket to enjoy the benefits of many tax-saving ideas and procedures. For example, the interest income on Series EE bonds is free from state income tax, and the holder can elect to delay payment of federal taxes until (1) the year the bonds are redeemed for cash or (2) the year in which they finally mature, whichever occurs first. This feature makes Series EE bonds an excellent vehicle for earning tax-deferred income.

There are other strategies that can cut your tax bill. Accelerating or bunching deductions into a single year may permit itemizing deductions. Shifting income from one year to another is one way to cut your tax liability. If you expect to be in the same or a higher income tax bracket this year than you will be next year, defer income until next year and shift expenses to this year so you can accelerate your deductions and reduce taxes this year.

Maximizing Deductions Review a comprehensive list of possible deductions for ideas, because even small deductions can add up to big tax savings. Accelerate or bunch deductions into one tax year if this allows you to itemize rather than take the standard deduction. For example, make your fourth-quarter estimated state tax payment before December 31 rather than on January 15 to deduct it in the current taxable year. Group miscellaneous expenses—and schedule unreimbursed elective medical procedures—to fall into one tax year so that they exceed the required "floor" for deductions (2 percent of AGI for miscellaneous expenses; 10 percent of AGI for medical expenses). Increase discretionary deductions such as charitable contributions.

Income Shifting One way of reducing income taxes is to use a technique known as income shifting. Here the taxpayer shifts a portion of his or her income, and thus taxes, to relatives in lower tax brackets. This can be done by creating trusts or custodial accounts or by making outright gifts of income-producing property to family members. For instance, parents with $125,000 of taxable income (28 percent marginal tax rate) and $18,000

income shifting a technique used to reduce taxes in which a taxpayer shifts a portion of income to relatives in lower tax brackets

tax deferred income that is not subject to taxes immediately but that will later be subject to taxes

in corporate bonds paying $2,000 in annual interest might give the bonds to their 15-year-old child—with the understanding that such income is to be used ultimately for the child's college education. The $2,000 would then belong to the child, who would presumably pay $100 (0.10 × [$2,000 − $1,000 minimum standard deduction for a dependent]) in taxes on this income, while the parents' taxable income would be reduced by $2,000, reducing their taxes by $560 (0.28 × $2,000).

Unfortunately, this strategy is not as simple as it seems. A number of restrictions surround the strategy for children under 19, so it's possible to employ such techniques with older children (and with other older relatives, such as elderly parents). Parents also need to recognize that shifting assets into a child's name to save taxes could affect the amount of college financial aid for which the child qualifies. Additional tax implications of gifts to dependents are discussed in Chapter 15.

Tax-Free and Tax-Deferred Income Some investments provide tax-free income; in most cases, however, the tax on the income is only deferred (or delayed) to a later date. Although there aren't many forms of tax-free investments left today, probably the best example would be the *interest* income earned on *municipal bonds.* Such income is free from federal income tax and possibly state income taxes. (Tax-free municipal bonds are discussed in Chapter 12.)

Earnings on money put into a Roth IRA are also tax-free. Income that is tax deferred, in contrast, only delays the payment of taxes to a future date. Yet until that time arrives, tax-deferred investment vehicles allow you to *accumulate tax-free earnings*. This results in much higher savings than would occur in a taxed account. A good example of tax-deferred income would be income earned in a *traditional IRA*. Chapter 14 provides a detailed discussion of this and other similar arrangements.

Most wage earners can open an IRA and contribute up to $5,500 (or possibly $6,500, depending on an age qualification) each year to the account (in 2015). *All the income you earn in your IRA accumulates tax free*. This is a *tax-deferred* investment and so you'll eventually have to pay taxes on these earnings, but not until you start drawing down your account. *Roth IRAs* provide a way for people to contribute after-tax dollars where, not only do earnings grow tax free, but withdrawals are non-taxable if the account has been open for five or more years and the individual is over 59½. However, keep in mind that using after-tax dollars for a Roth IRA means that the contribution is not tax-deductible. In addition to IRAs, tax-deferred income can also be obtained from other types of pension and retirement plans and annuities. Chapter 14 provides more information on these financial products and strategies.

PLANNING OVER A LIFETIME

Tax Preparation and Planning

Here are some key considerations for tax planning in each stage of the life cycle.

PRE-FAMILY INDEPENDENCE: 20s

▸ Manage your withholding amount so that it is about equal to your tax bill. Avoid large amounts owed or refunded.

▸ Maintain a careful record of income and tax-deductible expenses.

▸ Consider using tax preparation software.

FAMILY FORMATION/CAREER DEVELOPMENT: 30–45

▸ When you marry and/or have family changes, revise your withholding amount accordingly.

▸ Acquire tax shelters like a mortgage, which has tax-deductible interest expenses.

▸ Make regular contributions to your employer's tax-sheltered retirement plan and consider IRAs.

PRE-RETIREMENT: 45–65

▸ As your income grows, consider tax-exempt investments like municipal bonds.

▸ Consider increasing your average contributions to tax-sheltered retirement plans.

▸ Consider larger, "catch-up" retirement plan contributions.

RETIREMENT: 65 AND BEYOND

▸ Estimate Social Security benefits and plan when you will start receiving payments.

▸ Plan orderly withdrawals from tax-sheltered retirement accounts and for the associated tax bill.

▸ Consider the use of life insurance to manage potential estate taxes. This is covered in more detail in Chapter 15.

Gabriel and Lydia's Tax Management Strategy

Gabriel and Lydia Hamilton are a married couple in their late 20s. Lydia is an electrical engineer, and Gabriel is a freelance computer programmer. They recently saw a newscast about the budget deficit in the United States and believe it likely that tax rates will increase significantly by the time they retire. Gabriel expects to finish a large programming job toward the end of this year and is preparing to bill his client. The couple expects their marginal tax rate to increase from 15 percent to 25 percent next year. What tax management strategies should they pursue?

Lydia and Gabriel decided that they should get more serious about retirement planning given the prospect of a larger tax bite next year and going forward. So they each invested $3,000 in an IRA this year and plan to invest the maximum next year. Lydia invested in a traditional IRA that reduces their taxable income by $3,000 this year. Her plan to invest more next year will provide even more of a benefit given their higher expected tax rate. Gabriel invested in a Roth IRA, which provides no tax benefit this year but will shield the future value of the IRA from ever being taxed. This addresses their long-term concerns. Finally, Gabriel decided to bill his client immediately to speed the receipt of the consulting income to this year, when their tax rate is expected to be lower than next year. Gabriel and Lydia are well on their way to managing their taxes effectively.

Tom Saga/Shutterstock.com

STUDY TOOLS 3

LOCATED AT BACK OF THE TEXTBOOK
☐ Chapter Review Card

LOCATED AT WWW.CENGAGE.COM/LOGIN
☐ Review Key Term flashcards and create your own cards.

☐ Track your knowledge and understanding of key concepts in personal finance.
☐ Complete practice and graded quizzes to prepare for tests.
☐ Complete interactive content at PFIN6 Online.
☐ View the chapter highlight boxes at PFIN6 Online.

Financial Planning Exercises

LO2 1. **Calculating marginal tax rates.** Piper Wells is single and received the items and amounts of income shown below during 2015, as shown below. Determine the marginal tax rate applicable to each item. Note that if the item is not taxable, the marginal rate is 0.

Salary	$30,000
Dividends	800
Gift from mother	500
Child support from ex-husband	3,600
Interest on savings account	250
Rental property	900
Loan from bank	2,000
Interest on state government bonds	300

LO2, 3 2. **Estimating taxable income, tax liability, and potential refund.** Hannah Owens is 24 years old and single, lives in an apartment, and has no dependents. Last year she earned $55,000 as a sales assistant for Business Solutions: $3,910 of her wages was withheld for federal income taxes. In addition, she had interest income of $142. She takes the standard deduction. Calculate her taxable income, tax liability, and tax refund or tax owed for 2015.

LO2 3. **Calculating taxes on security transactions.** If Julia Murray is single and in the 28 percent tax bracket, calculate the tax impact of each of the following security transactions. (Use the IRS regulations for capital gains in effect in 2015.) Treat each of the following cases as independent of the others.

   a. She sold stock for $1,200 that she purchased for $1,000 5 months earlier.

   b. She sold bonds for $4,000 that she purchased for $3,000 3 years earlier.

   c. She sold stock for $1,000 that she purchased for $1,500 15 months earlier.

LO2 4. **Bill's son, Joe, is 26 and a full-time graduate student at State U.** For 2015, Bill provided Joe with $10,000 of support. Joe also received a scholarship of $10,000 which he used to pay his $8,000 tuition and provided some living expenses with the remainder ($2,000).

   a. Can Bill claim Joe as a dependent using the qualified child rule?

   b. Can Bill claim Joe as a dependent using the qualified relative rule?

LO2, 3 5. **Calculating taxable income for a married couple filing jointly.** Sam and Kate Coleman are married and have one child. Sam is putting together some figures so that he can prepare the Colemans' joint 2015 tax return. He can claim three personal exemptions (including himself). So far, he's been able to determine the following with regard to income and possible deductions:

Total unreimbursed medical expenses incurred	$1,155
Gross wages and commissions earned	50,770
IRA contribution	5,000
Mortgage interest paid	5,200
Capital gains realized on assets held *less than* 12 months	1,450
Income from limited partnership	200
Job expenses and other allowable deductions	875
Interest paid on credit cards	380
Qualified dividend income earned	610

Sales taxes paid	2,470
Charitable contributions made	1,200
Capital losses realized	3,475
Interest paid on a car loan	570
Alimony paid by Ross to his first wife	6,000
Social Security taxes paid	2,750
Property taxes paid	700
State income taxes paid	1,700

Given this information, how much taxable income will the Colemans have in 2015? (**Note:** Assume that Sam is not covered by a pension plan where he works, the standard deduction of $12,600 for married filing jointly applies, and each exemption claimed is worth $4,000.)

LO3 6. Choosing and preparing an individual tax form. Use Worksheets 3.1 and 3.2. Mark Huang is single, graduated from college in 2015 and began work as a systems analyst in July of that year. He is preparing to file his income tax return for 2015 and has collected the financial information shown below for that calendar year.

Scholarship used to pay tuition	$ 5,750
Scholarship used to pay room and board	1,850
Salary	30,250
Interest income	185
Itemized deductions	3,000
Income taxes withheld	2,600

a. Prepare Mark's 2015 tax return, using a $6,300 standard deduction, a personal exemption of $4,000, and the tax rates given in Exhibit 3.3. Which tax form should Mark use, and why? (You may obtain tax forms on the IRS web site, **www.irs.gov**. Either leave blank or make up information not provided, such as social security number and address.)

b. Prepare Mark's 2015 tax return using the data in part a along with the following information:

IRA contribution	$5,000
Cash dividends received	150

Which tax form should he use in this case? Why?

LO3 7. Effect of tax credit vs. tax deduction. Explain and calculate the differences resulting from a $1,000 tax credit versus a $1,000 tax deduction for a single taxpayer in the 25 percent tax bracket with $40,000 of pre-tax income.

LO4 8. Preparing for a tax audit. Colin and Sophie Griffin have been notified that they are being audited. What should they do to prepare for the audit?

LO5 9. Getting help with tax form preparation. Lewis Olson busy job doesn't leave him much spare time. Consequently, he would like some help preparing his federal tax forms. What advice would you give Lewis?

LO6 10. **Effective tax planning.** Explain the key elements of effective tax planning. What are some of the most popular tax management strategies?

LO6 11. **Effective tax planning.** Mary Hall reports the following data from her 2015 tax return. Analyze the data and suggest tax planning ideas that she should consider.

Salary	$150,000
Interest income	30,000
Qualified dividends	1,000
Total Adjusted Gross Income	$181,000

Note: The interest income is from a bank savings account earning 1%. The dividends are from utility stock paying 3 percent dividends.

4 | Managing Your Cash and Savings

LEARNING OBJECTIVES

After studying this chapter, you will be able to...

LO1 Understand the role of cash management in the personal financial planning process.

LO2 Describe today's financial services marketplace, both depository and nondepository financial institutions.

LO3 Select the checking, savings, electronic banking, and other bank services that meet your needs.

LO4 Open and use a checking account.

LO5 Calculate the interest earned on your money using compound interest and future value techniques.

LO6 Develop a cash management strategy that incorporates a variety of savings plans.

After finishing this chapter, go to **PAGE 107** for **STUDY TOOLS**

rCarner/Shutterstock.com

How Will This Affect Me? Finding the best mix of alternative cash management accounts and assets requires careful cost/benefit analysis in light of personal objectives and constraints.

This chapter presents a variety of different alternatives and focuses on key characteristics that include liquidity, minimum balances, interest rate returns and costs, and safety. Cash management alternatives examined include checking and savings accounts as well as money market deposit accounts, certificates of deposit, money market mutual funds, U.S. Treasury bills, and U.S. and U.S. Series I bonds. This chapter will prepare you to design an effective cash management strategy, which is an integral part of a comprehensive financial plan.

4-1 THE ROLE OF CASH MANAGEMENT IN PERSONAL FINANCIAL PLANNING

LO1 Establishing good financial habits involves managing cash as well as other types of assets. In this chapter, we focus our attention on **cash management**—the routine, day-to-day administration of cash and near-cash resources, also known as *liquid assets*. These assets are considered liquid because they're either held in cash or can be readily converted into cash with little or no loss in value.

There are several other kinds of liquid assets beyond cash, including checking accounts, savings accounts, money market deposit accounts, money market mutual funds, and other short-term investments. Near term needs are usually met with cash on hand, and unplanned or future needs are met using some type of savings or short-term investment. Exhibit 4.1

> Efficient cash management ensures adequate funds for both household use and an effective savings program.

briefly describes some popular types of liquid assets and the representative rates of return they earned in the fall of 2016. The rates reflect the Federal Reserve's (the Fed's) policy goal of keeping rates low to help stimulate the economy during the fragile period following the global financial crisis of 2008–2009.

In personal financial planning, efficient cash management ensures adequate funds for both household use and an effective savings program. Write checks only at certain times of the week or month and, just as important, avoid carrying your checkbook (or debit card) when you might be tempted to spend money for unplanned purchases. If you're going shopping, set a maximum spending limit beforehand—an amount consistent with your cash budget. This system not only helps you avoid frivolous, impulsive expenditures but also documents how and where you spend your money.

cash management the routine, day-to-day administration of cash and near-cash resources, also known as *liquid assets*, by an individual or family

Exhibit 4.1

Representative Rates of Return

Type	Fall 2016	Description
Cash	0%	Pocket money; the coin and currency in one's possession.
Interest checking account	0.31%	A substitute for cash. Offered by commercial banks and other financial institutions such as savings and loans and credit unions.
Savings account/Money market deposit	0.49%	Savings accounts are available at any time, but funds cannot be withdrawn by check. Money market deposit accounts (MMDAs) require a fairly large (typically $1,000 or more) minimum deposit, and offer check-writing privileges.
Certificate of deposit (CD)	1.18% (1-year)	A savings instrument where funds are left on deposit for a stipulated period (one week to one year or more); imposes a penalty for withdrawing funds early. Market yields vary by size and maturity; no check-writing privileges.
U.S. Treasury bill (T-bill)	0.328 (3-month)	Short-term, highly marketable security issued by the U.S. Treasury (originally issued with maturities of 13 and 26 weeks); smallest denomination is $100.
U.S. Savings bond (EE)	0.10%	Issued at a discount from face value by the U.S. Treasury; rate of interest is tied to U.S. Treasury securities. Long a popular savings vehicle (widely used with payroll deduction plans). Matures to face value in approximately five years; sold in denominations of $25 and more.

Another aspect of cash management is establishing an ongoing savings program, which is an important part of personal financial planning. Savings are not only a cushion against financial emergencies but also a way to accumulate funds to meet future financial goals. You may want to put money aside so that you can go back to school in a few years to earn a graduate degree, or buy a new home, or take a vacation. Savings will help you meet these specific financial objectives.

4-1a The Problem with Low Interest Rates

Just how low did interest rates fall in the wake of the financial crisis under the Fed's policies? Consider how some key interest rates in the fall of 2016 compare with their historical averages from 2000 to the fall of 2016. The average interest rates on 5- and 10-year Treasury bonds over this time period were 2.90 percent and 3.63 percent, respectively. In the fall of 2016 these rates had fallen to only 1.18 percent and 1.63 percent! And a prudent saver looking for a short-term return on a 3-month negotiable CD could only get about 0.08 percent in the fall of 2016.

These drops in interest rates have important implications for your personal finances. For a sense of the significance of the drop in interest rates, consider the effect of investing $25,000 for five years at the low rate of only 1.18 percent in September 2016 vs. investing at the historical average rate of 2.90 percent. After five years, you would have about $28,841 at the average rate and only about $26,510 at the lower rate.

There are benefits and costs to the unprecedentedly low interest rates that have persisted since the financial crisis of 2008–2009. Whether they are a net benefit or a net cost depends on your perspective. As of the fall of 2016 the Fed had continued to keep interest rates low. However, there were increasing signs that an improving economy would moderate the Fed's efforts to keep rates so low. While financial markets generally reacted positively to this low rate policy by pushing up asset prices, low interest rates also tend to signal sluggish economic growth and the risk of deflation.

The benefits of lower interest rates include the reduced costs of financing the massive federal budget deficit, which is a significant savings given that interest on the federal debt was $402.4 billion in 2015. And lower rates have helped support the "too big to fail" banks. Indeed, the Fed's low interest rate policy allowed banks to pay less than 1 percent interest on savings. But the costs are equally impressive. Low interest rates reduce income to retirees and to pension funds. Some retirees have had to dip into their principal, which could put more stress on welfare programs for the elderly and may prompt the government to increase its financial support of underfunded pension funds.

Extremely low interest rates favor borrowers and dampen the incentive to save. While keeping big banks afloat is important, some argue that low interest rates have helped protect banks from absorbing the consequences of their actions and redistribute wealth away from prudent savers. Indeed, the inflation-adjusted real interest rate has been negative, which means that savers are not keeping up with inflation and will either have to tap into their principal or cut their spending. This is bad for retirees and for the overall economy. People tend to give less to charity as they seek to cover income shortfalls resulting from lower interest rates. The percentage of savings out of disposable income fell from a 8.2 percent in 1985 to a low of only 1.5 percent in 2005 and settled around 5.7 percent in the mid-2016.

Low interest rates create a variety of economic distortions, especially when real, inflation-adjusted interest rates are negative. Such rates discourage savings and discourage the reduction of overall debt levels in the economy. Low interest rates also encourage investors to search for investments that pay income, which increases the demand for stocks paying high dividends and for lower-grade, riskier bonds. Unfortunately, low interest rates do not seem to increase the supply of credit materially. Being fearful of taking much risk in the wake of the financial crisis, banks have tended to invest more in government securities and less in risky loans.

So what's a prudent saver to do in such a low-interest-rate environment? Unfortunately, the search for higher current returns leads many people to make investments that are too risky for them. Some move into higher-quality corporate bonds. But when rates are so low, they are likely to go up. And bond prices fall when rates rise, which poses substantial price risk to longer-term bonds. More moderate strategies involve buying stocks that pay higher dividends and buying preferred stocks, which will be discussed more in Chapter 12. But stocks are generally riskier than bonds, so the pursuit of higher returns in a low-interest-rate environment must be tempered by careful consideration of the suitability of the likely higher risk.

4-2 TODAY'S FINANCIAL SERVICES MARKETPLACE

LO2 Stella Patterson hasn't been inside her bank in years. Her company deposits her salary into her checking account each month, and she regularly does all her banking from her home computer: with the click of a mouse, she can check her account balances, pay her bills, even search for the best rates on savings instruments. And by making a few simple entries, she is able to withdraw money from her U.S. bank account using an automated teller machine (ATM) in Rome!

The financial services industry continues to evolve, thanks in large part to advanced technology and changing regulations. Today, consumers can choose from many different types of financial institutions, all competing for their business. No longer must you go to one place for your checking account, another for credit cards or loans, and yet another for brokerage services. Instead, financial institutions are expanding services and competitively pricing their products by bundling different accounts. For example, if you have $25,000 worth of funds in several Bank of America/Merrill Lynch accounts, you're eligible for reduced or zero-cost commissions on stock trades, free checking, free bill-pay, a credit card, and free

Capricorn Studio/Shutterstock.com

ATM debit card transactions. And online banking gives you easy access to all of these services.

The *financial services industry* as we know it today comprises all institutions that market various kinds of *financial products* (such as checking and savings accounts, credit cards, loans and mortgages, insurance, and mutual funds) and *financial services* (such as financial planning, securities brokerage, tax filing and planning, estate planning, real estate, trusts, and retirement). What 30 years ago were several distinct (though somewhat related) industries are now, in essence, one industry in which firms are differentiated more by organizational structure than by name or product offerings. This is good news – we have more choices!

4-2a Types of Financial Institutions

Financial institutions can be classified into two broad groups—depository and nondepository—based on whether or not they accept deposits as traditional banks do.

Go to Smart Sites

Looking for a fee-free Internet bank? *PC Magazine* lists five good ones to choose from, and why. A highlight box in each chapter of PFIN Online includes "Smart Sites," a list of resources and sites that offer additional information on topics in the PFIN text. Log in at www.cengagebrain.com.

Depository Financial Institutions The vast majority of financial transactions take place at *depository financial institutions*—commercial banks (both brick-and-mortar and Internet), savings and loan associations (S&Ls), savings banks, and credit unions. Although they're regulated by different agencies, depository financial institutions are commonly referred to as "banks" because of their similar products and services. What sets these institutions apart from others is their ability to accept deposits; most people use them for their checking and savings account needs. These depository financial institutions are described in Exhibit 4.2.

Nondepository Financial Institutions Other types of financial institutions that offer banking services, *but don't accept deposits like traditional banks*, are considered *nondepository institutions*. Today you can hold a credit card issued by a stock brokerage firm or have an account with a mutual fund that allows you to write a limited number of checks.

4-2b How Safe Is Your Money?

Almost all commercial banks, S&Ls, savings banks, and credit unions are federally insured by U.S. government agencies. The few that are not federally insured usually obtain insurance through either a state-chartered or a private insurance agency. Most experts believe that these privately insured institutions have less protection against loss than those that are federally insured. Exhibit 4.3 lists the insuring agencies and the maximum insurance

BEHAVIOR MATTERS

Why Can't I Seem to Save More—and What Can I Do About It?

There's a well-worn joke about meaning to read a book about procrastination … but you just can't get around to it. Similarly, procrastination is a common behavioral bias that often keeps us from saving more because we just keep putting it off. People are particularly likely to procrastinate when they make decisions that are perceived as complex. For example, if you view the saving decision more broadly as a set of subsequent, complex investment decisions, you're more likely to put off the decision to save more. So what's the best way to proceed if you

want to save more? Simplify the decision by adopting an easy plan like saving 10 percent of your income by directing your bank to automatically transfer the money each month from your checking to savings account. Putting basic decisions like this on autopilot combats our natural tendency to procrastinate. That's a start that you can build on before approaching more complex investing decisions. Because no savings means nothing to invest, it's best to act now and not worry about specific savings decisions every month in the beginning.

Exhibit 4.2

Depository Financial Institutions

Depository financial institutions differ from their nonbank counterparts, such as stock brokerages and mutual funds, in their ability to accept deposits. Most consumers use these institutions to meet their checking and savings account needs.

Institution	Description
Commercial bank	Offers checking and savings accounts and a full range of financial products and services; the only institution that can offer *noninterest-paying checking accounts (demand deposits)*. The most popular of the depository financial institutions. Most are traditional *brick-and-mortar banks*, but Internet banks—online commercial banks—are becoming more popular because of their convenience, lower service fees, and higher interest paid on account balances.
Savings and loan association (S&L)	Channels the savings of depositors primarily into mortgage loans for purchasing and improving homes. Also offers many of the same checking, saving, and lending products as commercial banks. Often pays slightly higher interest on savings than do commercial banks.
Savings bank	Similar to S&Ls, but located primarily in the New England states. Most are *mutual* associations—their depositors are their owners and thus receive a portion of the profits in the form of interest on their savings.
Credit union	A nonprofit, member-owned financial cooperative that provides a full range of financial products and services to its *members*, who must belong to a common occupation, religious or fraternal order, or residential area. Generally small institutions when compared with commercial banks and S&Ls. Offer interest-paying checking accounts—called share draft accounts—and a variety of saving and lending programs. Because they are run to benefit their members, they pay higher interest on savings and charge lower rates on loans than do other depository financial institutions.

Exhibit 4.3

Federal Deposit Insurance Programs

Insurance on checking and savings accounts at federally insured institutions covers up to $250,000.

Savings Institution	Insuring Agency	Basic Insurance Amounts
Commercial bank	Federal Deposit Insurance Corporation (FDIC)	$250,000/depositor through the Bank Insurance Fund (BIF)
Savings and loan association	FDIC	$250,000/depositor through the Savings Association Insurance Fund (SAIF)
Savings bank	FDIC	$250,000/depositor through the Bank Insurance Fund (BIF)
Credit union	National Credit Union Administration (NCUA)	$250,000/depositor through the National Credit Union Share Insurance Fund (NCUSIF)

amounts provided under the various federal deposit insurance programs.

Deposit insurance protects the funds you have on deposit at banks and other depository institutions against institutional failure. In effect, the insuring agency stands behind the financial institution and guarantees the safety of your deposits up to a specified maximum amount. The Dodd-Frank Wall Street Reform and Consumer Protection Act was signed into law in late 2010 and increased the maximum deposit insurance amount from $100,000 to $250,000.

It's important to understand that deposit insurance is provided to the *depositor, per insured* bank rather than to a *deposit account*. Thus, the checking *and* savings accounts of each depositor are insured and, *as long as the maximum insurable amount*

Internet banks an online commercial bank

share draft accounts an account offered by credit unions that is similar to interest-paying checking accounts offered by other financial institutions

deposit insurance a type of insurance that protects funds on deposit against failure of the institution; can be insured by the FDIC and the NCUA *per bank is not exceeded*, the depositor can have any number of accounts and still be fully protected. This is an important feature to keep in mind because many people mistakenly believe that the maximum insurance applies to *each* of their accounts.

Now that banks are offering a greater variety of products, including mutual funds, it's important to remember that only deposit accounts, including CDs, are covered by deposit insurance. *Securities purchased through your bank are not protected by deposit insurance.*

As a depositor, it's possible to increase your $250,000 of traditional deposit insurance if necessary by opening accounts in different depositor names at the same institution. For example, a married couple can obtain as much as $1,500,000 in coverage by setting up several accounts:

▶ One in the name of each spouse ($500,000 in coverage)

▶ A *joint account* in both names (good for another $500,000, which is $250,000 per account owner)

▶ *Separate trust or self-directed retirement (IRA, Keogh, etc.) accounts* in the name of each spouse (good for an additional $250,000 per spouse)

In this case, each depositor name is treated as a separate legal entity, receiving full insurance coverage—the husband alone is considered one legal entity, the wife another, and the husband and wife as a couple a third. The trust and self-directed retirement accounts are also viewed as separate legal entities.

demand deposit an account held at a financial institution from which funds can be withdrawn on demand by the account holder; same as a *checking account*

4-3 A FULL MENU OF CASH MANAGEMENT PRODUCTS

LO3 As a student on a tight budget, working his way through college, Julian Olson knew how important it was to plan his saving and spending. By using a checking account comparison chart like the one in Exhibit 4.4, Julian could compare information on daily balance requirements, service fees, interest rates, and the services his bank offers to college students and others.

4-3a Checking and Savings Accounts

People hold cash and other forms of liquid assets, such as checking and savings accounts, for the convenience that they offer in making purchase transactions, meeting normal living expenses, and providing a safety net, or cushion, to meet unexpected expenses. Because of the federal *Truth in Savings Act of 1993*, all depository financial institutions must clearly disclose fees, interest rates, and terms on both checking and savings accounts. In addition, banks must use a standard *annual percentage yield (APY)* formula that takes compounding (discussed later) into account when stating the interest paid on accounts. This makes it easier for consumers to compare each bank's offerings.

The law also requires banks to pay interest on a customer's full daily or monthly average deposit balance. And it strictly prohibits them from paying interest on only the lowest daily balance or paying no interest if the account balance falls below the minimum balance for just one day. In addition, banks must notify customers 30 days in advance before lowering rates on deposit accounts or CDs.

Checking Accounts A checking account held at a financial institution is known as a **demand deposit**, meaning that the bank must permit these funds to be withdrawn whenever the account holder demands. You put money into your checking account by *depositing* funds; you withdraw it by *writing a check*, *using a debit card*, or *making a cash withdrawal*. As long as you have sufficient funds in your account, the bank, when presented with a valid check or an electronic debit, must immediately pay the amount indicated by deducting it from your account.

Regular checking is the most common type of checking account. Traditionally, it pays no interest, but any service charges can be waived if you maintain a minimum balance (usually between $500 and $1,500), though many banks are moving away from such minimum balance

Exhibit 4.4

Checking Accounts Comparison Chart

Most banks offer a variety of checking account options, which are typically differentiated by minimum balances, fees, and other services.

Representative Bank USA

Features	College Checking	Custom Checking	Advantage Checking	Advantage Plus Checking
Minimum daily balance (to waive monthly service fee)	None	$750 in checking	$5,000 in checking	$7,500 combined balance
Monthly service fee	$5.95	$9 with direct deposit	$11 without direct deposit; no fee with Homeowner's Option	$12 ($2 discount with direct deposit)
Interest	No	No	Yes	Yes
Online statements	Free	Free	Free	Free
Check safekeeping	Free	Free	Free	Free
Monthly check return	$3.00	$3.00	$3.00	Free
ATM and check card	Free	Free	Free	Free
Bank by phone	Free automated calls	Free automated calls	Free automated calls	Free banker-assisted calls
Overdraft protection	Credit card	Credit card	Credit card, line of credit account, and select deposit accounts	Credit card, line of credit account, and select deposit accounts
Direct deposit advance service	Not available	Yes, with a direct deposit of $100 a month or more	Yes, with a direct deposit of $100 a month or more	Yes, with a direct deposit of $100 a month or more

requirements. Technically, only commercial banks can offer non-interest-paying, regular checking accounts. Savings banks, S&Ls, and credit unions also offer checking accounts; but these accounts, which must pay interest, are called *NOW (negotiable order of withdrawal) accounts* or, in the case of credit unions, *share draft accounts.*

Savings Accounts A savings account is another form of liquid asset available at commercial banks, S&Ls, savings banks, credit unions, and other types of financial institutions. Savings deposits are referred to as **time deposits**, since they are expected to remain on deposit for longer periods of time than demand deposits. Because savings deposits earn higher rates of interest, they are typically preferable to checking accounts when the depositor's goal is to accumulate money for a future expenditure or to maintain balances for meeting unexpected expenses.

Most banks pay higher interest rates on larger savings account balances. For example, a bank might pay 0.25 percent on balances up to $2,500, 0.40 percent on balances between $2,500 and $10,000, and 0.60 percent on balances of more than $10,000. In addition to withdrawal policies and deposit insurance, the stated interest rate and the method of calculating interest paid on savings accounts are important considerations when choosing the financial institution in which to place your savings. As noted above, current interest rates are extremely low by historical standards due to the Fed's post-crisis policies.

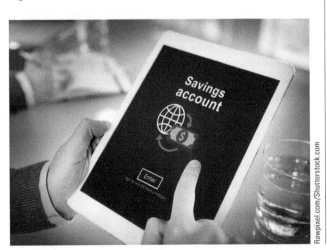

Rawpixel.com/Shutterstock.com

time deposits a savings deposit at a financial institution; remains on deposit for a longer time than a demand deposit

Interest-Paying Checking Accounts Depositors can choose from NOW accounts, money market deposit accounts, and money market mutual funds.

Now Accounts Negotiable order of withdrawal (NOW) accounts are checking accounts on which the financial institution pays interest. There is no legal minimum balance for a NOW, but many institutions impose their own requirement, often between $500 and $1,000. Some pay interest on any balance in the account, but most institutions pay a higher rate of interest for balances above a specified amount.

Money Market Deposit Accounts Money market deposit accounts (MMDAs) are offered at banks and other financial institutions and compete with money market mutual funds for deposits. MMDAs are popular with savers and investors because of their convenience and safety and because deposits in MMDAs (unlike those in money market mutual funds) are *federally insured*. Most banks require a minimum MMDA balance of $1,000 or more.

Depositors can use check-writing privileges or ATMs to access MMDA accounts. They receive a limited number (usually six) of free monthly checks and transfers but pay a fee on additional transactions. Although this reduces the flexibility of these accounts, most depositors view MMDAs as savings and so do not consider these restrictions to be a serious obstacle. Moreover, MMDAs pay the highest interest rate of any bank account on which checks can be written.

Money Market Mutual Funds Money market mutual funds have become the most successful type of mutual fund ever offered. A **money market mutual fund (MMMF)** pools the funds of many small investors to purchase high-return, short-term marketable securities offered by the U.S. Treasury, major corporations, large commercial banks, and various government organizations. (Mutual funds are discussed in detail in Chapter 13.)

MMMFs have historically paid interest at rates of 1 percent to 3 percent above those paid on regular savings accounts. Moreover, investors have instant access to their funds through check-writing privileges, although these must be written for a stipulated minimum amount (often $500). The checks look like, and are treated like, any other check drawn on a demand deposit account. And as with all interest-bearing checking accounts, you continue to earn interest on your money while the checks make their way through the banking system.

Asset Management Accounts Perhaps the best example of a banking service also offered by a nondepository financial institution is the **asset management account (AMA)**, or *central asset account*. The AMA is a comprehensive deposit account that combines checking, investing, and borrowing activities and is offered primarily by brokerage houses and mutual funds. AMAs appeal to investors because they can consolidate most of their financial transactions at one institution and on one account statement.

A typical AMA account includes an MMDA with unlimited free checking, a *Visa* or *MasterCard* debit card, use of ATMs, and brokerage and loan accounts. Annual fees and account charges (e.g., a per-transaction charge for ATM withdrawals) vary, so it pays to shop around. The distinguishing feature of these accounts is that they automatically "sweep" excess balances—for example, amounts over $500—into a higher-return MMMF on a daily or weekly basis. When the account holder needs funds to purchase securities or cover checks written on the MMDA, the funds are transferred back to the MMDA. And if the amount of securities purchased or checks presented for payment exceeds the account balance, the needed funds are supplied automatically through a loan.

Although AMAs are an attractive alternative to a traditional bank account, they do have some drawbacks. For example, compared with banks, there are fewer physical "branch" locations. However, AMAs are typically affiliated with ATM networks, making it easy to withdraw funds. Yet ATM transactions are more costly; checks can take longer to clear; and some bank services may not be offered. Moreover, AMAs are not covered by deposit insurance, although these deposits are protected by the *Securities Investor Protection Corporation* (SIPC) and the firm's private insurance.

4-3b Electronic Banking Services

An important area in cash management today is *electronic banking services*. Whether you're using an ATM or checking your account balance online, electronic banking services make managing your money easier and more convenient. Electronic funds transfer systems

---

negotiable order of withdrawal (NOW) accounts a checking account on which the financial institution pays interest; NOWs have no legal minimum balance

money market deposit accounts (MMDAs) a federally insured savings account, offered by banks and other depository institutions, that competes with money market mutual funds

money market mutual fund (MMMF) a mutual fund that pools the funds of many small investors and purchases high-return, short-term marketable securities

asset management account (AMA) a comprehensive deposit account; offered primarily by brokerage houses and mutual funds allow you to conduct many types of banking business at any hour of the day or night.

Electronic Funds Transfer Systems Electronic funds transfer systems (EFTSs) allow depositors to conduct a variety of different types of bank transactions at any time by using the latest telecommunications and computer technology to electronically transfer funds into and out of their accounts. For example, your employer may use an EFTS to electronically transfer your pay from the firm's bank account directly into your personal bank account at the same or a different bank. This eliminates the employer's need to prepare and process checks and the employee's need to deposit them. Electronic transfer systems make possible such services as debit cards and ATMs, preauthorized deposits and payments, bank-by-phone accounts, and online banking.

Debit Cards and Automated Teller Machines This form of EFTS uses specially coded plastic cards, called debit cards, to transfer funds from the customer's bank account (a debit) to the recipient's account. A debit card may be used to make purchases at any place of business set up with the point-of-sale terminals required to accept debit card payments. The personal identification number (PIN) issued with your debit card verifies that you are authorized to access the account.

Visa and *MasterCard* issue debit cards linked to your checking account that give you even more flexibility. In addition to using the card to purchase goods and services, you can use it at ATMs, which have become a popular way to make banking transactions. Automated teller machines (ATMs) are remote computer terminals that customers of a bank or other depository institution can use to make deposits, withdrawals, and other transactions such as loan payments or transfers between accounts—24 hours a day, 7 days a week. Most banks have ATMs outside their offices, and some place freestanding

ATMs in shopping malls, airports, and grocery stores; at colleges and universities; and in other high-traffic areas to enhance their competitive position.

If your bank belongs to an EFTS network, such as Cirrus, Star, or Interlink, then you can get cash from the ATM of any bank in the United States or overseas that is a member of that network. (In fact, the easiest way to get foreign currency when you travel overseas is through an ATM on your bank's network! It also gives you the best exchange rate for your dollar.) Banks charge an average per-transaction fee of over $4.50 for using the ATM of another bank, and some also charge when you use your ATM card to pay certain merchants. However, to be more competitive, some banks now reimburse the fees associated with using the ATMs of other banks.

Security concerns are increasing pressure for financial institutions to replace the common magnetic strip on credit cards with EMV chips, named for its developers—*Europay, MasterCard, Visa*. The cardholder information is entered on a chip embedded in the card in an encrypted form. Card issuers now require the use of EMV cards. However, many ATMs and merchants' credit card readers have not been converted yet. In the interim, cards with both a magnetic strip and the EMV chip are being offered by issuers.

Debit card use is increasing because these cards are convenient both *for retailers*, who don't have to worry about bounced checks, and *for consumers*, who don't have to write checks. These cards are so popular, in fact, that the total dollar volume of purchases made using *Visa's* branded debit cards actually surpassed their credit-card purchases in 2008. Indeed, the convenience of debit cards may be their biggest drawback: *they make it easier to overspend.* To avoid such problems, make sure you record all debit card purchases immediately in your checkbook ledger and deduct them from your checkbook balance. Also be aware that, if there's a problem with a purchase, you can't stop payment—an action you could take if you had paid by check or credit card.

> The convenience of debit cards may be their biggest drawback: *they make it easier to overspend.*

electronic funds transfer systems (EFTSs) systems using the latest telecommunications and computer technology to electronically transfer funds into and out of customers' accounts

debit cards specially coded plastic cards used to transfer funds from a customer's bank account to the recipient's account to pay for goods or services

automated teller machines (ATMs) remote computer terminals that customers of depository institutions can use to make basic transactions, 24 hours a day, 7 days a week

Financial Planning Tips

USING ONLINE BANKING SAFELY

- **Confirm that the online bank site is legitimate.** Watch out for fake Internet sites that use a name or Internet address similar to, but not the same as, that of your bank. These sites try to trick you into entering their Internet site and providing your account number and password. Make sure that you have typed the correct Internet address for your specific bank before entering any account information. Read the "About Us" section that describes the institution and confirm that its deposits are insured by the FDIC. Look for the FDIC logo or "Member FDIC." It is wise to check the FDIC's online database of insured institutions, which is found by searching "Bank Find" at http://research.fdic.gov/bankfind/.

- **Protect your personal Information.** Banks are required to inform you of their privacy policy. This describes what personal information the bank keeps and what information, if any, it shares with other companies. When logging onto a bank site, make sure that the Internet site is encrypted. This is indicated by a browser icon that looks like a "lock" or a "key," along with "https" in the address line. Passwords or PINs should be unique to you and changed regularly.

Source: Adapted from "Safe Internet Banking," www.fdic.gov/bank/individual/online/safe.html, accessed October 2016.

Preauthorized Deposits and Payments Two related EFTS services are *preauthorized deposits and payments*. They allow you to receive automatic deposits or make payments that occur regularly. For example, you can arrange to have your paycheck or monthly benefits deposited directly into your account. Regular, fixed-amount payments, such as mortgage and consumer loan payments or monthly retirement fund contributions, can be preauthorized to be made automatically from your account. You can also preauthorize regular payments of varying amounts such as monthly utility bills.

Bank-by-Phone Accounts Bank customers can make various types of transactions by telephone, either by calling a customer service operator who handles the transaction or by using the keypad on a touch-tone telephone to provide instructions to the bank. After the customer provides a passcode to access the account, the system provides the appropriate prompts to perform various transactions, such as obtaining an account balance, finding out what checks have cleared, transferring funds to other accounts, and dispatching payments to participating merchants. However, online banking options are replacing bank-by-phone accounts.

Online and Mobile Banking and Bill Payment Services A recent Federal Reserve survey found that 74 percent of consumers relied on online banking services and 35 percent used mobile banking. These percentages have grown steadily as banks make online and mobile services easier to use and as people become more comfortable using the Internet and mobile phones for financial transactions. Many individuals do little more than check their balances, but more than half use the Internet to transfer funds as well. Today, most banks aggressively compete for your online banking business because it's in their best financial interests to do so. A recent study showed that the cost of a full-service teller transaction is about $1.00, an ATM transaction is less than 30 cents, and an Internet transaction is less than 1 cent.

Although computer-based, bank-at-home systems and mobile banking don't replace the use of an ATM to obtain cash or deposit money, they can save both time and postage when you're paying bills. Other benefits include convenience and the potential to earn higher interest rates and pay lower fees. But online banking doesn't always live up to its promises. You can't make cash deposits and you don't always know when the funds will reach your account.

4-3c Regulation of EFTS Services

The federal *Electronic Fund Transfer Act of 1978* describes your rights and responsibilities as an EFTS user. Under this law, you cannot stop payment on a defective or questionable purchase, although individual banks and state laws often have more lenient provisions. If there's an error, you must notify the bank within 60 days of its occurrence. The bank must then investigate and advise you of the results within 10 days. The bank can then take up to 45 more days to investigate the error but must return the disputed money to your account until the issue is resolved.

If you fail to notify the bank of an error within 60 days, the bank has no obligation under federal law to conduct an investigation or return your money. You must notify the bank immediately about the theft, loss, or unauthorized use of your EFTS card. Notification within two business days after you discover the card missing limits your loss to $50. After two business days, you may lose up to $500 (but never more than the amount that was withdrawn by the thief). If you don't report the loss within 60 days after your periodic statement was mailed, you can lose all the money in your account.

When reporting errors or unauthorized transactions, it's best to notify your bank by telephone and follow up with a letter; then keep a copy of the letter. These safeguards notwithstanding, *your best protection is to guard carefully the PIN used to access your accounts.* Don't write the PIN on your EFTS card, and be sure to check your statements for possible errors or unauthorized transactions.

4-3d Other Bank Services

In addition to the services described earlier in this chapter, many banks offer other types of money management services, such as safe-deposit boxes and trust services.

▶ **Safe-deposit boxes:** A *safe-deposit box* is a rented drawer in a bank's vault. Boxes can be rented for an average of about $30 per year, depending on their size. When you rent a box, you receive one key to it and the bank keeps another key. The box can be opened only when both keys are used. This arrangement protects items in the box from theft and serves as an excellent storage place for jewelry, contracts, stock certificates, titles, and other important documents. Keeping valuables in a safe-deposit box may also reduce your homeowner's insurance preimium by eliminating the "riders" that are often needed to cover such items.

▶ **Trust services:** Bank trust departments provide investment and estate planning advice. They manage and administer the investments in a trust account or from an estate.

4-4 MAINTAINING A CHECKING ACCOUNT

LO4 By the time George Simpson started college, he had a thriving car-detailing business that earned him several hundred dollars per week. Some customers paid him in advance, some paid after the fact, and some forgot (or otherwise neglected) to pay at all. But by depositing each check or cash payment into his checking account, George was able to keep track of his earnings without complicated bookkeeping.

A checking account is one of the most useful cash management tools. It's a safe and convenient way to hold money and streamline point-of-sale purchases, debt payments, and other basic transactions. You can have regular or interest-paying checking accounts at commercial banks, S&Ls, savings banks, credit unions, and even brokerage houses through asset management accounts. For convenience, we'll focus on commercial bank checking accounts, although our discussion applies also to checking accounts maintained at other types of financial institutions.

4-4a Opening and Using Your Checking Account

Factors that typically influence the choice of where to maintain a checking account are convenience, services, and cost. Many people choose a bank based solely on convenience factors: location, business hours, number of drive-thru windows, and number and location of branch offices and ATMs. Ease of access is obviously an important consideration because most people prefer to bank near home or work. But in addition to convenience and safety, you should also consider the interest rates the bank offers, types of accounts (including special accounts that combine such features as credit cards, free checks, and reduced fees), structure and level of fees and charges, and quality of customer service.

The Cost of a Checking Account Bank service charges have increased sharply for a variety of reasons, including the growth of interest-bearing checking accounts. Today few, if any, banks and other depository institutions allow unlimited free, check-writing privileges. Most banks levy monthly and per-check fees when your checking account balance drops below a required minimum, and some may charge for checking no matter how large a balance you carry.

While some banks are moving away from minimum balance requirements, a common requirement is to maintain a minimum balance of $500 to $1,000 or more to avoid service charges. Although some banks use the *average*

If you're looking for a bank, here are some important factors to consider:

- **Convenient location and useful online and mobile services.** Find a bank that is conveniently located *and* has online services, because such banks tend to pay more competitive savings rates.

- **Free checking and free money transfers.** "Free checking" usually means that you aren't required to keep a minimum balance in your account and can write as many checks each month as you like. Even if it isn't labeled as such, look for free checking. Also look for banks that let you transfer funds between different accounts for free.

- **Convenient ATMs.** The average fee for using the ATM of another bank is about over $5. Although some banks are starting to refund such fees, by visiting only ATMs that belong to your bank, you can avoid all surcharges and the hassle of refunds. It is best to have an ATM close to your work and home.

- **Overdraft and FDIC protection.** Given that fees for bounced checks averages over $30, it is important to know what the charges are and what kind of overdraft protection is offered. Also make sure that your deposits are insured by the FDIC.

- **Competitive interest income.** Find out if the bank pays interest on your balance. You can shop for the most competitive rates in your zip code at www.bankrate.com and www.bankingmyway.com.

monthly balance in an account to determine whether to levy a service charge, most use the *daily* balance procedure. This means that if your account should happen to fall just $1 below the minimum balance *just once* during the month, you'll be hit with the full service charge—even if your average balance is three times the minimum requirement. Service charges take two forms: (1) a base service charge of, say, $7.50 a month, and (2) additional charges of, say, 25 cents for each check you write and 10 cents for each ATM or bank-by-phone transaction.

In addition to the service charges on checking accounts, banks have increased most other check-related charges and raised the minimum balances required for free checking and waivers of specified fees. The average charge on a returned check is between $25 and $30, and stop-payment orders typically cost $20 to $35. Some banks charge fees for ATM or bank-by-phone transactions that exceed a specified number. Most also charge for using the ATM of another bank that is not a member of the same network. It's not surprising that smart consumers use cost as the single most important variable when choosing where to set up a checking account.

Individual or Joint Account? A couple or partners wishing to open a checking account may do so in one of three ways:

1. They can each open individual checking accounts (on which the other cannot write checks).

2. They can open a joint account that requires both signatures on all checks.

3. They can open a joint account that allows either one to write checks (the most common type of joint account).

One advantage of the joint account over two individual accounts is lower service charges. In addition, the account has rights of survivorship: for a married couple, this means that if one spouse dies, the surviving spouse, after fulfilling a specified legal requirement, can draw checks on the account. If account owners are treated as tenants in common rather than having rights of survivorship, then the survivor gets only his or her share of the account. Thus, when you're opening a joint account, be sure to specify the rights you prefer.

General Checking Account Procedures After you select the bank that meets your needs, it's a simple matter to open an account. The application form asks for basic personal information such as name, date of birth, Social Security number, address, phone, and place of employment. You'll also have to provide identification, sign signature cards, and make an initial deposit. The bank will give you a supply of checks to use until your personalized checks arrive.

After opening a checking account, follow these basic procedures:

▶ Always write checks in ink.

▶ Include the name of the person being paid, the date, and the amount of the check—written in both numerals and words for accuracy.

- Sign the check the same way as on the signature card you filled out when opening the account.

- Note the check's purpose on the check—usually on the line provided in the lower-left corner. This information is helpful for both budgeting and tax purposes.

Make sure to enter all checking account transactions—checks written, deposits, point-of-sale debit purchases, ATM transactions, and preauthorized automatic payments and deposits—in the **checkbook ledger** provided with your supply of checks. Then, *subtract* the amount of each check, debit card purchase, ATM cash withdrawal, or payment, and *add* the amount of each deposit to the previous balance to keep track of your current account balance. Good transaction records and an accurate balance prevent overdrawing the account.

Prepare a deposit slip with each deposit (such slips are generally included with your checks and also available at your bank) listing the currency, coins, and checks being deposited. List checks by the *transit ID number* printed on the check, usually at the top right. Also properly endorse all checks that you're depositing. To protect against possible loss of endorsed checks, it's common to use a special endorsement, such as "Pay to the order of XYZ Bank," or a restrictive endorsement, such as "For deposit only." When depositing checks, you may encounter a delay in funds' availability due to the time required for them to clear. To avoid overdrawing your account, know your bank's "hold" policy on deposits—it generally takes between one and five business days for funds to become available.

Overdrafts When a check is written for an amount greater than the current account balance, the result is an **overdraft**. If the overdraft is proven to be intentional, the bank can initiate legal proceedings against the account holder. The action taken by a bank on an overdraft depends on the strength of its relationship with the account holder and the amount involved. In the vast majority of cases, the bank simply stamps the overdrawn check with the words "insufficient balance (or funds)" and returns it to the party to whom it was written. This is often called a "bounced check." The account holder is notified of this action, and the holder's bank deducts an average overdraft fee of $35 from his checking account. The depositor of a "bad check" may also be charged a fee by her bank, which explains why merchants typically charge bad check writers $15 to $25 per bounced check and often refuse to accept future checks from them.

When you have a strong relationship with your bank or arrange **overdraft protection**, the bank will pay a check that overdraws the account. In cases where overdraft protection has not been prearranged but the bank pays the check, the account holder is usually notified by the bank and charged a penalty fee for the inconvenience. However, the check does not bounce, and the check writer's creditworthiness is not damaged.

There are several ways to arrange overdraft protection. Many banks offer an overdraft line of credit that automatically extends a loan to cover the amount of an overdraft. In most cases, however, the loans are made only in specified increments, such as $50 or $100, and interest (or a fee) is levied against the loan amount, not the actual amount of the overdraft. This can be an expensive form of protection, particularly if you do not promptly repay the loan.

Another way to cover overdrafts is with an *automatic transfer program*, which automatically transfers funds from your savings account into your checking account in the event of an overdraft. Under this program, some banks charge both an annual fee and a fee on each transfer. Of course, *the best form of overdraft protection is to use good cash management techniques and regularly balance your checking account.*

Stopping Payment Occasionally it's necessary to **stop payment** on a check if it was issued as part of a contract that was not carried out, or because a good or service paid for by check is found to be faulty (note that some states prohibit you from

JohnKwan/Shutterstock.com

checkbook ledger a booklet, provided with a supply of checks, used to maintain accurate records of all checking account transactions

overdraft the result of writing a check for an amount greater than the current account balance

overdraft protection an arrangement between the account holder and the depository institution wherein the institution automatically pays a check that overdraws the account

stop payment an order made by an account holder instructing the depository institution to refuse payment on an already issued check stopping payment on faulty goods or services). To stop payment on a check, you must notify the bank and fill out a form indicating the check number and date, amount, and the name of the party to whom it was written. You can initiate stop-payment orders online or by phone. Once you place a stop-payment order, the bank refuses payment on the affected check, and the check will be rejected if another bank presents it in the check-clearing process. Banks typically charge a fee ranging from $25 to $35 per check to stop payment. There's one big exception to all this, and that is, *if your checks or checkbook are lost or stolen, there's no need to stop payment on them* because you have no personal liability. Stopping payment in this case only incurs expense; it doesn't change your personal liability.

4-4b Monthly Statements

Once a month, your bank provides a statement—an itemized listing of all transactions in your checking account (checks written, ATM transactions, debit purchases, automatic payments, and deposits made). Also included are bank service charges and interest earned (see John Webb's May 2017 bank statement in Exhibit 4.5). Some banks include your original canceled checks with your bank statement, although most are abandoning this practice as we move toward a "paperless" society. Banks that don't return canceled checks will usually provide photocopies of them on request, generally for a fee. Many banks now let you view canceled checks online, free of charge.

It's important to review your monthly bank statement to verify the accuracy of your account records and to reconcile any differences between the statement balance and the balance shown in your checkbook ledger. The monthly statement is also a valuable source of information for your tax records.

Account Reconciliation You should reconcile your bank account as soon as possible after receiving your monthly statement. The **account reconciliation** process, or *balancing the checkbook*, can uncover errors in recording checks or deposits, in addition or subtraction, and, occasionally, in the bank's processing of a check. It can also help you avoid overdrafts by forcing you to verify your account balance monthly. Assuming that neither you nor the bank has made any

account reconciliation verifying the accuracy of your checking account balance in relation to the bank's records as reflected in the bank statement, which is an itemized listing of all transactions in the checking account

---

YOU CAN DO IT NOW: Reconcile Your Checkbook In this era of online and mobile banking, it's easy to keep up with the *current* balance in your checking account. So many people don't bother to reconcile their checking accounts. But it's all too easy to forget about outstanding checks, delayed payments, and ATM withdrawals when you just focus on your current balance. And reconciling your checkbook provides insight into how you spend your money each month, which will inform your budgeting and overall financial planning. So pick up your most recent bank statement and get reconciled—you can **do it now**.

---

errors, discrepancies between your checkbook ledger account balance and your bank statement can be attributed to one of four factors:

1. Checks that you've written, ATM withdrawals, debit purchases, or other automatic payments subtracted from your checkbook balance haven't yet been received and processed by your bank and therefore remain outstanding.

2. Deposits that you've made and added to your checkbook balance haven't yet been credited to your account.

3. Any service (activity) charges levied on your account by the bank haven't yet been deducted from your checkbook balance.

4. Interest earned on your account (if it's a NOW or an MMDA account) hasn't yet been added to your checkbook balance.

The reverse side of your bank statement usually provides a form for reconciling your account, along with step-by-step instructions. As an illustration, Worksheet 4.1 includes an account reconciliation form that John Webb completed for the month of May 2017 using the reconciliation procedures described in "Make that Checkbook Balance." You can use this form to reconcile either regular or interest-paying checking accounts.

4-4c Special Types of Checks

In some circumstances, sellers of goods or services may not accept personal checks because they can't be absolutely sure that the check is good. This is common for large purchases or when the buyer's bank is not located in the same area where the purchase is

Exhibit 4.5

A Bank Statement

Each month, you receive a statement from your bank or depository financial institution that summarizes the month's transactions and shows your latest account balance. This sample statement for May 2017 for John Webb not only shows the checks that have been paid, it also lists all ATM transactions, point-of-sale transactions using his ATM card (the Interlink payments at Lucky Stores), and direct payroll deposits.

```
    YOUR BANK                          #240
    P.O. BOX 516   ANY CITY, USA   90000-0000

       JOHN C. WEBB
       1765 SHERIDAN DRIVE              N        CALL (800) 222-0000
       YOUR CITY, STATE 12091           21       24 HOURS/DAY, 7 DAYS/WEEK
                                                 FOR ASSISTANCE WITH
                                                 YOUR ACCOUNT.

   PAGE 1 OF 1      THIS STATEMENT COVERS: 4/30/2017 THROUGH 5/29/2017
```

PREMIUM ACCOUNT	SUMMARY				
	PREVIOUS BALANCE	473.68		MINIMUM BALANCE	21.78
0123-45678	DEPOSITS	1,302.83+			
	WITHDRAWALS	1,689.02−			
	SERVICE CHARGES	7.50−			
	DIRECT DEPOSIT DISCOUNT	1.00+			
	NEW BALANCE	80.99			

CHECKS AND WITHDRAWALS	CHECK	DATE PAID	AMOUNT	CHECK	DATE PAID	AMOUNT
	203	5/01	10.00	213	5/08	40.00
	204	4/30	15.00	214	5/09	9.58
	205	5/10	635.00	215	5/20	66.18
	206	5/08	25.00	216	5/20	64.92
	207	5/07	19.00	217	5/21	25.03
	208	5/07	50.00	218	5/21	37.98
	209	5/08	15.00	219	5/22	35.00
	210	5/10	83.00	220	5/22	105.00
	211	5/10	10.00	222*	5/22	100.00
	212	5/08	70.00	223	5/21	40.00
				224	5/29	40.82

	PREMIUM ACCOUNT FEE LESS $1.00 DISCOUNT	4/30	6.50
ATM TRANSACTIONS	INTERLINK PURCHASE #572921 ON 04/30 AT LUCKY STORE NO 043	5/01	50.00
	WITHDRAWAL #08108 AT 00165A ON 05/04	5/06	20.00
	INTERLINK PURCHASE #807409 ON 05/11 AT LUCKY STORE NO 056	5/13	12.51
	WITHDRAWAL #01015 AT 00240C ON 05/17	5/17	20.00
	WITHDRAWAL #04792 AT 00167C ON 05/20	5/20	20.00
	WITHDRAWAL #04386 AT 00240D ON 05/21	5/21	40.00
	INTERLINK PURCHASE #880318 ON 05/28 AT LUCKY STORE #043	5/29	30.00

DEPOSITS		DATE POSTED	AMOUNT
	AVS RNT CAR SYST PAYROLL G2 000000035382	5/03	618.69
	AVS RNT CAR SYST PAYROLL G2 000000035382	5/17	83.39
	AVS RNT CAR SYST PAYROLL G2 000000035382	5/17	600.75

ATM LOCATIONS USED	
00165A:	249 PRIMROSE RD, ANY CITY, USA
00240C:	490 BROADWAY, ANY CITY, USA
00167C:	1145 BROADWAY, ANY CITY, USA
00240D:	490 BROADWAY, ANY CITY, USA

John Webb used this form to reconcile his checking account for the month of May 2017. Because line A equals line B, he has fully reconciled the difference between the $80.99 bank statement balance and his $339.44 checkbook balance. Accounts should be reconciled each month—as soon as possible after receiving the bank statement.

CHECKING ACCOUNT RECONCILIATION

For the Month of ___May___ , 20 _17_

Accountholder Name (s) ___John C. Webb___

Type of Account ___Regular Checking___

1. Ending balance shown on bank statement _____ **$ 80.99**

Add up checks and withdrawals still outstanding:

Check Number or Date	Amount	Check Number or Date	Amount
221	$ 81.55		
225	196.50		
Lucky—5/28	25.00		
ATM—5/29	40.00		
TOTAL	**$ 343.05**		

2. Deduct total checks/withdrawals still outstanding from bank balance _____ **− $343.05**

Add up deposits not shown on bank statement:

Date	Amount	Date	Amount
5/29/17	595.00		
TOTAL	**$ 595.00**		

3. Add total deposits still outstanding to bank balance _____ **+ $595.00**

A **Adjusted Bank Balance (1 − 2 + 3)** _____ **$332.94**

4. Ending balance shown in checkbook _____ **$339.44**

5. Deduct any bank service charges for the period ___(−$7.50 + $1.00)___ **− $ 6.50**

6. Add interest earned for the period _____ **+ $ 0**

B **New Checkbook Balance (4 − 5 + 6)** _____ **$332.94**

Note: Your account is reconciled when line A equals line B.

being made. A form of check that guarantees payment may be required instead; these include cashier's checks, traveler's checks, and certified checks.

▶ **Cashier's check:** Anyone can buy a cashier's check from a bank. These checks are often used by people who don't have checking accounts. They can be purchased for the face amount of the check plus a service fee averaging around $9, although occasionally they're issued at no charge to bank customers. The bank issues a check payable to a third party and drawn on itself, not you—the best assurance you can give that the check is good.

▶ **Traveler's check:** Some large financial organizations—such as Citibank, American Express, *MasterCard*, *Visa*, and Bank of America—issue traveler's checks, which can be purchased at commercial banks and most other financial institutions. They typically come in denominations ranging from $20 to $100, and any amount—in multiples of $20 to $100—can be purchased at a time. A fee of 1 to 2 percent or more can be charged on the purchase, which is often waived for good customers. Properly endorsed and countersigned traveler's checks are accepted by most U.S. businesses and can be exchanged for local currencies in most parts of the world. Because they're insured against loss or theft, they provide a safe, convenient, and popular form of money for travel. However, the large number of counterfeit traveler's checks has made them less popular with many businesses, which is making them less commonly used.

▶ **Certified check:** A certified check is a personal check that the bank certifies, with a stamp, to guarantee that the funds are available. The bank immediately deducts the amount of the check from your account. There's usually only a minimal (or no) charge for this service if you are the bank's customer for this service.

4-5 ESTABLISHING A SAVINGS PROGRAM

LO5, LO6 The vast majority of American families have some form of savings, making it clear that most of us understand the value of saving for the future. In the wake of the recent financial crisis, the U.S. personal saving rate increased to an average of about 5 percent of after-tax income after hitting a low of around 1 percent in 2005. Saving is intended to preserve the value of money, ensure liquidity, and earn a competitive rate of return. Almost by definition, *smart savers are smart investors.* They regard saving as more than putting loose change into a piggy bank; rather, they recognize the importance of saving and know that savings must be managed as astutely as any security. After all, what we normally think of as "savings" is really a form of investing—albeit in short-term, highly liquid, low-risk investments. Establishing and maintaining an ongoing savings program is a vital element of personal financial planning. To get the most from your savings, however, you must understand your options and how different savings vehicles pay interest.

> Establishing and maintaining an ongoing savings program is a vital element of personal financial planning.

4-5a Starting Your Savings Program

Careful financial planning dictates that you hold a portion of your assets to meet liquidity needs and accumulate wealth. Although opinions differ as to how much you should keep as liquid reserves, the post-crisis consensus is that most families should have an amount equal to at least six months of after-tax income. Therefore, if you take home $3,000 a month, you should have at least $18,000 in liquid reserves. If your employer has a strong salary continuation program covering extended periods of illness, or if you have a sizable line of credit available, then a somewhat lower amount is probably adequate.

A specific savings plan should be developed to accumulate funds. Saving should be a priority item in your budget, not something that occurs only when income happens to exceed expenditures. Some people manage this by arranging to have savings directly withheld from their paychecks. Not only do direct deposit arrangements help your savings effort, they also enable your funds to earn interest sooner. Or you

cashier's check A check payable to a third party that is drawn by a bank on itself in exchange for the amount specified plus, in most cases, a service fee (of $5 to $10)

traveler's checks a check sold (for a fee of 1 to 2 percent) by many large financial institutions, typically in denominations ranging from $20 to $100, that can be used for making purchases and exchanged for local currencies in most parts of the world

certified check a personal check that is guaranteed (for a fee of $10 to $15 or more) by the bank on which it is drawn can transfer funds on a regular basis to other financial institutions, such as commercial banks, savings and loans, savings banks, credit unions, and even mutual funds. But the key to success is to establish a *regular* pattern of saving.

You should make it a practice to set aside an amount you can comfortably afford *each month*, even if it's only $50 to $100. (Keep in mind that $100 monthly deposits earning 4 percent interest will grow to more than $36,500 in 20 years!)

You must also decide which savings vehicles best meet your needs. Many savers prefer to keep their emergency funds in a regular savings or money market deposit account at an institution with federal deposit insurance. Although these accounts are safe, convenient, and highly liquid, they tend to pay relatively low rates of interest. Other important considerations include your risk tolerance, the length of time you can leave your money on deposit, and the level of current and anticipated interest rates.

Suppose that one year from now, you plan to use $5,000 of your savings to make the down payment on a new car, and you expect interest rates to drop during that period. In such a case, you might want to lock in today's higher rate by purchasing a one year certificate of deposit (CD). On the other hand, if you're unsure about when you'll actually need the funds or believe that interest rates will rise, you may be better off with an MMDA or MMMF because their rates change with market conditions, and you can access your funds at any time without penalty.

Many financial planning experts recommend keeping a minimum of 10 percent of your investment portfolio in savings-type instruments, in addition to the six months of liquid reserves noted earlier. Thus, someone with $50,000 in investments should probably have a minimum of $5,000—and possibly more—in short-term vehicles such as MMDAs, MMMFs, or CDs. At times, the amount invested in short-term vehicles could far exceed the recommended minimum, approaching 50 percent or more of the portfolio. This generally depends on expected interest rate movements. If interest rates are relatively high and you expect them to fall, you would invest in long-term vehicles in order to lock in the attractive interest rates. On the other hand, if rates are relatively low and you expect them to rise, you might invest in short-term vehicles so that you can more quickly reinvest when rates do rise.

4-5b Earning Interest on Your Money

Interest earned is the reward for putting your money in a savings account or short-term investment vehicle, and it's important for you to understand how that interest is earned. Unfortunately, even in the relatively simple world of savings, not all interest rates are created equal.

The Effects of Compounding Interest can be earned in one of two ways. First, some short-term investments are sold on a *discount basis*. This means the security is sold for a price that's lower than its redemption value. The difference between the purchase price and redemption value is the amount of interest earned on the investment. Treasury bills, for instance, are issued on a discount basis. The second way to earn interest on short-term investments is by *direct payment,* which occurs when interest is applied to a regular savings account. The amount of interest earned is added to the amount invested, so at maturity you get your money back, plus whatever you earned in interest. However, determining the actual rate of return can be a bit daunting.

The first complication is in the method used to determine the amount and rate of **compound interest** earned annually. You've probably seen advertisements by banks or other depository institutions declaring that they pay daily, rather than annual, interest. Consider an example to understand what this means. Assume that you invest $1,000 in a savings account advertised as paying annual **simple interest** at a rate of 5 percent; that means the interest is paid only on the initial amount of the deposit. Thus, if you leave the $1,000 on deposit for one year, you'll earn $50 in interest, and the account balance will total $1,050 at year's end. In this case, the **nominal (stated) rate of interest** is 5 percent. In contrast, the **effective rate of interest** is the annual rate of return that's *actually earned* (or *charged*) during the period the funds are held (or borrowed). You can calculate it with the following formula:

$$\text{Effective rate of interest} = \frac{\text{Amount of interest earned}}{\text{Amount of money invested or deposited}}$$

In our example, because $50 was earned during the year on an investment of $1,000, the effective rate is $50/$1,000 or 5 percent, which is the same as the nominal rate of interest. (Notice in the preceding formula that

EXAMPLE: Calculating Earnings when Interest is Compounded Semiannually Suppose Hugo can invest $1,000 at 5 percent, compounded *semiannually.* Because interest is applied midyear, his dollar earnings will be:

First 6 months' interest	$= \$1,000 \times 0.05 \times 6/12$
	$= \$25.00$
Second 6 months' interest	$= \$1,025 \times 0.05 \times 6/12$
	$= \$25.63$
Total annual interest	$= \$50.63$

it's interest earned during the *year* that matters. If you wanted to calculate the effective rate of interest on an account held for six months, you'd double the amount of interest earned.)

Interest is generated on a larger investment in the second half of the year because the amount of money on deposit has increased by the amount of interest earned in the first half ($25). Although the nominal rate on this account is still 5 percent, the effective rate is 5.06 percent ($50.63/$1,000). As you may have guessed, *the more frequently interest is compounded, the greater the effective rate for any given nominal rate.* Exhibit 4.6 shows these relationships for a sample of interest rates and compounding periods. Note that with a 7 percent nominal rate, daily compounding adds one-fourth of a percent to the total return—not a trivial amount.

Compound Interest Generates Future Value Compound interest is part of the *future value* concept introduced in Chapter 2. You can use the procedures described

CALCULATOR

Inputs	Functions
1000	PV
4	N
5	I
	CPT
	FV
	Solution
	$1,215.51

See Appendix E for details.

compound interest when interest earned in each subsequent period is determined by applying the *nominal (stated) rate of interest* to the sum of the initial deposit and the interest earned in each prior period

simple interest interest that is paid only on the initial amount of the deposit

nominal (stated) rate of interest the promised rate of interest paid on a savings deposit or charged on a loan

effective rate of interest the annual rate of return that is actually earned (or charged) during the period the funds are held (or borrowed)

Exhibit 4.6

The Magic of Compounding

The effective rate of interest you earn on a savings account will exceed the nominal (stated) rate if interest is compounded more than once a year (as are most savings and interest-paying accounts).

Nominal Rate (%)	Annually (%)	Semiannually (%)	Quarterly (%)	Monthly (%)	Daily (%)
		Effective Rate			
3	3.00	3.02	3.03	3.04	3.05
4	4.00	4.04	4.06	4.07	4.08
5	5.00	5.06	5.09	5.12	5.13
6	6.00	6.09	6.14	6.17	6.18
7	7.00	7.12	7.19	7.23	7.25
8	8.00	8.16	8.24	8.30	8.33
9	9.00	9.20	9.31	9.38	9.42
10	10.00	10.25	10.38	10.47	10.52
11	11.00	11.30	11.46	11.57	11.62
12	12.00	12.36	12.55	12.68	12.74

EXAMPLE: Calculating the Future Value of a Savings Deposit   David would like to know how much $1,000 will be worth in 4 years if he deposits it into a savings account paying 5 percent interest per year compounded annually. Using the future value formula and the future value factor from Appendix A (see Chapter 2 if you need a reminder):

Future value = Amount deposited
            × Future value factor
        = $1,000 × 1.216
        = $1,216

EXAMPLE: Calculating the Future Value of Ongoing Savings   Zoe deposits $1,000 a year into a savings account paying 5% per year, compounded annually. Using the future value interest factor for an annuity in Appendix B, in 4 years Zoe will have:

Future value = Amount deposited yearly
            × Future value annuity factor
        = $1,000 × 4.310
        = $4,310

 Go to Smart Sites

If you're not satisfied with the CD rate at your local bank, go to Bankrate.com. There you'll find not only the highest rates on CDs nationwide but also the checking and savings account fees at banks in your city.

there to find out how much an investment or deposit will grow over time at a compounded rate of interest. You can use the same basic procedure to find the future value of an *annuity*.

4-5c A Variety of Ways to Save

There has been a huge growth of savings and short-term investment vehicles, particularly for people of modest means. Today, investors can choose from savings accounts, money market deposit accounts, money market mutual funds, NOW accounts, CDs, U.S. Treasury bills, Series EE bonds, Series I savings bonds, and asset management accounts. We examined several of these savings vehicles earlier in this chapter. Let's now look at the four remaining types of deposits and securities.

Before opening a deposit account, investigate the following factors that determine the amount of interest you'll earn on your savings or interest-bearing checking account:

- **Frequency of compounding.** The more often interest is compounded, the higher your return.

- **Balance on which interest is paid.** For balances that qualify to earn interest, most banks use the actual balance method, or day of deposit to day of withdrawal, method. The actual balance method is fairest because it pays depositors interest on all funds on deposit for the actual amount of time they remain there.

- **Interest rate paid.** The Truth in Savings Act standardized the way that banks calculate the rate of interest they pay on deposit accounts. This makes it easy to compare each bank's annual percentage yield (APY) and to choose the bank offering the highest APY.

Certificates of Deposit Certificates of deposit (CDs) differ from the savings instruments discussed earlier in that CD funds (except for CDs purchased through brokerage firms) must remain on deposit for a specified period (from seven days to as long as seven or more years). Although it's possible to withdraw funds prior to maturity, an interest penalty usually makes withdrawal somewhat costly. The bank or other depository institution is free to charge whatever penalty it likes, but most require you to forfeit some interest.

Banks, S&Ls, and other depository institutions can offer any rate and maturity CD they wish. As a result, a wide variety of CDs are offered by most banks, depository institutions, and other financial institutions such as brokerage firms. Most pay higher rates for larger deposits and longer periods of time. CDs are convenient to buy and hold because they offer attractive and highly competitive yields plus federal deposit insurance protection.

U.S. Treasury Bills The U.S. Treasury bill (T-bill) is considered the ultimate safe haven for savings and investments. T-bills are issued by the U.S. Treasury as part of its ongoing process of funding the national debt. They are sold on a discount basis in minimum denominations of $100 and are issued with 1-month (4-week), 3-month (13-week), 6-month (26-week), or 1-year (52-week) maturities. The bills are auctioned off every Monday. Backed by the full faith and credit of the U.S. government, T-bills pay an attractive and safe return that is free from state and local income taxes.

Go to Smart Sites

At the T-bill page of Treasury Direct's Internet site, you can learn about T-bills and then buy them online.

T-bills are almost as liquid as cash because they can be sold at any time (in a very active secondary market) with no interest penalty. However, should you have to sell before maturity, you may lose some money on your investment if interest rates have risen, and you'll have to pay a broker's fee. As noted earlier, Treasury bills pay interest on a *discount basis* and thus are different from other savings or short-term investment vehicles—that is, their interest is equal to the difference between the purchase price paid and their stated value at maturity. For example, if you paid $980 for a bill that will be worth $1,000 at maturity, you'll earn $20 in interest ($1,000–$980).

An individual investor may purchase T-bills directly by participating in the weekly Treasury auctions, or indirectly through a commercial bank or a securities dealer who buys bills for investors on a commission basis. T-bills may now be purchased over the Internet (**www.treasurydirect.gov**).

Series EE Bonds Although they are issued by the U.S. Treasury on a discount basis and are free of state and local income taxes, Series EE bonds are quite different from T-bills. Savings bonds are *accrual-type securities*, which means that interest is paid when they're cashed in or before maturity, rather than periodically during their lives. Also known as "Patriot Bonds"—in recognition of September 11, 2001—Series EE bonds are backed by the full faith and credit of the U.S. government and can be replaced without charge in case of loss, theft, or destruction. You can purchase them at banks or other depository institutions or through payroll deduction plans. Issued

certificate of deposit (CD) a type of savings instrument issued by certain financial institutions in exchange for a deposit; typically requires a minimum deposit and has a maturity ranging from seven days to as long as seven or more years

U.S. Treasury bill (T-bill) a short-term (3-, 6-, or 12-month maturity) debt instrument issued at a discount by the U.S. Treasury in its ongoing process of funding the national debt

Series EE bonds a savings bond issued in various denominations by the U.S. Treasury

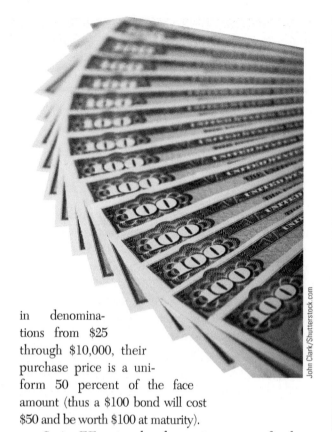

John Clark/Shutterstock.com

in denominations from $25 through $10,000, their purchase price is a uniform 50 percent of the face amount (thus a $100 bond will cost $50 and be worth $100 at maturity).

Series EE savings bonds earn interest at a fixed rate for 30 years. Their long life lets investors use them for truly long-term goals like education and retirement. The higher the rate of interest being paid, the shorter the time it takes for the bond to accrue from its discounted purchase price to its maturity value. Bonds can be redeemed any time after the first 12 months, although redeeming EE bonds in less than five years results in a penalty of the last three months of interest earned. The interest rate is set every six months in May and November and changes with prevailing Treasury security market yields. EE bonds increase in value every month, and the stipulated interest rate is compounded semiannually.

In addition to being exempt from state and local taxes, Series EE bonds give their holders an appealing tax twist: *Savers need not report interest earned on their federal tax returns until the bonds are redeemed.* A second attractive tax feature—available to qualified bond holders—allows partial or complete tax avoidance of EE bond earnings when proceeds are used to pay education expenses, such as college tuition, for the bond purchaser, a spouse, or another IRS-defined dependent.

I Savings Bonds I savings bonds are similar to Series EE bonds in several ways. For starters, both are issued by the

I savings bonds a savings bond issued at face value by the U.S. Treasury; its practically fixed rates provides some inflation protection

PLANNING OVER A LIFETIME

Managing Cash and Savings

Here are some key considerations for managing your cash and savings in each stage of the life cycle.

PRE-FAMILY INDEPENDENCE: 20s

▸ Build up savings in general and emergency fund in particular.

▸ Pay off any outstanding college loans.

▸ Find best mix of financial institution accounts based on fees, returns, and convenience. Make comparisons across banks.

FAMILY FORMATION/CAREER DEVELOPMENT: 30–45

▸ Increase savings to fund future financial goals.

▸ Broaden variety of cash management vehicles and reliance on financial planners for strategy development.

▸ Carefully relate savings program to funding childrens' future educational needs.

PRE-RETIREMENT: 45–65

▸ Maintain emergency fund.

▸ Relate savings strategies more directly to retirement planning.

▸ Start being sensitive to the presence of "senior" discounts.

▸ Get an estimate of your Social Security benefits based on your expected retirement date.

RETIREMENT: 65 AND BEYOND

▸ Maintain list of bank accounts that are easily accessible by spouse and family.

▸ Take advantage of bank accounts with senior discounts on fees.

▸ Integrate cash management and savings with retirement spending and estate plan.

U.S. Treasury, they're both accrual-type securities, and interest on both of them compounds semiannually over a 30-year period. And like Series EE bonds, I savings

Isabel Likes Cash—Too Much?

Jason Stitt/Shutterstock.com

Isabel has a good job that pays $65,000 a year. She invests the maximum amount allowable in her work-based retirement plan. During the financial crisis a few years ago, her retirement investments fell about 40 percent in value! While her investments have more than recovered, Isabel is very risk conscious and has consequently built up an emergency fund of $60,000, which she keeps in a savings account that pays 0.5 percent, compounded monthly. Is Isabel approach to handling her emergency funds the best way to go?

Isabel has done a great job setting aside a $60,000 emergency fund. And contributing the maximum will serve her well. However, the recommended emergency fund for a maximum of 6 months of income for her $65,000 annual income is only $32,500. So she has set aside $27,500 more than is recommended. Further, Isabel is leaving it in a savings account only paying 0.5 percent a year, which generates interest income of only about $300.69 a year. It would make sense for Isabel to invest the excess $27,500 more aggressively—even a CD would provide a higher return with comparable risk. And she should at least shop around for a better savings rate than 0.5 percent for her hopefully reduced emergency fund. Isabel could find another savings account with a rate of at least 1 percent a year, which would about double her return. Isabel is doing great—but she likes cash too much for her own good. She could do even better.

---

bonds' interest remains exempt from state and local income taxes but does face state and local estate, inheritance, gift, and other excise taxes. In addition, interest earnings are subject to federal income tax but may be excluded when used to finance education, with some limitations.

There are some major differences between the two savings vehicles, however. I bonds are available in smaller denominations (between $25 and $10,000). And while Series EE bonds are sold at a discount, I bonds are sold at face value. I savings bonds also differ from Series EE bonds in that their annual interest rate combines a fixed rate that remains the same for the life of the bond with a semiannual inflation rate that changes with the Consumer Price Index for all Urban Consumers (CPI-U). In contrast, the rate on Series EE bonds is based on the six-month averages of five-year Treasury security market yields. Thus, *the key difference between Series EE bonds and I bonds is that I bond returns are adjusted for inflation.* Note in particular that the earnings rate cannot go below zero, and that the value of I bonds cannot drop below their redemption value.

STUDY TOOLS 4

LOCATED AT BACK OF THE TEXTBOOK
☐ Chapter Review Card

LOCATED AT WWW.CENGAGEBRAIN.COM
☐ Review Key Term flashcards and create your own cards.
☐ Track your knowledge and understanding of key concepts in personal finance.
☐ Complete practice and graded quizzes to prepare for tests.
☐ Complete interactive content at PFIN6 Online.
☐ View the chapter highlight boxes at PFIN6 Online.

©viphotos/Shutterstock 140785408

Financial Planning Exercises

LO1

1. **Adapting to a low interest rate environment.** A retired couple has expressed concern about the really low interest rates they're earning on their savings. They've been approached by an adviser who says he has a "sure-fire" way to get them higher returns. What would you tell this retired couple about the low-interest-rate environment, and how would you recommend them to view the adviser's new prospective investments?

LO2, 3, 4

2. **Comparing banks online.** What type of bank serves your needs best? Visit the Internet sites of the following institutions and prepare a chart comparing the services offered, such as traditional and online banking, investment services, and personal financial advice. Which one would you choose to patronize, and why?

   a. Wells Fargo (https://www.wellsfargo.com)—a nationwide, full-service bank

   b. A leading, local commercial bank in your area

   c. A local savings institution

   d. A local credit union

LO2, 3, 4

3. **Choosing a new bank.** You're getting married and believe your present bank is not a good fit. Discuss how you should go about choosing a new bank and opening an account. Consider the factors that are important to you in selecting a bank—such as the type and ownership of new accounts and bank fees and charges.

LO3

4. **Exposure from stolen ATM card.** Suppose that someone stole your ATM card and withdrew $1,000 from your checking account. How much money could you lose (according to federal legislation) if you reported the stolen card to the bank: (a) the day the card was stolen, (b) 6 days after the theft, (c) 65 days after receiving your periodic statement?

LO4

5. **Calculating the net costs of checking accounts.** Determine the annual net cost of these checking accounts:

   a. Monthly fee $4, check-processing fee of 20 cents, average of 23 checks written per month

   b. Annual interest of 1.5 percent paid if balance exceeds $750, $8 monthly fee if

account falls below minimum balance, average monthly balance $815, account falls below $750 during four months

LO4

6. **Checking account reconciliation.** Use Worksheet 4.1. Carlos Alvarez has a an interest-paying (NOW) checking account at the First State Bank. His checkbook ledger lists the following checks:

Check Number	Amount
654	$206.05
658	55.22
662	103.00
668	99.00
670	6.10
671	50.25
672	24.90
673	32.45
674	44.50
675	30.00
676	30.00
677	111.23
678	38.04
679	97.99
680	486.70
681	43.50
682	75.00
683	98.50

Carlos also made the following withdrawals and deposits at an ATM near his home:

Date	Amount	Transaction
11/1	$50.00	Withdrawal
11/2	$525.60	Deposit
11/6	$100.00	Deposit
11/14	$75.00	Withdrawal
11/21	$525.60	Deposit
11/24	$150.00	Withdrawal
11/27	$225.00	Withdrawal
11/30	$400.00	Deposit

Carlos' checkbook ledger shows an ending balance of $286.54. He has just received

Financial Planning Exercises

his bank statement for the month of November. It shows an ending balance of $622.44; it also shows that he earned interest for November of $3.28, had a check service charge of $8 for the month, and had another $20 charge for a returned check. His bank statement indicates the following checks have cleared: 654, 662, 672, 674, 675, 676, 677, 678, 679, and 681. ATM withdrawals on 11/1 and 11/14 and deposits on 11/2 and 11/6 have cleared; no other checks or ATM activities are listed on his statement, so anything remaining should be treated as outstanding. Use a checking account reconciliation form like the one in Worksheet 4.1 to reconcile Carlos' checking account.

LO5, 6   7.   **Calculating interest earned and future value of savings account.** If you put $6,000 in a savings account that pays interest at the rate of 3 percent, compounded annually, how much will you have in five years? (Hint: Use the future value formula.) How much interest will you earn during the five years? If you put $6,000 each year into a savings account that pays interest at the rate of 4 percent a year, how much would you have after five years?

LO5, 6   8.   **Determining the right amount of short-term, liquid investments.** Leo and Ava Bryant together earn approximately $92,000 a year after taxes. Through an inheritance and some wise investing, they also have an investment portfolio with a value of almost $200,000.

     a.   How much of their annual income do you recommend the Bryants hold in some form of liquid savings as reserves? Explain.

     b.   How much of their investment portfolio do you recommend they hold in savings and other short-term investment vehicles? Explain.

     c.   How much, in total, should they hold in short-term liquid assets?

LO6   9.   **Short-term investments and inflation.** Describe some of the short-term investments that can be used to manage your cash resources. What factors would you focus on if you were concerned that inflation will increase significantly in the future?

5 | Making Automobile and Housing Decisions

LEARNING OBJECTIVES

After studying this chapter, you will be able to…

LO1 Design a plan to research and select a new or used automobile.

LO2 Decide whether to buy or lease a car.

LO3 Identify housing alternatives, assess the rental option, and perform a rent-or-buy analysis.

LO4 Evaluate the benefits and costs of homeownership and estimate how much you can afford to pay for a home.

LO5 Describe the home-buying process.

LO6 Choose mortgage financing that meets your needs.

After you finish this chapter, go to **PAGE 141** for **STUDY TOOLS**

Katsiaryna Pleshakova/Shutterstock.com

How Will this Affect Me? A home is typically the largest single investment you'll ever make and a car is usually the second largest. The decisions to buy and finance these assets are consequently important, personal, and complicated.

This chapter presents frameworks for deciding when to buy a first home, how to finance a home, and when to rent rather than purchase a home. It also discusses how to best go about buying a new or used car, and how to decide between leasing and purchasing a car. Given the large costs of such assets, the frameworks provided in this chapter can significantly improve your short- and long-term financial well-being.

5-1 BUYING AN AUTOMOBILE

LO1 Buying an automobile is probably the first major expenditure that many of us make. The car purchase is second only to housing in the amount of money the typical consumer spends. Because you'll likely buy a car many times during your life—most people buy one every two to five years—a systematic approach to selecting and financing a vehicle can mean significant savings. Before making any major purchase, consider some basic guidelines to wise purchasing decisions:

► *Research* your purchase thoroughly, considering not only the market but also your personal needs.

► *Select* the best vehicle for your needs.

► *Buy* the asset after negotiating the best price and arranging financing on the best terms. Be sure you understand all the terms of the sale before signing any contracts.

▶ *Maintain* your purchase and make necessary repairs promptly.

Exhibit 5.1 summarizes the steps in the new car-buying process.

> A systematic approach to selecting and financing a vehicle can mean significant savings.

5-1a Choosing a Car

Hybrid, diesel, or gas? Sport utility vehicle (SUV) or pickup truck? Sedan, convertible, or coupe? Car buyers today have more choices than ever before, so being an informed buyer is more important than ever. A good place to start your research is by tapping into the many available sources of information about cars, their prices, features, and reliability. Industry resources include manufacturers' brochures and dealer personnel. Car magazines such as *Car and Driver*, *Motor Trend*, and *Road and Track*, and consumer magazines such as *Consumer Reports* and *Consumer Guide*, regularly compare and rate cars. In addition, *Consumer Reports* and *Kiplinger's Personal Finance* magazines publish annual buying guides that include comparative statistics and ratings on most domestic and foreign cars.

The Internet has made it especially easy to do your homework before ever setting foot in a dealer's showroom. It's so easy to visit one of the many comprehensive Internet sites for car shoppers, where you'll find pricing and model information, as well as links to other useful sites. Don't forget the Internet sites of the automobile companies themselves. For example, Ford Motor Company is online at www.ford.com and Toyota is at www.toyota.com.

 ## Go to Smart Sites

With Edmunds.com's auto loan calculators, you can evaluate auto financing options and check rates to find the lowest auto loan rates in your area. A highlight box in each chapter of PFIN Online includes "Smart Sites," a list of resources and sites that offer additional information on topics in the PFIN text.

Exhibit 5.1

Key Steps in Buying a New Car

These steps summarize the car-buying process discussed in this chapter.

- Research which car best meets your needs and determine how much you can afford to spend on it. Choose the best way to pay for your new car—cash, financing, or lease. Ask your insurance agent for annual premium quotes for insuring various cars, as auto insurance is another significant expense of owning a car.

- Check web sites like **Edmunds.com** and TV and newspapers for incentives and rebates on the car you would like to buy. This could include a cash rebate or low-cost financing.

- Decide on a price based on dealer's cost for the car and options, plus a markup for the dealer's profit, minus rebates and incentives.

- Find the exact car for you in terms of size, performance, safety, and styling. Choose at least three "target cars" to consider buying. Get online quotes from multiple car dealers.

- Test-drive the car—and the car salesperson. Test-drive the car at least once, both on local streets and on highways. Determine if the car salesperson is someone you want to do business with. Is he or she relaxed, open, and responsive to your questions?

- If you are trading in your old car, you are not likely to get as high a price as if you sell it yourself. Look up your car's trade-in value at Edmunds.com or **kbb.com**. Get bids from several dealers.

- Negotiate the lowest price on your new car by getting bids from at least three dealers. Hold firm on your target price before closing the deal.

- Close the deal after looking not just at the cost of the car but also the related expenses. Consider the sales tax and various fees. Get the salesperson to fax you a worksheet and invoice before you go to the dealership.

- Review and sign the paperwork. If you have a worksheet for the deal, the contract should match it. Make sure the numbers match and there are no additional charges or fees.

- Inspect the car for scratches and dents. If anything is missing—like floor mats, for example—ask for a "Due Bill" that states it in writing.

Source: Adapted from Philip Read, "10 Steps to Buying a New Car," www.edmunds.com/car-buying/10-steps-to-buying-a-new-car.html, accessed October 2016.

5-1b Affordability

Before shopping for a car, determine how much you can afford to spend. You'll need to calculate two numbers unless you plan to pay cash for the entire cost of the car:

▶ **Amount of down payment:** This money will likely come from savings, so be sure not to deplete your emergency fund.

▶ **Size of the monthly loan payment you can afford:** Carefully consider the amount of money you can afford to spend, along with your basic transportation needs. Don't forget to include insurance. And remember: your monthly car payment should be no more than 20 percent of your monthly gross income.

Operating Costs The out-of-pocket cost of operating an automobile includes not only car payments but also insurance, license, fuel, oil, tires, and other operating and maintenance outlays. Some of these

EXAMPLE: Calculating How Much Can You Afford to Pay for a Car You can use the down payment and monthly payment amounts to calculate the total amount that you can afford for a car. For example, suppose you have $3,000 for a down payment, you can pay $500 a month, and your bank is offering four-year (48-month) car loans at 6 percent annual (6%/12 = 0.5%, monthly) interest. How much of a loan can you afford? Using a financial calculator and the keystrokes shown on the next page, you'll find that you can take out a loan of about $21,300. Add that to the $3,000 down payment, and you'll be able to afford a car costing $24,300.

costs are *fixed* regardless of how much you drive; others are *variable*, depending on the number of miles you drive. The biggest fixed cost is likely to be the *installment payments* associated with the loan (or lease) used to acquire the car. The biggest variable cost will probably be fuel.

Another significant cost is **depreciation**, which is the loss in value that occurs over the period of ownership. If you paid $20,000 for an automobile that can be sold three years later for $14,000, the car will cost you $6,000 in depreciation. Although depreciation may not be a recurring out-of-pocket cash cost, it's an important expense that shouldn't be overlooked.

Gas, Diesel, or Hybrid? It's increasingly important to consider the type of fuel you prefer to use in your car. If you're concerned about the environmental impact of the fuel your car uses, you may be interested only in a hybrid car. Although you'll want to consider fuel economy when car shopping, comparable gas-fueled, internal combustion engines and diesel-powered cars tend to have similar fuel economy. Generally, diesels are a bit noisier, have less acceleration but more power, and have longer engine lives than do traditional gas-powered cars.

Hybrids, which blend gas and battery power, have experienced rapid sales growth due to historically increasing gas prices, improved technology and availability, and greater public awareness of environmental issues. Although they're more economical and less polluting than gas- and diesel-powered vehicles, hybrids do have some disadvantages: high cost of battery replacement, generally higher repair costs, and typically higher initial purchase prices. It's important to consider the differences between the costs and performance of differently fueled vehicles and decide on the vehicle you want before shopping for a specific new or used car.

New, Used, or "Nearly New"? One decision you must make is whether to buy a new, used, or "nearly new" car. If you can't afford to buy a new car, the decision is made for you. Some people who can afford to buy a new car choose to buy a used car so they can have a better model—a used luxury car such as a BMW, Lexus, or Mercedes—rather than a less-expensive brand of new car, such as a Ford. With the increasing popularity of used cars, car dealers are trying to dispel the negative image associated with buying a used, or "pre-owned," car.

Once you know what you want, shop at these places:

▶ **Franchise dealerships:** Offer the latest-model used cars, provide financing, and will negotiate on price.

▶ **Superstores:** AutoNation, CarMax, and similar dealers offer no-haggle pricing and a large selection. They certify their cars and may offer a limited, short-term warranty.

▶ **Independent used car lots:** Usually offer older (four- to six-year-old) cars and have lower overhead than franchise dealers. There are no industry standards, so be sure to check with the Better Business Bureau before buying.

▶ **Private individuals:** Generally cost less because there's no dealer overhead; may have maintenance records. Be sure that the seller holds the title to the car.

Size, Body Style, and Features Your first consideration should be what type of car you prefer. More than one style category may work for you. For example,

Tom Wang/Shutterstock.com

depreciation the loss in the value of an asset such as an automobile that occurs over its period of ownership; calculated as the difference between the price initially paid and the subsequent sale price a family of five can buy a mid-size or full-size sedan, station wagon, minivan, or compact or full-size SUV. When considering size, body style, and features, think about your needs, likes, and dislikes as well as the cost. There's usually a direct relationship between size and cost: the larger the car, the more expensive it will be to purchase and to operate. Also consider performance, handling, appearance, fuel economy, reliability, repair problems, and the resale value of the car. And don't try to adapt your needs to fit the car you want—a two-passenger sports car may not be appropriate if you need the car for business or if you have children.

By listing all of the options you want before shopping for a new car, you can avoid paying for features you really don't need. Literally hundreds of options—ranging in price from a few dollars up to $2,000 or more—are available, including automatic transmission, a bigger engine, air conditioning, high-performance brakes, an audio player, clock, power windows, power seats, electric door locks, leather seats, navigation systems, a rear-window defroster, and special suspension. Some appearance-related options are two-tone or metallic paint, electric sunroof, special tires, sport wheels, and various interior and exterior trim packages. On new cars, window stickers detail each option and its price. In contrast, you're usually on your own with used cars.

Other Considerations Here are some other factors that affect affordability:

▶ **Trading in or selling your existing car:** Although trading in is convenient, it's generally a better deal to sell your old car outright. If you're willing to take the time, you can usually sell your car for more than the wholesale price typically offered by a dealer on a trade-in.

▶ **Fuel economy:** The *Environmental Protection Agency (EPA) mileage ratings* are especially useful on new vehicles, which carry a sticker indicating the number of miles per gallon each model is expected to get for both city and highway driving. You can check out those ratings at www.fueleconomy.gov.

▶ **Safety features:** Government regulations ensure that these features are likely to be similar in new cars, but older used cars may not have some features such as side-impact airbags. And don't forget to include the cost of *auto insurance*, which is discussed in detail in Chapter 10.

anchoring a behavioral bias in which an individual tends to allow an initial estimate (of value or price) to dominate the subsequent assessment (of value or price) regardless of new information to the contrary

5-1c The Purchase Transaction

Once you've determined what you can afford to spend and the features that you want, you're ready to begin car shopping. If you plan to buy a new car, visit more than one dealer with cars that meet your requirements. Look the cars over and ask questions—but don't make any offers until you've found two or three cars with the desired features that are priced within your budget. Also, if you can be flexible about the model and options you want, you can sometimes negotiate a better deal than if you're determined to have a particular model and options. Be sure to do some comparison shopping, because a dealer selling the same brand as another may give you a better deal. And watch out for lowballing, where the salesperson quotes a low price to get you to make an offer, and then negotiates the price upward prior to your signing the sales contract. Exhibit 5.2 lists some other factors to consider once you begin looking at cars.

Negotiating Price Choosing among various makes, models, and options can make comparisons difficult. Consequently, the price you pay for a car, whether new or

BEHAVIOR MATTERS

"Anchoring" and the Used Car Salesperson Strategy

While we try to be logical and objective in making purchases, psychologists find that people start with an initial estimate of value. We often anchor on that initial value and have a hard time moving away from it in negotiating transactions.

Consider a common strategy of used-car salespeople. Why do you think that they start negotiating with a high price and then work their way down? Some salespeople try to get the consumer anchored on the initial high price so that when a lower price is offered, the consumer tends to view the lower price as a good value, even if that is not the case. Combine this behavioral bias with our tendency to be overconfident about our negotiating skills, and you have a potential problem.

So what should you do about the anchoring behavioral bias? Recognize the tendency, do your homework about a reasonable price for a used car, and take into account the used-car salesperson's strategy.

Exhibit 5.2

Finding the Best Car for You

Start by inspecting the key points of the car. Don't overlook the obvious:

- *How easy is it to get people and things into and out of the car?*

  Do the doors open easily?

  Is the trunk large enough for your needs?

  Does the car offer a pass-through or fold-down rear seat to accommodate larger items?

- *Comfort and visibility:*

  Are the seats comfortable?

  Can you adjust the driver's seat and steering wheel properly?

  What are the car's blind spots for a person of your height?

  Can you see all the gauges clearly?

  Can you reach the controls for the radio, audio player, heater, air conditioner, and other features easily while driving?

  Does it have the options you want?

Then take the car for a test drive.

- Set aside at least 20 minutes and drive it on highways and local roads.

- To test acceleration, merge into traffic getting onto the freeway and try passing another car.

- If possible, drive home and make sure the car fits into your garage—especially if you're interested in a large SUV or truck!

- For a used car, test the heater and air conditioner. Then turn the fan off and listen for any unusual engine noises.

- Check out overall handling. Parallel park, make a U-turn, and brake hard. Do the gears shift smoothly? If testing a standard transmission, try to determine if the clutch is engaging too high or too low, which might indicate excessive wear or a problem.

As soon as you return to the car lot, take notes on how well the car handled and how comfortable you felt driving it.

- This is especially important if you are test driving several cars.

---

used, can vary widely. The more you narrow your choices to a particular car, the easier it is to get price quotes from dealers to make an "apples-to-apples" comparison.

The "sticker price" on a new car represents the manufacturer's *suggested retail price* for that particular car with its listed options. This price means very little. The key to negotiating a good price is knowing the *dealer's cost* for the car. The easiest and quickest way to find the dealer's invoice cost is going to the Edmunds (**www.edmunds.com**) or Kelley Blue Book (**www.kbb.com**) Internet sites. Try to negotiate the lowest acceptable markup above dealer invoice (3 percent to 4 percent for cars priced under $20,000; 6 percent to 7 percent for higher-priced models), then push for a firm quote, and make it clear that you are comparison shopping.

If you want to avoid negotiating entirely, you can buy your car through a buying service, either by phone or over the Internet. These include independent companies—such as AutoVantage (**www.autovantage.com**), Autobytel (**www.autobytel.com**), and AutoWeb (**www.autoweb**

.com)—or services offered through credit unions, motor clubs, and discount warehouses such as Costco.

Buying services work in a variety of ways. They may have an arrangement with a network of dealers to sell cars at a predetermined price above invoice, provide you with competitive bids from several local dealers, find the car you want and negotiate the price with the dealer, or place an order with the factory for a made-to-order car. You'll get a good price through a service—although you shouldn't assume that it will be the best price.

It's best not to discuss your plan to finance the purchase or the value of your trade-in until after you've settled the question of price. These should be separate issues. Salespeople typically want to find out how much you can afford monthly and then offer financing deals with payments close to that amount. In the case of trade-ins, the dealer might offer you a good price for your old car and raise the price of the new car to compensate. The dealer may offer financing terms that sound attractive, but be sure to compare them with the cost of bank loans.

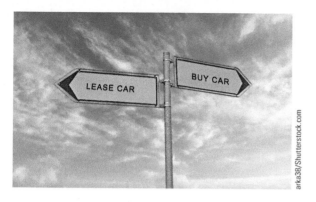
arka38/Shutterstock.com

Sometimes dealers increase the price of the car to make up for a low interest rate, or attractive financing may apply only to certain models. Financing charges can include unneeded extras such as credit life insurance, accident insurance, an extended warranty, or a service package.

Manufacturers and dealers often offer buyers special incentives, such as rebates and cut-rate financing, particularly when car sales are slow. In some cases, you may have a choice between a rebate and low-cost financing. To determine which is the better deal, calculate the difference between the monthly payments on a market-rate bank loan and the special dealer loan for the same term. Multiply the payment difference by the loan maturity, in months, and compare it with the rebate.

> **EXAMPLE: Determining If a Rebate Is a Good Deal** A car dealer offers either a $1,000 rebate or a 4 percent interest rate on a $10,000, four-year loan. Your monthly payments would be $226 with dealer financing and $234 on a 6 percent bank loan with similar terms. The payment savings over the life of the loan are $384 ($8 per month × 48 months), which is less than the $1,000 rebate. In this case, you would be better off with the rebate.

Closing the Deal Whether you're buying a new or used car, to make a legally binding offer you must sign a **sales contract** that specifies the offering price and all the conditions of your offer. The sales contract also specifies whether the offer includes a trade-in. If it does, the offering price will include both the payment amount and the trade-in allowance. Because this agreement

sales contract an agreement to purchase an automobile that states the offering price and all conditions of the offer; when signed by the buyer and seller, the contract legally binds them to its terms

lease an arrangement in which the lessee receives the use of a car (or other asset) in exchange for making monthly lease payments over a specified period

contractually binds you to purchase the car at the offering price, be sure that you want and can afford the car before signing the agreement. You may be required to include a deposit of around $200 or more with the contract to show that you're making an offer in good faith.

Once the dealer accepts your offer, you complete the purchase transaction and take delivery of the car. If you're not paying cash for the car, you can arrange financing through the dealer, at your bank, a credit union, or a consumer finance company. The key aspects of these types of installment loans, which can be quickly negotiated if your credit is good, are discussed in Chapter 7.

> **YOU CAN DO IT NOW: What's Your Car Worth?** If you have a car, it's good to know what it's worth from time to time. That way you'll have a better sense of your net worth and you'll know how much your car is depreciating over time. Just go to the Kelley Blue book site at **http://www.kbb.com** and go to the "Price New/Used Cars" – you can **do it now**.

5-2 LEASING A CAR

LO2 Don't worry about temperamental engines or transmissions—just get a new car every few years using a leasing arrangement. Put a small amount down, make easy payments. No wonder leasing is popular, accounting for about 25 percent of all new vehicles delivered. When you **lease**, you (the lessee) receive the use of a car in exchange for monthly lease payments over a specified period of time, usually two to four years.

Leasing appeals to a wide range of car users, even though the total cost of leasing is generally more than buying a car with a loan, and at the end of the lease you have nothing. The car—and the money you paid to rent it—is gone. So why do so many car buyers lease their cars? Reasons include rising new car prices, the nondeductibility of consumer loan interest, lower monthly payments, driving a more expensive car for the same monthly payment, and minimizing the down payment to preserve cash.

With all the advertisements promising low monthly lease payments, it's easy to focus on only the payment. Unlike a loan purchase, with a lease you're paying not for the whole car but only for its use during a specified period. Leasing is a more complex arrangement than borrowing money to buy a car. Until you understand how leasing works, and compare lease terms with bank financing, you won't know if leasing is the right choice for you.

5-2a The Leasing Process

The first step is the same for leasing as it is for purchasing: research car types and brands, comparison shop at several dealers, and find the car you want at the best price. Don't ask the dealer about leasing or any financing incentives until *after* you've negotiated the final price. Then compare the lease terms offered by the dealer to those of at least one independent leasing firm. As with a purchase, try to negotiate lower lease payments—a payment reduction of $20 a month saves nearly $1,000 on a four-year lease. And don't reveal what you can afford to pay per month; doing so can lead you to a poor lease deal.

The vast majority of car lessees choose the **closed-end lease**, often called the *walk-away lease*, because at the end of its term you simply turn in the car and walk away, assuming that you have neither exceeded the preset mileage limit nor abused the car. Under the less popular **open-end (finance) lease**, if the car is worth less than the estimated **residual value**—the remaining value of the car at the end of the lease term—then you must pay the difference. These leases are used primarily for commercial business leasing.

A commonly cited benefit of leasing is the absence of a down payment. However, today most leases require a "capital cost reduction," which is a type of down payment that lowers the potential depreciation and therefore your monthly lease payments.

Given the one-time, up-front capital cost reduction payment, the size of the monthly lease payment is based on four variables:

1. The **capitalized cost** of the car (the price of the car you are leasing)

2. The forecast *residual value* of the car at the end of the lease

3. The **money factor**, or financing rate on the lease (similar to the interest rate on a loan)

4. The *lease term*

Terminating a lease early is often difficult and costly, so be reasonably certain that you can keep the car for the full lease term. The lease contract should outline any costs and additional fees associated with early termination. Early termination clauses also apply to cars that are stolen or totaled in an accident. Some leases require "gap insurance" to cover the lost lease payments that would result from early termination caused by one of these events.

Under most leases, you are responsible for insuring and maintaining the car. Also, be aware that at the end of the lease, you are obligated to pay for any "unreasonable wear and tear." A good lease contract should clearly define what is considered unreasonable. In addition, most leases require the lessee to pay a disposition fee of about $150 to $250 when the car is returned.

The annual mileage allowance—typically, about 10,000 to 15,000 miles per year for the lease term—is another important lease consideration. Usually the lessee must pay between 10 and 25 cents per mile for any miles over the limit. For example, if the lease allows 15,000 miles per year and you put 50,000 miles on a car over the three-year term of the lease, then you'd exceed the limit by 5,000 miles ($3 \times 15,000 = 45,000 < 50,000$); at 20 cents per mile, you'd be liable for $0.20 \times 5,000 = \$1,000$. If you expect to exceed the allowable mileage, you would be wise to negotiate a more favorable rate for extra miles before signing the lease contract.

Most auto leases include a **purchase option** (either a fixed price, the market price at the end of the lease term, or the residual value of the car) that specifies the price at which the lessee can buy the car at the end of the lease term. A lower residual results in a lower purchase price but raises monthly payments.

5-2b The Lease versus Purchase Analysis

To decide whether it is less costly to lease rather than purchase

closed-end lease the most popular form of automobile lease; often called a *walk-away lease*, because at the end of its term the lessee simply turns in the car (assuming the preset mileage limit has not been exceeded and the car hasn't been abused)

open-end (finance) lease an automobile lease under which the estimated *residual value* of the car is used to determine lease payments; if the car is actually worth less than this value at the end of the lease, the lessee must pay the difference

residual value the remaining value of a leased car at the end of the lease term

capitalized cost the price of a car that is being leased

money factor the financing rate on a lease; similar to the interest rate on a loan

purchase option a price specified in a lease at which the lessee can buy the car at the end of the lease term a car, you need to perform a *lease versus purchase analysis* to compare the total cost of leasing to the total cost of purchasing a car over equal periods. In this analysis, the purchase is assumed to be financed with an installment loan over the same period as the lease.

For example, Eleanor Clark is considering either leasing or purchasing a new Toyota Prius costing $29,900. The four-year, closed-end lease that she is considering requires a $2,900 down payment (capital cost reduction), a $500 security deposit, and monthly payments of $440, including sales tax. If she purchases the car, she will make a $4,500 down payment and finance the balance with a four-year, 4 percent loan requiring monthly payments of about $576. She will also have to pay 5 percent sales tax ($1,500) on the purchase, and she expects the car to have a residual value of $16,500 at the end of four years. Eleanor can earn 3 percent interest on her savings with short-term CDs.

After filling in Worksheet 5.1, Eleanor concludes that purchasing is better because its *total cost* of $17,665.42 is $6,762.58 less than the $24,428.00 total cost of leasing—even though the monthly lease payment is about $136 lower. All else being equal, the least costly alternative is preferred.

foreclosures the process whereby lenders attempt to recover loan balances from borrowers who have quit making payments by forcing the sale of the home pledged as collateral

5-2c When the Lease Ends

At the end of the lease, you'll be faced with a major decision. Should you return the car and walk away, or should you buy the car? If you turn in the car and move on to a new model, you may be hit with "excess wear and damage" and "excess mileage" charges and disposition fees. If you can't return the car without high repair charges or greatly exceeded mileage allowances, you may come out ahead by buying the car. Whether the purchase option makes sense depends on the residual value. Sometimes, with popular cars, the residual value in your lease agreement is below the car's trade-in value. Buying the car then makes sense. Even if you want a different car, you can exercise the purchase option and sell the car on the open market and net the difference, which could be $1,000 or more. If the reverse is true and the residual is higher than the price of a comparable used car, just let the lease expire.

5-3 MEETING HOUSING NEEDS: BUY OR RENT?

5-3a Housing Prices and the Recent Financial Crisis

LO3 Before considering how and when to buy or rent a home, it is important to consider the recent rough history of housing prices during and after the financial crisis of 2008–2009. After examining this context in which housing decisions are made, we'll consider how to know when you should buy your first home. In the remainder of this chapter, we'll explore some of the decision variables and discuss how to approach the home-buying and renting process.

The pre-crisis bubble in real estate prices had important side effects. It encouraged a massive increase in construction and the extraction of a lot of home equity through home equity loans and refinancings, about two-thirds of which went into increased consumption. Net worth increased with home prices as well. Yet those side effects went in the opposite direction during the financial crisis. Between 2007 and 2009, the crisis reduced the average family's net worth by about 23 percent and dampened consumption, which slowed the macroeconomy. Home **foreclosures**, the process whereby lenders attempt to recover loan balances from borrowers who have quit making payments by forcing the sale of the home pledged as collateral, increased significantly.

This worksheet illustrates Eleanor Clark's lease versus purchase analysis for a new Toyota Prius costing $29,990. The four-year, closed-end lease requires an initial payment of $3,400 ($2, 900 down payment + $500 security deposit) and monthly payments of $440. Purchasing requires a $4,500 down payment, sales tax of 5 percent ($1,499.50), and 48 monthly payments of $575.45. The trade-in value of the new car at the end of four years is estimated to be $16,500. *Because the total cost of leasing of $24,428 is greater than the $17,665.42 total cost of purchasing, Eleanor should purchase rather than lease the car.*

AUTOMOBILE LEASE VERSUS PURCHASE ANALYSIS*

Name _Eleanor Clark_   Date _Sept. 6, 2017_

Item Description		Amount
LEASE		
1	Initial payment:	
	a. Down payment (capital cost reduction):	$ 2,900.00
	b. Security deposit:	500.00 $ 3,400.00
2	Term of lease and loan (years)*	4
3	Term of lease and loan (months) (Item 2 × 12)	48
4	Monthly lease payment	$ 440.00
5	Total payments over term of lease (Item 3 × Item 4)	$ 21,120.00
6	Interest rate earned on savings (in decimal form)	0.030
7	Opportunity cost of initial payment (Item 1 × Item 2 × Item 6)	$ 408.00
8	Payment/refund for market value adjustment at end of lease ($0 for closed-end leases) and/or estimated end-of-term charges	$ 0.00
9	**Total cost of leasing (Item 1a + Item 5 + Item 7 + Item 8)**	$ 24,428.00
PURCHASE		
10	Purchase price	$ 29,990.00
11	Down payment	$ 4,500.00
12	Sales tax rate (in decimal form)	0.05
13	Sales tax (Item 10 × Item 12)	$ 1,499.50
14	Monthly loan payment (Terms: _25,490.00_, _48_ months, _4_ %)	$ 575.54
15	Total payments over term of loan (Item 3 × Item 14)	$ 27,625.92
16	Opportunity cost of down payment (Item 2 × Item 6 × Item 11)	$ 540.00
17	Estimated value of car at end of loan	$ 16,500.00
18	**Total cost of purchasing (Item 11 + Item 13 + Item 15 + Item 16 − Item 17)**	$ 17,665.42

DECISION

If the value of Item 9 is less than the value of Item 18, leasing is preferred; otherwise, the *purchase alternative is preferred.*

*Note: This form is based on equal terms (periods) for the lease and the installment loan, which is assumed to be used to finance the purchase.

Did the Real Estate Bubble Result from Behavioral Biases?

There's a tendency for us to sometimes exhibit herding behavior. Well-known Yale behavioral economist and Nobel laureate Professor Robert Shiller argues that after the rapid run-up in real estate prices between 2001 and 2006, a "social epidemic" encouraged the belief that housing was a critical investment opportunity that shouldn't be missed. And there is a behavioral bias, known as the *conservatism bias*, which encourages us to rely too heavily on past experience and to revise our expectations for the future too slowly in light of new information. These psychological biases only fed additional housing price increases apart from the underlying real estate investment fundamentals, which supported the development of the real estate bubble.

Households often have trouble distinguishing between real (inflation-adjusted) and nominal (unadjusted for inflation) changes in interest rates and rents. Thus, when expected inflation drops, consumers buy homes to take advantage of apparently low nominal financing costs without realizing that future home price and rent appreciation rates will fall by comparable amounts. Falling inflation and the associated "inflation illusion" in the early 2000s consequently brought unjustified real estate price spikes, which culminated in the housing bubble and its subsequent dramatic pop.

From early 2001 through 2006, home prices in the United States rose rapidly. The median nominal sales price of existing homes rose from $141,600 to $230,400. Existing home prices started dropping and fell to a median price of $154,600 in early 2012. Prices had fallen because the real estate bubble had popped and the financial crisis of 2008–2009 had vastly depressed home sales. This period of recession brought high unemployment, low consumer confidence, and tighter credit. Indeed, at the worst point about one in seven American homeowners had *negative equity* in their homes, meaning they owed more on their mortgage than their homes were worth.

condominium (condo) a form of direct ownership of an individual unit in a multiunit project in which lobbies, swimming pools, and other common areas and facilities are jointly owned by all property owners in the project

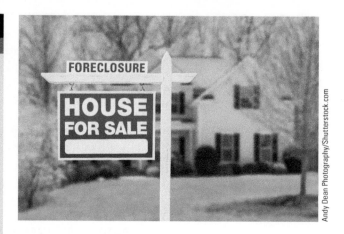

Andy Dean Photography/Shutterstock.com

5-3b What Type of Housing Meets Your Needs?

Knowing when to buy your first home is not always clear-cut. There are many factors to consider before taking on such a large financial responsibility. In the remainder of this chapter, we'll explore some of these factors and discuss how to approach the home-buying process.

Because you have your own unique likes and dislikes, the best way to start your search for housing is to list your preferences and classify them according to whether their satisfaction is essential, desirable, or merely a "plus." This exercise is important for three reasons. First, it screens out housing that doesn't meet your minimum requirements. Second, it helps you recognize potential trade-offs—seldom will you find a single home that meets all your needs. Third, it will help you focus on those needs for which you are willing and able to pay.

As a potential homeowner, one of the first decisions you'll have to make is the type of housing unit that you want and need. Several of the following may be suitable:

▶ **Single-family homes:** These are the most popular choice. They can be stand-alone homes on their own legally defined lots or *row houses* or *townhouses* that share a common wall. Single-family homes typically offer buyers privacy, prestige, pride of ownership, and maximum property control.

▶ **Condominiums:** The term condominium, or condo, describes a form of ownership rather than a type of building. Condominiums can be apartments, townhouses, or cluster housing. The condominium buyer receives title to an individual residential unit and joint ownership of common areas and facilities such as lobbies, swimming pools, lakes, and tennis courts. Buyers arrange their own mortgages and pay their own taxes for their units. They are assessed a monthly *homeowner's fee* for their proportionate share of common facility maintenance costs. Many home buyers are attracted to condominiums because they don't want the responsibility of maintaining and caring for a large property.

▶ **Cooperative apartments:** In a cooperative apartment, or co-op, building, each tenant owns a share of the nonprofit corporation that owns the building. Residents lease their units from the corporation and pay a monthly assessment in proportion to ownership shares, based on the space they occupy. These assessments cover the cost of services, maintenance, taxes, and the mortgage on the entire building, and they are subject to change depending on the actual costs of operating the building and the actions of the board of directors, which determines the corporation's policies.

▶ **Rental units:** Some individuals and families choose to *rent* or *lease* their place of residence rather than own it. They may be just starting out and have limited funds for housing, they may be uncertain as to where they want to live, or they just may prefer renting. Rental units range from duplexes, fourplexes, and even single-family homes to large, high-rise apartment complexes containing several hundred units. Renting does come with restrictions, however. For example, you may not be allowed to have a pet or make changes to the unit's appearance.

Gauging the General Attractiveness of Renting versus Buying a Home You can get a general sense of the relative cost of renting versus buying a home by considering the so-called rent ratio, which is the ratio of the average house price to the average annual rent in the area that you are considering. Given the bursting of the housing bubble in the late 2000s, the inflation-adjusted rent ratio steadily fell to around late-1990 levels. Thus, the relative attractiveness of renting has decreased in recent years. Exhibit 5.3 relies on nominal rent ratios to show the percentage by which it is cheaper to buy versus rent across the United States in the last few years. Based on data from 2015, buying was on average 23 percent cheaper than renting in the overall the United States. You may want to consider this type of analysis when evaluating where to relocate or in forming some basic expectations if you've decided where to move.

Analyzing the Rent-or-Buy Decision Many people choose to rent rather than buy their home. For example, young adults usually rent for one or more of the following reasons: (1) they don't have the funds for a down payment and closing costs, (2) they're unsettled in their jobs and family status, (3) they don't want the additional responsibilities associated with homeownership, (4) they believe they can invest the down payment so they can afford a nicer home later, or (5) they believe they should rent now and buy later when the housing market conditions or mortgage rates are more attractive.

The economics of renting or buying a place to live depends on four main factors: (1) housing prices and mortgage interest rates, (2) tax write-offs for homeowners, (3) the expected increase or decrease in home values over time, and (4) how many years you expect to stay in your home. To choose the lowest-cost alternative, compare the cost of renting with the cost of buying, as illustrated by the rent-or-buy analysis in Worksheet 5.2. Note that because the interest deduction nearly always exceeds the amount of the standard deduction ($6,300 for single and $12,600 for married filing jointly in 2016), the form assumes that the taxpayer will itemize deductions.

Suppose you're deciding between renting an apartment for $850 a month or buying a similar-sized condominium for $150,000. Purchasing the condo involves a $30,000 down payment; taking out a $120,000, 6 percent, 30-year mortgage with monthly mortgage payments of $719 (See Calculator); $4,500 in closing costs; and property taxes, insurance, and maintenance. With renting, the only costs are the $850 monthly rental payment and an annual renter's insurance premium of $600. Assume that you're in the 25 percent ordinary income tax bracket and that you'll itemize deductions if you purchase the home. Substituting the appropriate values into Worksheet 5.2 and making the required calculations results in the total cost of each alternative.

The cost of renting in Part A of Worksheet 5.2 is simply the annual rent (monthly rent multiplied by 12)

CALCULATOR

Inputs	Functions
120000	PV
360	N
6	÷
12	=
	I
	CPT
	PMT
Solution	
719.46	

See Appendix E for details.

cooperative apartment (co-op) an apartment in a building in which each tenant owns a share of the nonprofit corporation that owns the building

rent ratio the ratio of the average house price to the average annual rent, which provides insight into the relative attractiveness of buying a house versus renting in a given area of potential interest

Exhibit 5.3

Relative Attractiveness of Renting versus Buying a House

The Trulia Rent vs. Buy Index portrays the average asking price of homes versus the average annual rent for properties listed on Trulia. While the cost of renting versus buying varies, home purchase continues to be cheaper than renting in 98 out of the 100 largest U.S. metro areas.

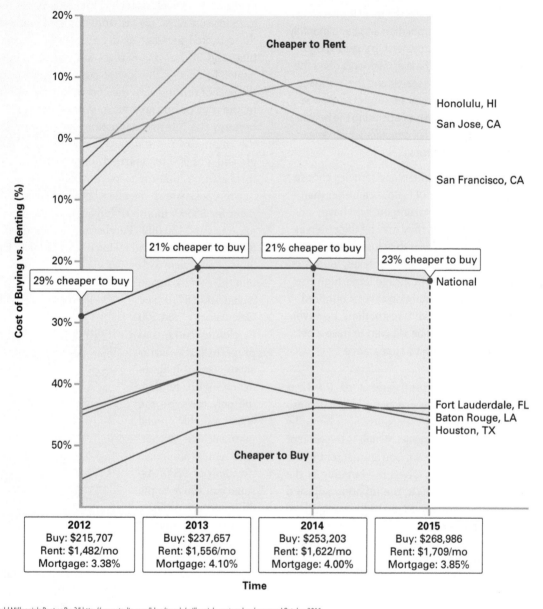

Source: "Should Millennials Rent or Buy?," http://www.trulia.com/blog/trends/millennials-rent-or-buy/, accessed October 2016.

plus the annual renter's insurance premium of $600, plus the $40 opportunity cost of the security deposit, all of which results in a total annual cost of $10,840.

The annual cost of buying in Part B includes mortgage payments, property taxes, homeowner's insurance, annual maintenance, and closing costs to arrive at total costs of $14,964 in Item 6. Then, subtract the portion of the mortgage payment going to pay off the loan balance because it's not part of the interest cost. Subtract the tax savings derived from interest and property taxes to arrive at Item 11, which is the after-tax cost of homeownership of $10,980. But as a homeowner, you also enjoy the benefits

With this procedure for making the rent-or-buy decision, you should *rent* if the total cost of renting is less than the total cost of buying or *buy* if the total cost of renting is more than the total cost of buying. In this example, the rental option requires monthly payments of $850. The purchase option is a $150,000 condo, financed with a $30,000 down payment and a $120,000, 6 percent, 30-year mortgage, with additional closing costs of $4,500.

RENT-OR-BUY ANALYSIS

A. COST OF RENTING

1. Annual rental costs
   (12 × monthly rental rate of $850) $ 10,200

2. Renter's insurance   600

3. Opportunity cost of security deposit: $ 1,000 × after-tax savings rate 0.040   40

   Total cost of renting (line A.1 + line A.2 + line A.3) $ 10,840

B. COST OF BUYING

1. Annual mortgage payments (Terms: $ 120,000 , 360 months, 6 %) $ 8,634
   (12 × monthly mortgage payment of $ 719)

2. Property taxes   3,000
   (2.0% of price of home)

3. Homeowner's insurance   750
   (0.5% of price of home)

4. Maintenance   1,200
   (0.8% of price of home)

5. After-tax cost of interest on down payment and closing costs   1,380
   ($ 34,500 × 4.0 % after-tax rate of return)

6. Total costs (sum of lines B.1 through B.5) $ 14,964

Less:

7. Principal reduction in loan balance (see note below) $ 1,434

8. Tax savings due to interest deductions*   1,800
   (Interest portion of mortgage payments $ 7,200 × tax rate of 25 %)

9. Tax savings due to property tax deductions*   750
   (line B.2 × tax rate of 25 %)

10. Total deductions (sum of lines B.7 through B.9)   3,984

11. Annual after-tax cost of homeownership   10,980
    (line B.6 − line B.10)

12. Estimated annual appreciation in value of home   3,000
    (2 % of price of home)

    Total cost of buying (line B.11 − line B.12) $ 7,980

Note: Find monthly mortgage payments using a calculator or from Exhibit 5.5. An easy way to approximate the portion of the annual loan payment that goes to interest (line B.8) is to multiply the interest rate by the size of the loan (in this case, $120,000 × .06 = $7,200). Then, to find the principal reduction in the loan balance (line B.7), simply subtract the amount that goes to interest from total annual mortgage payments ($8,634−$7,200 = $1,434).

*Tax shelter items.

of home value appreciation. Assuming a modest 2 percent appreciation in the value of the home reduces the annual cost to $7,980. Thus, buying is better than renting because the total cost of renting is $2,860 ($10,840 − $7,980) a year more than the total cost of buying.

Recall that one of the factors to consider in the rent or buy decision is how many years you expect to stay in your home. A common rule of thumb is that you shouldn't buy a home unless you expect to stay in it at least three years. This is, in part, based on a typical average real estate sales commission of about 6 percent. Consider how this relates to the example in Worksheet 5.2, which assumes the value of the home will appreciate at 2 percent per year. Thus, if you sell the home in three years using a real estate agent, the 6 percent selling costs will just equal the 6 percent increase in value. In contrast, if you sell in less than three years, the advantage to buying will be erased. So this example shows that buying is cheaper than renting under the implicit assumption that you would stay in your home longer than three years. By implication, it would likely be cheaper to rent than to buy if you planned to be in the home for less than three years.

> A common rule of thumb is that you shouldn't buy a home unless you expect to stay in it at least three years.

It's important *not* to base the rent-or-buy decision solely on the numbers. Your personal needs and the general condition of the housing market are also important considerations. If you think you may want to move to a different city in a few years and pay the moving costs yourself or if you're worried about job security, renting may make sense even if the numbers favor buying. Think of this as the intangible value of flexibility. Further, for some people, factors such as the need for privacy, the desire to personalize one's home, and the personal satisfaction gained from homeownership outweigh the financial considerations. You should look at the rent-or-buy decision over a timeline of several years, using different assumptions regarding rent increases, mortgage rates, home appreciation

rates in the area, and the rate of return that you can earn on the funds you could invest (if you rent) rather than use toward a down payment on a house (if you buy).

5-4 HOW MUCH HOUSING CAN YOU AFFORD?

LO4 Buying a home obviously involves a lot of careful planning and analysis. Not only must you decide on the kind of home you want (its location, number of bedrooms, and other features), you must also consider its cost, what kind of mortgage to get, how large a monthly payment you can afford, what kind of homeowner's insurance coverage to have, and so forth.

Sound financial planning dictates caution when buying a home or any other major item. Spending too much for a home can have a detrimental effect not only on your current budget and lifestyle but also on your long-term savings and investment plans and thus possibly even your retirement plans. Knowing how much housing you can afford goes a long way toward helping you achieve balanced financial goals.

5-4a Benefits of Owning a Home

Homeownership offers the security and peace of mind derived from living in one's own home and the feeling of permanence and sense of stability. This so-called psychological reward is not the only reason people enjoy owning their home. There are also some significant financial payoffs from homeownership:

▶ **Tax shelter:** As explained in Chapter 3, you can deduct both mortgage interest and property taxes when calculating your federal and, in most states, state income taxes, thereby reducing your taxable income and thus your tax liability. The only requirement is that you itemize your deductions. This tax break is so good that people who have never itemized usually begin doing so after they buy their first house.

▶ **Inflation hedge:** Not only does homeownership offer a place to live, it also represents an

Peshkov Daniil/Shutterstock.com

investment that provides a valuable inflation hedge. That's because homes generally appreciate in value at a rate equal to or greater than the rate of inflation. For example, from 2001 through 2006, a home became one of the best investments you could make, generating a far better return than stocks, bonds, or mutual funds. However, for longer term planning, you should expect that housing prices will roughly keep pace with the rate of inflation.

5-4b The Costs of Homeownership

Although there are some strong emotional and financial reasons for owning a home, there's still the question of whether you can afford to own one. There are two important aspects to consider when it comes to affordability: (1) you must be able to come up with the down payment and other closing costs, and (2) you must be able to meet the cash-flow requirements associated with monthly mortgage payments and other home maintenance expenses. In particular, there are five types of costs to consider: the down payment, points and closing costs, mortgage payments, property taxes and insurance, and maintenance and operating expenses.

The Down Payment The first major hurdle is the **down payment**. Most buyers finance a major part of the purchase price of the home, but they're required by lenders to invest money of their own, called *equity*. The actual amount of down payment required varies among lenders, mortgage types, and properties. To determine the amount of down payment required in specific instances, lenders use the **loan-to-value ratio**, which specifies the maximum percentage of the value of a property that the lender is willing to loan. For example, if the loan-to-value ratio is 80 percent, the buyer will have to come up with a down payment equal to the remaining 20 percent.

Lenders often base the required down payment on a home on the lower of the sale price and the appraised value. Thus, if a house is selling for $250,000 and its

appraised value is $260,000, it is common for lenders to use $250,000 in calculating the required down payment in light of the loan-to-value ratio.

First-time home buyers typically spend several years accumulating enough money to afford the down payment and other costs associated with a home purchase. You can best save these funds if you plan ahead, using future value techniques to determine the monthly or annual savings necessary to have a stated amount by a specified future date. A detailed demonstration of this process is included in Chapter 11 (see Worksheet 11.1, Part B). A disciplined savings program is the best way to obtain the funds needed to come up with the down payment and other closing costs on a home.

If you don't have enough savings to cover the down payment and closing costs, you can consider several other sources. The Federal National Mortgage Association ("Fannie Mae") has programs to help buyers who have limited cash for a down payment and closing costs. The "Fannie 3/2" Program is available from local lenders to limit required down payments for qualified buyers. "Fannie 97" helps the home buyer who can handle monthly mortgage payments but doesn't have cash for the down payment. It requires only a 3 percent down payment from the borrower's own funds, and the borrower needs to have only one month's mortgage payment in cash savings, or reserves, after closing.

Programs have also developed to help banks liquidate homes owned by Fannie Mae because of the foreclosures resulting from the financial crisis of 2008–2009. The HomePath Mortgage Financing program is available from local and national lenders. Borrowers who meet certain income criteria may qualify for a 97 percent loan-to-value mortgage and may obtain their down payment from a gift, grant or loan from a nonprofit organization, state or local government, or employer. The HomePath Renovation Mortgage Financing program is a comparable program available only on homes that will be a primary residence and are in need of light renovations.

When the down payment is less than 20 percent, the lender usually requires the buyer to obtain **private mortgage insurance (PMI)**, which protects the lender from loss if the borrower defaults on the loan. Usually

Hasloo Group Production Studio/Shutterstock.com

down payment a portion of the full purchase price provided by the purchaser when a house or other major asset is purchased; often called *equity*.

loan-to-value ratio the maximum percentage of the value of a property that the lender is willing to loan

private mortgage insurance (PMI) an insurance policy that protects the mortgage lender from loss in the event the borrower defaults on the loan; typically required by lenders when the down payment is less than 20 percent

PMI covers the lender's risk above 80 percent of the house price. Thus, with a 10 percent down payment, the mortgage will be a 90 percent loan, and mortgage insurance will cover 10 percent of the home's price. The cost of mortgage insurance can be included in your monthly payment, and the average cost ranges from about $40 to $70 per month. Under federal law, PMI on most loans made on or after mid-1999, ends automatically once the mortgage is paid down to 78 percent of the original value of the house.

Points and Closing Costs A second hurdle to homeownership relates to mortgage points and closing costs. **Mortgage points** are fees charged by lenders at the time that they grant a mortgage loan. Points are like interest in that they are a charge for borrowing money. They're related to the lender's supply of loanable funds and the demand for mortgages; the greater the demand relative to the supply, the more points you can expect to pay. One point equals 1 percent of the amount borrowed.

pogonici/Shutterstock.com

Points increase the *effective rate of interest* or APR on a mortgage. The amount you pay in points and the length of time you hold a mortgage determine the increase in the effective interest rate. For example, on an 8 percent, 30-year, fixed-rate mortgage, each point increases the annual percentage rate by about 0.11 percent if the loan is held for 30 years or 0.17 percent if held 15 years. You pay the same amount in points regardless of how long you keep your home. So, the longer you hold the mortgage, the longer the period over which you *amortize* (spread out) the fixed cost of the points and the smaller the effect of the points on the effective annual interest rate.

For tax purposes, the points paid on a mortgage at the time a home is originally purchased are usually considered immediately tax deductible. However, the same points are *not* considered immediately tax deductible if they're incurred when *refinancing* a mortgage; in this case, the amount paid in points must be written off (amortized) over the life of the new mortgage loan.

Closing costs are all expenses that borrowers ordinarily pay when a mortgage loan is closed and they receive title to the purchased property. Closing costs are like down payments: they represent money that you must come up with *at the time you buy the house*. Closing costs are made up of such items as loan application and loan origination fees, mortgage points, title search and insurance fees, attorneys' fees, appraisal fees, and other miscellaneous fees. Exhibit 5.4 provides a list of these fees and shows that they can total 50 percent or more of the down payment amount. For example, as can be seen in the exhibit, with a 10 percent down payment on a $200,000 home, the closing costs are about 56 percent of the down payment, or $11,130.

> **EXAMPLE: Calculating Mortgage Points** If you borrow $100,000 and loan fees equal three points, the amount of money you'll pay in points is:
>
> $$\$100,000 \times 0.03 = \$3,000$$

Lenders typically use points as an alternative way of charging interest on their loans. They can vary the interest rate along with the number of points they charge to create loans with comparable effective rates. For example, a lender might be willing to give you a 5 percent rather than a 6 percent mortgage if you're willing to pay more points. That is, you choose between a 6 percent mortgage rate with one point or a 5 percent mortgage rate with three points. If you choose the 5 percent loan, you'll pay a lot more *at closing* (although the amount of interest paid *over the life of the mortgage* may be considerably less).

mortgage points fees (one point equals 1 percent of the amount borrowed) charged by lenders at the time they grant a mortgage loan; they are related to the lender's supply of loanable funds and the demand for mortgages

closing costs all expenses (including mortgage points) that borrowers ordinarily pay when a mortgage loan is closed and they receive title to the purchased property

Mortgage Payments The monthly mortgage payment is determined using a standard but fairly detailed formula. Each mortgage payment is made up partly of principal repayment on the loan and partly of interest charges on the loan. However, as Exhibit 5.5 shows, for most of the life of the mortgage the vast majority of each monthly payment goes to *interest*. The loan illustrated in the exhibit is a $100,000, 30-year, 5 percent mortgage with monthly payments of $536.82, for a total of $6,441.84 per year. Note that it is not until the 16th year of this 30-year mortgage that the principal portion of the monthly loan payment exceeds the amount that goes to interest.

Exhibit 5.4

Closing Costs: The Hidden Costs of Buying a Home

The closing costs on a home mortgage loan can be substantial—as much as 5 percent to 7 percent of the price of the home. Except for the real estate commission (generally paid by the seller), the buyer incurs the biggest share of the closing costs and must pay them—in addition to the down payment—when the loan is closed and title to the property is conveyed.

Item	Size of Down Payment	
	20%	**10%**
Loan application fee	$ 300	$ 300
Loan origination fee	1,600	1,800
Points	4,160	5,400
Mortgage and homeowner's insurance	—	675
Title search and insurance	665	665
Attorneys' fees	400	400
Appraisal fees	425	425
Home inspection	350	350
Mortgage tax	665	725
Filing fees	80	80
Credit reports	35	35
Miscellaneous	200	200
Total closing costs	$9,530	$11,130

Note: Typical closing costs for a $200,000 home—2.6 points charged with 20 percent down, 3 points with 10 percent down. Actual amounts will vary by lender and location.

Most mortgage lenders and realtors use their calculator to obtain monthly payments. Yet some of them still use *comprehensive mortgage payment tables*, which provide monthly payments for virtually any combination of loan size, interest rate, and maturity. Exhibit 5.6 provides an excerpt from one such comprehensive mortgage payment table (with values rounded to the nearest cent). It lists the *monthly payments* associated with a $10,000, fixed-rate loan for selected maturities of 10 to 30 years and for various interest rates ranging from 5 percent to 10 percent. This table can be used to find the monthly payment for a loan of any size.

The calculator keystrokes shown in the margin can be used with a financial calculator to more easily and precisely calculate mortgage payments in the above example. Note that the mortgage payment of $1,079.19 is a more accurate figure than the value calculated using the table.

Affordability Ratios

The key issue regarding mortgage payments is *affordability*: How large a monthly mortgage payment can you afford, given your budget? This amount determines how much you can borrow to finance the purchase of a home.

To obtain a mortgage, a potential borrower must be "qualified"—that is, demonstrate that he or

---

EXAMPLE: Calculating Monthly Mortgage Payments You'd like to use the mortgage payment tables to find the monthly loan payment on a $180,000, 6 percent, 30-year mortgage.

Divide the amount of the loan ($180,000) by $10,000 and then multiply this factor (18.0) by the payment amount shown in Exhibit 5.6 for a 6 percent, 30-year loan ($59.96):

$180,000/$10,000 = 18.0 and 18.0 × $59.96
= $1,079.28

Thus, the resulting monthly mortgage payment is $1,079.28. See the Calculator in the right column.

CALCULATOR

Inputs	Functions
180000	PV
360	N
6	÷
12	=
	I
	CPT
	PMT
Solution	
1,079.19	

See Appendix E for details.

By using the following variables in the home affordability analysis form, the Wrights estimate a maximum home purchase price of $201,000: their combined annual income of $75,200; the $30,000 available for a down payment and paying all closing costs; estimated monthly property taxes and homeowner's insurance of $375; the lender's 28 percent monthly mortgage payment affordability ratio; an average interest rate of 6 percent and expected loan maturity of 30 years, and a minimum down payment of 10 percent.

HOME AFFORDABILITY ANALYSIS*

Name __James and Cora Wright__ Date __August 14, 2017__

Item	Description	Amount
1	Amount of annual income	$ 75,200
2	Monthly income (Item 1 ÷ 12)	$ 6,267
3	Lender's affordability ratio (in decimal form)	0.28
4	Maximum monthly mortgage payment (PITI) (Item 2 × Item 3)	$ 1,755
5	Estimated monthly prop tax and homeowner's insurance payment	$ 375
6	Maximum monthly loan payment (Item 4 − Item 5)	$ 1,380
7	Approximate average interest rate on loan	6 %
8	Planned loan maturity (years)	30
9	Monthly mortgage payment per $10,000 (using Item 7 and Item 8 and Table of Monthly Mortgage Payments in Exhibit 5.6)	$ 59.96
10	Maximum loan based on monthly income ($10,000 × Item 6 ÷ Item 9)	$230,000
11	Funds available for making a down payment and paying closing costs	$ 30,000
12	Funds available for making a down payment (Item 11 × .67)	$ 20,100
13	Maximum purchase price based on available monthly income (Item 10 + Item 12)	$250,100
14	Minimum acceptable down payment (in decimal form)	0.10
15	Maximum purchase price based on down payment (Item 12 ÷ Item 14)	$201,000
16	Maximum home purchase price (lower of Item 13 and Item 15)	$201,000

*Note: This analysis assumes that one-third of the funds available for making the down payment and paying closing costs are used to meet closing costs and that the remaining two-thirds are available for a down payment. This means that closing costs will represent an amount equal to about 50 percent of the down payment.

so obtain estimates of utilities when evaluating a home for purchase.

5-4c Performing a Home Affordability Analysis

Worksheet 5.3 helps you determine the maximum price for a home purchase based on your monthly income and down payment amount after meeting estimated closing costs. In our example, James and Cora Wright have a combined annual income of $75,200 and savings of $30,000 for a down payment and closing costs. They estimate monthly property taxes and homeowner's insurance at $375, and expect the mortgage lender to use a 28 percent monthly mortgage payment affordability ratio, to lend at an average interest rate of 6 percent on a

30-year (360-month) mortgage, and to require a 10 percent minimum down payment. The Wrights' analysis shows that they can afford to purchase a home for about $201,000.

Worksheet 5.3 walks us through the steps that the Wright family took to reach this conclusion. The maximum purchase price is determined from two perspectives: the maximum based on monthly income and the maximum based on the minimum acceptable down payment. The lower of the two estimates determines the maximum purchase price. Based on their monthly income and a 28 percent affordability ratio, their monthly payment could be $1,755 ($6,267 × 0.28), shown as Item 4. After deducting taxes and insurance, the maximum monthly mortgage payment amount is $1,380 (Item 6).

EXAMPLE: Calculating the Maximum Affordable Mortgage Loan The Wrights want to determine the maximum loan they can carry given that they can afford a maximum monthly mortgage payment of $1,380. Exhibit 5.6 indicates that a $10,000 loan for 30 years at 6 percent would result in a monthly payment of $59.96, as indicated in Item 9 of Worksheet 5.3. This would support loan of:

$$\$10,000 \times \$1,380/\$59.96 = \$230,153.44$$

The calculator result in the margin indicates a maximum purchase price of $230,172.43, which is more precise than the approximation provided using Exhibit 5.6.

CALCULATOR

Inputs	Functions
1380	PMT
360	N
6	÷
12	=
	I
	CPT
	PMT
	Solution
	230,172.43

See Appendix E for details.

With a down payment of $30,000 and monthly income of $6,267, the Wright family can afford a home costing $250,100 (Item 13). The Wrights then look at the maximum purchase price based on their $30,000 down payment, or $150,000 (Item 15). Their maximum home purchase price is the lower of Items 13 and 15, or $201,000 (Item 16), and is limited by the amount available for a down payment.

5-5 THE HOME-BUYING PROCESS

LO5 Buying a home requires time, effort, and money. You'll want to educate yourself about available properties and prevailing prices by doing a systematic search and careful analysis. And you'll also need a basic understanding of the role of a real estate agent, the mortgage application process, the real estate sales contract, and other documents required to close a deal.

5-5a Shop the Market First

Most people who shop the housing market rely on real estate agents for information, access to properties, and advice. Many of them also shop via the Internet, visiting various real estate sites to learn about available properties. Going online, you can specify preferences such as location, price, and size and then obtain descriptions and color photos of all properties that meet your needs.

As noted earlier, you must begin your home search project by figuring out what *you* require for your particular lifestyle needs—in terms of living space, style, and other special features. The property's location, neighborhood,

Bloomberg/Getty Images

and school district are important considerations as well. It's helpful to divide your list into *necessary* features, such as the number of bedrooms and baths, and *optional*—but desirable—features, such as fireplaces, whirlpool tubs, and so on. And of course, an affordability analysis is a critical part of the housing search.

Keep an open mind as you start looking. Be flexible and look at a variety of homes in your price range. This can be invaluable in helping to define your wants and needs more clearly.

> The property's location, neighborhood, and school district are important considerations.

Real Estate Short Sales The bursting of the real estate bubble associated with the financial crisis of 2008–2009 increased the use of real estate short sales. A **real estate short sale** is the sale of property in which *the proceeds are less than the balance owed on the mortgage* used to secure the property. This procedure is an effort by a mortgage lender to come to terms with homeowners who are about to default or are defaulting on their mortgage loans. A broker's price opinion or an appraisal is obtained to estimate the probable selling price of the property for the purposes of the short sale.

A short sale typically occurs to prevent home foreclosure by finding

the most economic means for the mortgage lender to recover as much of the loan balance owed on the property as possible. In contrast, in a foreclosure the borrower typically cannot make scheduled mortgage payments and the lender repossesses the property in an effort to recover the loan balance owed. Mortgage holders will agree to a short sale only if they believe the proceeds generated by the sale will produce a smaller loss than foreclosing on the property. A real estate short sale may consequently be viewed as a negotiated effort to mitigate the mortgage lender's losses.

While a short sale can reduce a lender's losses, *it can also be beneficial for the homeowner.* A real estate short sale will avoid having a foreclosure appear on the homeowner's credit history. Short sales should also help homeowners manage the costs that got them into trouble in the first place. Finally, a short sale is usually faster and cheaper for the homeowner than a foreclosure.

5-5b Using an Agent

Real estate agents are professionals who are in daily contact with the housing market. Once you describe your needs to an agent, he or she can begin to search for appropriate properties. Your agent will also help you negotiate with the seller, obtain satisfactory financing, and, although not empowered to give explicit legal advice, prepare the real estate sales contract. Most real estate firms belong to a local **Multiple Listing Service (MLS)**, a comprehensive listing, updated daily, of properties for sale in a given community or metropolitan area. A brief description of each property and its asking price are included; many of which are accompanied by photos of the property.

Buyers should remember that *agents typically are employed by sellers*. Unless you've agreed to pay a fee to a sales agent to act as a buyer's agent, a realtor's primary responsibility, by law, is to sell listed properties at the highest possible prices. Agents are paid only if they make a sale, so some might pressure you to "sign now or miss the chance of a lifetime." But most agents will listen to your needs and work to match you with the right property and under terms that will benefit both you and the seller. Good agents recognize that their interests are best served when all parties to a transaction are satisfied.

real estate short sale sale of real estate property in which the proceeds are less than the balance owed on a loan secured by the property sold

Multiple Listing Service (MLS) a comprehensive listing, updated daily, of properties for sale in a given community or metropolitan area; includes a brief description of each property with a photo and its asking price but can be accessed only by realtors who work for an MLS member of the real estate commission, the buyer probably absorbs some or even all of the commission.

5-5c Prequalifying and Applying for a Mortgage

Before beginning your home search, it's wise to meet with one or more mortgage lenders to prearrange a mortgage loan. **Prequalification** can work to your advantage in several ways. You'll know ahead of time the specific mortgage amount that you qualify for—subject, of course, to changes in rates and terms—and can focus your search on homes within an affordable price range.

Prequalification also provides estimates of the required down payment and closing costs for different types of mortgages. It identifies in advance any problems, such as credit report errors, that might arise from your application, and allows you time to correct them. Finally, prequalification enhances your bargaining power with the sellers of a house by letting them know that the deal won't fall through because you can't afford the property or obtain suitable financing. And since you will have already gone through the mortgage application process, the time required to close the sale should be relatively short.

5-5d The Real Estate Sales Contract

After selecting a home to buy, you must enter into a sales contract. State laws generally specify that, to be enforceable in court, real estate buy–sell agreements must be in writing and contain certain information, including (1) the names of buyers and sellers, (2) a description of the property sufficient for positive identification, (3) specific price and other terms, and (4) usually the signatures of the buyers and sellers. Real estate sales transactions often take weeks and sometimes months to complete. Contract requirements help keep the facts straight and reduce the chance for misunderstanding, misrepresentation, or fraud.

> **prequalification** the process of arranging with a mortgage lender, in advance of buying a home, to obtain the amount of mortgage financing the lender deems affordable for the home buyer

Real estate commissions typically average between 5 percent and 6 percent. It may be possible to negotiate a lower commission with your agent or to find a discountbroker, or one who charges a flat fee. Commissions are usually explicitly paid only by the seller. However, because the price of a home is often inflated by the size

Ratana21/Shutterstock.com

Exhibit 5.7

Effective Home-Buying Strategies

Keeping in mind the following advice will improve your chances of becoming a happy, successful homeowner:

- **Don't wipe out your savings.** While it makes sense to put down the largest down payment you can afford, it is important to keep your emergency reserves intact, hold money for closing costs, and set aside funds to handle possible repairs and future maintenance.

- **Pick the right neighborhood.** You've heard that the three most important factors in valuing real estate are location, location, and location. This is no joke. Drive through a neighborhood, ask the police department about crime statistics, and talk to neighbors before you buy. If they don't want to talk, that tells you something too!

- **Stay away from the most expensive home in the neighborhood.** While having the largest and most expensive home in the neighborhood might be appealing, it doesn't bode well for resale value. If you need three bedrooms, don't consider a five-bedroom that looks good but costs more and meets your needs less.

- **Interview your agent and ask hard questions.** Make sure that he or she is experienced. Consider signing a buyer's broker agreement, which gives both you and the broker responsibilities and reasonable performance expectations.

- **Rely on professional advice.** Pay attention to what your agent or mortgage broker tells you. Look up information on the Internet, read real estate books, and ask for a second opinion. Lawyers and accountants are excellent resources.

- **Use traditional financing.** One of the biggest lessons of the financial crisis a few years ago is that real estate prices don't always go up. And what you don't know about your mortgage can hurt you! Don't sign off on your mortgage until you understand every detail. Terms like indexes, margins, caps, and negative amortization should make you nervous.

- **Don't change the financial picture before closing.** While waiting for loan funding, there is no need to buy a new car to match your new home. Your excellent credit report does not give you free rein to buy whatever you want. Borrowing too much more at this time could adversely affect the funding of a mortgage.

- **Be sure to do the home inspection.** Home inspections are *not* a waste of time and money. Qualified home inspectors can find problems that most of us would miss.

- **Be careful about taking on additional debt after closing.** After you become a homeowner, you'll be offered many deals on a home equity loan. Although it may be tempting to pull out all your equity and use this newfound money to buy all sorts of new toys, you should stick to a reasonable financial plan. It is critically important to cover the contingency of losing a job or an emergency by setting aside some money.

Source: Based on Elizabeth Weintraub, "Top 10 Ways to Lose Your Home," www.homebuying.about.com/od/buyingahome/tp/072007LoseHome.htm, accessed October 2016.

Although these requirements fulfill the minimums necessary for court enforcement, in practice real estate sales contracts usually contain several other contractual clauses relating to earnest money deposits, contingencies, personal property, and closing costs. An **earnest money deposit** is the money you pledge to show good faith when you make an offer. If, after signing a sales contract, you withdraw from the transaction without a valid reason, you might have to forfeit this deposit. A valid reason for withdrawal would be stated in the contract as a contingency clause. With a **contingency clause**, you can condition your agreement to buy on such factors as obtaining financing, a satisfactory termite inspection or other physical inspection of the property, or the advice of a lawyer or real estate expert.

5-5e Closing the Deal

After you obtain financing and your loan is approved, the closing process begins. The **Real Estate Settlement Procedures Act (RESPA)** governs closings on owner-occupied houses, condominiums, and apartment buildings of four units or fewer. The Act reduced closing costs by prohibiting kickbacks made to real estate agents and others from lenders or title insurance companies. It also requires clear, advance disclosure of all closing costs to home buyers. Exhibit 5.7 provides some tips to help you sail through the home-buying process in general and the closing process in particular.

earnest money deposit money pledged by a buyer to show good faith when making an offer to buy a home

contingency clause a clause in a real estate sales contract that makes the agreement conditional on such factors as the availability of financing, property inspections, or obtaining expert advice

Real Estate Settlement Procedures Act (RESPA) a federal law requiring mortgage lenders to give potential borrowers a government publication describing the closing process and providing clear, advance disclosure of all closing costs to home buyers

5-6 FINANCING THE TRANSACTION

JohnKwan/Shutterstock.com

LO6 Earlier in this chapter, we saw that mortgage terms can dramatically affect the amount you can afford to spend on a home. The success of a real estate transaction often hinges on obtaining a mortgage with favorable terms. A **mortgage loan** is secured by the property: If the borrower defaults, the lender has the legal right to liquidate the property to recover the funds it is owed. Before you obtain such a loan, it's helpful to understand the sources and types of mortgages and their underlying economics.

5-6a Sources of Mortgage Loans

The major sources of home mortgages today are commercial banks, thrift institutions, and mortgage bankers or brokers. Commercial banks are also an important source of *interim construction loans,* providing short-term financing during the construction phase for individuals who are building or remodeling a home. After the home is completed, the homeowner obtains *permanent financing,* in the form of a standard mortgage loan, and then uses the proceeds from it to repay the construction loan.

Another way to obtain a mortgage loan is through a mortgage banker or mortgage broker. Both solicit borrowers, originate loans, and place them with traditional mortgage lenders as well as life insurance companies and pension funds. Although **mortgage bankers** often use their own money to initially fund mortgages they later resell, **mortgage brokers** take loan applications and then seek lenders willing to grant the mortgage loans under the desired terms. Most brokers also have ongoing relationships with different lenders, thereby increasing your chances of finding a loan even if you don't qualify at a commercial bank or thrift institution. Brokers can often simplify the financing process by cutting through red tape, negotiating more favorable terms, and reducing the amount of time to close the loan. Mortgage brokers earn their income from commissions and origination fees paid by the lender, costs that are typically passed on to the borrower in the points charged on a loan.

Shopping for the best mortgage rate and terms has become a lot easier due to the Internet. Many sites allow you to search for the best fixed-rate or adjustable-rate mortgage in your area. HSH Associates, a mortgage consulting firm with an Internet site at www.hsh.com, lists mortgages offered by banks, mortgage companies, and brokerage firms across the country along with information on prevailing interest rates, terms, and points. Bankrate, www.bankrate.com, and similar sites also offer mortgage comparisons.

5-6b Types of Mortgage Loans

For our purposes here, we'll group mortgages in two catagories based on (1) terms of payment and (2) whether they're conventional, insured, or guaranteed.

There are literally dozens of different types of home mortgages from which to choose. The most common types of mortgage loans are fixed-rate and adjustable-rate mortgages.

Fixed-Rate Mortgages The **fixed-rate mortgage** accounts for a large portion of all home mortgages. Both the rate of interest and the monthly mortgage payment are fixed over the full term of the loan. The most common type of fixed-rate mortgage is the *30-year fixed-rate* loan, although *10- and 15-year loans* are becoming

mortgage loan a loan secured by the property: If the borrower defaults, the lender has the legal right to liquidate the property to recover the funds it's owed

mortgage banker a firm that solicits borrowers, originates primarily government-insured and government-guaranteed loans, and places them with mortgage lenders; often uses its own money to initially fund mortgages it later resells

mortgage broker a firm that solicits borrowers, originates primarily conventional loans, and places them with mortgage lenders; the broker merely takes loan applications and then finds lenders willing to grant the mortgage loans under the desired terms

fixed-rate mortgage the traditional type of mortgage in which both the rate of interest and the monthly mortgage payment are fixed over the full term of the loan more popular as homeowners recognize the advantages of paying off their loan over a shorter period of time. Because of the risks that the lender assumes with a 30-year loan, it's usually the most expensive form of home financing.

The *15-year fixed-rate* loan is becoming increasingly popular. Even though it is repaid twice as fast (15 years versus 30), the monthly payments don't increase excessively. To pay off a loan in less time, the homeowner must pay more each month, but monthly payments don't have to be doubled to pay off the loan in half the time. The monthly payment on a 15-year loan is generally only about 20 percent to 30 percent larger than the payment on a 30-year loan. The following table shows the difference in monthly payment and total interest paid for 30- and 15-year fixed-rate mortgages. In both cases the purchaser borrows $160,000 at a 5 percent fixed rate of interest.

Term of Loan	Regular Monthly Payment	Total Interest Paid over Life of Loan
30 years	$ 858.91	$149,209.25
15 years	$1,265.27	$ 67,748.56

Perhaps the most startling feature is the substantial difference in the total amount of interest paid over the term of the loan. Note in the example above that you can save *$81,460.69* ($149,209.25 − $67,748.56) just by financing your home with a 15-year mortgage rather than over the traditional 30 years. And keep in mind this savings is possible even though monthly payments differ by only about $406 ($1,265.27 − $858.91). The difference in the monthly payment is usually even less because 15-year mortgages are usually available at interest rates that are about half a percentage point below otherwise comparable 30-year loans.

Another way to shorten the mortgage term without committing to an initially shorter-term mortgage is by making extra principal payments regularly or when you have extra funds. This approach can save you a lot

in interest payments over time. You could effectively replicate a 15-year loan using a 30-year mortgage while preserving the option to quit making extra payments whenever you like.

Adjustable-Rate Mortgages (ARMs) Another popular form of home loan is the adjustable-rate mortgage (ARM). In this case, the rate of interest, and therefore the size of the monthly payment, is adjusted based on market interest rate movements. The mortgage interest rate is linked to a specific *interest rate index* and is adjusted at specific intervals (usually once or twice a year) based on changes in the index. When the index moves up, so does the interest rate on the mortgage and, in turn, the size of the monthly mortgage payment increases. The new interest rate and monthly mortgage payment remain in effect until the next adjustment date.

The term of an ARM can be 15 or 30 years. Because the size of the monthly payments will vary with interest rates, there's no way to tell what your future payments will be. However, because the borrower assumes most or all of the interest rate risk in these mortgages, the *initial rate of interest* on an adjustable-rate mortgage is normally well below—typically by 2 to 3 percentage points—the rate of a standard 30-year fixed-rate loan. Of course, whether the borrower actually ends up paying less interest depends on the behavior of market interest rates during the term of the loan.

Features of ARMs It's important for home buyers to understand the basic features of an ARM:

▶ **Adjustment period**: Although the period of time between rate changes is typically six months to one year, adjustment periods can range from three months to three years or more.

▶ **Index rate**: A baseline rate that captures the movement in interest rates, usually tied to six-month U.S. Treasury securities, six-month CDs, or the average cost of funds to savings institutions.

▶ **Margin**: The percentage points that a lender *adds to the index* to determine the rate of interest on an ARM, usually a fixed amount over the life of the loan.

▶ **Interest rate caps**: Limits the amount the interest rate can increase over a given period. *Periodic caps* limit interest rate increases from one adjustment to the next (typically lenders cap annual rate adjustments at 1 to 2 percentage points), and *overall caps*

adjustable-rate mortgage (ARM) a mortgage on which the rate of interest, and therefore the size of the monthly payment, is adjusted based on market interest rate movements

adjustment period on an adjustable-rate mortgage, the period of time between rate or payment changes

index rate on an adjustable-rate mortgage, the baseline index rate that captures interest rate movements

margin on an adjustable-rate mortgage, the percentage points a lender adds to the *index rate* to determine the rate of interest

interest rate cap on an adjustable-rate mortgage, the limit on the amount that the interest rate can increase each adjustment period and over the life of the loan limit the interest rate increase over the life of the loan (lifetime interest rate caps are typically set at 5 to 8 percentage points). Many ARMs have both periodic and overall interest rate caps.

▶ **Payment caps**: Limits on monthly payment increases that may result from a rate adjustment—usually a percentage of the previous payment. If your ARM has a 5 percent payment cap, your monthly payments can increase no more than 5 percent from one year to the next—regardless of what happens to interest rates.

Because most ARMs are 30-year loans (360 payments), you can determine the initial monthly payment in the same manner as for any other 30-year mortgage. For example, for an $100,000 loan at 6.5 percent (4.5 percent index rate + 2 percent margin), we can use a calculator as shown here to find the first-year monthly payments of $632.07. Assuming a one-year adjustment period, if the index rate rises to 5.5 percent, then the interest rate for the second year will be 7.5 percent (5.5 percent + 2 percent = 7.5 percent). The size of the monthly payment for the next 12 months will then be adjusted upward to about $697.83. This process is repeated each year thereafter until the loan matures.

CALCULATOR

Inputs	Functions
100000	PV
360	N
6.5	÷
12	=
	I
	CPT
	PMT
	Solution
	632.07

See Appendix E for details.

Beware of Negative Amortization

Some ARMs are subject to **negative amortization**—an increase in the principal balance resulting from monthly loan payments that are lower than the amount of monthly interest being charged. In other words, you could end up with a larger mortgage balance on the next anniversary of your loan than on the previous one. This occurs when the payment is set below the interest charge, or when the ARM has *interest rates* that are adjusted *monthly*—with monthly *payments* that adjust *annually*. In the latter case, when rates are rising on these loans, the current monthly payment can be less than the interest being charged, and the difference is added to the principal, thereby increasing the size of the loan. When

considering an ARM, be sure to learn whether negative amortization could occur. Generally, loans without the potential for negative amortization are available, although they tend to have slightly higher initial rates and interest rate caps.

Here are a couple of other types of ARMs lenders may sometimes offer:

▶ **Convertible ARMs** allow borrowers to convert from an adjustable-rate to a fixed-rate loan during a specified time period, usually any time between the 13th and 60th month. Although these loans seldom provide the lowest initial rate, they allow the borrower to convert to a fixed-rate loan if interest rates decline. A conversion fee of about $500 is typical, and the fixed rate is normally set at 0.25 percent to 0.5 percent above the going rate on fixed-rate loans at the time you convert.

▶ **Two-step ARMs** have just two interest rates, the first for an initial period of five to seven years, and a higher one for the remaining term of the loan.

Fixed or Adjustable Rate? Fixed-rate mortgages are popular with home buyers who plan to stay in their homes for at least five to seven years and want to know what their payments will be. Of course, the current level of interest rates and your expectations about future interest rates will influence your choice of a fixed-rate or adjustable-rate mortgage. When the average interest rate on a 30-year mortgage loan is high, people often choose adjustable-rate mortgages to avoid being locked into prevailing high rates. In sharp contrast, when interest rates are low, many home buyers opt for fixed-rate mortgages to lock in these attractive rates. In such situations, many homeowners with adjustable-rate mortgages will often refinance them with fixed-rate loans to take advantage of the favorable fixed rates.

payment cap on an adjustable-rate mortgage, the limit on the monthly payment increase that may result from a rate adjustment

negative amortization when the principal balance on a mortgage loan increases because the monthly loan payment is lower than the amount of monthly interest being charged; some ARMs are subject to this undesirable condition

convertible ARM an adjustable-rate mortgage loan that allows borrowers to convert from an adjustable-rate to a fixed-rate loan, usually at any time between the 13th and the 60th month

two-step ARM an adjustable-rate mortgage with just two interest rates: one for the first five to seven years of the loan, and a higher one for the remaining term of the loan

Other Mortgage Payment Options. In addition to standard fixed-rate and adjustable-rate mortgage loans, some lenders offer variations designed to help first-time home buyers:

▶ **Interest-only mortgages** are loans requiring the borrower to pay only the interest portion of the loan. Rather than amortizing the loan with equal monthly payments, the borrower merely pays the accrued interest each month—the option to pay interest only lasts for a specified period, often 5 to 10 years, after which time all future loan payments will also include principal. These mortgages allow the borrower to make lower payments (early on in the life of the loan) that are still fully tax deductible. Most interest-only mortgages are offered as ARMs.

▶ **Graduated-payment mortgages** are loans offering low payments for the first few years, gradually increasing until year three or five, and then remaining fixed. The low initial payments appeal to people who are just starting out and expect their income to rise. If this doesn't occur, however, it could result in a higher debt load than the borrower can handle.

▶ **Growing-equity mortgages** are fixed-rate mortgages with payments that increase over a specific period. The extra funds are applied to the principal, so a conventional 30-year loan can be paid off in about 20 years.

▶ **Biweekly mortgages** are loans on which payments equal to half

interest-only mortgage a mortgage that requires the borrower to pay only interest; typically used to finance the purchase of more expensive properties

graduated-payment mortgage a mortgage that starts with unusually low payments that rise over several years to a fixed payment

growing-equity mortgage fixed-rate mortgage with payments that increase over a specific period. Extra funds are applied to the principal so that the loan is paid off more quickly

biweekly mortgage a loan on which payments equal to half the regular monthly payment that are made every two weeks

buydown financing made available by a builder or seller to a potential new-home buyer at well below market interest rates, often only for a short period

conventional mortgage a mortgage offered by a lender who assumes all the risk of loss; typically requires a down payment of at least 20 percent of the value of the mortgaged property

FHA mortgage insurance a program under which the Federal Housing Administration (FHA) offers lenders mortgage insurance on loans having a high loan-to-value ratio; its intent is to encourage loans to home buyers who have very little money available for a down payment and closing costs

YOU CAN DO IT NOW: Current Mortgage Rates
If you're considering buying a home, you need to know current mortgage rates to determine prospective monthly payments and the implied price you can afford to pay for the home. Up-to-date market rates for different maturities of fixed and adjustable rate mortgages are available at **http://www.bankrate.com**. And you can also obtain refinancing rates there if you already have a mortgage and are considering refinancing it. It's so easy – you can **do it now**.

of a regular monthly payment are made every two weeks rather than once a month. Because you make 26 payments (52 weeks/2), which is the equivalent of 13 monthly payments, the principal balance declines faster and so you pay less interest over the life of the loan.

▶ **Buydowns** are a type of seller financing sometimes offered on new homes. A builder, for example, arranges for mortgage financing with a financial institution at interest rates well below market rates. For example, a builder may offer 5 percent financing when the market rate of interest is around 6 or 6.5 percent. Be careful, though, because the reduced rate may only be good for a short period, or the buyer may actually end up paying for the reduced interest in the form of a higher purchase price.

Conventional, Insured, and Guaranteed Loans
A **conventional mortgage** is a mortgage offered by a lender who assumes all the risk of loss. To protect themselves, lenders usually require a down payment of at least 20 percent of the value of the mortgaged property. For lower down payments, the lender usually requires *private mortgage insurance (PMI)*, as described earlier in the chapter. High borrower equity greatly reduces the likelihood of default on a mortgage and subsequent loss to the lender. However, a high down payment requirement makes home buying more difficult for many families and individuals.

The **FHA mortgage insurance** program helps people buy homes even when they have very little money available for a down payment and closing costs; these are known as *insured loans*. In 2016, the up-front mortgage insurance premium for a 15- or 30-year mortgage was 1.75 percent of the loan amount—paid by the borrower at closing or included in the mortgage—plus another 0.45 percent to 1.05 percent annual renewal premium, paid monthly, depending on the amount and maturity of the loan and the

Using this form, the Sanchez family finds that—by refinancing the $70,180 balance on their 10-year-old, $80,000, 8 percent, 30-year mortgage (which has no prepayment penalty and requires payments of $587 per month) with a 5 percent, 20-year mortgage requiring $463 monthly payments and $2,400 in total after-tax closing costs—it will take 26 months to break even. Because the Sanchez family plans to stay in their home for at least 60 more months, the refinancing is easily justified.

MORTGAGE REFINANCING ANALYSIS

Name Felix and Anna Sanchez   Date October 8, 2017

Item	Description	Amount
1	Current monthly payment (Terms: $ 80,000, 8%, 30 years)	$ 587
2	New monthly payment (Terms: $ 70,180, 5%, 20 years)	463
3	Monthly savings, pretax (Item 1 + Item 2)	$ 124
4	Tax on monthly savings [Item 3 × tax rate (25 %)]	31
5	Monthly savings, after-tax (Item 3 − Item 4)	$ 93
6	Costs to refinance:	
	a. Prepayment penalty	$ 0
	b. Total closing costs (after-tax)	2,400
	c. Total refinancing costs (Item 6a + Item 6b)	$ 2,400
7	Months to break even (Item 6c ÷ Item 5)	26

amount of the down payment. The FHA agrees to reimburse lenders for losses up to a specified maximum amount if the buyer defaults. The interest rate on an FHA loan is generally about 0.5 percent to 1 percent lower than that on conventional fixed-rate loans. The affordability ratios that are used to qualify applicants for these loans are typically less stringent than those used for conventional loans. To learn more about FHA mortgages, visit www.fha.com.

Guaranteed loans are similar to insured loans, but better—if you qualify. **VA loan guarantees** are provided by the U.S. Veterans Administration to lenders who make qualified mortgage loans to eligible veterans of the

VA loan guarantee a guarantee offered by the U.S. Veterans Administration to lenders who make qualified mortgage loans to eligible veterans of the U.S. Armed Forces and their unmarried surviving spouses

U.S. armed forces and their unmarried surviving spouses. This program, however, does not require lenders or veterans to pay a premium for the guarantee. In many instances, an eligible veteran must pay only closing costs. Thus, under such a program, a veteran can effectively buy a home with no down payment. (This can be done *only once* with a VA loan.) The mortgage loan—subject to a usual maximum of about $417,000 (or much more in high-cost counties) for a no-money-down loan (as of 2016)—can amount to as much as 100 percent of a purchased property's appraised value.

It is important to note that there are some regional differences in VA loan requirements. VA loans include a funding fee of about 2 percent on first-time, no-down-payment loans for regular military members (the fee is lower if the down payment is 10 percent or more). The VA sets the maximum interest rate, which (as with FHA loans) is usually about 0.5 percent *below* the rate on conventional fixed-rate loans. To qualify, the veteran must meet VA credit guidelines. You can find more information at **www.homeloans.va.gov**.

5-6c Refinancing Your Mortgage

After you've purchased a home and closed the transaction, interest rates on similar loans may drop. If rates drop by 1 percent to 2 percent or more, then you should consider the economics of refinancing after carefully comparing the terms of the old and new mortgages, the anticipated number of years you expect to remain in the home, any prepayment penalty on the old mortgage, and the closing costs associated with the new mortgage.

Worksheet 5.4 provides a form for analyzing the impact of refinancing. The data for the Sanchez family's analysis is shown. Their original $80,000, 10-year-old, 8 percent mortgage has a current balance of $70,180 and monthly payments of $587 for 20 more years. If they refinance the $70,180 balance at the prevailing rate of 5 percent, then the monthly payment would drop to $463 over the remaining 20-year life of the current mortgage. The Sanchez family plans to live in their house for at least five more years. They won't have to pay a penalty for prepaying their current mortgage, and closing and other costs associated with the new mortgage are $2,400 after taxes. Entering these values into Worksheet 5.4 reveals (in Item 7) that it will take the Sanchez family 26 months to break even with the new mortgage. Because 26 months is considerably less than their anticipated minimum five years (60 months) in the home, *the economics easily support refinancing their mortgage under the specified terms.* Most families decide to refinance in order to lower their monthly

mortgage payments—it is, after all, almost like getting a raise in pay! In such cases, the analysis is relatively simple: determine how long it will take for the monthly savings to equal any closing costs (as spelled out in Worksheet 5.4).

PLANNING OVER A LIFETIME

Auto and Housing Decisions

Here are some key considerations in making auto and housing decisions in each stage of the life cycle.

PRE-FAMILY INDEPENDENCE: 20s

» Start saving for a downpayment on a house.

» Compare renting versus buying a house.

» Familiarize yourself with the various types of mortgages.

FAMILY FORMATION/CAREER DEVELOPMENT: 30–45

» Compare current mortgage rates with yours and evaluate the value of refinancing.

» Budget to make additional payments on your mortgage to gain greater financial flexibility in the future.

» Save to finance the replacement of your current car.

PRE-RETIREMENT: 45–65

» Periodically re-evaluate the attractiveness of refinancing your mortgage.

» Budget to pay off your mortgage prior to retirement.

» Consider whether different type of car(s) appropriate.

RETIREMENT: 65 AND BEYOND

» Re-evaluate housing choices and location. Consider downsizing but watch transactions costs.

» Pay off mortgage.

» Consider whether more than one family car is needed in retirement.

Lucy Wants to Buy a House but Doesn't Want a Roommate Now

Lucy Allen has saved $10,000 toward a $20,000 down payment on buying a home. She puts aside $300 a month in her house fund and is currently renting a one-bedroom apartment on her own for $1,300 a month. If she rented a two-bedroom apartment with a roommate, she could reduce her rent to $900 a month. While having a roommate is not Lucy's favorite solution, she'd be able to build up her down payment for buying a house a lot faster if she were able to save an extra $400 a month. If Lucy stays on her own and her finances remain the same, it will take her about 2 ¾ years to put aside the needed additional $10,000. In contrast, if she set aside the rent saved by getting a roommate, she would have the needed $10,000 in about only 14 months. Doing without a roommate at this stage in Lucy's life is costly.

wavebreakmedia/Shutterstock.com

STUDY TOOLS 5

LOCATED AT BACK OF THE TEXTBOOK
- ☐ Chapter Review Card

LOCATED AT WWW.CENGAGEBRAIN.COM
- ☐ Review Key Term flashcards and create your own cards.
- ☐ Track your knowledge and understanding of key concepts in personal finance.

- ☐ Complete practice and graded quizzes to prepare for tests.
- ☐ Complete interactive content at PFIN6 Online.
- ☐ View the chapter highlight boxes at PFIN6 Online.

©viphotos/Shutterstock1407785408

Financial Planning Exercises

LO1, 2 1. **Planning a new car purchase.** Olivia Green has just graduated from college and needs to buy a car to commute to work. She estimates that she can afford to pay about $450 per month for a loan or lease and has about $2,000 in savings to use for a down payment. Develop a plan to guide her through her first car-buying experience, including researching car type, deciding whether to buy a new or used car, negotiating the price and terms, and financing the transaction.

LO2 2. **Lease versus purchase car decision. Use Worksheet 5.1.** Everett Adams is trying to decide whether to lease or purchase a new car costing $18,000. If he leases, he'll have to pay a $600 security deposit and monthly payments of $450 over the 36-month term of the closed-end lease. On the other hand, if he buys the car, then he'll have to make a $2,400 down payment and will finance the balance with a 36-month loan requiring monthly payments of $515; he'll also have to pay a 6 percent sales tax ($1,080) on the purchase price, and he expects the car to have a residual value of $6,500 at the end of three years. Use the automobile lease versus purchase analysis form in Worksheet 5.1 to find the total cost of both the lease and the purchase, and then recommend the best strategy for Everett.

LO3 3. **Interpreting rent ratios.** Henry Roberts has equally attractive job offers in San Jose and Houston. Henry would really like to buy rather than rent a home after he moves. Explain the relative attractiveness of moving to Houston rather than San Jose based on the data portrayed in Exhibit 5.3 and in light of Henry's stated goal.

LO3, 4 4. **Rent versus buy home. Use Worksheet 5.2.** Amelia Flores is currently renting an apartment for $725 per month and paying $275 annually for renter's insurance. She just found a small townhouse she can buy for $185,000. She has enough cash for a $10,000 down payment and $4,000 in closing costs. Amelia estimated the following costs as a percentage of the home's price: property taxes, 2.5 percent; homeowner's insurance, 0.5 percent; and maintenance,

0.7 percent. She is in the 25 percent tax bracket. Using Worksheet 5.2, calculate the cost of each alternative and recommend the least costly option—rent or buy—for Amelia.

LO4 5. **Maximum affordable mortgage payment.** Using the maximum ratios for a conventional mortgage, how big a monthly payment could the Clinton family afford if their gross (before-tax) monthly income amounted to $3,500? Would it make any difference if they were already making monthly installment loan payments totaling $750 on two car loans?

LO4 6. **Changes in mortgage principal and interest over time.** Explain how the composition of the principal and interest components of a fixed-rate mortgage change over the life of the mortgage. What are the implications of this change?

LO4 7. **Calculating required down payment on home purchase.** How much would you have to put down on a house with an appraised value of $105,000 when the lender required an 80 percent loan-to-value ratio?

LO4 8. **Calculating monthly mortgage payments.** Find the *monthly* mortgage payments on the following mortgage loans using either your calculator or the table in Exhibit 5.6:

a. $90,000 at 6.5 percent for 30 years

b. $125,000 at 5.5 percent for 20 years

c. $97,500 at 5 percent for 15 years

LO4, 5 9. **Estimating closing costs on home purchase.** How much might a home buyer expect to pay in closing costs on a $220,000 house with a 10 percent down payment? How much would the home buyer have to pay at the time of closing, taking into account closing costs, down payment, and a loan fee of three points?

LO5 10. **Using a real estate broker.** Describe the ways in which a real estate broker represents buyers versus sellers. What's a typical real estate commission?

LO6 11. **Adding to monthly mortgage payments.** What are the pros and cons of adding $100 a month to your fixed-rate mortgage payment?

Financial Planning Exercises

LO6 12. **Refinancing a mortgage. Use Worksheet 5.4.** Lily Nguyen purchased a condominium four years ago for $200,000, paying $1,250 per month on her $162,000, 8 percent, 25-year mortgage. The current loan balance is $152,401. Recently, interest rates dropped sharply, causing Lily to consider refinancing her condo at the prevailing rate of 6 percent. She expects to remain in the condo for at least four more years and has found a lender that will make a 6 percent, 21-year, $152,401 loan, requiring monthly payments of $1,065. Although there is no prepayment penalty on her current mortgage, Lily will have to pay $1,500 in closing costs on the new mortgage. She is in the 15 percent tax bracket. Based on this information, use the mortgage refinancing analysis form in Worksheet 5.4 to determine whether Lily should refinance her mortgage under the specified terms.

6 | Using Credit

LEARNING OBJECTIVES

After studying this chapter, you will be able to...

LO1 Describe the reasons for using consumer credit and identify its benefits and problems.

LO2 Develop a plan to establish a strong credit history.

LO3 Distinguish among the different forms of open account credit.

LO4 Apply for, obtain, and manage open forms of credit.

LO5 Choose the right credit cards and recognize their advantages and disadvantages.

LO6 Avoid credit problems, protect yourself against credit card fraud, and understand the personal bankruptcy process.

After finishing this chapter, go to **PAGE 168** for **STUDY TOOLS**

Mark Viker/Getty Images

How Will This Affect Me? The ability to borrow funds to buy goods and services is as convenient as it is seductive. It is important to understand how to get and maintain access to credit via credit cards, debit cards, lines of credit, and other means. This chapter reviews the common sources of consumer credit and provides a framework for choosing among them. It also discusses the importance of developing a good credit history, achieving and maintaining a good credit score, and protecting against identity theft and credit fraud. The chapter will help you understand the need to use credit intentionally, in a way that is consistent with your overall financial objectives.

6-1 THE BASIC CONCEPTS OF CREDIT

LO1, LO2 It's so easy—just slide that credit card through the reader and you can get gas for your car, buy a laptop at Best Buy, or furnish an apartment. It happens *several hundred million times a day* across the United States. Credit, in fact, has become an entrenched part of our everyday lives, and we as consumers use it in one form or another to purchase just about every type of good or service imaginable. Indeed, because of the ready availability and widespread use of credit, our economy is often called a "credit economy." And for good reason: as of the end of 2015, households in this country had run up about $12.12 trillion in debt—and that doesn't even include home mortgages.

Consumer credit is important in the personal financial planning process because of the impact it can have on (1) attaining financial goals and (2) cash budgets. For one thing, various forms of consumer credit can help you reach your financial objectives by enabling you to acquire some of the more expensive items in a systematic fashion without throwing your whole budget into disarray. But there's another side to consumer credit: it has to be paid back. Unless credit is used intelligently, the "buy now, pay later" attitude can quickly turn an otherwise orderly budget into a nightmare and lead to some serious problems—even bankruptcy! Consumers need to know how to establish credit and how to avoid the dangers of using it improperly.

6-1a Why We Use Credit

People typically use credit as a way to pay for goods and services that cost more than they can afford to take from their current income. This is particularly true for those in the 25–44 age group, who have not had time to accumulate the liquid assets required to pay cash outright for major purchases and expenditures. As people begin to approach their mid-40s, however, their savings and investments start to build up and their debt loads tend to decline—which is unsurprising when you consider that the median household net worth for those in the 45–54 age group is considerably higher than for those aged 35 to 44.

Whatever their age group, people tend to borrow for several major reasons:

▶ **To avoid paying cash for large outlays.** Rather than pay cash for large purchases such as houses and cars, most people borrow part of the purchase price and then repay the loan on some scheduled basis. Spreading payments over time makes big-ticket items more affordable, and consumers get the use of an expensive asset right away.

▶ **To meet a financial emergency.** For example, people may need to borrow to cover living expenses during a period of unemployment or to purchase plane tickets to visit a sick relative.

▶ **For convenience.** Merchants as well as banks offer a variety of charge accounts and credit cards that allow consumers to charge just about anything—from gas or clothes and stereos to doctor and dental bills and even college tuition. Further, in many places— restaurants, for instance—using a credit card is far easier than writing a check.

▶ **For investment purposes.** As we'll see in Chapter 11, it's relatively easy for an investor to partially finance the purchase of many different kinds of investments with borrowed funds.

6-1b Improper Uses of Credit

Many people use consumer credit to live beyond their means. For some people, overspending becomes a way of life, and it is perhaps the biggest danger in borrowing— especially because it's so easy to do. And nowhere did that become more apparent than in the wake of the credit crisis of 2008–2009. Indeed, as credit became more readily available and easier to obtain, it also became increasingly clear that many consumers were, in fact, severely overusing it. Whether or not the consumer deserved the credit was really not an issue—the only thing that seemed to matter was that it was there for the taking. All this resulted in a credit meltdown unlike anything this country had ever seen.

Some people use their credit cards to make even routine purchases, and all too often don't realize they have overextended themselves until it's too late. And by making only the minimum payment, borrowers pay a huge price in the long run. Exhibit 6.1 shows the amount of time

> Some people use their credit cards to make even routine purchases, and all too often don't realize they have overextended themselves until it's too late.

and interest charges required to repay credit card balances if you make only minimum payments of 3 percent of the outstanding balance.

> **EXAMPLE:** Paying Only the Minimum on Your Credit Card If you carry a $3,000 balance—which is about *one-fifth* of the national average—on a credit card that charges 15 percent annually, it would take you 14 years to retire the debt, and your interest charges would total some $2,000—*or more than 66 percent of the original balance!*

Some cards offer even lower minimum payments of just 2 percent of the outstanding balance. Although such small payments may seem like a good deal, clearly they don't work to your advantage and only increase the time and amount of interest required to repay the debt. Indeed, by making minimum, 2 percent payments, it would take *more than 32 years* to pay off a $5,000 balance on a credit card that carries a 15 percent rate of interest. In contrast, that same $5,000 balance could be paid off in *just 16.4 years* if you had made 3 percent minimum payments. Just think, making an additional 1 percent payment can save you nearly 16 years of interest! That's why federal banking regulators issued guidelines stating that minimum monthly credit card payments should cover at least 1 percent of the outstanding balance plus all monthly finance charges and any other fees.

Exhibit 6.1

Minimum Payments Mean Maximum Years

Paying off credit card balances at the minimum monthly amount required by the card issuer will take a long time and cost you a great deal of interest, as this table demonstrates. *The calculations here are based on a minimum 3% payment and 15% annual interest rate.*

Original Balance	Years to Repay	Interest Paid	Total Interest Paid as Percentage of Original Balance
$5,000	16.4	$3,434	68.7%
4,000	15.4	2,720	68.0
3,000	14.0	2,005	66.8
2,000	12.1	1,291	64.5
1,000	8.8	577	57.7

The best way to steer clear of future repayment shock is to avoid using your credit card in the following situations:

▶ Meeting basic living expenses.

▶ Making impulse purchases, especially expensive ones.

▶ Purchasing nondurable (short-lived) goods and services.

Except in situations where credit cards are used occasionally for convenience, or where payments on recurring credit purchases are built into the monthly budget, a good rule to remember when considering the use of credit is that *the product purchased on credit should outlive the payments*.

Unfortunately, people who overspend must eventually choose to either become delinquent in their payments or sacrifice necessities, such as food or a cell phone. If payment obligations aren't met, the consequences are likely to be a damaged credit rating, lawsuits, or even personal bankruptcy. *Ignoring the telltale signs that you are overspending can only lead to more serious problems.*

6-1c Establishing Credit

The willingness of lenders to extend credit depends on their assessment of your creditworthiness—that is, your ability to repay the debt promptly. Lenders look at various factors in making this decision, such as your present earnings and net worth. Equally important, they look at your current debt position and your credit history. Thus, it's worth your while to do what you can to build a strong credit rating.

First Steps in Establishing Credit First, open checking and savings accounts. They signal stability to lenders and indicate that you handle your financial affairs in a businesslike way. Second, use credit: open one or two charge accounts and use them periodically, even if you prefer paying cash. You might pay an annual fee or interest on some (or all) of your account balances, but in the process, you'll build a record of being a reliable credit customer. Third, obtain a small loan, even if you don't need one. If you don't actually need the money, put it in a liquid investment, such as a money market account or certificate of deposit. The interest you earn should offset some of the interest expense on the loan; you can view the difference as a cost of building good credit. You should repay the loan promptly, perhaps even a *little* ahead of schedule, to minimize the difference in interest rates. Keep in mind that your ability to obtain a significant loan in the future will depend, in part, on how you managed smaller ones in the past.

Build a Strong Credit History From a financial perspective, maintaining a strong credit history is just as important as developing a solid employment record. Don't take credit lightly, and don't assume that getting the loan or the credit card is the toughest part. It's not. That's just the first step; making payments in a prompt and timely fashion—month in and month out—is the really tough part of the consumer credit process. And in many respects, it's the most important element of consumer credit because it determines your creditworthiness. By using credit wisely and repaying it on time, you're establishing a *credit history* that tells lenders you're a dependable, reliable, and responsible borrower. When you take on credit, you have an *obligation* to live up to the terms of the loan, including how and when the credit will be repaid.

If you foresee difficulty in meeting a monthly payment, let the lender know. Usually arrangements can be made to help you through the situation. This is especially true with installment loans that require fixed monthly payments. Don't just skip a payment, because that will put your account into *late status until you make up the missed payment*. Instead, try to work out an extension with your lender.

ESB Professional/Shutterstock.com

THE 5 C'S OF CREDIT

Lenders often use the "5 C's of Credit" to assess the willingness and ability of a borrower to repay a loan.

1. **Character:** A key factor in defining the borrower's willingness to live up to the terms of the loan.

2. **Capacity:** The ability of the borrower to service the loan in a timely fashion.

3. **Collateral:** Something of value that's used to secure a loan and that the lender can claim in case of default.

4. **Capital:** The amount of unencumbered assets owned by the borrower, used as another indicator of the borrower's ability to repay the loan.

5. **Condition:** The extent to which prevailing economic conditions could affect the borrower's ability to service a loan.

If you expect to be late on a payment, explain the situation to the loan officer and ask for an extension of one (or two) months on your loan. In most cases, as long as this hasn't occurred before, the extension is almost automatically granted. The maturity of the loan is formally extended for a month (or two), and the extra interest of carrying the loan for another month (or two) is either added to the loan balance or, more commonly, paid at the time the extension is granted (such an extension fee generally amounts to a fraction of the normal monthly payment). Then, in a month or two, you pick up, where you left off and resume your normal, monthly payments on the loan. This is the most sensible way of making it through those rough times because it doesn't harm your credit record. You just shouldn't do it too often.

Go to Smart Sites

How Much Credit Can You Handle? Sound financial planning dictates that you have a good idea of how much credit you can comfortably tolerate. The easiest way to avoid repayment problems and ensure that your borrowing won't place an undue strain on your monthly budget is to *limit the use of credit to your ability to repay the debt.* A useful guideline widely used by lenders is to make sure your monthly repayment burden doesn't exceed 20 percent of your monthly *take-home pay.* Most experts, however, regard the 20 percent figure as the *maximum* debt burden and strongly recommend a **debt safety ratio** closer to 10 percent or 15 percent—perhaps even lower if you plan on applying for a new mortgage in the near future. Note that the monthly

debt safety ratio the proportion of total monthly consumer credit obligations to monthly take-home pay

repayment burden here *does include* payments on your credit cards, but it *excludes* your monthly mortgage obligation.

For example, consider someone who takes home $2,500 a month. Using a 20 percent ratio, she should have monthly consumer credit payments of no more than $500—that is, $2,500 × 0.20 × $500. This is the maximum amount of her monthly disposable income that she should need to pay off both personal loans and other forms of consumer credit (such as credit cards and education loans). This, of course, is not the maximum amount of consumer credit that she can have outstanding. In fact, her total consumer indebtedness can, and likely would, be considerably larger. The key factor is that with her income level, her *payments* on this type of debt should not exceed $500 a month. Obviously, *the lower the debt safety ratio, the better shape you're in, creditwise, and the easier it should be for you to service your outstanding consumer debt.*

You can compute the debt safety ratio as follows:

$$\text{Debt safety ratio} = \frac{\text{Total monthly consumer credit payments}}{\text{Monthly take-home pay}}$$

This measure is the focus of Worksheet 6.1, which you can use for keeping close tabs on your own debt safety ratio. It shows the impact that each new loan you take out, or credit card you sign up for, can have on this important measure of creditworthiness. Consider, for example, Max and Nina Carter. As seen in Worksheet 6.1, they have five outstanding consumer loans and they're carrying balances on three credit cards. All totaled, these eight obligations require monthly payments of almost $740, which accounts for about one-fifth of their combined take-home pay and gives them a debt safety ratio of 18 percent. And note the information at the bottom of the worksheet that says if the Carters want to lower this ratio to, say, 15 percent, then they'll either have to reduce their monthly payments to $615 or increase their take-home pay to at least $4,927 a month.

A worksheet like this one will help a household stay on top of their monthly credit card and consumer loan payments as well as their debt safety ratio—an important measure of creditworthiness. The key here is to keep the debt safety ratio as low as (reasonably) possible, something that can be done by keeping monthly loan payments in line with monthly take-home pay.

MONTHLY CONSUMER LOAN PAYMENTS & DEBT SAFETY RATIO

Name _Max and Nina Carter_ **Date** _June 21, 2017_

■ Type of Loan*	Lender	Current Monthly (or Min.) Payment
• *Auto and personal loans*	Ford Motor Credit	$ 360.00
	Bank of America	115.00
• *Education loans*	U.S. Dept. of Education	75.00
• *Overdraft protection line*	Bank of America	30.00
• *Personal line of credit*		
• *Credit cards*	Bank of America Visa	28.00
	Fidelity MC	31.00
	JC Penney	28.00
• *Home equity line*	Bank of America	72.00
	TOTAL MONTHLY PAYMENTS	$ 739.00

*__Note:__ List only those loans that require regular monthly payments.

■ Monthly Take-Home Pay	Max	$ 1,855.00
	Nina	2,250.00
	TOTAL MONTHLY TAKE-HOME PAY	$ 4,105.00

■ **Debt Safety Ratio:**

$$\frac{\text{Total monthly payments}}{\text{Total monthly take-home pay}} \times 100 = \frac{\$739.00}{\$4,105.00} \times 100 = \underline{18.0\ \%}$$

• *Changes needed to reach a new debt safety ratio*

1. New (Target) debt safety ratio: _15.0_ %

2. At current take-home pay of _$ 4,105.00_, total monthly payments must equal:

Total monthly take-home pay × Target debt safety ratio**

$$\underline{\$4,105.00} \times \underline{0.150} = \underline{\$615.75}$$
New monthly payments

OR

3. With current monthly payments of _$ 739.00_, total take-home pay must equal:

$$\frac{\text{Total monthly payments}}{\text{New (target) debt safety ratio}} \times 100 = \frac{\$739.00}{0.150} = \underline{\$4,926.67}$$
New take-home pay

**__Note:__ Enter debt safety ratio as a decimal (e.g., 15% = 0.15).

6-2 CREDIT CARDS AND OTHER TYPES OF OPEN ACCOUNT CREDIT

LO3 **Open account credit** is a form of credit extended to a consumer in advance of any transactions. Typically, a retail outlet or bank agrees to allow the consumer to buy or borrow up to a specified amount on open account. Credit is extended so long as the consumer does not exceed the established **credit limit** and makes payments in accordance with the specified terms. Open account credit issued by a retail outlet, such as a department store or oil company, is usually usable only in that establishment or one of its locations. In contrast, open account credit issued by banks, such as *MasterCard* and *Visa* accounts, can be used to make purchases at a wide variety of businesses. Having open account credit is a lot like having your own personal line of credit—it's there when you need it. Open account credit generally is available from two broadly defined sources: financial institutions and retail stores/merchants. *Financial institutions* issue general-purpose credit cards, as well as secured and unsecured revolving lines of credit and overdraft protection lines. *Retail stores and merchants* make up the other major source of open account credit. They provide this service as a way to promote the sales of their products, and their principal form of credit is the charge (or credit) card. Let's now take a look at these two forms of credit, along with *debit cards* and *revolving lines of credit*.

Feng Yu/Shutterstock.com

open account credit a form of credit extended to a consumer in advance of any transaction

credit limit a specified amount beyond which a customer may not borrow or purchase on credit

bank credit card a credit card issued by a bank or other financial institution that allows the holder to charge purchases at any establishment that accepts it

line of credit the maximum amount of credit a customer is allowed to have outstanding at any point in time

cash advance a loan that can be obtained by a bank credit card holder at any participating bank or financial institution

6-2a Bank Credit Cards

Probably the most popular form of open account credit is the **bank credit card**, issued by commercial banks and other financial institutions—*Visa* and *MasterCard* being the two dominant types. These cards allow their holders to charge purchases worldwide at literally millions of stores, restaurants, shops, and gas stations, as well as at state and municipal governments, colleges and universities, medical groups, and mail-order houses—not to mention the Internet, where they've become the currency of choice. They can be used to pay for almost anything—groceries, doctor bills, college tuition, airline tickets, and car rentals. They can also be used to borrow money. In fact, by 2003, the amount of transactions completed with credit and debit cards had actually surpassed those made with cash or check.

The financial crisis in 2008–09 brought tougher credit standards and sharply reduced credit lines to the bank credit card business. Standards tend to tighten quickly in a crisis, and it can take several years before they move back to their pre-crisis levels. As a result, consumers find it harder to get new credit cards, and the limits on existing cards are often slashed.

Line of Credit The **line of credit** provided to the holder of a bank credit card is set by the issuer. It's the maximum amount that the cardholder can owe at any given time. The size of the credit line depends on both the applicant's request and the results of the issuer's investigation of the applicant's credit and financial status. Lines of credit can reach $50,000 or more, but for the most part, they range from about $500 to $2,500. Although card issuers fully expect you to keep your credit within the specified limits, most won't take any real action until you extend your account balance by a certain percentage. For example, if you had a $1,000 credit limit, you probably wouldn't hear a peep out of the card issuer until your outstanding balance exceeded, say, $1,200 (i.e., 20 percent above the $1,000 line of credit). On the other hand, don't count on getting off for free, because most card issuers assess *over-the-limit* fees whenever you go over your credit limit (more on this later).

Cash Advances In addition to purchasing merchandise and services, the holder of a bank credit card can obtain a **cash advance** from any participating bank. Cash advances are loans on which interest begins to accrue immediately. They're transacted in the same way as merchandise purchases, except they take place at a commercial bank or some other financial institution and involve the receipt of cash (or a check) instead of goods and services. Another way to get a cash advance is to use the "convenience checks" that you receive from the card issuer to pay for purchases. You can even use your credit card to draw cash from an ATM, any time of the day or night. Usually, the size of the cash advance from an ATM is limited to some nominal amount (a common amount is $500 or less), although the amount you can obtain from the teller window at a bank is limited only by the unused credit in your account.

Interest Charges *The interest rates on credit cards are usually higher than any other form of consumer credit.* The average annual rate of interest charged on bank credit cards was around 15 percent in the fall of 2016. You'll find that most bank cards have one rate for merchandise purchases and a much higher rate for cash advances. For example, the rate on merchandise purchases might be 15 percent, while the rate on cash advances could be 20 percent or more. And when shopping for a credit card, watch out for those *special low introductory rates* that many banks offer. Known as "teaser rates," they're usually only good for the first 6 to 12 months. Then, just as soon as the introductory period ends, so do the low interest rates.

Most of these cards have variable interest rates that are tied to an index that moves with market rates. The most popular is the prime or **base rate**: the rate a bank uses as a base for loans to individuals and small or mid-size businesses. These cards adjust their interest rate monthly or quarterly and usually have minimum and maximum rates.

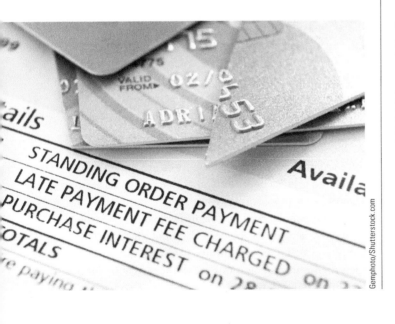
Gemphoto/Shutterstock.com

> **EXAMPLE:** Bank Credit Card Index Interest Rates Consider a bank card whose terms are *prime plus 7.5 percent*, with a minimum of 10 percent and a maximum of 15.25 percent. If the prime rate is 3.25 percent, then the rate of interest charged on this card would be 3.25 percent + 7.5 percent = 10.75 percent.

Bank credit card issuers must disclose interest costs and related information to consumers *before* extending credit. In the case of purchases of merchandise and services, the specified interest rate may not apply to charges until after the **grace period**. During this short period, usually 20 to 30 days, you have historically been able to pay your credit card bill in full and avoid any interest charges. However, once you carry a balance—that is, when you don't pay your card in full during the grace period—the interest rate is usually applied to any unpaid balances carried from previous periods as well as to any new purchases made. Interest on cash advances, in contrast, *begins the day that the advance is taken out.*

Other Fees Besides the interest charged on bank credit cards, there are other fees you should be aware of. To begin with, many (though not all) bank cards charge *annual fees* just for the "privilege" of being able to use the card. In most cases, the fee is around $25 to $40 a year, though it can amount to much more for prestige cards. As a rule, the larger the bank or S&L, the more likely it is to charge an annual fee for its credit cards. What's more, many issuers also charge a *transaction fee* for each (non-ATM) cash advance. This fee usually amounts to about $5 per cash advance or 3 percent of the amount obtained in the transaction, whichever is more.

Card issuers have come up with many ways to squeeze additional revenue from you. These include late-payment fees, over-the-limit charges, foreign transaction fees, and balance transfer fees. For example, if you're a bit late in making your payment some banks will hit you with a late-payment fee, which is really a redundant charge because you're already paying interest on the unpaid balance. Similarly, if you happened to go over your credit limit you'd be hit with a charge for that, too (again, this is in addition to the interest you're already paying). Regardless of when or why any of these fees are levied, the net effect is that *they add to the true cost of using bank credit cards.*

base rate the rate of interest a bank uses as a base for loans to individuals and small to midsize businesses

grace period a short period of time, usually 20 to 30 days, during which you can pay your credit card bill in full and not incur any interest charges

Behavioral Biases and Credit Card Use

Be wary of the minimum payment on your monthly credit card statement. Many people focus unduly or "anchor" on the stated minimum payment and as a result, pay a lower amount than they would otherwise. And the effect is obvious—they end up paying more interest.

Another tendency is to fall victim to "mental accounting," which refers to inappropriately viewing interdependent decisions as independent. For example, some people hold short-term, low-yield investments *and* costly credit card debt at the same time. It would obviously make sense to liquidate such investments and use the proceeds to pay off the credit card debt, which reduces interest charges. But many people don't do this because they view these as separate and unrelated transactions.

You should always consider how your financial decisions relate to one another and take into account common behavioral biases like anchoring and mental accounting and how they relate to managing credit card debt.

These onerous credit card issuer practices and extra fees led to the passage of the Credit Card Act of 2009. In the past, credit card companies could change interest rates and other aspects of the agreement without notice. They could even change terms retroactively such that they applied months before you were notified. The law requires credit card companies to give 45 days' notice before changing your agreement. Similarly, credit card companies previously could raise your interest rate if your credit report deteriorated, or if you were late on just one payment. The law allows credit card companies to apply a new interest rate only to new balances after you are 60 days delinquent paying on your account. And just as important is that your outstanding balance can only be charged your old interest rate.

reward (co-branded) credit card a bank credit card that combines features of a traditional bank credit card with an additional incentive, such as rebates and airline mileage

affinity cards a standard bank credit card issued in conjunction with some charitable, political, or other nonprofit organization

6-2b Special Types of Bank Credit Cards

Bank credit cards sure aren't what they used to be. Today, in addition to standard, "plain vanilla"

bank cards, you can obtain cards that offer rebates and special incentive programs, cards that are sponsored by nonprofit organizations, even credit cards aimed specifically at college students.

Reward Cards One of the fastest-growing segments of the bank card market is the **reward (co-branded) credit card**, which combines features of a traditional bank credit card with an incentive: cash, merchandise rebates, airline tickets, or even investments. About half of credit cards are rebate cards, and new types are introduced almost every day. Here are some of the many incentive programs:

▶ **Frequent flyer programs.** The cardholder earns free frequent flyer miles for each dollar charged on his or her credit card. These frequent flyer miles can then be used with airline-affiliated programs for free tickets, first-class upgrades, and other travel-related benefits.

▶ **Automobile rebate programs.** Some credit cards allow the cardholder to earn annual rebates of up to 5 percent that can be used, up to specified limits, for new car purchases, leases, or auto maintenance programs. Indeed, most of the major car companies offer some kind of rewards-related credit card that can be used to buy a car or related items.

▶ **Other merchandise rebates.** An increasing number of companies are participating in bank card reward programs, including, for example, Norwegian Cruise Line, Harrah's casino, NASCAR, Starbucks, and Marriott Hotels. Several regional phone companies even offer rebates on phone calls. (A good site for finding information about rebate card offers is **www.cardtrak.com.**)

Are rebate cards a good deal? Well, yes and no. To see if they make sense for you, evaluate these cards carefully by looking at your usage patterns and working out the annual cost of the cards before and after the rebate. Don't get so carried away with the gimmick that you lose sight of the total costs. Most incentive cards carry higher interest rates than regular bank cards do. These cards generally work best for those who can use the rebates, charge a lot, and don't carry high monthly balances.

Affinity Cards "Credit cards with a cause" is the way to describe **affinity cards**. These cards are nothing more than standard *Visa* or *MasterCards* that are issued in conjunction with a sponsoring group—most commonly some type of charitable, political, or professional organization. So-named because of the bond between the sponsoring group and its members, affinity cards are sponsored by such nonprofit organizations as Mothers Against Drunk Driving (MADD), the American Wildlife Fund, and the

Special Olympics. In addition, they are issued by college and university alumni groups, labor organizations, religious and fraternal groups, and professional societies.

Why even bother with one of these cards? Well, unlike traditional bank cards, affinity cards make money for the group backing the card because the sponsoring groups receive a share of the profits. But to cover the money that goes to the sponsoring organization, the issuer/bank usually charges higher fees or higher interest rates. Even so, some may view these cards as a great way to contribute to a worthy cause. Others, however, may feel it makes more sense to use a traditional credit card and then write a check to their favorite charity.

Yaping/Shutterstock.com

> **YOU CAN DO IT NOW:** Is Your Credit Card a Good Deal? While your credit card might have been a good deal when you first got it, that may not still be the case. Go to a credit card Internet site like http://www.creditcards.com, which allows you to evaluate numerous credit cards by type. For example, you can focus on 0% APR, rewards, cash back, travel and airline, cards for students, and more types of cards. It's worth a look – you can **do it now.**

Secured Credit Cards You may have seen the ads on TV where the announcer says that no matter how bad your credit, you can still qualify for one of their credit cards. The pitch may sound too good to be true; and in some respects, it is because there's a catch. Namely, the credit is "secured"— meaning you have to put up *collateral* in order to get the card. These are so-called **secured**, or **collateralized credit cards** where the amount of credit is determined by the amount of liquid collateral you're able to put up.

These cards are targeted at people with no credit or bad credit histories, who don't qualify for conventional credit cards. Issued as *Visa* or *MasterCard*, they're like any other credit card except for the collateral. To qualify, a customer must deposit a certain amount (usually $500 or more) into a 12- to 18-month certificate of deposit that the issuing bank holds as collateral. The cardholder then gets a credit line equal to the deposit. If the customer defaults, the bank has the CD to cover its losses. By making payments on time, it's hoped that these cardholders will establish (or reestablish) a credit history that may qualify them for a conventional (unsecured) credit card. Secured credit cards normally carry annual fees and finance charges that are equal to, or greater than, those of regular credit cards.

Student Credit Cards Some large banks, through their *Visa* and *MasterCard* programs, have special credit cards that specifically target college students. These student credit cards often come packaged with special promotional programs that are meant to appeal to this segment of the market—such as free music, movie tickets, and the like. Except for these features, there's really nothing unusual about these cards or their terms. Most simply require that you be enrolled in a two- or four-year college or university and have some source of income, whatever that may be. In particular, they usually *do not require* any parental or guardian guarantees, nor do they require that you hold a full-time (or even a part-time) job. From the student's perspective, these cards not only offer convenience but are also great for building a solid credit history.

6-2c Retail Charge Cards

Retail charge cards are issued by department stores, oil companies, car rental agencies, and so on. These cards are popular with merchants because they build consumer loyalty and enhance sales; consumers like them because they offer a convenient way to shop. These cards carry a preset credit limit—a line of credit—that varies with the creditworthiness of the cardholder. This form of credit is most common in department and clothing stores and other high-volume outlets, where customers are likely to make several purchases each month. Most large oil companies also offer charge cards that allow customers to buy gas and oil products, *but they're expected to pay for such purchases*

> **secured (collateralized) credit cards** a type of credit card that's secured with some form of collateral, such as a bank CD
>
> **student credit card** a credit card marketed specifically to college students
>
> **retail charge card** a type of credit card issued by retailers that allows customers to charge goods and services up to a preestablished amount

in full upon receipt of the monthly bill. Interest on retail charge cards is typically fixed at 1.5 percent to 1.85 percent monthly, or about 18 percent to 22 percent per year—considerably more than what most bank cards charge.

Tuan_Azizi/Shutterstock.com

6-2d Debit Cards

It looks like a credit card, it works like a credit card, it even has the familiar *MasterCard* and *Visa* credit card markings. But it's not a *credit* card—rather, it's a *debit* card. Simply put, a **debit card** provides direct access to your checking account and, thus, *works like writing a check*. That is, when you use a debit card to make a purchase, the amount of the transaction is charged directly to your checking account. Using a debit card isn't the same thing as buying on credit; it may appear that you're charging it, but actually *you're paying with cash*. Accordingly, there are no finance charges to pay.

Debit cards are becoming more popular, especially with consumers who want the convenience of a credit card but not the high cost of interest that comes with them. In fact, in 2006, debit card use exceeded credit card use for the first time. Debit cards are accepted at most establishments displaying the *Visa* or *MasterCard* logo but function as an alternative to writing checks. If you use a debit card to make a purchase at a department store or restaurant, the transaction will show up on your next monthly *checking account* statement.

Needless to say, to keep your records straight, you should enter debit card transactions directly into your checkbook ledger as they occur and treat them as withdrawals, or checks, by subtracting them from your checking account balance. Debit cards can also be used to gain access to your account through 24-hour teller machines or ATMs, which is the closest thing to a cash advance that these cards have to offer.

A big disadvantage of a debit card, of course, is that it doesn't provide a line of credit. In addition, it can cause overdraft

debit card a card used to make transactions for *cash* rather than credit; replaces the need for cash or checks by initiating charges against the *checking* account

revolving line of credit a type of open account credit offered by banks and other financial institutions that can be accessed by writing checks against demand deposit or specially designated credit line accounts

overdraft protection line a line of credit linked to a checking account that allows a depositor to overdraw the account up to a specified amount

problems if you fail to make the proper entries to your checkbook or inadvertently use it when you think you're using a credit card. Also, some debit card issuers charge a transaction fee or a flat annual fee; and some *merchants* may even charge you just for using your debit card. On the plus side, a debit card enables you to avoid the potential credit problems and high costs of credit cards.

Further, if convenience is the major reason you use a credit card, you might want to consider switching to a debit card for at least some transactions. For example, some gas stations give discounts for cash purchases and consider a debit card to be as good as cash.

Another difference between debit and credit cards involves the level of protection for the user when a card is lost or stolen. When a credit card is lost or stolen, federal banking laws ensure that the cardholder is not liable for any fraudulent charges if the loss or theft is reported before that card is used. If reported after the card is used, the cardholder's maximum liability is $50. Unfortunately, *this protection typically does not extend to debit cards.* Instead, your liability resulting from a lost or stolen debit card is typically limited to $50 up to a maximum of $500, "depending on the circumstances of the loss." In practice, however, most banks provide the same level of protection for debit cards as for credit cards, but check with your bank to be sure.

6-2e Revolving Credit Lines

Revolving lines of credit are offered by banks, brokerage houses, and other financial institutions. These credit lines normally don't involve the use of credit cards. Rather, they're accessed by writing checks on regular checking accounts or specially designated credit line accounts. They are a form of open account credit and often represent a far better deal than credit cards, not only because they offer more credit but also because they can be a lot less expensive. And there may even be a tax advantage to using one of these other kinds of credit. These lines provide their users with ready access to borrowed money (through cash advances) using revolving lines of credit. The three major forms of open (non–credit card) credit are overdraft protection lines, unsecured personal lines of credit, and home equity credit lines.

Overdraft Protection An **overdraft protection line** is simply a line of credit linked to a checking account that enables a depositor to overdraw his or her checking

Financial Planning Tips

Yes, debit cards are convenient to use and generally accepted by most establishments. But unlike credit cards, debit cards provide a thief with direct access to your checking account. If you find a fraudulent charge on your credit card bill, you can just decline or dispute the charge. In contrast, by the time you find a fraudulent charge on your debit card, your money—*not the bank's money*—is already gone, and it's up to *you* to get it back, not the bank. While it usually takes only a few days to deal with fraudulent credit card transactions, it can take months to get your money back from fraudulent debit transactions.

You are most vulnerable to debit card fraud in the following situations:

- **Be careful using outdoor ATMs.** "Skimming" is the capturing of card information by a magnetic strip reader. Skimmers can be placed over the real card slots at ATMs. Watch for apparently beaten-up or odd-looking ATMs, which might indicate that a skimmer has been added. Surprisingly, outdoor ATMs are among the most dangerous places to use a debit card. Public places provide criminals with the ability to add skimmers, point cameras at the ATM, or even watch transactions with binoculars. It's much safer to use ATMs inside retail stores or other well-lighted, high-traffic areas.

- **Protect your personal identification number (PIN) at gas stations.** Gas stations are another vulnerable spot when using debit cards. Given that there's not much supervision, it's easy for a criminal to install a skimmer or point a camera at the gas pump. Credit cards are much safer to use.

- **The Internet is a dangerous place to use a debit card.** Your debit card information is vulnerable to capture at many points: malware could be on your computer, your data could be intercepted by wireless eavesdropping on the way to the vendor, or your merchant's database could be compromised. The site may *claim* it's safe, but so what? You have no idea how many people are handling your private debit card data, or who they are.

- **Some restaurants keep debit card data on file.** And restaurants routinely take your card out of your sight to process a transaction, which creates the opportunity for someone to inappropriately keep the information. Ethical or not, few small businesses take adequate steps to protect your private data.

Source: Adapted from Claes Bell, CFA, "4 Risky Places to Swipe Your Debit Card," www.bankrate.com/finance/checking/risky-places-swipe-debit-card-1.aspx, accessed October 2016.

---

account up to a predetermined limit. These lines are usually set up with credit limits of $500 to $1,000, but they can be for as much as $10,000 or more. The consumer taps this line of credit by simply writing a check, and if that particular check happens to overdraw the account, the overdraft protection line will automatically advance funds in an amount necessary to put the account back in the black. In some cases, overdraft protection is provided by *linking the bank's credit card to your checking account*. These arrangements act like regular overdraft lines except that, when the account is overdrawn, the bank automatically taps your credit card line and transfers the money into your checking account. It's treated as a cash advance from your credit card, but the result is the same as a regular overdraft protection line; it automatically covers overdrawn checks.

> It's best to view an overdraft protection line strictly as an *emergency* source of credit.

If you're not careful, you can quickly exhaust this type of credit by writing a lot of overdraft checks. As with any line of credit, there's a limit to how much you can obtain.

Routinely overdrawing your account is a signal that you're probably mismanaging your cash and/or living beyond your budget. It's best to view an overdraft protection line strictly as an *emergency* source of credit—and any funds advanced should be repaid as quickly as possible.

Unsecured Personal Lines Another form of revolving credit is the **unsecured personal credit line**, which basically makes a line of credit available to an individual on an as-needed basis.

In essence, it's a way of borrowing money from a bank, S&L, credit union, savings

> **unsecured personal credit line**
> a line of credit made available to an individual on an as-needed basis

bank, or brokerage firm any time you wish but without going through all the hassle of setting up a new loan.

Here's how it works. Suppose that you apply for and are approved for a personal line of credit at your bank. Once you've been approved and the credit line is established, you'll be issued *checks* that you can write against it. If you need a cash advance, all you need to do is write a check (against your credit line account) and deposit it into your checking account. Or, if you need the money to buy some big-ticket item—say, an expensive computer system—you can just make the credit line check out to the dealer and, when it clears, it will be charged against your unsecured personal credit line as an advance. Personal lines of credit are usually set up for minimums of $2,000 to $5,000 and often amount to $25,000 or more. As with an overdraft protection line, once an advance is made, repayment is set up on a monthly installment basis. Depending on the amount outstanding, repayment is normally structured over a period of two to five years. In order to keep the monthly payments low, larger amounts of debt are usually given longer repayment periods.

Although these credit lines do offer attractive terms to the consumer, they come with their share of problems, perhaps the biggest of which is how easily the cash advances can be obtained. These lines also normally involve *substantial* amounts of credit and are nearly as easy to use as credit cards. This combination can have devastating effects on a family's budget if it leads to overspending or excessive reliance on credit. As such, systematic repayment of the debt should be built into the budget, and every effort should be made to ensure that using this kind of credit will not overly strain the family finances.

Home Equity Credit Lines Consider this: A couple buys a home for $285,000; 10 years later, it's worth $365,000. The couple now has an asset worth $365,000 on which all they owe is the original mortgage, which may now have a balance of, say, $220,000. The couple clearly has built up a substantial amount of equity in their home: $365,000 − $220,000 = $145,000. But how can they tap that equity without having to sell their home? The answer is a **home equity credit line**. Such lines are much like unsecured personal credit lines except that they're *secured with a second mortgage on the home*. These lines of credit allow you to tap up to 100 percent (or more) of the equity in your home by merely writing a check. Although some banks and financial institutions allow their customers to borrow up to 100 percent of the *equity* in their homes—or, in some cases, even more—most lenders set

home equity credit line a line of credit issued against the existing equity in a home

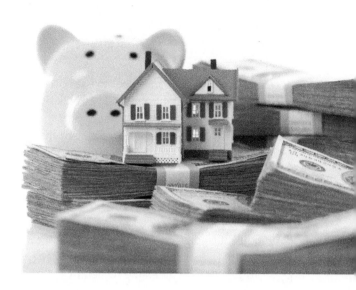

their maximum credit lines at 75 percent to 80 percent *of the market value* of the home, which reduces the amount of money they'll lend.

Here's how these lines work. Recall that the couple in our example that has built up equity of $145,000 in their home—equity against which they can borrow through a home equity credit line. Assuming they have a good credit record and using a 75 percent loan-to-market-value ratio, a bank would be willing to lend up to $273,750; that is, 75 percent of the value of the house is $0.75 \times \$365,000 = \$273,750$. Subtracting the $220,000 still due on the first mortgage, we see that our couple could qualify for a home equity credit line of $53,750. Note, in this case, that if the bank had been willing to lend the couple *100 percent of the equity* in their home, then it would have given them a (much higher) credit line of $145,000, which is the difference between what the house is worth and what they still owe on it. Most lenders don't do this because it results in very large credit lines and, more importantly, it doesn't provide the lender with much of a cushion should the borrower default.

Home equity lines also have an attractive tax feature: The annual interest charges on such lines may be fully deductible for those who itemize. This is the only type of consumer loan that still qualifies for such tax treatment. According to the latest provisions of the tax code, a homeowner is allowed to *fully deduct the interest charges on home equity loans up to $100,000*, regardless of the original cost of the house or use of the proceeds. Indeed, the only restriction is that *the amount of total indebtedness on the house cannot exceed its fair market value*, which is highly unlikely because homeowners usually cannot borrow more than 75 percent to 80 percent of the home's market value anyway.

EXAMPLE: Tax Deductibility of Home Equity Credit Line Interest The homeowners in the prior discussion could take out the full amount of their credit line ($53,750), and every dime that they paid in interest would be tax deductible. If they paid, say, $3,225 in interest, and if they were in the 28 percent tax bracket, then this feature would reduce their tax liability by some $903 ($3,225 × 0.28)—assuming, of course, they itemize their deductions.

Not only do home equity credit lines offer shelter from taxes, they're also among *the cheapest forms of consumer credit*. For example, while the average rate on credit cards in the fall of 2015 was about 15 percent, the average rate on home equity credit lines was about 4.62 percent. To see what that can mean to you as a borrower, assume you have $10,000 in consumer debt outstanding. If you had borrowed that money through a standard consumer loan at 15 percent, you'd pay interest of $1,500 per year—none of which would be tax deductible. Borrow the same amount through a home equity credit line at 4.62 percent and you'll pay only $462 in interest. And because that's all tax deductible, if you're in the 28 percent tax bracket, the after-tax cost to you would be $462 × (1 − 0.28) = $332.64.

Home equity credit lines are offered by a variety of financial institutions, from banks and S&Ls to major brokerage houses. All sorts of credit terms and credit lines are available, and most of them carry repayment periods of 10 to 15 years or longer. Perhaps most startling is the maximum amount of credit available under these lines—indeed, $100,000 figures are not at all unusual. And it's precisely because of the enormous amount of money available that this form of credit should be used with caution. *Having equity in your home does not necessarily mean you have the cash flow necessary to service the debt such a credit line allows.* Remember that your home serves as the collateral on this line of credit, and if you can't repay the loan, you could lose it.

> Having equity in your home does not necessarily mean you have the cash flow necessary to service the debt that such a credit line allows.

6-3 OBTAINING AND MANAGING OPEN FORMS OF CREDIT

LO4 Consumers love to use their charge cards. In 2015, *Visa* alone handled about $7.4 trillion in transactions and had about 2.4 billion cards outstanding.

For the sake of convenience, people often maintain several different kinds of open credit. Nearly every household, for example, uses 30-day charge accounts to pay their utility bills, phone bills, and so on. In addition, most families have one or more retail charge cards and a couple of bank cards; some people, in fact, may have as many as 15 to 20 cards or more. And that's not all—families can also have revolving credit lines in the form of overdraft protection or a home equity line. When all these cards and lines are totaled together, a family conceivably can have tens of thousands of dollars of readily available credit. It's easy to see why consumer credit has become such a popular way of making relatively routine purchases.

6-3a Opening an Account

What do retail charge cards, bank credit cards, and revolving lines of credit all have in common? They all require you to go through a formal credit application. Let's now look at how you'd go about obtaining open forms of credit, including the normal credit application, investigation, and decision process. We'll couch our discussion in terms of credit cards, but keep in mind that similar procedures apply to other revolving lines of credit as well.

The Credit Application Credit applications are usually available at the store or bank involved. Sometimes they can be found at the businesses that accept these cards or obtained on request from the issuing companies. The type of information requested in a typical credit card application covers little more than personal/family matters, housing, employment and income, and existing charge accounts. Such information is intended to give the lender insight about the applicant's creditworthiness. In essence, the lender wants to determine whether the applicant has the *character* and *capacity* to handle the debt in a prompt and timely manner.

The Credit Investigation Once the credit application has been completed and returned to the establishment issuing the card—or more commonly today, submitted online—it is subject to a **credit investigation**. The purpose is to evaluate the kind of credit risk that you pose to the lender. So be sure to fill out your credit application carefully. Believe

credit investigation an investigation that involves contacting credit references or corresponding with a credit bureau to verify information on a credit application it or not, lenders really do look at it closely. The key items they look at are how much money you make, how much debt you have outstanding and how well you handle it, and how stable you are economically (e.g., your age, employment history, and whether you own or rent a home). Obviously, the higher your income and the better your credit history, the greater the chance that your credit application will be approved. During the investigation, the lender will verify much of the information you've provided—obviously, false or misleading information will almost certainly result in outright rejection of your application.

YOU CAN DO IT NOW: **How Does Your Credit Report Look?** When did you last check your credit report? It's a good idea look at it at least once a year to know where you stand and to ensure that there are no errors. The Fair Credit Reporting Act (FCRA) requires each of the national credit reporting firms – Experian, Equifax, and TransUnion – to provide a free copy of your credit report once a year. These three companies have set up an Internet site where you can get your free annual report at **https://www.annualcreditreport.com.** Be careful not to use other Internet sites that offer free credit reports, free credit monitoring, or free credit scores. Such sites are not authorized to meet the legal requirements of the FCRA and often have strings attached. Just go to the authorized site — you can **do it now.**

The Credit Bureau A **credit bureau** is a type of reporting agency that collects and sells information about individual borrowers. If, as is often the case, the lender doesn't know you personally, it must rely on a cost-effective way of verifying your employment and credit history. And that's where credit bureaus come into play, as they maintain basic credit files on current and potential borrowers.

Contrary to popular opinion, your credit file does *not* contain everything anyone would ever want to know about you—there's nothing on your lifestyle, friends, habits, or religious or political affiliations. Instead, most of the information is pretty dull stuff and covers such things as name, Social Security number, age, number of dependents, employment record and salary data, public records of bankruptcies, and the names of those who recently requested copies of your file.

credit bureau an organization that collects and sells credit information about individual borrowers

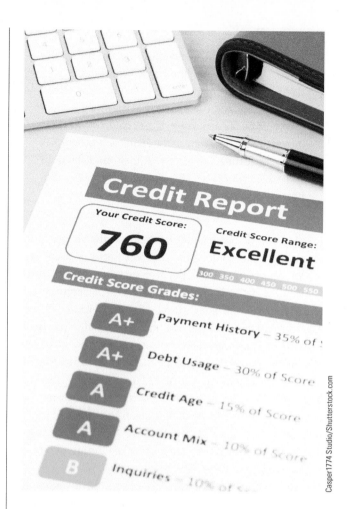

Although one late credit card payment probably won't make much of a difference on an otherwise clean credit file, a definite pattern of delinquencies (consistently being 30 to 60 days late with your payments) or a personal bankruptcy certainly will. Unfortunately, poor credit traits will stick with you for a long time, because delinquencies remain on your credit file for as long as 7 years, and bankruptcies for 10 years. An example of an actual credit bureau report (or at least a part of one) is provided in Exhibit 6.2.

Local credit bureaus are established and mutually owned by local merchants and banks. They collect and store credit information on people living within the community and make it available, for a fee, to members who request it. Local bureaus are linked together nationally through one of the "big three" national bureaus—TransUnion, Equifax Credit Information Services, and Experian—each of which provides the mechanism for obtaining credit information from almost any place in the United States. Traditionally, credit bureaus did little more than collect and provide credit information. They neither analyzed the information nor used it to make final credit decisions. In 2006, however, the three major credit bureaus announced that they had jointly developed

Exhibit 6.2

An Example of a Credit Bureau Report

Credit bureau reports have been revised and are now easier to understand. Notice that, in addition to some basic information, the report deals strictly with credit information—including payment records, past-due status, and types of credit.

Your Credit Report as of 04/09/2017

This Credit Report is available for you to view for 30 days. If you would like a current Credit Report, you may order another from MyEquifax.

ID # XXXXXXXXXXXX

• Personal Data

Social Security Number: 022-22-2222
Date of Birth: 1/11/1986

John Q. Public
2351 N 85th Ave
Phoenix, AZ 85037

• Previous Address(es):

133 Third Avenue
Phoenix, AZ 85037

• Employment History

Cendant Hospitality FR

	Location:	Employment Date:	Verified Date:
	Phoenix, AZ	2/1/2006	1/3/2008

Previous Employment(s):

SOFTWARE Support Hospitality Franch

	Location:	Employment Date:	Verified Date:
	Atlanta, GA	1/3/2008	1/3/2008

• Public Records

No bankruptcies on file
No liens on file
No foreclosures on file

• Collection Accounts

No collections on file.

• Credit Information

Company Name	Account Number and Whose Account	Date Opened	Last Activity	Type of Account and Status	High Credit	Items as of Date Reported Terms Balance		Past Due	Date Reported
Americredit Financial Services	40404XXXX JOINT ACCOUNT	03/2016	02/2017	Installment REPOSSESSION	$16933	$430	$9077	$128	2/2017

Prior Paying History
30 days past due 07 times; 60 days past due 05 times; 90+ days past due 03 times
INVOLUNTARY REPOSSESSION AUTO

| Capital One | 412174147128XXXX INDIVIDUAL ACCOUNT | 10/2015 | 01/2017 | Revolving PAYS AS AGREED | $777 | 15 | $514 | | 01/2017 |

Prior Paying History
30 days past due 02 times; 60 days past due 1 times; 90+ days past due 00 times
CREDIT CARD

| Desert Schools FCU | 423325003406XXXX INDIVIDUAL ACCOUNT | 07/2004 | 06/2014 | Revolving PAYS AS AGREED | $500 | | $0 | | 07/2014 |

Prior Paying History
30 days past due 02 times; 60 days past due 00 times; 90+ days past due 00 times
ACCOUNT PAID   CLOSED ACCOUNT

• Credit Inquiries

Companies that Requested your Credit File

04/09/2016 EFX Credit Profile Online
06/30/2016 Automotive
01/18/2015 Desert Schools Federal C.U.
07/02/2014 Time Life, Inc.

a new credit-scoring system, called *VantageScore*, that would incorporate data from all three bureaus—Equifax, Experian, and TransUnion. Thus, for the first time, each of the three national bureaus began assigning uniform credit ratings to individual credit files—though they're still obligated to report other credit scores, such as the widely used FICO scores.

Credit bureaus in the past were heavily criticized because of the large numbers of reporting errors they made and their poor record in promptly and efficiently correcting these errors. Fortunately, things have changed dramatically in recent years as the major bureaus have taken a more consumer-oriented approach. Even so, you should ensure that your credit report accurately reflects your credit history. The best way to do that is to obtain a copy of your own credit report—by law, you're entitled to receive *a free copy of your credit report once a year* (to get yours, go to the Internet site set up by the Federal Trade Commission at www.annualcreditreport.com)—and then go through it carefully. If you do find a mistake, let the credit bureau know immediately—and by all means, put it writing; *then request a copy of the corrected file to make sure that the mistake has been eliminated.* Most consumer advisors recommend that you review your credit files annually.

Here are the Internet sites for the three national credit bureaus:

▶ Equifax Credit Information Services www.equifax.com

▶ TransUnion LLC Consumer Disclosure Center www.tuc.com

▶ Experian National Consumer Assistance Center www.experian.com

6-3b The Credit Decision

Using the data provided by the credit applicant, along with any information obtained from the credit bureau, the store or bank must decide whether to grant credit. Very likely, some type of **credit scoring** scheme will be used to make the decision. An overall credit score is developed for you by assigning values to such factors as your annual income, whether you rent or own your home, number and types of credit cards you hold, level of your existing debts, whether you have savings accounts, and general credit references. Fifteen or 20 different factors or characteristics may be considered, and each characteristic receives a score based on some predetermined standard. For example, if you're

credit scoring a method of evaluating an applicant's creditworthiness by assigning values to such factors as income, existing debts, and credit references

---

IMPROVING YOUR FICO SCORES

Improving your FICO score is a lot like working out to get healthier: It takes time and there's no quick fix. But here are some tips you might want to follow to reach a high score:

- Pay your bills on time.
- If you've missed payments, get current and stay current.
- If you're having trouble making ends meet, contact your creditors and work out a payment plan.
- Keep credit card balances low.
- Pay off debt rather than move it around.
- Don't open new credit cards just to increase your available credit.
- Re-establish your credit history if you've had problems in the past.

Source: Adapted from "How to Repair My Credit and Improve My FICO Scores," www.myfico.com/crediteducation/improveyourscore.aspx, accessed October 2016.

---

26 years old, single, earn $32,500 a year (on a job that you've had for only two years), and rent an apartment, you might receive the following scores:

Age (25–30)	5 points
Marital status (single)	−2 points
Annual income ($30–$35 thousand)	12 points
Length of employment (2 years or less)	4 points
Rent or own a home (rent)	0 points
	19 points

Similar scores would be assigned to another 10 to 15 factors and, other things being equal, the stronger your personal traits or characteristics, the higher the score you'll receive. Statistical studies show that certain personal and financial traits can be used to determine your creditworthiness. Indeed, the whole credit scoring system is based on extensive statistical studies that identify the characteristics to look at and the scores to assign.

The biggest provider of credit scores is, by far, Fair Isaac & Co.—the firm that produces the widely used *FICO scores*. Unlike some credit score providers, *Fair Isaac uses only credit information in its calculations*. There's nothing in them about your age, marital status, salary, occupation, employment history, or where you live. Instead, FICO scores are derived from the following five major components, which are listed along with their respective weights: payment history (35 percent), amounts owed (30 percent), length of credit history (15 percent), new credit (10 percent), and types of credit used (10 percent). FICO scores, which are reported by all three of the major credit bureaus, range from a low of 300 to a max of 850. These scores are meant to be an indication of a borrower's credit risk; the higher the score, the lower the risk. While few, if any, credit decisions are based solely on FICO scores, you can be sure that higher scores are likely to result in lower interest rates on loans and therefore lower loan payments.

Go to Smart Sites

To learn more about FICO scores—including what's in your FICO score, what's not in it, and what you can do to improve it—visit the Fair Isaac & Co. Internet site. Find it at PFIN Online.

6-3c Computing Finance Charges

Because card issuers don't know in advance how much you'll charge on your account, they cannot specify the dollar amount of interest you will be charged. But they can—and must, according to the Truth in Lending Act—disclose the *rate of interest* that they charge and their method of computing finance charges. This is the **annual percentage rate (APR)**, the true or actual rate of interest paid, which must include all fees and costs and be calculated as defined by law. Remember, it's your right as a consumer to know—and it is the lender's obligation to tell you—the dollar amount of charges (where applicable) and the APR on any financing you consider.

The amount of interest you pay for open credit depends partly on the method the lender uses to calculate the balances on which they apply finance charges. Most bank and retail charge card issuers use one of two variations of the **average daily balance (ADB) method**, which applies the interest rate to the ADB of the account over the billing period. The most common method (used by an estimated 95 percent of bank card issuers) is the *ADB including new purchases*. An alternative is the ADB method *excluding new purchases*. Balance calculations under each of these methods are as follows:

▶ **ADB including new purchases.** For each day in the billing cycle, take the outstanding balance, including new purchases, and subtract payments and credits; then divide by the number of days in the billing cycle.

DenisNata/Shutterstock.com

▶ **ADB excluding new purchases.** Same as the first method but *exclude* new purchases.

These different calculations can obviously affect a card's credit balance and therefore the amount of finance charges you'll have to pay. Also be aware that the finance charges on two cards with the same APR but different methods of calculating balances may differ dramatically. It's important to know the method your card issuer uses. For active card users, the ADB procedure that *includes new purchases* will usually produce considerably more interest income for the issuer and, in turn, is *far more expensive* from the cardholder's perspective.

annual percentage rate (APR) the actual or true rate of interest paid over the life of a loan; includes all fees and costs

average daily balance (ADB) method a method of computing finance charges by applying interest charges to the average daily balance of the account over the billing period

Exhibit 6.3

Finding the Average Daily Balance and Finance Charge

The ADB including new purchases is the method most widely used by credit card issuers to determine the monthly finance charge on an account.

	Number of Days (1)	Balance (2)	Calculation (1) × (2) (3)
	5	$1,582	$ 7,910
	7	$2,332	16,324
	15	$2,732	40,980
	4	$2,457	9,828
Total	31		$75,042

$$ABD = \frac{\$75,042}{31} = \$2,420.71$$

Finance charge: $2,420.71 × 0.015 = $36.31

6-3d Managing Your Credit Cards

Congratulations! You have applied for and been granted a bank credit card, as well as a retail charge card from your favorite department store. You carefully reviewed the terms of the credit agreement and have at least a basic understanding of how finance charges are computed for each account. Now you must manage your accounts efficiently, using the monthly statements to help you make the required payments on time, as well as to track purchases.

The Statement If you use a credit card, you'll receive monthly statements similar to the sample bank card statement in Exhibit 6.4, showing billing cycle and payment due dates, interest rate, minimum payment, and all account activity during the current period. Retail charge cards have similar monthly statements, but without a section for cash advances. The statement summarizes your account activity: the previous balance (the amount of credit outstanding at the beginning of the month—not to be confused with past-due, or late, payments); new charges made (four, in this case) during the past month; any finance charges (interest) on the unpaid balance; the preceding period's payment; any other credits (such as those for returns); and the new balance (previous balance plus new purchases and finance charges, less any payments and credits).

You should review your statements every month. Save your receipts and use them to verify statement entries for purchases and returns *before* paying. If you find any errors or suspect fraudulent use of your card, first use the issuer's toll-free number to report any problems; then follow up *in writing* within 60 days of the postmark on the bill.

Although merchandise and cash transactions are separated on the statement, the finance charge in each case is calculated at the rate of 1.5 percent per month (18 percent annually). This procedure works fine for illustration, but it's a bit out of the ordinary because most card issuers charge a higher rate for cash advances than for purchases.

Payments Credit card users can avoid *future* finance charges by paying the total new balance shown on their statement each month. For example, if the $534.08 total new balance shown in Exhibit 6.4 is paid by the due date of September 21, 2017, then no additional finance charges will be incurred. (The cardholder, however, is still liable for the $4.40 in finance charges incurred to date.) If cardholders cannot pay the total new balance, they can pay any amount that is equal to or greater than the **minimum monthly payment** specified on the statement. If they do this, however, they will incur additional finance charges in the following months.

Note that the account in Exhibit 6.4 has a minimum payment of 5 percent of the new balance, rounded to the nearest full dollar. As shown at the bottom of the statement, this month's minimum payment is $27.00 (i.e., $534.08 × 0.05 = $26.70 ≈ $27.00). This $27.00 includes a *principal payment* of $22.60; that is: $27.00 − $4.40

minimum monthly payment in open account credit, a minimum specified percentage of the new account balance that must be paid in order to remain current

Exhibit 6.4

A Bank Credit Card Monthly Statement

Each month, a bank credit card holder receives a statement that provides an itemized list of charges and credits as well as a summary of previous activity and finance charges.

Please detach the above portion and return it with your payment to insure proper credit.

Bank Card Statement
Retain this statement for your records.

Account Number	Name(s)	Statement Date	Payment Due Date
123-XYZ-45678	Mr. Joshua Garrett Mrs. Phoebe Garrett	8-24-2017	09-21-2017

ACCOUNT ACTIVITY

Previous Balance	203.64	
Payments −	119.89	
Credits −	.00	
Subtotal	83.75	
New Transaction +	445.93	
Finance Charge +	4.40	
Late Charge +	.00	
NEW BALANCE	534.08	

Credit Status
Your Credit Limit is: **2000.00**
Your Available Credit is: **1465.92**

FINANCE CHARGE CALCULATION

Amounts Subject to Finance Charge		This Month's Charge
A. *Average Daily Balance	293.25	4.40
B. *Cash Advance	.00	.00
C. *Loan Advance	.00	.00
		4.40

*Finance Charges explained on reverse side

ENTIRE BAL.	
1.5%	18.00%
Monthly Periodic Rate	Nominal Annual Rate
18.00%	

Finance Charge — Annual Percentage Rate

Mail Billing Inquiries to: Post Office Box 7890, Van Niles, California, 85258, or call 800/000-0000
For Inquiries on Past Due Accounts, Overlimits or Credit Line Increase, call 800/000-0000

Posted Mo./Day	Transaction Description or Merchant Name and Location		Purchase Mo./Day	Bank Reference Number	Purchases/ Advances/Debits	Payments Credits
8-08	AMERICA WEST AIRLINES	LOS ANGELES	07-25	850000008823395192	42.00	
8-13	HACIENDA MOTORS	COSTA MESA	08-05	015400018537022316	166.86	
8-15	RICOS RESTAURANT	PALM SPRG	08-10	114500018856161722	132.47	
8-12	PAYMENT—THANK YOU		08-11	4501000182MD02139		119.89
8-24	RENEES RESTAURANT	NEWPORT	08-13	114500068201632483	104.60	

Notice See reverse side for important information

					Total Debits	Total Credits
MIN. PAYMENT: 27.00	NEW BALANCE: 534.08				445.93	119.89

(in interest charges) = $22.60. That's actually about 4.25 percent of the "new balance." If the new balance had been less than $200, the bank would have required a payment of $10 (which is the absolute minimum dollar payment) or of the total new balance, if less than $10. Cardholders who fail to make the minimum payment are considered to be in default on their account, and the bank issuing the card can take action against the cardholder.

 Go to Smart Sites

Use About.com's Credit Card Calculators to find out how interest rate changes affect your balance, if debt consolidation makes sense, and answers to similar questions.

6-4 USING CREDIT WISELY

LO5, LO6 As we've discussed, credit cards and revolving lines of credit can simplify your life financially. Unfortunately, you can also get into real trouble with these forms of credit unless you use them wisely. That's why you should carefully shop around to choose the right credit cards for your personal situation, understand the advantages and disadvantages of credit cards, learn how to resolve credit problems, and know how to avoid the ultimate cost of credit abuse—bankruptcy.

6-4a Shop Around for the Best Deal

They say it pays to shop around, and when it comes to credit cards, that's certainly true. With all the fees and high interest costs, it pays to get the best deal possible. So, where do you start? Most credit experts suggest the first thing you should do is step back and take a look at yourself. What kind of "spender" are you, and how do you pay your bills? The fact is, no single credit card is right for everyone. If you pay off your card balance each month, then you'll want a card that's different from the one that's right for someone who carries a credit balance from month to month and may only pay the minimum due. Regardless of which category you fall into, there are basically four card features to look for:

> The fact is, no single credit card is right for everyone.

- ▶ Annual fees
- ▶ Rate of interest charged on account balance
- ▶ Length of the grace period
- ▶ Method of calculating balances

If you normally pay your account balance in full each month, get a card with *no annual fees and a long grace period.* The rate of interest on the card is irrelevant because you don't carry account balances from month to month anyway. In sharp contrast, if you don't pay your account in full, then look for cards that charge *a low rate of interest on unpaid balances.* The length of the grace period isn't all that important here, but obviously, other things being equal, you're better off with low (or no) annual fees.

Sometimes, however, "other things aren't equal" and you have to decide between interest rates and annual fees. If you're not a big spender and don't build up big balances on your credit card, then *avoid* cards with annual fees and get one with as *low* a rate of interest as possible. (This situation applies to most college students.) On the other hand, if you do carry big balances (say, $1,000 or more), then you'll probably be better off *paying an annual fee* (even a relatively high one) *to keep the rate of interest on the card as low as possible.*

EXAMPLE: Credit Card Choice Trade-offs
Sometimes in choosing between credit cards there is a trade-off between interest rates and annual fees. For example, with a $2,000 average balance, your total yearly finance charges (including annual fees) will be *less* with a card that has, say, a $50 annual fee and an interest rate of 15 percent than with one that has no annual fee but charges a higher (19 percent) rate of interest.

The bottom line is this: Don't take the first credit card that comes along. Instead, get the one that's right for you. Learn as much as you can about the credit cards you've been offered or are considering. To do that, go to Internet sites like www.bankrate.com; www.creditcards.com; or www.cardtrak.com, to mention just a few. These sites provide all sorts of information about fees, rates, credit terms, and so forth on a wide array of different types of credit cards. Another alternative is to go to publications like *Money* magazine and *Kiplinger's Personal Finance,* whose respective Internet sites are located at www.money.com and www.kiplinger.com. These magazines and Internet sites regularly publish information about banks and other financial institutions that offer low-cost credit cards nationally; see Exhibit 6.5 for an example.

One final point: Some people spend a lot of time and energy shopping for deals, jumping from one card to another to take advantage of low introductory rates. Although a strategy like this may result in lower interest payments, it can backfire if the low rates rise significantly after the introductory period or if you miss a payment. A wiser approach is to shop around, check for better deals from time to time, and then *direct the rest of your energy toward reducing (or even eliminating) any monthly balances.*

6-4b Avoiding Credit Problems

Unfortunately, it's not unusual to find people using credit cards to solve cash-flow problems. Even the most careful

Exhibit 6.5

Average Interest Rates for Different Types of Credit Cards

Information about low-cost credit cards is readily available in the financial media. Pay particular attention to the *cards with the lowest rates* (probably best for people who regularly carry an account balance) and *no-fee cards with the lowest rates* (probably best for people who pay their accounts in full each month).

Type of Credit Card	Average Annual Percentage Rate (APR)
Balance transfer cards	14.41%
Cash back cards	15.33%
Low interest cards	12.00%

These rates are as of October 17, 2016; are adjustable. Banks sometimes offer lower introductory rates, many charge no annual fee, and the cards vary in credit score requirements. Most of these cards have variable rates. Data compiled from www.bankrate.com, accessed October 2016.

consumers occasionally find themselves with mounting credit card debt, especially after the year-end holiday buying season. The real problems occur when the situation is no longer temporary and the debt continues to increase. If overspending is not curtailed, then the size of the unpaid balance may seriously strain the budget. Essentially, people who let their credit balances build up are *mortgaging their future*. By using credit, they're actually committing a part of their future income to make debt payments.

The best way to avoid credit problems is to be disciplined when using credit. Reduce the number of cards you carry, and don't rush to accept the tempting preapproved credit card offers that you may get in the mail. A wallet full of cards can work against you in two ways. Obviously, the ready availability of credit can tempt you to overspend and incur too much debt. But there's another, less obvious, danger: when you apply for a loan, lenders look at the *total amount* of credit you have available, as well as at the outstanding balances on your credit cards. If you have a lot of unused credit capacity, it may be harder to get a loan because of lender concerns that you could become overextended. Also, your FICO score will be reduced because of the amount of potential credit represented by the cards.

You really don't need three or four bank cards. Two credit cards is the most financial advisors suggest you carry. And should you decide to start using a new card (because their offer was just too good to pass up), then *get rid of one of your old cards*—physically cut up the old card and inform the issuer in writing that you're canceling your account.

6-4c Credit Card Fraud

Despite all the efforts of law enforcement officials, there are still people out there who are doing their best to rip you off! In fact, plastic has become the vehicle of choice among crooks. No doubt about it: Credit card crime is big business, with annual losses in the United States estimated to run in the billions of dollars a year. Basically, "it's us against them," and the first thing you have to understand is that the credit card you're carrying around is a powerful piece of plastic. To reduce your chances of being defrauded, here are some suggestions you should follow:

▶ Never, ever, give your account number to people or organizations *who call you*, no matter how legitimate it sounds.

▶ If you initiated the call, it's okay to give your account number over the phone when ordering or purchasing something from a major catalog house, airline, hotel, and so on.

▶ Use the same precautions *when purchasing something over the Internet with* your credit card—don't do it *unless* you're dealing with a major retailer who uses state-of-the-art protection against fraud and thievery.

▶ When paying for something *by check*, don't put your Social Security or credit card account number on the check, and don't let the store clerk do it.

▶ Don't put your phone number or address (and certainly not your Social Security number) on credit/charge slips, even if the merchant asks for it—they're not entitled to it.

▶ When using your card to make a purchase, *always keep your eye on it.* If the clerk wants to make another

PROTECT AGAINST IDENTITY THEFT

Watch out for the following methods that thieves use to get your information:

- **Dumpster diving.** Don't leave bills or anything with personal information in your trash.

- **Skimming.** Watch for unusual "additions" to credit and debit card readers that can steal your numbers.

- **Phishing.** Thieves can pretend to be financial institutions or companies and can use Internet pop-ups or send e-mail messages that ask you to disclose personal information.

- **Changing your address.** Thieves can reroute your bills to them by completing a change of address form.

- **Old-fashioned stealing.** Simple still works. Thieves continue to steal wallets and purses, mail, and new checks or tax information. Also, they sometimes bribe employees to provide access to your personal information.

- **Pretexting.** Thieves can obtain your personal information from financial institutions, telephone companies, and other sources under false pretenses.

So what should you do?

- **Deter** thefts by protecting your information. Be aware of the abovementioned ways in which information is stolen.

- **Detect** suspicious activity by consistently checking your financial and billing statements.

- **Defend** against identity theft as soon as you suspect a possible problem. Place a "fraud alert" on your credit reports by contacting one of the consumer reporting companies noted earlier in this chapter (Experian, TransUnion, or Equifax). Contact the security departments of each company where an unauthorized account was opened.

Source: Adapted from http://www.utica.edu/academic/institutes/cimip /idcrimes/schemes.cfm, https://www.commonwealth.com/RepSiteContent /identity_theft_ftc.htm, and https://www.consumer.ftc.gov/articles/0216 -protecting-against-credit-card-fraud, accessed October 2016.

---

imprint, ask for the first one and tear it up on the spot.

▶ Always draw a line on the credit slip through any blank spaces above the total.

▶ *Destroy* all old credit slips; and when you receive your monthly statement, be sure to *go over it promptly* to make sure there are no errors. If you find a mistake, call or send a letter immediately, detailing the error.

▶ If you lose a card or it's stolen, *report it to the card issuer immediately*—the most you're ever liable for with a lost or stolen card is $50 (per card), but if you report the loss before the card can be used, you won't be liable for any unauthorized charges.

▶ Destroy old cards or those you no longer use.

personal bankruptcy a form of legal recourse open to insolvent debtors, who may petition a court for protection from creditors and arrange for the orderly liquidation and distribution of their assets

6-4d Bankruptcy: Paying the Price for Credit Abuse

It certainly isn't an overstatement to say that, during the 1980s and 1990s, *debt was in.* In fact, the explosion of debt that has occurred since 1980 is almost incomprehensible. The national debt rose from less than a trillion dollars when the 1980s began to over $18.2 trillion by the end of 2015. Businesses also took on debt rapidly. Not to be outdone, consumers were using credit like there was no tomorrow. So it should come as no surprise that when you couple this heavy debt load with a serious economic recession like that in 2008–2009, you have all the ingredients of a real financial crisis. And that's just what happened, as personal bankruptcies soared in the wake of the crisis—indeed, in 2015, about 819,200 people filed for **personal bankruptcy**.

When too many people are too heavily in debt, a recession (or some other economic reversal) can come along and push many of them over the edge. But let's

PLANNING OVER A LIFETIME

Using Credit

Here are some key considerations for using credit in each stage of the life cycle.

PRE-FAMILY INDEPENDENCE: 20s

» Obtain a credit card to start building a credit history. Consider a secured card first.

» Plan to pay all consumer credit bills in full.

» Carefully monitor all charges and financial statements for unauthorized transactions.

FAMILY FORMATION/CAREER DEVELOPMENT: 30–45

» Watch consumer credit use carefully to avoid overspending.

» Periodically evaluate credit card costs, and change cards if you are not getting the best deal.

» Continue to monitor all accounts for unauthorized transactions and possible identity theft.

PRE-RETIREMENT: 45–65

» Re-evaluate use of consumer credit in light of revised expenditures and income.

» Check your credit score periodically.

» Continue to watch for unauthorized transactions and identity theft.

RETIREMENT: 65 AND BEYOND

» Budget to eliminate reliance on consumer credit in retirement.

» Maintain credit score to assure credit access.

» Be particularly careful about releasing personal financial information.

The only way a recession can push you over the edge is if you're already sitting on it!

taken, this is followed by repossession of property and, eventually, even bankruptcy. Two of the most widely used bankruptcy procedures (employed by well over 95 percent of those individuals who file for bankruptcy) are (1) the Wage Earner Plan and (2) straight bankruptcy.

Wage Earner Plan The Wage Earner Plan (as defined in *Chapter 13* of the U.S. Bankruptcy Code) is a workout procedure involving some type of debt restructuring—usually by establishing a debt repayment schedule that's more compatible with the person's income. It may be a viable alternative for someone who has a steady source of income, in 2016 not more than $1,184,200 in secured debt and $394,725 in unsecured debt, and a reasonably good chance of being able to repay the debts in three to five years. A majority of creditors must agree to the plan, and interest charges (along with late-payment penalties) are waived for the repayment period. Creditors usually will go along with this plan because they stand to lose more in a straight bankruptcy.

Straight Bankruptcy Straight bankruptcy, which is allowed under *Chapter 7* of the bankruptcy code, can be viewed as a legal procedure that results in "wiping the slate clean and starting anew." About 70 percent of those filing personal bankruptcy choose this route. However, straight bankruptcy does not eliminate all the debtor's obligations, nor does the debtor necessarily lose all of his or her assets. For example, the debtor must make certain tax payments and keep up alimony and child-support payments but is allowed to retain certain payments from Social Security, retirement, veterans', and disability benefits. The debtor also may retain the equity in a home, a car, and some other personal assets. Minimum values are established by federal regulations, though state laws are generally much more generous regarding the amount the debtor is allowed to keep.

> **Wage Earner Plan** an arrangement for scheduled debt repayment over future years that is an alternative to straight bankruptcy; used when a person has a steady source of income and there is a reasonable chance of repayment within three to five years
>
> **straight bankruptcy** a legal proceeding that results in "wiping the slate clean and starting anew"; most of a debtor's obligations are eliminated in an attempt to put the debtor's financial affairs in order

face it, recessions are not the main culprit here. The only way a recession can push you over the edge is if you're already sitting on it! The real culprit is excess debt. Some people simply abuse credit by taking on more than they can afford. Then, sooner or later, these debtors start missing payments and their credit rating begins to deteriorate. Unless corrective actions are

Ryan Has Had It and Files for Bankruptcy

Ryan Booth is overwhelmed by his bills. While making $60,000 a year, he has amassed credit card debt of $24,000, has an $80,000 college loan, holds a $150,000 mortgage, and pays monthly on his leased Jetta. He's having trouble paying the mortgage monthly and can never seem to pay more than the minimum on his credit card debt. Ryan's wife, Helen, is currently unemployed. Ryan has heard that declaring bankruptcy can eliminate some of his debt commitments and give him extra time to deal with others. He's had it and just filed for bankruptcy. What can Ryan look forward to as a result of his decision?

Ryan can expect some cash flow relief in the short-term, and filing for bankruptcy will likely prevent or at least delay foreclosure on his home. However, the bankruptcy filing will adversely affect his credit report for up to the next 10 years. Ryan will probably have trouble getting a loan or a new credit card. And if he can bor-

TheaDesign/Shutterstock.com

row money or get a new credit card, he'll probably have to pay the highest allowable interest rate. By not having managing his family's indebtedness, Ryan has exercised the bankruptcy "nuclear option." This provides short-term relief at the expense of longer-term access to credit on reasonable terms.

STUDY TOOLS 6

© viphotos/Shutterstock140785408

LOCATED AT BACK OF THE TEXTBOOK
☐ Chapter Review Card

LOCATED AT WWW.CENGAGEBRAIN.COM
☐ Review Key Term flashcards and create your own cards.
☐ Track your knowledge and understanding of key concepts in personal finance.

☐ Complete practice and graded quizzes to prepare for tests.
☐ Complete interactive content at PFIN6 Online.
☐ View the chapter highlight boxes at PFIN6 Online.

Financial Planning Exercises

LO1 1. **Establishing credit history.** After graduating from college last fall, Elsa Crawford took a job as a consumer credit analyst at a local bank. From her work reviewing credit applications, she realizes that she should begin establishing her own credit history. Describe for Elsa several steps that she could take to begin building a strong credit record. Does the fact that she took out a student loan for her college education help or hurt her credit record?

LO2 2. **Evaluating debt burden.** Carter Barnes has monthly take-home pay of $1,685; he makes payments of $410 a month on his outstanding consumer credit (excluding the mortgage on his home). How would you characterize Carter's debt burden? What if his take-home pay were $850 a month and he had monthly credit payments of $150?

LO2 3. **Evaluating debt safety ratio. Use Worksheet 6.1.** Diana Wade is evaluating her debt safety ratio. Her monthly take-home pay is $3,320. Each month, she pays $380 for an auto loan, $120 on a personal line of credit, $60 on a department store charge card, and $85 on her bank credit card. Complete Worksheet 6.1 by listing Diana's outstanding debts, and then calculate her debt safety ratio. Given her current take-home pay, what is the maximum amount of monthly debt payments that Diana can have if she wants her debt safety ratio to be 12.5 percent? Given her current monthly debt payment load, what would Diana's take-home pay have to be if she wanted a 12.5 percent debt safety ratio?

LO3 4. **Comparing credit and debit cards.** Diego Ortega is trying to decide whether to apply for a credit card or a debit card. He has $8,500 in a savings account at the bank and spends his money frugally. What advice would you have for Diego? Describe the benefits and drawbacks of each type of card.

LO3 5. **Home equity lines.** Aaron and Laura Pearson have a home with an appraised value of $180,000 and a mortgage balance of only $90,000. Given that an S&L is willing to lend money at a loan-to-value ratio of 75 percent, how big a home equity credit line can Aaron and Laura obtain? How much, if any, of this line would qualify as tax-deductible interest if their house originally cost $200,000?

LO4 6. **Using overdraft protection line.** Sloane Chen has an overdraft protection line. Assume that her October 2017 statement showed a latest (new) balance of $862. If the line had a minimum monthly payment requirement of 5 percent of the latest balance (rounded to the nearest $5 figure), what would be the minimum amount that she'd have to pay on her overdraft protection line?

LO4 7. **Choosing between credit cards.** Otis Hopkins recently graduated from college and is evaluating two credit cards. Card A has an annual fee of $75 and an interest rate of 9 percent. Card B has no annual fee and an interest rate of 16 percent. Assuming that Otis intends to carry no balance and pay off his charges in full each month, which card represents the better deal? If Otis expected to carry a significant balance from one month to the next, which card would be better? Explain.

LO4 8. **Calculating credit card interest.** Lola Schneider a student at State College, has a balance of $380 on her retail charge card. If the store levies a finance charge of 21 percent per year, how much monthly interest will be added to Lola's account?

LO4 9. **Balance transfer credit cards.** Rebecca Holland has several credit cards, on which she is carrying a total current balance of $14,500. She is considering transferring this balance to a new card issued by a local bank. The bank advertises that, for a 2 percent fee, she can transfer her balance to a card that charges a 0 percent interest rate on transferred balances for the first nine months. Calculate the fee that Rebecca would pay to transfer the balance, and describe the benefits and drawbacks of balance transfer cards.

LO5 10. **Credit card liability.** Willow Xu was reviewing her credit card statement and noticed several charges that didn't look familiar to her. Willow is unsure whether she should "make some noise," or simply pay the bill in full and forget about the unfamiliar charges. If some of these charges aren't hers, is she still liable for the full amount? Is she liable for any part of these charges—even if they're fraudulent?

LO6 11. **Protecting against credit card fraud.** Wyatt Scott takes pride in managing his finances carefully with great attention to detail. He recently received a phone call in which he was asked to confirm his credit card account number and social security number. Wyatt was pleased he had the information handy and appreciated the caller's thoroughness. He gladly provided the information. What advice would you give Wyatt concerning his response?

7 | Using Consumer Loans

LEARNING OBJECTIVES

After studying this chapter, you will be able to...

LO1 Know when to use consumer loans and be able to differentiate between the major types.

LO2 Identify the various sources of consumer loans.

LO3 Choose the best loans by comparing finance charges, maturity, collateral, and other loan terms.

LO4 Describe the features of, and calculate the finance charges on, single-payment loans.

LO5 Evaluate the benefits of an installment loan.

LO6 Determine the costs of installment loans and analyze whether it is better to pay cash or to take out a loan.

After finishing this chapter, go
to **PAGE 192** for
STUDY TOOLS

Jupiterimages/Getty Images

How Will This Affect Me? Consumer loan sources abound, and their terms vary significantly. The primary types are single-payment and installment consumer loans. It's important to understand when to use each credit source, to be able to calculate and compare their costs, and to determine the circumstances in which it is best to take out a loan or pay cash. Practical examples considered in this chapter include taking out a car loan and borrowing to pay for a college education. The chapter provides you with an applied framework for evaluating the best ways to choose among and obtain consumer loans.

7-1 BASIC FEATURES OF CONSUMER LOANS

LO1, LO2 In previous chapters, we've discussed the different types of financial goals that individuals and families can set for themselves. These goals often involve large sums of money and may include such things as a college education or the purchase of a new car. One way to reach these goals is to systematically save the money. Another is to use a loan to at least partially finance the transactions. Consumer loans are important to the personal financial planning process because they can help you reach certain types of financial goals. The key, of course, is to successfully manage the credit by keeping both the amount of debt used and the debt repayment burden *well within your budget*.

7-1a Using Consumer Loans

As we saw in Chapter 6, using open or revolving credit can be helpful to those who plan and live within their personal financial budgets. More important to the achievement of long-term personal financial goals, however, are *single-payment* and *installment loans*. These long-term liabilities are widely used to finance the purchase of goods that are far too expensive to buy from current income, to help fund a college education, or to pay for certain nondurable items, such as expensive vacations.

They differ from open forms of credit in several ways, including the formality of their lending arrangements. That is, while open account credit results from a rather informal process, **consumer loans** are *formal, negotiated contracts* that specify both the terms for borrowing and the repayment schedule. Another difference is that an open line of credit can be used again and again, but consumer loans are one-shot transactions made for specific purposes. Because there's no revolving credit with a consumer loan, no more credit is available (from that particular loan) once it's paid off. Furthermore, no credit cards or checks are issued with this form of credit. Finally, whereas open account credit is used chiefly to make repeated purchases of relatively low-cost *goods*

> Consumer loans are important because they can help you reach certain types of financial goals.

and services, consumer loans are used mainly to *borrow money* to pay for big-ticket items.

7-1b Different Types of Loans

Although they can be used for just about any purpose imaginable, most consumer loans fall into one of the following categories:

▶ **Auto loans.** Financing a new car, truck, SUV, or mini-van is the single most common reason for borrowing money through a consumer loan. Indeed, auto loans account for about 35 percent of all consumer credit outstanding. Generally speaking, about 80 percent to 90 percent of the cost of a new vehicle (somewhat less with used cars) can be financed with credit. The buyer must provide the rest through

consumer loans loans made for specific purposes using formally negotiated contracts that specify the borrowing terms and repayment

pathdoc/Shutterstock.com

a *down payment*. The loan is *secured* with the auto, meaning that the vehicle serves as collateral for the loan and can be repossessed by the lender should the buyer fail to make payments. These loans generally have maturities ranging from 36 to 60 months.

▶ **Loans for other durable goods.** Consumer loans can also be used to finance other kinds of *costly durable goods*, such as furniture, home appliances, TVs, home computers, recreational vehicles, and even small airplanes and mobile homes. These loans are also secured by the items purchased and generally require some down payment. Maturities vary with the type of asset purchased: 9- to 12-month loans for less costly items, such as TVs and computers, versus a 10- to 15-year loan for (say) a mobile home.

▶ **Education loans.** Getting a college education is another important reason for taking out a consumer loan. Such loans can be used to finance either undergraduate or graduate studies, and special, government-subsidized loan programs are available to students and parents. We'll discuss student loans in more detail in the following section.

▶ **Personal loans.** These loans are typically used for nondurable expenditures, such as an expensive European vacation, or to cover temporary cash shortfalls. Many personal loans are *unsecured*, which means there's no collateral with the loan other than the borrower's good name.

collateral an item of value used to secure the principal portion of a loan

single-payment loan a loan made for a specified period, at the end of which payment is due in full

interim financing the use of a single-payment loan to finance a purchase or pay bills in situations where the funds to be used for repayment are known to be forthcoming in the near future

installment loan a loan that is repaid in a series of fixed, scheduled payments rather than a lump sum

▶ **Consolidation loans.** This type of loan is used to straighten out an unhealthy credit situation, which often occurs when consumers overuse credit cards, credit lines, or consumer loans and can no longer promptly service the debt. By borrowing money from one source to pay off other forms of credit, borrowers can replace, say, five or six monthly payments that total $400 with one payment amounting to $250. *Consolidation loans are usually expensive, and people who use them should be careful to stop using credit cards and other forms of credit until they repay the loans. Otherwise, they may end up right back where they started.*

Single-Payment or Installment Loans Consumer loans can also be broken into categories based on the type of repayment arrangement—single-payment or installment. **Single-payment loans** are made for a specified period, at the end of which time payment in full (principal plus interest) is due. They generally have maturities ranging from 30 days to a year or so. Sometimes single-payment loans are made to finance purchases or pay bills when the cash to be used for repayment is known to be forthcoming in the near future; in this case, they serve as a form of interim financing. In other situations, single-payment loans are used by consumers who want to avoid being strapped with monthly installment payments.

Installment loans, in contrast, are repaid in a series of fixed, scheduled payments rather than in one lump sum. The payments are almost always set up on a monthly basis, with each installment made up partly of principal and partly of interest. For example, out of a $75 monthly payment, $50 might be credited to principal and the balance to interest. These loans are typically made to finance the purchase of a good or service for which current resources are inadequate. The repayment period can run from six months to six years or more. Installment loans have become a way of life for many consumers. They're popular because they provide a convenient way to "buy now and pay later."

Student Loans Today, the average annual total cost of tuition, fees, books and supplies, and room and board ranges from about $24,000 at four-year public colleges for state residents to over $47,000 at private colleges. Alarmingly, after adjusting for inflation, students are paying about three times what they paid 30 years ago for a public college education, and about two-and-a-half times what they paid for a private college education. Many families, even those who started saving for college when their children were young, are faced with higher-than-expected bills. Fortunately, there are many types of financial aid programs available, including some federal programs as well as state, private, and college-sponsored programs.

Paying for a college education is one of the most legitimate reasons for going into debt. Although you could borrow money for college through normal channels—that is, take out a regular consumer loan from your bank and use the proceeds to finance an education—there are better ways to go about getting education loans. Indeed, in 2010, Congress significantly modified the federal college-funding system. The new legislation ends the bank-based student loan system by preventing private financial institutions from making profits as intermediaries between students and federal education aid dollars. All federal student loans must now go through a direct lending program, so private lending companies such as Sallie Mae are now out of that business. The federal government (and some state governments) have available several different types of subsidized educational loan programs. The federally sponsored programs are:

▶ Stafford loans (Direct and Federal Family Education Loans—FFEL)

▶ Perkins loans

▶ Parent Loans for Undergraduate Students (PLUS)

The Stafford and Perkins loans have the best terms and are the foundation of the government's student loan program. In contrast, PLUS (which stands for *Parent Loans for Undergraduate Students*) loans are *supplemental loans* for *undergraduate students* who demonstrate a need but, for one reason or another, don't qualify for Stafford or Perkins loans or who need more aid than they're receiving. Under this program, parents can take out loans to meet or supplement the costs of their children's college education, *up to the full cost of attendance*. Although Stafford and Perkins loans are made directly to students, PLUS loans are made to the parents or legal guardians of college students.

The best place to start looking for information about these and other programs is the Internet. For example, look up FASTWEB (which stands for *Financial Aid Search Through the Web*). This site, which is free, not only provides details on all the major, and some of the not-so-major, student loan programs but also has a service that matches individuals with scholarships and loans—even going so far as to provide form letters to use in requesting more information. (The address is www.fastweb.com.)

Let's look at the Stafford loan program to see how student loans work. There are two types of Stafford loans. In the subsidized loan program, the U.S. Department of Education pays interest while the student is in school and also during certain grace and deferment periods. In the unsubsidized program, the borrower is responsible for all interest, whether in or out of school. Stafford loans carry low, government-subsidized interest rates.

The whole process—which really is quite simple—begins with a visit to the school's financial aid office, where a financial aid counselor will help you determine your eligibility. To be eligible, you must demonstrate a *financial need*, where the amount of your financial need is defined as the cost of attending school *less* the amount that can be paid by you or your family. Thus, in these programs, students are expected to contribute something to covering their educational expenses regardless of their income. You must also be making *satisfactory progress in your academic program*, and you cannot be in default on any other student loans. Each academic year, you'll have to fill out a Free Application for Federal Student Aid (FAFSA) statement to attest that these qualifications are being met (you can complete and submit the form on the Internet at **www.fafsa.ed.gov**).

 Go to Smart Sites

To find advice on financing college (loans and scholarships) and helpful online calculators, check out the Princeton Review's financing section. A highlight box in each chapter of PFIN Online includes "Smart Sites," a list of resources and sites that offer additional information on topics in the PFIN text.

Obtaining a Student Loan All you have to do to obtain a (Stafford) loan is complete a simple application form. The latest innovation in this procedure involves transmitting the application electronically to the necessary parties, thus reducing paperwork and speeding up the processing (for example, see www.staffordloan.com).

Each program has specific loan limits. For example, with subsidized Stafford loans for *dependent* undergraduate students, you can borrow up to $3,500 for first-year studies, $4,500 for the second year, and $5,500 per academic year thereafter, up to a subsidized loan maximum of $23,000 for undergraduate studies—you can obtain even more if you can show that you're no longer dependent on your parents; in other words, that you're an *independent* undergraduate student paying for your college education on your own. Subsidized Stafford loans are no longer available to graduate and professional students. However, unsubsidized Stafford loans of up to $20,500 per school year are still available to these students. Exhibit 7.1 compares the major loan provisions of the three federally sponsored student loan programs: Stafford, Perkins, and PLUS loans.

Each year, right on through graduate school, a student can take out a loan from one or more of these government programs. Over time, that can add up to a lot of loans, and a substantial amount of debt—all of which must be repaid. But here's another nice feature of these loans: *loan repayment doesn't begin until after you're out of school* (for the Stafford and Perkins programs only; repayment on PLUS loans normally begins within 60 days of loan disbursement). In addition, except for PLUS loans, interest doesn't begin accruing until you get out of school. Once repayment begins, you start paying interest on the loans; this interest may be tax deductible, depending on your income.

Student loans usually require monthly (principal and interest) payments over a period of 5 to 10 years. To help you service the debt, if you have several student loans

outstanding, you can *consolidate* the loans at a single, blended rate and extend the repayment period to as long as 20 years. You also can ask for either: (1) an *extended repayment* for a longer term of up to 30 years; (2) a *graduated repayment schedule*, which will give you low payments in the early years and then higher payments later on; or (3) an *income-contingent repayment plan*, with payments that fluctuate annually according to your income and debt levels. But no matter what you do, *take the repayment provisions seriously because defaults will be reported to credit bureaus and become a part of your credit file.* Furthermore, you can't get out of repaying your student loans by filing for bankruptcy: whether you file under Chapter 7 or Chapter 13, *student loans are not dischargeable in a bankruptcy proceeding.*

Are Student Loan Programs "Too Big to Fail"? During the recent financial crisis, some banks were deemed "too big to fail" by virtue of their importance to the operation of the entire financial system. Their size consequently became the rationale for providing massive public financial assistance. Education is important to the economy, and, as discussed in this chapter, the federal government provides loans to finance undergraduate and graduate education. The financial crisis obviously put more pressure on households seeking to pay the increasing cost of

Exhibit 7.1

Federal Government Student Loan Programs at a Glance

More and more college students rely on loans subsidized by the federal government to finance all or part of their educations. There are three types of federally subsidized loan programs, the basic loan provisions of which are listed here. These loans all have low interest rates and provide various deferment options and extended repayment terms. (*Note*: Loan rates and terms shown here are for the 2016–2017 school year.)

Loan Provisions	Type of Federal Loan Program		
	Stafford Loans*	Perkins Loans	PLUS Loans
Borrower	Student	Student	Parent
Interest rate	3.76% (undergrad subsidized) 5.31% (grad/professional)	5%	4.276%
Cumulative borrowing limits	*Dependent and independent undergrad students:* $23,000; *Grad/professional students:* $138,500 (including a maximum of $65,500 in subsidized loans), or $224,000 for medical school/health professionals	$27,500 (undergrad) $60,000 (grad/professional)	No total dollar limit: Cost of attendance minus any other financial aid received
Loan fees	1.069% of loan amount	None	4.272% of loan amount
Loan term	Up to 10 years	10 years	10 years

*Data are subsidized undergraduate Stafford loans and unsubsidized graduate or professional Stafford loans, and interest rates are as of October 2016. Stafford loans can be subsidized or unsubsidized and the lifetime limits can differ. Subsidized Stafford loans also have annual borrowing limits. Perkins loans have annual limits of $5,500 per year of undergraduate study and $8,000 per year of graduate school.
Source: www.fastweb.com and www.staffordloan.com, accessed October 2016.

college educations. So how large have student loans grown? Student loans now total more than $1.3 trillion, which is greater than overall U.S. credit card debt! So the federal government has taken on a significant liability to support higher education that is important to the overall economy. This prompted a representative of the Consumer Finance Protection Bureau (CFPB) to observe that the student loan program has possibly become "too big to fail" as well.

While this chapter discusses the limits on public loans, there is no limit on private student loans. The average undergraduate student loan for graduating college students in 2016 was about $37,100. Yet about 5 percent of student borrowers owe more than $100,000. And about 25 percent of all student borrowers have a past-due balance. This level of indebtedness takes on particular significance given that the average starting salary of a recent college graduate in 2016 was about $50,200.

A survey by the Young Invincibles, a nonprofit group focusing on issues affecting 18- to 34-year-olds, found that about two-thirds of student borrowers with private loans did not understand the differences between public and private student loans. This is significant because public lenders are often more flexible than private lenders in providing financial relief when borrowers are under pressure. For example, federal programs provide public service loan forgiveness, income-based repayment, and loan repayment assistance programs.

Strategies for Reducing Student Loan Costs It's important to borrow as little as possible to cover college costs. This common-sense goal can be quantified by borrowing in light of the student's expected future salary. Based on that expected future salary, figure out what monthly payment the student will be able to afford and then use a loan repayment calculator to determine the maximum amount that can be borrowed at the expected interest rate on the loan. For example, consider using the online student loan calculator at **www.bankrate.com/calculators /college-planning/loan-calculator.aspx**. The analysis should also include looking for the lowest interest rate.

Before borrowing, it makes sense to explore all possibly available grants and scholarships and to apply for federal student aid. And upon graduation it is wise to explore the Public Service Loan Forgiveness and Loan Repayment Assistance programs. There could also be the option to consolidate federal student loans

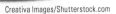

Creativa Images/Shutterstock.com

and to participate in an income-based repayment program.

Fixed- or Variable-Rate Loans Most consumer loans are made at fixed rates of interest—that is, the interest rate charged and the monthly payments remain the same over the life of the obligation. However, variable-rate loans are also being made with increasing frequency, especially on *longer-term installment loans*. As with an adjustable-rate home mortgage, the rate of interest charged on such loans changes periodically in keeping with prevailing market conditions. If market interest rates go up, the rate of interest on the loan goes up accordingly, as does the monthly loan payment. These loans have periodic adjustment dates (e.g., monthly, quarterly, or semiannually), at which time the interest rate and monthly payment are adjusted as necessary. Once an adjustment is made, the new rate remains in effect until the next adjustment date (sometimes the payment amount remains the same but the number of payments changes). Many variable-rate loans limit the maximum increase per adjustment period as well as over the life of the loan. Typically, variable-rate loans are desirable *if interest rates are expected to fall* over the course of the loan. In contrast, fixed-rate loans are preferable *if interest rates are expected to rise.*

7-1c Where Can You Get Consumer Loans?

Consumer loans can be obtained from a number of sources, including commercial banks, consumer finance companies, credit unions, S&Ls, sales finance companies, and life insurance companies. They can even be provided by brokerage firms, pawnshops, or friends and relatives. *Commercial banks* dominate the field and provide nearly half of all consumer loans. Second to banks are *consumer finance companies* and then *credit unions*. Altogether, about 75 percent of consumer loans are originated by these three types of financial institutions.

Commercial Banks Because they offer various types of loans at attractive rates of interest, commercial banks are a popular source of consumer loans. One attractive thing about commercial banks is that they typically charge lower rates than most other lenders, largely because they take only the best credit risks and are able to obtain relatively inexpensive funds from their depositors. The demand for their loans is generally high, and they can be selective in making consumer loans. Commercial banks usually lend only to customers with good credit ratings who can readily demonstrate an ability to repay a loan according to the specified terms. They also give preference to loan applicants who are account holders. Although banks prefer to make loans secured by some type of collateral, they also make unsecured loans to lower risk customers.

Consumer Finance Companies Sometimes called *small loan companies*, consumer finance companies make secured and unsecured (signature) loans to qualified individuals. These companies do not accept deposits but obtain funds from their stockholders and through open market borrowing. Because they don't have the inexpensive sources of funds that banks and other deposit-type institutions do, their interest rates are generally quite high. Actual rates charged by consumer finance companies are regulated by interest-rate ceilings (or usury laws) set by the states in which they operate. The maximum allowable interest rate may vary with the size of the loan, and the state regulatory authorities may also limit the length of the repayment period. Loans made by consumer finance companies typically are for $5,000 or less and are secured by some type of collateral. These lenders specialize in small loans to high-risk borrowers. As such, they are quite costly, but they may be the only alternative for people with poor credit ratings.

Rawpixel.com/Shutterstock.com

⬤ Go to Smart Sites

America's Credit Unions provides information to help you find a credit union in your area.

Credit Unions A credit union is a cooperative financial institution that is owned by the people ("members")

consumer finance company a firm that makes secured and unsecured personal loans to qualified individuals; also called a *small loan company*

sales finance company a firm that purchases notes drawn up by sellers of certain types of merchandise, typically big-ticket items

captive finance company a sales finance company that is owned by a manufacturer of big-ticket merchandise GMAC is a captive finance company

who use its services. Only the members can obtain installment loans and other types of credit from these institutions, but credit unions can offer membership to just about anyone they want, not merely to certain groups of people. Because they are nonprofit organizations with minimal operating costs, credit unions charge

relatively low rates on their loans. They make either unsecured or secured loans, depending on the size and type of loan requested. Membership in a credit union provides the most attractive borrowing opportunities available because their interest rates and borrowing requirements are usually more favorable than other sources of consumer loans.

Savings and Loan Associations S&Ls, as well as savings banks, primarily make mortgage loans. While they aren't major players in the consumer loan field, S&Ls can make loans on such consumer durables as automobiles, televisions, refrigerators, and other appliances. They can also make certain types of home improvement and mobile-home loans as well as some personal and educational loans. Rates of interest on consumer loans at S&Ls are fairly close to the rates charged by commercial banks. If anything, they tend to be a bit more expensive. Like their banking counterparts, the rates charged at S&Ls will, in the final analysis, depend on such factors as type and purpose of the loan and the borrower's overall creditworthiness.

Sales Finance Companies Businesses that sell relatively expensive items—such as automobiles, furniture, and appliances—often provide installment financing to their customers. Because dealers can't afford to tie up their funds in installment loans, they sell them to a sales finance company. This procedure is often called "selling paper" because the merchants are, in effect, selling their loans to a third party. When the sales finance company purchases these notes, customers are usually notified to make payments directly to it.

The largest sales finance organizations are the captive finance companies owned by the manufacturers of big-ticket items. Ford Motor Credit Corporation

The Paradox of More Financial Choices

More choices are better than fewer choices, right? That sounds like common sense. Yet behavioral finance studies show that when presented with too many financial choices, many people get overwhelmed and fall back on what they already know, or just make the simplest choice by default. This is called the *paradox of choice*. Our brains are just not wired to analyze lots of choices. The best defense is to be financially literate: do your homework, develop a framework for making such decisions, and be prepared to ask for help.

Consider the complicated choice among various mortgage types and terms. You have to choose between 15- and 30-year maturities and between fixed- and adjustable-rate mortgages; decide on the amount of the down payment, the amount of "points" (percent of the loan amount) to pay in order to reduce your mortgage rate, and when to "lock in" your rate; and you must choose the best array of up-front fees. Some consumers, when facing so many decisions, end up borrowing too much or holding mortgages that are inconsistent with their best interests. And research shows that lower financial literacy and analytical abilities are directly related to higher mortgage default rates.

This book in general, and the chapters on managing credit in particular, should help you make these complicated financial decisions.

(FMCC) and General Electric Credit Corporation (GECC) are just two examples of captive finance companies that purchase the installment loans made by the dealers of their products. Most commercial banks also act as sales finance companies by buying paper from auto dealers and other businesses. The cost of financing through a sales finance company is often higher than the rates charged by banks and S&Ls, particularly when you let the dealer do all the work in arranging the financing (dealers normally get a cut of the finance income, so it's obviously in their best interest to secure as high a rate as possible).

Life Insurance Companies Life insurance policyholders may be able to obtain loans from their insurance companies. That's because certain types of policies not only provide death benefits but also have a savings function, so they can be used as collateral for loans. Life insurance companies are required by law to make loans against the **cash value**—the amount of accumulated savings—of certain types of life insurance policies. The rate of interest on this type of loan is stated in the policy and usually carries a variable rate that goes up and down with prevailing market conditions. Although you'll be charged interest for as long as the policy loan is outstanding, these loans don't have repayment dates—in other words, *you don't have to pay them back.*

When you take out a loan against the cash value of your life insurance policy, you're really borrowing from yourself. Thus, the amount of the loan outstanding, plus any accrued interest, is deducted from the amount of coverage provided by the policy—*effectively lowering your insurance coverage.* The chief danger in life insurance loans is that they don't have a firm maturity date, so *borrowers may lack the motivation to repay them.*

Friends and Relatives Sometimes, rather than going to a bank or some other financial institution, you may have a close friend or relative who is willing to lend you money. Such loans often are attractive because little or no interest is charged. *Still, given the potential for disagreement and conflict, borrowing from friends or relatives is not advisable.* Consider doing so only when there are no other viable alternatives. Remember, a loan to or from a friend or family member is far more than a regular financial transaction: The interest is emotional, and at risk is the relationship itself.

7-2 MANAGING YOUR CREDIT

LO3 Choose the best loans by comparing finance charges, maturity, collateral, and other loan terms. Borrowing money to make major purchases—and, in genral, using consumer loans—is a sound way to conduct

> **cash value** an accumulation of savings in a life insurance policy that can be used as a source of loan collateral

your financial affairs. From a financial planning perspective, you should ask yourself two questions when considering the use of a consumer loan: (1) does this transaction fit into your financial plans? and (2) do the required debt payments on the loan fit into your monthly cash budget?

When *full consideration is given not only to the need for the asset in question, but also to the repayment of the ensuing debt*, sound credit management results. In contrast, if the expenditure in question will seriously jeopardize your financial plans, or if repaying the loan is likely to strain your cash budget, then you should definitely reconsider the purchase. Perhaps it can be postponed, or you can liquidate some other assets in order to come up with more down payment. Whatever route you choose, the key point is to make sure that the debt will be fully compatible with your financial plans and cash budget *before* the loan is taken out and the money spent.

7-2a Shopping for Loans

Once you've decided to use credit, it's equally important that you shop around and evaluate the various costs and terms available. You may think the only thing you need do to make a sound credit decision is to determine which source offers the lowest finance charge. But this could not be farther from the truth—as we'll see below, finance charges are just one of the factors to consider when shopping for a loan.

Finance Charges What's it going to cost me? That's one of the first things most people want to know when taking out a loan. And that's appropriate because borrowers should know what they'll have to pay to get the money. Lenders are required by law to explicitly state all finance charges and other loan fees.

Find out the *effective* (or true) *rate* of interest you'll have to pay on the loan, as well as whether the loan carries a fixed or variable rate. Ask the lender what the annual rate of

> When full consideration is given not only to the need for the asset in question, but also to the repayment of the ensuing debt, sound credit management results.

interest on the loan will be because it's far more relevant to compare percentage rates on alternative borrowing arrangements than the dollar amount of the loan charges. This rate of interest, known as the *annual percentage rate (APR)*, includes not only the stated cost of money but also any additional fees that might be required on the loan (APR is more fully discussed later). Also, if it's a variable-rate loan, find out what the interest rate is pegged to, how many "points" are added to the base rate, how often the loan rate can be changed, and if rate caps exist. Just as important is how the lender makes the periodic adjustments: Will the *size* of the monthly payment change, or the *number* of monthly payments?

Loan Maturity Try to make sure that the size and number of loan payments will fit comfortably into your spending and savings plans. The cost of credit generally increases with the length of the repayment period. Thus, to lower your cost, you should consider shortening the loan maturity—but only to the point where doing so won't place an unnecessary strain on your cash flow. Although a shorter maturity may reduce the cost of the loan, it also increases the size of the monthly loan payment. Indeed, finding a monthly loan payment that you'll be comfortable with is a critical dimension of sound credit management.

Lengthening the loan maturity is just one way of coming up with an affordable monthly payment. Fortunately, there are scores of Internet sites where you can quickly run through all sorts of alternatives to find the monthly payment that will best fit your monthly budget. The "tools" section of most major financial services sites on the Internet have calculators that enable you to quickly and easily figure interest rates and monthly loan payments for all sorts of loans. Generally, all you need to do is plug in a few key pieces of information—such as the interest rate and loan term—and then hit "calculate."

Maxx-Studio/Shutterstock.com

For example, go to **www.finaid.org** and try out their "Loan Calculator."

Total Cost of the Transaction When comparison shopping for credit, always look at the total cost of *both* the price of the item purchased *and* the price of the credit. Retailers often manipulate both sticker prices and interest rates, so it's hard to know what kind of deal you're getting until you look at the total cost of the transaction. Comparing *monthly payments* is a good way to get a handle on total cost. It's easy to compare total costs: *just add the amount put down on the purchase to the total of all the monthly loan payments.* Other things being equal, the one with the lowest total is the one you should pick.

Collateral Make sure you know up front what collateral (if any) you'll have to pledge on the loan and what you stand to lose if you default on your payments. If it makes no difference to you and if it's not too inconvenient, using collateral often makes sense because it may result in *lower* finance charges—perhaps half a percentage point or so.

Other Loan Considerations In addition to following the guidelines just described, here are some questions you should also ask:

▶ Can you choose a *payment date* that will be compatible with your spending patterns?

▶ Can you obtain the loan *promptly and conveniently*?

▶ What are the charges for late payments, and are they reasonable?

▶ Will you receive a refund on credit charges if you prepay your loan, or are there prepayment penalties?

Taking the time to look around for the best credit deal will pay off, not only in reducing the cost of such debt but also in keeping the burden of credit in line with your cash budget and financial plans. In the long run, you're the one who has the most to gain (or lose). Thus, *you should see to it that the debt you undertake does, in fact, have the desired effects on your financial condition.* You're paying for the loan, so you might as well make the most of it!

7-2b Keeping Track of Your Consumer Debt

To stay abreast of your financial condition, it's a good idea to periodically take inventory of your outstanding consumer debt. Ideally, you should do this every three or four months but at least once a year. To take inventory of what you owe, simply list all your outstanding consumer debt. Include *everything except your home mortgage*—installment loans, student loans, single-payment loans, credit cards, revolving

---

Financial Planning Tips

IS A 0 PERCENT APR LOAN REALLY A GREAT DEAL? WATCH THE REBATE …

Many 0 percent APR loan deals also give you the alternative of a cash-back rebate. You can have one or the other, but not both. Taking the cash-back rebate means that you finance your loan at a normal interest rate. However, accepting the rebate will allow you to borrow less, although you pay a higher interest rate.

Consider an example in which you buy a car and finance $15,000 for 48 months at a 6.7 percent APR interest rate, which requires a monthly payment of $357.11. Your total payments over the life of the loan are $17,141. Interest is $17,141 − $15,000 = $2,141. Alternatively, a 0 percent APR loan deal for the same car at the same price would cost you only $312.50 per month, which is a savings of $2,141 over the life of the loan. Assume that both loans are for 48 months and that your down payment is the same.

Now, assume that the car dealer offers a $2,000 cash-back rebate as an alternative to the 0 percent APR loan deal. This would reduce the loan amount to $13,000, which would mean a monthly payment of $309.49 at 6.7 percent APR. So the cash-back rebate provides a lower monthly payment than the 0 percent APR loan.

What can you take away from this example? If you have the choice, it is almost always better to accept a rebate than a 0 percent APR loan. This is especially the case if you don't have much down payment money, because the rebate effectively acts as a down payment.

Source: Adapted from "0% APR Loan Deals—Good Deal or Not?" http://www.best-car-deals.buyerreports.org/0-apr-loan-deals, accessed October 2016.

---

credit lines, overdraft protection lines, even home equity credit lines.

Worksheet 7.1 should be helpful in preparing a list of your debts. To use it, simply list the current monthly payment and the latest balance due for each type of consumer credit outstanding; then, total both columns to see how much you're paying each month and how large a debt load you have built up. Hopefully, when you've totaled all the numbers, you won't be surprised to learn just how much you really do owe.

An easy way to assess your debt position is to compute your *debt safety ratio* (we discussed this ratio in Chapter 6) by dividing the total monthly payments (from the worksheet) by your monthly take-home pay. If 20 percent or more of your take-home pay is going to monthly credit payments, then you're relying too heavily on credit; if your debt safety ratio works out to 10 percent or less, you're in a strong credit position. *Keeping track of your credit and limiting the amount of outstanding debt to a reasonable level is the surest way to maintain your creditworthiness.*

WORKSHEET 7.1 TRACKING YOUR CONSUMER DEBT

Use a worksheet like this one to keep track of your outstanding credit along with your monthly debt service requirements. Such information is a major component of sound credit management.

AN INVENTORY OF CONSUMER DEBT

Name: Hugh and Ruth Bates

Date: June 14, 2017

Type of Consumer Debt	Creditor	Current Monthly Payment*	Latest Balance Due
Auto loans	Ford	$ 342.27	$ 13,796.00
Education loans	U.S. Dept of Education	117.00	7,986.00
Personal installment loans	Chase Bank	183.00	5,727.00
	Bank of America	92.85	2,474.00
Home improvement loan			
Other installment loans			
Single-payment loans			
Credit cards (retail charge cards, bank cards, T&E cards, etc.)	CapitalOne Visa	42.00	826.00
	Amex	35.00	600.00
	Lowe's	40.00	1,600.00
Overdraft protection line	Hill County Schools Credit Union	15.00	310.00
Personal line of credit			
Home equity credit line	Wells Fargo	97.00	9,700.00
Loan on life insurance			
Margin loan from broker			
Other loans	Mom & Dad		2,500.00
	Totals	$ 964.12	$ 45,519.00

$$\text{Debt safety ratio} = \frac{\text{Total monthly payments}}{\text{Monthly take-home pay}} \times 100 = \frac{\$ \ 964.12}{\$ \ 5,200.00} \times 100 = \underline{18.5} \%$$

*Leave the space blank if there is *no* monthly payment required on a loan (e.g., as with a single-payment or education loan).

7-3 SINGLE-PAYMENT LOANS

LO4 Unlike most types of consumer loans, a single-payment loan is repaid in full with a single payment on a given due date. The payment usually consists of principal and all interest charges. Sometimes, however, interim interest payments must be made (e.g., every quarter), in which case the payment at maturity is made up of principal plus any unpaid interest. Although installment loans are far more popular, single-payment loans still have their place in the consumer loan market.

Single-payment loans can be secured or unsecured and can be taken out for just about any purpose. They're often most useful when the funds needed for a given purchase or transaction are temporarily unavailable but are expected in the near future. By helping you cope with a temporary cash shortfall, these loans can serve as a form of interim financing until other, permanent arrangements can be made.

7-3a Important Loan Features

When applying for either a single-payment or an installment loan, you must first submit a **loan application**, an example of which is shown in Exhibit 7.2. The loan application gives the lending institution information about the purpose of the loan, whether it will be secured or unsecured, and the applicant's financial condition. The loan officer uses this document, along with other information (such as a credit report from the local credit bureau and income verification) to determine whether you should be granted the loan. Here again, some type of *credit scoring* (as discussed in Chapter 6) may be used to make the decision. When applying for a loan, you should also consider various features of the debt, the three most important of which are loan collateral, loan maturity, and loan repayment.

Loan Collateral Most single-payment loans are secured by certain, specified assets. For *collateral*, lenders prefer items they feel are readily marketable at a price that's high enough to cover the principal portion of the loan—for example, an automobile, jewelry, or stocks and bonds. If a loan is obtained to purchase some personal asset, then that asset may be used to secure it. In most cases, lenders don't take physical possession of the collateral but instead file a **lien**, which is a legal claim that permits them to liquidate the collateral to satisfy the loan if the borrower defaults. If the borrowers maintain possession or title to *movable* property—such as cars, TVs, and jewelry—then the instrument that gives lenders title to the property in event of default is called a **chattel mortgage**. If lenders hold title to the collateral—or

take possession of it, as is often the case with stocks and bonds—then the agreement giving them the right to sell these items in case of default is a **collateral note**.

Loan Maturity As indicated previously, the maturity (or term) on a single-payment loan is usually one year or less; it very rarely extends to two years or longer. When you request a single-payment loan, be sure that the term is long enough to allow you to obtain the funds for repaying the loans *but* not any longer than necessary. Don't stretch the maturity out too far because the amount of the finance charges paid increases with time. Because the loan is retired in a single payment, the lender must be confident that you'll be able to repay it even if unexpected events occur in the future. So, the term of your single-payment loan must be reconciled with your budget, as well as with your ability to pay.

Loan Repayment Repayment of a single-payment loan is expected at a single point in time: on its maturity date. Occasionally, the funds needed to repay this type of loan will be received prior to maturity. Depending on the lender, the borrower might be able to repay the loan early and thus reduce the finance charges. Many credit unions actually permit early repayment of these loans with *reduced* finance charges. However, commercial banks and other single-payment lenders may not accept early repayments or, if they do, may charge a **prepayment penalty** on them. This penalty normally amounts to a set percentage of the interest that would have been paid over the remaining life of the loan. The Truth in Lending Act requires lenders to disclose in the loan agreement whether, and in what amount, prepayment penalties are charged on a single-payment loan.

Occasionally, an individual borrows money using a single-payment loan and then discovers that he or she is short of money when the loan comes due. Should this happen to you, don't just let the payment go past due. Instead, *inform the lender in advance so that a partial payment, loan extension, or some other arrangement needs to*

> **loan application** gives a lender information about the purpose of the loan as well as the applicant's financial condition
>
> **lien** a legal claim permitting the lender, in case the borrower defaults, to liquidate the items serving as collateral to satisfy the obligation
>
> **chattel mortgage** a mortgage on personal property given as security for the payment of an obligation
>
> **collateral note** a legal note giving the lender the right to sell collateral if the borrower defaults on the obligation
>
> **prepayment penalty** an additional charge you may owe if you decide to pay off your loan prior to maturity

Exhibit 7.2

A Consumer Loan Credit Application

A typical loan application, like this one, contains information about the person(s) applying for the loan, including source(s) of income, current debt load, and a brief record of employment.

CONSUMER CREDIT APPLICATION

LOAN INFORMATION

Amount Requested $	Purpose		Application Type ☐Individual ☐Joint

COLLATERAL INFORMATION

☐Motor Vehicle: Year____ Make_____ Model_____ Miles____
☐Personal Property   ☐Other (Describe)

APPLICANT INFORMATION

Name (Last, First, M.I.)	E-mail Address

Social Security # - -	Date of Birth / /	☐Married ☐Unmarried ☐Separated	# of Dependents

CO-APPLICANT INFORMATION

Name (Last, First, M.I.)	E-mail Address

Social Security # - -	Date of Birth / /	☐Married ☐Unmarried ☐Separated	# of Dependents

---

APPLICANT RESIDENCE INFORMATION

Address (Number, St, and Apt. or Lot # if applicable)	Telephone #
City, State, Zip Code	Time At Residence Years / Months /
Previous Address	Time At Residence Years / Months /

☐Rent ☐Live with Parents ☐Own ☐Other____	Landlord or Mortgage Holder Name: Phone #:	Monthly Payment $

CO-APPLICANT RESIDENCE INFORMATION

Address (Number, St, and Apt. or Lot # if applicable)	Telephone #
City, State, Zip Code	Time At Residence Years / Months /
Previous Address	Time At Residence Years / Months /

☐Rent ☐Live with Parents ☐Own ☐Other____	Landlord or Mortgage Holder Name: Phone #:	Monthly Payment $

APPLICANT EMPLOYMENT INFORMATION

Employer	Employer Telephone
Employer Address	Position
Gross Income: $ ☐Weekly ☐Bi-weekly ☐Monthly	Time At Job Years / Months /
Other Income: $ Source	
Previous Employer & location	Previous Emp. Phone #
Position	Time At Job Years / Months /

CO-APPLICANT EMPLOYMENT

Employer	Employer Telephone
Employer Address	Position
Gross Income: $ ☐Weekly ☐Bi-weekly ☐Monthly	Time At Job Years / Months /
Other Income: $ Source	Alimony, Child support, or separate maintenance income need not be revealed if you do not wish to have it considered as a basis for repaying this obligation.
Previous Employer & Location	Previous Emp. Phone #
Position	Time At Job Years / Months /

APPLICANT CREDIT REFERENCES

Creditor	Payment	Balance

CO-APPLICANT CREDIT REFERENCES

Creditor	Payment	Balance

☐Checking Bank Name_____ Acct#_____ ☐Savings Bank Name_____ Acct#_____	☐Checking Bank Name_____ Acct#_____ ☐Savings Bank Name_____ Acct#_____

AUTHORIZATION AND SIGNATURES

By signing this application, you promise that all information provided is true and complete. You also promise that you have revealed any pending lawsuits or unpaid judgements against you. You intend the lender and/or assignee to rely upon these promises in deciding whether to extend credit to you. You authorize a full investigation of your credit record and your employment history. You also authorize the seller and/or assignee to release information about your credit experience with them. You understand that the lender will retain this application whether or not it is approved. I understand that if the application is for a secured loan additional information may be required.

Applicant Signature	Date	Co-Applicant Signature	Date

be made. Under such circumstances, the lender will often agree to a **loan rollover**, in which case the original loan is paid off by taking out another loan. The lender will usually require that all the interest and at least part of the principal be paid at the time of the rollover.

For example, if you originally borrowed $5,000 for 12 months, then the bank might be willing to lend you a lower amount, such as $3,500 for another 6 to 9 months, as part of a loan rollover. In this case, you'll have to "pay down" $1,500 of the original loan, along with all interest due. However, you can expect the interest rate on a rollover loan to go up a bit; that's the price you pay for falling short on the first loan. Also, you should not expect to get more than one, or at the most two, loan rollovers—a bank's patience tends to grow short after a while.

7-3b Finance Charges and the Annual Percentage Rate

As indicated in Chapter 6, lenders are required to disclose both the dollar amount of finance charges and the APR of interest. A sample **loan disclosure statement** applicable to either a single-payment or installment loan can be seen in Exhibit 7.3. Note that such a statement discloses not only interest costs, but also other fees and expenses that may be tacked onto the loan. Although disclosures like this one allow you to compare the various borrowing alternatives, you still need to understand the methods used to compute finance charges because similar loans with the same *stated* interest rates may have different finance charges and APRs. The two basic procedures used to calculate the finance charges on single-payment loans are the *simple interest method* and the *discount method*.

Simple Interest Method Interest is charged only on the *actual loan balance outstanding* in the **simple interest method**. This method is commonly used on revolving credit lines and installment loans made by commercial banks, S&Ls, and credit unions. To see how it's applied to a single-payment loan, assume that you borrow $1,000 for two years at an 8 percent annual rate of interest. On a single-payment loan, the actual loan balance outstanding for the two years will

APR
Annual Percentage Rate

masuti/Shutterstock.com

be the full $1,000 because no principal payments will be made until this period ends. With simple interest, the finance charge is obtained by multiplying the *principal* outstanding by the stated annual rate of interest and then multiplying this amount by the term of the loan:

Finance Charge (Simple Interest) =
Amount of loan × Interest rate × Term of loan

Note that the term of the loan is stated in years. For example, the term would equal 0.5 for a 6-month loan, 1.25 for a 15-month loan, and 2.0 for a 2-year loan.

> **EXAMPLE: Calculating the Total Finance Charge on a Simple Interest Loan** You have taken out a $1,000, 8 percent, two-year simple interest loan. Using the above expression, the finance charge on the loan equals $160 ($1,000 × 0.08 per year × 2 years). With this type of credit arrangement, the loan payment is found by adding the finance charges to the principal amount of the loan, so you'd have to make a loan payment of $1,000 + $160 = $1,160 at maturity to pay off this debt.

To calculate the true, or annual, percentage rate on this loan, the average annual finance charge is divided by the average loan balance outstanding, as follows:

$$APR = \frac{\text{Average annual finance charge}}{\text{Average loan balance outstanding}}$$

The average annual finance charge is found by dividing the total finance charge by the life of the loan (in years). In the above example, the result is $160/2 = $80. Because no principal payments are made on these loans, the outstanding

loan rollover the process of paying off a loan by taking out another loan

loan disclosure statement a document, which lenders are required to supply borrowers, that states both the dollar amount of finance charges and the APR applicable to a loan

simple interest method a method of computing finance charges in which interest is charged on the actual loan balance outstanding

Exhibit 7.3

A Loan Disclosure Statement

The loan disclosure statement informs the borrower of all charges (finance and otherwise) associated with the loan and the annual percentage rate (APR). It also specifies the payment terms as well as the existence of any balloon payments.

FEDERAL TRUTH IN LENDING DISCLOSURE STATEMENT

Creditor: YOUR FAVORITE MORTGAGE CORPORATION
Borrower(s):

Account Number: 1111111

ANNUAL PERCENTAGE RATE	FINANCE CHARGE	Amount Financed	Total of Payments
The cost of your credit as a yearly rate	The dollar amount the credit will cost you	The amount of credit provided to you or on your behalf	The amount you will have paid after you have made all payments as scheduled
7.337 %	$ 205,017.52	$ 138,796.50	$ 343,814.02

Your payment schedule will be:

NUMBER OF PAYMENTS	AMOUNT OF PAYMENTS	WHEN PAYMENTS ARE DUE
359	$955.05	Monthly beginning 09/01/17
1	951.07	Monthly beginning 08/01/48

Variable Rate: If checked, your loan contains a variable rate feature. Disclosures about the variable rate feature have been provided to you earlier.

Demand Feature: If checked, this obligation has a demand feature.

Insurance: You may obtain property insurance from anyone you want that is acceptable to the creditor.

If checked, you can get insurance through Your Favorite Mortgage Corporation. You will pay $_____ for 12 months hazard insurance coverage. You will pay $ _____ for 12 months flood insurance coverage.

Security: You are giving a security interest in   property being purchased   property located at
1234 118TH STREET, NW, WASHINGTON, DC 20009
   Assignment of brokerage account and pledge of securities   Personal property: stocks and lease
   Assignment of life insurance policy   Other:
Late Charges: If a payment is late, you will be charged **5.000** % of the payment.

Prepayment: If you pay off early, you may will not have to pay a penalty. You may will not be entitled to a refund of part of the finance charge.

Assumption: Someone buying your house may, subject to conditions, be allowed to cannot assume the remainder of the mortgage on the original terms.

See your contract documents for any additional information about nonpayment, default, any required repayment in full before the scheduled date, prepayment refunds and penalties and assumption policy.

<u>ACKNOWLEDGMENT</u>
By signing below you acknowledge that you have received a completed copy of this Federal Truth in Lending Statement prior to the execution *of* any closing documents.

_____   _____
Borrower/Date of Acknowledgment   Borrower/Date of Acknowledgment

---

Source: Adapted from www.entitledirect.com/sites/default/files/fed_truth_in_lending.pdf, accessed October 2016.

When you're planning to take out a loan for a purchase (large or small), it's important to understand how lenders will evaluate your loan application. Here are some items they look at and what you can do to make them as good as possible:

- **Credit report.** Lenders will review your credit report from two or three of the credit reporting companies (Experian, Equifax, and TransUnion) to assure that they have all the facts. Make sure to check at least one of your reports so you'll know what the lender is seeing and can fix any potential errors that could delay or prevent the approval of your loan.

- **Debt history.** The lender will carefully evaluate how much debt you already owe, how much unused credit is available to you, how promptly you pay your bills, and whether you've applied for more credit lately.

- **Job history.** Lenders will look at your job history in order to evaluate your financial stability and associated capacity to repay the loan.

- **Savings.** The lender will want to know if you have enough money for a down payment, funds to cover an emergency, and where these funds are (e.g., savings account, checking account, and mutual funds).

- **Pre-approval.** Whether you're hoping to finance a house or a new car, you'll be in the best bargaining position when shopping if you have obtained a pre-approval (pre-qualification) for a specific loan amount.

---

loan balance is fixed at $1,000, as is the average loan balance.

> **EXAMPLE: Calculating the Annual Percentage Rate on a Simple Interest Loan** Continuing the prior simple loan example, because the loan balance outstanding remains at $1,000 over the life of the loan, the average balance outstanding is $1,000. Interest per period is $160/2 = $80. Thus, the APR is:
>
> $$\$80/\$1,000 = 8 \text{ percent}$$

The APR and the stated rate of interest are equivalent when the simple interest method is used to calculate finance charges regardless of whether loans are single-payment or installment.

Discount Method The **discount method** calculates total finance charges on the full principal amount of the loan, *which is then subtracted from the amount of the loan.* The difference between the amount of the loan and the finance charge is then disbursed (paid) to the borrower. In other words, the finance charges are paid in advance and represent a discount from the principal portion of the loan. The finance charge on a single-payment loan using the discount method is calculated in exactly the same way as for a simple interest loan:

$$\text{Finance charge (discount)} = \text{Amount of loan} \times \text{Interest rate} \times \text{Term of loan}$$

Using this approach, the finance charge on the $1,000, 8 percent, two-year, single-payment discount loan is (of course) the same $160 that we calculated earlier. However, in sharp contrast to simple interest loans, the loan repayment with a discount loan is based on the original amount of the loan, and the finance charges are deducted up front from the loan proceeds. Thus, for the $1,000 loan, the borrower will receive $840 ($1,000 less $160), and in two years will be required to pay back $1,000. The discount method consequently yields a much higher APR on single-payment loans than does the simple interest method. The Bonus Exhibit "Finance Charges and APRs for a Single-Payment Loan ($1,000 Loan for Two Years at 8 Percent Interest)" contrasts the results from both methods for the single-payment loan example discussed here. (Visit PFIN6 Online. Log in at **www.cengagebrain.com.**)

discount method a method of calculating finance charges in which interest is computed and then subtracted from the principal, with the remainder being disbursed to the borrower

> **EXAMPLE: Calculating the Annual Percentage Rate on a Discount Loan** You have taken out a $1,000, 8 percent, two-year discount loan. To find the APR on this discount loan, substitute the appropriate values into the APR expression shown previously. For this 2-year loan, the average annual finance charge is $160/2 = $80. However, because this is a discount loan, the borrower will receive only $840. And because this is a single-payment loan, the average amount of debt outstanding is also $840. When these figures are used in the APR equation, we find the true rate for this 8 percent discount loan is:
>
> $$\$80/\$840 = 9.52 \text{ percent}$$
>
> Clearly, the discount method yields a much higher APR on single-payment loans than does the simple interest method.

7-4 INSTALLMENT LOANS

LO5, LO6 Installment loans differ from single-payment loans in that they require the borrower to repay the debt in a series of installment payments (usually monthly) over the life of the loan. Installment loans have long been one of the most popular forms of consumer credit—right up there with credit cards! This is because most people find it easier on their checkbooks to make a series of small payments than to make one big payment.

Installment loans can be used to finance just about any type of big-ticket item imaginable.

Go to Smart Sites

It's easier than ever to keep track of your debt, and do it wherever you are. Mint.com's free site can help you track all your cards and even features a free app.

7-4a A Real Consumer Credit Workhorse

As a financing vehicle, installment loans can be used to finance just about any type of big-ticket item imaginable. New car loans are the dominant type of installment loan, but this form of credit is also used to finance home furnishings, appliances and entertainment centers, camper trailers and other recreational vehicles, and even expensive vacations. Also, more and more college students are turning to this type of credit as one way to finance their education. Not only can installment loans be used to finance all sorts of things, they can also be obtained at many locations. You'll find them at banks and other financial institutions as well as at major department stores and merchants that sell relatively expensive products.

These loans can be taken out for just a few hundred dollars, or they can involve thousands of dollars—indeed, installment loans of $25,000 or more are not that uncommon. In addition, installment loans can be set up with maturities as short as six months or as long as 7 to 10 years or even 15 years.

Most installment loans are secured with some kind of collateral. For example, the car or home entertainment center you purchased with the help of an installment loan usually serves as collateral on the loan. Even personal loans used to finance things like expensive vacations can be secured. In these cases, the collateral could be securities, CDs, or most any other type of financial asset. One rapidly growing segment of this market consists of installment loans secured by second mortgages. These so-called *home equity loans* are similar to the home equity credit lines discussed in Chapter 6, except they involve a set amount of money loaned over a set period of time (often as long as 15 years) rather than a revolving credit line from which you can borrow, repay, and reborrow.

For example, if a borrower needs $25,000 to help pay for an expensive, new boat, he can simply take out a loan in that amount and *secure it with a second mortgage on his home*. This loan would be like any other installment loan in the sense that it'll be repaid over a set period of time in monthly installments. Besides their highly competitive interest rates, a big

karen roach/Shutterstock.com

attraction of *home equity loans* is that the interest paid on them usually can be taken as a tax deduction. Thus, borrowers get the double benefit of *lower interest rates and tax deductibility*.

7-4b Finance Charges, Monthly Payments, and the APR

We previously discussed the simple interest and discount methods of determining finance charges on single-payment loans. In this section, we look at the two procedures—*simple and add-on interest*—that are usually used to compute finance charges and monthly payments on installment loans. (Technically, discount interest can also be used with installment loans, but because this is rare we don't cover it here.) To illustrate, we'll use an 8 percent, $1,000 installment loan that is to be paid off in 12 monthly payments. As in the earlier illustration for single-payment loans, we assume that interest is the only component of the finance charge; there are no other fees and charges.

Using Simple Interest When simple interest is used with installment loans, interest is charged only on the outstanding balance of the loan. Thus, as the loan principal declines with monthly payments, the amount of interest being charged also decreases. Because finance charges change each month, the procedure used to find the interest expense is mathematically complex. Fortunately, this isn't much of a problem in practice because of the widespread use of computers, handheld financial calculators (which we'll illustrate later), and interest rate factor tables—an example of which is provided in Exhibit 7.4. The tables show the *monthly payment* that would be required to retire an installment loan carrying a given simple rate of interest with a given term to maturity. Because these tables (sometimes referred to as *amortization schedules*) have interest charges built right into them, the monthly payments shown cover both principal and interest.

Notice that the loan payments shown in Exhibit 7.4 cover a variety of interest rates (from 6 percent to 18 percent) and loan maturities (from 6 to 60 months). The values in the table represent the monthly payments

Exhibit 7.4

A Table of Monthly Installment Loan Payments*

You can use a table like this to find the monthly payments on a wide variety of simple interest installment loans. Although it's set up to show payments on a $1,000 loan, with a little modification, you can easily use it with any size loan (the principal can be more or less than $1,000).

Rate of Interest	Loan Maturity						
	6 Months	12 Months	18 Months	24 Months	36 Months	48 Months	60 Months
6.0%	$169.60	$86.07	$58.23	$44.32	$30.42	$23.49	$19.33
6.5	169.84	86.30	58.46	44.55	30.65	23.71	19.57
7.0	170.09	86.53	58.68	44.77	30.88	23.95	19.80
7.5	170.33	86.76	58.92	45.00	31.11	24.18	20.05
8.0	170.58	86.99	59.15	45.23	31.34	24.42	20.28
8.5	170.82	87.22	59.37	45.46	31.57	24.65	20.52
9.0	171.07	87.46	59.60	45.69	31.80	24.89	20.76
9.5	171.32	87.69	59.83	45.92	32.04	25.13	21.01
10.0	171.56	87.92	60.06	46.15	32.27	25.37	21.25
11.0	172.05	88.50	60.64	46.73	32.86	25.97	21.87
12.0	172.50	88.85	60.99	47.08	33.22	26.34	22.25
13.0	173.04	89.32	61.45	47.55	33.70	26.83	22.76
14.0	173.54	89.79	61.92	48.02	34.18	27.33	23.27
15.0	174.03	90.26	62.39	48.49	34.67	27.84	23.79
16.0	174.53	90.74	62.86	48.97	35.16	28.35	24.32
17.0	175.03	91.21	63.34	49.45	35.66	28.86	24.86
18.0	175.53	91.68	63.81	49.93	36.16	29.38	25.40

*To repay a $1,000, simple interest loan.

CALCULATOR KEYSTROKES

Instead of using a table like the one in Exhibit 7.4, you could also use a handheld financial calculator to *find the monthly payments on an installment loan*. Here's what you'd do. First, set the payments per year (P/Y) key to 12 to put the calculator in a monthly payment mode. Now, to find the monthly payment needed to pay off an 8 percent, 12-month, $1,000 installment loan, use the keystrokes shown here, where

N = length of the loan, in *months*

I/Y = the *annual* rate of interest being charged on the loan

PV = the amount of the loan, entered as a *negative* number

As seen, to pay off this installment loan, you will have to make payments of $86.99 per month for the next 12 months.

required to retire a $1,000 loan. Although it's assumed that you're borrowing $1,000, you can use the table with any size loan. For example, if you're looking at a $5,000 loan, just multiply the monthly loan payment from the table by 5; or, if you have a $500 loan, multiply the loan payment by 0.5. In many respects, this table is just like the mortgage loan payment schedule introduced in Chapter 5, except we use much shorter loan maturities here than with mortgages.

EXAMPLE: Determining Installment Loan Payment Amounts Using Financial Tables Suppose you want to find the monthly installment payment required on our $1,000, 8 percent, 12-month loan using Exhibit 7.4. Looking under the 12-month column and across from the 8 percent rate of interest, we find a value of $86.99. That is the monthly payment it will take to pay off the $1,000 loan in 12 months. Multiplying the monthly payments ($86.99) by the term of the loan in months (12) results in total payments of $86.99 × 12 = $1,043.88. The difference between the total payments on the loan and the principal portion represents the *total finance charges on the loan*—in this case, $1,043.88 − $1,000 = $43.88 in interest charges.

From each monthly payment (of $86.99 in the example given earlier), a certain portion goes to interest, and the balance is used to reduce the principal. Because the principal balance declines with each payment, the amount that goes to interest also *decreases*, while the amount that goes to principal *increases*.

CALCULATOR

Inputs	Functions
12	N
8	I/Y
−1,000	PV
	CPT
	PMT
Solution	
86.99	

See Appendix E for details.

Add-On Method Some installment loans, particularly those obtained directly from retail merchants or made at finance companies and the like, are made using the **add-on method**. Add-on loans are very expensive. Indeed, they generally rank as one of the most costly forms of consumer credit, with APRs that are often well above the rates charged even on many credit cards. With add-on interest, the finance charges are calculated using the *original* balance of the loan. This amount (the total finance charges) is then added on to the original loan balance to determine the total amount to be repaid. The amount of finance charges on an add-on loan can be found by using the familiar simple interest formula:

$$\text{Finance charge (add-on)} = \text{Amount of loan} \times \text{Interest rate} \times \text{Term of loan}$$

Given the $1,000 loan that we've been using for illustrative purposes, the total finance charges on an 8 percent, one-year add-on loan would be

$$\text{Finance charge (add-on)} = \$1,000 \times 0.08 \times 1 = \$80$$

Compared to the finance charges for the same loan on a simple interest basis ($43.88), *an add-on installment loan is a lot more expensive*. Keep in mind that both of these loans would be quoted as 8 percent loans. Thus, you may think you're getting an 8 percent loan, but looks can be deceiving—especially when you're dealing with add-on interest.

Because the effective rate of interest with an add-on loan is expected to be considerably higher than the stated rate, it's especially important to determine the loan's APR. That can easily be done with a financial calculator,

Exhibit 7.5

Comparative Finance Charges and APRs*

In sharp contrast to simple interest loans, the APR with add-on installment loans is much higher than the stated rate.

	Simple Interest	Add-on Interest
Stated rate on loan	8%	8%
Finance charges	$43.88	$80.00
Monthly payments	$86.99	$90.00
Total payments made	$1,043.88	$1,080.00
APR	8%	14.45%

* Assumes a $1,000, 8 percent, 12-month installment loan.

EXAMPLE: Calculating Monthly Payments on an Add-On Installment Loan You want to calculate the monthly payments on a $1,000, 8 percent, 12-month add-on interest loan. The previously calculated finance charge is $80. Thus,

Monthly payment = ($1,000 + $80)/12 = $90

As expected, these monthly payments are higher than those on an otherwise comparable simple interest installment loan.

CALCULATOR KEYSTROKES

Here's how you *find the APR on an add-in installment loan* using a financial calculator. First, make sure the payments per year (P/Y) key is set to 12 so that the calculator is in the monthly payment mode. Then, to find the APR on a $1,000, 12-month, 8 percent add-on installment loan, use the following keystrokes, where

N = Length of the loan, in months

PV = Size of the loan, entered as a negative number

PMT = Size of the monthly installment loan payments

You'll find that the APR on the 8 percent add-on loan is a whopping 14.45 percent!

as shown next. As you can see in the below Calculator Keystrokes, the APR on this 8 percent add-on loan is more like 14.45 percent. Clearly, when viewed from an APR perspective, the add-on loan is an expensive form of financing. This is because when add-on interest is applied to an installment loan, the interest included in each payment is charged on the *initial principal*, even though the outstanding loan balance is reduced as installment payments are made. A summary of comparative finance charges and APRs for simple interest and add-on interest methods is presented in Exhibit 7.5.

Federal banking regulations require the exact APR (accurate to the nearest 0.25 percent) be disclosed to borrowers. And note that not only interest but also any other fees required to obtain a loan are considered part of the finance charges and must be included in the computation of APR.

Prepayment Penalties Another type of finance charge that's often found in installment loan contracts is the *prepayment penalty*, which is an additional charge you may owe if you decide to pay off your loan prior to

maturity. When you pay off a loan early, you may find that you owe quite a bit more than expected, especially if the lender uses the **Rule of 78s** (or **sum-of-the-digits method**) to calculate the amount of interest paid and the principal balance to date. You might think that paying off a $1,000, 8 percent, one-year loan at the end of six months would mean that you've paid about half of the principal and owe somewhere around $500 to the lender. Well, that's just not so with a loan that uses the Rule of 78s. You would actually owe $518.46 using the Rule of 78s while you

add-on method a method of calculating interest by computing finance charges on the original loan balance and then adding the interest to that balance

Rule of 78s (sum-of-the-digits method) a method of calculating interest that has extra-heavy interest charges in the early months of the loan

Using a worksheet like this, you can decide whether to buy on time or pay cash by comparing the after-tax cost of interest paid on a loan with the after-tax interest income lost by taking the money out of savings and using it to pay cash for the purchase.

BUY ON TIME OR PAY CASH

Name_ Paul Sandoval _____ Date_ 2/28/2017 _____

■ Cost of Borrowing		
1. Terms of the loan		
a. Amount of the loan	$ 12,000.00	
b. Length of the loan (in years)	3.00	
c. Monthly payment	$ 376.04	
2. Total loan payments made (monthly loan payment × length of loan in months) $ _376.04_ per month _36_ months		$ 13,537.44
3. Less principal amount of the loan		$ 12,000.00
4. Total interest paid over life of loan (line 2 − line 3)		$ 1,537.44
5. Tax considerations: • Is this a home equity loan (where interest expenses can be deducted from taxes)? . . . . □ yes ☑ no • Do you itemize deductions on your federal tax returns? ☑ yes □ no • If you answered yes to BOTH questions, then proceed to line 6; if you answered no to *either one* or *both* of the questions, then proceed to *line 8* and use *line 4* as the after-tax interest cost of the loan.		
6. What federal tax bracket are you in? (use either 10, 15, 25, 28, 33, or 35%)	_28_%	
7. Taxes saved due to interest deductions (line 4 × tax rate, from line 6: $ _____ × ____%)		$ 0.00
8. Total after-tax interest cost on the loan (line 4 − line 7)		$ 1,537.44
■ Cost of Paying Cash		
9. Annual interest earned on savings (annual rate of interest earned on savings × amount of loan: _4_ % × _12,000.00_)		$ 480.00
10. Annual after-tax interest earnings (line 9 × [1 − tax rate] — e.g., 1 − 28% = 72%: $ _480.00_ × _72_%)		$ 346.00
11. Total after-tax interest earnings over life of loan (line 10 × line 1b: $ _346.00_ × _3_ years)		$ 1,038.00
■ Net Cost of Borrowing		
12. Difference in cost of borrowing vs. cost of paying cash (line 8 − line 11)		$ 499.44

BASIC DECISION RULE: *Pay cash* if line 12 is positive; *borrow the money* if line 12 is negative.

Note: For simplicity, compounding is ignored in calculating *both* the cost of interest and interest earnings.

would only owe $509.97 with the same loan under simple interest.

The Rule of 78s method charges more interest in the early months of the loan under the rationale that the borrower has use of more money in the loan's early stages and so should pay higher finance charges in the early months and progressively less later. There's nothing wrong with that, of course. It's how all loans operate. But what *is* wrong is that *the Rule of 78s front-loads an inordinate amount of interest charges to the early months of the loan, thereby producing a much higher principal balance than you'd normally expect.* (Remember: The more of the loan payment that goes to interest, the less that goes to principal). Thus, the Rule of 78s benefits the lender at the expense of the borrower.

7-4c Buy on Time or Pay Cash?

When buying a big-ticket item, you often have little choice but to take out a loan—the item being purchased is just so expensive that you can't afford to pay cash. And even if you do have the money, you may still be better off using an installment loan *if the cash purchase would end up severely depleting your liquid reserves.* But don't just automatically take out a loan. Rather, take the time to find out if, in fact, that is the best thing to do.

Such a decision can be made by using Worksheet 7.2, which considers the cost of the loan relative to the after-tax earnings generated from having your money in some type of short-term investment. Here, it's assumed that the consumer has an adequate level of liquid reserves and that these reserves are being held in some type of savings account. (Obviously, if this is not the case, then there's little reason to go through the exercise because you have no choice but to borrow the money.) Essentially, it all boils down to this: *If it costs more to borrow the money than you can earn in interest, then withdraw the money from your savings to pay cash for the purchase. If not, you should probably take out a loan.*

Consider this situation: You're thinking about buying a second car (a low-mileage, used vehicle), but after the normal down payment, you still need to come up with $12,000. This balance can be taken care of in one of two ways: (1) you can take out a 36-month, 8 percent installment loan (with a monthly payment of $376.04), or (2) you can pay cash by drawing the money from a money fund (paying 4 percent interest today and for the foreseeable future). We can now run the numbers to decide whether to buy on time or pay cash—see Worksheet 7.2 for details. In this case, we assume the loan is a standard installment loan (where

the interest does not qualify as a tax deduction) and that you're in the 28 percent tax bracket. The worksheet shows that by borrowing the money you'll end up paying about $1,537 in interest (line 4), none of which is tax deductible. In contrast, by leaving your money on deposit in the money fund, you'll receive only $1,038 in interest, after taxes (see line 11). Taken together, we see the net cost of borrowing (line 12) is

PLANNING OVER A LIFETIME

Using Consumer Loans

Here are some key considerations for using credit in each stage of the life cycle.

PRE-FAMILY INDEPENDENCE: 20s

▸ Make sure your emergency fund is adequate.

▸ If you are married, maintain your individual credit history by not borrowing exclusively as a couple.

▸ Review your credit report at least once a year.

FAMILY FORMATION/CAREER DEVELOPMENT: 30–45

▸ Start selectively relying on savings rather than credit for large purchases.

▸ Budget to keep credit account balances easy to pay each month.

▸ Monitor your credit report at least once a year.

PRE-RETIREMENT: 45–65

▸ If you must make credit payments late, inform the lender.

▸ Monitor your credit card and bank statements for unauthorized transactions.

▸ Monitor your credit report at least once a year.

RETIREMENT: 65 AND BEYOND

▸ Consider a second mortgage or home equity line of credit to reduce borrowing costs.

▸ Budget to limit dependence on consumer credit.

▸ Monitor your credit report at least once a year.

nearly $500—so you'll be paying $1,537 to earn only $1,038, which certainly doesn't make much sense! It's far more cost-effective in this case to take the money from savings and pay cash for the car, because you'll save nearly $500.

Although $500 is a convincing reason for avoiding a loan, sometimes the actual dollar spread between the cost of borrowing and interest earned is small, perhaps only $100 or less. Being able to deduct the interest on a loan can lead to a relatively small spread, but it can also occur, for example, if the amount being financed is relatively small—say, you want $1,500 or $2,000 for a ski trip to Colorado. In this case—and as long as the spread stays small enough—you may decide it's still worthwhile to borrow the money in order to maintain a higher level of liquidity. Although this decision is perfectly legitimate when very small spreads exist, it makes less sense as the gap starts to widen.

FINANCIAL IMPACT OF PERSONAL CHOICES

Jake and Agnes Calculate their Auto Loan Backwards

Jake and Agnes Barnett budget and spend their money carefully. Their Honda CRV has over 150,000 miles and needs to be replaced. Because they drive their cars so long, Jake and Agnes have decided to buy a new car and have saved a $5,000 down payment. They are willing to make a monthly car payment of about $350 while 48 month loans are at 3 percent. Before they choose a new car, they want to determine how much they can afford to spend on it given their budget constraints.

Jake and Agnes do their auto loan calculations backwards to figure out the size of the auto loan implied by a 48 month maturity and 3 percent interest rate. Using a calculator and the approach explained in this chapter, that loan amount is about $15,813. Thus, given their down payment of $5,000, Jake and Agnes can afford a car selling for about $20,813 net of tax, title and licensing fees. They are indeed careful, if not "backward," car shoppers who explore the angles.

Filmfoto/Shutterstock.com

STUDY TOOLS 7

LOCATED AT BACK OF THE TEXTBOOK
☐ Chapter Review Card

LOCATED AT WWW.CENGAGEBRAIN.COM
☐ Review Key Term flashcards and create your own cards.
☐ Track your knowledge and understanding of key concepts in personal finance.

☐ Complete practice and graded quizzes to prepare for tests.
☐ Complete interactive content at PFIN6 Online.
☐ View the chapter highlight boxes at PFIN6 Online.

8-1 BASIC INSURANCE CONCEPTS

LO1 As most people discover, life is full of unexpected events that can have far-reaching consequences. Your car is sideswiped on the highway and damaged beyond repair. A family member falls ill and can no longer work. A fire or other disaster destroys your home. Your spouse dies suddenly. Although people don't like to think about such possibilities, protecting yourself and your family against unforeseen events is part of sound financial planning. Insurance plays a central role in providing that protection.

Life insurance helps replace lost income if premature death occurs, providing funds so your loved ones can keep their home, maintain an acceptable lifestyle, pay for education, and meet other needs. *Health insurance* covers medical costs when you get sick or become disabled. Property insurance reimburses you if, for example, your car or home are destroyed or damaged.

> Protecting yourself and your family against unforeseen events is part of sound financial planning.

These various types of insurance are intended *to protect you and your family from the financial consequences of losing assets or income when an accident, illness, or death occurs.* By anticipating the potential risks to which your assets and income could be exposed, and by weaving insurance protection into your financial plan, you lend a degree of certainty to your financial future. This chapter introduces important insurance concepts and then focuses on life insurance decisions.

8-1a The Concept of Risk

In insurance terms, *risk* is the chance of economic loss. Whenever you and your family have a financial interest in something—your life, health, home, car, or business—there's a risk of significant financial loss. To protect against such losses, you must use strategies such as risk avoidance, loss prevention and control, risk assumption, and insurance.

Risk Avoidance The simplest way to deal with risk is to avoid the act that creates it. For example, people who are afraid they might lose everything as a result of an automobile accident could avoid driving. Similarly, avid skydivers or bungee jumpers might want to choose another recreational activity. But **risk avoidance** has its costs. People who avoid driving experience considerable inconvenience, and the retired skydiver may suffer from stress-related health risks. Risk avoidance is attractive when the cost of avoidance is less than the cost of handling it some other way.

Loss Prevention and Loss Control **Loss prevention** is any activity that reduces the chance that a loss will occur (such as driving within the speed limit to lessen the chance of being in a car accident). **Loss control**, in contrast, is any activity that lessens the severity of loss once it occurs (such as wearing a safety belt or buying a car with air bags). Loss prevention and loss control should be important parts of all risk management programs.

Risk Assumption **Risk assumption** involves bearing the risk of loss. Risk assumption is an effective way to handle small exposures to loss when insurance is too expensive. For example, the risk of having your *PFIN6* text stolen probably doesn't justify buying insurance.

Risk assumption is also a reasonable approach for dealing with large, uninsurable risks, such as a nuclear holocaust. Unfortunately, people often assume risks while unaware of their exposure to loss or thinking that their insurance policy offers adequate protection when it doesn't.

Insurance An **insurance policy** is a contract between you (the insured) and an insurance company (the insurer) under which the insurance company agrees to reimburse you for any losses you suffer according to specified terms. From your perspective, *you are transferring your risk of loss to the insurance company.* You pay a relatively small *certain* amount (the insurance premium) in exchange for the insurance company's promise that it will reimburse you if you suffer a covered loss.

Why are insurance companies willing to accept this risk? They combine the loss experiences of large numbers of people and use statistical information, called *actuarial data*, to estimate the risk—frequency and magnitude—of loss for the given population. They set and collect premiums, which they invest and use to pay out losses and expenses. If they pay out less than the sum of the premiums and the earnings on them, they make a profit.

8-1b Underwriting Basics

Insurance companies take great pains in **underwriting**, deciding whom they will insure and the applicable premiums they will charge. Underwriters design rate-classification schedules so that people pay premiums that reflect their chance of loss. Through underwriting, insurance companies try to guard against *adverse selection*, which happens when only high-risk clients apply for and get insurance coverage. Insurers are always trying to improve their underwriting capabilities in order to set premium rates that will protect policyholders adequately and yet be attractive and reasonable. Because underwriting practices and standards vary among insurance companies, you can often save money by shopping around for the company offering the most favorable underwriting policies for your specific characteristics and needs.

8-2 WHY BUY LIFE INSURANCE?

LO2 Life insurance planning is an important part of every successful financial plan. Its primary purpose is to *protect your dependents from financial loss in the event of your untimely death.* Life insurance protects the assets you've accumulated during your life and provides funds to help your family reach important financial goals, even after you die. The key idea

---

risk avoidance avoiding an act that would create a risk

loss prevention any activity that reduces the probability that a loss will occur

loss control any activity that lessens the severity of loss once it occurs

risk assumption the choice to accept and bear the risk of loss

insurance policy a contract between the insured and the insurer under which the insurer agrees to reimburse the insured for losses suffered according to specified terms

underwriting the process used by insurers to decide who can be insured and to determine applicable rates that will be charged for premiums

Mega Pixel/Shutterstock.com

is that life insurance helps protect your family from the potentially catastrophic financial damage caused by the premature death of the major breadwinner(s).

> Life insurance helps protect your family from the potentially catastrophic financial damage caused by the premature death of the major breadwinner(s).

8-2a Benefits of Life Insurance

People don't like to talk about death or the things associated with it, so they often delay addressing their life insurance needs. Life insurance is intangible, and its benefits typically occur after you die. The key benefits of life insurance include the following:

▶ **Financial protection for dependents.** If your family or loved ones depend on your income, will they be able to maintain their current lifestyle, stay in their home, or afford a college education after you die? Life insurance can help replace that lost income. The most important benefit of life insurance is providing financial protection for your dependents after your death.

EXAMPLE: Using Life Insurance to Protect Dependents If you were to die prematurely, your spouse could use your life insurance proceeds to pay off the mortgage on your home. Your family could consequently continue living there comfortably, or set aside funds for your childen's college education.

▶ **Protection from creditors.** A life insurance policy can be structured so that death benefits are paid directly to a named beneficiary, which means that creditors cannot claim the cash benefits from your life insurance policy.

▶ **Tax benefits.** Life insurance proceeds paid to your heirs are not usually subject to state or federal income taxes, and under certain circumstances, they can pass to named beneficiaries free of any *estate* taxes.

▶ **Savings vehicle.** Some types of life insurance policies can serve as a savings vehicle, particularly for those who are looking for safety of principal.

Just as with other aspects of personal financial planning, life insurance decisions can be made easier by following a step-by-step approach. You will need to answer following questions:

▶ Do you need life insurance?

▶ If so, how much life insurance do you need?

▶ Which type of life insurance is best, given your financial objectives?

▶ What factors should be considered in making the final purchase decision?

8-2b Do You Need Life Insurance?

In general, life insurance should be considered if you have dependents counting on you for financial support. Neither a single adult without children or other relatives to support typically needs life insurance, nor does a child. Life insurance requirements of married couples depend on their earning potential and assets—such as a house—that they want to protect. The need for life insurance increases with children because they will suffer the greatest financial hardship from the premature death of a parent. Even non–wage-earning parents often need life insurance to ensure that children are cared for adequately if the parent dies. As families accumulate assets, their life insurance requirements continue to change. Life changes, such as divorce, also affect life insurance needs.

8-3 HOW MUCH LIFE INSURANCE IS RIGHT FOR YOU?

LO3 After confirming your need for life insurance, you must determine the appropriate amount of life insurance coverage to buy. You can use one of two methods to estimate how much insurance is needed: the *multiple-of-earnings method* and the *needs analysis method*.

The **multiple-of-earnings method** multiplies your gross annual earnings by some selected (often arbitrary) number to arrive at an estimate of adequate life insurance coverage. A rough rule of thumb used by many insurance agents is that your insurance coverage should equal 5 to 10 times your current income. Because the multiple-of-earnings method fails to consider your specific financial obligations and resources, it should be considered only a loose approximation of life insurance needs.

multiple-of-earnings method a method of determining the amount of life insurance coverage needed by multiplying gross annual earnings by some selected number

Exhibit 8.1

How Much Life Insurance Do You Need?

The needs analysis method uses three steps to estimate life insurance needs.

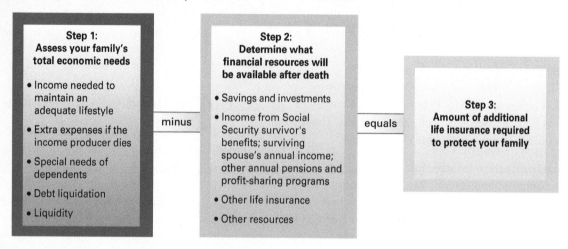

Step 1: Assess your family's total economic needs		Step 2: Determine what financial resources will be available after death		Step 3: Amount of additional life insurance required to protect your family
• Income needed to maintain an adequate lifestyle • Extra expenses if the income producer dies • Special needs of dependents • Debt liquidation • Liquidity	**minus**	• Savings and investments • Income from Social Security survivor's benefits; surviving spouse's annual income; other annual pensions and profit-sharing programs • Other life insurance • Other resources	**equals**	

EXAMPLE: Determining the Amount of Life Insurance Using the Multiple-of-Earnings Method You rely on the rule that your life insurance coverage should be between 5 and 10 times your current income. Thus, if you currently earn $70,000 a year, using the multiple-of-earnings method you'd need between $350,000 and $700,000 worth of life insurance.

The second, more detailed, approach is the **needs analysis method**. This method considers both the financial obligations and resources of the insured and involves the three steps illustrated in Exhibit 8.1 and then described.

8-3a Step 1: Assess Your Family's Total Economic Needs

The first step in needs analysis asks: *What financial resources will my survivors need should I die tomorrow?* The following five items can guide you in answering this question:

1. **Income needed to maintain an adequate lifestyle.** If you died, how much money would your dependents need monthly in order to live a comfortable life? Estimate this amount by reviewing your family's current monthly budget, including expenses for housing costs, utilities, food, clothing, and medical and dental needs. Also consider other expenses such as property taxes, insurance, recreation and travel, and savings. Recognize that the amount needed may change over time due to inflation and the needs at different stages in the life cycle.

2. **Extra expenses if an income producer dies.** These expenses include funeral costs and any expenses, such as child care and housekeeping, that might be incurred to replace services currently provided by the insured or surviving spouse, who must give up those responsibilities and find a job.

3. **Special needs of dependents.** In addition to daily economic needs, you may want to provide for special needs of your dependents, such as long-term nursing care for a disabled or chronically ill child, an emergency fund for unexpected financial burdens, or a college education fund for your children.

4. **Debt liquidation.** To leave the insured's family relatively debt free, it's necessary to determine the average amount needed to pay off outstanding bills and other similar obligations, possibly including the home mortgage.

5. **Liquidity.** If a high percentage of your wealth is in illiquid assets, the cash proceeds from life insurance can be used to pay bills and maintain assets until they can be sold at a fair market value.

needs analysis method a method of determining the amount of life insurance coverage needed by considering a person's financial obligations and available financial resources *in addition to life insurance*

8-3b Step 2: Determine What Financial Resources Will Be Available After Death

The second step is to list all current resources that will be available for meeting economic needs. The resources typically include money from savings, investments, Social Security survivor's benefits, proceeds from employer-sponsored group life insurance policies, death benefits payable from accumulated pension plans and profit-sharing programs, as well as proceeds from selling a home and other real estate, jewelry, stocks, bonds, and other assets that can be liquidated. Another important resource is income that can be earned by the surviving spouse or children. After identifying these resources, reasonable estimates of value should be made and totaled.

8-3c Step 3: Subtract Resources from Needs to Calculate How Much Life Insurance You Require

Finally, subtract the total available resources (from Step 2) from the total economic needs (from Step 1). If available resources are greater than anticipated needs, then no additional life insurance is required. If the resources are less than the needs—as is the case in most families with children—then the difference is the amount of life insurance necessary to protect the family.

The needs analysis method may seem complex, but insurance companies and Internet sites have software that can be used to quickly determine the insurance needs of individuals and families. Because *life insurance needs will likely change over time*, you should review and adjust life insurance programs (as necessary) at least every five years or after any major family changes occur, such as the birth of a child, the purchase of a home, or a job change.

Needs Analysis in Action: The Reed Family We can demonstrate the needs analysis method by considering the hypothetical case of Parker and Marie Reed. Parker Reed is 37 and the primary breadwinner in the family; he currently earns $95,000 per year. Parker and his wife, Marie, use Worksheet 8.1 to estimate the amount of life insurance needed to provide for Marie and their two children, ages 6 and 8, if he should die prematurely.

Financial Resources *Needed* after Death (Step 1) Parker and Marie Reed review their budget and decide that monthly living expenses for Marie and the two children would be about $3,500 in current dollars while the children are still living at home, or $42,000 annually. After both children leave home, Marie, now 35, will need

Syda Productions/Shutterstock.com

a monthly income of $3,000—or $36,000 a year—until she retires at age 65. At that point, the Trimble family estimates that Marie's living expenses would fall to $2,750 a month, or $33,000 annually. The life expectancy of a woman Marie's age is 87 years, so the Reed family calculates that Isabel will spend about 22 years in retirement. Therefore, as shown in the first section of the worksheet, the total income necessary for the Reed family's living expenses over the next 52 years is $1,878,000.

Although Marie previously worked as a stockbroker, they are concerned that her previous education may be somewhat outdated if she needed to reenter the workforce. So they include $25,000 for Marie to update her education and skills. Parker and Marie also want to fund their children's college educations and decide to establish a college fund of $100,000 for this purpose. Last, they estimate final expenses (i.e., funeral costs and estate taxes) of $15,000.

The Reed family uses credit sparingly, so their outstanding debts total $155,000 (a current mortgage balance of $150,000, an automobile loan of $4,000, and miscellaneous charge account balances of $1,000).

All these estimates are shown in the top half of Parker and Marie's insurance calculations in Worksheet 8.1. Note that $2,173,000 is the total amount of financial resources needed to meet their financial goals if Parker were to die prematurely.

Financial Resources *Available* after Death (Step 2) If Parker died, Marie would be eligible to receive Social Security survivor's benefits for both her children and herself. Social Security survivor's benefits, discussed in more detail in Chapter 14, are intended to provide basic, minimum

Social Security survivor's benefits benefits under Social Security intended to provide basic, minimum support to families faced with the loss of a principal wage earner

Financial Planning Tips

BUYING THE RIGHT LIFE INSURANCE FOR YOU

The following tips will help you get the right insurance policy at the right price.

- **Don't let an insurance agent tell you how much insurance you need.** Use the methods in this chapter to determine the right amount of insurance for you. Agents often have a strong motivation to sell large policies—the larger, the better.

- **Consult an independent insurance broker.** Independent brokers have access to more products than the representative of any single company.

- **Just say no to one-meeting recommendations.** A broker who makes a recommendation in the first meeting is moving too fast and probably is not considering all of your best options.

- **Know how your agent is compensated.** Is he or she compensated by a commission-alone, fee-plus-commission, or fee-only structure? If you don't know how your broker is paid, you cannot recognize possible conflicts of interest.

- **Keep your insurance and investment decisions separate.** Term insurance provides protection against premature death alone, without a savings element. Whole life and universal life policies provide both insurance and savings; consequently, they cost much more. If you combine insurance and investing, make sure you understand why and the costs of doing so. Most people buy separate insurance and investment products.

- **Always do some comparison shopping.** There are lots of alternatives, with major price differences for essentially the same product.

- **Avoid replacing old whole-life insurance policies.** After holding a whole-life policy for years, you may lose the premiums that you've paid and pay more administration fees if you replace it. Just buy more insurance if your circumstances warrant doing so.

- **Avoid buying expensive riders.** Insurance agents often try to sell riders that provide special, extra coverage. Make sure that you need any riders that you buy.

- **Consider your budget when buying insurance.** Make sure you understand and can afford new insurance before you buy it.

Source: Adapted from J. D. Roth, "14 Tips for Purchasing Life Insurance," www.getrichslowly.org/blog/2009/04/28/14-tips-for-purchasing-life-insurance/, accessed October 2016.

support to families faced with the loss of the principal wage earner. Parker and Marie visit the Social Security Administration's Internet site and estimate that Marie will receive approximately $3,200 a month, or $38,400 a year, in Social Security survivor's benefits for herself and the children until the youngest child graduates from high school in 12 years.

In the 18 years between the time the children leave home and Marie retires, the Reed family expects that Marie will be employed full-time and earn about $35,000 after taxes. After Marie turns 65, she'd receive approximately $2,250 a month ($27,000 a year) from Parker's survivor's benefits, her own Social Security benefits, and her own retirement benefits. However, Marie will have some other resources available if Brent should die. The couple has saved $65,000 in a mutual fund, and Parker's employer provides a $100,000 life insurance policy for him. Adding these amounts to Marie's expected income means that she'd have $1,849,800 in total resources available.

Additional Life Insurance Needed (Step 3) To determine the amount of life insurance that the Reed family should buy for Parker they subtract the total financial resources available ($1,849,800) from the total financial resources needed ($2,173,000) and get $323,200. Thus, Parker should buy an additional $325,000 or so of life insurance to protect his family. Now the Reed family can begin to consider which type of policy is best.

8-3d Life Insurance Underwriting Considerations

Insurance companies use *underwriting* to determine whom they will insure and what they will charge for the coverage. It begins by asking potential insureds to complete an application designed to gather information for use in estimating the likelihood that the insured will die while the life insurance policy is in effect. Underwriters use life expectancy figures to look at overall longevity for various age groups and also consider specific factors

LIFE INSURANCE NEEDS ANALYSIS METHOD

Insured's Name Parker and Marie Reed   **Date** April 12, 2017

Step 1: Financial resources needed after death

1. Annual living expenses and other needs

		Period 1	Period 2	Period 3	
a.	Monthly living expenses	$ 3,500	$ 3,000	$ 2,750	
b.	Net yearly income needed (a × 12)	$ 42,000	$ 36,000	$ 33,000	
c.	Number of years in time period	12	18	22	
d.	Total living need per time period (b × c)	$504,000	$648,000	$726,000	
TOTAL LIVING EXPENSES (add line d for each period)					$1,878,000

2. Special needs

a.	Spouse education fund		$ 25,000
b.	Children's college fund		$ 100,000
c.	Other needs		0
3. Final expenses (funeral, estate costs, etc.)			$ 15,000
4. Debt liquidation			
a.	House mortgage	$ 150,000	
b.	Other loans	$ 5,000	
c.	Total debt (4a + 4b)		$ 155,000
5. Other financial needs			0
TOTAL FINANCIAL RESOURCES NEEDED (add right column)			$2,173,000

Step 2: Financial resources available after death

1. Income

		Period 1	Period 2	Period 3	
a.	Annual Social Security survivor's benefits	$ 38,400	0	0	
b.	Surviving spouse's annual income	0	$ 35,000	0	
c.	Other annual pensions and Social Security benefits	0	0	$ 27,000	
d.	Annual income	$ 38,400	$ 35,000	$ 27,000	
e.	Number of years in time period	12	18	22	
f.	Total period income (d × e)	$460,800	$630,000	$594,000	
TOTAL INCOME					$1,684,800
2.	Savings and investments				$ 65,000
3.	Other life insurance				$ 100,000
4.	Other resources				0
TOTAL FINANCIAL RESOURCES AVAILABLE (Total income + 2 + 3 + 4)					$1,849,800

Step 3: Additional Life Insurance needed

Step 1: Total financial resources needed	$2,173,000
Step 2: Total financial resources available	$1,849,800
ADDITIONAL LIFE INSURANCE NEEDED	$ 323,200

related to the applicant's health, habits, and experiences. This information is used to determine whether to accept you and what premium to charge. For example, someone in excellent health is usually considered "preferred" and pays the lowest premium. If you have any of the risks commonly considered in life insurance underwriting—such as obesity, heart disease, or a high-risk hobby or job—then it's particularly important to shop carefully and compare the cost implications of different types of insurance policies and the underwriting standards used by different companies. For example, an overweight, hang-gliding enthusiast with a history of heart disease who walks tightropes for a living should expect to pay more for life insurance.

8-4 WHAT KIND OF POLICY IS RIGHT FOR YOU?

LO4 After determining the amount of life insurance that you need, your next step is to choose the correct type of insurance policy. Three major types of policies account for 90 to 95 percent of life insurance sales: term life, whole life, and universal life.

8-4a Term Life Insurance

Term life insurance, which provides a specified amount of insurance protection for a set period, is the simplest type of insurance policy. If you die while the policy is in force, your beneficiaries will receive the full amount specified in your policy. Term insurance can be bought for many different time periods, such as 5 years, 10 years, or even 30 years. Premiums typically can be paid annually, semiannually, or quarterly.

term (level) life insurance insurance that provides only death benefits, for a specified period, and does not provide for the accumulation of cash value

straight term policy a term insurance policy written for a given number of years, with coverage remaining unchanged throughout the effective period

decreasing term policy a term insurance policy that *maintains a level premium* throughout all periods of coverage while *the amount of protection decreases*

Types of Term Insurance The most common types of term insurance are *straight (or level) term* and *decreasing term*.

Straight Term A straight term life insurance policy is written for a set number of years during which the amount of coverage remains unchanged. The *annual premium* on a straight term policy can increase each year on an annual renewable term policy or remain level throughout the policy period on a *level premium term policy*. Exhibits 8.2 and 8.3 list representative annual premiums for annual renewable term and level premium term life policies, respectively. (*Note:* The premiums are for nonsmokers; rates for similar smoker policies would be higher in view of the greater risk and generally shorter life expectancies of smokers.) Annual renewable term policies aren't popular today. Because people now live longer, the rates for level premium term are now well below those on annual renewable term from the first year on, so they're a better value.

Decreasing Term Because the death rate increases with each year of life, the premiums on annual renewable straight term policies for each successive period of coverage will also increase. As a result, some term policies *maintain a level premium* throughout all periods of coverage, while *the amount of death benefit protection decreases*. Such a policy is called a decreasing term policy because the amount of protection decreases over its life. Decreasing term is used when the amount of needed coverage declines over time. For example, a homeowner can match her life insurance coverage with the declining balance on her home mortgage. And families with young children can match coverage with the declining level of family income needed as their kids grow up and become independent.

The type and length of term policy that you choose affects the amount of premiums that you'll pay over time. The annual premium for a specified initial amount of coverage, say $250,000, would be lowest for straight term, higher for decreasing term, and highest for annual renewable term. The premium on decreasing term is higher than the premium on straight term because most major insurance companies don't offer decreasing term policies, so there is less competition between companies offering decreasing term policies and they can therefore charge high premiums.

Advantages and Disadvantages of Term Life One of the biggest advantages of term life is that its initial premiums are lower than other types of insurance, especially for younger people. Term life is an economical way to buy a large amount of life insurance protection over a relatively short period to cover needs that will disappear over time.

The main disadvantage, however, is that term insurance offers only temporary coverage. If you need more coverage when the policy expires, renewal can be a problem if you then have factors that make it difficult to qualify

Exhibit 8.2

Representative Annual Renewable Term Life Insurance Premiums: $100,000 Policy, Preferred Nonsmoker Rates

When you buy term life insurance, you're buying a product that provides life insurance coverage and nothing more. This table shows representative rates for several age categories and selected policy years; actual premiums increase every year. As you can see, females pay less than males for coverage, and premiums increase sharply with age.

Policy Year	Age 25		Age 40		Age 60	
	Male	Female	Male	Female	Male	Female
1	$164	$143	$188	$178	$595	$471
5	167	150	228	225	920	685
10	174	163	297	264	1,579	1,108
15	186	176	388	330	2,704	1,811
20	228	225	550	443	Not available	Not available

Exhibit 8.3

Representative Level Premium Term Life Rates: $100,000 Preferred Nonsmoker Policy

This table shows representative annual premiums for $100,000 of level premium term life insurance. Although level premium costs less than annual renewable term for the same period, you must requalify at the end of each term to retain the low premium.

Age	10 Year		15 Year		20 Year		30 Year	
	Male	Female	Male	Female	Male	Female	Male	Female
25	$120	$108	$120	$108	$125	$108	$161	$139
35	125	120	131	122	142	133	180	157
40	144	135	154	145	174	161	242	195
50	216	185	257	213	315	259	523	399
60	450	324	567	412	744	545	Not available	Not available

EXAMPLE: Appropriate Use of Term Life Insurance Term life insurance is particularly useful for covering needs that will disappear over time. For example, should you die prematurely you'd like for your family to be able to pay off the mortgage. Term insurance can help achieve that goal. Yet some day in the future the mortgage will be paid off and the associated need for term insurance will end.

for insurance. Term policies that offer a **renewability** provision give you the option to renew your policy at its expiration, even if you have become uninsurable due to an accident or other illness during the original policy period. Of course, the premium will increase to reflect the greater chance of death at older ages. Renewable term policies

renewability a term life policy provision allowing the insured to renew the policy at the end of its term without having to show evidence of insurability are renewable at the end of each term until the insured reaches age 65 or 70.

Another option that overcomes some of the limitations of term insurance is a convertibility provision, which at stated times allows you to convert your term policy into a comparable whole life policy. A whole life policy, as we'll discuss next, provides lifelong protection, eliminating the need to continually renew your life insurance. Convertibility, which is standard on most term policies, is particularly useful if you need a large amount of relatively low-cost, short-term protection immediately, but in the future you expect to have greater income that will allow you to purchase permanent insurance.

One way to overcome the drawback of having to pay increased premiums at the end of each term is to purchase a longer term policy. The insurance industry has begun to offer 30-year straight term policies that lock in a set premium. For example, a 35-year-old man who qualifies for preferred rates could lock in a $250,000 death benefit for 30 years in a row and pay only a set premium of $360 a year. As with all insurance policies, however, make sure before signing up that the rate is fully locked in for the duration of the policy.

Who Should Buy Term Insurance? Because most young families on limited budgets have a high need for death protection, they should focus on guaranteed renewable and convertible term insurance. This will preserve financial resources for meeting immediate and future consumption and savings goals. Healthy older people with adequate financial resources may tend to use term policies to meet only specific coverage needs. For example, they may want to leave a legacy for their grandchildren or a charity.

One strategy is to buy term insurance and invest in a retirement plan the difference between the premium for whole life and the premium for term insurance. This is referred to as "buying term and investing the difference." As the cost of term insurance increases, the value of the investment also increases—hopefully to the level needed at one's stage of life. That is, the investment replaces the need for lifetime insurance.

convertibility a term life policy provision allowing the insured to convert the policy to a comparable whole life policy

whole life insurance life insurance designed to offer ongoing insurance coverage over the course of an insured's entire life

cash value the accumulated refundable value of an insurance policy; results from the investment earnings on paid-in insurance premiums

nonforfeiture right a life insurance feature giving the whole life policyholder, upon policy cancellation, the portion of those assets that were set aside to provide payment for the future death claim

8-4b Whole Life Insurance

Unlike term insurance, whole life insurance provides permanent insurance coverage during an individual's entire life. In addition to death protection, whole life insurance has a *savings* feature, called cash value, that results from the investment earnings on paid-in insurance premiums. Thus, *whole life provides not only insurance coverage, but also a modest return on your investment.* The savings rates on whole life policies are normally *fixed* and *guaranteed* to be more than a certain rate (historically 4 to 6 percent). Exhibit 8.4 illustrates how the cash value in a whole life policy builds up over time. Obviously, the longer the insured keeps the policy in force, the greater the cash value. Whole life can be purchased through several different payment plans, all providing for accumulation of cash values.

If a policyholder cancels his or her contract prior to death, then that portion of the assets set aside to provide payment for the death claim is available to him. This right to a cash value is termed the policyholder's nonforfeiture right. By terminating their insurance contracts, policyholders forfeit their rights to death benefits.

Types of Whole Life Policies Three major types of whole life policies are available: continuous premium, limited payment, and single premium.

Continuous Premium Under a *continuous premium whole life* policy—or *straight life,* as it's more commonly called—individuals pay a level premium each year until they either die or exercise a nonforfeiture right. The earlier in life the coverage is purchased, the lower the annual premium. Whole life should seldom be purchased by anyone simply because the *annual* premium will be lower now than if it's purchased later. Of course, the sooner people purchase whole life, the longer they have coverage in force, but (all other things being equal) the *more* they pay in total.

Of the various whole life policies available, continuous premium/straight life offers the greatest amount of permanent death protection and the least amount of savings per premium dollar. To develop a sense of the costs of this type of policy, consider the representative rates shown in Exhibit 8.5.

Limited Payment A *limited payment whole life* policy covers your entire life but the premium payment is based on a specified period—for example, 20 or 30 years—during which you pay a level premium. For stipulated age policies, such as those paid up at age 55 or 65, you pay premiums until you reach the stated age. In all cases, upon completion of the scheduled payments, *the insurance remains in force, at its face value, for the rest of the insured's life.*

Exhibit 8.4

Illustration of the Cash Value and Pure Death Protection in a Whole Life Policy

Here is an example of the projected cash value for an actual $200,000 whole life policy issued by a major life insurer to a male, age 30. For *each year* of the illustration, the difference between the $200,000 death benefit and the projected cash value represents the *death protection* offered by the insurer.

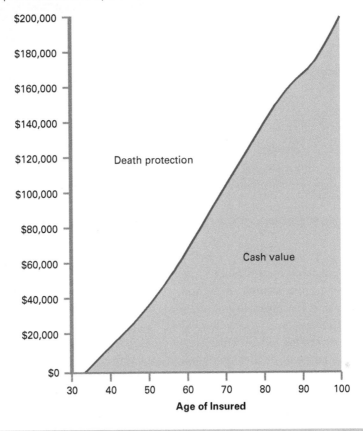

If lifelong death protection is the primary aim of the life insurance policy, then the insured should purchase continuous premium whole life instead of a limited payment policy. Because more continuous premium whole life insurance can be purchased with the same number of dollars as limited payment whole life, people who need whole life insurance are probably better off using straight life insurance to get the most for their life insurance dollars. Then, once their insurance needs are reduced, they can convert the policy to a smaller amount of paid-up life insurance. On the other hand, if people have life insurance already in force that is sufficient to protect against income loss, then they can use limited payment policies as part of their savings or retirement plans.

Single Premium *Single premium whole life insurance* is purchased with one cash premium payment at the inception of the contract, thus buying life insurance coverage for the rest of your life. Because of its investment attributes, single premium life insurance (SPLI) has limited usefulness for most families but appeals to those looking for a *tax-sheltered investment vehicle*. Like any whole life insurance policy, interest/investment earnings within the policy are tax-deferred. However, any cash withdrawals or loans taken against the SPLI cash value before age 59½ are taxed as capital gains and subject to the 10 percent penalty for early withdrawal.

Advantages and Disadvantages of Whole Life The most noteworthy advantage of whole life insurance is

Exhibit 8.5

Representative Whole Life Insurance Annual Premiums: $100,000 Policy, Preferred Nonsmoker Rates

Like any life insurance product, whole life is more expensive the older you are. Also, whole life is more costly than term because you're getting an investment/savings account, represented by the "total cash value" column, in addition to life insurance coverage.

Age	Annual Premium		Premiums Paid through Year 20		Cash Value at Year 20*		Dividend Value at Year 20**		Paid-Up Insurance at Year 20***	
	Male	Female	Male	Female	Male	Female	Male	Female	Male	Female
25	$1,057	$956	$21,140	$19,120	$17,116	$15,073	$5,439	$5,240	$17,964	$19,728
30	1,218	1,099	24,360	21,980	20,749	18,163	5,807	5,582	16,320	17,830
35	1,454	1,278	29,080	25,560	24,980	21,651	7,079	6,167	16,964	16,783
40	1,749	1,499	34,980	29,980	29,696	25,496	7,964	6,439	16,365	14,965
50	1,260	2,183	53,600	43,660	40,574	34,797	16,765	12,028	26,055	20,945
60	4,569	3,562	91,380	71,240	53,494	47,083	45,169	29,183	54,996	39,221

*Guaranteed cash value position only.

**Non-guaranteed accumulated dividend values—currently earning 4.0% on accumulated cash dividend values.

***Non-guaranteed paid-up additions dividend option—paid-up life insurance.

that premium payments contribute toward building an estate, regardless of how long the insured lives. And the insured can borrow against the policy or withdraw cash value when the need for insurance protection has expired. Another benefit (except for SPLI) is that individuals who need coverage can budget their premium payments over a relatively long period, thereby avoiding affordability and uninsurability problems. Also, earnings build up on a tax-sheltered basis, which means that the underlying cash value of the policy increases at a much faster rate than it otherwise would. Other valuable options include the ability to continue coverage after the policy lapses because premiums were not paid (nonforfeiture option) and the ability to revive an older, favorably priced policy that has lapsed (policy reinstatement).

Additional benefits of whole life policies are shown in the "Dividend Value at Year 20" and "Paid-Up Insurance at Year 20" columns of Exhibit 8.5. The dividend value column indicates the dividends available for distribution to the insured as cash, as a means of reducing premiums, or to purchase a small amount of paid-up insurance. Similarly, the paid-up insurance column indicates how much insurance coverage the policyholder can retain if the policy premiums are no longer paid beyond that point and the total cash value at that time is exchanged for the indicated amount of coverage. For example, Exhibit 8.5 shows that a male buying insurance at the age of 40 would pay a premium of $1,749 a

year. After 20 years, the cash value of the policy would be $29,696 and the accumulated value of unreceived dividends would be $7,946. If he decided to quit paying the premiums from then on, he could sacrifice the $29,696 cash value in return for life insurance coverage of $16,365 up to a maximum age specified in the policy, which is often 65. This flexibility of whole life policies is viewed as a benefit by some insurance buyers.

Dotshock/Shutterstock.com

One disadvantage of whole life insurance is its cost. It provides less death protection per premium dollar than does term insurance. Compare the premiums paid for various whole life products with those of term insurance by inspecting Exhibits 8.2, 8.3, and 8.5. You can readily see how much more expensive whole life is than term life. Another disadvantage of whole life is that its investment feature provides lower yields than many otherwise comparable vehicles. *A whole life policy should not be used to obtain the best return on investment.* However, if a person wishes to combine a given amount of death protection for the entire life of the insured (or until the policy is terminated) with a savings plan that provides a *moderate* tax-sheltered rate of return, then whole life insurance may be a wise purchase.

One way to keep the cost of whole life down is to purchase *low-load whole life insurance.* This is sold directly by insurers to consumers, sometimes via a toll-free number or over the Internet, thereby eliminating sales agents and large commissions from the transaction. As a result, cash values of low-load policies grow much more quickly than traditional policies sold by agents.

> **EXAMPLE:** Using Low-Load Whole Life Insurance—Building Cash Value Consider the case of a 50-year-old male who purchased a low-load policy with a $500,000 death benefit for an annual premium of $7,500. Within five years, his cash surrender value was projected to be more than $36,000. In contrast, a comparable, fully loaded policy was projected to produce a cash value of only $24,000.

Who Should Buy Whole Life Insurance? Some financial advisors recommend that you use cash-value insurance to cover your *permanent need for insurance*—the amount that your dependents will need regardless of the age at which you die. Such needs may include final expenses and either the survivor's retirement needs (Period 3 in Worksheet 8.1) or additional insurance coverage, whichever is less. This amount is different for every person. Using these guidelines, the Reed family in our earlier example would need about $147,000 in whole life insurance (in Worksheet 8.1: $15,000 final expenses [Step 1, line 3] plus about $132,000 of Period 3 living expenses [Step 1, line 1d for Period 3 minus Step 2, line 1f

for Period 3—$726,000 − $594,000]) and about another $151,000 in term life (in Worksheet 8.1: about $298,000 [Step 3] minus about $147,000 in permanent insurance just calculated). Limited payment whole life and single premium whole life policies should be purchased only when the primary goal is savings or additional tax-deferred investments and not protection against financial loss resulting from death.

8-4c Universal Life Insurance

Universal life insurance is permanent, cash-value insurance that combines term insurance, which provides death benefits, with a tax-sheltered savings/investment account that pays interest, usually at competitive money market rates. The death protection (or pure insurance) portion and the savings portion are identified separately in its premium. This is referred to as *unbundling.* Exhibit 8.6 shows representative annual outlays, premiums, and cash values for a $100,000 universal life policy.

With universal life, part of your premium pays administrative fees, and the remainder is put into the cash-value (savings) portion of the policy, where it earns a certain rate of return. This rate of earnings varies with market yields but is guaranteed to be more than some stipulated minimum rate (say, 4 percent). Then, each month, the cost of one month's term insurance is withdrawn from the cash value to purchase the required death protection. As long as there's enough in the savings portion to buy death protection, the policy will stay in force. Should the cash value grow to an unusually large amount, the amount of insurance coverage must be increased in order for the policy to retain its favorable tax treatment (tax laws require that the death benefits in a universal life policy *must always exceed the cash value* by a stipulated amount).

Universal life policies enjoy the same favorable tax treatment as do other forms of whole life insurance: death benefits are tax free and, prior to the insured's death, amounts credited to the cash value (including investment earnings) accumulate on a tax-deferred basis. The insurance company sends the insured an annual statement summarizing the monthly credits of interest and deductions of expenses.

Advantages and Disadvantages of Universal Life As with any insurance policy, universal life has its pros and cons. There are two primary advantages:

universal life insurance permanent cash-value insurance that combines term insurance (death benefits) with a tax-sheltered savings/investment account that pays interest, usually at competitive money market rates

Whole Life vs. Term Life Insurance and Behavioral Biases

Term life insurance is "pure" insurance, which means that if you don't die during the term, the policy pays nothing. In contrast, a whole (permanent) life insurance policy insures against death in general. The insurance company knows it will eventually pay out on the policy but does not know exactly when. A whole life insurance policy also accumulates cash value over time based on the difference in the premiums on whole life and term life policies for a given individual. A whole life policy may be viewed as life insurance with an internal investment feature. Whole life policies are consequently more expensive than term life.

Consider how whole life insurance policies can be marketed to exploit behavioral biases. Whole life insurance can be presented to appeal to the mental accounting behavioral bias. Many people think of life insurance and saving for retirement as separate though related "mental accounts," both of which have merit. Yet it's easy to confound the investment and life insurance components of a whole life policy when an agent pitches it as an automatic savings plan. Thus, the policy is marketed as offering both protection for your family in the event of premature death as well as providing an automatic savings plan that helps you consistently pursue retirement savings goals. Some agents will even argue that the whole life policy will

eventually be "free" when the cash value has grown large enough to cover the insurance premium. Many cannot resist the apparent appeal of protecting their family today in the event of premature death combined with a disciplined savings plan that helps you save for retirement and will provide "free" insurance in the future.

A rational decision maker knows that there is no such thing as "free" insurance. And such a person would separate the need to have a savings plan from the need to have adequate life insurance coverage. So what causes people to confound these decisions? The concept of premature death, protecting one's family, and planning for retirement are emotional issues. A fully aware person would likely commit to a savings plan, buy term life insurance, and invest the difference between the whole life and term life premiums. Saving and investing for retirement are separate issues that need not be combined in a whole life insurance policy. This is not to say that there are no people for whom whole life insurance is appropriate. However, life insurance and investing for retirement should not be considered without separate analyses.

Source: Adapted from Justin Reckers and Robert Simon, "Behavioral Finance and Life Insurance," www.morningstar.com /advisor/t/42987554/behavioral-finance-and-life-insurance .htm#axzz2i25ZJlmG, accessed October 2016.

▶ **Flexibility.** The annual premium that you pay can be increased or decreased from year to year because the cost of the death protection *may be covered from either the annual premium or the accumulation account* (i.e., the cash value). If the accumulation account is adequate, you can use it to pay the annual premium. The death benefit also can be increased (subject to evidence of insurability) or decreased, and you can change from the level benefit type of policy to the cash value plus a stated amount of insurance.

▶ **Savings feature.** A universal life insurance policy credits cash value at the "current" rate of interest, and this *current* rate of interest may well be higher than the *guaranteed* minimum rate.

Universal life's flexibility in making premium payments, although an attractive feature, is also one of its two major drawbacks:

▶ **Changing premiums and protection levels.** A policyholder who economizes on premium payments in early years may find that premiums must be higher than originally planned in later policy years to keep the policy in force. Indeed, some policyholders expect their premiums to vanish once cash value builds to a certain level, but often the premiums never disappear, or they reappear when interest rates fall.

▶ **Charges or fees.** Universal life usually carries heavy fees compared to other policy types. Most states require the insurance company to issue an annual disclosure statement spelling out premiums paid,

Exhibit 8.6

Representative Universal Life Insurance Annual Outlays: $100,000 Policy, Preferred Nonsmoker Rates

Universal life premiums are lower than whole life and can vary over the policy's life. After deducting the cost of the death benefit and any administrative fees from your annual contribution, the rest goes into an accumulation account and builds at a variable rate. In this example, the current rate is 2.95 percent and the guaranteed rate is only 2 percent.

Age	Annual Premium Outlay		Premiums Paid through Year 20		Cash Surrender Value at Year 20*		Cash Surrender Value at Year 20**	
	Male	Female	Male	Female	Male	Female	Male	Female
25	$864	$772	$17,280	$15,440	$13,435	$12,099	$16,838	$15,248
30	1,001	895	20,020	17,900	15,753	14,106	19,913	17,881
35	1,172	1,048	23,440	20,960	18,144	16,185	23,560	21,111
40	1,390	1,234	27,800	24,680	20,352	18,060	27,821	25,012
50	2,016	1,761	40,320	35,220	22,187	20,743	38,846	35,175
60	3,104	2,670	62,154	53,400	10,817	19,835	52,341	47,593

*Based on an minimum guaranteed annual interest rate of 2.00%.

**Based on the current annual interest rate of 2.95%.

all expenses and mortality costs, interest earned, and beginning and ending cash values.

Go to Smart Sites

What is your life worth? Interactive apps for Android and iOS devices allow you to determine how much life insurance you need. A highlight box in each chapter of PFIN Online includes "Smart Sites," a list of resources and sites that offer additional information on topics in the PFIN text.

Who Should Buy Universal Life Insurance? Universal life is a suitable choice if you're looking for a savings vehicle with greater potential returns than offered by a whole life policy. Its flexible nature makes it particularly useful for people anticipating changes, such as the birth of a child, that require changes in death protection.

8-4d Other Types of Life Insurance

Besides term, whole life, and universal life, you can buy several other types of life insurance products, including variable life insurance, group life, and other special-purpose life policies such as credit life, mortgage life, and industrial life insurance. These insurance products serve diverse needs.

Variable Life Insurance A **variable life insurance** policy goes further than universal life policies in combining death benefits and savings. The policyholder decides how to invest the money in the savings (cash-value) component. The investment accounts are set up just like *mutual funds*, and most firms that offer variable life policies let you choose from a full menu of different types of funds. Variable life insurance does not guarantee a *minimum return*. And as the name implies, the amount of insurance coverage provided varies with the profits (and losses) generated in the investment account. Exhibit 8.7 demonstrates how two possible investment return scenarios would affect the cash value and death benefits of a variable life insurance policy for a 45-year-old, nonsmoking male over a 20-year period.

Variable life is more of an investment vehicle than a life insurance policy. If you want the benefits of higher investment returns, then you must also be willing to assume the risks of reduced insurance coverage. Therefore, *you should use extreme care when buying variable life insurance.* Indeed, variable life insurance has become less popular since the financial crisis of 2008–2009.

Group Life Insurance Under **group life insurance**, one master policy is issued, and each eligible group member

variable life insurance life insurance in which the benefits are a function of the returns being generated on the investments selected by the policyholder

group life insurance life insurance that provides a master policy for a group; each eligible group member receives a certificate of insurance

Exhibit 8.7

Representative Variable Life Insurance Values: $100,000 Policy, Preferred Nonsmoker, Male, Age 45

Variable life insurance pays a death benefit whose amount is tied to the policy's investment returns. The cash value created over the life of the policy is also related to investment returns. This table shows the effects of 6 percent and 12 percent annual returns over a 20-year period. Lower returns result in lower cash value and death benefits; higher returns result in higher cash value and death benefits.

Policy Year	Total Premiums Paid	6% Return		12% Return	
		Cash Value	Death Benefit	Cash Value	Death Benefit
1	$1,575	$995	$100,995	$1,064	$101,064
5	8,705	5,244	105,244	5,705	105,705
10	19,810	10,592	110,592	15,365	115,365
15	33,986	15,093	115,093	27,688	127,688
20	52,079	17,080	117,080	43,912	143,912

receives a certificate of insurance. Group life is nearly always term insurance, and the premium is based on the group's characteristics as a whole rather than the characteristics of any specific individual. Employers often provide group life insurance as a fringe benefit for their employees. However, just about any type of group (e.g., a labor union, a professional association, or an alumni organization) can secure a group life policy, as so long as the insurance is only incidental to the reason for the group's existence.

Accounting for about one-third of all life insurance in the United States, group life is one of the fastest-growing areas of insurance. Group life policies generally provide that individual members who leave the group may continue the coverage by converting their protection to individually issued whole life policies. It is important to note that conversion normally doesn't require evidence of insurability, as long as it occurs within a specified period. Of course, after conversion, the individual pays all premiums.

The availability of group coverage through employee benefit programs should be considered when developing a life insurance program. Because of its potentially temporary nature and relatively low benefit amount (often equal to about one year's salary), only in rare cases should a family rely solely on group life insurance to fulfill its primary income-protection requirements.

Other Special-Purpose Life Policies Use caution before buying any of the following types of life insurance:

▶ **Credit life insurance.** Banks, finance companies, and other lenders generally sell credit life insurance in conjunction with installment loans. Usually credit life is a term policy of less than five years and with a face value corresponding to the outstanding balance on the loan. Although liquidating debts on the death of a family breadwinner is often desirable, it's usually preferable to do so with term or whole life insurance because credit life is an expensive form of life insurance.

▶ **Mortgage life insurance.** Mortgage life insurance is a term policy designed to pay off the mortgage balance on a home in the event of the borrower's death. As in the case of credit life, this need can usually be met less expensively by shopping the market for a suitable decreasing term policy.

▶ **Industrial life insurance.** Sometimes called home service life insurance, this whole life insurance is issued in policies with small face amounts, often $1,000 or less. Agents call on policyholders weekly or monthly to collect the premiums. Industrial life insurance costs much more per $1,000 of coverage than regular whole life policies, primarily because of its high marketing costs. Even so, some insurance authorities believe that industrial life insurance offers the only practical way to deliver coverage to low-income families.

credit life insurance life insurance sold in conjunction with installment loans

mortgage life insurance a term policy designed to pay off the mortgage balance in the event of the borrower's death

industrial life insurance (home service life insurance) whole life insurance issued in policies with relatively small face amounts, often $1,000 or less

8-5 BUYING LIFE INSURANCE

LO5 Once you have evaluated your personal financial needs and have become familiar with the basic life insurance options, you're ready to begin shopping for a life insurance policy. Exhibit 8.8 summarizes the major advantages and disadvantages of the most popular types of life insurance we've discussed in this chapter. The key activities involved in shopping for life insurance include: (1) comparing costs and features of competitive policies, (2) selecting a financially healthy insurance company, and (3) choosing a good agent.

> The costs of similar life insurance policies can vary considerably from company to company.

8-5a Compare Costs and Features

The costs of similar life insurance policies can vary considerably from company to company. Comparison shopping can save thousands of dollars over the life of a policy. For example, the total cost for a 10-year, $250,000, term life policy at preferred rates for a 25-year-old can range from $1,170 to more than $2,000. The Bonus Exhibit, "Major Insurance Rating Agencies," summarizes differences in the key features of various types of life insurance. (Visit PFIN6 Online. Log in at **www.cengagebrain.com.**) If you have an unusual health problem or some other type of complication, then spending time checking out several companies can really pay off.

It is not enough, however, to look only at current rates. You'll also need to know how long the rates are locked in and find out about guaranteed rates—the maximum you can be charged when you renew. A guaranteed policy may cost another $20 a year, but you won't be hit with unexpected, larger rate increases later. Establish for how long you'll need the coverage, and then find the best rates for the total period; low premiums for a five-year policy may jump when you renew for additional coverage. Also be sure that you're getting the features you need, such as convertibility of term policies.

Exhibit 8.8

Major Advantages and Disadvantages of the Most Popular Types of Life Insurance

Major advantages and disadvantages of the most popular types of life insurance are summarized here. They should be considered when shopping for life insurance.

Type of Policy	Advantages	Disadvantages
Term	• Low initial premiums • Simple, easy to buy	• Provides only temporary coverage for a set period. • May have to pay higher premiums when policy is renewed.
Whole life	• Permanent coverage • Savings vehicle: cash value builds as premiums are paid • Some tax advantages on accumulated earnings	• Cost: provides less death protection per premium dollar than term. • Often provides lower yields than other investment vehicles. • Sales commissions and marketing expenses can increase costs of fully loaded policy.
Universal life	• Permanent coverage • Flexible: lets insured adapt level of protection and cost of premiums • Savings vehicle: cash value builds at current rate of interest • Savings and death protection identified separately	• Can be difficult to evaluate true cost at time of purchase; insurance carrier may levy costly fees and charges
Variable life	• Investment vehicle: insured decides how cash value will be invested	• Higher risk

Financial Planning Tips

BREEZING THROUGH YOUR LIFE INSURANCE MEDICAL EXAM

You're more likely to pass your life insurance medical exam if you keep the following tips in mind:

- **Know what to expect.** The examiner will measure and record your height, weight, blood pressure, and pulse rate, and may collect blood and urine samples. Also, expect the examiner to confirm the answers that you provided on your life insurance application. The test results will be sent to the insurance company and the underwriter, which will assess your risk and determine your life insurance premiums.

- **Drink water before the exam.** This makes it easier to draw blood.

- **Fast before the exam.** Eating within four to eight hours before the exam could elevate your glucose levels.

- **Don't do a rigorous workout for at least 12 hours prior to the exam.** Take it easy, and avoid even a fast walk or a workout on an aerobic machine. Strenuous exercise before a physical can elevate the protein found in your urine to a point of concern.

- **Avoid alcohol for at least 12 hours before the exam.** Drinking too much alcohol can dehydrate you and possibly elevate liver function test flags, which can push you into a riskier category.

- **Avoid caffeine and nicotine for at least a couple of hours prior to the exam.** Caffeine and nicotine tend to elevate blood pressure. If you simply cannot make it without coffee, be sure to drink it black—no cream or sugar.

- **Bring a list of your medications.** Examiners typically take a medical history during the exam, which requires a list of your current prescriptions and over-the-counter medications.

- **Be sure to get to bed early the night before the exam.** While it might not directly affect your test results, you'll be more relaxed and this should help moderate your blood pressure if you have "white coat anxiety."

Source: Adapted from Jeffrey Steele, "Ace Your Life Insurance Medical Exam," www.insurance.com/life-insurance/life-insurance-basics /life-insurance-medical-exam.aspx, accessed October 2016.

Finally, be sure the insurance policies that you are comparing *have similar provisions and amounts.* In other words, don't compare a $100,000 term life policy from one company with a $150,000 universal life policy from another. Instead, *first decide how much and what kind of policy you want, and then compare costs.* For similar cash-value policies, you may find it useful to compare interest-adjusted cost indexes that are often shown on policy illustrations.

It's easy to gather information that allows you to compare costs and features. Term life quote services, available over the phone or on the Internet, can streamline the selection process by providing you, free of charge, with the names of several companies offering the lowest-cost policies based on your specifications. Probably the fastest-growing source of life insurance quotes and policies in recent years is the Internet. You not only can obtain quick, real-time quotes but also can buy insurance electronically. Buying on the Internet allows you to avoid dealing with insurance salespeople, and you can purchase the policies (usually term insurance only) on cost-effective terms. For example, one major life insurer offers discounts of up to 20 percent for term life policies purchased online. Of course, you'll still need a physical exam, but often the insurance company will send a qualified technician/nurse to your home or office to take a blood sample and other basic readings. Efinancial (**www .efinancial.com**), Select Quote Insurance Services (**www.selectquote.com**), Insure.com (**www.insure .com**), and Matrix Direct Insurance Services (**http:// matrixdirect.com**) maintain databases of life insurance policy costs for various companies and will also act as your agent to buy a policy if you wish. Insure. com and MatrixDirect.com provide quotes for both term insurance and whole life. Also, don't overlook companies that sell directly to the public or offer low-load policies, such as Ameritas, Lincoln Benefit, and USAA (for the military and their families).

8-5b Select an Insurance Company

Selecting a life insurance company is an important part of shopping for life insurance. You want to be sure that the company will be around and have the assets to pay your beneficiaries. Factors to consider before making the final choice include the firm's reputation, its financial history, commissions and other fees, and the specifics of their policy provisions. If you're choosing a company for a cash-value life insurance policy, the company's investment performance and dividend history are also important considerations.

Unless there's a good reason to do otherwise, you should probably limit the companies that you consider to those that have been doing business for 25 years or more and that have annual premium volume of more than $100 million. These criteria will rule out a lot of smaller firms, but there are still plenty of companies left to choose from. You may also find that one company is preferable for your term protection and another for your whole life needs.

Private rating agencies—A.M. Best, Fitch, Moody's, Standard & Poor's, and Weiss—have done much of the work for you. These agencies use publicly available financial data to evaluate the insurance companies' ability to pay future claims made by policyholders, known as their *claims paying ability*. The Bonus Exhibit "Key Features of Various Types of Life Insurance" provides detailed contact information for each of these agencies. (To view this exhibit, go to CourseMate for PFIN6. Log in at **www.cengagebrain.com**.) The ratings agencies then give each insurance firm a "grade" based on their analysis of the firm's financial data.

Most experts agree that it's wise to purchase life insurance only from insurance companies that are assigned ratings by at least two of the major rating agencies and are consistently rated in the top two or three categories (e.g., rated Aaa, Aa1, or Aa2 by Moody's) by each of the major agencies from which they received ratings. Most public libraries and insurance agents have these ratings, and each of the agencies mentioned previously have an Internet presence where insurance company ratings may be found.

The easiest way to comprehensively evaluate an insurance company is to rely on the Comdex ranking, which considers the ratings established by A. M. Best, Standard & Poor's, Moody's Investors Services, and Fitch. (See **http://www.ebixlife.com/vitalsigns/comdexcalc.aspx** for more information.)

8-5c Choosing an Agent

There's an old axiom in the life insurance business that life insurance is sold, not bought. Life insurance agents play a major role in most people's decision to buy life insurance. Unless you plan to buy all your life insurance via the Internet, selecting a good life insurance agent is important because you'll be relying on him or her for guidance in making some important financial decisions.

When seeking a good life insurance agent, try to obtain recommendations from other professionals who work with agents. Bankers in trust departments, attorneys, and accountants who are specialists in estate planning are usually good sources. In contrast, be a bit wary of selecting an agent simply because of the agent's aggressiveness in soliciting your patronage.

Don't assume that just because agents are licensed, they are competent and will serve your best interests. Consider an agent's formal and professional level of educational attainment. Does the agent have a college degree with a major in business or insurance? Does the agent have a professional designation, such as Chartered Life Underwriter (CLU), Chartered Financial Consultant (ChFC), or Certified Financial Planner® (CFP®)? These designations are awarded only to those who meet experience requirements and pass comprehensive examinations in such fields as life and health

YOU CAN DO IT NOW: Check Out the Best Life Insurance Companies The ratings of the best life insurance companies and an overall ranking, known as the Comdex rank, are provided online at **http://toplifeinsurancereviews.com/comdex-ranking-life-insurance/**. Go to the site and jot down the top five life insurance companies. Now you have a great start when you are ready to shop for life insurance—you can **do it now**.

tubartstock/Shutterstock.com

insurance, estate and pension planning, investments, and federal income tax law.

Observe how an agent reacts to your questions. Does the agent use fancy buzzwords and generic answers, or does she really listen attentively and, after some thought, logically answer your questions? These and other personal characteristics should be considered. In most cases, you should talk with more than one agent and discuss the pros and cons of each with your spouse or other trusted person before making a commitment.

Go to Smart Sites

Looking for an insurance agent? Link to the Web site sponsored by the Independent Insurance Agents and Brokers of America, Inc.

8-6 KEY FEATURES OF LIFE INSURANCE POLICIES

LO6 A life insurance policy is a contract that spells out the policyholder's and the insurer's rights and obligations and policy features. There's no such thing as a standard life insurance policy, and policies can vary from state to state. Even so, certain elements are common in most life insurance contracts.

8-6a Life Insurance Contract Features

Key features found in most life insurance contracts are the beneficiary clause, settlement options, policy loans, premium payments, grace period, nonforfeiture options, policy reinstatement, and change of policy.

Beneficiary Clause The **beneficiary** is the person who will receive the death benefits of the policy on the insured's death. All life insurance policies should have one or more beneficiaries. An insured should name both a *primary beneficiary* and various *contingent beneficiaries*. The

> **beneficiary** a person who receives the death benefits of a life insurance policy after the insured's death

primary beneficiary receives the entire death benefit if he or she is surviving when the insured dies. If the primary beneficiary does not survive the insured, the insurer will distribute the death benefits to the contingent beneficiaries. If neither primary nor contingent beneficiaries are living at the death of the insured, then the death benefits pass to the insured's estate and are distributed by the probate court according to the insured's will or, if no will exists, according to state law.

The identification of named beneficiaries should be clear. For example, if a man designating his beneficiary as "my wife," later divorces and remarries, there could be a controversy as to which wife is entitled to the benefits. Obviously, you should change your named beneficiary if circumstances such as marital status change. The person you name as a beneficiary can be changed at any time by notifying the insurance company, so as long as you didn't indicate an *irrevocable beneficiary* when you took out the policy.

Settlement Options Insurance companies generally offer several ways of paying life insurance policy death proceeds. The distribution method can either be permanently established by the policyholder before death or left up to the beneficiary when the policy proceeds are paid out:

▶ **Lump sum.** This is the most common settlement option, chosen by more than 95 percent of policyholders. The entire death benefit is paid in a single amount, allowing beneficiaries to use or invest the proceeds soon after death occurs.

▶ **Interest only.** The insurance company keeps policy proceeds for a specified time; the beneficiary receives interest payments, usually at some guaranteed below-market rate. This option is used when there's no current need for the principal—for example, proceeds could be left on deposit until children go to college, with interest supplementing family income. However, it's important to be aware that the interest received is normally taxable.

▶ **Fixed period.** The face amount of the policy, along with interest earned, is paid to the beneficiary over a fixed time period. For example, a 55-year-old beneficiary may need additional income until Social Security benefits start.

Skylines/Shutterstock.com

Most insurance agents are ethical and professional. However, in order to protect yourself from the few who are not, it's important to keep in mind some potential conflicts of interest between you and insurance agents and brokers. Most have to do with sales commission incentives that can conflict with you getting the best advice.

- Agents only rarely disclose their commissions—and likely will do so only if you ask. Ask agents about the commissions that they receive on competing insurance products. If they balk at the request, it's time to find another agent.

- Agents often avoid bringing up the negative aspects of a policy to make the sale. This also tempts some agents to oversimplify policy features. You need to ask the hard questions.

- While some existing policies should be kept and some replaced, agents only get paid for giving advice when it leads to commissions. So agents can be unreliable sources of advice about the performance of an existing policy. Getting a second opinion from an agent with another firm is always a good idea.

- Watch out when agents present company illustrations and projections of future policy performance. It's hard to make good decisions solely on the basis of comparing one illustration with another. Don't accept the projections and assumptions uncritically.

- Be aware that some lawyers, accountants, and financial planners don't ask hard questions about life insurance proposals because they depend on life insurance agents for business referrals. Thus, it can be hard to find objective sources of advice concerning life insurance proposals. Consider using a fee-only insurance advisor.

Notwithstanding these potential conflicts of interest, you can accomplish a lot by doing your own homework and by relying on recommended advisors who are true fiduciaries that put their clients first.

Source: Life Insurance Advisors, Inc., "Conflicts and Limitations of Life Insurance Agents," www.lifeinsuranceadvisorsinc.com/conflicts.html, accessed October 2016.

▶ **Fixed amount.** The beneficiary receives policy proceeds in regular payments of a fixed amount until the proceeds run out.

▶ **Life income.** The insurer guarantees to pay the beneficiary a certain amount for the rest of his or her life, based on the beneficiary's sex, age when benefits start, life expectancy, policy face value, and interest rate assumptions. This option appeals to beneficiaries who don't want to outlive the income from policy proceeds and then become dependent on others for support. An interesting variation of this settlement option is the *life-income-with-period-certain option,* which guarantees a specified number of payments that would pass to a secondary beneficiary if the original beneficiary dies before the period ends.

Policy Loans An advance made by a life insurance company to a policyholder against a whole life policy is called a **policy loan**. These loans are secured by the cash value of the life insurance policy. Although these loans do *not* have to be repaid, any balance plus interest on the loan remaining at the insured's death is *subtracted from the proceeds of the policy.* Typically, policies offer either a fixed-rate loan or a rate that varies with market interest rates on high-quality bonds. Policy loans should be used only if the insured's estate is large enough to cover the accompanying loss of death proceeds when the loan is not repaid. A word of caution: *Be careful with these loans. Unless certain conditions are met, the IRS may treat them as withdrawals, meaning they could be subject to tax penalties.*

Premium Payments All life insurance contracts specify when premiums, which are normally paid in advance, are due. Most insurers allow the policyholder to elect to pay premiums annually, semiannually, quarterly, or monthly, but they typically charge a fee to those paying more often than annually.

Grace Period The *grace period* permits the policyholder to retain full death protection for a short period (usually 31 days) after missing a premium payment date. In other words, you won't lose your insurance protection just because you're a little late in making the premium payment.

> **policy loan** an advance, secured by the cash value of a whole life insurance policy, made by an insurer to the policyholder

Nonforfeiture Options As noted earlier, a *nonforfeiture option* pays a cash value life insurance policyholder the policy's cash value when a policy is terminated before its maturity. State laws require that all permanent whole, universal, or variable life policies contain a nonforfeiture provision. Rather than receiving the policy's cash value, insurance companies usually offer the following two options—*paid-up insurance* and *extended term insurance*:

▶ **Paid-up insurance.** The policyholder uses the cash value to buy a new, single premium policy with a lower face value. For example, a policy canceled after 10 years might have a cash value of $90.84 per $1,000 of face value, which will buy $236 of paid-up whole life insurance. This paid-up insurance is useful because the cash value would continue to grow from future interest earnings, even though the policyholder makes no further premium payments. This option is useful when a person's income and need for death protection decline, but he or she still wants some coverage.

▶ **Extended term insurance.** The insured uses the accumulated cash value to buy a term life policy for the same face value as the lapsed policy and a coverage period determined by the amount of term protection that the single premium payment buys at the insured's present age. This option usually goes into effect automatically if the policyholder quits paying premiums and gives no instructions to the insurer.

multiple indemnity clause a clause in a life insurance policy that typically doubles or triples the policy's face amount if the insured dies in an accident

disability clause a clause in a life insurance contract containing a *waiver-of-premium benefit* alone or coupled with *disability income*

guaranteed purchase option an option in a life insurance contract giving the policyholder the right to purchase additional coverage at stipulated intervals without providing evidence of insurability

Policy Reinstatement As long as a whole life policy is under the reduced paid-up insurance option or the extended term insurance option, the policyholder may reinstate the original policy, usually within three to five years of its lapsing, by paying all back premiums, plus interest at a stated rate, and by providing evidence that he or she can pass a physical examination and meet any other insurability requirements. *Reinstatement* revives the original contractual relationship between the company and the policyholder. Before exercising a reinstatement option, a policyholder should determine whether buying a new policy would be less costly.

Change of Policy Many life insurance contracts contain a provision that permits the insured to switch from one policy form to another. For instance, a policyholder may decide that he'd rather have a policy that is paid up at age 65 rather than his current, continuous premium whole life policy. A change-of-policy provision allows this change without penalty. When policyholders change from lower- to higher-coverage policies, they may need to prove insurability.

8-6b Other Policy Features

Along with the key contractual features described earlier, here are some other policy features to consider:

▶ **Multiple indemnity clause.** Multiple indemnity clauses increase the face amount of the policy, most often doubling or tripling it, if the insured dies in an accident. This benefit is usually offered to the policyholder at a small additional cost. This coverage should be ignored as a source of funds when determining insurance needs because it offers no protection if the insured's death is due to illness.

▶ **Disability clause.** A disability clause may contain a waiver-of-premium benefit alone or coupled with disability income. A *waiver-of-premium benefit* excuses the payment of premiums on the life insurance policy if the insured becomes totally and permanently disabled prior to age 60 (or sometimes age 65). Under the *disability income portion*, the insured not only is granted a waiver of premium, but also receives a monthly income equal to $5 or $10 per $1,000 of policy face value. Some insurers will continue these payments for the life of the insured; others terminate them at age 65. Disability riders for a waiver of premium and disability income protection are relatively inexpensive and can be added to most whole life policies but generally not to term policies.

▶ **Guaranteed purchase option.** The policyholder who has a guaranteed purchase option may purchase additional coverage at stipulated intervals without providing evidence of insurability. This option is frequently offered to buyers of a whole life policy who are under age 40. Increases in coverage usually can be purchased every

Steven Frame/Shutterstock.com

the death benefits from a whole or universal life policy prior to death. Some insurers offer this option at no charge to established policyholders if the insured suffers a terminal illness that is expected to result in death within a specified period (such as six months to a year) or needs an expensive treatment (such as an organ transplant) to survive. These benefits can also be added as a *living benefit rider* that pays a portion of a policy's death benefit in advance, usually about 2 percent per month, for long-term health care such as nursing home expenses. This rider can add an extra 5 to 15 percent to the normal life insurance premium, and benefits are capped at some fixed percentage of the death benefit.

▶ **Viatical settlement.** Like a living benefits feature, this option allows a terminally ill insurance holder to receive a percentage of the insurance policy's death benefit for immediate use. But unlike the living benefits feature, this isn't handled through the insurance company but rather through a third-party investor. The insured sells an interest in the life insurance policy to the investor, who then becomes the policy's beneficiary, and then receives a cash amount from that investor—most commonly 60 percent of the policy value. After the insured dies, the investor receives the balance from the policy.

Approach viatical settlements carefully because they mean giving up all future claims on the life insurance policy and can also affect the insured's Medicare eligibility in some cases. Note also that some viatical settlement companies—the firms that arrange the transfer between insureds and investors—have been scrutinized by government agencies for unethical practices.

8-6c Understanding Life Insurance Policy Illustrations

A **life insurance policy illustration** is a hypothetical representation of a policy's performance that reflects the most important assumptions that the company relies on when presenting the policy results to a prospective client. Insurance illustrations are complicated and often contain more than 20 pages of numbers

three, four, or five years in sums equal to the amount of the original policy or $10,000, whichever is lower. This option should be attractive to individuals whose life insurance needs and ability to pay are expected to increase over a 5- to 15-year period.

▶ **Suicide clause.** Nearly all life insurance policies have a *suicide clause* that voids the contract if an insured commits suicide within a certain period, typically two years after the policy's inception. In these cases, the company simply returns the premiums that have been paid. If an insured commits suicide after this initial period has elapsed, the policy proceeds are paid regardless.

▶ **Exclusions.** Although all private insurance policies exclude some types of losses, life policies offer broad protection. Other than the suicide clause, the only common exclusions are aviation, war, and hazardous occupation or hobby. However, a company would rarely be able to modify the premium charged or coverage offered should the insured take up, say, bull riding or wingsuit flying *after* a policy is issued.

▶ **Participation.** In a **participating policy**, the policyholder is entitled to receive *policy dividends* reflecting the difference between the premiums that are charged and the amount of premium necessary to fund the actual mortality experience of the company. When the base premium schedule for participating policies is established, a company estimates what it believes its mortality and investment experience will be and then adds a generous margin of safety to these figures. The premiums charged the policyholder are based on these conservative estimates.

▶ **Living benefits.** Also called *accelerated benefits*, this feature allows the insured to receive a percentage of

participating policy a life insurance policy that pays *policy dividends* reflecting the difference between the premiums that are charged and the amount of premium necessary to fund the actual mortality experience of the company

life insurance policy illustration a hypothetical representation of a life insurance policy's performance that reflects the most important assumptions that the insurance company relies on when presenting the policy to a prospective client and legal disclaimers. The insurance illustration specifies the inflows from premiums paid and interest credits, both of which increase the cash value of the policy. The illustration also states mortality charges and expenses, both of which decrease the cash value. An illustration typically consists of two main parts:

▶ **Guaranteed illustration.** The insurance company is required by law to disclose the worst-case scenario, which shows the effects of the insurer crediting the minimum interest and charging the maximum amount based on standard mortality tables. It's safe to assume that the benefits, cash surrender value, and accumulated values will never be lower than what this scenario presents.

▶ **Current illustration.** This is the insurance company's representation of policy performance based on the credit rates and mortality charges *currently* in effect.

When you look at an insurance illustration, focus first on the basic assumptions that the company used to compute it, including your age, sex, and underwriting health status. As noted above, the illustration will indicate the premiums, cash surrender value, and death benefits. Double-check all of the information. Ask the insurance agent to provide an *inforce reprojection* that shows any changes in credits or charges that the insurance company has declared for the next policy year. These changes in credits and charges will affect premiums or benefits. Most agents will not provide this unless you ask them. Watch for any unanticipated premium increases.

Check to make sure that all of the following sections are present in the narrative summary of the illustration and that no pages are missing:

▶ **Policy description, terms, and features.** This section overviews the main components of the policy. Double-check that the policy's premiums and benefit projections match your needs.

▶ **Underwriting discussion.** This provides a detailed description of the policy's benefits, premiums and tax information.

▶ **Column definitions and key terms.** This defines the terms used in the illustration. Make sure that you understand all the definitions and terms.

▶ **Disclaimer.** This section informs the prospective client that the illustration's portrayal of future values could vary from actual results.

▶ **Signature page.** This section provides a numerical summary of the illustration in 5- and 10-year increments. The insurance agent's signature here

PLANNING OVER A LIFETIME

Life Insurance

Here are some key considerations for life insurance use in each stage of the life cycle.

PRE-FAMILY INDEPENDENCE: 20s

▸ Term life insurance is needed only if you have dependents relying on you financially.

FAMILY FORMATION/CAREER DEVELOPMENT: 30–45

▸ If you marry, add life insurance to cover the financial needs of your spouse and other dependents.

▸ Consider increasing insurance coverage as additional children are born.

PRE-RETIREMENT: 45–65

▸ Re-evaluate insurance coverage if you change jobs or move to a higher-paying job.

▸ Consider reducing insurance coverage as children leave home and graduate from college. More insurance coverage may be needed if you are supporting aging parents. Consider possible use of life insurance in estate planning, which is covered in detail in Chapter 15.

▸ Evaluate the magnitude of your accumulated assets relative to needs of dependents. Insurance may no longer be needed or could be dramatically decreased.

RETIREMENT: 65 AND BEYOND

▸ Assure the adequate financial protection of your surviving spouse.

▸ Consider possible use of life insurance in estate planning, which is covered in detail in Chapter 15.

▸ It may be possible to discontinue coverage for grown dependents. You may need to maintain some life insurance to help dependents with special needs and for estate planning.

acknowledges that he or she has explained that the nonguaranteed elements are subject to change, and your signature acknowledges that you understand this.

Quinn and Celia Consider "Buying Term and Investing the Rest"

Quinn and Celia Hansen have two young children and believe it's time to buy a life insurance policy to protect their family. They've both heard the life insurance advice to "buy term and invest the rest." In order to evaluate this advice they've collected quotes for 20-year term and whole life policies on Quinn, both with a payoff of $250,000. The whole life policy premium is $347 a month, while the term policy premium is only $23 a month. In 20 years, the whole life policy will have a guaranteed cash value of $70,018 but at current rates would be worth $105,721. The death benefit will have grown to $326,352. If the Hansens buy the term policy and invest the $324 difference in monthly premiums at 8 percent for 20 years, they could have a portfolio worth about $190,843!

The Hansens wonder about the financial consequences of their decision. It looks like buying term and investing the difference leaves them better off. Yet the financial consequences can only be fully evaluated in light of the Hansens' objectives and attitudes towards risk. The whole life insurance policy provides a *guaranteed* cash value in 20 years, while the invested difference produces a higher expected, but *risky*, nonguaranteed payoff. And the hansens must consider whether they will have the discipline to keep "investing the difference" over the next 20 years. Once the whole life policy's cash value builds up, they could stop paying the premium by accepting some trade-offs in the value of the policy. In 20 years, the term life insurance coverage will go away,

Jeanie333/Shutterstock.com

which might be fine if the kids are gone and the mortgage is paid off. In contrast, the Hansens could stop paying the whole life policy premiums then and accept a reduced paid-up amount of coverage.

The personal financial consequences of "buy term and invest the rest" suggest the advice may well work for the Hansens. The best decision depends on their objectives, discipline, and attitudes towards the risks of "investing the rest."

Source: Adapted from Chris Arnold, "Life Insurance: Is Buying Term and Investing the Difference Your Best Approach?" www.nerdwallet.com/blog/finance/advisorvoices/difference-term-life-insuranc/, accessed October 2016.

STUDY TOOLS 8

LOCATED AT BACK OF THE TEXTBOOK
☐ Chapter Review Card

LOCATED AT WWW.CENGAGEBRAIN.COM
☐ Review Key Term flashcards and create your own cards.
☐ Track your knowledge and understanding of key concepts in personal finance.

☐ Complete practice and graded quizzes to prepare for tests.
☐ Complete interactive content at PFIN6 Online.
☐ View the chapter highlight boxes at PFIN6 Online.

©viphotos/Shutterstock140785408

Financial Planning Exercises

LO2, 3, 4 1. **Deciding if additional life insurance is needed and, if so, appropriate type. Use Worksheet 8.1.** Mark Hawkins 45, is a recently divorced father of two children, ages 10 and 7. He currently earns $95,000 a year as an operations manager for a utility company. The divorce settlement requires him to pay $1,500 a month in child support and $400 a month in alimony to his ex-wife. She currently earns $35,000 a year as a schoolteacher. Mark is now renting an apartment, and the divorce settlement left him with about $100,000 in savings and retirement benefits. His employer provides a $75,000 life insurance policy. Mark's ex-wife is currently the beneficiary listed on the policy. What advice would you give to Mark? What factors should he consider in deciding whether to buy additional life insurance at this point in his life? If he does need additional life insurance, what type of policy or policies should he buy? Use Worksheet 8.1 to help answer these questions for Mark.

LO2, 3, 4 2. **Estimating life insurance needs. Use Worksheet 8.1.** Margo Schmidt is a 72-year-old widow who has recently been diagnosed with Alzheimer's disease. She has limited financial assets of her own and has been living with her daughter Esther for two years. Her income is $850 a month in Social Security survivor's benefits. Esther wants to make sure that her mother will be taken care of if Esther should die prematurely. Esther, 40, is single and earns $55,000 a year as a human resources manager for a small manufacturing firm. She owns a condo with a current market value of $100,000 and has a $70,000 mortgage. Other debts include a $5,000 auto loan and $500 in various credit card balances. Her 401(k) plan has a current balance of $24,500, and she keeps $7,500 in a money market account for emergencies. After talking with her mother's doctor, Esther believes that her mother will be able to continue living independently for another two to three years. She estimates that her mother would need about $2,000 a month to cover her living expenses and medical costs during this time. After that, Esther's mother will probably need nursing home care. Esther calls several local nursing homes and finds that it will cost about $5,000 a month when her mother enters a nursing home. Her mother's doctor says it is difficult to estimate her mother's life expectancy but indicates that, with proper care, some Alzheimer's patients can live 10 or more years after diagnosis. Esther also estimates that her personal final expenses would be around $5,000, and she'd like to provide a $25,000 contingency fund that would be used to pay a trusted friend to supervise her mother's care if Esther were no longer alive. Use Worksheet 8.1 to calculate Esther's total life insurance requirements, and recommend the type of policy that she should buy.

LO2, 3, 4, 5 3. **Appropriateness of whole life insurance policy.** Malcolm and Ainsley Weaver are a dual-career couple who just had their first child. Malcolm, age 30, already has a group life insurance policy, but Ainsley's employer does not offer a life insurance benefit. A financial planner is recommending that the 27-year-old Ainsley buy a $250,000 whole life policy with an annual premium of $1,670 (the policy has an assumed rate of earnings of 5 percent a year). Help Ainsley evaluate this advice and decide on an appropriate course of action.

LO2, 3, 4, 6 4. **Appropriateness of variable life insurance.** While at lunch with a group of coworkers, one of your friends mentions that he plans to buy a variable life insurance policy because it provides a good annual return and is a good way to build savings for his five-year-old's college education. Another colleague says that she's adding coverage through the group plan's additional insurance option. What advice would you give them?

LO3, 4, 5 5. **Choosing among types of life insurance.** Sofia Fernandez, a 38-year-old widowed mother of three children (ages 12, 10, and 4), works as a product analyst for a major consumer products company. Although she's covered by a group life insurance policy at work, she feels, based on some rough calculations, that she needs additional protection. Eric Hart, an insurance agent from Insurance Advisers, has been trying to persuade her to buy a $150,000, 25-year, limited payment whole life policy. However, Sofia favors a variable life policy. To further complicate matters, Sofia's father feels that term life insurance is more suitable to the needs of her young family.

a. Explain to Sofia the differences between (i) a whole life policy, (ii) a variable life policy, and (iii) a term life policy.

b. What are the major advantages and disadvantages of each type of policy?

c. In what way is a whole life policy superior to either a variable life or term life policy? In what way is a variable life policy superior? How about term life insurance?

d. Given the limited information in the case, which type of policy would you recommend for Sofia? Explain your recommendations.

LO4 6. **Life insurance premiums and comparison of types.** Using the premium schedules provided in Exhibits 8.2, 8.3, and 8.5, how much in *annual* premiums would a 25-year-old male have to pay for $100,000 of annual renewable term, level premium term, and whole life insurance? (Assume a 10-year term or period of coverage.) How much would a 25-year-old woman have to pay for the same coverage? Consider a 40-year-old male (or female): Using annual premiums, compare the cost of 10 years of coverage under annual renewable and level premium term options and whole life insurance coverage. Relate the advantages and disadvantages of each policy type to their price differences.

LO6 7. **Using insurance policy illustrations.** Describe the key elements of an insurance policy illustration, and explain what a prospective client should focus on in evaluating an illustration.

9 | Insuring Your Health

LEARNING OBJECTIVES

After studying this chapter, you will be able to...

LO1 Discuss why having adequate health insurance is important, and identify the factors contributing to the growing cost of health insurance.

LO2 Differentiate among the major types of health insurance plans, and identify major private and public health insurance providers and their programs.

LO3 Analyze your own health insurance needs and explain how to shop for appropriate coverage.

LO4 Explain the basic types of medical expenses covered by the policy provisions of health insurance plans.

LO5 Assess the need for and features of long-term-care insurance.

LO6 Discuss the features of disability income insurance and how to determine your need for it.

After you finishing this chapter, go

to **PAGE 249** for

STUDY TOOLS

Ojo Images/Getty Images

How Will This Affect Me? Having adequate health insurance is critically important to your financial plan. Health care costs have grown dramatically in recent years, and a major illness or accident could wipe you out financially if you are uninsured. Yet health insurance policies are complicated to price and to compare. This chapter explains the importance of health insurance and the key determinants of its costs. The various types of public and private health insurance are described, and a framework for decision making is provided. This includes discussions of how to analyze your health insurance needs, how to make sense of common policy features, and policy buying tips. The implications of the Patient Protection and Affordable Care Act and the Reconciliation Act of 2010 (ACA) on your decisions are considered. This chapter also discusses how to determine whether you need long-term-care insurance or disability income insurance. After reading this chapter, you should understand how to insure your health most effectively and economically.

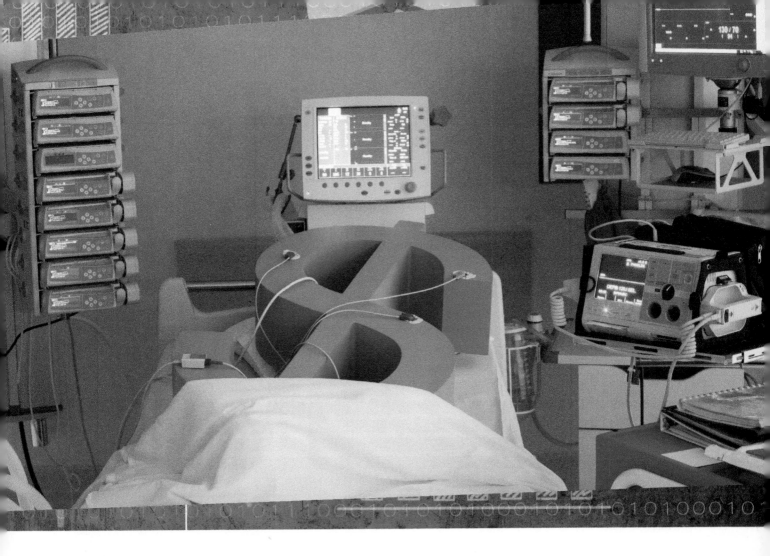

9-1 THE IMPORTANCE OF HEALTH INSURANCE COVERAGE

LO1 The next best thing to good health is a good health insurance plan. In recent years, the price of medical treatment has risen dramatically. The cost of a major illness can easily total tens (or even hundreds) of thousands of dollars in expense due to hospital, medical care, and loss of income. Health insurance helps you pay both routine and major medical care costs. Indeed, a significant number of U.S. personal bankruptcies are due, at least in part, to medical costs.

Despite the financial importance of health insurance, over 10 percent of the population don't have health insurance. And about 14 percent of the uninsured are children.

Exhibit 9.1 helps explain why so many are uninsured; from 1999 to 2015, the average annual premium for families experienced more than a two-fold increase! In 2015, the average total annual premium was $6,251

> The next best thing to good health is a good health insurance plan.

for single coverage and $17,545 for family coverage. The average percentage of health care premiums paid by covered workers was about 28 percent for family plans.

Costly advances in medical technology, an aging U.S. population, and a poor demand-and-supply distribution of health care facilities and services have fueled rapidly rising health care costs. In addition, administrative costs, excessive paper work, increased regulation, and insurance fraud are also contributing to rising health care costs.

Go to Smart Sites

Healthcare.gov has a state-specific interactive guide to help walk you through you choices in health care plans and providers. A highlight box in each chapter of PFIN Online includes "Smart Sites," a list of resources and sites that offer additional information on topics in the PFIN text.

Exhibit 9.1

Average Annual Worker and Employer Contributions to Premiums and Total Premiums for family Coverage, 1999–2015

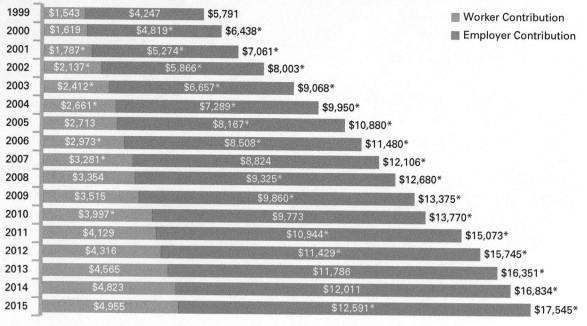

Year	Worker Contribution	Employer Contribution	Total
1999	$1,543	$4,247	$5,791
2000	$1,619	$4,819*	$6,438*
2001	$1,787*	$5,274*	$7,061*
2002	$2,137*	$5,866*	$8,003*
2003	$2,412*	$6,657*	$9,068*
2004	$2,661*	$7,289*	$9,950*
2005	$2,713	$8,167*	$10,880*
2006	$2,973*	$8,508*	$11,480*
2007	$3,281*	$8,824	$12,106*
2008	$3,354	$9,325*	$12,680*
2009	$3,515	$9,860*	$13,375*
2010	$3,997*	$9,773	$13,770*
2011	$4,129	$10,944*	$15,073*
2012	$4,316	$11,429*	$15,745*
2013	$4,565	$11,786	$16,351*
2014	$4,823	$12,011	$16,834*
2015	$4,955	$12,591*	$17,545*

* Estimate is statistically different from estimate for the previous year shown (p <.05).

Source: Kaiser/HRET Survey of Employer-Sponsored Health Benefits, 1999–2015.

It can be risky to go without adequate health insurance coverage. Concern over health care costs and the number of uninsured Americans has made health care reform a major priority of Congress and the administration. Policy solutions concerning the proper mix between government-run and privately run health insurance programs continue to prompt vigorous debate even after the passage of the ACA, which is discussed below. Becoming familiar with current health insurance options and issues should help you make better decisions as well as provide a useful perspective on the ongoing health care reform debate.

9-2 HEALTH INSURANCE PLANS

LO2 Health insurance coverage can be obtained from private sources and government-sponsored programs. Regardless of the source of the plan, the ACA has significantly affected the expenses covered, the method of purchasing health insurance plans,

group health insurance
health insurance consisting of contracts written between a group, (employer, union, etc.) and the health care provider

and the related taxes. In recent years, 28 percent of national health care expenditures were paid for by households, private businesses paid 21 percent, state and local governments paid 16 percent, the federal government paid 27 percent, and the rest was presumably paid by the self-insured.

9-2a Private Health Insurance Plans

Private companies sell a variety of health insurance plans to both groups and individuals. **Group health insurance** is a contract written between a group (such as an employer, union, credit union, or other organization) and the health care provider: a private insurance company, Blue Cross/Blue Shield plan, or managed care organization. Typically, group plans provide comprehensive medical expense coverage and may also offer prescription drug, dental, and vision care services.

If your employer has more than just a few employees, you'll probably have access to some type of group health plan. To control rising costs, many employers underwrite employee health care coverage much the way insurers do. In addition, many employers are shifting a larger percentage of health care costs to employees. So be sure to

Exhibit 9.2

How the Most Common Types of Health Plans Compare

This table highlights some of the key differences among the three most common types of health plans.

Type	Choice of Service Providers	Premium Cost	Out-of-Pocket Costs	Annual Deductible
Indemnity	Yes	Low if high-deductible plan, high if low-deductible plan	Usually 20 percent of medical expenses plus deductible	Yes
HMO	No	Low	Low co-pay	No
PPO	Some	Higher than HMO	Low if using network providers, higher if provider is outside the network	No

compare group and individual policies before deciding which coverage to buy.

Most private health insurance plans fall into one of two categories: traditional *indemnity (fee-for-service) plans* and *managed care plans*, which include health maintenance organizations (HMOs), preferred provider organizations (PPOs), and similar plans. Both categories of plans cover, in somewhat different ways, the medical care costs arising from illness or accidents. Exhibit 9.2 compares the key differences among the three most common types of health plans.

Traditional Indemnity (Fee-for-Service) Plans

With a traditional indemnity (fee-for-service) plan, the health care provider is separate from your insurer. Your insurer either pays the provider directly or reimburses your expenses when you submit claims for medical treatment. Typically, indemnity plans pay 80 percent of the eligible health care expenses, and the insured pays the other 20 percent. The health insurance company will begin paying its share after you pay a deductible amount of expenses, which typically ranges from $100 to over $2,000. The lower your deductible, the higher your premium.

The amount the insurance company pays is commonly based on the usual, customary, and reasonable (UCR) charges—what the insurer considers to be the prevailing fees within your area, not what your doctor or hospital actually charges. If your doctor charges more than the UCR, you may be responsible for the full amount of the excess. UCR charges vary significantly among insurers, so you should compare your doctor's fees with what a plan pays. Under many indemnity plans, physicians who accept the insurance agree to accept the UCR payments set by the insurer. Importantly, it should be noted that there are few indemnity plans left in the United States.

Managed Care Plans Today, employers are moving toward managed care plans under which subscribers/users contract with and make monthly payments directly to the organization that provides the health care service. Most major health insurance companies offer both indemnity and managed care plans. Managed care plan members receive comprehensive health care services from a designated group of doctors, hospitals, and other providers.

Under a managed care plan, the insured pays no deductibles and only a small fee, or co-payment, for office visits and medications. Most medical services—including preventive and routine care that indemnity plans may not cover—are fully covered when obtained from plan providers. Managed care plans include health maintenance organizations (HMOs), preferred provider organizations (PPOs), exclusive provider organizations (EPOs), and point-of-service (POS) plans.

Health Maintenance Organizations

A health maintenance organization (HMO) is an organization of hospitals, physicians, and other health care providers that provides comprehensive health care services to its members. HMO members pay a monthly fee

indemnity (fee-for-service) plan health insurance plan in which the health care provider is separate from the insurer, who pays the provider or reimburses you for a specified percentage of expenses after a deductible amount has been met

managed care plan a health care plan in which subscribers/users contract with the provider organization, which uses a designated group of providers meeting specific selection standards to furnish health care services for a monthly fee

health maintenance organization (HMO) an organization of hospitals, physicians, and other health care providers who have joined to provide comprehensive health care services to its members, who pay a monthly fee

Financial Planning Tips

STUDENT HEALTH CARE INSURANCE UNDER THE ACA

Active students have a high injury rate, and viruses often move quickly through college campuses and dorms. It is essential to be insured, even when you are young and generally healthy. No one knows when an expensive medical procedure may be required. For these reasons, colleges often require students to have health insurance. And being a student does not allow anyone to avoid the uninsured fee under the ACA, whichever was the higher of 2.5% of household income or $695 in 2016. Under the ACA, many parents can meet that requirement by keeping their children on their health insurance plan until the age of 26 (and this actually applies whether they are in school or not). Here are some key trends and issues to consider in arranging student health care insurance.

- **Escalating costs.** The ACA requires students to have a level of coverage that exceeds the plans historically offered by most colleges. Consequently, premiums can be expensive. Indeed, some colleges are dropping student health insurance plans due to their higher costs. Students who are not covered under their parents' health care plan should consider buying an individual health insurance plan.

You can compare prices and coverage using an Internet provider like www.eHealthInsurance.com or http://www.StudentHealthPlan.com.

- **Network coverage.** If you are a student relying on your parents' policy, be careful if your college is in another state. Make sure that your plan's network of preferred doctors and hospitals extends there. If not, the highest level of coverage may not be available.

- **Parent policy choices.** Parents should choose a family plan that covers their children for all medical emergencies and associated care. Most plans have basic out-of-state coverage for children. However, if out-of-state coverage is limited, as noted earlier, consider a high-deductible, catastrophic student health plan. It makes sense for students to return home for all routine care and prescriptions.

- **Good effects of the law.** The ACA may make some student health plans more appealing. It prohibits all plans from having "lifetime coverage limits" that put a cap on the maximum coverage in the case of a serious illness or accident. The law also prohibits insurers from excluding students for pre-existing conditions.

---

that varies according to the number of people in their family. A co-payment typically of $5 to $40 is charged each time services are provided by the HMO or a prescription is filled. The services provided to HMO members include doctors' office visits, imaging and laboratory services, preventive care, health screenings, hospital inpatient care and surgery, maternity care, mental health care, and drug prescriptions.

The advantages of HMO membership include a lack of deductibles, few or no exclusions, and not having to file insurance claims. In the past, the primary disadvantage was that HMO members couldn't always choose their physicians and might face limitations if they needed care outside of the geographic area of their HMO. However, in recent years, many HMOs don't require members to pick one primary care physician, some don't require referrals, and almost all offer some flexibility to get coverage out of network.

There are two main types of HMOs: group and individual practice associations. A **group HMO** employs a group of doctors to provide health care services to members *from a central facility*. Often, the group HMO's hospital facilities are located in the same facility. Group HMOs are most prevalent in larger cities.

An **individual practice association (IPA)** is the most popular type of HMO. IPA members receive medical care from individual physicians practicing *from their own offices and from community hospitals* that are affiliated with the IPA. As a member of an IPA, you have some choice of which doctors and hospitals to use.

Preferred Provider Organizations A **preferred provider organization (PPO)** is a managed care plan that has the characteristics of both an IPA and an indemnity plan.

group HMO a HMO that provides health care services *from a central facility*; most prevalent in larger cities

individual practice association (IPA) a form of HMO in which subscribers receive services from physicians practicing *from their own offices and from community hospitals* affiliated with the IPA

preferred provider organization (PPO) a health provider that combines the characteristics of the IPA form of HMO with an indemnity plan to provide comprehensive health care services to its subscribers within a network of physicians and hospitals

An insurance company or provider group contracts with a network of physicians and hospitals that agree to accept a negotiated fee for medical services provided to the PPO members. Unlike the HMO, however, a PPO also provides insurance coverage for medical services not provided by the PPO network, so you can choose to go to other doctors or hospitals. However, you will pay a higher price for medical services provided by out-of-network doctors and hospitals.

Other Managed Care Plans You may encounter two other forms of managed care plans. An **exclusive provider organization (EPO)** contracts with medical providers to offer services to members at reduced costs, but it reimburses members only when affiliated providers are used. Plan members who use a nonaffiliated provider must bear the entire cost. The **point-of-service (POS) plan** is a hybrid form of HMO that allows members to go outside of the HMO network for care. Payment for nonaffiliated physician services is similar to indemnity plan payments: The plan pays a specified percentage of the cost after your medical costs reach an annual deductible.

Blue Cross/Blue Shield Plans In a technical sense, **Blue Cross/Blue Shield plans** are not insurance policies but rather prepaid hospital and medical expense plans. Today, there are about 36 independent local Blue Cross/Blue Shield organizations, all of them for-profit corporations, which cover about 106 million people.

Blue Cross contracts with hospitals that agree to provide specified hospital services to members of subscriber groups in exchange for a specified fee or payment. Blue Cross also contracts for surgical and medical services. Blue Cross serves as the intermediary between the groups that want these services and the physicians who contractually agree to provide them.

Pressmaster/Shutterstock.com

Many Blue Cross and Blue Shield plans have combined to form one provider, and they compete for business with other private insurance companies. Blue Cross/Blue Shield payments for health care services are seldom made to the subscriber but rather directly to the participating hospital or physician.

9-2b Government Health Insurance Plans

In addition to health insurance coverage provided by private sources, federal and state agencies provide health care coverage to eligible individuals. About 36 percent of the U.S. population is covered by some form of government health insurance program. For example, prior to the implementation of the ACA, the government offered the Pre-Existing Condition Insurance Plan (PCIP), which provided health coverage to U.S. citizens or others residing in the United States legally who have been denied health insurance because of a pre-existing condition, as long as the person had been uninsured for at least six months. The program was administered by states and the federal government. In addition, some states provide health insurance for children who do not qualify for Medicaid (discussed below), but whose family still has very low income.

Medicare Medicare is a health insurance program administered by the Social Security Administration. It's primarily designed to help persons 65 and over meet their health care costs, but it also covers many people under 65 who receive monthly Social Security disability benefits. Funds for Medicare benefits come from Social Security taxes paid by covered workers and their employers. Medicare provides basic hospital insurance, supplementary medical insurance, and prescription drug coverage:

▶ **Basic hospital insurance.** This coverage (commonly called *Part A*) provides inpatient hospital services such as

exclusive provider organization (EPO) a managed care plan that is similar to a PPO but reimburses members only when affiliated providers are used

point-of-service (POS) plan a hybrid form of HMO that allows members to go outside the HMO network for care and reimburses them at a specified percentage of the cost

Blue Cross/Blue Shield plans prepaid hospital and medical expense plans under which health care services are provided to plan participants by member hospitals and physicians

Medicare a health insurance plan administered by the federal government to help persons age 65 and over, and others receiving monthly Social Security disability benefits, to meet their health care costs room, board, and other customary inpatient service for the first 90 days of illness. A deductible is applied during the first 60 days of illness. Co-insurance provisions, applicable to days 61–90 of the hospital stay, can further reduce benefits. Medicare also covers all or part of the cost of up to 100 days in post-hospital extended-care facilities that provide skilled care, such as nursing homes. However, it doesn't cover the most common types of nursing home care—intermediate and custodial care. Medicare basic hospital insurance also covers some posthospital medical services such as intermittent nursing care, therapy, rehabilitation, and home health care. Medicare deductibles and co-insurance amounts are revised annually to reflect changing medical costs.

▶ **Supplementary medical insurance.** The supplementary medical insurance (SMI) program (commonly called *Part B*) covers the services of physicians and surgeons in addition to the costs of medical and health services such as imaging, laboratory tests, prosthetic devices, rental of medical equipment, and ambulance transportation. It also covers some home health services (such as in-home visits by a registered nurse) and limited psychiatric care. Unlike Medicare's basic hospital insurance, SMI is a *voluntary program* for which participants pay premiums, which are then matched with government funds. Anyone age 65 or over can enroll in SMI.

▶ **Medicare Advantage plans.** Medicare Advantage plans (commonly called *Plan C*) provide Medicare benefits to eligible people, but they differ in that they are administered by private providers rather than by the government. Common supplemental benefits include vision, hearing, dental, general checkups, and health and wellness programs. These supplemental benefits are a major reason for interest in these plans. Medicare pays the private health plan a fixed amount every month for each member. The members may pay a monthly premium in addition to the Medicare Part B premium. However, many of the private providers don't charge a premium beyond the Medicare Part B premium, which the member pays directly to Medicare. Members usually pay a fixed amount (e.g., a co-payment of $30), every time they visit a doctor, rather than pay a deductible and buy co-insurance (typically 20 percent) under original Medicare.

Private plans may use some of the excess payments that they receive from the government to offer supplemental benefits. Most plans also include Medicare prescription drug coverage, discussed next. Because Medicare Advantage plans cost the federal government more than standard Medicare, the subsidies paid to these plans will start to decline under the ACA, which may lead to higher premiums or reduced benefits. However, the benefits cannot be reduced if they could normally be received from standard Medicare.

▶ **Prescription drug coverage.** The prescription drug coverage program (commonly called *Part D*) is insurance covering both brand-name and generic prescription drugs at participating pharmacies. It's intended to provide protection for people who have very high drug costs. All Medicare recipients are eligible for this coverage, regardless of their income and resources, health status, or existing prescription expenses. There are several ways to obtain this coverage. Participants in this *voluntary program* pay a monthly fee and a yearly deductible, which vary by provider. In 2016, average monthly premium was about $42 and some paid up to $100. Most plans had a deductible of $360. They also pay part of the cost of prescriptions, including a co-payment or co-insurance. The plan provides extra help—paying almost all prescription drug costs—for the one in three Medicare recipients who have limited income and resources.

supplementary medical insurance (SMI) a voluntary program under Medicare (commonly called *Part B*) that provides payments for services not covered under basic hospital insurance (*Part A*)

Medicare Advantage plans commonly called *Plan C*, these plans provide Medicare benefits to eligible people, but they differ in that they are administered by private providers rather than by the government. Common supplemental benefits include vision, hearing, dental, general checkups, and health and wellness programs

prescription drug coverage a voluntary program under Medicare (commonly called *Part D*), insurance that covers both brand-name and generic prescription drugs at participating pharmacies. Participants pay a monthly fee and a yearly deductible and must also pay part of the cost of prescriptions, including a co-payment or co-insurance

Although Medicare pays for many health care expenses for the disabled and those over 65, there are still gaps in its coverage. Many Medicare enrollees buy private insurance policies to fill in these gaps.

Medicaid Medicaid is a state-run, public assistance program providing health insurance benefits only to those who are unable to pay for health care. Each state has its own Medicaid regulations, eligibility requirements, and covered medical services. Although Medicaid is primarily funded by each state, the federal government also contributes funds. About 70 million people are covered by Medicaid.

Workers' Compensation Insurance Workers' compensation insurance is designed to compensate workers who are injured on the job or become ill through work-related causes. Although mandated by the federal government, each state is responsible for workers' compensation legislation and regulation. Specifics vary from state to state, but typical workers' compensation benefits include medical and rehabilitation expenses, disability income, and scheduled lump-sum amounts for death and certain injuries, such as dismemberment. Employers bear nearly the entire cost of workers' compensation insurance in most states. Premiums are based on historical usage; employers who file the most claims pay the highest rates. Self-employed people are required to contribute to workers' compensation for themselves and their employees.

Affordable Health Care Act of 2010 The Patient Protection and Affordable Care Act and the Reconciliation Act of 2010 (usually just called the Affordable Health Care Act, or ACA) is extensive and remains controversial. Its legality was contested, and the U.S. Supreme Court affirmed its constitutionality in June 2012. In making health care insurance decisions, it's important to understand the broad strokes of the law.

The ACA has two key goals:

▶ Reduce the number of uninsured citizens in the country

▶ Reduce the increases in health care costs by providing a government-based health insurance exchange in each state

The ACA is designed to reach these goals by requiring the purchase of health insurance and by assuring that health insurance provides "essential health benefits." All individuals who are not covered by Medicaid or Medicare are required to purchase health insurance or pay a penalty that will amount to the greater of $695 per adult (and $347.50 per child) or 2.5 percent of the family income in 2016. Businesses employing more than 50 full-time employees must provide health insurance for their employees, or else pay a penalty of $2,000 per employee in excess of 30 employees. For example, if a business has 130 full-time employees but does not provide insurance, the penalty would be $2,000 × (130 − 30), or $200,000 per year.

The essential health benefits required by the ACA include the following:

▶ Ambulatory patient services

▶ Emergency services

▶ Hospitalization

▶ Maternity and newborn care

▶ Mental health and substance use disorder services, including behavioral health treatment

▶ Prescription drugs

▶ Rehabilitative and habilitative services and devices

▶ Laboratory services

▶ Preventive and wellness services and chronic disease management

▶ Pediatric services, including oral and vision care

In addition, the ACA requires that health insurance plans provide the following features:

▶ Cover pre-existing conditions

▶ Parents must have the option to carry their children on their plan until age 26

▶ Lifetime dollar limits on total insurance coverage are prohibited

▶ Plans must cover preventive care and medical screenings

▶ Insurers must spend at least 80 percent of premiums on claims

Under the ACA health care insurance exchanges are available in each state. The exchanges are competitive marketplaces where health insurance may be purchased by individuals and small firms. All insurance plans listed on the insurance exchanges must provide the essential health benefits described above. Similarly, all plans offered by employers must provide the indicated

Medicaid a state-run, public assistance program that provides health insurance benefits only to those who are unable to pay for health care

workers' compensation insurance health insurance required by state and federal governments and paid nearly in full by employers in most states; it compensates workers for job-related illness or injury essential health benefits. The ACA provides four levels of benefits, each of which is identified by a "metal label."

Metal Label	Percent of Benefit Costs
Bronze	60%
Silver	70%
Gold	80%
Platinum	90%

The areas where insurance companies can compete are quite limited. The rates that companies charge vary largely depending upon the geographical area and whether or not the insured uses tobacco products. The hope is that, by increasing competition among insurers, the cost of insurance will decrease.

The ACA's expenditures are to be financed by several sources of revenue. These include higher Medicare taxes, fees on insurers, and an excise tax levied on the insurance companies providing "Cadillac" policies. It is hoped that changes in the Medicare program will provide some offsetting cost savings. The long-term net effect of the ACA on the federal budget deficit remains a hotly debated topic. However, the above key provisions of the law will influence the coverage and cost of your health insurance. Therefore, it's important to understand how health insurance policies are currently structured so that you'll be in a good position to appreciate the significance of the changes as the law is phased in.

> **YOU CAN DO IT NOW: Compare Policies on an ACA Health insurance Exchange** It's worth taking the time to survey the policies and premiums available to you on an ACA health insurance marketplace. Just go to **https://www.healthcare.gov/see-plans.** All you have to do is put in your zip code and some basic information about yourself. If you're shopping, it provides useful information. And if you already have a plan through your job, it'll be interesting to see how it compares. It's easy—and you can **do it now.**

9-3 HEALTH INSURANCE DECISIONS

LO3 How can you systematically plan your health insurance purchases? As with other insurance decisions, you'll need to consider potential areas of loss, types of coverage and other resources available to you and your family, and any gaps in protection. Then you can choose a health insurance plan that's best for you.

9-3a Evaluate Your Health Care Cost Risk

Most people need protection against two costs resulting from illness or accidents: (1) expenses for medical care and rehabilitation and (2) loss of income or household services. The cost of medical care can't be estimated easily; but in cases of long-term, serious illness, medical bills and related expenses can easily run into hundreds of thousands of dollars. An adequate amount of protection against these costs for most people would be at least $300,000 and, with a protracted illness or disability, as much as $1 million. In contrast, lost income is typically calculated as a percentage of your (or your spouse's) current monthly earnings, generally 60 to 75 percent.

A good health insurance plan embodies more than financing medical expenses, lost income, and replacement services. It should incorporate other means of risk reduction such as risk avoidance, loss prevention and control, and risk assumption:

▶ **Risk avoidance.** Look for ways to avoid exposure to health care loss before it occurs. For example, people who don't take illegal drugs never have to worry about disability from overdose, people who refuse to ride on motorcycles avoid the high risk of injury, and people who don't smoke in bed are a lot less likely to doze off and start a fire in their house.

▶ **Loss prevention and control.** Accept responsibility for your own well-being and live a healthier lifestyle to prevent illness and reduce high medical costs. Smoking, alcohol and drug dependency, improper diet, inadequate sleep, and lack of regular exercise contribute to more than 60 percent of all diagnosed illnesses. Eliminating some or all of these factors from your lifestyle can reduce your chances of becoming ill. Similarly, following highway safety laws, not driving while intoxicated, and wearing a seat belt help prevent injury from car accidents.

▶ **Risk assumption.** Consider the health risks that you're willing to retain. Some risks pose relatively small loss potential, and you can budget for them rather than insure against them. For example, choosing insurance plans with deductibles and waiting periods is a form of risk assumption because it's more economical to pay small amounts from savings than to consistently pay higher premiums to cover them.

9-3b Determine Available Coverage and Resources

Some employers providing health insurance as an employee benefit offer only one plan and pay either all or part of the premiums. If you work for an employer who provides health insurance this way, you should evaluate the plan's benefits and costs to determine if additional coverage—either for yourself or your dependents—is necessary.

Some employers offer a *flexible-benefit ("cafeteria") plan* that allows them to choose fringe benefits. Typically, the menu of benefits includes more than one health insurance option, as well as life insurance, disability income insurance, and other benefits. The employer specifies a set dollar amount that it will provide, and employees choose a combination of benefits. If the employee wants or needs additional insurance benefits, most employers will set up a salary reduction agreement with the employee. The employee agrees to reduce his or her salary by the amount of the additional cost of the desired benefit.

Some employers offer consumer-directed health plans that go one step beyond a flexible-benefit plan. These plans combine a high-deductible health insurance policy with a tax-free **health reimbursement account (HRA)**, a plan funded by employers for each participating employee. When the account balance is used up, you must pay the remaining deductible of the health insurance policy before insurance begins to pay. You can "roll over" the amount of unused money annually.

Another similar type of account is the **health savings account (HSA)**. The HSA is also a tax-free account, but the money is contributed by employees or employers (or both) for use in paying routine medical costs. An HSA is also combined with a high-deductible insurance policy to pay for catastrophic care in case of major accident or illness, and—as with an HRA—any unused money can be rolled over each year. If you change jobs, the money in your HSA belongs only to you and is yours to keep. In addition to the HSA and HRA, there are many other consumer-directed health plans.

Tom Saga/Shutterstock.com

If you're married and your spouse is employed, you should evaluate his or her benefit package before making any decisions. You may, for example, already be covered under your spouse's group health insurance plan or be able to purchase coverage for yourself and family members at a cheaper rate than through your own employer's plan.

If you're laid off from or leave a job where you've had health benefits, then you are legally eligible to continue your coverage for a period of 18 months under federal COBRA regulations (discussed later in this chapter). You'll be responsible for paying the full cost of the insurance if you decide to continue your coverage during this time, but you'll still pay group insurance rates that are often less expensive than buying individual insurance. However, you must arrange to continue your coverage before leaving your former employer. Importantly, under the ACA, losing your job triggers a "qualifying life event" allowing you to obtain health insurance under COBRA or you can buy a policy in the private health insurance market. But there are critical enrollment windows and policy coverage details to compare. You'll need to do the math to determine the best option for you.

Another important aspect of group coverage to consider is retiree benefits. Some companies provide health insurance to retirees, but most don't, so you probably shouldn't count on receiving employer-paid benefits once you retire. Know what your options are to ensure continued coverage for both you and your family after you retire. Medicare will cover basic medical expenses, but you'll probably need to supplement this coverage with one of the 12 standard Medigap plans, which are termed plans "A" through "L."

There are several other possible sources of health care coverage. Homeowner's and automobile insurance policies often contain

health reimbursement account (HRA) an account into which employers place contributions that employees can use to pay for medical expenses. Usually combined with a high-deductible health insurance policy

health savings account (HSA) a tax-free savings account—funded by employees, employer, or both—to spend on routine medical costs. Usually combined with a high-deductible policy to pay for catastrophic care limited amounts of medical expense protection. For example, your automobile policy may cover your medical expenses if you're involved in an auto accident regardless of whether you're in a car, on foot, or on a bicycle when the accident occurs. In addition to Social Security's Medicare program, various other government programs help pay medical expenses. For instance, medical care is provided for people who've served in the armed services and were honorably discharged. Public health programs exist to treat communicable diseases, children with disabilities, and mental health disorders.

If you need or want to purchase additional medical insurance coverage on an individual basis, you can purchase a variety of policies from a private insurance company such as Aetna, CIGNA, or United Healthcare. You should buy health care plans from an insurance agent who will listen to your needs and provide well-thought-out responses to your questions. You should also research carriers and choose one that is rated highly by at least two of the major ratings agencies and that has a reputation for settling claims fairly and promptly. The National Committee for Quality Assurance (NCQA) is a non profit, unbiased organization that issues annual "report cards" that rate the service quality of various health plans.

9-3c Choose a Health Insurance Plan

After familiarizing yourself with the different health insurance plans and providers and reviewing your needs, you must choose one or more plans to provide coverage. If you're employed, first review the various health insurance plans that your company offers. If you can't get coverage from an employer, get plan descriptions and policy costs from several providers—including a group plan from a professional or trade organization, if available—for both indemnity and managed care plans. You should also check the state or federal insurance exchange available to you. Then take your time and carefully read the plan materials to understand exactly what is covered and at what cost. Next, review your past medical costs, estimate your future costs, and use them to compare your costs under various plans.

You'll have to ask yourself some important questions when choosing your particular plan:

community rating approach to health insurance premium pricing policyholders in a community (area) pay the same premium without regard to their personal health, age, gender, or other factors

▶ **How important is cost compared with having freedom of choice?** You may have to pay more to stay with your current doctor if he or

Go to Smart Sites

What grade did your health plan get on its quality "report card" this year? The National Committee for Quality Assurance (NCQA) can tell you.

she is not part of a managed care plan that you're considering. Also, you have to decide if you can tolerate the managed care plan's approach to health care.

Some states have experimented in recent years with the **community rating approach to health insurance premium pricing**, which prohibits insurance companies from varying rates based on health status or claims history. The community is defined as the area in which the insurance is offered. In the "pure" approach, all policyholders in an area pay the same premium without regard to their personal health, age, gender, or other factors. Under the adjusted (modified) community rating approach, insurers can adjust premiums based only on your family size, where you live, whether you use

CHOOSING A HEALTH INSURANCE PLAN

Ask the following questions when choosing among health care insurance plans:

- Can I choose to use any doctor, hospital, clinic, or pharmacy?

- What coverage, if any, is provided for seeing specialists like eye doctors and dentists?

- Does the plan cover special conditions or treatments like psychiatric care, pregnancy, and physical therapy?

- Does the plan cover home care or nursing home care?

- What kind of limitations are there on the coverage of prescribed medications?

- What are the deductible and any co-payment amounts?

- What is the maximum I would have to pay out of health care expenses, either in a calendar year or during my lifetime?

- How are billing or service disputes handled under the plan?

Source: Adapted from "Choosing a Health Insurance Plan," www.usa.gov/topics/health/health-insurance/choosing.shtml, accessed October 2016.

Behavioral Biases in Making Health Insurance Decisions

Research in behavioral economics indicates that individuals have difficulty making decisions involving uncertainty, trade-offs between current and future benefits and costs, or significant complexity. This analysis requires estimating the probabilities, financial costs, and quality of life and happiness associated with possible future health events such as having cancer or a heart attack. This is hard to do.

Research shows that individuals tend to make systematic mistakes in estimating probabilities. For example, they are inclined to overestimate the likelihood of low-probability events, such as dying in a plane crash. And it's almost impossible for most people to estimate the financial costs associated with various health conditions. This is because, for the most part, there is no place to look up health service prices. And people tend to overestimate how much their quality of life and happiness will decline if they become sick.

Health care choices often require bearing costs today in the hope of future benefits. This is as much the case for preventive care as it is for more costly and invasive procedures designed to reduce the probability of cancer among high-risk patients. Yet research shows that people tend to invest too little in such activities because they put too much weight on current costs and too little weight on future benefits.

Health care insurance decisions can be quite complex. Insurance policies include many facets such as deductibles, co-payments, and different levels of coverage for different providers. The many trade-offs are hard to work through. For example, employees may not fully appreciate that they are sacrificing some wages in return for employer health care insurance premium subsidies.

What are the implications of the above biases?

- It's important to be aware of common behavioral biases when making health insurance decisions. For example, realize that most people don't pay sufficient attention to the importance of preventive health care measures.

- Most of us would be better off if our health insurance plans were mediated by some entity that would screen and restrict health insurance choices down to a manageable number. Research suggests that employers would perform this role better than the government or private insurance agents, which is a provocative finding in light of the ACA.

Source: "Lessons for Health Care from Behavioral Economics," www .nber.org/bah/2008no4/w14330.html (see referenced study by Jeffrey Liebman and Richard Zeckhauser, "Simple Humans, Complex Insurance, Subtle Subsidies," Working Paper 14330, www.nber.org/papers/w14330, 2008), accessed October 2016.

---

tobacco, and your age. The ACA requires insurance companies to adhere to the adjusted community rating approach for individuals and small businesses.

▶ **Will you be reimbursed if you choose a managed care plan and want to see an out-of-network provider?** For most people, the managed care route is cheaper—even if you visit a doctor only once a year—because of indemnity plans'"reasonable charge" provisions.

▶ **What types of coverage do you need?** Everyone has different needs; one person may want a plan with good maternity and pediatric care, whereas

another may want outpatient mental health benefits. Make sure the plans that you consider offer what you want.

▶ **How good is the managed care network?**
Research participating doctors and hospitals to see how many of your providers are part of the plan. Check out the credentials of participating providers; a good sign is accreditation from the NCQA. Are the providers' locations convenient for you? What preventive medical programs does it provide? Has membership grown? Talk to friends and associates to see what their experiences have been with the plan.

- **How old are you, and how is your health?** Many financial advisors recommend buying the lowest-cost plan—which may be an indemnity plan with a high deductible—if you're young and healthy.

After considering all of the coverages and resources available to you, identify any gaps in your health insurance coverage and determine how best to fill them. Doing this requires an understanding of the features, policy provisions, and coverage provided by various insurance carriers and policies. We'll discuss these in detail in the next section.

9-4 MEDICAL EXPENSE COVERAGE AND POLICY PROVISIONS

LO4 To evaluate different health insurance plan options, you should compare and contrast what they cover and how each plan's policy provisions may affect you and your family. By doing so, you can decide which health plan offers the best protection at the most reasonable cost. Worksheet 9.1 provides a convenient checklist for comparing the costs and benefits of competing health insurance plans.

> To evaluate different health insurance plan options, you should compare and contrast what they cover and how each plan's policy provisions may affect you and your family.

9-4a Types of Medical Expense Coverage

The medical services covered vary among health plans. You can purchase narrowly defined plans that cover only what you consider to be the most important medical services or, if you want the comfort of broader coverage and can afford it, you can purchase insurance that covers most or all of your health care needs. Here, we describe the medical expenses most commonly covered by health insurance.

Hospitalization A *hospitalization insurance policy* reimburses you for the cost of your hospital stay. Hospitalization policies usually pay for a portion of (1) the hospital's daily semiprivate room rate, which typically includes meals, nursing care, and other routine services,

major medical plan an insurance plan designed to supplement the basic coverage of hospitalization, surgical, and physicians expenses; used to finance more catastrophic medical costs

and (2) the cost of ancillary services such as laboratory tests, imaging, and medications you receive while hospitalized. Many hospitalization plans also cover some outpatient and out-of-hospital services once you're discharged, such as in-home rehabilitation, diagnostic treatment, and preadmission testing. Some hospitalization plans merely pay a flat, daily amount for each day the insured is in the hospital, regardless of actual charges. Most policies limit the number of days of hospitalization and place a maximum dollar amount on ancillary services that they will pay for.

Surgical Expenses *Surgical expense insurance* covers the cost of surgery in or out of the hospital. Usually, surgical expense coverage is provided as part of a hospitalization insurance policy or as a rider to such a policy. Most plans reimburse you for *reasonable and customary* surgical expenses based on a survey of surgical costs during the previous year. They may also cover anesthesia, nonemergency treatment using imaging, and a limited allowance for diagnostic tests.

Some plans still pay according to a *schedule of benefits*, reimbursing up to a fixed maximum for a particular surgical procedure. For example, the policy might state that you would receive no more than $1,500 for an appendectomy or $1,200 for diagnostic arthroscopic surgery on a knee. Scheduled benefits are often inadequate when compared with typical surgical costs. Most elective cosmetic surgeries, such as a "nose job" or other cosmetic surgeries, are typically excluded from reimbursement unless they are deemed medically necessary.

Physician Expenses *Physician expenses insurance*, also called *regular medical expense insurance*, covers the cost of visits to a doctor's office or for a doctor's hospital visits, including consultation with a specialist. Also covered are imaging and laboratory tests performed outside of a hospital. Plans are offered on either a *reasonable and customary* or *scheduled benefit* basis. Sometimes, the first few visits with the physician for any single cause are excluded. This exclusion serves the same purpose as the deductible and waiting period features found in other types of insurance. Often, these plans specify a maximum payment per visit, as well as a maximum number of visits per injury or illness.

Major Medical Insurance Major medical plans provide broad coverage for nearly all types of medical expenses resulting from either illnesses or accidents. In the

Here is a convenient checklist that you can use to compare the costs and benefits of competing health care plans.

Check those services listed in the first column that are most important to you, determine how these services are handled in each policy, and then write in the co-insurance or co-payment rate and any limits on service under each of the different policy columns. The most important covered service is hospitalization.

Service	Policy #1	Policy #2	Policy #3
Hospital care			
Surgery (inpatient and outpatient)			
Office visits to your doctor			
Maternity/well-baby care			
Pediatric care			
Immunizations			
Mammograms			
Medical tests, X-rays			
Mental health care			
Dental care, braces, and cleaning			
Vision care, eyeglasses, and exams			
Prescription drugs			
Home health care			
Nursing home care			
Services you need that are excluded			
Choice of doctors			
Location of doctors and hospitals			
Ease of getting an appointment			
Minimal paperwork			
Waiting period for coverage			

Source: Adapted from www.pahealthoptions.com/docs/compare_coverage_checklist.pdf, accessed October 2016.

past, it was common to have lifetime limits of $500,000 or $1,000,000. However, the ACA eliminates lifetime limits on total health care insurance payments by insurers. Because hospitalization, surgical, and physicians expense coverage meets the smaller medical costs, major medical is used to finance more catastrophic medical costs. Many people buy major medical with a high deductible to protect against a catastrophic illness.

Comprehensive Major Medical Insurance A com-prehensive major medical insurance plan combines basic hospitalization, surgical, and physician expenses coverage with major medical protection into a single policy, usually with a low deductible. Comprehensive major medical insurance is often written under a group contract, although efforts have been taken to make this type of coverage available to individuals.

Dental Services *Dental insurance* covers necessary dental care and some dental injuries sustained through accidents. (Expenses for accidental damage to natural teeth are normally covered under standard surgical expense and major medical policies.) Covered services may include examinations, X-rays, dental

comprehensive major medical insurance a health insurance plan that combines into a single policy the coverage for basic hospitalization, surgical, and physician expense along with major medical protection cleanings, fillings, extractions, dentures, root canal therapy, orthodontics, and oral surgery. The maximum coverage under most dental policies is often low—$1,000 to $2,500 per patient—so these plans don't fully protect against high dental work costs.

Limited Protection Policies The types of health plans discussed so far are sufficient to meet the protection needs of most individuals and families. But insurance companies offer other options that provide limited protection against certain types of perils:

▶ *Accident policies* that pay a specified sum to an insured injured in a certain type of accident

▶ *Sickness policies*, sometimes called *dread disease policies*, that pay a specified sum for a named disease, such as cancer

▶ *Hospital income policies* that guarantee a specific daily, weekly, or monthly amount as long as the insured is hospitalized

Sound insurance planning seldom dictates the purchase of limited protection policies. The cost of purchasing these insurance options typically outweighs the limited coverage they provide. The problem with buying policies that cover only a certain type of accident, illness, or financial need is that major gaps in coverage will often occur. The financial loss can be just as great if the insured falls down a flight of stairs or if contracts cancer, lung disease, or heart disease. Most limited-peril policies should be used only to supplement a comprehensive insurance program if the coverage is not overlapping.

9-4b Policy Provisions of Medical Expense Plans

To compare the health insurance plans offered by different insurers, evaluate whether they contain liberal or restrictive provisions. Generally, policy provisions can be divided into two groups: terms of payment and terms of coverage.

Terms of Payment Four provisions govern how much your health insurance plan will pay:

deductible the initial amount *not* covered by an insurance policy and thus the insured's responsibility; usually determined on a calendar-year basis or on a per-illness or per-accident basis

participation (co-insurance) clause a provision in many health insurance policies stipulating that the insurer will pay some portion—say, 80 or 90 percent—of the amount of the covered loss in excess of the deductible

internal limits a feature commonly found in health insurance policies that limits the amounts that will be paid for certain specified expenses, even if the claim does *not* exceed overall policy limits

(1) deductibles, (2) participation (co-insurance), (3) internal limits, and (4) coordination of benefits.

Deductibles Because major medical insurance plans are designed to supplement basic hospitalization, surgical, and physicians expense plans, those offered under an indemnity (fee-for-service) plan often have a relatively large *deductible*, typically $500 or $1,000. The **deductible** represents the initial amount that's *not* covered by the policy and thus must be paid by the insured. Comprehensive major medical plans tend to offer lower deductibles, sometimes $100 or less. Most plans offer a calendar-year, all-inclusive deductible, which allows the insured to accumulate the deductible from more than one incident of use. Some plans also include a *carryover provision*, whereby any part of the deductible that occurs during the final three months of the year can be applied to the current year's deductible and can *also* be applied to the following calendar year's deductible. In a few plans, the deductible is on a per-illness or per-accident basis.

> **EXAMPLE:** Effect of Per-Illness or Per-Accident Deductible You're covered by a health insurance policy that has a $1,000 per-illness or per-accident deductible. How much would the policy pay if you suffered three separate accidents in one year, each requiring $1,000 of medical expenses? None! Unfortunately, you wouldn't be eligible to collect any benefits from the major medical plan.

Participation (Co-insurance) A **participation**, or **co-insurance**, **clause** stipulates that the company will pay some portion—say, 80 percent or 90 percent—of the amount of the covered loss in excess of the deductible rather than the entire amount. Co-insurance helps reduce the incentive for policyholders to fake illness and discourages them from incurring unnecessary medical expenses. Many major medical plans also have a *stop-loss provision* that places a cap on the amount of participation required. Without a stop-loss provision, a $1 million medical bill could leave the insured responsible for, say, $200,000 of costs. Often such provisions limit the insured's participation to less than $10,000 and sometimes to as little as $2,000.

Internal Limits Most major medical policies are written with **internal limits** that control the amounts paid for certain specified expenses—even if the claim *doesn't* exceed overall policy limits. Charges commonly subject to internal limits are hospital room and board, surgical fees, mental and nervous conditions, and nursing services. If an insured chooses an expensive physician or medical facility, then he or she is responsible for paying the portion of the charges that are above a "reasonable and customary" level or beyond a specified maximum amount. The following example shows how deductibles, co-insurance, and internal limits constrain the amount a company is obligated to pay under a major medical plan.

Major Medical Policy: An Example Assume that Alonso Ramirez a graduate student, has coverage under a major medical insurance policy that specifies a $1,000 deductible, an 80 percent co-insurance clause, internal limits of $350 per day on hospital room and board, and $6,000 as the maximum payable surgical fee. When Alonso was hospitalized for three days to remove a small tumor, he incurred these costs:

Hospitalization: 3 days at $500 a day	$ 1,500
Surgical expense	5,800
Other covered medical expenses	3,800
Total medical expenses	$11,100

By the terms of the policy's co-insurance clause, the maximum the company must pay is 80 percent of the covered loss in excess of the deductible. Without internal limits, the company would pay $8,080 (0.80 × [$11,100 − $1,000]). The internal limits further restrict the payment. Even though 80 percent of the $500-per-day hospitalization charge is $400, the most the company would have to pay is $350 per day. Thus, Alonso, the insured, becomes liable for $50 per day for three days, or $150. The surgical expense is below the $6,000 internal limit, so the 80 percent co-insurance clause applies, and the insurer will pay $4,640 (0.80 × $5,800). The company's total obligation is reduced to $7,930 ($8,080 − $150), and Alonso must pay a total of $3,170 ($1,000 deductible + 0.20 × [$11,100 − $1,000] co-insurance + $150 excess hospital room and board charges). This example shows that, even though major medical insurance can offer large amounts of reimbursement, the in-sured may still be responsible for substantial payments.

Coordination of Benefits Health insurance policies are not contracts of *indemnity*. This means that the insured party can collect multiple payments for the same illness or accident unless health insurance policies include a **coordination of benefits provision**. This clause prevents you from collecting more than 100 percent of covered charges by collecting benefits from more than one policy. For example, many private health insurance policies coordinate benefit provisions with medical benefits paid under workers' compensation. Others widely advertise that their policies will pay claims regardless of the policyholder's other coverage and, of course, often charge more per dollar of protection. Using policies with coordination of benefits clauses can help you prevent coverage overlaps and, ideally, reduce your premiums.

Considering the complexity of medical expense contracts, the various clauses limiting payments, and coordination of benefits with other policies, one might expect that insurers often pay only partial claims and sometimes completely deny claims. However, if you make a claim and don't receive satisfactory payment, don't give up.

Terms of Coverage Several contract provisions affect a health insurance plan's value to you. Some important provisions address (1) the persons and places covered, (2) cancellation, (3) pre-existing conditions, (4) pregnancy and abortion, (5) mental illness, (6) rehabilitation coverage, and (7) continuation of group coverage.

Persons and Places Covered Some health insurance policies cover only the named insured; others offer protection to all family members. Historically, of those that offer family coverage, some have terminated benefits payable on behalf of children at age 18 and others continued them to age 24 as long as the child remains in school or is single. *The health reform bill allows young adults to remain on their parents' insurance until they turn 26 years old.* Some policies protect you only while you're in the United States or Canada. Others offer worldwide coverage but exclude specified countries.

Cancellation Many health insurance policies are written to permit *cancellation* at the insurer's option at any time. Some policies explicitly state this; others don't. To protect yourself against premature cancellation, buy policies that specifically state that the insurer won't cancel coverage so long as premiums are paid.

Pre-existing Conditions In the past, most health insurance policies sold to individuals (as opposed to group/employer-sponsored plans) contained a **pre-existing condition clause**. This means the policy might exclude coverage for physical or mental problems you had at the time you bought it. In some

> **coordination of benefits provision** a provision often included in health insurance policies to prevent the insured from collecting more than 100 percent of covered charges; it requires that benefit payments be coordinated if the insured is eligible for benefits under more than one policy

> **pre-existing condition clause** a clause included in most individual health insurance policies permitting permanent or temporary exclusion of coverage for any physical or mental problems the insured had at the time the policy was purchased. The Patient Protection and Affordable Care Act of 2010 prohibits such exclusions

policies, the exclusion was permanent; in others, it lasted only for the first year or two that the coverage was in force. Some group insurance plans have also historically had pre-existing condition clauses, but they tended to be less restrictive than those in individually written policies. The ACA has changed this. The new legislation prohibits insurers from denying coverage due to the presence of pre-existing conditions.

Employees who have recently left a job or retired are covered by the *Health Insurance Portability and Accountability Act, (HIPAA).* This federal law, implemented in 1996, is designed to protect people's ability to obtain continued health insurance after they leave a job or retire, even if they have a serious health problem. Under HIPAA, if you've already been covered by a health plan without a break in coverage of more than 63 days and you apply for new insurance, insurers cannot turn you down, charge you higher premiums, or enforce an exclusionary period because of your health status. HIPAA doesn't guarantee you group coverage, but it does protect your ability to buy individual health insurance. HIPAA now applies only to "grandfathered" plans that existed when the ACA went into effect in March 2010. The ACA deals with some of the issues previously addressed by HIPAA.

Pregnancy and Abortion Many individual and group health insurance plans include special clauses for medical expenses incurred through pregnancy or abortion. Some liberal policies pay for all related expenses, including sickleave pay during the final months of pregnancy, whereas others pay for medical expenses that result from pregnancy or abortion complications, but not for routine procedure expenses. In the most restrictive cases, policies offer no coverage for any costs of pregnancy or abortion.

Mental Illness Many health insurance plans omit or offer only reduced benefits for treatment of mental disorders.

Nednapa/Shutterstock.com

For example, a health insurance policy may offer hospitalization benefits that continue to pay so long as you remain hospitalized— except for mental illness. It may restrict payment for mental illness to one-half the normally provided payment amounts and for a period not to exceed 30 days. Unfortunately, mental illness is the number one sickness requiring long-term hospital care. Because coverage for mental illness is an important insurance protection, check your policies to learn how liberal—or how restrictive—they are regarding this feature.

Rehabilitation Coverage Health insurance plans focus primarily on meeting reasonable and necessary medical expenses. But many policies also include *rehabilitation coverage* for counseling, occupational therapy, and even some educational or job training programs for insureds who are partially or totally disabled because of an illness or accident. This is a good feature to look for in major medical and disability income policies.

Continuation of Group Coverage Under the **Consolidated Omnibus Budget Reconciliation Act (COBRA)**, passed by Congress in 1986, an employee who leaves the insured group voluntarily or involuntarily (except in the case of "gross misconduct") may elect to continue coverage for up to 18 months by paying premiums to his or her former employer on time (up to 102 percent of the company cost). The employee retains all benefits previously available, except for disability income coverage.

Similar continuation coverage is available for retirees and their families for up to 18 months or until they become eligible for Medicare, whichever occurs first. An employee's dependents may be covered for up to 36 months under COBRA under special circumstances, such as divorce or death of the employee. After COBRA coverage expires, most states provide for conversion of the group coverage to an individual policy regardless of the insured's current health and without evidence of insurability. As noted earlier, under the ACA, losing your job triggers a "qualifying life event" that allows you to obtain health insurance under COBRA. Or, you can buy a policy in the private health insurance market.

Consolidated Omnibus Budget Reconciliation Act (COBRA) federal law that allows an employee who leaves the insured group to continue coverage for up to 18 months by paying premiums to his or her former employer on time; the employee retains all benefits previously available, except for disability income coverage

Wavebreakmedia/Shutterstock.com

9-4c Cost Containment Provisions for Medical Expense Plans

In response to the ongoing inflation in medical costs, insurers and employers that sponsor medical expense plans try to control their costs. Cost containment provisions are included in almost all medical expense plans and include the following:

▶ **Preadmission certification.** This requires you to receive approval from your insurer before entering the hospital for a scheduled stay. Such approval is not normally required for emergency stays.

▶ **Continued stay review.** To receive normal reimbursement, the insured must secure approval from the insurer for any stay that exceeds the originally approved limits.

▶ **Second surgical opinions.** Many plans require second opinions on specific nonemergency procedures and, in their absence, may reduce the surgical benefits paid. Most surgical expense plans now fully reimburse the cost of second opinions.

▶ **Waiver of co-insurance.** Because insurers can save money on hospital room-and-board charges by encouraging outpatient surgery, many now agree to waive the co-insurance clause and pay 100 percent of surgical costs for outpatient procedures. A similar waiver is sometimes applied to generic pharmaceuticals. For example, the patient may choose between an 80 percent payment for a brand-name pharmaceutical costing $35 or 100 percent reimbursement for its $15 generic equivalent.

▶ **Limitation of insurer's responsibility.** Many policies also have provisions limiting the insurer's financial responsibility to reimbursing only for costs that are considered "reasonable and customary." This provision can sometimes place limitations on the type and place of medical care for which the insurer will pay.

9-5 LONG-TERM-CARE INSURANCE

LO5 **Long-term care** involves the delivery of medical and personal care, other than hospitalization, to persons with chronic medical conditions in a nursing home, in an assisted living community, or in the patient's home. Long-term care is expensive. For example, a year's stay in a private room in a nursing home averages $92,376 according to a 2016 cost-of-care survey by Genworth Financial, which is up from an average of $67,525 in 2008. About 44 percent of men and 58 percent of women over 65 are expected to need long-term care at some time. And yet, less than 3 percent of American adults have purchased long-term care insurance. This is a potential concern because the average long-term stay is over one year.

> Long-term care insurance is an important part of health insurance and retirement financial planning.

Consumers directly pay about 25 percent of long-term care costs, and government programs such as Medicare and Medicaid cover less than half of the total cost for those meeting their strict eligibility requirements. Major medical insurance plans also exclude most of the costs related to long-term care. Fortunately, long-term-care insurance policies are available that are indemnity policies paying a fixed dollar amount for each day you receive specified care either in a nursing home or at home. The decision to buy long-term-care insurance is an important part of health insurance and retirement financial planning.

The ACA has provisions that relate to long-term care. It includes the Community Living Assistance Services and Support Program (CLASS), which is a voluntary, consumer-financed insurance plan designed to cover long-term care expenses. This is similar to long-term-care programs currently available in the private market. However, it differs in that the program will be administered by the government. Further, any working adult who is 18 or older will be able

long-term care the delivery of medical and personal care, other than hospital care, to persons with chronic medical conditions resulting from either illness or frailty to enroll, regardless of any pre-existing medical condition. And the benefits will be good for as long as someone needs long-term care. However, the fate of the long-term-care parts of the ACA remain unclear. The U.S. Department of Health and Human Services has questioned the financial viability of implementing the long-term-care program presented in the ACA.

Most individual long-term-care products are purchased either through organizations like the American Association of Retired Persons (AARP) or directly from the more than 100 insurance companies that offer them. Employer-sponsored long-term-care insurance is also growing in popularity. Usually, however, employees pay the full cost of premiums, although employer-sponsored plans can often cost less than purchasing long-term care on an individual basis. Whether you purchase long-term-care insurance as an individual or through an employer-sponsored plan, however, it's important to evaluate policy provisions and costs.

9-5a Do You Need Long-Term-Care Insurance?

The odds of needing more than a year of nursing home care before you reach age 65 are 1 in 33, and the expense of a prolonged nursing home stay can cause severe financial hardship. Answer the following questions to decide if you need long-term-care insurance:

▶ **Do you have many assets to preserve for your dependents?** Because you must deplete most of your assets before Medicaid will pay for nursing home care, some financial advisors recommend that people over 65 whose net worth is more than $100,000 and income exceeds $50,000 a year consider long-term-care insurance—*if* they can afford the premiums. The very wealthy, however, may prefer to self-insure.

▶ **Can you afford the premiums?** Premiums of many good-quality policies can be 5 percent to 7 percent of annual income or even more. Such high premiums may cause more financial hardship than the cost of a potential nursing home stay. You may be better off investing the amount you'd spend in premiums; it would then be available for *any* future need, including long-term health care.

▶ **Is there a family history of disabling disease?** This factor increases your odds of needing long-term care. If there's a history of Alzheimer's, neurological disorders, or other potentially debilitating diseases, the need for long-term-care insurance may increase.

▶ **What is your gender?** Women tend to live longer than men and are more likely to require long-term

care. They're also the primary caregivers for other family members, which may mean that when they need care, help won't be available.

▶ **Do you have family who can care for you?** The availability of relatives or home health services to provide care can reduce the cost of long-term care.

9-5b Long-Term-Care Insurance Provisions and Costs

When purchasing long-term-care insurance, it is important to evaluate and compare policy provisions, which are important factors in determining the premium for each policy. Exhibit 9.3 summarizes the typical provisions of policies offered by leading insurers. Let's take a closer look at the most important policy provisions to consider when purchasing long-term-care insurance:

▶ **Type of care.** Some long-term-care policies offer benefits only for nursing home care, whereas others pay only for services in the insured's home, such as skilled or unskilled nursing care, physical therapy, homemakers, and home health aides. Because it's hard to predict whether a person might need to be in a nursing home, most financial planners recommend policies covering both. Many of these policies focus on nursing home care, and any expenses for health care in the insured's home are covered in a rider to the basic policy. Many policies also cover assisted living, adult day care and other community care programs, alternative care, and respite care for the caregiver.

▶ **Eligibility requirements.** Some important *gatekeeper provisions* determine whether the insured will receive payment for claims. The most liberal policies state that the insured will qualify for benefits as long as his or her physician orders the care. A popular and much more restrictive provision pays only for long-term care that's medically necessary because of sickness or injury. One common gatekeeper provision requires the insured's inability to perform a given number of *activities of daily living (ADLs)* such as bathing, dressing, or eating. Some policies also provide care for cognitive impairment or when medically necessary and prescribed by the patient's physician. In the case of an Alzheimer's patient who remains physically healthy, inclusion of cognitive abilities as ADLs would be extremely important.

▶ **Services covered.** Most policies today cover several levels of service in state-licensed nursing homes: skilled, intermediate, and custodial care. *Skilled care* is needed when a patient requires constant attention from a medical professional, such as a physician or registered nurse. *Intermediate care* is provided when

Exhibit 9.3

Typical Provisions in Long-Term-Care Insurance Policies

Long-term-care insurers offer a wide range of provisions in their policies. A typical policy includes the following.

Services covered	Skilled, intermediate, and custodial care; home health care; adult day care (often)
Benefit eligibility	Physician certification and/or medically necessary
Daily benefit	$100–$500/day, nursing home; $50–$250/day, home health care
Benefit period	3–4 years
Maximum benefit period	5 years; unlimited
Waiting period	0–100 days
Renewability	Guaranteed
Pre-existing conditions	Conditions existing 6–12 months prior to policy coverage
Inflation protection	Yes, for an additional premium
Deductibility periods	0, 20, 30, 90, 100 days
Alzheimer's disease coverage	Yes
Age limits for purchasing	40–84

the patient needs medical attention or supervision but not the constant attention of a medical professional. *Custodial care* provides assistance in the normal activities of daily living but no medical attention or supervision; a physician or nurse may be on call, however. Most long-term-care policies also cover home care services, such as skilled or unskilled nursing care, physical therapy, homemakers, and home health aides provided by state-licensed or Medicare-certified home health agencies.

▶ **Daily benefits.** Long-term-care policies reimburse the insured for the cost of services incurred up to a daily maximum. For nursing home care policies, the daily maximums generally range from $100 to $500, depending on the amount of premium that the insured is willing to pay. For combination nursing home and home care policies, the maximum home care benefit is normally half the nursing home maximum.

▶ **Benefit duration.** The maximum duration of benefits ranges from one year to the insured's lifetime. Lifetime coverage is expensive, however. Most financial planners recommend the purchase of a policy with a duration of three to six years to give the insured protection for a longer-than-average period of care.

▶ **Waiting period.** Even if the policy's eligibility requirements are met, the insured must pay long-term-care expenses during the waiting, or elimination, period. Typical waiting periods are 90 to 100 days. Although premiums are much lower for policies with longer waiting periods, the insured must have liquid assets to cover his

or her expenses during that period. An insured who still requires care after the waiting period expires will begin to receive benefits for the duration of the policy, as long as its eligibility requirements continue to be met.

▶ **Renewability.** Most long-term-care insurance policies now include a guaranteed renewability provision to ensure continued coverage for your lifetime as long as you continue to pay the premiums. This clause does not ensure a level premium over time, however. Nearly all policies allow the insurer to raise premiums if the claims experience for your peer group of policyholders is unfavorable. Watch out for policies with an optional renewability clause because they are renewable *only at the insurer's option.*

▶ **Pre-existing conditions.** Some policies once included a pre-existing conditions clause, similar to those described previously. If someone has already been diagnosed with Parkinson's or Alzheimer's disease, takes memory drugs, needs any type of assistance in walking, has had a stroke, or has osteoporosis,

waiting period (elimination period) the period, after an insured meets the policy's eligibility requirements, during which he or she must pay expenses out-of-pocket; when the waiting period expires, the insured begins to receive benefits

guaranteed renewability policy provision ensuring continued insurance coverage for the insured's lifetime as long as the premiums continue to be paid

optional renewability contractual clause allowing the insured to continue insurance *only at the insurer's option* an insurance company may not be willing to sell that person a long-term insurance policy.

▶ **Inflation protection.** Many policies offer inflation protection riders that, for an additional premium, let you increase benefits by a flat amount, often 5 percent, per year. Others offer benefits linked to the rise in the consumer price index (CPI). Most policies discontinue inflation adjustments after either 10 or 20 years. Inflation protection riders can add between 25 and 40 percent to the basic premium for a long-term-care insurance policy.

▶ **Premium levels.** Long-term-care insurance is rather expensive, and premiums vary widely among insurance companies. For example, an average healthy 55-year-old couple may pay about $4,000 per year for a policy that pays for three years' care at $150 per day for nursing home care with a 90-day waiting period and a 3 percent inflation rider. The cost of the same coverage drops substantially with the ages of the insured. Given the significant rise in premium with age, some financial planners recommend buying long-term-care insurance when you are fairly young. But keep in mind that, although the annual premiums are lower, you'll be paying for a lot longer time before you would likely need the benefits.

9-5c How to Buy Long-Term-Care Insurance

When buying long-term-care insurance, make sure the insurer is a financially sound company (based on ratings from the major ratings agencies) with a proven track record in this market segment. Here are some additional guidelines to help you choose the right policy:

▶ **Buy the policy when you're healthy.** Once you have a disease, such as Alzheimer's or multiple sclerosis, or have a stroke, you become uninsurable. So the best time to buy is when you're in your mid-50s or 60s.

▶ **Buy the right types of coverage—but don't buy more coverage than you need.** Your policy should cover skilled, intermediate, and custodial care as well as adult day care centers and assisted living facilities. If you have access to family caregivers or home health services, opt for only nursing home coverage; if not, select a policy with generous home health care benefits. To reduce costs, increase the waiting period before benefits begin; the longer you can cover the costs yourself,

disability income insurance insurance that provides families with weekly or monthly payments to replace income when the insured is unable to work because of a covered illness, injury, or disease

Monkey Business Images/Shutterstock.com

the lower your premiums. You may also choose a shorter benefit payment period; three years is a popular choice, but the average nursing home stay is about one year. Lifetime coverage increases the premium for a 65-year-old by as much as 40 percent.

▶ **Understand what the policy covers and when it pays benefits.** The amounts paid, benefit periods, and services covered vary among insurers. One rule of thumb is to buy a policy covering 80 to 100 percent of current nursing home costs in your area. Some policies pay only for licensed health care providers, whereas others include assistance with household chores. Know how the policy defines benefit eligibility.

9-6 DISABILITY INCOME INSURANCE

LO6 When a family member becomes sick for an extended period, the effect on the family goes beyond medical bills. About one-third of people between the ages of 35 and 65 will be disabled for 90 days or longer before age 65, and about one in seven people between the ages of 35 and 65 will become disabled for five years or more. During the working years, becoming disabled is more likely than death. For a 35-year-old male, the odds are nearly two to one, and for a 35-year-old female, the odds are nearly three to one. Although most Americans have life insurance, few have taken steps to protect their family should a serious illness or accident prevent them from working for an extended period.

The best way to protect against the potentially devastating financial consequences of a health-related disability is with disability income insurance. **Disability income insurance** provides families with weekly or monthly payments to replace income when the insured is unable to work because of a covered illness, injury, or disease. Some companies also offer disability income protection for a spousal homemaker; such coverage helps pay for the services that the spouse would normally provide.

Almost all employers offer disability income insurance at attractive rates, but it is often voluntary, and you may have to pay the entire premium yourself. Group coverage is usually a good buy because the premiums average $300 to $500 a year depending on age and income—about one-third less than the cost of comparable private coverage. Of course, if you change jobs then you may lose the coverage. The benefits received from a group plan for which you pay the premiums are tax free (unless paid through a flexible spending account).

Social Security offers disability income benefits, but you must be unable to do *any* job whatsoever to receive benefits. Benefits are payable only if your disability is expected to last at least one year (or to be fatal), and they don't begin until you've been disabled for at least five months. The actual amount paid is a percentage of your previous monthly earnings, with some statistical adjustments. The percentage is higher for people with low earnings. The average benefit amount in 2016 was $1,166 per month, with a maximum monthly payment of $2,639 per month.

There is a significant need for disability income coverage. Although most workers receive some disability insurance benefits from their employer, in many cases the group

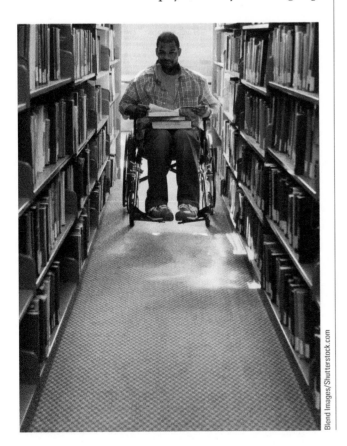

Blend Images/Shutterstock.com

plan falls short and pays only about 60 to 70 percent of salary for a limited period. The first step in considering disability income insurance is to determine the dollar amount that your family would need (typically monthly) if an earner becomes disabled. Then you can buy the coverage that you need or supplement existing coverage if necessary.

9-6a Estimating Your Disability Insurance Needs

The main purpose of disability income insurance is to replace all (or most) of the income—that is, earnings—that would be lost if you became disabled and physically unable to hold a job. In essence, it should enable you to maintain a standard of living at or near your present level. To help decide how much disability income insurance is right for you, use Worksheet 9.2 to estimate your monthly disability benefit needs. Here is all you have to do:

1. **Calculate take-home pay.** Disability benefits are generally (but not always) tax free, so you typically need to replace only your *take-home (after-tax) pay.* Benefits from employer-paid policies are fully or partially taxable. To estimate take-home pay, subtract income and Social Security taxes paid from your gross earned income (salary only). Divide this total by 12 to get your monthly take-home pay.

2. **Estimate the monthly amounts of disability benefits from government or employer programs.**

   a. *Social Security disability benefits.* Obtain an estimate of your benefits by using the online calculators provided by the Social Security Administration at www.ssa.gov/planners/benefitcalculators.htm.

   b. *Other government program disability benefits* for which you qualify (armed services, Veterans Administration, civil service, the Federal Employees Compensation Act, state workers' compensation systems). There are also special programs for railroad workers, longshoremen, and people with black-lung disease.

   c. *Company disability benefits.* Ask your company benefits supervisor to help you calculate company-provided benefits, including sick pay or wage continuation plans (these are essentially short-term disability income insurance) and plans formally designated as disability insurance. For each benefit that your employer offers, check on its tax treatment.

   d. *Group disability policy benefits.* A private insurer provides the coverage and you pay for it, often through payroll deduction.

3. **Add up your existing monthly disability benefits.**

Using this worksheet makes the job of estimating disability benefit insurance needs a lot easier.

DISABILITY BENEFIT NEEDS

Name(s) _____ Date _____

1. Estimate current monthly take-home pay .... $ _____
2. Estimate existing monthly benefits
   a. Social Security benefits .... $ _____
   b. Other government program benefits .... _____
   c. Company disability benefits .... _____
   d. Group disability policy benefits .... _____
3. Total existing monthly disability benefits (2a + 2b + 2c + 2d) .... _____
4. **Estimated monthly disability benefits needed ([1] – [3])** .... $ _____

4. **Subtract your existing monthly disability benefits from your current monthly take-home pay.** The result shows the estimated monthly disability benefits that you'll need in order to maintain your present after-tax income. Note that investment income and spousal income (if the spouse is presently employed) are ignored because it's assumed that this income will continue and is necessary to maintain your current standard of living. If your spouse is now unemployed but would enter the workforce if you ever became disabled, then his or her estimated monthly income (take-home pay) could be subtracted from Item 4 of Worksheet 9.2 to determine your net monthly disability benefit needs.

9-6b Disability Income Insurance Provisions and Costs

The scope and cost of your disability income coverage depend on its contractual provisions. Although disability income insurance policies can be complex, certain features are important: (1) definition of disability, (2) benefit amount and duration, (3) probationary period, (4) waiting period, (5) renewability, and (6) other provisions.

Definition of Disability Disability policies vary in the standards that you must meet to receive benefits. Some pay benefits if you're unable to perform the duties of your customary occupation—the *own occupation* (or "Own Occ") definition—whereas others pay only if you can engage in no gainful employment at all—the *any occupation* (or "Any Occ") definition. Under the "Own Occ" definition, a professor who lost his voice—yet could still

be paid to write or do research—would receive full benefits because he couldn't lecture, a primary function of his occupation. With a *residual benefit option*, you would be paid partial benefits if you can work only part-time or at a lower salary. The "Any Occ" definition is considerably less expensive because it gives the insurer more leeway in determining whether the insured should receive benefits.

Benefit Amount and Duration Most individual disability income policies pay a flat monthly benefit, which is stated in the policy, whereas group plans pay a fixed percentage of gross income. In either case, insurers normally won't agree to amounts of more than 60 to 70 percent of the insured's gross income. Insurers won't issue policies for the full amount of gross income because this would give some people an incentive to fake a disability (e.g., "bad back") and collect more in insurance benefits than they normally would receive as take-home pay.

Monthly benefits can be paid for a few months or a lifetime. If you're assured a substantial defined-benefit pension, Social Security, or other benefits at retirement, then a policy that pays benefits until age 65 is adequate. Many people, however, will need to continue working for many more years and should consider a policy offering lifetime benefits. Some policies offer benefits for periods as short as two or five years. Although these policies may be better than nothing, they don't protect against the major financial losses associated with long-term disabilities.

Probationary Period Both group and individual disability income policies are likely to include a probationary period, usually 7 to 30 days, which is a time delay from the date the

Financial Planning Tips

BUYING DISABILITY INCOME INSURANCE

Consider the following tips in evaluating disability income insurance policies:

- **Know what the government can do for you.** Social Security disability benefits are available only to those with a condition that makes them unable to work for at least a year or that is terminal. The average benefit payout is only about 40 percent of pre-disability income. Qualified applicants should expect to wait between three and five months to get Social Security disability benefits. Only a few states provide additional benefits, although it's worth checking that. If you buy a private disability income insurance policy, be aware that most require you to apply for Social Security benefits, which will be subtracted from the benefit that you receive from the insurer.

- **Buying a policy at work is usually cheapest.** Many employers provide disability income insurance and pay part of the premiums. If you go this route, make sure that you have both short- and long-term coverage. Short-term coverage usually lasts for a few months and long-term coverage often starts paying after 90 to 180 days. Make sure that you're not exposed to a significant gap

between the two. If you buy a policy through your employer, you may be able to pay the premiums directly out of your paycheck on a pretax basis. However, this means that your benefits would be taxable.

- **Determine if a policy purchased through your employer is portable.** It's good to know if you can keep the policy if you leave your current company.

- **Understand the circumstances in which the disability insurance benefit will be paid.** The best trigger is when you cannot do your current job. However, some policies pay only if you cannot do any comparable job, which is a much more complicated constraint.

- **Read the fine print.** It's important to know what percentage of pre-disability income is paid out by the policy. And does it include just base salary or additional compensation like commissions or bonuses? Are there limits on benefit payouts for certain conditions like mental illness? You'll want to know the ins and outs of each policy that you consider.

Source: Anna Wilde Matthews, "Just in Case: The Skinny on Buying Disability Insurance," http://online.wsj.com/news/articles/SB1000142 4052748704561004575013073100310794, accessed October 2016.

policy is issued until benefit privileges are available. Any disability stemming from an illness, injury, or disease that occurs during the probationary period is *not* covered—even if it continues beyond this period. This feature keeps costs down.

Waiting Period The waiting period (elimination period) provisions in a disability income policy are similar to those discussed for long-term-care insurance. Typical waiting periods range from 30 days to a year. If you have an adequate emergency fund to provide family income during the early months of disability, you can choose a longer waiting period and substantially reduce your premiums, as shown in Exhibit 9.4.

With most insurers, you can trade an increase in the waiting period—say, from 60 days to 90 days—for an increase in the duration of benefits from five years to age 65 or later. In fact, as Exhibit 9.4 shows, the premium charged by this insurer for a policy covering a 35-year-old male with a 30-day waiting period and one-year benefit period ($389) is comparable to one charged for a five-year benefit period with a three-month waiting period ($343). Accepting this type of trade-off usually makes sense

because the primary purpose of insurance is to protect the insured from a catastrophic loss, not from smaller losses that are better handled through proper budgeting and saving.

Renewability Most individual disability income insurance is either *guaranteed renewable* or *noncancelable*. As with long-term-care policies, guaranteed renewability ensures that you can renew the policy until you reach the age stated in the clause, usually between 65 and 67. Premiums can be raised over time if justified by the loss experience of all those in the same class (usually based on age, sex, and occupational category). Noncancelable policies offer guaranteed renewability, but they also guarantee that future premiums will remain the same as those stated in the policy at issuance. Because of this stable premium guarantee, noncancelable policies generally are more expensive than those with only a guaranteed renewability provision.

Other Provisions The purchasing power of income from a long-term disability policy that pays, say, $2,000 per month could be severely affected by inflation. In fact,

Exhibit 9.4

Representative Disability Income Insurance Premium Costs

The cost of disability income insurance varies with the terms of payment, as well as the length of the waiting period. Women pay substantially higher rates than men do. This table shows premiums for basic disability income coverage for a 35-year-old that pays $2,000 per month in benefits and has guaranteed premiums to age 67. The quotes assume the best occupation class, which is professional office. The policy also includes a 3 percent inflation rider.

Benefit Period:	1 Years		5 Years		To Age 67	
Waiting Period	**Male**	**Female**	**Male**	**Female**	**Male**	**Female**
30 Days	$389	$566	$596	$907	$901	$1,532
60 Days	266	403	415	621	673	1,167
90 Days	Not available	Not available	343	490	590	963
180 Days	Not available	Not available	283	437	521	846
365 Days	Not available	Not available	na	na	490	781

PLANNING OVER A LIFETIME

Insuring Your Health

Here are some key ideas concerning how insuring your health changes over the stages in the life cycle.

INDEPENDENT LIFESTYLE (20s)

▸ Assess your health and take steps to stay healthy: exercise, eat well, and avoid smoking and drinking too much alcohol.

▸ While in school or unemployed, take advantage of your opportunity to stay on your parents' health insurance until the age of 26.

▸ When employed, take out health care insurance coverage with your employer and/or check out policies available on the ACA insurance exchange.

▸ Evaluate the appropriateness of disability income insurance.

▸ Consider pre-tax accounts like flexibility spending to save money.

FAMILY AND CAREER DEVELOPMENT (30s–40s)

▸ Consider HMOs and PPOs to lower deductibles and to maximize flexibility of choices.

▸ Re-evaluate the need for disability income insurance.

▸ Re-evaluate your health insurance policy and its premiums.

MATURE LIFESTYLE (50s–60s)

▸ Evaluate the need for long-term-care insurance.

▸ Re-evaluate the need for long-term-care insurance.

▸ Familiarize yourself with Medicare benefits.

RETIREMENT (65+)

▸ Consider the best way to get prescription benefits in light of Medicare options.

▸ Re-evaluate the need for long-term-care insurance.

a 3 percent inflation rate would reduce the purchasing power of this $2,000 benefit to less than $1,500 in 10 years. To counteract such a reduction, many insurers offer a *cost-of-living adjustment (COLA)*. With a COLA provision, the monthly benefit is adjusted upward each year, often in line with the CPI, although these annual adjustments are often capped at a given rate (say, 8 percent).

Although some financial advisors suggest buying COLA riders, others believe that the 10 to 25 percent additional premium is too much to pay for this protection.

Although the COLA provision applies only once the insured is disabled, the *guaranteed insurability option (GIO)* can allow you to purchase additional disability income insurance in line with inflation increases while you're still healthy. Under the GIO, the price of this additional insurance is fixed at the contract's inception, and you don't have to prove insurability.

A *waiver of premium* is standard in disability income policies. If you're disabled for a minimum period, normally 60 or 90 days, the insurer will waive any future premiums that come due while you remain disabled. In essence, the waiver of premium gives you additional disability income insurance in the amount of your regular premium payment.

Remember that disability income insurance is just one part of your overall personal financial plan. You'll need to find your own balance between cost and coverage.

Trevor Expands His Health Insurance Coverage

Trevor Wilson is 27 years old. He works for a company with a good health insurance plan. Indeed, Trevor has heard it's priced better than most plans and has consequently taken out the optional expanded dental and vision plans. While he doesn't currently wear glasses or contact lenses, he does go for an annual eye exam and wants the extra vision plan in case he ends up needing corrective lens or has any eye problems. His plan has a $40 co-payment for an annual eye exam and pays $100 toward eyeglass frames, plus 20 percent of the rest of the cost. Contacts lenses have similar coverage. Trevor pays just an additional $15 monthly premium for the vision plan. He feels more comfortable having expanded health insurance coverage.

While Trevor feels better having expanded health insurance coverage in general and vision coverage in particular, it isn't currently a cost-effective decision. He makes a $40 co-payment for an annual eye exam, which is probably cheaper than the full cost of an eye exam. But Trevor doesn't wear glasses or contacts. His $15 monthly premium costs him $180 per year. It's extremely unlikely that he saves anywhere near that much on the cost of his exam under the vision plan. And if Trevor has a significant medical problem with his eyes, his major medical insurance plan should cover the costs well. It could make sense for him to have expanded vision coverage in

Anteromite/Shutterstock.com

the future, if corrective lenses are needed, but for now it appears that Trevor's comfort in having expanded vision coverage is costly.

STUDY TOOLS 9

©viphotos/Shutterstock 140785408

LOCATED AT BACK OF THE TEXTBOOK
☐ Chapter Review Card

LOCATED AT WWW.CENGAGEBRAIN.COM
☐ Review Key Term flashcards and create your own cards.

☐ Track your knowledge and understanding of key concepts in personal finance.
☐ Complete practice and graded quizzes to prepare for tests.
☐ Complete interactive content at PFIN6 Online.
☐ View the chapter highlight boxes at PFIN6 Online.

Financial Planning Exercises

LO1, 2, 3, 4   **1.**   **Evaluating current health insurance.** Assess your current health insurance situation. What does your policy cover? What is excluded? Are there any gaps that you think need to be filled? Are there any risks in your current lifestyle or situation that might make additional coverage necessary? If you were to purchase health insurance for yourself in the near future, what type of plan would you select, and why? What steps can you take to keep your health costs down?

LO2, 3, 4   **2.**   **Comparing health insurance policies.** *Use Worksheet 9.1.* Sylvia Lewis a recent college graduate, has decided to accept a job offer from a nonprofit organization. She'll earn $34,000 a year but will receive no employee health benefits. Sylvia estimates that her monthly living expenses will be about $2,000 a month, including rent, food, transportation, and clothing. She has no health problems and expects to remain in good health in the near future. Using the Internet or other resources, gather information about three health insurance policies that Sylvia could purchase on her own. Include at least one HMO. Use Worksheet 9.1 to compare the policies' features. Should Sylvia buy health insurance? Why or why not? Assuming that she does decide to purchase health insurance, which of the three policies would you recommend and why?

LO2, 3, 4   **3.**   **Choosing a health insurance plan.** Tim and Lena Wallace have two children, a six-year-old and a five-month old. Their younger child, Justin, was born with a congenital heart defect that will require several major surgeries in the next few years to correct fully. Tim is employed as a salesperson for a major pharmaceutical firm, and Lena is not currently working outside of the home. Tim's employer offers a choice between two health benefit plans:

- An indemnity plan that allows the Wallaces to choose health services from a wide range of doctors and hospitals. The plan pays 80 percent of all medical costs, and the Wallaces are responsible for the other 20 percent. There's a deductible of $500 per person. Tim's employer will pay 100 percent of the cost of this plan for Tim, but the Wallaces will be responsible for paying $380 a month to cover Lena and the children under this plan.

- A group HMO. If the Wallaces choose this plan, the company still pays 100 percent of the plan's cost for Tim, but insurance for Lena and the children will cost $295 a month. They'll also have to make a $20 co-payment for any doctor's office visits and prescription drugs. They will be restricted to using the HMO's doctors and hospital for medical services.

Which plan do you recommend the Wallaces choose? Why? What other health coverage options should they consider?

LO2, 3, 4   **4.**   **Out-of-pocket health care insurance costs.** Brian Nam was seriously injured in a skiing accident that broke both his legs and an arm. His medical expenses included five days of hospitalization at $900 a day, $6,200 in surgical fees, $4,300 in physician's fees (including time in the hospital and eight follow-up office visits), $520 in prescription medications, and $2,100 for physical therapy treatments. All of these charges fall within customary and reasonable payment amounts.

a. If Brian had a health insurance plan that pays 80 percent of his charges with a $500 deductible and a $5,000 stop-loss provision, how much would he have to pay out of pocket?

b. What would Brian's out-of-pocket expenses be if he belonged to an HMO with a $20 co-pay for office visits?

c. Monthly premiums are $155 for the standard plan and $250 for the HMO. If he had no other medical expenses this year, which plan would have provided more cost-effective coverage for Brian? What other factors should be considered when deciding between the two plans?

Managing Credit Exercises

LO2, 3, 4, 5, 6 **5.** *Evaluating health care coverage.* Blake Wright was a self-employed window washer earning approximately $700 per week. One day, while cleaning windows on the eighth floor of the First National Bank Building, he tripped and fell from the scaffolding to the pavement below. He sustained multiple severe injuries but miraculously survived the accident. He was immediately rushed to the local hospital for surgery. Blake remained there for 60 days of treatment, after which he was allowed to go home for further recuperation. During his hospital stay, he incurred the following expenses: surgeon, $2,500; physician, $1,000; hospital bill for room and board, $250 per day; nursing services, $1,200; anesthetics, $600; wheelchair rental, $100; ambulance, $150; and drugs, $350. Blake has a major medical policy that has a $3,000 deductible clause, an 80 percent co-insurance clause, internal limits of $180 per day on hospital room and board, and $1,500 as a maximum surgical fee. The policy provides no disability income benefits.

a. Explain the policy provisions as they relate to deductibles, co-insurance, and internal limits.

b. How much should Blake recover from the insurance company? How much must he pay out of his own pocket?

c. Would any other policies have offered Blake additional protection? What about his inability to work while recovering from his injury?

d. Based on the information presented, how would you assess Blake's health care insurance coverage? Explain.

LO5 **6.** *Pros and cons of long-term care insurance.* Discuss the pros and cons of long-term-care insurance. Does it make sense for anyone in your family right now? Why or why not? What factors might change this assessment in the future?

LO6 **7.** *Calculating need for disability income insurance.* Use Worksheet 9.2. Fabio Rampulia, a 35-year-old computer programmer, earns $76,000 a year. His monthly take-home pay is $3,800. His wife, Regina, works part-time at their children's elementary school but receives no benefits. Under state law, Fabio's employer contributes to a workers' compensation insurance fund that would provide $2,250 per month for six months if he were disabled and unable to work.

a. Use Worksheet 9.2 to calculate Fabio's disability insurance needs assuming that he won't qualify for Medicare under his Social Security benefits.

b. Based on your answer in part a, what would you advise Fabio about his need for additional disability income insurance? Discuss the type and size of disability income insurance coverage that he should consider, including possible provisions that he might want to include. What other factors should he take into account if he decides to purchase a policy?

LO6 **8.** *Calculating need for disability income insurance.* Use Worksheet 9.2. Do you need disability income insurance? Calculate your need using Worksheet 9.2. Discuss how you'd go about purchasing this coverage.

10 | Protecting Your Property

LEARNING OBJECTIVES

After studying this chapter, you will be able to...

LO1 Discuss the importance and basic principles of property insurance, including types of exposure, indemnity, and co-insurance.

LO2 Identify the types of coverage provided by homeowner's insurance.

LO3 Select the right homeowner's insurance policy for your needs.

LO4 Analyze the coverage in a personal automobile policy (PAP) and choose the most cost-effective policy.

LO5 Describe other types of property and liability insurance.

LO6 Choose a property and liability insurance agent and company, and settle claims.

After you finish this chapter, go to **PAGE 273** for **STUDY TOOLS**

George White/Getty Images

How Will This Affect Me? The chapter explains the key property insurance concepts of indemnity, subrogation, and co-insurance. It then describes the common sources of property and liability risk exposures and the insurance coverage available to address them. The main characteristics of homeowner's and auto insurance are covered, as well as how to choose the version of each policy type that's best for you. Supplemental insurance to protect against floods and earthquakes and personal liability umbrella policies are also described. Especially practical tips can be found in the discussions of how to choose an insurance agent and how to settle property and liability insurance claims. When you finish this chapter you should understand the best and most cost-effective ways to use insurance to protect your property and associated liability exposures.

10-1 BASIC PRINCIPLES OF PROPERTY INSURANCE

LO1 Suppose that a severe storm destroyed your home. Could you afford to replace it? Most people couldn't. To protect yourself from this and other similar types of property loss, you need property insurance. What's more, every day you face some type of risk of negligence. For example, you might be distraught over a personal problem and unintentionally run a red traffic light, seriously injuring a pedestrian. Could you pay for the medical and other costs? Because consequences like this and other potentially negligent acts could cause financial ruin, having appropriate liability insurance is essential.

Property and liability insurance should be as much a part of your personal financial plan as life and health insurance. Such coverage protects the assets that you've already acquired and safeguards your progress toward financial goals. **Property insurance** guards against catastrophic losses of real and personal property caused by such perils as fire, theft, vandalism, windstorms, and other calamities. **Liability insurance** offers protection against the financial consequences that may arise from the insured's responsibility for property loss or personal injuries to others.

Inefficient or inadequate insurance protection is at odds with the objectives of personal financial planning. It is consequently important to become familiar with the principles of property and liability insurance. We begin this chapter with a discussion of the basic principles of property and liability insurance.

> Property and liability insurance should be as much a part of your personal financial plan as life and health insurance.

property insurance insurance coverage that protects real and personal property from catastrophic losses caused by a variety of perils such as fire, theft, vandalism, and windstorms

liability insurance insurance that protects against the financial consequences that may arise from the insured's responsibility for property loss or injuries to others

10-1a Types of Exposure

Most individuals face two basic types of exposure: physical loss of property and loss through liability.

Exposure to Property Loss Most property insurance contracts define the property covered and name the **perils**—the causes of loss—for which the insured will be compensated in case of a claim against their policy. As a rule, most property insurance contracts impose two obligations on the property owner: (1) developing a complete inventory of the property being insured and (2) identifying the perils against which protection is desired. Some property contracts limit coverage by excluding certain types of property and perils, while others offer more comprehensive protection.

Property Inventory Inventorying property is part of the financial planning process. It is especially important in the case of a total loss—if your home is destroyed by fire, for example. Because all property insurance companies require you to show *proof of loss* when making a claim, your personal property inventory, along with corresponding values, can provide this information. A comprehensive property inventory not only helps you settle a claim when a loss occurs but also serves as a useful guide for selecting the most appropriate coverage for your particular needs.

Most families have a home, household furnishings, clothing and personal belongings, lawn and garden equipment, and motor vehicles, all of which need to be insured. Fortunately, most homeowner's and automobile insurance policies provide coverage for these types of belongings. But many families also own such items as motorboats and trailers, various types of off-road vehicles, business property and inventories, jewelry, stamp or coin collections, guns, musical instruments, antiques, paintings, bonds, securities, and other items of special value, such as cameras, golf clubs, electronic equipment, and personal computers. Coverage for these belongings (and those that accompany you when you travel) often require special types of insurance.

Many insurance companies have easy-to-complete personal property inventory forms available to help policyholders prepare inventories. Part of one such form is shown in Exhibit 10.1. These inventory forms can be supplemented with photographs or videos of household contents and belongings. *Every effort should be made to keep these documents in a safe place*, where they can't be destroyed—such as a bank safe-deposit box. You might also consider keeping a *duplicate copy* with a parent or trusted relative. Remember that you may need inventories and photographs to authenticate any property losses that may occur.

Identifying Perils Many people feel a false sense of security after buying insurance because they believe that they're safeguarded against all contingencies. The fact is, however, certain *perils* cannot be reasonably insured. For example, most homeowner's or automobile insurance policies limit or exclude damage or loss caused by flood (such as that caused by Hurricane Katrina in New Orleans in 2005), earthquake, backing up of sewers and drains, mudslides, mysterious disappearance, war, nuclear radiation, and ordinary wear and tear. In addition, property insurance contracts routinely limit coverage based on the location of the property, time of loss, persons involved, and types of hazards to which the property is exposed. See Exhibit 10.2 for a list of perils that are typically covered.

Liability Exposures We all encounter a variety of liability exposures daily. Driving a car, entertaining guests at home, volunteer activities, or being careless in performing professional duties are some common liability risks. Loss exposures result from **negligence**, which is failing to act in a reasonable manner or take necessary steps to protect others from harm. Even if you're never negligent and always prudent, someone might *believe* that you are the cause of a loss and bring a costly lawsuit against you. Losing the judgment could cost you thousands—or even millions—of dollars, and it could result in bankruptcy or financial ruin.

Fortunately, *liability insurance* protects you against losses resulting from these risks, *including the high legal fees* required to defend yourself against lawsuits. It's important to obtain adequate liability insurance through your homeowner's and automobile policies or through a separate umbrella policy.

10-1b Principle of Indemnity

The **principle of indemnity** states that the insured may not be compensated by the insurance company in an amount exceeding the insured's economic loss. Most property and liability insurance contracts are based on this principle—although this *principle does not apply*

peril a cause of loss

negligence failing to act in a reasonable manner or to take necessary steps to protect others from harm

principle of indemnity an insurance principle stating that an insured may not be compensated by the insurance company in an amount exceeding the insured's economic loss

Exhibit 10.1

A Personal Property Inventory Form

Using a form like this will help you keep track of your personal property, including its date of purchase, original purchase price, and replacement cost.

Living Room

Stereo System

Brand	
Model	
Serial #	Date purchased
Purchase price $	Replacement cost $

Large-Screen TV

Brand	
Model	
Serial #	Date purchased
Purchase price $	Replacement cost $

Computer

Brand	
Model	
Serial #	Date purchased
Purchase price $	Replacement cost $

Home Theater System

Brand	
Model	
Serial #	Date purchased
Purchase price $	Replacement cost $

DVD Player

Brand	
Model	
Serial #	Date purchased
Purchase price $	Replacement cost $

Living Room

Article	Qty.	Date Purchased	Purchase Price	Replacement Cost
Air conditioners (window)				
Blinds/shades				
Bookcases				
Books				
Cabinets				
Carpets/rugs				
Chairs				
Chests				
Clocks				
Couches/sofas				
Curtains/draperies				
Fireplace fixtures				
Lamps/lighting fixtures				
Mirrors				
Pictures/paintings				
Audio recordings				
Planters				
Stereo equipment				
Tables				
Television sets				
Other				
Other				

to life and health insurance. Several important concepts relate to the principle of indemnity.

Actual Cash Value versus Replacement Cost The principle of indemnity limits the amount that an insured may collect to the **actual cash value** of the property: the replacement cost minus the value of physical depreciation. Some insurers pay replacement cost without taking depreciation into account—for example, most homeowner's policies cover building losses on a replacement cost basis if the proper type and amount of insurance is purchased. If an insured property is damaged and there is no replacement cost

actual cash value a value assigned to an insured property that is determined by subtracting the amount of physical depreciation from its replacement cost

Dale A Stork/Shutterstock.com

provision, then the insurer is obligated to pay no more than the property would cost new today (its replacement cost) less the amount of depreciation from wear and tear.

> **EXAMPLE: Recovery of Replacement Cost** A fire has destroyed furniture that was 6 years old with an estimated useful life of 10 years. The replacement cost is $5,000. At the time of loss, the furniture was subject to an assumed physical depreciation of 60 percent (6 years ÷ 10 years)—in this case, $3,000. Because the actual cash value is estimated at $2,000 ($5,000 replacement cost minus $3,000 of depreciation), the maximum that the insurer would have to pay is $2,000. Importantly, the original cost of the property has no bearing on the settlement.

Subrogation After an insurance company pays a claim, its **right of subrogation** allows it to request reimbursement from either the person who caused the loss or that person's insurance company. For example, if you're in an automobile accident in which the other party damages your car, you may collect the amount of the loss from your insurer, or from the at-fault party's insurer, but not from both. This is because collecting the full amount of the loss from both parties would violate the principle of indemnity by leaving you better off after the loss than before it. So if your insurer pays you and the other party is at fault, your insurance company can go after the responsible party to recover the amount it paid out to you.

right of subrogation the right of an insurer, who has paid an insured's claim, to request reimbursement from either the person who caused the loss or that person's insurer

co-insurance in property insurance, a provision requiring a policyholder to buy insurance in an amount equal to a specified percentage of the replacement value of their property

Other Insurance Nearly all property and liability insurance contracts have an *other-insurance clause*, which normally states that if a person has more than one insurance policy on a property, each company is liable for only a prorated amount of the loss based on its proportion of the total insurance covering the property. Without this provision, insured persons could use duplicate property insurance policies to collect from multiple companies and actually profit from their losses.

10-1c Co-insurance

Co-insurance, a provision commonly found in property insurance contracts, requires policyholders to buy insurance in an amount equal to a specified percentage of the replacement value of their property. The provision stipulates that if a property isn't properly covered, the property owner will become the "co-insurer" and bear part of the loss. If the policyholder has the stipulated amount of coverage (usually 80 percent of the value of the property), then the insurance company will reimburse for covered losses, dollar-for-dollar, up to the amount of the policy limits. Obviously, you should evaluate closely the co-insurance clause of any property insurance policy so you won't have an unexpected additional burden in the case of a loss.

> **EXAMPLE: Effect of Co-insurance** Tony and Vera have a fire insurance policy on their $300,000 home with an 80 percent co-insurance clause. The policy limits must equal or exceed 80 percent of the replacement value of their home. They ran short of money and decided to save by buying a $180,000 policy instead of $240,000 (80 percent of $300,000), as required by the co-insurance clause. If a loss occurs, the company would be obligated to pay only 75 percent (180,000/240,000) of the loss, up to the amount of the policy limit. Thus, on damages of $40,000, the insurer would pay only $30,000 (75 percent of $40,000).

 Go to Smart Sites

A highlight box in each chapter of *PFIN Online* includes "Smart Sites," a list of resources and sites that offer additional information on topics in the PFIN text. For basic coverage questions, check out "About Coverage" choices under the Auto and Home/Renter tabs at insurance.com's Internet site.

HOMEOWNER'S INSURANCE

LO2, LO3 Homeowners can choose from five different forms (HO-1, HO-2, HO-3, HO-5, and HO-8). Two other forms (HO-4 and HO-6) meet the needs of renters and owners of condominiums (see Exhibit 10.2). An HO-4 renter's policy offers essentially the same broad protection as an HO-2 homeowner's policy, but the coverage doesn't apply to the rented dwelling unit because the tenant usually doesn't own it.

All HO forms are divided into two sections. Section I applies to the dwelling, accompanying structures, and personal property of the insured. Section II deals with comprehensive coverage for personal liability and for medical payments to others. The scope of coverage under Section I is least with an HO-1 policy and greatest with an HO-5 policy. HO-8 is a modified coverage policy

Exhibit 10.2

A Guide to Homeowner's Policies

The amount of insurance coverage you receive depends on the type of homeowner's (HO) policy you buy. You can also obtain coverage if you're a renter or a condominium owner.

Form	Coverages*	Covered Perils
Basic Form (HO-1)	A—$15,000 minimum; B—10% of A; C—50% of A; D—10% of A; E—$100,000; F—$1,000 per person	Fire, smoke, lightning, windstorm, hail, volcanic eruption, explosion, glass breakage, aircraft, vehicles, riot or civil commotion, theft, vandalism, or malicious mischief
Broad Form (HO-2)	Minimum varies; other coverages in same percentages or amounts except D—20% of A	Covers all basic-form risks plus weight of ice, snow, sleet; freezing; accidental discharge of water or steam; falling objects; accidental tearing, cracking, or burning of heating/cooling/sprinkler system or appliance; damage from electrical current
Special Form (HO-3)	Minimum varies; other coverages in same percentages or amounts except D—20% of A	Dwelling and other structures covered against risks of direct physical loss to property except losses specifically excluded; personal property covered by same perils as HO-2 plus damage by glass or safety glazing material that is part of a building, storm door, or storm window
Renter's Form (HO-4)	Coverages A and B—Not applicable C—Minimum varies by company D—20% of C E—$100,000 F—$1,000 per person	Covers same perils covered by HO-2 for personal property
Comprehensive Form (HO-5)	Coverages A and B—Not applicable C—Minimum varies by company D—20% of C E—$100,000 F—$1,000 per person	Covers same perils as HO-4 but covered perils are dwelling, other structures, and personal property covered against risks of direct physical loss, except losses as specifically excluded
Condominium Form (HO-6)	Coverage A—Minimum $1,000 B—Not applicable C—Minimum varies by company D—40% of C E—$100,000 F—$1,000 per person	Covers same perils covered by HO-2 for personal property
Modified Coverage Form (HO-8)	Same as HO-1, except losses are paid based on the amount required to repair or replace the property using common construction materials and methods	Same perils as HO-1, except theft coverage applies only to losses on the residence premises up to a maximum of $1,000; certain other coverage restrictions also apply

* Coverages:
A. Dwelling
B. Other structures
C. Personal property
D. Loss of use
E. Personal liability
F. Medical payments to others

David Huntley/Shutterstock.com

for older homes, which is used to insure houses that have market values well below their cost to rebuild. The coverage in Section II is the same for all forms.

In the following paragraphs, we'll explain the important features of homeowner's forms HO-3 and HO-5, the most common policies. (As Exhibit 10.2 shows, HO-1 is a basic, seldom-used policy with relatively narrow coverage.) The key difference in coverage under the HO-3 and HO-5 forms is the number of perils against which protection applies to the personal property coverage.

10-2a Perils Covered

Some property and liability insurance agreements, called **comprehensive policies**, cover all perils except those specifically excluded, whereas **named peril policies** name particular, individual perils covered.

comprehensive policy property and liability insurance policy covering all perils unless they are specifically excluded

named peril policy property and liability insurance policy that individually names the perils covered

Section I Perils The perils against which the home and its contents are insured are shown in Exhibit 10.2. Coverage on the dwelling is the same for the HO-3 and HO-5 forms, but coverage on the house itself and other structures (e.g., a detached garage) is comprehensive under HO-3 and HO-5 but is a named peril in HO-2. An HO-5 provides comprehensive coverage on the personal property where the HO-3 provides only named perils. Whether homeowners should buy an HO-5 or an HO-3 form depends primarily on how much they're willing to spend to secure the additional protection. The size of premiums for HO-5 and HO-3 policies can differ substantially among insurance companies and states. Buying an HO-1 or HO-2 policy is not recommended because of its more limited coverage.

Note in Exhibit 10.2 that the types of Section I perils covered include just about every situation, from fire and explosions to lightning and wind damage to theft and vandalism. Some perils are specifically excluded from most homeowner's contracts—in particular, *most policies (even HO-5 and HO-3 forms) exclude earthquakes and floods*, even if you live in an area where the risk of an earthquake or a flood is relatively high and the catastrophic nature of such events causes widespread and costly damage. Of course, you can obtain coverage for earthquakes and floods under a separate policy or a rider.

Section II Perils The coverage under Section II of the homeowner's contract is called *comprehensive personal liability coverage* because it offers protection against personal liability (major exclusions are noted later) resulting from *negligence*. It does not insure against other losses for which one may become liable, such as libel, slander, defamation of character, and contractual or intentional wrongdoing. For example, coverage would apply if you unintentionally knocked someone down your stairs. If you purposely struck and injured another person, however, or deliberately harmed someone's reputation either orally or in writing, then homeowner's liability coverage would not protect you.

Section II also provides a limited amount of medical coverage, irrespective of negligence or fault, for persons other than the homeowner's family in certain types of minor accidents on or off the insured's premises. This coverage helps homeowners to meet their moral obligations and helps deter possible lawsuits.

10-2b Factors Affecting Home Insurance Costs

Several influences affect premiums for home and property insurance:

► **Type of structure.** The construction materials used as well as the style and age of your home affect the cost of insuring it. For example, a home built from brick

Behavioral Biases in Buying Property Insurance

What are the best property insurance policies for you? The answer to that question depends on your various risk exposures, your attitude toward risk, and the costs of competing insurance policies. There are some well-known behavioral biases that can lead you to make decisions that aren't in your best interest. It's a good idea to keep the following in mind when buying property insurance:

- **Don't just automatically renew your property insurance.** *Anchoring* is the behavioral bias in which people tend to rely unduly on past prices or estimates without considering new information. Just because your property insurance premiums were competitive in the past does not mean that they're still that way when your policy comes up for renewal. Be sure to shop around—don't just renew your current policy.

- **Be careful to weigh recent evidence properly before buying insurance.** The *representativeness bias* is the tendency to place too much weight on recent experience when making financial decisions. Guess what happens the day after an area is hit by an earthquake? Despite the relative rarity of the event almost everywhere, many people run out to get it, and the price of earthquake insurance goes up! So be careful about buying insurance right after an adverse event occurs. Weigh the evidence carefully, assess your true risk exposures, and buy insurance accordingly.

---

costs less to insure than a similar home made of wood, yet the reverse is true when it comes to earthquake insurance—brick homes are more expensive to insure.

- ▶ **Location of home.** Local crime rates, weather, and proximity to a fire hydrant all affect your home's insurance premium costs. If many claims are filed from your area, insurance premiums for all the homeowners there will be higher.

- ▶ **Credit score.** Research shows that people with lower credit scores tend to file more insurance claims. Credit scores affect premiums more than any other factor. If you have a poor credit score, you may pay two or three times more than an otherwise comparable person with an excellent credit score.

- ▶ **Other factors.** If you have a swimming pool, trampoline, aggressive dog, or other potentially hazardous risk factors on your property, your homeowner's premiums will be higher. Deductibles and the type and amount of coverage also affect the cost.

YOU CAN DO IT NOW: Check Out the Best Homeowner's Insurance Companies When you're considering buying new homeowners insurance, it's good to know how the various insurance companies are rated. A good Internet site is **http://www.consumeraffairs .com/insurance/home.html#buyers-guide**, which summarizes industry ratings by A. M. Best, Standard & Poors, and J. D. Power & Associates. You can **do it now.**

10-2c Property Covered

The homeowner's policy offers property protection under Section I for the dwelling unit, accompanying structures, and personal property of homeowners and their families. Coverage for certain types of loss also applies to lawns, trees, plants, and shrubs. However, the policy excludes structures on the premises used for business purposes (except incidentally), animals (pets or otherwise), and motorized vehicles not used in maintaining the premises (such as autos, motorcycles, golf carts, or snowmobiles). *Business inventory* (e.g., goods held by an insured who is a traveling salesperson, or other goods held for sale) is not covered. Although the policy doesn't cover business inventory, it does cover *business property* (such as books, computers, copiers, office furniture, and supplies), typically up to a maximum of $2,500, while it is on the insured premises.

10-2d Personal Property Floater

Because your homeowner's policy may not protect your expensive personal property adequately, you can either add the **personal property floater (PPF)** as an endorsement to your homeowner's policy or take out a separate floater policy. *The PPF provides either blanket or scheduled coverage of items that are not covered adequately in a standard homeowner's policy.*

> **personal property floater (PPF)** an insurance endorsement or policy providing either blanket or scheduled coverage of expensive personal property not adequately covered in a standard homeowner's policy

A *blanket*, or *unscheduled*, *PPF* provides the maximum protection available for virtually all the insured's personal property. *Scheduled PPFs* list the items to be covered and provide supplemental coverage under a homeowner's contract. This coverage is especially useful for expensive property, such as jewelry, fine art, guns, and collections, that is valued at more than coverage C limits (discussed later), and it includes loss, damage, and theft. For example, you should itemize a diamond ring valued at $7,500 because it's worth more than the standard $1,000 coverage C allowance for all jewelry stolen.

10-2e Renter's Insurance: Don't Move In Without It

If you live in an apartment (or some other type of rental unit), be aware that although the building you live in is likely to be fully insured, *your furnishings and other personal belongings are not*. As a renter (or even the owner of a condominium unit), you need a special type of HO policy to obtain insurance coverage on your personal possessions.

Consider, for example, Nicole Palmer's predicament. She never got around to insuring her personal possessions in the apartment she rented in Boston. One wintry night, a water pipe ruptured and the escaping water damaged her furniture, rugs, and other belongings. When the building owner refused to pay for the loss, Nicole hauled him into court—and lost. Why did she lose her case? Simple: *Unless a landlord can be proven negligent—and this one wasn't—he or she isn't responsible for a tenant's property*. The moral of this story is clear: Once you've accumulated valuable personal belongings (from clothing and home furnishings to stereo equipment, TVs, computers, and DVD players), make sure that they're covered adequately by insurance, even if you're only renting a place to live! Otherwise, you could risk losing everything you own.

Renter's insurance, Form HO-4, is a scaled-down version of homeowner's insurance that is available at reasonable rates. It covers the contents of a house, apartment, or cooperative unit, but not the structure itself, against the same perils as Form HO-2. Owners of condominium units need Form HO-6; it's similar but includes a minimum of $1,000 in protection for any building alterations, additions, and decorations paid for by the policyholder. HO-4 and HO-6 policies include liability coverage and protect you at home and away. For example, if somebody is injured and sues you, the policy would pay for damages

up to a specified limit—generally $100,000, although some insurers go as high as $500,000.

A standard renter's insurance policy covers furniture, carpets, appliances, clothing, and most other personal items for their cash value at the time of loss. Expect to pay around $150 to $250 a year for about $30,000 in personal coverage and $100,000 in liability coverage, depending on where you live. For maximum protection, you can pay about 10 percent more and buy *replacement-cost insurance*, which pays the actual cost of replacing articles with comparable ones. The standard renter's policy provides limited coverage of such valuables as jewelry, furs, and silverware, although some insurers pay up to $1,000 for the loss of watches, gems, and furs and up to $2,500 for silverware.

> A standard renter's insurance policy covers furniture, carpets, appliances, clothing, and most other personal items for their cash value at the time of loss.

10-2f Coverage: What Type, Who, and Where?

Homeowners' policies define the types of losses they cover and the people and locations covered.

Types of Losses Covered There are three types of property-related losses when misfortune occurs:

1. Direct loss of property
2. Indirect loss occurring due to loss of damaged property
3. Additional expenses resulting from direct and indirect losses

Homeowner's insurance contracts offer compensation for each type of loss.

Section I Coverage. When a house is damaged by an insured peril, the insurance company will pay reasonable

Exhibit 10.3

Calculating Replacement Cost

Here's a typical example of how an insurance company calculates replacement cost. It would take $374,400 to fully replace this home today.

Dwelling cost: 2,400 sq ft at $125 per sq ft	$300,000
Extra features: built-in appliances, mahogany cabinets, 3 ceiling fans	15,000
Porches, patios: screened and trellised patio	3,700
Two-car garage: 900 sq ft at $55 per sq ft	49,500
Other site improvements: driveway, storage, landscaping	6,200
Total replacement cost	$374,400

living expenses, such as the cost of renting alternative accommodations, while the insured's home is being repaired or rebuilt. The insurer will also pay for damages caused by perils other than those mentioned in the policy if a named peril is determined to be the underlying cause of the loss. For example, if lightning (a covered peril) strikes a house while a family is away and knocks out the power, causing $400 worth of food in the freezer and refrigerator to spoil, then the loss will be paid even though temperature change (the direct cause) is not mentioned in the policy.

Section II Coverage. In addition to paying successfully pursued liability claims against an insured, a homeowner's policy covers (1) the cost of defending the insured, (2) reasonable expenses incurred by an insured in helping the insurance company's defense, and (3) the payment of court costs. This coverage applies even when the liability suit is found to be without merit.

Persons Covered A homeowner's policy covers the persons named in the policy and members of their families who are residents of the household. A person, such as a college student, can be a resident of the household even while temporarily living away from home. The parents' homeowner's policy may cover the college student's belongings at school—including such items as stereo equipment, TVs, personal computers, and microwave ovens—but there could be limits and exceptions to the coverage. The standard homeowner's contract also extends limited coverage to guests of the insured.

Locations Covered Most homeowner's policies offer coverage worldwide when off premises temporarily. For example, an insured's personal property is fully covered when lent to the next-door neighbor or kept in a hotel room in Paris. The only exception is property left at a

second home where coverage is reduced unless the loss occurs while the insured is residing there.

Homeowners and their families have liability protection for their negligent acts wherever they occur. Excluded are negligent acts involving certain types of motorized vehicles (such as large boats and aircraft) and those occurring in the course of employment or professional practice.

10-2g Limitations on Payment

Other factors that influence the amount an insurance company will pay for a loss include replacement-cost provisions, policy limits, and deductibles.

Replacement Cost The amount necessary to repair, rebuild, or replace an asset at today's prices is the **replacement cost**. When replacement-cost coverage is in effect, a homeowner's reimbursement for damage to a house or accompanying structures is based on the cost of repairing or replacing those structures, without taking any deductions for depreciation. Exhibit 10.3 illustrates a replacement-cost calculation for a 2,400-square-foot home with a two-car garage.

Homeowners are eligible for reimbursement on a full replacement-cost basis only if they keep their homes insured for at least 80 percent of the amount that it would cost to build them today, not including the value of the land. Because inflation could cause coverage to fall below the 80 percent requirement, homeowners can purchase an inflation protection rider that automatically adjusts the amount of coverage

> **replacement cost** the amount necessary to repair, rebuild, or replace an asset at today's prices

Financial Planning Tips

LOWERING YOUR HOMEOWNER'S INSURANCE PREMIUMS

Having the right amount of homeowner's insurance is important. But there's no need to overpay. Here are some ways to reduce your insurance premiums:

- **Increase your deductible.** A primary goal of insurance is to protect your family's financial resources from cataclysmic losses, not to totally insulate you from having to pay out much of anything under any circumstances. Think of your insurance as risk sharing, not risk elimination. Increasing your deductible from $500 to $1,000 could reduce your insurance premiums by 25 percent! And if you file a claim, many insurers will increase your premiums so much that it's often not worth filing the claim.

- **Bundle your homeowner's and auto insurance.** Buying your homeowner's and auto insurance from the same insurer can provide a discount of 5 to 15 percent. First, get quotes from separate companies for each policy and then compare them with bundled quotes.

- **Check on the discounts that you may get from insurers.** Some relatively minor improvements to your home can earn you discounts. Examples include discount for smoke detectors, deadbolt locks, security and fire alarms, and fire extinguishers. Often, seniors also can get an additional 10 percent discount.

- **Ask your insurance agent what you can do to reduce the risk of your home from the insurer's perspective.** For example, updating an old heating system or replacing old wiring can reduce your insurance premiums.

- **Avoid risks that insurers don't like to insure.** Owning dogs that are more frequently involved in claims (such as pit bulls) can limit or void your policy. Similarly, having a swimming pool or a trampoline can increase your insurance premium. You may have to buy additional coverage to protect yourself against certain risk exposures.

- **Manage your credit score.** Allowing your credit score to get too low can increase your insurance premium.

- **Shop carefully for homeowner's insurance.** While it's worthwhile to shop around from time to time, keep in mind that you may be getting a longevity discount if you've been with your insurer for a few years. It's common to get a 5 percent discount if you've been with your company for three to five years, and to get a 10 percent discount if you've been with the company for at least six years.

Source: Adapted from www.aisinsurance.net/ten-ways-to-cut-the-costs-of-homeowners-insurance/, accessed October 2016.

---

based on prevailing inflation rates. Without the rider, maximum compensation for losses would be based on a specified percentage of loss.

Even if a home is in an excellent state of repair, its market value may be reduced by functional obsolescence within the structure—as, for example, when a house that doesn't have enough electrical power to run a dishwasher, microwave, and hair dryer at the same time. The HO-8 homeowner's form (for older homes) was adopted as a partial response to this problem. A 2,200-square-foot home in an older neighborhood might have a market value (excluding land) of $195,000, yet the replacement cost might be $260,000. The HO-8 policy solves this problem by covering property in full up to the amount of the loss or up to the property's market value, whichever is less.

Policy Limits In Section I of the homeowner's policy, the amount of coverage on the dwelling unit (coverage A)

establishes the amounts applicable to the accompanying structures (coverage B), the unscheduled personal property (coverage C), and the temporary living expenses (coverage D). Generally, the limits under coverage B, C, and D are 10 percent, 50 percent, and 10 to 20 percent, respectively, of the amount of coverage under A.

> **EXAMPLE: Homeowner's Policy Coverage Limits**
> If a house is insured for $150,000, then the respective limits for coverage B, C, and D would be $15,000, $75,000, and $30,000 (i.e., 10 percent of $150,000, 50 percent of $150,000, and 20 percent of $150,000). Each of these limits can be increased if it's considered insufficient to cover the exposure. Also, for a small reduction in premium, some companies will permit a homeowner to reduce coverage on unscheduled personal property up to 40 percent of the amount on the dwelling unit.

Remember that homeowner's policies usually specify limits for certain types of personal property included under the coverage C category. These coverage limits are *within the total dollar amount* of coverage C and in no way act to increase that total. For example, a common dollar limit for losses of money, bank notes, bullion, and related items is $200; securities, accounts, deeds, evidences of debt, manuscripts, passports, tickets, and stamps have a $1,000 limit. Loss from jewelry theft is limited to $1,000, and payment for theft of silverware, goldware, and pewterware has a $2,500 limit. Some policies also offer $5,000 coverage for home computer equipment. You can increase these limits by increasing coverage C.

In Section II, the personal liability coverage (coverage E) often starts out at $100,000, and the medical payments portion (coverage F) normally has a limit of $1,000 per person. Additional coverage included in Section II consists of claim expenses, such as court costs and attorney fees; first aid and medical expenses, including ambulance costs; and damage to others' property of up to $500 per occurrence.

Although these are the most common limits, most homeowners need additional protection, especially liability coverage. In these days of high damage awards by juries, a $100,000 liability limit may not be adequate. The cost to increase the liability limit with most companies is small. For example, the annual premium difference between a $100,000 personal liability limit and a $300,000 limit is likely to be only $20 to $30. You can also increase personal liability coverage by purchasing a personal liability umbrella policy.

Deductibles Each of the preceding limits on recovery constrains the maximum amount an insurance company must pay under the policy. *Deductibles*, which limit what a company must pay for small losses, help reduce insurance premiums by doing away with the frequent, small-loss claims that are proportionately more expensive to administer. The standard deductible in most states is $250 on the physical damage protection covered in Section I. However, choosing higher deductible amounts of $500 or $1,000 results in considerable premium savings—as much as 10 to 20 percent in some states. Deductibles don't apply to liability and medical payments coverage because insurers want to be notified of all claims in order to investigate properly and prepare adequate defenses for resulting lawsuits.

10-2h Homeowner's Insurance Premiums

As you might expect, insurance premiums vary widely depending on the insurance provider (company) and the location of the property (neighborhood/city/state).

It pays to shop around! When you're shopping, be sure to state clearly the type of insurance you're looking for and to obtain and compare the cost, net of any discounts, offered by a number of agents or insurance companies. Remember that each type of property damage coverage is subject to a deductible of $250 or more.

Most people need to modify the basic package of coverage by adding an inflation rider and increasing the coverage on their homes to 100 percent of the replacement cost. Changing the contents protection from actual cash value to replacement cost and scheduling some items of expensive personal property may be desirable. Most insurance professionals also advise homeowners to increase their liability and medical payments limits. Each of these changes results in an additional premium charge.

And to reduce your total premium, you can increase the amount of your deductibles. Because it's better to budget for small losses than to insure against them, larger deductibles are a popular strategy. You may also qualify for discounts for deadbolt locks, monitored security systems, and other safety features such as smoke alarms and sprinkler systems.

10-3 AUTOMOBILE INSURANCE

LO4 Automobiles involve risk because damage to them or negligence in their use can result in significant loss. Fortunately, insurance can protect individuals against a big part of these costs. Automobile insurance includes several types of coverage packaged together. We begin by describing the major features of a private passenger automobile policy. Then we briefly explain no-fault laws, followed by discussions of auto insurance premiums and financial responsibility laws.

10-3a Types of Auto Insurance Coverage

The **personal automobile policy (PAP)** is a comprehensive automobile insurance policy designed to be easily understood by the "typical" insurance purchaser. Made up of six parts, the policy's first four parts identify the coverage provided:

▶ Part A: Liability coverage

▶ Part B: Medical payments coverage

> **personal automobile policy (PAP)** a comprehensive automobile insurance policy designed to be easily understood by the "typical" insurance purchaser

Robert Crum/Shutterstock.com

▶ Part C: Uninsured motorists coverage

▶ Part D: Coverage for damage to your vehicle

Part E pertains to your duties and responsibilities if you're involved in an accident, and Part F defines basic provisions of the policy, including the policy coverage period and the right of termination.

You're almost sure to purchase liability, medical payments, and uninsured motorists protection, but you may *not* buy protection against damage to your automobile if it's an older vehicle of relatively little value. On the other hand, if your vehicle is leased or you have a loan against it, then you'll probably be required to have a specified amount of physical damage coverage—part D.

Exhibit 10.4 illustrates how the four basic parts of a PAP might be displayed in a typical automobile insurance policy and shows the premium for a six-month period. Here we will take a closer look at the coverage provided by parts A through D.

Part A: Liability Coverage Most states require you to buy at least a minimum amount of liability insurance. Under the typical PAP, the insurer agrees to:

▶ Pay damages for bodily injury and/or property damage for which you are legally responsible as a result of an automobile accident

bodily injury liability losses a PAP provision that protects the insured against claims made for bodily injury

▶ Settle or defend any claim or suit asking for such damages

The provision for legal defense is important and could save thousands of dollars, even if you're not at fault in an automobile accident. The policy does *not* cover defense of criminal charges against the insured due to an accident (such as a drunk driver who's involved in an accident). Part A also provides for certain supplemental payments (not restricted by the applicable policy limits) for expenses incurred in settling the claim, reimbursement of premiums for appeal bonds, bonds to release attachments of the insured's property, and bail bonds required as a result of an accident.

Policy Limits. Although the insurance company provides both bodily injury and property damage liability insurance under part A, it typically sets *a dollar limit up to which it will pay for damages from any one accident*. Typical limits are $50,000, $100,000, $300,000, and $500,000. You'd be well advised to consider no less than $300,000 coverage in today's legal liability environment. Damage awards are increasing, and the insurer's duty to defend you *ends when the coverage limit has been exhausted*. It's easy to "exhaust" $50,000 or $100,000, leaving you to pay any additional costs above the policy limit. So be sure to purchase adequate coverage—*regardless of the minimum requirements in your state*. Otherwise, you place your personal assets at risk. As Exhibit 10.4 shows, the Rivera family obtained fairly high coverage limits.

Some insurers make so-called *split limits* of liability coverage available, with the first amount in each combination the per-individual limit, and the second the per-accident limit. Some policy limit combinations for protecting individuals against claims made for **bodily injury liability losses** are $25,000/$50,000, $50,000/$100,000, $100,000/$300,000, $250,000/$500,000, and $500,000/$1,000,000. Because the Rivera family purchased the $250,000/$500,000 policy limits, the maximum amount that any one person negligently injured in an accident could receive from the insurance company would be $250,000. Further, the total amount that the insurer would pay to all injured victims in one accident would not exceed $500,000. If a jury awarded a claimant $80,000, the defendant whose insurance policy limits were $50,000/$100,000 could be required to pay $30,000 out of his or her pocket ($80,000 award minus $50,000 paid by insurance). For the defendant, this could mean loss of home, cars, bank

Exhibit 10.4

The Four Parts of a Personal Automobile Policy (PAP)

This automobile insurance statement for six months of coverage shows how the four major parts of a PAP might be incorporated. Notice that the premium for collision/comprehensive damage is relatively low because of the age and type of car (a 2013 Honda CRV); these drivers also enjoyed a premium reduction of more than $130 for the six months due to having other insurance with the same provider, a car alarm system, and a good driving record.

ANYSTATE INSURANCE COMPANIES   **AUTO RENEWAL**

Anystate Automobile Insurance Company
1665 West Anywhere Drive
Yourtown, CO 80209   2013 Honda CRV

POLICY NUMBER	PERIOD COVERED	DATE DUE	PLEASE PAY THIS AMOUNT
ABC-123-XYZ-456	MAY 26, 2017 to NOV 26, 2017	MAY 26, 2017	$424.56

1 H -1582   A

Rivera, Carlos A. & Emma R.
1643 Thunder Rd. #32
Yourtown, CO 80209

Coverages and Limits			Premiums
Part A	A	Liability	
		Bodily Injury 250,000/500,000	$178.40
		Property Damage 100,000	
Part B	M	Medical 5,000	31.95
Part C	U	Uninsured Motor Vehicle	
		Bodily Injury 250,000/500,000	39.92
Part D	G	500 Deductible Collision	122.28
	D-WG	500 Deductible Comprehensive	33.46
	R	Rental Reimbursement	$16
	H	Emergency Road Service	2.55
Amount Due			**$424.56**

Your premium is based on the following …
If not correct, contact your agent.

2013 Honda CRV
Serial number: 4 ABCD12M3NP456789

Drivers of vehicle in your household …
There are no male or unmarried female
drivers under age 25.
Younger drivers included if rated on another
car insured with us.

Ordinary use of vehicle …
To and from work or school, more than
100 miles weekly.
Driven more than 7,500 miles annually.
(National average is 10,000 miles
annually.)

Source: Adapted from a major automobile insurance company quote.

accounts, and other assets. In many states, if the value of these assets is too little to satisfy a claim, the defendant's wages may be garnished (taken by the court and used to satisfy the outstanding debt).

The policy limits available to cover **property damage liability losses** are typically $10,000, $25,000, $50,000, and $100,000. In contrast to bodily injury liability limits, property damage limits are stated as a per-accident limit,

without specifying limits applicable on a per-item or per-person basis.

Persons Insured. Two basic definitions in the PAP determine who is covered under part A: insured person and covered auto.

property damage liability losses a PAP provision that protects the insured against claims made for damage to property

Essentially, an *insured person* includes you (the named insured) and any family member, any person using a covered auto, and any person or organization that may be held responsible for your actions. The *named insured* is the person named in the declarations page of the policy. The spouse of the person named is considered a named insured if he or she resides in the same household. Family members are persons related by blood, marriage, or adoption and residing in the same household. An unmarried college student living away from home usually is considered a family member. *Covered autos* are the vehicles shown in the declarations page of your PAP, autos acquired during the policy period, any trailer owned, and any auto or trailer used as a temporary substitute while your auto or trailer is being repaired or serviced. An automobile that you lease for an extended time can be included as a covered automobile.

The named insured and family members have part A liability coverage regardless of the automobile they are driving. However, for persons other than the named insured and family members to have liability coverage, they must be driving a covered auto.

Part B: Medical Payments Coverage

Medical payments coverage insures a covered individual for reasonable and necessary medical expenses incurred within three years of an automobile accident in an amount not to exceed the policy limits. It provides for reimbursement even if other sources of recovery, such as health or accident insurance, also make payments. What's more, in most states, the insurer reimburses the insured for medical payments even if the insured proves that another person was negligent in the accident and receives compensation from that party's liability insurer.

A person need not be occupying an automobile when the accidental injury occurs to be eligible for benefits. Injuries sustained as a pedestrian, or on a bicycle in a traffic accident, are also covered. (Motorcycle accidents are normally not covered.) Part B insurance also pays on an excess basis. For instance, if you're a passenger in a friend's automobile during an accident and suffer $8,000 in medical expenses, you can collect under his medical payments insurance up to his policy limits. Further, you can collect (up to the amount of your policy limits) from your insurer the amount exceeding what the other medical payments provide.

uninsured motorists coverage automobile insurance designed to meet the needs of "innocent" victims of accidents who are negligently injured by uninsured, underinsured, or hit-and-run motorists

underinsured motorists coverage optional automobile insurance coverage, available in some states, that protects the insured against damages caused by being in an accident with an underinsured motorist who is found liable

Policy Limits. Medical payments insurance usually has per-person limits of $1,000, $2,000, $3,000, $5,000, or $10,000. Thus, an insurer could conceivably pay $60,000 or more in medical payments benefits for one accident involving a named insured and five passengers. Most families are advised to buy the $5,000 or $10,000 limit because, even though they may have other health insurance available, they can't be sure that their passengers are as well protected.

Persons Insured. Coverage under an automobile medical payments insurance policy applies to the named insured and to family members who are injured while occupying an automobile (whether owned by the named insured or not) or when struck by an automobile or trailer of any type. Part B also applies to any other person occupying a covered automobile.

Part C: Uninsured Motorists Coverage

Uninsured motorists coverage is available to meet the needs of "innocent" victims of accidents who are negligently injured by uninsured, underinsured, or hit-and-run motorists. Nearly all states require uninsured motorists insurance to be included in each liability insurance policy issued, but the coverage can be rejected in most of these states. Rejecting uninsured motorists coverage is not a good idea. Under uninsured motorists coverage, an insured is legally entitled to collect an amount equal to the sum that could have been collected from the negligent motorist's liability insurance, had such coverage been available, up to a maximum amount equal to the policy's stated *uninsured motorists limit.*

Three points must be proven to receive payment through uninsured motorists insurance: (1) another motorist must be at fault, (2) the motorist has no available insurance or is underinsured, and (3) damages were incurred. With uninsured motorists coverage, you generally can collect only for losses arising from bodily injury.

Policy Limits. Because uninsured motorists insurance is fairly low in cost (usually no more than $150 per year), drivers should purchase at least its minimum available limits. The Riveras purchased $250,000/$500,000 coverage for just $39.92 per six months. This means that the maximum payout per person is $250,000 and the maximum payout for all people injured in one accident is $500,000.

Persons Insured. Uninsured motorists protection covers the named insured, family members, and any other person occupying a covered auto.

Underinsured Motorists Coverage. In addition to *uninsured motorists,* in some states, for a small premium, you can obtain underinsured motorists coverage, which protects against damages caused by being in an accident with an underinsured motorist who is found liable. Underinsured motorists insurance has become increasingly popular and *can be purchased for both bodily injury and property damage*. If an at-fault driver causes more damage to you than the limit of her liability, your insurance company makes up the difference (up to the limits of your coverage) and then goes after the negligent driver for the deficiency. If it's available in your state, you should consider purchasing this optional coverage.

> **EXAMPLE: Underinsured Motorists Coverage** If you have underinsured motorists coverage of $50,000 for bodily injury and incur medical expenses of $40,000 because of an accident caused by an at-fault insured driver with the minimum compulsory bodily injury limit of $25,000, your insurer will cover the $15,000 gap ($40,000 medical expenses minus $25,000 liability limit of at-fault driver).

Part D: Coverage for Physical Damage to a Vehicle

This part of the PAP provides coverage for damage to your auto. The two basic types of coverage are collision and comprehensive (or "other than collision").

Collision Insurance. Collision insurance is automobile insurance that pays for collision damage to an insured automobile *regardless of who is at fault*. The amount of insurance payable is the actual cash value of the loss in excess of your deductible. Remember that *actual cash value is defined as replacement cost minus depreciation*. So, if a car is demolished, the insured is paid an amount equal to the car's depreciated value minus any deductible. Deductibles typically range between $50 and $1,000, and selecting a higher deductible, as did the Riveras, will reduce your premium.

Lenders and lessors typically require collision insurance on cars they finance. In some cases, especially when the auto dealer is handling the financing, it will try to sell you this insurance. *Avoid buying automobile insurance from car dealers or finance companies*. It is best to buy such insurance from your regular insurance agent and include collision insurance as part of your full auto insurance policy (i.e., the PAP). A full-time insurance agent is better able to assess and meet your insurance needs. The collision provision of your insurance policy often fully protects you in a rental car, so be sure to check before purchasing supplemental collision insurance when renting a car.

Go to Smart Sites

Is there ever a time to drop comprehensive coverage? eHow's site helps you decide.

Comprehensive Automobile Insurance. Comprehensive automobile insurance protects against loss to an insured automobile caused by any peril (with a few exceptions) *other than collision*. The maximum compensation provided under this coverage is the actual cash value of the automobile. Coverage includes, but is not limited to, damage caused by fire, theft, glass breakage, falling objects, malicious mischief, vandalism, riot, and earthquake. The automobile insurance policy normally does *not* cover the theft of personal property left in the insured vehicle. However, this may be covered by the off-premises coverage of the homeowner's policy if the auto was locked when the theft occurred.

10-3b No-Fault Automobile Insurance

No-fault automobile insurance is a system under which each insured party is compensated by his or her company, regardless of which party caused the accident. In return, legal remedies and payments for pain and suffering are restricted. Under the concept of *pure* no-fault insurance, the driver, passengers, and injured pedestrians are reimbursed by the insurer of the car for economic losses stemming from

> **collision insurance** automobile insurance that pays for collision damage to an insured automobile *regardless of who is at fault*
>
> **comprehensive automobile insurance** coverage that protects against loss to an insured automobile caused by any peril (with a few exceptions) *other than collision*
>
> **no-fault automobile insurance** automobile insurance that reimburses the parties involved in an accident without regard to negligence

bodily injury. The insurer doesn't have to cover claims for losses to other motorists who are covered by their own policies.

Advocates of no-fault automobile insurance apparently forget that the sole purpose of liability insurance is to protect the assets of the insured—not to pay losses, *per se*. State laws governing no-fault insurance vary widely, but most states provide from $2,000 to $10,000 in personal injury protection and restrict legal recovery for pain and suffering to cases where medical or economic losses exceed some threshold level, such as $500 or $1,000. In all states, recovery based on negligence is permitted for economic loss exceeding the amount payable by no-fault insurance.

10-3c Automobile Insurance Premiums

The cost of car insurance depends on many factors, including your age, where you live, the car you drive, your driving record, the coverage you have, and the amount of your deductible. Consequently, car insurance premiums—even for the same coverage—vary all over the map.

Factors Affecting Premiums Factors that influence how auto insurance premiums are set include (1) rating territory, (2) amount of use the automobile receives, (3) personal characteristics of the driver, (4) type of automobile, and (5) insured's driving record.

▶ **Rating territory.** Rates are higher in geographic areas where accident rates, number of claims filed, and average cost of claims paid are higher. Rates reflect auto repair costs, hospital and medical expenses, jury awards, and theft and vandalism in the area. Even someone with a perfect driving record will be charged the going rate for the area where the automobile is garaged. Exhibit 10.5 gives some helpful tips for protecting your vehicle wherever you live. Some jurisdictions prohibit the use of rating territories, age, and gender factors because they believe these factors unfairly discriminate against the urban, the young, and the male.

▶ **Use of the automobile.** Rates are also lower if the insured automobile isn't usually driven to work or is driven less than 3 miles one way. Premiums rise slightly if you drive more than 3 but fewer than 15 miles to work and increase if your commute exceeds 15 miles each way.

▶ **Drivers' personal characteristics.** The insured's age, sex, and marital status can also affect automobile insurance premiums. Insurance companies base their premium differentials on the number of accidents involving certain age groups. For example, drivers

aged 25 and under make up only about 15 percent of the total driving population, but they are involved in nearly 30 percent of auto accidents and in 26 percent of all fatal accidents. Male drivers are involved in a larger percentage of fatal crashes, so unmarried males under age 30 (and married males under age 25) pay higher premiums than do older individuals. Females over age 24, as well as married females of any age, are exempt from the youthful operator classification and pay lower premiums.

▶ **Type of automobile.** Insurance companies charge higher rates for automobiles classified as intermediate-performance, high-performance, and sports vehicles and also for rear-engine models. Some states even rate four-door cars differently from two-door models.

▶ **Driving record.** The driving records—traffic violations and accidents—of those insured and the people who live with them affect premium levels. More severe traffic convictions—driving under the influence of alcohol or drugs, leaving the scene of an accident, homicide or assault arising from the operation of a motor vehicle, and driving with a revoked or suspended driver's license—result in higher insurance premiums. Any conviction for a moving traffic violation that results in the accumulation of points under a state point system also may incur a premium surcharge. In most states, accidents determined to be the insured's fault also incur points and a premium surcharge.

> Nearly all insurance companies give discounts to families with two or more automobiles insured by the same company.

YOU CAN DO IT NOW: Evaluate the Best Auto Insurance Companies When you're considering buying new car insurance, it's helpful to know which insurance companies are considered the best. A good Internet site is **http://www.consumeraffairs.com /insurance/car.html**. The site discusses the key elements of auto insurance policies, which include liability, comprehensive coverage, uninsured motorist protection, collision coverage, and personal injury protection. You can **do it now**.

Driving Down the Cost of Auto Insurance One of the best ways to reduce the cost of auto insurance is to take advantage of the insurer's discounts, which can knock from 5 to 50 percent off your annual premium. Some give overall *safe-driving (accident-free) discounts*,

Exhibit 10.5

Preventing Your Car from Being Stolen

You can help prevent your car from being stolen by taking the following precautions:

- Never leave your keys in an unattended car.
- Never leave your car running and unattended.
- Avoid leaving valuables visible inside your car.
- Keep your car doors locked, even while driving. Close all windows.
- Do not leave your vehicle title or proof of insurance in the car.
- Avoid high-crime areas even if the alternate route takes more time.
- Install antitheft devices like a burglar alarm or a steering-wheel lock.
- Etch your car's vehicle identification number (VIN) on more than one of the windows.
- When parking on an incline, turn the wheels turned toward the curb and set the emergency brake.
- Do not resist a carjacker. You can't be replaced; your car can.

Source: Adapted from "How to Prevent Your Car from Being Stolen," www.geico.com/information/safety/auto/preventing-auto-theft/, accessed October 2016.

and most give youthful operators lower rates if they've had *driver's training*. High school and college students may also receive *good-student discounts* for maintaining a B average or making the dean's list at their school.

Nearly all insurance companies give discounts to families with two or more automobiles insured by the same company (the *multicar discount*). Most insurers also offer discounts to owners who install *antitheft devices* in their cars. Likewise, some insurers offer *nonsmoker* and *nondrinker discounts*. Some insurers accept only persons who are educators or executives; others accept only government employees. Through more selective underwriting, these companies are able to reduce losses and operating expenses, which results in lower premiums.

It's to your advantage to look for and use as many of these discounts as you can. Take another look at the auto insurance statement in Exhibit 10.4, which has a total 6-month premium of $424.56. While not shown, if more than one car was insured with the company the premium could be reduced to $360.83. And if multiple cars are insured and homeowners and liability umbrella insurance policies were also held, the auto insurance premium could be reduced even further to $286.39.

Another effective way to drive down the cost of car insurance is to *raise your deductibles* (as discussed earlier in this chapter). For example, the premium difference between a $100 deductible and a $500 deductible may be as much as 25 percent on collision coverage and 30 percent on comprehensive coverage; and a $1,000 deductible may save you as much as 50 percent on both collision and comprehensive coverage.

10-3d Financial Responsibility Laws

Most states have **financial responsibility laws**, whereby motorists *must buy a specified minimum amount of automobile liability insurance* or provide other proof of comparable financial responsibility. The required limits are low in most states—well below what you should carry. Financial responsibility laws fall into two categories. *Compulsory auto insurance laws* require motorists to show evidence of insurance coverage *before* receiving their license plates. Penalties for not having liability insurance include fines and suspension of your driver's license. The second category requires motorists to show evidence of their insurance coverage only *after* being involved in an accident. If they then fail to demonstrate compliance with the law, their registrations and driver's licenses are suspended.

10-4 OTHER PROPERTY AND LIABILITY INSURANCE

LO5 Homeowner's and automobile insurance policies provide the basic protection needed by most families, but some need other, more specialized types of insurance. Popular forms of other insurance include supplemental property insurance—earthquake, flood, and other forms of transportation—as well as the personal liability umbrella policy.

financial responsibility laws laws requiring motorists to buy a specified minimum amount of automobile liability insurance, or to provide other proof of comparable financial responsibility

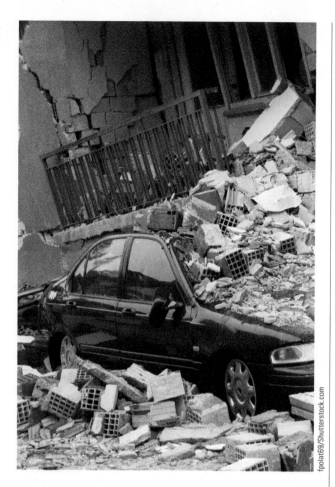

fpolat69/Shutterstock.com

10-4a Supplemental Property Insurance Coverage

Because homeowner's policies exclude certain types of damage, you may want to consider some of the following types of supplemental coverage:

▶ **Earthquake insurance.** In addition to California, areas in other states are also subject to this type of loss. Very few homeowners buy this coverage because these policies typically carry a 15 percent deductible on the replacement cost of a home damaged or destroyed by earthquake.

▶ **Flood insurance.** The federal government has established a subsidized flood insurance program in cooperation with private insurance agents, who can sell this low-cost coverage to homeowners and tenants living in designated communities. The flood insurance program also encourages communities to initiate land-use controls to reduce future flood losses.

▶ **Other forms of transportation insurance.** In addition to automobiles, you can buy policies to insure other types of vehicles such as mobile homes, recreational vehicles, or boats.

10-4b Personal Liability Umbrella Policy

Persons with moderate to high levels of income and net worth may want to purchase a **personal liability umbrella policy**, which provides added liability coverage for homeowner's and automobile insurance. Umbrella policies often include limits of $1 million or more. Some also provide added amounts of coverage for a family's major medical insurance. The premiums are usually quite reasonable for the broad coverage offered—$150 to $300 a year for as much as $1 million in coverage. The insured party must already have relatively high liability limits ($100,000 to $300,000) on their homeowner's and auto coverage in order to purchase a personal liability umbrella policy.

10-5 BUYING INSURANCE AND SETTLING CLAIMS

LO6 The first step when buying property and liability insurance is to develop an inventory of exposures to loss and then arrange them from highest to lowest priority. Losses that lend themselves to insurance protection are those that seldom occur but are potentially substantial—for example, damage to a home and its contents, or liability arising from a negligence claim. Somewhat less important, but still desirable, is insurance to cover losses that could disrupt a family's financial plans, even if the losses might not result in insolvency. Such risks include physical damage to automobiles, boats, and other personal property of moderate value. Lowest-priority exposures can be covered by savings or from current income.

10-5a Property and Liability Insurance Agents

A good property insurance agent can make the purchase process much easier. Most property insurance agents fall into either the captive or independent category. A **captive agent** represents only one insurance company and is more or less an employee of that company. Allstate, Nationwide, and State Farm are major insurance companies that

personal liability umbrella policy an insurance policy providing excess liability coverage for homeowner's and automobile insurance as well as additional coverage not provided by either policy

captive agent an insurance agent who represents only one insurance company and who is, in effect, an employee of that company market their products through captive agents. In contrast, **independent agents** typically represent from 2 to 10 different insurance companies. These agents may place your coverage with any of the companies with whom they have an agency relationship. Some well-known companies that operate through independent agents include The Hartford, Kemper, Chubb, and Travelers. Either type of agent can serve your needs well and should take the time to do the following:

▶ Review your total property and liability insurance exposures

▶ Inventory property and identify exposures

▶ Determine appropriate covered perils, limits, deductibles, and floater policies

Because of large variations in premiums and services, it pays to comparison shop.

Property insurance agents who meet various experiential and educational requirements, including passing a series of written examinations, qualify for the *Chartered Property and Casualty Underwriter (CPCU)* or *Certified Insurance Counselor (CIC)* designation. Another alternative to consider is companies that sell directly to the consumer through an 800 number or online. Generally, their premiums are lower. Examples of direct sellers are Amica, Erie, GEICO, and USAA.

10-5b Property and Liability Insurance Companies

When selecting an agent, you should ask questions about the company, including its financial soundness, its claims-settlement practices, and the geographic range of its operations (this could be important if you're involved in an accident 1,000 miles from home). As with any form of insurance, you should check the company's ratings (see Chapter 8) and stick with those rated in the top categories. Friends and acquaintances often can provide insight into its claims settlement policy. Many insurance companies now have elaborate home pages on the Internet containing information about the provider and its products, directions to local agents, or calculators to crunch the numbers and generate sample premiums.

10-5c Settling Property and Liability Claims

Insurance companies typically settle claims promptly and fairly—especially life and health care claims. But in settling property

independent agent an insurance agent who may place coverage with any company with which he or she has an agency relationship, as long as the insured meets that company's underwriting standards and liability claims, there is often some claimant–insurer disagreement. Here we review the claims settlement process, beginning with what you should do immediately following an accident.

First Steps Following an Accident After an accident, record the names, addresses, and phone numbers of all witnesses, drivers, occupants, and injured parties, along with the license numbers of the automobiles involved. *Never leave the scene of an accident, even if the other party says it's all right* or *if no one is injured*. Immediately notify law enforcement officers and your insurance agent of the accident. Never discuss liability at the scene of an accident, or with anyone other than the police and your insurer. The police are responsible only for assessing the probability of a law violation and maintaining order at the scene of an accident—not for making liability judgments.

Steps in Claims Settlement If you're involved in an accident, one of the first things to decide is whether you want to file a claim. Most experts agree that unless it's a very minor or insignificant accident, the best course of action is to file a claim. Be aware, though, that if you've made several claims then your insurance company may decide to drop you after settling the most recent one. The claims settlement process typically involves these steps:

1. **Notice to your insurance company.** You must notify your insurance company that a loss (or potential for loss) has occurred. Timely notice is extremely important.

2. **Investigation.** Insurance company personnel may talk to witnesses or law enforcement officers and gather physical evidence to determine whether the claimed loss is covered by the policy. And they'll check to make sure that the date of the loss falls within the policy period. If you delay filing your claim, you hinder the insurer's ability to check the facts. All policies specify the period within which you must give notice. Failure to report an accident can result in losing your right to collect on it.

3. **Proof of loss.** This proof requires you to give a sworn statement. You may have to show medical bills, submit an inventory, and certify the value of lost property (e.g., a written inventory, photographs, and purchase receipts). You may also have to submit an employer

claims adjustor an insurance specialist who works for the insurance company, as an independent adjustor, or for an adjustment bureau to investigate claims

PLANNING OVER A LIFETIME

Protecting Your Property

Here are some suggested ways to insure your property and protect against liability exposures over the different stages of your life.

INDEPENDENT LIFESTYLE (20s)

» Evaluate renter's insurance to protect your personal property and to limit liability exposure.

» Make sure to get adequate auto insurance. Don't try to save by buying too little liability coverage.

FAMILY AND CAREER DEVELOPMENT (30s–40s)

» Buy homeowner's insurance with appropriate property and liability coverage.

» Document your personal items with photos and purchase receipts.

» Re-evaluate auto insurance coverage.

MATURE LIFESTYLE (50s–60s)

» Review homeowner's insurance coverage. Keep in mind the possible need for riders on expensive, otherwise insufficiently uncovered personal items.

» Consider bundling your homeowner's and auto policies with the same insurer for a discount.

» Consider getting policy discounts by buying antitheft systems for your home and/or car.

RETIREMENT (65+)

» Revise homeowner's and liability coverage in light of retirement situation.

» Revise auto insurance in light of your retirement situation.

statement of lost wages and, if possible, physical evidence of damage (e.g., X-rays if you claim a back injury; a broken window or pried door if you claim a break-in and theft at your home). After reviewing your proof of loss, the insurer may (1) pay you the amount you asked for, (2) offer you a lesser amount, or (3) deny that the company has any legal responsibility under the terms of your policy.

If the amount is disputed, most policies provide for some form of claims arbitration. You hire a third party, the company hires a third party, and these two arbitrators jointly select one more person. When any two of the three arbitrators reach agreement, their decision binds you and the company to their solution. When a company denies responsibility, you do not get the right of arbitration. In such cases, the company is saying the loss does not fall under the policy coverage. You must then either forget the claim or bring in an attorney or, perhaps, a public adjustor (discussed next).

Claims Adjustment Usually the first person to call when you need to file a claim is your insurance agent. If your loss is relatively minor, the agent can process it quickly and, in fact, often gives you a check right on the spot. If your loss is more complex, your company probably will assign a claims adjustor to the case. A **claims adjustor** is an insurance specialist who works for the insurance company either as an independent adjustor or for an adjustment bureau. The adjustor investigates claims, looking out for the company's interests—which might very well be to keep you, its customer, satisfied. However, many claimants are out to collect all they can from insurance companies, which they think have "deep pockets." Thus, adjustors walk a fine line: They must diligently question and investigate while at the same time offering service to minimize settlement delays and financial hardship. To promote your own interest in the claim, cooperate with your adjustor and answer inquiries honestly—keeping in mind that the insurance company signs the adjustor's paycheck.

STUDY TOOLS 10

©viphotos/Shutterstock140785408

LOCATED AT BACK OF THE TEXTBOOK
☐ Chapter Review Card

LOCATED AT WWW.CENGAGEBRAIN.COM
☐ Review Key Term flashcards and create your own cards.
☐ Track your knowledge and understanding of key concepts in personal finance.

☐ Complete practice and graded quizzes to prepare for tests.
☐ Complete interactive content at PFIN6 Online.
☐ View the chapter highlight boxes at PFIN6 Online.

Financial Planning Exercises

LO1 1. **Co-insurance clauses.** Isla Potter had a homeowner's insurance policy with $175,000 of coverage on the dwelling. Would a 90 percent co-insurance clause be better than an 80 percent clause in such a policy? Give reasons to support your answer.

LO2 2. **Evaluating homeowner's policy coverage.** Last year, Nash and Eve Hodges bought a home with a dwelling replacement value of $350,000 and insured it (via an HO-5 policy) for $310,000. The policy reimburses for actual cash value and has a $500 deductible, standard limits for coverage C items, and no scheduled property. Recently, burglars broke into the house and stole a two-year-old television set with a current replacement value of $600 and an estimated useful life of eight years. They also took jewelry valued at $1,850 and silver flatware valued at $3,000.

    a. If the Hodges' policy has an 80 percent co-insurance clause, do they have enough insurance?

    b. Assuming a 50 percent coverage C limit, calculate how much the Hodges family would receive if they filed a claim for the stolen items.

    c. What advice would you give the Hodges family about their homeowner's coverage?

LO3 3. **Need for renter's insurance.** Ian and Elena Ballard, both graduate students, moved into an apartment near the university. Elena wants to buy renter's insurance, but Ian thinks they don't need it because their furniture isn't worth much. Elena points out that, among other things, they have some expensive computer and stereo equipment. To help the Ballards resolve their dilemma, suggest a plan for deciding how much insurance to buy, and give them some ideas for finding a policy.

LO4 4. **Collecting on a homeowner's insurance claim.** Sasha Underwood's home in Los Angeles was recently gutted in a fire. Her living and dining rooms were completely destroyed, and the damaged personal property had a replacement value of $25,000. The average age of the damaged personal property was 5 years, and its useful life was estimated to be 15 years. What is the maximum amount the insurance company would pay Sasha assuming that it reimburses losses on an actual cash-value basis?

LO4 5. **Evaluating personal automobile policy features.** Tucker Carson of Pittsburgh, Pennsylvania is a single, 40-year-old loan officer at a large regional bank; he has a 16-year-old son. He has decided to use his annual bonus as a down payment on a new car. One Saturday afternoon in late September, Tucker visits Decker Motors and buys a new car for $32,000. To obtain insurance on the car, he calls his agent, Valerie Hurst who represents Shepard's Insurance Agency, and explains his auto insurance needs. Valerie says that she'll investigate the various options for him. Three days later, Tucker and Valerie get together to review his coverage options. Valerie offers several proposals, including various combinations of the following coverages: (i) basic automobile liability insurance, (ii) uninsured motorists coverage, (iii) automobile medical payments insurance, (iv) automobile collision insurance, and (v) comprehensive automobile insurance.

    a. Describe the key features of these insurance coverages.

    b. Are there any limitations on these coverages? Explain.

    c. Indicate the persons who would be protected under each type of coverage.

    d. What kind of insurance coverages would you recommend that Tucker purchase? Explain your recommendation.

LO5 6. **Personal automobile policy coverage.** Brandon Dougherty has a personal automobile policy (PAP) with coverage of $25,000/$50,000 for bodily injury liability, $25,000 for property damage liability, $5,000 for medical payments, and a $500 deductible for collision insurance. How much will his insurance cover in each of the following situations? Will he have any out-of-pocket costs?

    a. Brandon loses control and skids on ice, running into a parked car and causing $3,785 damage to the unoccupied vehicle and $2,350 damage to his own car.

    b. Brandon runs a stop sign and causes a serious auto accident, badly injuring two

The only other thing they need to determine at this point is the *expected rate of return* they can reasonably earn on their money. The Finleys know that the amount of money they'll have to put into their investment program largely depends on *how much they can earn from their investments*: the higher their rate of return, the less they'll have to put up. Let's say they feel comfortable using a 6 percent rate of return. That's a fairly conservative number—one that won't require them to put all or most of their money into high-risk investments—and they're reasonably certain they can reach that level of return, *on average*, over the long haul. It's important to use some care in coming up with a projected rate of return. Don't saddle yourself with an unreasonably high rate because that will only reduce the chance of reaching your targeted financial goal.

There are two ways of coming up with the capital needed to reach a targeted sum of money: (1) you can make a lump-sum investment right up front and let that amount grow over time; or (2) you can set up a systematic savings plan and put away a certain amount of money each year. Worksheet 11.1 indicates the amount of investment capital needed to reach a given financial goal. It employs the *compound value* concept discussed in Chapter 2 and is based on a given financial target (of $330,000, line 1) and a projected average rate of return on your investments (of 6 percent, line 2). By way of brief review of the Chapter 2 framework, the yearly savings required to fund the target goal is computed as:

$$\text{Yearly savings} = \frac{\text{Future amount of money desired}}{\text{Future value annuity factor}}$$

You can use this worksheet to find either a required lump-sum investment (Part A of the worksheet) or an amount that will have to be put away each year in a savings plan (Part B). We'll assume that the Finleys have $10,000 to start with (this comes mostly from gifts their daughter received from her grandparents). Because they know they'll need a lot more than that to reach their target, the Finleys decide to use Part B of the worksheet to find out how much they'll have to save annually.

Stargazer/Shutterstock.com

The first thing to do is find the future value of the $10,000 initial investment. The specific question here is: How much will that initial, lump-sum investment grow to over an 18-year period? Using the compound value concept and the appropriate "future value factor" (from Appendix A), we see in line 7 that this deposit will grow to about $28,540. But that's only about 9 percent of the target amount of $330,000. Indeed, by subtracting the terminal value of the initial investment (line 7, $28,540) from our target (line 1, $330,000), we find the amount that must be generated from some sort of annual savings plan—see line 8. Again, using the appropriate future value factor (this time from Appendix B), we find that the Finleys will have to put away about $9,754 a year in order to reach their target of $330,000 in 18 years. That is, the $9,754 a year will grow to $301,460, and this amount plus $28,540 (the amount to which the initial $10,000 will grow) equals the Finleys' targeted financial goal of $330,000.

As you might have suspected, the last few steps in the worksheet can just as easily be done on a financial calculator. That is, after determining the size of the nest egg (as in Step 8), you can use a financial calculator to find the amount of money that must be put away each year to fund the nest egg.

An Investment Plan Provides Direction Now that the Finleys know how much they have to save each year, their next step is deciding how they'll save it. It's best to follow a *systematic savings plan*—for example, build a set amount of savings each month or quarter into the household budget and then stick with it. But whatever procedure is followed, keep in mind that all we're doing here is *accumulating the required initial investment capital.*

That money still has to be put to work in an investment program, and that's where an investment plan enters the picture. An investment plan is a preferably written statement explaining how the accumulated investment capital will be invested in order to reach the targeted goal. In the Finleys' case, their capital accumulation plan calls for a 6 percent rate of return as a target they feel they can achieve. Now they need to find a way to obtain that 6 percent return on their money—meaning that they must specify, in general terms at least, the kinds of investment vehicles that they intend to use. When completed, *an investment plan is a way of translating an abstract investment target* (in this case, a 6 percent return) *into a specific investment program.*

11-1c What Are Your Investment Objectives?

Some people buy securities largely for the protection they provide from taxes. Others put money aside for that proverbial rainy day or, perhaps, to build up a nice retirement nest egg. *Your goals set the tone for*

your investment program, and they play a major role in determining how conservative (or aggressive) you're likely to be in making investment decisions. These goals define the purpose for your investments. The most frequent investment objectives are to (1) enhance current income, (2) save for a major purchase, (3) accumulate funds for retirement, and (4) seek shelter from taxes.

Current Income The idea with current income is to put your money into investments that will enable you to supplement your income. In other words, it's for people who want to live off their investment income. A secure source of high current income, from dividends or interest, is the primary concern of such investors. Retired people, for example, often choose investments offering higher current income at lower risk.

Major Expenditures People often put money aside, sometimes for years, to save up enough to make just one major expenditure. Here are the most common ones:

▶ Down payment on a home

▶ Money for a child's college education

▶ Capital for going into business

▶ Expensive (perhaps once-in-a-lifetime) vacation

▶ Purchase of a special, expensive item

▶ Funds for retirement

Whatever your goal, the idea is to set your sights on something and then go about building your capital with that objective in mind. Once you know about how much money you'll need to attain one of these goals (following a procedure like the one illustrated in Worksheet 11.1), you can specify the types of investment vehicles that you intend to use. For example, you might follow a lower-risk approach by making a single, lump-sum investment in a high-grade bond that matures the same year you'll need the funds; or you could follow a riskier investment plan that calls for investing a set amount of money over time in something like a growth-oriented mutual fund. Of course, for some purposes—such as the down payment on a home, or a child's education—you'll probably want to take a lot less risk than for others, because attaining these goals should not be jeopardized by the types of investments you choose to employ.

Retirement Accumulating funds for retirement is *the single most important reason for investing.* Too often, though, retirement planning occupies only a small amount of our time because we tend to rely too heavily on employers and Social Security for our retirement needs. As many people learn too late in life, that can be a serious mistake. A much better approach is to review

You can use a worksheet like this one to find out how much money you must come up with to reach a given financial goal. This worksheet is based on the same future value concepts introduced in Chapter 2.

DETERMINING AMOUNT OF INVESTMENT CAPITAL

Financial goal: _Accumulate $330,000 in 18 years for the purpose of meeting the cost of daughter's college education._

1. Targeted Financial Goal (see Note 1)	$ 330,000
2. Projected Average Return on Investments	6%
A. Finding a Lump-Sum Investment:	
3. Future Value Factor, from Appendix A ■ based on _____ years to target date and a projected average return on investment of ___%___	0.000
4. Required Lump-Sum Investment ■ line 1 ÷ line 3	$ 0
B. Making a Series of Investments over Time:	
5. Amount of Initial Investment, if any (see Note 2)	$ 10,000
6. Future Value Factor, from Appendix A ■ based on __18__ years of target date and a projected average return on investment of __6%__	2.854
7. Terminal Value of Initial Investment ■ line 5 × line 6	$ 28,540
8. Balance to Come from Savings Plan ■ line 1 − line 7	$ 301,460
9. Future Value Annuity Factor, from Appendix B ■ based on __18__ years to target date and a projected average return on investment of __6%__	30.906
10. Series of Annual Investments Required over Time ■ line 8 ÷ line 9	$ 9,754

Note 1: The "targeted financial goal" is the amount of money you want to accumulate by some target date in the future.

Note 2: If you're starting from scratch—i.e., there is *no* initial investment—enter zero on line 5, *skip* lines 6 and 7, and then use the total targeted financial goal (from line 1) as the amount to be funded from a savings plan; now proceed with the rest of the worksheet.

the amounts of income that you can realistically expect to receive from Social Security and your employee pension plan, and then to decide, based on your retirement goals, *whether they'll be adequate to meet your needs*. You'll probably find that you'll have to supplement them through personal investing. (Retirement plans are discussed in Chapter 14.)

Shelter from Taxes As explained in Chapter 3, federal income taxes do not treat all sources of income equally. For example, if you own real estate, then you may be able to take depreciation deductions against certain other sources of income, thereby reducing the amount of your final taxable income. This tax write-off feature can make real estate an attractive investment for some investors, even though its pre-tax rate of return may not appear very high. The goal of sheltering income from taxes is a legitimate one that, for some investors, often goes hand in hand with the goals of saving for a major outlay or for retirement. If you can avoid paying taxes on the income from an investment, then all other things considered, you will have more funds available for reinvestment during the period.

11-1d Different Ways to Invest

After establishing your investment objectives, you can use a variety of investment vehicles to fulfill those goals. In this section, we'll briefly describe the key types of investments that are popular with (and widely used by) individual investors.

Common Stock *Common stocks* are a form of *equity*—each share of stock represents a fractional ownership position in a corporation. A share of stock typically entitles the holder to equal participation in the corporation's earnings and dividends as well as an equal vote to elect the management of the corporation. From the investor's perspective, the return to stockholders comes from dividends and/or appreciation in share price. Common stock has no maturity date and, as a result, remains outstanding indefinitely (common stocks are discussed in Chapter 12).

Bonds In contrast to stocks, *bonds* are *liabilities*—they're IOUs of the issuer. Governments and corporations issue bonds that pay a stated return, called *interest*. An individual who invests in a bond receives a stipulated interest income, typically paid every six months, plus the return of the principal (face) value of the bond at maturity. For example, if you purchased a $1,000 bond that paid 10 percent interest in semiannual installments, you could expect to receive $50 every six months (10 percent × 0.5 years × $1,000) and at maturity recover the $1,000

face value of the bond. Of course, a bond can be bought or sold prior to maturity at a price that may differ from its face value because bond prices, like common stock prices, fluctuate in the marketplace (see Chapter 12).

Preferreds and Convertibles These are *hybrid securities* in that each has the characteristics of both stocks and bonds. *Preferred securities* are issued as stock and, as such, represent an equity position in a corporation. But unlike common stock, preferreds have a stated (fixed) dividend rate that is paid before the dividends to holders of common stock are paid. Like bonds, preferred stocks are usually purchased for the current income (dividends) that they pay.

A *convertible security*, in contrast, is usually a fixed-income obligation (typically a bond but sometimes a preferred stock) that carries a conversion feature permitting the investor to convert it into a specified number of shares of common stock. Thus, convertible securities provide the fixed-income benefits (interest) of a bond while offering the price appreciation (capital gains) potential of common stock. (Convertibles are discussed in Chapter 12.)

Mutual Funds, Exchange Traded Funds, and Exchange Traded Notes An organization that invests in and professionally manages a diversified portfolio of securities is called a *mutual fund*. A mutual fund sells shares to investors, who then become part owners of the fund's securities portfolio. Most mutual funds issue and repurchase shares at a price that reflects the underlying value of the portfolio at the time the transaction is made. Mutual funds have become popular with individual investors because they offer a wide variety of investment opportunities and a full array of services that many investors find particularly appealing.

Exchange traded funds (ETFs) are similar to mutual funds in that they, too, represent portfolios of securities. They are usually set up to track a basket or index of securities (e.g., the S&P 500) or a particular sector such as telecommunications or utility stocks. They also can include other types of investments, including bonds and real estate. Although mutual funds can only be bought or sold at the end of the day, investors can trade ETFs throughout the trading day, just like individual shares of stock. Further, ETFs provide more favorable tax treatment than mutual funds.

Exchange traded notes (ETNs) are more similar to ETFs than to mutual funds. They are senior, unsecured, unsubordinated debt securities issued by an underwriting bank. As such, ETNs are debt securities that have a maturity date and are backed only by the credit of the issuer. Like ETFs, most ETNs are designed to reproduce the returns on a market benchmark, net of investment management fees. Thus, the underwriting bank promises to pay an amount based on the value of the index, net of fees, upon maturity. It's important to realize that an ETN bears a different risk than an ETF. If the bank underwriting the ETN goes bankrupt, the ETN might lose value just as a senior debt security would. Consequently, ETFs only face the risk of market fluctuations, while ETNs face both market risk and the risk that the issuing bank will default. Unfortunately, this credit risk is hard for investors to evaluate. Like ETFs, ETNs are traded on an exchange. Also like ETFs, ETNs can provide tax advantages over mutual funds. (More information on these advantages and disadvantages will be discussed in Chapter 13.)

Real Estate Investments in *real estate* can take many forms, ranging from speculating in raw land to limited-partnership shares in commercial property; there are even mutual funds that specialize in real estate. The returns on real estate come from rents, capital gains, and certain tax benefits. (Various types of real estate investments are discussed in Chapter 13.)

11-2 SECURITIES MARKETS

LO2 The term securities markets generally describes the arena where stocks, bonds, and other financial instruments are traded. Such markets can be physical places, but they can just as easily be *electronic networks* that allow buyers and sellers to come together to execute trades. Securities markets can be broken into two parts: capital markets and money markets. The *capital market* is where long-term securities like stocks and bonds are traded. The *money market* is the marketplace for short-term, low-risk credit instruments with maturities of one year or less. These include U.S. Treasury bills, commercial paper, and so on. Each market provides a mechanism for bringing the buyers and sellers of securities together. Some of the more popular money market securities were discussed in Chapter 4. In this chapter, we'll concentrate on the capital markets.

11-2a Primary and Secondary Markets

In the *primary market,* new securities are sold to the public, and one party to the transaction is always the issuer. In contrast, previously issued (outstanding) securities are bought and sold in the *secondary market*, where the securities are "traded" between investors. A security is sold in the primary market just once, when it's originally issued by a corporation or a governmental body (e.g., a state or municipality). Subsequent transactions, in which securities are sold by one investor to another, take place in the secondary market.

Primary Markets When a corporation sells a new issue to the public, several financial institutions will participate in the transaction. To begin with, the corporation will probably use an *investment banking firm*, which specializes in *underwriting* (selling) new security issues. The investment banker will give the corporation advice on pricing and other aspects of the issue and will either sell the new security itself or arrange for a *selling group* to do so. The selling group is normally made up of several brokerage firms, each responsible for selling a certain portion of the new issue. On large issues, the originating investment banker will bring in other underwriting firms and form an *underwriting syndicate* in order to

> **securities markets** the marketplace in which stocks, bonds, and other financial instruments are traded

Exhibit 11.1

U.S. Broker and Dealer Markets

On a typical trading day, the secondary market is a beehive of activity where literally billions of shares change hands daily. This market consists of two parts, the broker market and the dealer market. As can be seen, each of these markets is made up of various exchanges and trading venues.

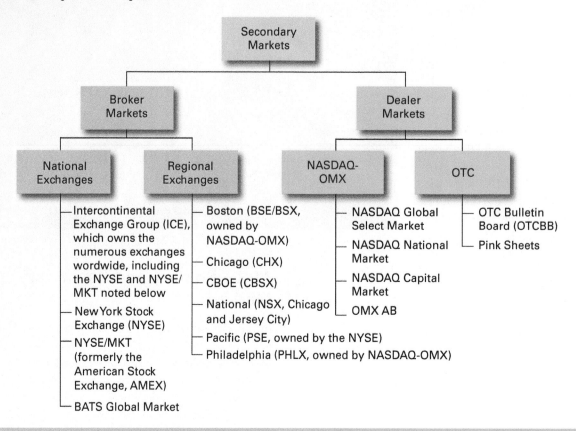

spread the risks associated with underwriting and selling the new securities. A potential investor in a new issue must be given a **prospectus**, which is a document describing the firm and the issue. Certain federal agencies are responsible for ensuring that all the information included in a prospectus accurately represents the facts.

Secondary Markets The secondary markets permit investors to execute transactions among themselves; it's the marketplace where an investor can easily sell his or her holdings to someone else. Unlike primary market transactions, the secondary market does not generate cash for the underlying company (issuer). Included among the secondary markets are the various *securities exchanges,* in which the buyers and sellers of securities are brought together for the purpose of executing trades. Another major

prospectus a document made available to prospective security buyers that describes the firm and a new security issue

segment of the market is made up of those securities that are listed and traded on the *National Association of Securities Dealers Automated Quotation System (NASDAQ)* market, which employs an all-electronic trading platform to execute trades. Finally, the *over-the-counter (OTC)* market deals in smaller, unlisted securities.

11-2b Broker Markets and Dealer Markets

By far, the vast majority of trades made by small individual investors take place in the secondary market, so we'll focus on that for the rest of this chapter. When you look at the secondary market *on the basis of how securities are traded,* you'll find that you can essentially divide the market into two segments: broker markets and dealer markets. Exhibit 11.1 shows the structure of the U.S. secondary market in terms of broker or dealer markets. As you can see, the *broker market* consists of national and regional "securities exchanges," while the *dealer market* is made up of both the NASDAQ market and the OTC market.

Probably *the biggest difference in these two markets is how the trades are executed.* When a trade occurs in a *broker market* (on one of the securities exchanges), then the two sides to the transaction—the buyer and the seller—are brought together and the trade takes place at that point: Party A sells his securities directly to the buyer, Party B. In a sense, with the help of a *broker*, the securities change hands right there on the floor of the exchange. In contrast, when trades are made in one of the *dealer markets*, the buyer and seller are never brought together directly; instead, their buy/sell orders are executed separately through *securities dealers*, who act as *market makers*. Essentially, two separate trades are made: Party A sells his securities (in, say, the XYZ Corp.) to one dealer, and Party B buys her securities (in the same XYZ Corp.) from the same or another dealer. Thus, there is always a dealer (market maker) on one side of the transaction.

Broker Markets When you think of the stock market, if you're like most individual investors then the first name to come to mind is the New York Stock Exchange. In 2007, the NYSE merged with Euronext, a combination of stock exchanges in Amsterdam, Brussels, Lisbon, and Paris. In late 2013, NYSE Euronext was acquired by the Intercontinental Exchange Group (ICE). ICE operates 11 regulated exchanges and five central clearing houses. In 2015, its listings included NYSE companies with an aggregate market value in excess of $25 trillion. It includes about 90 percent of the firms in the Dow Jones Industrial Average (DJIA) and about 80 percent of the firms in the S&P 500 index. ICE also owns the American Stock Exchange (AMEX), which was formerly the second-largest U.S. exchange. The AMEX has less restrictive listing requirements than the NYSE, so the acquisition allowed the NYSE to broaden the types of companies falling under its umbrella. The organization is also referred to as NYSE MKT. In mid-2014, ICE spun off Euronext as a standalone European company. The ICE entity is a part of the broker market—indeed, it's their biggest player. BATS Global Markets merged with Direct Edge in 2014. This created one of the largest stock exchange operators in the United States.

Besides ICE, a handful of *regional exchanges* are also part of the broker market. The number of securities listed on each of these exchanges typically ranges from about 100 to 500 companies. The best-known of these are the Boston, National, Pacific, and Philadelphia exchanges. These exchanges deal primarily in securities with local and regional appeal. To enhance their trading activity, regional exchanges often list securities that are also listed on the NYSE.

Dealer Markets A key feature of the dealer market is that, unlike the NYSE, it doesn't have centralized trading floors. Instead, it's made up of many market makers who are linked via a mass telecommunications network. Each market maker is actually a securities dealer who makes a market in one or more securities by offering to either buy or sell them at stated bid/ask prices. The **bid price** and **ask price** represent, respectively, the highest price offered to purchase a given security and the lowest price at which the security is offered for sale. In effect, an investor pays the ask price when *buying* securities and receives the bid price when *selling* them. Consisting of both the NASDAQ and OTC markets, dealer markets account for about 40 percent of all shares traded in the U.S. market—with NASDAQ accounting for the overwhelming majority of those trades.

The biggest dealer market, hands down, is made up of a select list of stocks that are listed and traded on NASDAQ. Founded in 1971, NASDAQ had its origins in the OTC market but today it is

bid price the price at which one can sell a security

ask price the price at which one can purchase a security considered *a totally separate entity that's no longer a part of the OTC market.* In fact, in 2006, the Securities and Exchange Commission (SEC) formally recognized NASDAQ as a "listed exchange," giving it much the same stature and prestige as the NYSE. To be traded on NASDAQ, all stocks must have at least two market makers—although the bigger, more actively traded stocks (such as Apple) will have many more than that. These dealers electronically post all their bid/ask prices so that, when investors place (market) orders, they're immediately filled at the best available price. In 2008, NASDAQ combined its business with OMX AB, which owned and operated the largest securities market in northern Europe. It also acquired the Philadelphia and Boston stock exchanges. Across its markets, NASDAQ lists about 3,100 companies with an aggregate market value of more than $9.3 trillion from all over the world.

NASDAQ sets various listing requirements in three-sub-markets: the *NASDAQ National Market*, the *NASDAQ Global Select Market*, and the *NASDAQ Capital Market*. These securities are widely quoted, and the trades, all executed electronically, are just as efficient as they are on the floor of the NYSE. Indeed, just as the NYSE has its list of big-name players (e.g., ExxonMobil, Wal-Mart, Pfizer, IBM, Coca-Cola, Home Depot, and UPS), so too does NASDAQ—including names like Apple, Microsoft, Facebook, Intel, Cisco Systems, eBay, and Google.

The other part of the dealer market is made up of securities that trade in the *over-the-counter (OTC) market.* This market is separate from NASDAQ and includes mostly small companies that either can't or don't wish to comply with NASDAQ listing requirements. They trade on either the *OTC Bulletin Board (OTCBB)* or in the so-called *Pink Sheets.* The OTCBB is an electronic quotation system that links the market makers who trade the shares of small companies. The OTCBB is regulated by the SEC, which requires (among other things) that all companies traded on this market file audited financial statements and comply with federal securities law. In sharp contrast, the OTC Pink Sheets represent the *unregulated* segment of the market, where companies aren't even required to file with the SEC.

11-2c Foreign Securities Markets

In addition to those in the United States, more than 100 other countries worldwide have organized securities exchanges. Indeed, actively traded markets can be found not only in such major industrialized nations as Japan, Great Britain, Germany, and Canada, but also in emerging economies. In terms of market capitalization (total market value of all shares traded), the NYSE is the biggest stock market in the world, followed by

---

Financial Planning Tips

IS IT TIME TO GET A ROBO INVESTMENT ADVISER?

Robo investment advisers are Internet-based platforms that typically use algorithms to recommend portfolios of low-cost, exchange-traded funds across multiple asset classes based on online questionnaires completed by investors. In the last few years, more than 200 companies have entered the market to help investors plan their portfolios online. These include fund giants Fidelity Investments and Vanguard Group, and brokerage firms such as Charles Schwab. While currently only a fraction of the wealth management market, digital wealth management assets are projected to reach $60 billion soon.

The average robo-adviser customer is millennial, self-directed, and comfortable with technology. Robo-advisers charge annual management fees usually ranging between 0.25 and 0.75 percent of assets plus fund expenses. In contrast, traditional advisers tend to charge an average of 1 percent. The primary rationale

for robo-advisers is that investors are best served by low fees and broadly diversified portfolios.

Should you be tempted to use a robo-adviser? Low expenses and simplified investment management are positives. However, surveys indicate that investors with the same investment objectives can receive markedly different advice from the broad array of robo-advisers. Keep in mind that you can get a bit of hand-holding from companies like Vanguard's Personal Advisor Services (**https://investor.vanguard.com/advice/personal -advisor**) and Personal Capital (**www.personalcapital .com/**). It makes sense to sample a number of robo-advisers' platforms and read their reviews carefully. And it's wise to do your homework before putting your investment portfolio on (semi-) automatic pilot.

Source: Adapted from Liz Moyer, "Putting Robo Advisers to the Test," *The Wall Street Journal,* www.wsj.com/articles/putting-robo-advisers -to-thetest-1429887456, accessed October 2016.

▶ **Read the auditor's report.** Look for phrases like "except for" or "subject to," as they mean just one thing: *There may be problems that you need to understand.*

11-4b The Financial Press

The most common sources of financial news are the Internet and the local newspaper. Other common sources of financial news include *The Wall Street Journal, Barron's,* and the "Money" section of *USA Today.* These are all national publications that include articles on the behavior of the economy, the market, various industries, and individual companies. The most comprehensive and up-to-date coverage of financial news is provided Monday through Saturday by *The Wall Street Journal.* Other excellent sources of investment information include magazines such as *Money, Forbes, Fortune, Bloomberg Businessweek,* and *Kiplinger's Personal Finance.* These publications are available online and as printed publications.

Market Data Usually presented in the form of averages, or indexes, *market data* describe the general behavior of the securities markets. The averages and indexes are based on the price movements of a select group of securities over an extended period. They're used to capture the overall performance of the market as a whole. You would want to follow one or more of these measures to get *a feel for how the market is doing over time* and, perhaps, an indication of what lies ahead. The absolute level of the index at a specific time (or on a given day) is far less important than *what's been happening to that index over a given period.* The most commonly cited market measures are those calculated by Dow Jones, Standard & Poor's, the NYSE, and NASDAQ. These measures are all intended to track the behavior of the stock market, particularly NYSE stocks (the Dow, S&P, and NYSE averages all follow stocks on the "big board," which is the NYSE).

Dow Jones Industrial Averages The granddaddy of them all, and probably the most widely followed measure of stock market performance, is the **Dow Jones Industrial Average (DJIA)**. Actually, the Dow Jones averages, which began in 1896, are made up of four parts: (1) an industrial average, the DJIA, which is based on 30 stocks; (2) a transportation average based on 20 stocks; (3) a utility average based on 15 stocks; and (4) a composite average based on all 65 industrial, transportation, and utility stocks. Most of the stocks in the DJIA are picked from the NYSE; but a few NASDAQ stocks, such as Intel and Microsoft, are included as well. Although these stocks are intended to represent a cross section of companies, there's a strong bias toward blue chips, which is a major criticism of the DJIA. The Bonus Exhibit found at PFIN6 Online titled "The Dow Jones Industrial Average" lists the 30 stocks currently in the DJIA.

Standard & Poor's Indexes The **Standard & Poor's (S&P) indexes** are similar to the Dow Jones averages in that both are used to capture the overall performance of the market. However, some important differences exist between the two measures. For one thing, the S&P has many more stocks. The popular S&P 500 composite index is based on 500 different stocks, whereas the DJIA uses only 30. What's more, the S&P index is made up of all large NYSE stocks in addition to some major AMEX and NASDAQ stocks, so there are not only more issues in the S&P sample, but also a greater breadth of representation. Finally, there are some technical differences in the mathematical procedures used to compute the two measures; the Dow Jones is a price-weighted average, whereas the S&P is a market value-weighted index.

Despite the technical differences, movements in the DJIA and the S&P 500 indices are *highly correlated.* Even so, the S&P has a much lower value than the DJIA—for example in October 2016 the Dow stood at about 18,145, whereas the S&P index of 500 stocks was around 2,141. This doesn't mean that the S&P consists of less valuable stocks; rather, the disparity is due solely to the different methods used to compute the measures. In addition to the S&P 500, two other widely followed S&P indices are the *MidCap 400* (made up of 400 medium-sized companies with an average market value of about $3.95 billion) and the *SmallCap 600* (consisting of companies with an average market cap of about $1.17 billion).

The NYSE, NASDAQ, and Other Market Indexes The most widely followed exchange-based indexes are those of the New York Stock Exchange (NYSE) and NASDAQ. The **NYSE index** includes all the stocks listed on the "big board" and provides a measure of performance in that market. Behavior in the NASDAQ market is measured by several indexes, the most comprehensive of which is the *NASDAQ Composite index,* which is

Dow Jones Industrial Average (DJIA) the most widely followed measure of stock market performance; consists of 30 blue-chip stocks listed mostly on the NYSE

Standard & Poor's (S&P) indexes indexes compiled by Standard & Poor's that are similar to the DJIA but employ different computational methods and consist of far more stocks

NYSE index an index of the performance of all stocks listed on the New York Stock Exchange calculated using virtually all the stocks traded on NASDAQ. In addition, there's the *NASDAQ 100 index*, which tracks the price behavior of the biggest 100 (nonfinancial) firms traded on NASDAQ—companies like Apple, Microsoft, Intel, Oracle, Cisco, and Staples. The NASDAQ Composite is often used as a benchmark in assessing the price behavior of *high-tech* stocks.

Besides these major indexes, there are a couple of other measures of market performance, one of which is the Dow Jones Wilshire 5000 index. It's estimated that the Wilshire index reflects the *total market value of 98 percent to 99 percent of all publicly traded stocks in the United States*. In essence, it shows what's happening in the stock market as a whole—the dollar amount of market value added or lost as the market moves up and down. Another widely followed measure is the *Russell 2000*, which tracks the performance of 2,000 relatively small companies and is widely considered to be a fairly accurate measure of the small-cap segment of the market.

Industry Data Local newspapers, *The Wall Street Journal, Barron's*, and various financial publications regularly contain articles and data about different industries. For example, Standard & Poor's *Industry Surveys* provides detailed descriptions and statistics for all the major industries; on a smaller scale, *Business Week* and other magazines regularly include indexes of industry performance and price levels.

Stock Quotes Stock price quotes appear daily on many sites, which include Yahoo! Finance (http://finance.yahoo.com), the *Wall Street Journal* (http://wsj.com), and CNN (www.cnn.com). Most online quotations provide not only current prices but a great deal of additional information as well.

Consider representative information available on numerous Internet sites. Exhibit 11.4 shows that Apple's stock price closed at $116.60 on October 21, 2016, which was a decrease of $0.46 from the prior day's closing price. The shares are shown as listed on the NASDAQ market. We see that Apple's trading symbol is AAPL. Its annual cash dividend yield is 1.95 percent, which is the annual dividend divided by the indicated market price. The firm's recent P/E ratio is also shown, which is the current market price divided by the per-share earnings for the most recent 12-month period; as can be seen, Apple is trading at a P/E of 13.6 times earnings, which is below that of the overall market. The average analyst's target forecast for Apple's stock price in one

> **Dow Jones Wilshire 5000 index** an index of the total market value of the approximately 6,000–7,000 or so most actively traded stocks in the United States

dennizn/Shutterstock.com

year is $128.32. And the exhibit shows that Apple's overall market capitalization (stock price times the number of shares) is $628.29 billion. This makes it the largest company in the world, as measured by market capitalization.

11-4c Advisory Services

Subscription advisory services provide information and recommendations on various industries and specific securities. The services normally cost from fifty to several hundred dollars a year, although you can usually review such material (for free) at your broker's office, at university and public libraries, or online. Probably the best-known investment advisory services are those provided by Value Line, Standard & Poor's, and Moody's Investors Service. An example of one of these reports is given in Exhibit 11.5. This report, prepared by Value Line, presents a concise summary of a company's financial history, current finances, and future prospects. Similar stock reports are also available from Standard & Poors and Morningstar.

11-5 ONLINE INVESTING

LO5 The Internet is a major force in the investing environment. It has opened the world of investing to individual investors, leveling the playing field and providing access to tools and market information formerly restricted to professionals. Not only can you trade all types of securities online, you can also find a wealth of information, from real-time stock quotes to securities analysts' research reports. However, online investing also carries risks. The Internet requires investors to exercise the same—and possibly more—caution as they would if they were getting information from and placing orders with a human broker. You don't have the safety net of a live broker suggesting that you rethink your trade. Online or off, the basic rules for smart investing are still the same: *Know what you're buying, from whom, and at what level of risk.*

Exhibit 11.4

Listed Stock Quote for Apple

This exhibit provides information on one day's trading activity and the price quote for Apple, which is traded on NASDAQ. Note that, in addition to the latest stock prices, a typical stock quote conveys an array of other information.

Apple Inc (AAPL)

116.60   −0.46 (−0.39%) At close: October 21 4:00 PM EST

Today's Trading

Previous close	117.06
Today's open	116.81
Beta	1.55
Volume	23,192,665
Average volume (3 months)	35,884,464
Market cap	$628.29B
Dividend yield	1.95%

Growth & Valuation

Quarterly Earnings Growth (yoy)	−27.00%
Quarterly Revenue Growth (yoy)	−14.60%
P/E ratio (trailing)	13.60
Price/Sales (ttm)	2.85
Price/Book (mrq)	4.97

Financials

Diluted EPS	$8.58
Total cash	$62.62B
Revenue (ttm)	$220.29B
Profit margin (ttm)	21.70%

Analysts' One-Year Price Forecast*

Mean target	$128.32
High target	$185.00
Low target	$85.00
Number of analysts in forecast	41

*Data provided by ThomsonFirstCall

Source: From http://finance.yahoo.com/q?s=AAPL, quotes from October 10, 2016; yoy = year over year (as of March 26, 2016); ttm = trailing 12 months (as of March 26, 2016.)

11-5a Online Investor Services

The Internet offers a full array of online investor services, from up-to-the-minute stock quotes and research reports to charting services and portfolio tracking. When it comes to investing, you name it and you can probably find it online. Unfortunately, although many of these are truly high-quality sites offering valuable information, many others are pure garbage, so be careful when entering the world of online investing. Let's now review the kinds of investor services you can find online, starting with investor education sites.

Exhibit 11.5

A *Value Line Investment Survey* Report

A Value Line report like this one provides a wealth of information about the operating results and financial condition of the company and is an invaluable source of information to investors.

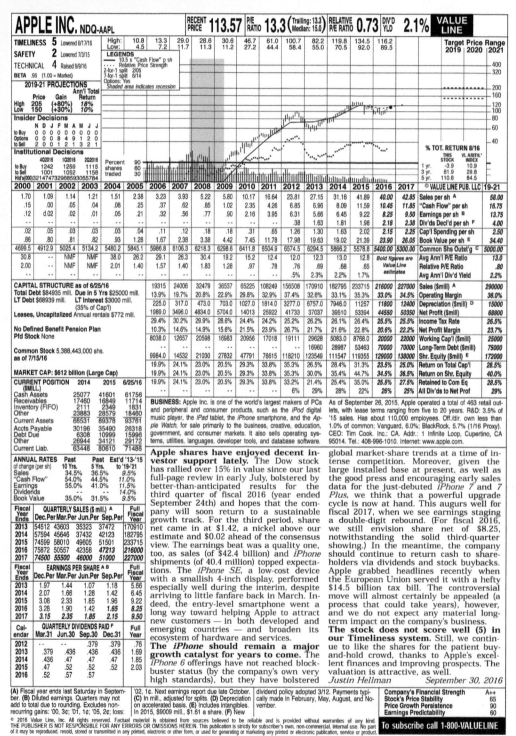

Investor Education The Internet offers a wide array of tutorials, online classes, and articles to educate the novice investor. Even experienced investors will find sites that expand their investing knowledge. Although most good investment-oriented Web sites include many educational resources, here are a few good sites featuring *investment fundamentals:*

▶ *The Motley Fool* (**www.fool.com**) *Fool's School* has sections on fundamentals of investing, mutual fund investing, choosing a broker, investment strategies and styles, lively discussion boards, and more.

▶ Morningstar (**www.morningstar.com**) provides comprehensive information on stocks mutual funds, ETFs, and more.

▶ Zacks Investment Research (**www.zacks.com**) is an excellent starting place to learn what the Internet can offer investors.

▶ NASDAQ (**www.nasdaq.com**) has Investing and Personal Finance sections with financial planning and choosing a broker.

Investment Tools Once you're familiar with the basics of investing, you can use the Internet to develop financial plans and set investment goals, find securities that meet your investment objectives, analyze potential investments, and organize your portfolio. Many of these tools, once used only by professional money managers, are free to anyone who wants to go online.

Investment Planning Online calculators and worksheets can help you find answers to your financial planning and investing questions. With them, you can figure out how much to save each month for a particular goal, such as the down payment for your first home, a college education for your children, or to be able to retire by the time you reach 55. For example, Fidelity (**www.fidelity.com**) and Vanguard (www.vanguard.com) have a wide selection of planning tools that deal with such topics as investment growth, college planning, and retirement planning. One of the best sites for financial calculators is *Kiplinger* (**www.kiplinger.com**). Go to their personal finance page, click on "Tools" and you'll find calculators dealing with everything from stocks, bonds, and mutual funds to retirement planning, home buying, and taxes.

Investment Research and Screening One of the best investor services offered online is the ability to conduct high-quality, in-depth research on stocks, bonds, mutual funds, and other types of investment vehicles. Go to a site like **www.kiplinger.com**, click on "Investing," and you can obtain literally dozens of pages of financial and market information about a specific stock or mutual fund. Many of these sites have links back to the company itself, so with a few mouse clicks, you can obtain the company's annual report, detailed financial statements, and historical summaries of a full array of financial and market ratios. In addition, you'll also find various *online screening tools* that can be used to identify attractive and potentially rewarding investment vehicles.

Financial Planning Tips

STARTING ONLINE INVESTING

- **Set aside some money to get started and choose a broker.** You don't need much—your initial deposit can be as little as $50. Choose an online broker with no minimum deposit. Consider the results of the online broker rankings provided in Exhibit 11.3 earlier in this chapter.

- **Learn the key investing jargon.** Some useful sources are Investopedia (www.investopedia.com) and InvestorWords (www.investorwords.com).

- **Practice with a paper account before investing real money.** Try out the Investing Simulator Center (www.investingonline.org/isc/index.html) and then practice with different investment strategies using online trading simulators like Icarra (www.icarra.com) or paperTrade (www.trademonster.com).

- **Gradually add more money to your account.** Add amounts regularly that are consistent with your investment goals.

- **Monitor your portfolio's performance.** Data can be obtained easily using Yahoo! Finance (finance.yahoo.com/) or Google Finance (www.google.com/finance).

- **Keep up with financial news.** In addition, read as much as you can on how to invest.

Source: Adapted from Matt Krantz, "How to Get Started Investing Online," www.dummies.com/how-to/content/investing-online-for -dummies-cheat-sheet.html, accessed October 2016.

These tools, available at sites like Quicken, Morningstar, or MSN Money Central, enable you to sort quickly through huge databases of stocks and mutual funds to find those that meet specific characteristics, such as stocks with low or high P/E multiples, small market capitalizations, high dividend yields, specific revenue growth, and low debt-to-equity ratios. You answer a series of questions to specify the type of stock or fund you're looking for, performance criteria you desire, cost parameters, and so on. The screen then provides a list of stocks (or funds) that meet the standards that you've set.

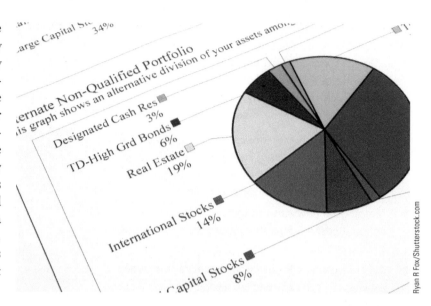

Go to Smart Sites

Tune your investment portfolio for retirement with E*TRADE's Easy Retirement Calculator.

Portfolio Tracking Almost every investment-oriented Internet site includes *portfolio tracking tools*. Simply enter the number of shares held, the purchase price, and the symbol for the stocks or mutual funds that you want to follow. The tracker then automatically updates the value of your portfolio in real time. What's more, you can usually click on one of the provided links and quickly obtain detailed information about each stock or mutual fund in your portfolio. Quicken.com, MSN MoneyCentral (**http://money.msn.com**), Google (**https:// google.com/finance/portfolio**), and E˚Trade (**www .etrade.com**) all have portfolio trackers that are easy to set up and use. For example, Quicken's tracker alerts you whenever an analyst changes the rating on one of your stocks or funds and tells you how well you're diversified among the major asset classes or sectors you hold.

11-6 MANAGING YOUR INVESTMENT HOLDINGS

LO6 Buying and selling securities is not difficult. The hard part is finding securities that will provide the kind of return you're looking for. Like most individual investors, you too will be buying, selling, and trading securities with ease in time. Eventually, your investment holdings will increase to the point where you're managing a whole portfolio of securities. In essence, a **portfolio** is a collection of investments assembled to meet a common investment goal. But a portfolio is far more than a collection of investments. It breathes life into your investment program, as it combines your personal and financial traits with your investment objectives to give some structure to your investments.

Seasoned investors often devote lots of attention to constructing diversified portfolios of securities. Such portfolios consist of stocks and bonds selected not only for their returns, but also for their combined risk–return behavior. The idea behind **diversification** is that by combining securities with dissimilar risk–return characteristics, you can produce a portfolio of reduced risk and more predictable levels of return.

Investment research shows you can achieve a noticeable reduction in risk simply by diversifying your investment holdings. For the small investor with a moderate amount of money to invest, this means that *investing in several securities rather than a single one should be beneficial*. The payoff from diversification comes in the form of reduced risk without a significant impact on return.

11-6a Building a Portfolio of Securities

In developing a portfolio of investment holdings, it's assumed that diversification is a desirable investment attribute that leads to improved returns and/or reduced risk. Again, as emphasized previously, holding a variety of investments is far more desirable than concentrating all your investments in a single security or industry. To get an idea of the kind of portfolio diversification employed by investors, look at the following numbers, which shows the types of investments held by *average individual investors*:

Type of Investment Product	Percentage of Portfolio October 2016
Stocks and stock funds	64.73%
Bonds and bond funds	16.59
Cash and short-term investments (CDs, money market deposit accounts, etc.)	18.68
Total	100.00%

This portfolio reflects the results of monthly asset allocation surveys conducted by the *American Association of Individual Investors*. Whether this is what your portfolio should look like depends on a number of factors, including your own needs and objectives.

Investor Characteristics To formulate an effective portfolio strategy, begin with an honest evaluation of your own financial condition and family situation. Pay particular attention to variables like these:

▶ Level and stability of income

▶ Family factors

▶ Investment horizon

▶ Net worth

▶ Investment experience and age

▶ Disposition toward risk

These variables set the tone for your investments. They determine the kinds of investments you should consider and how long you can tie up your money. For your portfolio to work, it must be tailored to meet your personal financial needs. For example, the size and predictability of an investor's employment income has a significant bearing on portfolio strategy. An investor with a secure job is more likely to embark on a more aggressive investment program than is an investor with a less secure position. Income taxes also bear on the investment decision. The higher an investor's income, the more important the tax ramifications of an investment program become.

In addition, an individual's investment experience will influence the type of investment strategy employed. It's best to "get your feet wet" in the investment market by slipping into it slowly, rather than leaping in head first. Investors who make risky initial investments often suffer heavy losses, damaging the long-run potential of their entire investment program. A cautiously developed

investment program will likely provide far more favorable long-run results than an impulsive, risky one. Finally, investors should consider risk carefully. High-risk investments have not only high return potential but also high risk of loss. A good rule to remember is that *an investor's exposure to risk should never exceed the capacity to bear that risk.*

Investor Objectives After developing a personal financial profile, the investor's next question is: "What do I want from my portfolio?" This seems like an easy question to answer. Ideally, we would all like to double our money every year by making low-risk investments. However, the realities of the highly competitive investment environment make this outcome unlikely, so the question must be answered more realistically. There's generally a trade-off between earning a high current income from an investment and obtaining significant capital appreciation from it. An investor must choose one or the other; it's hard to obtain both from a single investment. Of course, it's possible to have a *balance* of both income and growth (capital gains) in a portfolio; but most often, that involves "tilting" the portfolio in one direction (e.g., toward income) or the other (toward growth).

An investor's needs should determine which approach to pursue. For instance, a retired investor whose income depends partly on her portfolio will probably choose a lower-risk, current-income-oriented approach for financial survival. In contrast, a high-income, financially secure investor may be much more willing to make risky investments in hopes of improving her net worth. Likewise, a young investor with a secure job may be less concerned about current income and more able to bear risk. This type of investor will likely be more capital gains–oriented and may choose riskier investments.

> A portfolio should be built around an individual's needs, which in turn depend on income, family responsibilities, financial resources, age, retirement plans, and capacity to bear risk.

11-6b Asset Allocation and Portfolio Management

A portfolio should be built around an individual's needs, which in turn depend on income, family responsibilities, financial resources, age, retirement plans, and

portfolio a collection of securities assembled for the purpose of meeting common investment goals

diversification the process of choosing securities with dissimilar risk–return characteristics in order to create a portfolio that provides an acceptable level of return and an acceptable exposure to risk capacity to bear risk. These needs shape one's financial goals. But to create a portfolio geared to those goals, you need to develop an **asset allocation** strategy. Asset allocation focuses on the question of *how to divide your portfolio among different types of securities.* For example, what portion of your portfolio will be devoted to short-term securities, to long-term bonds and bond funds, and to individual common stocks and equity funds? The idea is to position your assets in such a way that you can protect your portfolio from negative developments in the market while still taking advantage of potential positive developments.

There's substantial evidence that over the long run, *the total return on a portfolio is influenced far more by its asset allocation plan than by specific security selections.* Asset allocation deals in broad categories and *does not tell you which individual securities to buy or sell.* It might look something like this:

Type of Investment	Asset Mix
Short-term securities	5%
Longer bonds (7- to 10-year maturities)	20
Equity funds	75
Total portfolio	100%

As you can see, all you're really doing here is deciding how to cut up the pie. You still have to decide which particular securities to invest in. Once you've decided that you want to put, say, 20 percent of your money into intermediate-term (7- to 10-year) bonds, your next step is to select those specific securities.

After establishing your asset allocation strategy, you should check it regularly to make sure that your portfolio is still in line with your desired asset mix and to see if that mix is still appropriate for your investment objectives. Here are some reasons to reevaluate your asset allocations:

▶ A major change in personal circumstances—marriage, birth of a child, loss of job, or family illness—that changes your investment goals.

▶ The proportion of an asset category rises or falls considerably and thereby deviates from your target allocation for that class by more than, say, 5 percent.

▶ You're close to reaching a certain goal (such as saving for your child's college education).

asset allocation a plan for dividing a portfolio among different classes of securities in order to preserve capital by protecting the portfolio against negative market developments

Periodically, you may find it necessary to *rebalance* your portfolio—that is, to reallocate the assets in your portfolio. For example, suppose that your asset allocation plan calls for 75 percent in equities but then the stock market falls, so stocks represent only 65 percent of your total portfolio value. If you're still bullish on the (long-term) market and if stocks are still appropriate for your portfolio, then you may view this as a good time to buy stocks and, in so doing, bring your portfolio back up to 75 percent in equities. But don't be too quick to rebalance every time your portfolio gets a little out of whack. You should allow for some variation in the actual allocations because market fluctuations will make it impossible to maintain exact percentages constantly. And don't forget to consider tax implications and the costs from trading commissions.

Portfolio management involves the buying, selling, and holding of various securities in order to meet a set of predetermined investment needs and objectives. To give you an idea of portfolio management in action, Exhibit 11.6 provides examples of four portfolios, each developed with a particular financial situation in mind. Notice that in each case, the asset allocation strategies and portfolio structures change with the different financial objectives. The first one is the *newlywed couple*; in their late 20s, they earn $65,000 a year and spend just about every cent. Next is the *two-income couple*; in their early 40s, they earn $115,000 a year and are concerned about college costs for their children, ages 17 and 12. Then there is the *single parent*; she is 34, has custody of her children, ages 7 and 4, and receives $50,000 a year in salary and child support. Finally, we have the *couple in their mid-50s*, who are planning for retirement in 10 years, when the husband will retire from his $95,000-a-year job.

> **YOU CAN DO IT NOW: Track Your Portfolio for Free** You can track your portfolio for free. And you can track a "paper" portfolio as well just to test out investment ideas. Go to https://www.google.com/finance/portfolio?action=view – you can **do it now**.

11-6c Keeping Track of Your Investments

Just as you need investment objectives to provide direction for your portfolio, so too do you need to *monitor* it by keeping track of what your investment

Exhibit 11.6

Four Model Portfolios

The type of portfolio you put together will depend on your financial and family situation as well as on your investment objectives. Clearly, what is right for one family may be totally inappropriate for another.

Family Situation	Portfolio
Newlywed couple in late 20s	80 to 90 percent in common stocks, with three-quarters of that in mutual funds aiming for maximum capital gains and the rest in growth-and-income or equity-income funds
	10 to 20 percent in a money market fund or other short-term money market securities
Two-income couple in early 40s	60 to 70 percent in common stocks, with three-quarters of that in blue chips or growth mutual funds and the rest in more aggressive issues or mutual funds aiming for maximum capital gains
	25 to 30 percent in discount Treasury notes whose maturities correspond with the bills for college tuition
	5 to 10 percent in money market funds or other short-term money market securities
Single parent in early 30s	50 to 60 percent in growth and income mutual funds
	40 to 50 percent in money market funds or other short-term money market securities
Couple in mid-50s	60 to 70 percent in blue-chip common stocks, growth funds, or value funds
	25 to 30 percent in municipal bonds or short-and intermediate-term discount bonds that will mature as the couple starts needing the money to live on
	5 to 10 percent in CDs and money market funds

holdings consist of, how they've performed over time, and whether they've lived up to your expectations. Sometimes investments don't perform the way that you thought they would. Their return may be well below what you'd like, or you may even have suffered a loss. In either case, it may be time to sell the investments and put the money elsewhere. A monitoring system should allow you to identify such securities in your portfolio. It should also enable you to stay on top of the holdings that are performing to your satisfaction. Knowing when to sell and when to hold can significantly affect the amount of return you're able to generate from your investments.

You can use a tool like Worksheet 11.2 to keep an inventory of your investment holdings. All types of investments can be included on this worksheet—from stocks, bonds, and mutual funds to real estate and savings accounts. To see how it works, consider the investment portfolio that has been built up since 2004 by Bill and Nora Crosby, a two-income couple in their early 40s. Worksheet 11.2 shows that, as of October 21, 2016. Bill and Nora hold common stock in three companies, two mutual funds, and a bond exchange-traded fund. Using a worksheet like this in conjunction with an *online portfolio tracker* would give an investor plenty of information about the performance of his or her portfolio—the *worksheet* providing long-term information from the date of purchase of an asset, and the *online portfolio tracker* providing year-to-date or annual returns. Note that the Crosbys' holdings have grown from $104,607.50 to $197,723.25. They have also received total dividends and coupon payments of $31,264.17. Thus, the latest market value of their portfolio including the dividends and coupons received is $228,988.01. The cumulative return on the Crosbys' overall portfolio, which includes price appreciation and dividends and coupons received, is an impressive-looking 89.01% percent. However, more insight into the risk of their investments would be needed before we could decide just how impressive the investment performance has been. A report like this should be prepared at least once a year; when completed, it provides a quick overview of your investment holdings and lets you know where you stand at a given point in time.

A worksheet like this one enables you to keep track of your investment holdings and to identify investments that aren't performing up to expectations.

AN INVENTORY OF INVESTMENT HOLDINGS

Name(s): Bill and Nora Crosby   Date: October 21, 2106

Type of Investment	Description of Investment	Date Purchased	Amount of Investment	Latest Market Value	Cumulative Return
Common stock	250 shares - McDonalds	12/7/2005	$8,815.00	$28,482.50	+223.11%
Common stock	300 shares - Disney	10/19/2007	$10,143.00	$27,909.00	+175.16%
Common stock	150 shares - Intel	8/11/2010	$2,914.50	$5,272.50	+80.91%
Exchange-traded fund	400 shares - Vanguard Total International Bond ETF	8/12/2014	20,444.00	$22,220.00	+8.69%
Mutual fund	200 shares - Vanguard Health Care	6/16/2004	$25,142.00	$40,056.00	+59.32%
Mutual fund	725 shares - Fidelity Contrafund	6/16/2004	$37,149.00	$73,783.25	+98.61%
	Market Value of Investments			$197,723.25	
	Total Dividends and coupons Received			$31,264.76	
	Portfolio Totals		$104,607.50	$228,988.01*	+89.01%

*Portfolio total value includes total dividends and coupon payments received.

PLANNING OVER A LIFETIME

Investing

Here are some key considerations for investment planning in each stage of the life cycle.

PRE-FAMILY INDEPENDENCE: 20s

» Describe specific, tangible investments goals concerning retirement, major purchases, ways to enhance current income, and tax shelters.

» Align your investment goals with an amount regularly set aside from your income.

» Establish an emergency fund equal to six months of income.

» Make paying off college loans a priority. They limit your financial flexibility.

FAMILY FORMATION/CAREER DEVELOPMENT: 30–45

» Revise investment plan to focus more on retirement and funding children's education, if applicable.

» Consider rebalancing investment portfolio consistent with long-term strategy.

» Gradually increase the amount set aside for investments and savings.

PRE-RETIREMENT: 45–65

» Revise investment plan in light of recent developments.

» Monitor portfolio performance and consider rebalancing asset exposures.

» Continue to gradually increase the amount you invest and save.

RETIREMENT: 65 AND BEYOND

» Revise investment plan to include more conservative assets.

» Monitor portfolio performance and match current income to expenditures.

» Integrate investment strategy with estate planning.

Cyrus and Lily Get Serious About Their Retirement Asset Allocation

Cyrus and Lily Dodson are married and are both 32 years old. While they want to save for their children's future college educations, they also want to be plan carefully for their retirement. They know it's important to be adequately diversified and to be properly positioned in the various asset categories in their 401(k) retirement plans and IRAs. So one recent Saturday afternoon they found a free online asset allocation calculator (**http://money.cnn.com /tools/assetallocwizard /assetallocwizard.html**) and got some initial guidance on their proper asset allocation.

The online survey asked them about their investment time horizon, how much risk they were comfortable with, the flexibility of their retirement dates, and whether they're tempted to sell stocks during a downturn or buy more. They indicated a 20+ year investment time horizon, medium risk

val lawless/Shutterstock.com

tolerance, flexible retirement dates, and an inclination to leave their investments alone during a downturn. The recommended asset allocation was:

- 10 percent bonds
- 50 percent large stocks
- 20 percent small stocks
- 20 percent foreign stocks

Given that this recommends they invest 90 percent of their money in stocks, Cyrus and Lily have decided to get some more recommendations for a broader perspective on their asset allocation decision. This recommendation strikes them as a bit too risky for their tastes. However, this recommendation confirms their interest in having a significant amount invested in stocks with decent international diversification for the long haul. Cyrus and Lily are well on their way to managing their retirement investments effectively.

STUDY TOOLS 11

LOCATED AT BACK OF THE TEXTBOOK
☐ Chapter Review Card

LOCATED AT WWW.CENGAGEBRAIN.COM
☐ Review Key Term flashcards and create your own cards.
☐ Track your knowledge and understanding of key concepts in personal finance.

☐ Complete practice and graded quizzes to prepare for tests.
☐ Complete interactive content at PFIN6 Online.
☐ View the chapter highlight boxes at PFIN6 Online.

©viphotos/Shutterstock140785408

Financial Planning Exercises

LO1 1. **Calculate amount to invest to meet objectives.** *Use Worksheet 11.1.* Mary Bender is now employed as the managing editor of a well-known business journal. Although she thoroughly enjoys her job and the people she works with, what she would really like to do is open a bookstore of her own. She would like to open her store in about eight years and figures she'll need about $50,000 in capital to do so. Given that Mary thinks she can make about 10 percent on her money, use Worksheet 11.1 to answer the following questions.

   a. How much would Mary have to invest today, in one lump sum, to end up with $50,000 in eight years?

   b. If she's starting from scratch, how much would she have to put away annually to accumulate the needed capital in eight years?

   c. If she already has $10,000 socked away, how much would she have to put away annually to accumulate the required capital in eight years?

   d. Given that Mary has an idea of how much she needs to save, explain how she could use an investment plan to help reach her objective.

LO2 2. **Rationale for stock exchange listings.** Why do you suppose that well-known companies such as Apple, Starbucks, and Facebook prefer to have their shares traded on the NASDAQ rather than on one of the major listed exchanges, such as the NYSE (for which they'd easily meet all listing requirements)? What's in it for them? What would they gain by switching over to the NYSE?

LO2 3. **Types of financial markets.** What is the difference between primary and secondary markets and between broker and dealer markets?

LO3 4. **Market and limit orders.** Victor Gould places an order to buy 100 shares of Google. Explain how the order will be processed if it's a market order. Would it make any difference if it had been a limit order? Explain.

LO4 5. **Finding and applying market index quotes.** Using resources like *The Wall Street Journal* or *Barron's* (either in print or online), find the latest values for each of the following market averages and indexes, and indicate how each has performed over the past six months:

   a. DJIA

   b. S&P 500

   c. NASDAQ Composite

   d. S&P MidCap 400

   e. Dow Jones Wilshire 5000

   f. Russell 2000

LO4 6. **Obtaining stock market quotes.** Using the Internet site for Yahoo! Finance (http://finance .yahoo.com), find the 52-week high and low for Coca-Cola's common stock (symbol KO). What is the stock's latest dividend yield? What was Coca-Cola's most recent closing price, and at what P/E ratio was the stock trading?

LO4 7. **Interpreting stock report information.** Using the *Value Line Investment Survey* report in Exhibit 11.5, find the following information for Apple.

   a. What was the amount of revenues (i.e., sales) generated by the company in 2015?

   b. What were the latest annual dividends per share and dividend yield?

   c. What is the earnings per share (EPS) projection for 2017?

   d. How many shares of common stock were outstanding?

   e. What were the book value per share and EPS in 2015?

   f. How much long-term debt did the company have in 2015?

LO5 8. **Choosing an online broker.** Based on Exhibit 11.3, which online broker do you believe would be best for you? Explain your rationale.

LO6 9. **Tracking portfolio performance.** *Use Worksheet 11.2* to help Grant and Elle Harding, a married

Financial Planning Exercises

couple in their early 30s, evaluate their securities portfolio, which includes these holdings.

a. *IBM.* (NYSE; symbol IBM): 100 shares bought in 2011 for $170.40 per share.

b. *Procter & Gamble* (NYSE; symbol PG): 150 shares purchased in 2010 at $61.85 per share.

c. *Google* (NASDAQ; symbol, GOOG): 200 shares purchased in 2014 at $519.98 per share.

d. The Hardings also have $8,000 in a one-year CD they bought one year ago, which pays 1.25 percent annual interest.

1. Based on the latest quotes obtained from the Internet, complete Worksheet 11.2. Consider using an online portfolio tracker like the one provided by Google (**www.google.com/finance/portfolio**). Note that Google accounts for dividends as cash received.

2. What's the total amount the Hardings have invested in these securities, the annual income they now receive, and the latest market value of their investments?

12 | Investing in Stocks and Bonds

LEARNING OBJECTIVES

After studying this chapter, you will be able to...

LO1 Describe the various types of risks to which investors are exposed, as well as the sources of return.

LO2 Know how to search for an acceptable investment on the basis of risk, total return, and yield.

LO3 Discuss the merits of investing in common stock and be able to distinguish among the different types of stocks.

LO4 Become familiar with the various measures of performance and how to use them in placing a value on stocks.

LO5 Describe the basic issue characteristics of bonds as well as how these securities are used as investment vehicles.

LO6 Distinguish between the different types of bonds, gain an understanding of how bond prices behave, and know how to compute different measures of yield.

After you finish this chapter, go to **PAGE 337** for **STUDY TOOLS**

William Potter/Shutterstock.com

How Will This Affect Me? Once you've figured out how much you need to invest to meet your financial goals, it's time to decide which specific investments to buy. This chapter describes the basic characteristics of stocks and bonds, explains their potential returns and risks, and provides a framework for choosing among stocks and bonds to meet your financial objectives. Care is taken to explore how stock and bond prices behave and how to evaluate their performance over time. After reading this chapter, you should be able to choose the most appropriate stocks and bonds for your portfolio in light of your goals and constraints.

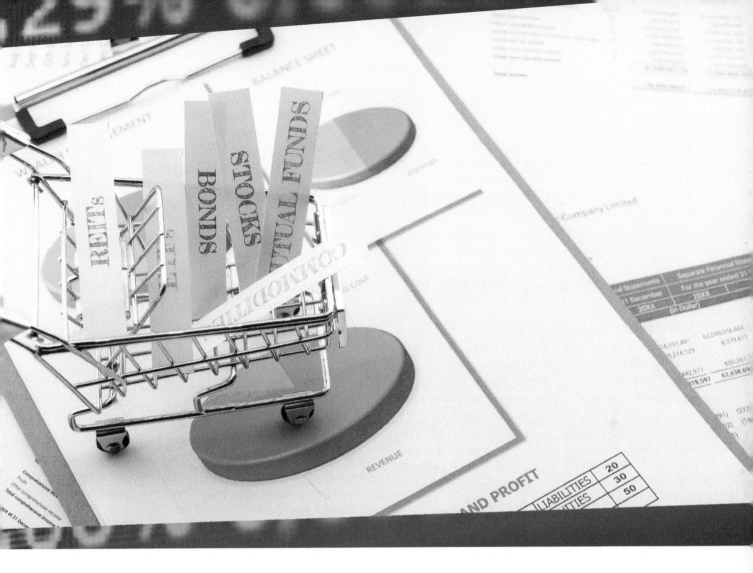

12-1 THE RISKS AND REWARDS OF INVESTING

LO1, LO2 Most rational investors are motivated to buy or sell a security based on its expected (or anticipated) return: buy if the return looks good, sell if it doesn't. But a security's return is just part of the story. You shouldn't consider the return on an investment without also looking at its *risk*—the chance that the actual return from an investment may differ from (i.e., fall short—you wouldn't mind if it exceeded expectations, after all) what was expected. You typically expect riskier investments to provide higher returns. Otherwise, what incentive is there for an investor to risk his or her capital? These two concepts (risk and return) are of vital concern to investors. So, before taking up the issue of investing in stocks and bonds, let's look more closely at the risks of investing and the various components of return. Equally

> You shouldn't consider the return on an investment without also looking at its risk.

important, we'll see how these two components can be used together to find potentially attractive investments.

12-1a The Risks of Investing

Just about any type of investment is subject to risk—some more so than others. The basic types of investment risk are business risk, financial risk, market risk, purchasing power

 Go to Smart Sites

risk, interest rate risk, liquidity risk, and event risk. Other things being equal, you'd like to reduce your exposure to these risks as much as possible.

Business Risk When investing in a company, you may have to accept the possibility that the firm will fail to maintain sales and profits or even to stay in business. Such failure is due either to economic or industry factors or, as is more often the case, to poor management decisions. **Business risk** is the variability surrounding the firm's cash flows and its ability to meet operating expenses in a timely fashion.

Financial Risk **Financial risk** concerns the amount of debt used to finance the firm, as well as the possibility that the firm will not have sufficient cash flows to meet these obligations on time. Look to the company's balance sheet in order to get a handle on a firm's financial risk.

Companies that have little or no long-term debt are often fairly low in financial risk. This is the case particularly if the company also has a healthy earnings picture. The problem with debt financing is that it creates principal and interest obligations that must be met regardless of how much profit the company is generating.

Market Risk **Market risk** results from the behavior of investors in the securities markets that can lead to swings in security prices. These price changes can be due to underlying intrinsic factors, as well as to changes in political and economic conditions or in investor tastes and preferences. Market risk is reflected in the *price volatility* of a security: the more

Dzmitry Kliapitski/Shutterstock.com

volatile the price of a security relative to the overall market, the greater its market risk.

Purchasing Power Risk Changes in the general level of prices within an economy produce **purchasing power risk**. In periods of rising prices (inflation), the purchasing power of the dollar declines. This means that a smaller quantity of goods and services can be purchased with a given number of dollars. In general, investments (like stocks or real estate) whose values tend to move with general price levels are most profitable during periods of rising prices, whereas investments (such as bonds) that pay fixed cash flows are preferred during periods of low or declining price levels.

Interest Rate Risk **Fixed-income securities**—which include notes, bonds, and preferred stocks—pay investors fixed periodic cash flows and, as such, are most affected by **interest rate risk**. As interest rates change, the prices of these securities fluctuate, decreasing with rising interest rates and increasing with falling rates. Changes in interest rates are due to fluctuations in the supply of or demand for money, which is heavily influenced by the monetary policy of the Federal Reserve in the United States.

Liquidity Risk The risk of not being able to liquidate (i.e., sell) an investment conveniently and at a reasonable price is called **liquidity risk**. In general, investment vehicles traded in *thin markets*, where supply and demand are small, tend to be less liquid than those traded in *broad markets*. However, to be liquid, an investment not only must be easy to sell, but also must be so *at a reasonable price*. Investments such as mutual funds, common stocks, and U.S. Treasury securities are generally highly liquid; others, such as raw land, are not.

Event Risk **Event risk** occurs when something substantial happens to a company and that event, in itself, has a sudden impact on the company's financial condition. It involves an unexpected event that has a significant and usually immediate effect on the underlying value of an investment. A good example of event risk was the action by the Food and Drug Administration (FDA) years ago to halt the use of silicone breast implants. The stock price of Dow Corning—the dominant producer of this product—quickly fell due to this single event! Another example is the tragedy of the terrorist attack in New York on September 11, 2001. Air travel declined substantially in the following months, with a related decline in airline stock prices. Fortunately, event risk is

business risk the variability associated with a firm's cash flows and its subsequent ability to meet its operating expenses

financial risk a type of risk associated with the mix of debt and equity financing used by the issuing firm, and its ability to meet its financial obligations

market risk a type of risk associated with the price volatility of a security

purchasing power risk a type of risk, resulting from possible changes in price levels, that can significantly affect investment returns

fixed-income securities securities such as bonds, notes, and preferred stocks that offer purchasers fixed periodic income

interest rate risk a type of risk, resulting from changing market interest rates, that mainly affects fixed-income securities

liquidity risk a type of risk associated with the inability to liquidate an investment conveniently and at a reasonable price

event risk the risk that some major, unexpected event will occur that leads to a sudden and substantial change in the value of an investment often confined to specific companies, securities, or market segments.

12-1b Returns from Investing

Any investment—whether it's a share of stock, a bond, real estate, or a mutual fund—has two basic sources of return: *current income* and *capital gains*. While some investments offer only one source of return (e.g., non–dividend-paying stocks provide only capital gains), many others offer both income and capital gains, which together make up what's known as the *total return* from an investment. When both elements of return are present, the relative importance of each will vary among investments. For example, while current income is more important with bonds, capital gains are usually a larger portion of the total return from common stocks.

Current Income Current income is generally received with some degree of regularity over the course of the year. It may take the form of dividends on stock, interest from bonds, or rents from real estate. People who invest to obtain income look for investments that will provide regular and predictable patterns of cash flows. Preferred stocks and bonds, which are expected to pay established amounts at specified times (e.g., quarterly or semiannually), are usually viewed as good income investments.

Capital Gains The other type of return available from investments is capital appreciation (or growth), which is reflected as an increase in the market value of an investment vehicle. Capital gains occur when you're able to sell a security for more than you paid for it. Investments that provide greater growth potential through capital appreciation normally have lower levels of

Financial Planning Tips

KEYS TO SUCCESSFUL INVESTING: ASSET ALLOCATION, DIVERSIFICATION, AND REBALANCING

Here are some key concepts that will help you manage your portfolio successfully:

- **Asset allocation.** This is the decision on how to divide your investments among the different major asset classes, which include stocks, bonds, and cash. The best mix depends on your *tolerance for risk* and on your *time horizon*. Longer-term investors, like someone in her 20s saving for retirement, are often more comfortable investing in riskier assets like stocks. In contrast, shorter-term investors, like someone saving for a house down payment or a child's education, often will be comfortable with less risk. Many such people will invest less in stocks and more in bonds. Most investors change their asset allocation as their time horizon changes—for instance, as they approach retirement. Thus, most investors tend to invest less in stocks and more in bonds and cash as they get older.

- **Diversification.** This is the strategy of spreading your money among different investments so that losses on some investments will be offset, at least somewhat, by gains on other investments in your portfolio. Your portfolio should be diversified both *among* and *within* asset classes. This means that your asset allocation strategy should spread out your money among stocks, bonds,

and cash and that your money should be spread out *among* different securities *within* each asset class. For example, within the equity asset class it's important to identify stocks that perform differently over various equity market conditions. This often involves investing in stocks in different sectors and industries.

- **Rebalancing.** Over time, changes in market values could make your portfolio inconsistent with your financial goals. For example, what if you have decided that your portfolio should consist of 70 percent stocks, but a market turndown has reduced the value of your stock holdings to only 60 percent of your portfolio? In order to rebalance your holdings, you'll need to buy more equities or sell some bonds and/or use some cash to fund the additional exposure to stocks. But before you rebalance, you should consider carefully the transaction costs and any possible tax consequences. Many financial advisors suggest that you consider rebalancing your portfolio every 6 to 12 months, and whenever the asset allocation gets out of kilter by a significant percentage, like 5 or 10 percent.

Source: "Beginners' Guide to Asset Allocation, Diversification, and Rebalancing," www.sec.gov/investor/pubs/assetallocation.htm, accessed October 2016.

current income because the firm achieves its growth by reinvesting its earnings instead of paying dividends to the owners. Many common stocks, for example, are bought for their capital gains potential.

Earning Interest on Interest: Another Source of Return When does a 4 percent investment end up yielding only 3 percent? Probably more often than you think! Obviously, it can happen when investment performance fails to live up to expectations. But it can also happen even when everything goes right. That is, as long as at least part of the return from an investment involves the periodic receipt of current income (such as dividends or interest payments), that income must be *reinvested* at a given rate of return in order to achieve the yield you thought you had going into the investment. Consider an investor who buys a 4 percent U.S. Treasury bond and holds it to maturity, a period of 20 years. Each year the

bondholder receives $40 in interest, and at maturity, the $1,000 in principal is repaid. There's no loss in capital, no default; everything is paid right on time. Yet this sure-fire investment ends up yielding only 3 percent. Why? Because the investor failed to reinvest the semiannual interest payments received at the original interest rate of 4 percent. By not plowing back all the investment earnings, the bondholder failed to earn any *interest on interest*.

Exhibit 12.1 shows the three elements of return for a 4 percent, 20-year bond: (1) the recovery of principal; (2) periodic interest income; and (3) the interest on interest earned from reinvesting the semiannual interest payments. Note that because the bond was originally bought at par ($1,000), you start off with a 4 percent investment. *Where you end up depends, in large part, on what you do with the interest earnings from this investment.* If you don't reinvest the interest income at the original 4 percent, then you'll end up on the 3 percent line—or even lower.

Exhibit 12.1

Three Elements of Return for a 4 Percent, 20-Year Bond

As seen here, the long-term return from an investment (in this case, a bond) is made up of three parts: recovery of capital, current income, and interest on interest; of the three components, interest on interest is particularly important, *especially for long-term investments.*

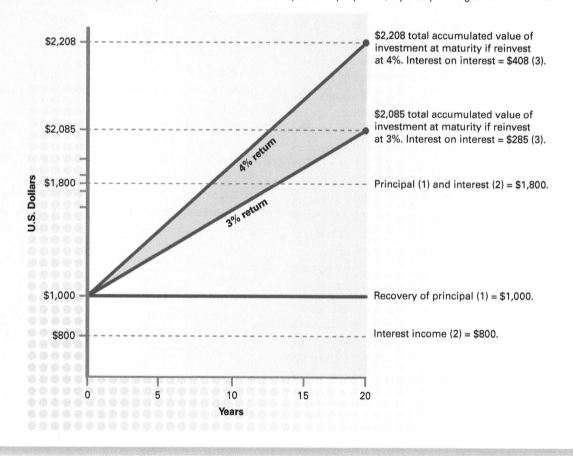

$2,208 total accumulated value of investment at maturity if reinvest at 4%. Interest on interest = $408 (3).

$2,085 total accumulated value of investment at maturity if reinvest at 3%. Interest on interest = $285 (3).

Principal (1) and interest (2) = $1,800.

Recovery of principal (1) = $1,000.

Interest income (2) = $800.

Exhibit 12.2

The Risk–Return Relationship

For investments, there's generally a direct relationship between risk and return: The more risk you face, the greater the return you should expect from the investment.

You have to earn interest on interest from your investments in order to move to the 4 percent line. Specifically, because you started out with a 4 percent investment, that's the rate of return that you need to earn when reinvesting your income. And keep in mind that even though we used a bond in our illustration, *this same concept applies to any type of long-term investment* as long as current income is part of an investment's return. This notion of earning interest on interest is what the market refers to as a fully *compounded rate of return*. The amount of interest on interest embedded in a security's return depends in large part on the length of your investment horizon. That is, *long-term investments* (e.g., 20-year bonds) are subject to a lot more interest on interest earnings than are short-term investments (e.g., six-month T-bills or dividend-paying stocks that you hold for only two or three years).

12-1c The Risk-Return Trade-Off

The amount of risk associated with a given investment is directly related to its expected return. This universal rule of investing means that if you want a higher level of return, you should expect greater risk exposure. While higher risk generally is associated with higher levels of return, this relationship doesn't necessarily work in the opposite direction. That is, you can't invest in a high-risk security and expect to earn a high rate of return automatically. Unfortunately, it doesn't work that way—risk isn't, by definition, that predictable!

Exhibit 12.2 portrays the risk-return trade-off for some popular investments. Note that it's possible to receive a positive return for zero risk, such as at point A. This is referred to as the **risk-free rate of return**, which is often measured by the return on a short-term government security, such as a 90-day Treasury bill (T-bill).

12-1d What Makes a Good Investment?

In keeping with the preceding risk-return discussion, it follows that the value of any investment depends on the amount and timing of benefits it's expected to provide relative to the amount of perceived risk involved. And this applies to all types of investments, including stocks, bonds, or

> **risk-free rate of return** the rate of return on government securities, such as Treasury bills, that is considered free from default risk

real estate and commodities. In this respect, they should all be treated the same.

Future Return In investments, it's the *expected future return on a security* that matters. Aside from the help that they can provide in getting a handle on future returns, *past returns are of little value to investors.* After all, it's not what the security did last year that matters but rather what it's expected to do next year. To get an idea of the future return on an investment, we must *formulate expectations of its future income and future capital appreciation.* As an illustration, assume you're thinking of buying some stock in Decision Analytics (DA) at the beginning of 2017. After reviewing several financial reports, you've estimated the future dividends and price behavior of DA as follows:

Expected average annual dividends, 2017–2019	$2.15/share
Expected market price of the stock, 2019	$95.00/share

Because the stock is now selling for $60 a share, the difference between its current and expected future market price ($95 – $60) represents the amount of *capital gains* you expect to receive over the next three years—in this case, $35 a share. The projected future price, along with expected average annual dividends, gives you an estimate of the stock's *future income stream*; what you need now is a way to measure the *expected return.*

Approximate Expected Yield Finding the exact expected rate of return on an investment involves an iterative mathematical procedure—one that's hard to solve without using a handheld financial calculator (which we'll demonstrate shortly). There is, however, a fairly easy way to obtain a reasonably close estimation of expected return, and that is to compute an investment's *approximate expected yield.* This approximation is useful when dealing with forecasted numbers (that are subject to some degree of uncertainty anyway). Note that we ignore taxes to focus on the basic approach to calculating yields. The measure considers not only current income and capital gains but interest on interest as well. Hence, *approximate expected yield provides a measure of the fully compounded rate of return* from an investment. Finding the approximate yield on an investment is shown in the nearby equation. If you briefly study the formula, you will see it's really not as formidable as it may appear. All it does is relate average current income and average capital gains to the average amount of the investment.

$$\text{Approximate expected yield} = \frac{\text{Average annual current income} + \left[\dfrac{\text{Future price of investment} - \text{Current price of investment}}{\text{Number of years in investment period}}\right]}{\left[\dfrac{\text{Current price of investment} + \text{Future price of investment}}{2}\right]}$$

EXAMPLE: Calculating the Approximate Expected Yield on a Stock To illustrate, let's use the DA example again. Given the average current income from annual dividends of $2.15, current stock price of $60, future stock price of $95, and an investment period of three years (you expect to hold the stock from the beginning of 2017 through the end of 2019), you can use this equation to find the expected approximate yield on DA as follows:

$$\text{Approximate expected yield} = \frac{\$2.15 + \left[\dfrac{\$95 - \$60}{3}\right]}{\left[\dfrac{\$60 + \$95}{2}\right]}$$

$$= \frac{\$2.15 + \left[\dfrac{\$35}{3}\right]}{\left[\dfrac{\$155}{2}\right]}$$

$$= \frac{\$2.15 + \$11.67}{\$77.50} = \frac{\$13.82}{\$77.50}$$

$$= 17.83 \text{ percent}$$

If your forecasts of annual dividends and capital gains hold up, an investment in DA should provide a return of around 17.83 percent per year.

Whether you should consider DA a viable investment candidate depends on how this expected return stacks up to the amount of risk you must assume. Suppose that you've decided the stock is moderately risky. To determine whether the expected rate of return on this investment will be satisfactory, you can compare

CALCULATOR

Inputs	Functions
3	N
−60	PV
2.15	PMT
95.00	FV
	CPT
	I/Y
	Solution
	19.66

See Appendix E for details.

CALCULATOR KEYSTROKES

You can easily find the *exact* expected return on this investment by using a financial calculator. First, put the calculator in the *annual compounding* mode. Then—to find the expected return on a stock that you buy at $60 a share, hold for three years (during which time you receive average annual dividends of $2.15 a share), and then sell at $95—use the keystrokes shown above, where:

N = number of *years* that you hold the stock

PV = the price that you pay for the stock (entered as a *negative* value)

PMT = *average* amount of dividends received *each year*

FV = the price that you expect to receive when you *sell* the stock (in three years)

You'll notice there is a difference in the computed yield measures (17.83 percent with the approximate procedure versus 19.66 percent here). That's to be expected because the former is only an approximate measure of performance, whereas this is an exact measure.

---

it to some benchmark. One of the best is the rate of return you can expect from a *risk-free* security such as a *U.S. T-bill* or a *U.S. T-bond*. The idea is that the return on a *risky* security should be greater than that available on a risk-free security. If, for example, U.S. T-bonds are yielding 4 or 5 percent, then you'd want to receive considerably more—perhaps 10 to 12 percent—to justify your investment in a moderately risky security like DA. In essence, the 10 to 12 percent is your **required rate of return**: the minimum rate of return you believe you should receive in compensation for the amount of risk that you must assume. *An investment is acceptable only if it's expected to generate a rate of return that meets (or exceeds) your required rate of return.* In the case of DA the stock should be considered a viable investment candidate because it provides more than the minimum or required rate of return.

> An investment is acceptable only if it's expected to generate a rate of return that meets (or exceeds) your required rate of return.

12-2 INVESTING IN COMMON STOCK

LO3, LO4 Common stocks appeal to investors for a variety of reasons. To some, investing in stocks is a way to hit it big if the issue shoots up in price. To others, it's the level of current income they offer. A share of common stock enables the investor to participate in the profits of the firm. Every shareholder is, in effect, a part owner of the firm and, as such, is entitled to a portion of its profit. Common stockholders are really the **residual owners** of the company, meaning that they're entitled to dividend income and a prorated share of the company's earnings, but only after all the firm's other obligations have been met.

12-2a Common Stocks as a Form of Investing

Given the nature of common stocks, if the market is strong, then investors can generally expect to benefit from steady price appreciation. A good example is the performance in 2013, when the market, as measured by the Dow Jones Industrial Average (DJIA), went up more than 26 percent. Unfortunately, when markets falter, so do investor returns. Look at what happened over the three-year period from early 2000 through late 2002, when the market (again, as measured by the DJIA) fell some 38 percent. Excluding dividends, a $100,000 investment would have declined in value to a little over $60,000. And in 2008, the Dow fell yet again, this time by almost 34 percent, while the S&P 500 Composite Index (S&P 500) fell by about 38 percent.

Make no mistake: The market does have its bad days, and sometimes those bad days seem to go on for months. It may not always appear that way, but those bad days *really are the exception, not the rule*. That was certainly the case over the 86-year period from 1929 through mid-2016, when the Dow went down (for the year) just 21 times.

required rate of return the minimum rate of return an investor feels should be earned in compensation for the amount of risk assumed

residual owners shareholders of the company; they are entitled to dividend income and a share of the company's profits only after all of the firm's other obligations have been met

Exhibit 12.3

Performance of Dow Jones Industrial Average and NASDAQ Composite, 2006 through 2016

The market entered one of the worst bear markets in history during 2008 and 2009, as the markets experienced the impact of the global financial crisis. Fortunately, the market recovered from 2009 to 2016. This graph shows how the value of a $10,000 investment changed between 2006 and October 2016.

Source: Morningstar 2016.

That's only about 25 percent of the time; the other 75 percent, the market was up—anywhere from around 2 percent on the year to nearly 40 percent! True, there's some risk and price volatility (even in good markets), but that's the price that you have to pay for all the upside potential.

Take a look at Exhibit 12.3, which tracks the behavior of the DJIA and the NASDAQ Composite from January 2006 to October 2016, and you'll quickly get a feel for just how volatile these markets were! As the exhibit shows, despite all those market gyrations, both the Dow and the NASDAQ—which track two totally different segments of the market—ended up with relatively decent returns 7.77 percent and 9.49 percent, respectively). Specifically, a $10,000 investment in the DJIA in January 2006 would have grown to about $22,438 by mid-October 2016, while $10,000 invested in the NASDAQ would have grown to about $26,634.

Issuers of Common Stock Shares of common stock can be issued by any corporation in any line of business. All corporations have stockholders, but not all of them have publicly traded shares. The stocks of interest to us in this book are the so-called

publicly traded issues—the shares that are readily available to the general public and that are bought and sold in the open market. Aside from the initial distribution of common stock when the corporation is formed, subsequent sales of additional shares may be made through a procedure known as a *public offering*. In a public offering, the corporation, working with its underwriter, simply offers the investing public a certain number of shares of its stock at a certain price.

Voting Rights The holders of common stock normally receive *voting rights*, which means that for each share of stock held, they receive one vote. In some cases, common stock may be designated as nonvoting at the time of issue, but this is the exception rather than the rule. Although different voting systems exist, small stockholders need not concern themselves with them because, regardless of the system used, their chances of affecting corporate control with their votes are quite slim.

Corporations have annual stockholders' meetings, at which time new directors are elected and special issues are voted on. Because most small stockholders can't attend these meetings, they can use a proxy to assign

Here are some myths that you should be aware of when investing:

- **During volatile markets it makes sense to sell your stocks and wait for calmer conditions.** While it sounds so reasonable, investors who remain in the market outperform those who move in and out to manage their market exposure. When trading in and out, you pay more commissions and, more important, you tend to miss the upturns in the market that can make you whole—or even more than whole—again.

- **Gold is a good addition to any portfolio.** It's true that gold can be a good asset to add because its returns tend to move opposite those of stocks, which is good for diversification. However, few advisors would recommend allocating more than 5 or 10 percent of a portfolio to gold in most cases. There have been long periods when gold has had poor returns.

- **The S&P 500 is the best place for long-term stock investors.** The large stocks in the S&P 500 do not always pay the best returns. Small-capitalization and value stocks tend to outperform the S&P 500 over the long haul.

- **Far less should be invested in stocks during retirement.** While it may make sense to reduce equity exposure as retirement *approaches*, there is evidence that gradually *increasing* equity exposure *during retirement* may best manage the risk of running out of money.

their votes to another person, who will vote for them. A **proxy** is a written statement assigning voting rights to another party.

Basic Tax Considerations Common stocks provide income in the form of dividends, usually paid quarterly, and/or capital gains, which occur when the price of the stock goes up over time. In 2016, dividends and capital gains were taxed at a rate between 0 and 20 percent based on the investor's income. There's a key difference between the taxes due on dividends and those due on capital gains: namely, there is no tax liability on any capital gains until the stock is actually sold (*paper gains*—that is, any price appreciation occurring on stock that you still own—accumulate tax free). *Bottom line: Taxes are due on any dividends and capital gains in the year in which the dividends are received or the stock is sold.*

Here's how it works. Assume you just sold 100 shares of common stock for $50 per share. Also assume the stock was originally purchased two years ago for $20 per share and that, during each of the past two years, you received $1.25 per share in cash dividends. Thus, for tax purposes, you would have received cash dividends of $125 (i.e., $1.25/share × 100 shares) *both* this year and last, plus you would have generated a capital gain, which is taxable this year, of $3,000 ($50/share − $20/share × 100 shares).

Suppose that you are in the 33 percent tax bracket. Even though you're in one of the higher brackets, both the dividends and capital gains earned on this investment qualify for the lower 15 percent tax rate. Therefore, on the dividends, you'll pay taxes of $125 × 0.15 = $18.75 (for each of the past two years), and on the capital gains, you'll owe $3,000 × 0.15 = $450 (for the current year only). Therefore, last year, your tax liability would have been $18.75 (for the dividends), and this year, it will be $468.75 (for the dividends and capital gains). Bottom line: out of the $3,250 that you earned on this investment over the past two years, you keep $2,762.50 after taxes.

12-2b Dividends

Corporations pay dividends to their common stockholders in the form of cash and/or additional stock. *Cash dividends* are most prevalent. Cash dividends are normally distributed quarterly in an amount determined by the firm's board of directors. For example, if the directors declared a quarterly cash dividend of 50 cents a share, and if you owned 200 shares of stock, then you'd receive a check for $100.

A popular way of assessing the amount

proxy a written statement used to assign a stockholder's voting rights to another person, typically one of the directors of dividends received is to measure the stock's dividend yield. **Dividend yield** is a measure of common stock dividends on a relative (percentage) basis—that is, the dollar amount of dividends received is compared to the market price of the stock. Dividend yield measures the rate of current income being earned on the investment. It's computed as follows:

$$\text{Dividend yield} = \frac{\text{Annual dividend received per share}}{\text{Market price per share of stock}}$$

For example, a company that pays $2 per share in annual dividends and has stock trading at $50 a share will have a dividend yield of 4 percent ($2/$50 = 0.04). Dividend yield is widely used by income-oriented investors looking for (reasonably priced) stocks with a long, sustained record of regularly paying higher-than-average dividends.

Occasionally, the directors may declare a stock dividend as a supplement to or in place of cash dividends. **Stock dividends** are paid in the form of additional shares of stock. That is, rather than receiving cash, shareholders receive additional shares of the company's stock—say, 1/10 of a share of new stock for each share owned (as in a *10 percent stock dividend*). For example, if you owned 100 shares of stock in a company that declared a 10 percent stock dividend, you'd receive 10 new shares of stock. Unfortunately, you'll be no better off after the stock dividend than you were before. That's because the total market value of the shares owned would be roughly the same after the stock dividend as before.

12-2c Some Key Measures of Performance

dividend yield the percentage return provided by the dividends paid on common stock

stock dividends new shares of stock distributed to existing stockholders as a supplement to or substitute for cash dividends

book value the amount of stockholders' equity in a firm; determined by subtracting the company's liabilities and preferred stock from its assets

net profit margin a key measure of profitability that relates a firm's net profits to its sales; shows the rate of return the company is earning on its sales

Seasoned investors use a variety of financial ratios and measures when making common stock investment decisions. Fortunately, most of the widely followed ratios can be found in published reports—like those produced by Value Line or Standard & Poor's (see Exhibit 11.5 in Chapter 11 for an example of a Value Line stock report)—so you don't have to compute them yourself. Even so,

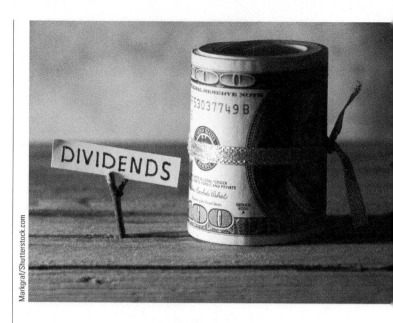

if you're thinking about buying a stock or already have some stocks, there are a few measures of performance that you'll want to keep track of, such as dividend yield (mentioned earlier), book value (or book value per share), net profit margin, return on equity, earnings per share, price/earnings ratio, and beta.

Book Value The amount of stockholders' equity in a firm is measured by **book value**. This accounting measure is found by subtracting the firm's liabilities and preferred stocks from the value of its assets. Book value indicates the amount of stockholder funds used to finance the firm. For instance, assume our example company (DA) had assets of $8 million, liabilities of $2 million, and preferred stock issued at $1 million. The book value of the firm's common stock would be $5 million ($8 million − $2 million − $1 million). When the book value is divided by the number of shares outstanding, the result is *book value per share*. So if DA had 100,000 shares of common stock outstanding, its book value per share would be $50 ($5,000,000/100,000 shares). Because of the impact that it can have on the firm's growth, you'd like to see book value per share steadily increasing over time. Also look for stocks whose market prices are comfortably above their book values.

Net Profit Margin As a yardstick of profitability, **net profit margin** is one of the most widely followed measures of corporate performance. Measured as a firm's net profit divided by its sales, this ratio indicates how well the company translates sales into profits. It also captures how well the company manages its cost structure. The higher the net profit margin, the more money the company earns. Look for a relatively stable—or even better, an increasing—net profit margin.

Return on Equity Another important and widely followed measure, **return on equity (ROE)** reflects the firm's overall profitability from the equityholders' perspective. Measured as net income divided by shareholders' equity, it captures, in a single ratio, the amount of success the firm is having in managing its assets, operations, and capital structure. ROE is important because it is significantly related to the profits, growth, and dividends of the firm. So long as a firm is not borrowing too much money, the better the ROE and the better the company's financial and competitive positions. Look for a stable or increasing ROE. Watch out for a falling ROE because that could spell trouble.

Earnings per Share With stocks, the firm's annual earnings are usually measured and reported in terms of **earnings per share (EPS)**. This metric translates total corporate profits into profits on a per-share basis and provides a convenient measure of the amount of earnings available to stockholders. EPS is found by using this simple formula:

$$EPS = \frac{\text{Net profit after taxes} - \text{Preferred dividends paid}}{\text{Number of shares of common stock outstanding}}$$

For example, if DA reported a net profit of $600,000, paid $100,000 in dividends to preferred stockholders, and had 100,000 shares of common stock outstanding, then it would have an EPS of $5.00 [($600,000 − $100,000)/100,000]. Note that preferred dividends are *subtracted* from profits because they must be paid before any monies can be made available to common stockholders. Stockholders follow EPS closely because it represents the amount the firm has earned on behalf of each outstanding share of common stock. Look for steady growth in EPS, too.

Price/Earnings Ratio When the prevailing market price of a share of common stock is divided by the annual earnings per share, the result is the **price/earnings (P/E) ratio**, a measure that's viewed as an indication of investor confidence and expectations. The higher the P/E multiple, the more confidence investors are presumed to have in a given security. In the case of DA, whose shares are currently selling for $60, the price/earnings ratio is 12 ($60.00 per share/$5.00 per share). In other words, DA stock is selling for 12 times its earnings. P/E ratios are important to investors because they reveal how aggressively the stock is being priced in the market. Watch out for very high P/Es—that is, P/Es that are

much higher than the market—because that could indicate the stock is overpriced. P/E ratios tend to move with the market. So when the market is soft, a stock's P/E will be lower; when the market heats up, the stock's P/E will typically rise.

Beta A stock's **beta** is an indication of its *price volatility*; it shows how responsive the stock is to changes in the overall stock market. Published betas are available from most brokerage firms and investment services. The market (often measured by the S&P index of 500 stocks) is used as a benchmark of performance and always has a beta of 1.0. From there, everything is relative: low-beta stocks—those with betas of less than 1.0—have low price volatility, whereas high-beta stocks—those with betas of more than 1.0—are considered to be volatile. In short, the higher a stock's beta, the riskier it is.

Beta is an *index* of relative price performance. So if DA has a beta of, say, 0.8, then it should rise (or fall) only 80 percent as much as the market. In contrast, if the stock had a beta of 1.8, then it would go up or down 1.8 times as much—the price of the stock would rise higher and fall harder than the general market. Other things being equal, if you're looking for a relatively

return on equity (ROE) a measure that captures the firm's overall profitability; it is important because of its impact on the firm's growth, profits, and dividends

earnings per share (EPS) the return earned by each share of common stock; calculated by dividing all earnings remaining after paying preferred dividends by the number of common shares outstanding

price/earnings (P/E) ratio a measure of investors' confidence in a given security; calculated by dividing market price per share by earnings per share

beta an index of the price volatility for a share of common stock; a reflection of how the stock price responds to market forces conservative investment, then you should stick with low-beta stocks. On the other hand, if it's potentially high capital gains and price volatility you're after, go with high-beta securities.

Go to Smart Sites

12-2d Types of Common Stock

Common stocks are often classified on the basis of their dividends or their rate of growth in EPS. Some popular types of common stock are blue-chip, growth, tech stocks, income, speculative, cyclical, defensive, large-cap, mid-cap, and small-cap stocks.

Blue-Chip Stocks Blue-chip stocks are the cream of the common stock crop. These stocks are unsurpassed in quality and have a long, stable record of earnings and dividends. They're issued by large, well-established firms that have impeccable financial credentials—firms like Apple, Walmart, IBM, Microsoft, and ExxonMobil. These companies hold important if not leading positions in their industries, and they often determine the standards by which other firms are measured. Blue chips are particularly attractive to investors who seek high-quality investments offering decent dividend yields and respectable growth potential.

Growth Stocks Stocks that have experienced—and are expected to continue experiencing—consistently high rates of growth in earnings and/or price are known as growth stocks. A good growth stock might exhibit a *sustained* rate of growth in earnings of 15 to 20 percent over a period when common stocks are averaging only 6 to 8 percent. In 2016, prime examples of large capitalization stocks expected to exhibit great growth included Pfizer, Tesla, United Therapeutics, CVS Health, and Delphi

Arek_malang/Shutterstock.com

Automotive. Growth stocks often reinvest a lot of their earnings. Because of their potential for dramatic price appreciation, they appeal mostly to investors who are seeking capital gains.

Tech Stocks Tech stocks represent the technology sector of the market and include all those companies that produce or provide technology-based products and services such as computers, semiconductors, computer software and hardware, peripherals, Internet services, and wireless communications. Thousands of companies fall into the tech stock category, including everything from very small firms providing some service on the Internet to huge multinational companies. Tech stocks may offer the potential for attractive, even phenomenal returns, but they also involve considerable risk and so are probably most suitable for investors with high tolerance for such risk. Included in the tech stock category are some big names—Apple, Microsoft, Cisco Systems, and Google—as well as many not-so-big names, such as Ininera, Baidu, Polycom, and Viavi Solutions.

---

blue-chip stock a stock generally issued by companies expected to provide an uninterrupted stream of dividends and good, long-term growth prospects

growth stock a stock whose earnings and/or market price have increased over time at a rate well above average

tech stock a stock that represents the technology sector of the market

Income Stocks versus Speculative Stocks Stocks whose appeal is based primarily on the dividends they pay are known as income stocks. They have a fairly stable stream of earnings, a large portion of which is distributed in the form of dividends. Income shares have relatively high dividend yields and thus are ideally suited for investors seeking a relatively safe and high level of current income from their investment capital. An added (and often overlooked) feature of these stocks is that, unlike bonds and preferred stock, holders of income stock can expect *the amount of dividends paid to increase over time*. Examples of income stocks include Philip Morris International, Johnson & Johnson, PepsiCo, and Procter & Gamble.

Rather than basing their investment decisions on a proven record of earnings, investors in speculative stocks gamble that some new information, discovery, or production technique will favorably affect the firm's growth and inflate its stock price. The value of speculative stocks and their P/E ratios tend to fluctuate widely as additional information about the firm's future is received. Investors in speculative stocks should be prepared to experience losses as well as gains because *these are high-risk securities*. In 2016, they included companies like Nevsun Resources, Dyax, Opthotech, and Chimerix.

Cyclical Stocks or Defensive Stocks Stocks whose price movements tend to follow the business cycle are called cyclical stocks. This means that when the economy is in an expansionary stage, the prices of cyclical stocks tend to increase; during a contractionary stage (recession), they decline. Most cyclical stocks are found in the basic industries—automobiles, steel, and lumber, for example—which are generally sensitive to changes in economic activity. Alcoa, eBay, Kohl's, Goodyear Tire & Rubber, Dow Chemical, and Ford Motor are all examples of cyclical stocks.

The prices and returns from defensive stocks, unlike those of cyclical stocks, are expected to remain stable during periods of contraction in business activity. For this reason, they're often called *countercyclical*. The shares of consumer goods companies, certain public utilities, and gold mining companies are good examples of defensive stocks. Because they're basically income stocks, their earnings and dividends tend to keep their market prices up during periods of economic decline. Coca-Cola, McDonald's, Walmart, Procter & Gamble, and Merck are all examples of defensive stocks.

Large-Caps, Mid-Caps, and Small-Caps In the stock market, a stock's size is based on its market value—or,

more commonly, on what's known as its *market capitalization* or *market cap*. A stock's market cap is found by multiplying its market price by the number of shares outstanding. The market can be broken into three major segments, as measured by a stock's market "cap":

Large-cap: Market caps of more than $10 billion

Mid-cap: Market caps of $2 to $10 billion

Small-cap: Stocks with market caps of less than $2 billion

Of the three major categories, the large-cap stocks are the real biggies—the Apples, Walmarts, GEs, and Microsofts of the world. Just because they're big, however, doesn't mean they're better. Indeed, both the small- and mid-cap segments of the market tend to hold their own with, or even outperform, large stocks over time.

Mid-cap stocks offer investors some attractive return opportunities as they provide much of the sizzle of small-stock returns but without all the price volatility. At the same time, because these are fairly good-sized companies and many of them have been around for a long time, they offer some of the safety of the big, established stocks. Among the ranks of the mid-caps are Accuity, Advance Auto Parts, Avery Dennison, Oshkosh, and USG. These securities offer a nice alternative to large stocks without all the drawbacks and uncertainties of small-caps, although they're probably most appropriate for investors who are willing to tolerate a bit more risk and price volatility.

Some investors consider small companies to be in a class by themselves. They believe these firms hold especially attractive return opportunities, and in many cases this has turned out to be true. Known as small-cap stocks, these companies often have annual revenues of less than $250 million. Because of their

income stock a stock whose appeal is the dividends it pays out; offers dividend payments that can be expected to increase over time

speculative stock stock that is purchased on little more than the hope that its price per share will increase

cyclical stock a stock whose price movements tend to parallel the various stages of the business cycle

defensive stock a stock whose price movements are usually contrary to movements in the business cycle

large-cap stock a stock with a total market value of more than $10 billion

mid-cap stock a stock whose total market value falls somewhere between $2 billion and $10 billion

small-cap stock a stock with a total market value of less than $2 billion small size, spurts of growth can dramatically affect their earnings and stock prices. Inovio Pharmaceuticals, Sequential Brand Group, M/I Homes, and Universal Electronics are just a few of the interesting small-cap stocks out there. Although some small-caps are solid companies with equally solid financials, that's definitely not the case with most of them! Because many of these companies are so small, they don't have a lot of stock outstanding and their shares aren't widely traded. These stocks may hold the potential for high returns, but investors should also be aware of the high-risk exposure associated with them.

12-2e Market Globalization and Foreign Stocks

Besides investing in many of the different types of stocks already mentioned, a growing number of American investors are turning to foreign markets as a way to earn attractive returns. Ironically, as our world is becoming smaller, our universe of investment opportunities is growing by leaps and bounds! Consider, for example, that in 1970, the U.S. stock market accounted for fully *two-thirds of the world market*. In essence, our stock market was twice as big as the rest of the world's stock markets *combined*. That's no longer true.

The U.S. share of the world equity market is around 53 percent, which is the highest it's been since 2003. Among the various ways of investing in foreign shares, two stand out: mutual funds and American Depositary Receipts (ADRs). Without a doubt, the best and easiest way to invest in foreign markets is through *international mutual funds* (we'll discuss such funds in Chapter 13). An alternative to mutual funds is to buy ADRs, which are *denominated in dollars and are traded directly on U.S. markets* (such as the NYSE). They're just like common stock, except that

each ADR represents a stated number of shares in a specific foreign company. The shares of more than 1,000 companies from some 50 foreign countries are traded on U.S. exchanges as ADRs; these companies include Honda Motor Co., Nestlé, Nokia, HSBC Holdings, Tata Motors, and Unilever. ADRs are a great way to invest in foreign stocks because their prices are quoted in dollars—not in British pounds, Swiss francs, or euros. What's more, all dividends are paid in dollars.

12-2f Investing in Common Stock

There are three basic reasons for investing in common stock: (1) to use the stock as a warehouse of value, (2) to accumulate capital, and (3) to provide a source of income. Some investors are more concerned about storage of value than others, and consequently put safety of principal first in their stock selection process. These investors are more quality conscious and tend to gravitate toward blue chips and other low-risk securities. Accumulation of capital generally is an important goal to individuals with long-term investment horizons. These investors use the capital gains and dividends that stocks provide to build up their wealth. Some use growth stocks for such purposes; others do it with income shares; still others use a little of both. Finally, some people use stocks as a source of income; to them, a dependable flow of dividends is essential. High-yielding, good-quality income shares are usually their preferred investment.

Advantages and Disadvantages of Stock Ownership Ownership of common stock has both advantages and disadvantages. Its advantages are threefold. First, the potential returns, in the form of both dividend income and price appreciation, can be substantial. Second, many stocks are actively traded and so are a highly liquid form of investment. Finally, market and company information about literally thousands of common stocks is widely published and readily available.

The disadvantages of owning common stock include risk, the problem of timing purchases and sales, and the uncertainty of dividends. Although potential common stock returns may be high, the risk associated with the actual receipt of that return is also great. Even though the careful selection of stocks may reduce the amount of risk to which the investor is exposed, a significant risk-return trade-off still exists. When it comes to common stock, not even dividends are guaranteed. If things turn bad, the company can always shut off the stream of dividends and suffer no legal ramifications. Finally, there's the timing of purchases and sales. Human nature being what it is, we don't always do it right. The goal is to buy low and sell high; but the problem of predicting price movements makes it difficult to achieve such a plan.

12-2g Making Investment Decisions

The first step in investing is to know *where* to put your money. The second is to know *when* to make your moves. This involves matching your risk and return objectives with the available investments. *A stock (or any other investment) should be considered a viable investment candidate as long as it looks likely to generate a sufficiently attractive rate of return* and, importantly, one that fully compensates you for the risks you take. Indeed, if you can't get enough return from the security to offset the risk, then you shouldn't invest in the stock!

Putting a Value on Stock Every investor will face one of the most difficult questions in the field of investments:

How much are you willing to pay for a stock? To answer this question, you must place a value on the stock. As noted earlier, we know that the value of a stock depends on its expected stream of future income, expected future market price appreciation, and the associated risk. Once you have a handle on the expected stream of future cash flows, you can use that information to find the *expected rate of return on the investment.* If the expected return from the investment exceeds your required rate of return, then you should make the investment. If the expected return is less than your required rate of return, then you should not buy the stock because it's currently "overpriced," and you won't be able to earn your required rate of return.

How do you go about finding a stock that's right for you? The answer is by doing a little digging and crunching a few numbers. Here's what you should do. First, find a company you like and then take a look at how it has performed *over the past three to five years.* Find out what kind of growth in sales it has experienced, if it has a strong ROE and has been able to maintain or improve its profit margin, and how much it has been paying out to stockholders in the form of dividends. This kind of information is readily available in publications like *Value Line Investment Survey* and *S&P Stock Reports* or from a number of Internet sites. The idea is to find stocks that are financially strong, have done well in the past, and continue to hold prominent positions in a given industry or market segment. But looking at the past is only the beginning. What's really important to stock valuation is the *future!*

Therefore, let's turn our attention to the expected future performance of a stock. The key items are future dividends and share price behavior. It generally doesn't make much sense to go out more than two or three years (five at the most) because the accuracy of most forecasts deteriorate rapidly with time. Thus, using a three-year investment horizon, you'd want to forecast annual dividends per share for each of the next three years *plus* the future price of the stock at the end of the three-year holding period. You can try to generate these forecasts yourself or you can check such publications as *Value Line Investment Survey* to obtain projections. (Value Line projects dividends and share prices three to five years into the future. See the example provided in Exhibit 11.5 in the prior chapter.) After projecting dividends and share price, you can use the approximate yield equation or a calculator to determine the expected return from the investment.

Consider the example of Apple using projections in the fall of 2016. The calculations in the example on the this page indicate that if Apple's stock performance lives up to the projections made in the *Value Line Investment Survey*, it should provide a return over 16 percent. In today's market, that would be an excellent return and one that likely meets or exceeds our risk-adjusted required rate of return. If that's the case, then this stock *should* be considered a possible investment candidate.

Timing Your Investments Once you find a stock that you think will give you the kind of return that you're looking for, then you're ready to deal with the matter of timing your investment. As long as the prospects for the market and the economy are positive, the time may be right to invest in stocks. Sometimes, however, investing in stocks makes no sense—in particular, *don't* invest in stocks under the following conditions:

▶ You believe *strongly* that the market is headed down in the short run. If you're confident the market's in for a

EXAMPLE: Calculating the Expected Return on Apple's Stock Consider the common shares of Apple, Inc., which provides hardware and software that includes Mac computers, iPod digital media players, iPhone smartphones, and iPad tablets. According to several financial reporting services, the company has strong financials; its sales have been growing at about 37 percent per year for the past five years, its net profit margin in 2016 was projected to be about 21 percent, and its ROE about 35 percent. Thus, the company has performed well and is definitely a market leader in its field. Indeed, it's currently the largest company in the world!

In the fall of 2016, the stock was trading at around $114 a share. Value Line was projecting dividends to be $2.18 a share in 2016, $2.38 in 2017, and an average of about $4 a share between 2019 and 2021. It was also estimating that the price of the stock could rise to an average of $177.50 a share over that period. For simplicity, we'll look at these forecasts as applying to a planned holding period of about three years and average the data accordingly.

Because the below approximate yield equation, as presented on page 314, uses "average annual current income" as one of the inputs, let's use a rough average of the projected dividends ($2.85 a share) as a proxy for average annual dividends. Because this stock was trading at about $114 a share and has a projected average future price of $177.50 a share, we can find the expected return (for our three-year investment horizon) as follows:

$$\text{Approximate expected yield (Expected return)} = \frac{\$2.85 + \left[\dfrac{\$177.50 - \$114.00}{3}\right]}{\left[\dfrac{\$177.50 + \$114.00}{2}\right]}$$

$$= \frac{\$2.85 + \$21.17}{\$145.75}$$

$$= 16.48 \text{ percent}$$

big fall (or will continue to fall, if it's already doing so), then wait until the market drops and buy the stock when it's cheaper.

▶ You feel uncomfortable with the general tone of the market—it lacks direction, or there's way too much price volatility to suit you. Once again, wait for the market to settle down before buying stocks.

Be Sure to Reinvest Your Dividends Unless you're living off the income, the basic investment objective

Exhibit 12.4

Cash or Reinvested Dividends

Participating in a dividend reinvestment plan is a simple yet highly effective way of building up capital over time. Over the long haul, it can prove to be a great way of earning a fully compounded rate of return on your money.

Situation: Buy 100 shares of stock at $25 a share (total investment $2,500); stock currently pays $1 a share in annual dividends. Price of the stock increases at 8 percent per year; dividends grow at 5 percent per year.

Investment Period	Number of Shares Held	Market Value of Stock Holdings	Total Cash Dividends Received
Take Dividends in Cash			
5 years	100	$ 3,672	$ 552
10 years	100	$ 5,397	$ 1,258
15 years	100	$ 7,930	$ 2,158
20 years	100	$ 11,652	$ 3,307
Participate in a DRP			
5 years	115.59	$ 4,245	$ 0
10 years	135.66	$ 7,322	$ 0
15 years	155.92	$12,364	$ 0
20 years	176.00	$20,508	$ 0

CALCULATOR KEYSTROKES

You can use a financial calculator—set in the *annual compounding mode*—to find the expected return on the Apple stock in our example that you purchase at $114 a share, hold for three years (during which time you receive average annual dividends of $2.85 a share), and then sell at $177.50 per share. Simply use the keystrokes shown below in the margin, where:

N = number of *years* you hold the stock

PV = the price you pay for the stock (entered as a *negative* value)

PMT = average amount of dividends received each *year*

FV = the price you expect to receive when you *sell* the stock (in three years)

The expected return (of 18.08 percent) is a bit higher here, but even so, it's still reasonably close to the return (of 16.48 percent) that we computed using the approximate yield method.

with stocks is the same as it is with any other security: to earn an attractive, fully compounded rate of return. This requires regular reinvestment of dividend income. And

there's no better way to accomplish such reinvestment than through a **dividend reinvestment plan (DRP)**. In a DRP, shareholders can sign up to have their cash dividends automatically reinvested in additional shares of the company's common stock—in essence, it's like taking your cash dividends in the form of more shares of common stock. Such an approach can have a tremendous impact on your investment position over time, as seen in Exhibit 12.4.

Many companies have DRPs, and each one gives investors a convenient and inexpensive way to accumulate capital. Stocks in most DRPs are acquired free of any brokerage commissions, and most plans allow *partial participation.* That is, rather than committing all their cash dividends to these plans, participants may

CALCULATOR

Inputs	Functions
3	N
−114.00	PV
2.85	PMT
177.50	FV
	CPT
	I/Y
Solution	
18.08	

See Appendix E for details.

dividend reinvestment plan (DRP) a program whereby stockholders can choose to take their cash dividends in the form of more shares of the company's stock specify a portion of their shares for dividend reinvestment and receive cash dividends on the rest. Some plans even sell their shares in their DRP programs at discounts of 3 to 5 percent. Most plans also credit fractional shares to the investors' accounts. There is a catch, however: even though these dividends take the form of additional shares of stock, *reinvested dividends are taxable, in the year they're received, just as if they had been received in cash.*

12-3 INVESTING IN BONDS

LO5, LO6 In contrast to stocks, *bonds are liabilities—* they're publicly traded IOUs where the bondholders are actually *lending money* to the issuer. Bonds are often referred to as *fixed-income securities* because the debt service obligations of the issuer are usually fixed—that is, the issuing organization agrees to pay a *fixed amount of interest periodically and to repay a fixed amount of principal at or before maturity.* U.S. bonds typically have face values of $1,000 or $5,000 and have maturities of 10 to 30 years or more.

12-3a Why Invest in Bonds?

Bonds provide investors with two kinds of income: (1) most provide current income, and (2) they can often generate substantial capital gains. The current income, of course, comes from the interest payments received periodically over the life of the issue. Indeed, this regular and predictable source of income is a key factor that draws investors to bonds. But these securities can also produce capital gains, which occurs whenever market interest rates fall. A basic trading rule in the bond market is that *interest rates and bond prices move in opposite directions:* when interest rates rise, bond prices fall. Conversely, when interest rates fall, bond prices rise. Thus, it's possible to buy bonds at one price and, if interest rate conditions are right, to sell them sometime later at a higher price.

Taken together, the current income and capital gains earned from bonds can lead to attractive investor returns. In addition, because of the general high quality of many bonds, they can also be used for the preservation and long-term accumulation of capital. In fact, some individuals commit all or a good deal of their investment funds to bonds because of this single attribute.

12-3b Bonds versus Stocks

Although bonds definitely do have their good points— lower risk and attractive levels of current income, along with *desirable diversification properties.* However, also have a significant downside: their *comparative* returns.

The fact is, *relative to stocks*, there's usually a big sacrifice in returns when investing in bonds—which, of course, is the price you pay for the even bigger reduction in risk! But just because there's a deficit in long-term returns, it doesn't mean that bonds are always the underachievers. Consider, for example, what's happened over the past 20 years or so. Starting in the 1980s, fixed-income securities held their own and continued to do so through the mid-1990s, only to fall far behind stocks for the rest of the decade. But then along came a couple of nasty bear markets in stocks (2000–2002 and 2007–2008), and the subsequent stock market recovery in 2009 and beyond. The net results of all this can be seen in Exhibit 12.5, which tracks the comparative returns of stocks (via the S&P 500 index) and bonds (using the Bank of America Merrill Lynch U.S. Treasuries 15+ year maturity total return index) from 1996 through 2016.

Over the roughly 20-year period from 1996 to October 2016. The S&P 500 outperformed long-term Treasury bonds by 0.77 percent (8.19 versus 7.42 percent). The net result was that a $10,000 investment in 1996 would have generated a terminal value in 2016 of about $51,435 for stocks, compared with about $44,358 for bonds. Although the long-term performance of stocks typically outstrips that of bonds, there have been times when that just wasn't so. And the margin was particularly small over this time period owing to the effects of the financial crisis.

Income tax tends to favor investing in stocks over bonds. This is because a major component of the return on bonds is interest. Interest is taxed as *ordinary income*, which was taxed at the top tax rate of 39.6 percent in 2016. In contrast, dividend income is taxed at the same rate as capital gains, which has a top rate of 20 percent Thus, bond interest is taxed at almost twice the rate as that for dividends from stock.

YOU CAN DO IT NOW: How Do Stock and Bond Market Returns Compare This Year? If you want a broad sense of how stock and bond returns compare so far this year, take a look at the returns on two broad-based exchange traded funds (ETFs, which we discuss in detail in Chapter 13). Vanguard's Total Stock Market ETF (ticker VTI) seeks to track the overall performance of U.S. stocks traded on the New York Stock Exchange and NASDAQ. And Vanguard's Total Bond Market ETF (ticker BND) seeks to track investment-grade U.S. bonds. Take a look at the year-to-date (YTD) returns, which were, for example, 8.25 percent for VTI and 5.88 percent for BND on October 21, 2016. Just go to **http://finance.yahoo.com/** and type VTI and then BND into the Quote Lookup box. You can **do it now.**

Exhibit 12.5

Comparative Performance of Stocks and Bonds: 1996 to 2016

This graph shows what happened to $10,000 invested in bonds over the (roughly) 20-year period from January 1996 through October 2016. Versus the same amount invested in stocks. It is clear that, although stocks held a commanding lead through early 2000 and then again in 2003–2006, the bear stock markets of 2000–2002 and 2008 limited the relative performance of stocks. Yet the bull market from 2009 to 2016 left stocks performing better than bonds for the entire period.

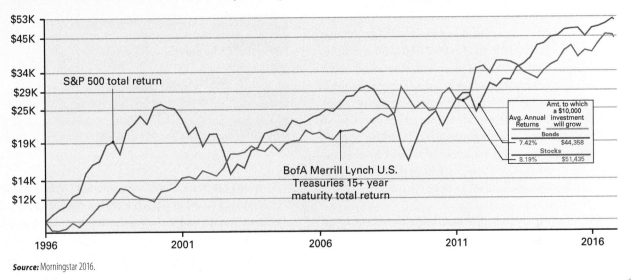

	Avg. Annual Returns	Amt. to which a $10,000 investment will grow
Bonds	7.42%	$44,358
Stocks	8.19%	$51,435

Source: Morningstar 2016.

12-3c Basic Issue Characteristics

A bond is a long-term debt instrument that carries certain obligations on the part of the issuer. Unlike the holders of common stock, bondholders have no ownership or equity position in the issuing firm or organization. This is so because bonds are debt and thus the bondholders, in a roundabout way, are only lending money to the issuer.

U.S. bonds typically pay interest every six months. The amount of interest paid depends on the **coupon**, which defines the annual interest that the issuer will pay to the bondholder. For instance, a $1,000 bond with an 8 percent coupon would pay $80 in interest every year ($1,000 × 0.08 = $80), generally in the form of two $40 semiannual payments. The principal amount of a bond, also known as its *par value*, specifies the amount of capital that must be repaid at maturity—there's $1,000 of principal in a $1,000 bond.

Debt securities regularly trade at market prices that differ from their principal (or par) values. This occurs whenever an issue's coupon differs from the prevailing market rate of interest; because the price of a bond will change until its yield is compatible with prevailing market yields. For example, such behavior explains why a 7 percent coupon issue will carry a market price of only $825 when the market yield is 9 percent. The drop in price is necessary to raise the expected yield on this bond from 7 to 9 percent. Issues with market values lower than par are known as *discount bonds* and carry coupons that are less than those on new issues. In contrast, issues with market values above par are called *premium bonds* and have coupons greater than those currently being offered on new issues.

> **coupon** a bond feature that defines the annual interest income that the issuer will pay the bondholder

Types of Issues In addition to their coupons and maturities, bonds can be differentiated from one another by the type of collateral behind them. In this regard, the issues can be viewed as having either junior or senior standing. *Senior bonds are secured obligations* because they're backed by a legal claim on some specific property of the issuer that acts as *collateral* for the bonds. Such issues include **mortgage bonds**, which are secured by real estate, and **equipment trust certificates**, which are backed by certain types of equipment and are popular with railroads and airlines. *Junior bonds*, on the other hand, are backed only with a promise by the issuer to pay interest and principal on a timely basis. There are several classes of *unsecured* bonds, the most popular of which is known as a **debenture**. Issued as either notes (with maturities of 2 to 10 years) or bonds (maturities of more than 10 years), debentures are totally unsecured in the sense that there's no collateral backing them up—other than the issuer's good name.

Sinking Fund Another provision that's important to investors is the **sinking fund**, which describes how a bond will be paid off over time. Not all bonds have these requirements. But for those that do, a sinking fund specifies the annual repayment schedule to be used in paying off the issue and indicates how much principal will be retired each year.

Sinking fund requirements generally begin one to five years after the date of issue and continue annually thereafter until all or most of the issue has been paid off. Any amount not repaid by maturity is then retired with a single balloon payment.

Call Feature Every bond has a **call feature**, which stipulates whether a bond can be called (i.e., retired) before its regularly scheduled maturity date and, if so, under what conditions. Basically, there are three types of call features:

- A bond can be *freely callable*, which means the issuer can retire the bond prematurely at any time.
- A bond can be *non-callable*, which means the issuer is prohibited from retiring the bond prior to maturity.
- The issue could carry a *deferred call*, which

Larry1235/Shutterstock.com

means the issue cannot be called until after a certain length of time has passed from the date of issue. The issue is not callable during the deferment period and then becomes freely callable thereafter.

Call features are normally used to retire a bond prematurely and replace it with one that carries a lower coupon. In this way, the issuer benefits from being able to reduce its annual interest costs. In an attempt to at least partially compensate investors who have their bonds called out from under them, a *call premium* (usually equal to about six months to 1 year of interest) is tacked onto the par value of the bond and paid to investors, along with the issue's par value, at the time the bond is called. For example, if a company decides to call its 7 percent bonds some 15 years before they mature, then it might have to pay $1,052.50 for every $1,000 bond outstanding (in this case, a call premium equal to nine months' interest—$70 × 0.75 = $52.50—would be added to the par value of $1,000). Although this might sound like a good deal, it's really not for the investor. The bondholder may indeed get a few extra bucks when the bond is called. But in turn, she loses a source of high current income. For example, the investor may have a 7 percent bond called away at a time when the best she can do in the market may be 4 or 5 percent.

12-3d The Bond Market

One thing that really stands out about the bond market is its size—the U.S. bond market is huge and getting bigger almost daily. Indeed, in 2016 the dollar value of bonds outstanding was about $41 trillion! Given such size, it's not surprising that today's bond market offers

mortgage bond a bond secured by a claim on real assets, such as a manufacturing plant

equipment trust certificate a bond secured by certain types of equipment, such as railroad cars and airplanes

debenture an unsecured bond issued on the general credit of the firm

sinking fund a bond provision specifying the annual repayment schedule to be used in paying off the issue

call feature a bond feature that allows the issuer to retire the security prior to maturity securities to meet just about any type of investment objective and suit virtually any type of investor, no matter how conservative or aggressive.

Treasury Bonds **Treasury bonds** (sometimes called *Treasuries* or *governments*) are a dominant force in the bond market and, if not the most popular, are certainly the best known. The U.S. Treasury issues bonds, notes, and other types of debt securities (such as the T-bills discussed in Chapter 4) as a means of meeting the federal government's ever-increasing borrowing needs. All Treasury obligations are high quality (backed by the full faith and credit of the U.S. government), a feature that—along with their liquidity—makes them extremely popular with individual and institutional investors both domestically and abroad.

Treasury notes are issued with maturities of 2, 3, 5, and 10 years, whereas *Treasury bonds* carry 20- and 30-year maturities. The Treasury issues its securities at regularly scheduled auctions, and it's through this process that the Treasury establishes the initial yields and coupons on the securities it issues. All Treasury notes and bonds are sold in minimum denominations of $1,000. Although interest income is subject to normal federal income tax, *it is exempt from state and local taxes.*

The newest type of Treasury issue is the **Treasury inflation-indexed bond**, or **TIPS** (which stands for "Treasury inflation-protected securities"). These securities—which are issued with maturities of 5, 10, or 20 years—give investors the opportunity to keep up with inflation by periodically adjusting their returns for any inflation that has occurred. Unfortunately, the coupons on these securities are set very low because they're meant to provide investors with *real (inflation-adjusted) returns.* So one of these bonds might carry a coupon of only 1.5 percent (when regular T-bonds are paying, say, 3.5 or 4 percent). But there's an upside even to this: The actual *size of the coupon payment will increase over time as the par value on the bond increases.*

Agency and Mortgage-Backed Bonds **Agency bonds** are an important segment of the U.S. bond market. Although issued by political subdivisions of the U.S. government, *these securities are not obligations of the U.S. Treasury.* An important feature of these securities is that they customarily provide yields that are comfortably above the market rates for Treasuries and thus offer investors a way to increase returns

> The U.S. bond market is huge and getting bigger almost daily.

EXAMPLE: Inflation-Adjustment of TIPS Bonds
Assume inflation is running at an annual rate of 3 percent. At the end of the year, the par (or maturity) value of your bond will increase by 3 percent (actually, adjustments to par value are made every six months). Thus, the $1,000 par value will grow to $1,030 at the end of the first year and, if the 3 percent inflation rate continues for the second year, the par value will once again move up, this time from $1,030 to $1,061 ($1,030 × 1.03).

with little or no real difference in risk. Some actively traded and widely quoted agency issues include those sold by the Federal Farm Credit Bank, the Federal National Mortgage Association (or Fannie Mae), the Student Loan Marketing Association, and the Federal Home Loan Mortgage Corporation (FHLMC, or Freddie Mac).

Although the various agencies issue traditional unsecured notes and bonds, they are perhaps best known for their **mortgage-backed securities**. Two of the biggest issuers of such securities, Fannie Mae and Freddie Mac, package and issue bonds backed by mortgages that have no government guarantee. The Government National Mortgage Association (or Ginnie Mae) is also active in the mortgage market. Owned by the U.S. government, it insures bonds that are backed by Veterans Administration (VA) and Federal Housing Administration (FHA) home loans.

Municipal Bonds **Municipal bonds** are the issues of states, counties, cities, and other political subdivisions such as school districts and water and sewer districts. They're unlike other bonds in that their interest income is usually free from federal income tax (which is why they're known as *tax-free bonds*). However, this tax-free status

Treasury bond a bond issued by and backed by the full faith and credit of the U.S. government

Treasury inflation-indexed bond (TIPS) a bond issued by the U.S. government that has principal payments that are adjusted to provide protection again inflation, as measured by the Consumer Price Index (CPI)

agency bond an obligation of a political subdivision of the U.S. government

mortgage-backed securities securities that are a claim on the cash flows generated by mortgage loans; bonds backed by mortgages as collateral

municipal bond a bond issued by state or local governments; interest income is usually exempt from federal taxes does not apply to any capital gains that may be earned on these securities; such gains are subject to the usual federal taxes. A tax-free yield is viewed by many as the most important feature of municipal bonds and is certainly a major reason why individuals invest in them.

The yields on municipal bonds are lower than the returns available from otherwise comparable fully taxable issues. So unless the tax effect is sufficient to raise the yield on a municipal to a level that equals or exceeds the yields on taxable issues, it obviously doesn't make sense to buy municipal bonds. You can determine the return that a fully taxable bond must provide in order to match the after-tax return on a lower-yielding tax-free bond by computing the **fully taxable equivalent yield**:

$$\text{Fully taxable equivalent yield} = \frac{\text{Yield on municipal bond}}{1 - \text{Tax rate}}$$

The Bonus Exhibit, "Table of Taxable Equivalent Yields" shows what a taxable bond (such as a corporate issue) would have to yield to equal the take-home yield of a tax-free municipal bond. (Visit PFIN6 Online. Log in at **www.cengagebrain.com.**) It demonstrates how the yield attractiveness of municipal bonds varies with an investor's income level. The higher the individual's tax bracket, the more attractive municipal bonds become.

Municipal bonds are generally issued as **serial obligations**. This means that the issue is broken into a series of smaller bonds, each with its own maturity date and coupon rate. Thus, instead of the bond having just one maturity date 20 years from now, it will have a series of (say) 20 maturity dates over the 20-year time frame. Although it may not seem that municipal issuers would default on either interest or principal payments, it does occur! Investors should be especially cautious when investing in **revenue bonds**, which are municipal bonds serviced from the income

generated by specific income-producing projects, such as toll roads. Unlike issuers of so-called **general obligation bonds**—which are backed by the full faith and credit of the municipality—the issuer of a revenue bond is obligated to pay principal and interest *only if a sufficient level of revenue* is generated. General obligation municipal bonds, in contrast, are required to be serviced in a prompt and timely fashion regardless of the level of tax income generated by the municipality.

Corporate Bonds The major nongovernmental issuers of bonds are corporations. The market for **corporate bonds** is customarily subdivided into several segments, which include *industrials* (the most diverse of the group), *public utilities* (the dominant group in terms of the volume of new issues), *rail and transportation bonds*, and *financial issues* (banks and finance companies). In this market, you'll find the widest range of different types of issues, from first mortgage and convertible bonds (discussed next) to debentures, subordinated debentures, and income bonds. Interest on corporate bonds is paid semiannually, and sinking funds are common. The bonds usually come in $1,000 denominations, and maturities usually range from 5 to 10 years but can be up to 30 years or more. Many of the issues carry call provisions that prohibit prepayment of the issue during the first 5 to 10 years. Corporate issues are popular with individuals because of their relatively high bond yields.

Convertible Bonds Another popular type of specialty issue, convertible bonds are found only in the corporate market. They are a *hybrid security* that possesses the features of both corporate bonds and common stocks. That is, although they are initially issued as debentures (unsecured debt), they carry a provision that enables them to be converted into a certain number of shares of the issuing company's common stock.

The key element of any convertible issue is its **conversion privilege**, which describes the conditions and specific nature of the conversion feature. First, it states exactly when the bond can be converted. Sometimes there'll be an initial waiting period of six months to perhaps two years after the date of issue, during which

---

EXAMPLE: Calculating the Fully-Taxable Equivalent Yield If a municipal bond offered a yield of 6 percent, an individual in the 35 percent federal tax bracket would have to find a fully taxable bond with a yield of more than 9 percent to reap the same after-tax return: 6 percent / (1 − 0.35) = 6 percent / 0.65 = 9.23 percent.

---

fully taxable equivalent yield the return a fully taxable bond must provide in order to match the after-tax return on a lower-yielding tax-free bond

serial obligation an issue that is broken down into a series of smaller bonds, each with its own maturity date and coupon rate

revenue bond a municipal bond serviced from the income generated by a specific project

general obligation bond a municipal bond backed by the full faith and credit of the issuing municipality

corporate bond a bond issued by a corporation

conversion privilege the provision in a convertible issue that stipulates the conditions of the conversion feature, such as the conversion period and conversion ratio time the issue cannot be converted. The *conversion period* then begins, during which the issue can be converted at any time. From the investor's point of view, the most important feature is the **conversion ratio**, which specifies the number of shares of common stock into which the bond can be converted. For example, one of these bonds might carry a conversion ratio of 20, meaning you can exchange one convertible bond for 20 shares of stock.

Given the significance of the price behavior of the underlying common stock to the value of a convertible security, another important measure is conversion value. **Conversion value** is an indication of what a convertible issue would trade for *if it were priced to sell based on its stock value*. Conversion value is easy to find: simply multiply the conversion ratio of the issue by the current market price of the underlying common stock. But convertibles seldom trade precisely at their conversion value; instead, they usually trade at **conversion premiums**, which means the convertibles are priced in the market at more than their conversion values. For example, a convertible that traded at $1,400 and had a conversion value of $1,200 would have a conversion premium of $200 (i.e., $1,400 − $1,200 = $200). Convertible securities appeal to investors who want *the price potential of a common stock along with the downside risk protection of a corporate bond*.

EMMANUEL DUNAND/Getty Images

> **EXAMPLE:** Calculating the Conversion Value of a Convertible Bond A convertible bond carrying a conversion ratio of 20 would have a conversion value of $1,200 if the firm's stock traded at a current market price of $60 per share (20 × $60 = $1,200).

12-3e Bond Ratings

Bond ratings are like grades: a letter grade is assigned to each bond that designates its investment quality. Ratings are widely used and are an important part of the municipal and corporate bond markets. The two largest and best-known rating agencies are Moody's and Standard & Poor's. Every time a large, new corporate or municipal issue comes to the market, a staff of professional bond analysts determine its default risk exposure and investment quality. The financial records of the issuing organization are thoroughly examined and its future prospects assessed. The result is the assignment of a bond rating at the time of issue that indicates *the ability of the issuing organization to service its debt in a prompt and timely manner*.

Exhibit 12.6 lists the various ratings assigned to bonds by each of the two major agencies. Note that the top four ratings (Aaa through Baa; or AAA through BBB) designate *investment-grade bonds*—such ratings are highly coveted by issuers because they indicate financially strong, well-run companies or municipalities. The next two ratings (Ba/B or BB/B) are where you'll find most **junk bonds**. These ratings indicate that, although any required principal and interest payments on the bonds are still being met, the risk of default is relatively high because the issuers lack the financial strength found with investment-grade issues.

Once a new issue is rated, the process doesn't stop there. Older, outstanding bonds are also regularly reviewed to ensure that their assigned ratings are still valid. Most issues will carry a single rating to maturity, but ratings can change over time as new

conversion ratio a ratio specifying the number of shares of common stock into which a convertible bond can be converted

conversion value a measure of what a convertible issue would trade for if it were priced to sell based on its stock value

conversion premium the difference between a convertible security's market price and its conversion value

junk bonds also known as *high-yield bonds*, these are highly speculative securities that have received low ratings from Moody's or Standard & Poor's

Exhibit 12.6

Moody's and Standard & Poor's Bond Ratings

Agencies like Moody's and Standard & Poor's rate corporate and municipal bonds; these ratings provide an indication of the bonds' investment quality (particularly regarding an issue's default risk exposure).

Bond Ratings*		
Moody's	S&P	Description
Aaa	AAA	*Prime-quality investment bonds*—This is the highest rating assigned, denoting extremely strong capacity to pay.
Aa A	AA A	*High-grade investment bonds*—These are also considered very safe bonds, though they're not quite as safe as Aaa/AAA issues; double A–rated bonds (Aa/AA) are safer (have less risk of default) than single A–rated issues.
Baa	BBB	*Medium-grade investment bonds*—These are the lowest of the investment-grade issues; they're felt to lack certain protective elements against adverse economic conditions.
Ba B	BB B	*Junk bonds*—With little protection against default, these are viewed as highly speculative securities.
Caa Ca C D	CCC CC C D	*Lower-quality bonds*—These are either in default or very close to it; they're often referred to as "zombie bonds."

* Some ratings may be modified to show relative standing within a major rating category; for example, Moody's uses numerical modifiers (1, 2, 3), whereas S&P uses plus (+) or minus (−) signs.

 Go to Smart Sites

If bonds are still a mystery to you, Investopedia's "Bond Basics" section site has an eight-part series that covers all the basics.

information becomes available. Finally, although it may appear that the issuing firm or municipality is receiving the rating, it's actually the *individual* issue that is being rated. As a result, a firm (or municipality) can have different ratings assigned to its issues. Most investors pay careful attention to ratings because they affect comparative market yields. Other things being equal, *the higher the rating, the lower the yield of an obligation.* Thus, whereas an A-rated bond might offer a 5 percent yield, a comparable AAA-rated issue would probably yield something like 4.25 or 4.50 percent.

12-3f Pricing a Bond

Unlike stocks, bonds aren't widely quoted in the financial press, not even in *The Wall Street Journal.* So, rather than looking at how bonds are quoted, let's look at how they're priced in the marketplace. Regardless of the type, *all bonds are priced as a percentage of par*; this means that a quote of, say, 85 translates into a price of 85 percent of the bond's par value. In the bond market, 1 point = $10; hence a quote of 85 does not mean $85 but rather $850. This is so because market convention assumes that bonds carry par values of $1,000. Keep in mind that the price of any bond is related to the issue's coupon and maturity—those two features are always a part of any listed price because of their effect on the price of a bond. (We'll explore more about the impact of coupons and maturities on bond price behavior in the section "Bond Prices and Yields" later in this chapter.)

In the corporate and municipal markets, bonds are priced in decimals, using three places to the right of the decimal point. Thus a quote of 87.562, as a percentage of a $1,000 par bond, converts to a price of $875.62. Similarly, a quote of 121.683 translates into a price of 1.21683 × $1,000 = $1,216.83. In contrast, U.S. Treasury and agency bond quotes are stated in *32s of a point* (where, again, 1 point = $10). For example, you might see the price of a T-bond listed at, "94:16." Translated, this means that the bond is being priced at $94\frac{16}{32}$, or 94.5 percent of par—in other words, it's being priced at $945.00. With government bonds, the figures to the right of the colon (:) show the number of 32s embedded in the price.

Bond Prices and Accrued Interest The price of a bond quoted on your favorite financial Internet site is unlikely to be the price that you would actually pay as a buyer. This is because such quoted prices usually do not include the interest that accrues between the coupon payment dates of the bond. **Accrued interest** is the amount of interest that's been earned since the last coupon payment date by the bond holder/seller, but which will be received by the new owner/buyer of the bond at the next regularly scheduled coupon payment date. When a bond is sold between coupon payment dates, the buyer pays the seller for the accrued interest, which is the prorated share of the upcoming coupon payment.

Consider a specific example of how accrued interest affects the price paid for a bond between coupon payments. Assume that you're selling a corporate bond with $1,000 par value and paying a 4 percent coupon semiannually, which is $20 every six months. The bond is quoted on the Internet at $1,000, and it's three months after the last coupon payment. Because the bond is half-way between coupon payments, accrued interest is $20 × 3/6 = $10. Thus, the buyer's actual price paid to the seller will be the $1,000 quoted price plus the accrued interest of $10, for a total of $1,010.

In market jargon, how accrued interest is treated in bond pricing is the basis for the distinction between **clean prices** and **dirty (full) prices**. This can be concisely summarized as:

Dirty (full) price = quoted price + accrued interest

Clean price = quoted price − accrued interest

So what's the significance of the distinction between dirty and clean prices for bond investors? It's important to realize that the commonly cited prices in the financial press and on the Internet are typically net of accrued interest and are so-called clean bond prices. The relevant sale or invoice price of a bond to the buyer is the dirty price, which adds the accrued interest to the quoted price. In terms of the earlier example, the buyer of the 4 percent coupon bond would pay the dirty price of $1,010, not the clean price of $1,000. In summary, the quoted clean price *understates* the true (dirty) price that must be paid to actually purchase the bond in the open market.

12-3g Bond Prices and Yields

The price of a bond depends on its coupon, maturity, and the movement of market interest rates. *When interest rates go down, bond prices go up*, and vice versa. The relationship of bond prices to market rates is captured in Exhibit 12.7. The graph serves to reinforce the *inverse* relationship between bond prices and market interest rates; note that *lower* rates lead to *higher* bond prices. The exhibit also shows the difference between premium and discount bonds. A **premium bond** is one that sells for more than its par value, which occurs whenever market interest rates drop below the coupon rate on the bond; a **discount bond**, in contrast, sells for less than par and is the result of market rates being greater than the issue's coupon rate. Thus the 4 percent bond in our illustration traded as a premium bond when market rates were at 2 percent but as a discount bond when rates stood at 6 percent.

What happens to the price of the bond over time is of considerable concern to investors who may wish to trade the bond

accrued interest the amount of interest that's been earned since the last coupon payment date by the bond holder/seller, but which will be received by the new owner/buyer of the bond at the next regularly coupon payment date

clean price the quoted price of a bond minus accrued interest

dirty (full) price the quoted price of a bond plus accrued interest

premium bond a bond whose market value is higher than par

discount bond a bond whose market value is lower than par

Exhibit 12.7

Price Behavior of a Bond with a 4 Percent Coupon

A bond sells at its par value so long as the prevailing market interest rate remains the same as the bond's coupon (e.g., when both coupon and market rates equal 4 percent). But if market rates drop, then bond prices rise, and vice versa; moreover, as a bond approaches its maturity, the issue price always moves toward its par value no matter what happens to interest rates.

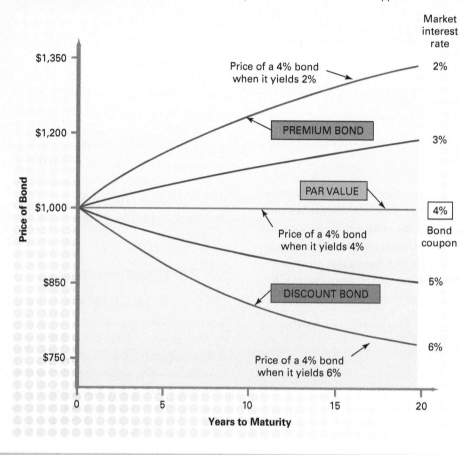

over the course of its life. We know that how much bond prices move depends not only on the *direction* of interest rates changes but also on the *magnitude* of such changes; the greater the moves in interest rates, the greater the swings in bond prices. Bond prices will also vary according to the coupon and maturity of the issue. Bonds with *lower coupons* and/or *longer maturities* will respond more vigorously to changes in market rates and undergo *greater price swings*. Thus, if interest rates are moving up, then the investor should seek high coupon bonds with short maturities because this will cause minimal price variation and *preserve as much capital as possible.*

current yield the amount of current income a bond provides relative to its market price

In contrast, if rates are heading down, that's the time to be in long-term bonds. If you're a speculator looking for a lot of capital gains, then go with long-term, *low coupon bonds.* And if you're trying to lock in a high level of coupon (interest) income, then stick with long-term, *high coupon* bonds that offer plenty of call protection.

Current Yield and Yield to Maturity The two most commonly cited bond yields are current yield and yield to maturity. **Current yield** reflects the amount of annual interest income the bond provides relative to its current market price. Here's the formula for measuring current yield:

$$\text{Current yield} = \frac{\text{Annual interest income}}{\text{Market price of bond}}$$

As you can see, the current yield on a bond is comparable to the dividend yield on a stock. This measure would be of interest to *investors seeking current income*. Other things being equal, the higher the current yield, the more attractive the bond would be.

> **EXAMPLE: Calculating the Current Yield on a Bond** A 6 percent bond with a $1,000 face value is currently selling for $910. Because annual interest income amounts to $60 (0.06 × $1,000), and because the current market price of the bond is $910, its current yield would be 6.59 percent ($60/$910).

The annual rate of return a bondholder would receive *if she held the issue to its maturity* is captured by the bond's **yield to maturity**. This measure captures both the annual interest income and the recovery of principal at maturity. It also includes the impact of interest on interest and therefore provides a fully compounded rate of return. If a bond is purchased at its face value, then its yield to maturity will equal the coupon, or stated, rate of interest. On the other hand, if the bond is purchased at a discount or premium, then its yield to maturity will vary according to the prevailing level of market yields.

You can find the yield to maturity on discount or premium bonds using the *approximate expected yield* formula introduced earlier in this chapter. Or you can use a handheld financial calculator (which we'll demonstrate soon) to obtain a yield to maturity that's a bit more accurate and is, in fact, very close to the measure used in the market. The only difference is that market participants normally use semi-annual compounding in their calculations whereas we use annual compounding for simplicity to illustrate the basic concept.

By setting the future maturity value of the investment equal to the bond's face value ($1,000), you can use the following version of the equation to find the *approximate yield to maturity on a bond*:

$$\text{Approximate yield to maturity} = \frac{\text{Annual coupon income} + \left[\dfrac{\$1,000 - \text{bond price}}{\text{Number of years to maturity}}\right]}{\left[\dfrac{\text{Current bond price} + \$1,000}{2}\right]}$$

> **EXAMPLE: Calculating the Approximate Yield to Maturity** Assume you're contemplating the purchase of a $1,000, 6 percent annual coupon income bond with 15 years remaining to maturity and that the bond is trading at a price of $910. The approximate yield to maturity on this bond will be:
>
> $$\text{Approximate yield to maturity} = \frac{\$60 + \left[\dfrac{\$1,000 - \$910}{15}\right]}{\left[\dfrac{\$910 + \$1,000}{2}\right]}$$
>
> $$= \frac{\$60 + \left[\dfrac{\$90}{15}\right]}{\left[\dfrac{\$1,910}{2}\right]} = 6.91 \text{ percent}$$
>
> Because this bond was purchased at a discount, its yield to maturity is above both the 6 percent stated coupon rate and the 6.59 percent current yield ($60/$910).

CALCULATOR KEYSTROKES

You can also find the yield to maturity on a bond using a financial calculator. Here's what you'd do. With the calculator in the *annual mode*, to find the yield to maturity on our 6 percent (annual pay), 15-year bond that's currently trading at $910, use the keystrokes shown below, where:

N = number of *years* to maturity

PV = the current market price of the bond (entered as a *negative* value)

PMT = the size of the annual coupon payments (in *dollars*)

FV = the par value of the bond

A value of 6.99 should appear in the calculator display, which is the bond's yield to maturity using annual compounding. Note that it's very close to the approximate yield of 6.91 percent that we just computed.

yield to maturity the fully compounded rate of return that a bond would yield if it were held to maturity

Measures of yield to maturity are used by investors to assess the attractiveness of a bond. The higher the yield to maturity, the more attractive the investment, other things being equal. *If a bond provided a yield to maturity that equaled or exceeded an investor's desired rate of return, then it would be considered a worthwhile investment candidate* because it would promise a yield that should compensate the investor adequately for the perceived amount of risk involved.

FINANCIAL IMPACT OF PERSONAL CHOICES

Jason and Serena Like High-Flying Stocks

Jason and Serena Maddox are both 33 years old and invest 15 percent of their after-tax annual income in stocks. They hate missing out on great returns when the stock of a company doing great things starts going through the roof. For example, Jason and Serena feel they should have invested in Electronic Arts in 2014 when it earned around a 60 percent return! So any time a company they know well earns more than 20 percent in a year, they try to invest in it. And because they believe in the stocks they buy, the Maddoxes always hold their stocks until they at least break even. What do you make of the Longorias' approach to stock investing?

The Maddoxes' decision to invest 15 percent of their after-tax income is great. However, Jason and Serena shouldn't invest just in stocks and should adopt an asset allocation strategy that provides diversified exposure to bonds, real estate, and more. Their current exclusive focus on stocks is likely too risky. Further, their rule to buy well-known stocks that earn more than a 20 percent return in a year likely leaves them insufficiently diversified. And their 20 percent return rule also focuses too much on *past* returns and not enough on a careful forecast of *future* returns. The Maddoxes could end up with overvalued stocks with their best performance behind them. Finally, their rule to not sell until they at least break even suggests the behavioral bias of unduly "anchoring" on purchase prices. It could be that a company has changed for the worse and it's simply time to sell, even if it implies a loss. Investing 15 percent of their income is great, but the Maddoxes could do even better.

SergeyP/Shutterstock.com

PLANNING OVER A LIFETIME

Investing in Stocks and Bonds

Here are some key considerations for investment planning in each stage of the life cycle.

PRE-FAMILY INDEPENDENCE: 20s

▸ Determine major investment goals and how much money needs to be invested each month to achieve them.

▸ Determine your asset allocation among stocks, bonds, and cash based on your time horizon and attitude toward risk.

▸ Make sure to participate in any employer-sponsored 401(k) retirement plan and match your asset allocation plan.

▸ Consider opening traditional and/or a Roth IRAs.

FAMILY FORMATION/CAREER DEVELOPMENT: 30–45

▸ Revise investment plan to focus more on retirement and funding children's education, if applicable.

▸ Review your asset allocation and rebalance if it is inconsistent with your goals.

▸ Gradually increase the amount invested in any employer-sponsored 401(k) retirement plan and re-evaluate how it relates to your asset allocation plan.

▸ Consider increasing your contribution to traditional and/or a Roth IRAs.

PRE-RETIREMENT: 45–65

▸ Revise investment plan in light of recent developments.

▸ Review your asset allocation and rebalance if it is inconsistent with your goals.

▸ Continue to gradually increase the amount you invest in any employer-sponsored 401(k) retirement plan and re-evaluate how it relates to your asset allocation plan.

▸ Consider increasing your contribution to traditional and/or a Roth IRAs.

RETIREMENT: 65 AND BEYOND

▸ Revise investment plan to lean more toward debt and cash instruments than to stocks.

▸ Review your asset allocation and rebalance if it is inconsistent with your goals.

▸ Integrate investment asset allocation strategy with estate planning.

▸ Carefully plan for mandatory withdrawals from tax shelter accounts and associated tax consequences.

STUDY TOOLS 12

LOCATED AT BACK OF THE TEXTBOOK
☐ Chapter Review Card

LOCATED AT WWW.CENGAGEBRAIN.COM
☐ Review Key Term flashcards and create your own cards.
☐ Track your knowledge and understanding of key concepts in personal finance.

☐ Complete practice and graded quizzes to prepare for tests.
☐ Complete interactive content at PFIN6 Online.
☐ View the chapter highlight boxes at PFIN6 Online.

©viphotos/Shutterstock140785408

Financial Planning Exercises

LO1, 2 1. **Ranking investments by expected returns.** What makes for a good investment? Use the approximate yield formula or a financial calculator to rank the following investments according to their expected returns.

    a. Buy a stock for $30 a share, hold it for three years, and then sell it for $60 a share (the stock pays annual dividends of $2 a share).

    b. Buy a security for $40, hold it for two years, and then sell it for $100 (current income on this security is zero).

    c. Buy a one-year, 5 percent note for $1,000 (assume that the note has a $1,000 par value and that it will be held to maturity).

LO3, 4 2. **Calculating expected return on an investment.** An investor is thinking about buying some shares of Sporting Metrics, Inc., at $75 a share. She expects the price of the stock to rise to $115 a share over the next three years. During that time, she also expects to receive annual dividends of $4 per share. Assuming that the investor's expectations (about the future price of the stock and the dividends that it pays) hold up, what rate of return can the investor expect to earn on this investment? (Hint: Use either the approximate yield formula or a financial calculator to solve this problem.)

LO3, 4 3. **Calculating expected return on a stock.** The price of Landscapes, Inc. is now $85. The company pays no dividends. Troy Compton expects the price four years from now to be $125 a share. Should Tucker buy Landscapes if he wants a 15 percent rate of return? Explain.

LO3, 4 4. **Calculating key stock performance metrics.** The Rivers Company recently reported net profits after taxes of $15.8 million. It has 2.5 million shares of common stock outstanding and pays preferred dividends of $1 million a year. The company's stock currently trades at $60 per share.

    a. Compute the stock's earnings per share (EPS).

    b. What is the stock's P/E ratio?

    c. Determine what the stock's dividend yield would be if it paid $1.75 per share to common stockholders.

LO3, 4 5. **Choosing appropriate stocks.** Assume that you've just inherited $500,000 and have decided to invest a big chunk of it ($350,000, to be exact) in common stocks. Your objective is to build up as much capital as you can over the next 15 to 20 years, and you're willing to tolerate a "good deal" of risk.

    a. What *types* of stocks (blue chips, income stocks, and so on) do you think you'd be most interested in, and why? Select at least three types of stocks and briefly explain the rationale for selecting each.

    b. Would your selections change if you were dealing with a smaller amount of money—say, only $50,000? What if you were a more risk-averse investor?

LO5, 6 6. **Calculating and interpreting current yield and yield to maturity.** Find the current yield of a 5.65 percent, 8-year bond that's currently priced in the market at $853.75. Now, use a financial calculator to find the yield to maturity on this bond (use annual compounding). What's the current yield and yield to maturity on this bond if it trades at $1,000? If it's priced at $750? Comment on your findings.

LO5, 6 7. **Tax treatment of bond returns.** An investor in the 28 percent tax bracket is trying to decide which of two bonds to select: one is a 5.5 percent U.S. Treasury bond selling at par; the other is a municipal bond with a 4.25 percent coupon, which is also selling at par. Which of these two bonds should the investor select? Why?

LO5, 6 8. **Calculating and interpreting current yield and yield to maturity.** Describe and differentiate between a bond's (a) current yield and (b) yield to maturity. Why are these yield measures important to the bond investor? Find the yield to maturity of a 20-year, 9 percent, $1,000 par value bond trading at a price of $850. What's the current yield on this bond?

Financial Planning Exercises

LO5, 6 9. **Calculating and comparing current yields.** Which of these two bonds offers the highest current yield? Which one has the highest yield to maturity?

   a. A 6.55 percent, 22-year bond quoted at 52.000

   b. A 10.25 percent, 27-year bond quoted at 103.625

LO6 10. **Clean and dirty bond prices.** You have decided to sell a 5 percent semiannual coupon bond two months after the last coupon payment. The bond is currently selling for $951.25. Answer the following questions about the bond:

   a. What is the clean price of the bond?

   b. What is the dirty (full) price of the bond?

   c. Explain how the clean and dirty prices of the bond are relevant to the buyer of the bond.

13 | Investing in Mutual Funds, ETFs, and Real Estate

LEARNING OBJECTIVES

After studying this chapter, you will be able to...

LO1 Describe the basic features and operating characteristics of mutual funds and exchange traded funds.

LO2 Differentiate between open- and closed-end mutual funds, as well as exchange traded funds, and discuss the various types of fund loads and charges.

LO3 Discuss the types of funds available to investors and the different kinds of investor services offered by mutual funds and exchange traded funds.

LO4 Gain an understanding of the variables that should be considered when selecting funds for investment purposes.

LO5 Identify the sources of return and calculate the rate of return earned on an investment in a mutual fund, as well as evaluate the performance of an exchange traded fund.

LO6 Understand the role that real estate plays in a diversified investment portfolio along with the basics of investing in real estate, either directly or indirectly.

After you finish this chapter, go to **PAGE 366** for **STUDY TOOLS**

How Will This Affect Me?

Having a financial plan and being aware that diversification is crucial is a great start to the task of investment planning. The next step is figuring out how to implement your plan by deciding what to invest in. For most people, diversification is best achieved using mutual funds and exchange traded funds (ETFs). This chapter describes the key characteristics of each type of fund, sorts through the various options you have, shows how to calculate rates of return and evaluate performance, and explains how to choose among funds. The essential elements of investing in real estate, and its role in diversifying your overall investment portfolio, are also covered. After reading this chapter, you should be in a good position to invest in mutual funds, ETFs, and real estate in a way that will help you achieve your financial objectives.

13-1 MUTUAL FUNDS AND EXCHANGE TRADED FUNDS: SOME BASICS

LO1, LO2 Sound investment planning involves finding investments with risk-return characteristics that are compatible with your financial objectives and risk tolerance. In this chapter, we'll look beyond stocks and bonds and consider other types of investments that enjoy widespread use among individual investors: mutual funds, exchange traded funds (ETFs), and real estate. These investments offer risk-return opportunities you may not be able to obtain from stocks or bonds. For example, investors interested in receiving the benefits of professional portfolio management, but who don't have the funds to purchase a diversified portfolio of securities, may find mutual fund and ETF shares attractive. Let's now take a closer look at each of these investments, starting with mutual funds. Keep in mind that many of the issues in analyzing and choosing mutual funds are essentially the same for ETFs.

A **mutual fund** is a financial services organization that receives money from its shareholders and invests those funds on their behalf in a diversified portfolio of securities. An **exchange traded fund (ETF)** is an investment company whose shares

> **mutual fund** a financial services organization that receives money from its shareholders and invests those funds on their behalf in a diversified portfolio of securities
>
> **exchange traded fund (ETF)** an investment company whose shares trade on stock exchanges; unlike mutual funds, ETF shares can be bought or sold (or sold short) throughout the day

Exhibit 13.1

Basic Mutual Fund Structure

A mutual fund brings together the funds from many individual investors and uses this pool of money to acquire a diversified portfolio of stocks, bonds, and other securities.

Mutual Fund Shareholders

Investors purchase shares in the mutual fund.

Mutual Fund

Money managers select and purchase securities.

Mutual Fund's Diversified Portfolio of Securities

---

trade on stock exchanges. Unlike mutual funds, ETF shares can be bought or sold (or sold short) throughout the day. ETFs are usually structured as an index fund that matches the performance of a certain market segment. Thus, when investors buy shares in a mutual fund, or an ETF they usually become *part owners of a widely diversified portfolio of securities*. A mutual fund or an ETF share can be thought of as the *financial product* that's sold to the public by an investment company. That is, the investment company builds and manages a portfolio of securities and sells ownership interests—shares of stock—in that portfolio through an investment known as a mutual fund. This concept underlies the whole mutual fund structure and is depicted in Exhibit 13.1.

For many individual investors today, mutual funds are the investment vehicle of choice. They're popular because they offer not only a variety of interesting investment opportunities, but also a wide array of services that many investors find appealing. They're an easy and convenient way to invest—one that's especially suited to beginning investors.

13-1a The Mutual Fund Concept

The first mutual fund in this country was started in Boston in 1924, and by 1980 there were some 564 mutual funds in operation. But that was only the beginning,

as assets under management in the United States grew to about $16.4 trillion by the in 2016. Indeed, *investors could choose from over 8,000 mutual funds*. (Counting duplicate or multiple fund offerings from the same portfolio, there were over *30,000 funds* available; such duplication occurs because sometimes two or three versions of the same fund are offered, with each "fund" having a different type of load charge or fee structure.) Clearly, mutual funds appeal to many investors, who all share one view: They've decided, for one reason or another, to turn the problems of security selection and portfolio management over to professional money managers.

 Go to Smart Sites

What is your fund's sector allocation, and past performance? The Street's Internet site has detailed fund breakdowns. A highlight box in each chapter of PFIN Online includes "Smart Sites," a list of resources and sites that offer additional information on topics in the PFIN text.

Pooled Diversification A mutual fund combines the investment capital of many people with similar investment goals and invests those funds in a wide variety of securities. Investors receive shares of stock in the mutual fund and, through the fund, enjoy much wider investment diversification than they could otherwise achieve. Indeed, a single mutual fund commonly holds hundreds of different securities! For example, in 2016, Fidelity Contrafund held 356 different securities, while the Dreyfus GNMA bond fund had almost 800 holdings. For all but the super-rich, that's far more diversification than most investors could ever hope to attain. Yet each investor who owns shares in a fund is, in effect, a part owner of that fund's diversified portfolio of securities. Regardless of the fund size, as the securities held by it move up and down in price, the market value of the mutual fund shares moves accordingly. And when the fund receives dividend and interest payments, they too are passed on to the mutual fund shareholders and distributed on the basis of prorated ownership. When a security held by the fund is sold for a profit, the capital gain is also passed on to fund shareholders. The whole mutual fund idea, in fact, rests on the concept of pooled diversification and works much like insurance, whereby individuals pool their resources for the collective benefit of all contributors.

> Opening a mutual fund account is as easy as opening a checking account.

13-1b Why Invest in Mutual Funds or ETFs?

Mutual funds and ETFs can be used by individual investors in various ways. One investor may buy a fund because of the substantial capital gains opportunities that it provides; another may buy a totally different fund not for its capital gains, but instead for its current income. Whatever kind of income a fund provides, individuals tend to use these investment vehicles for one or more of the following reasons:

▶ to achieve diversification in their investment holdings;

▶ to obtain the services of professional money managers;

▶ to generate an attractive rate of return on their investment capital, and

▶ for the convenience that they offer.

Diversification The ability to diversify allows investors to reduce their exposure to risk sharply by indirectly investing in many different securities and companies rather than just one or two. If you have only $500 or $1,000 to invest, you obviously won't achieve much diversification on your own. But if you invest that money in a mutual fund or an ETF, you'll end up owning part of a well-diversified portfolio of securities.

Professional Management Another major appeal of a mutual fund is the professional management that it offers. Though management is paid a fee for its services, the contributions of a full-time, expert manager should be worth the fee. These professionals know where to look for return and how to avoid unnecessary risk. At the minimum, their decisions should result in better long-run returns than the average individual investor can achieve.

Financial Returns Although professional managers *may* be able to achieve better returns than small investors can generate, the relatively high purchase fees, coupled with the management and operating costs, tend to reduce the returns actually earned on mutual fund investments. But the mutual fund industry hasn't attracted millions of investors by generating substandard returns. Quite the contrary; over the long haul, mutual funds have provided relatively attractive returns.

Convenience Mutual funds make it easy to invest, and most don't require much capital to get started. They handle all the paperwork and recordkeeping, their prices are widely quoted, and it's usually possible to deal in fractional shares. What's more, opening a mutual fund account is as easy as opening a checking account. Just fill in a few blanks, send in the minimum amount of money, and you're in business!

13-1c How Mutual Funds Are Organized and Run

Although it's tempting to think of a mutual fund as a monolithic entity, that's really not the case. Various functions—investing, recordkeeping, safekeeping, and others—are split among two or more companies. Besides the fund itself, which *is owned by the shareholders*, there are several other major players:

▶ The *management company* runs the fund's daily operations.

▶ The *investment advisor* buys and sells the stocks or bonds and otherwise oversees the portfolio.

▶ The *distributor* sells the fund shares, either directly to the public or through authorized dealers.

▶ The *custodian* (such as a bank) physically safeguards the securities and other assets of a fund.

▶ The *transfer agent* executes transactions, keeps track of shareholder trades, and maintains other records.

All this separation of duties is designed to

> **pooled diversification** a process whereby investors buy into a diversified portfolio of securities for the collective benefit of individual investors

protect the mutual fund investor/shareholder. Obviously, you can always lose money if your fund's stock or bond holdings go down in value. But that's really the only risk of loss that you face because the chance of ever losing money from fraud or a mutual fund collapse is almost nonexistent.

YOU CAN DO IT NOW: Objective Mutual Fund Resources Looking for information on mutual fund investing from a source that isn't trying to sell you a financial product? Then try the Mutual Fund Investor's Center at **http://mfea.com/**. It's sponsored by the Mutual Fund Education Alliance (MFEA), which is a national trade organization for mutual funds. You can **do it now**.

13-1d Open-End versus Closed-End Mutual Funds

It may seem that all mutual funds are organized in roughly the same way, but that's not the case. One way that funds differ is in how they are structured. Funds can be set up either as *open-end companies*, which can sell an unlimited number of ownership shares, or as *closed-end companies*, which can issue only a limited number of shares.

Open-End Investment Companies The term *mutual fund* commonly denotes an **open-end investment company**. Such organizations are the dominant type of investment company and account for well over 95 percent of assets under management. In an open-end investment company, investors actually buy their shares from, and sell them back to, the mutual fund itself. When they buy shares in the fund, the fund issues new shares of stock and fills the purchase order with these new shares. There's no limit, other than investor demand, to the number of shares the fund can issue. Further, all open-end mutual funds stand behind their shares and buy them back when investors decide to sell. So there's never any trading among individuals.

open-end investment company a firm that can issue an unlimited number of shares that it buys and sells at a price based on the current market value of the securities it owns; also called a *mutual fund*

net asset value (NAV) the current market value of all the securities the fund owns, less any liabilities, on a per-share basis

closed-end investment company an investment company that issues a fixed number of shares, which are themselves listed and traded like any other share of stock

Buy and sell transactions in an open-end mutual fund are carried out at prices based on the current value of all the securities held in the fund's portfolio. This is known as the fund's **net asset value (NAV)**, which is found by taking the total market value of all securities held by the fund, subtracting any liabilities, and dividing the result by the number of shares outstanding.

EXAMPLE: Calculating a Mutual Fund's NAV On a recent day, the market value of all the securities held by the XYZ mutual fund equaled $10 million, and XYZ had 500,000 shares outstanding. Consequently, the fund's NAV per share would amount to $20 ($10,000,000/500,000 = $20).

Closed-End Investment Companies The term *mutual fund* is supposed to be used only with open-end funds, but as a practical matter it's regularly used with closed-end investment companies as well. Basically, **closed-end investment companies** operate with a fixed number of shares outstanding and do *not* regularly issue new shares of stock. In effect, they are like any other corporation, except that the corporation's business happens to be investing in marketable securities. Like open-end funds, closed-end investment companies have enjoyed remarkable growth in the past decade or so. While only 34 of these funds existed in 1980, by 2016 there were about 550 closed-end funds with total net assets of around $260 billion—although this is just a fraction of the $16.4 trillion invested in the mutual fund industry. Shares in closed-end investment companies are actively traded in the secondary market just like any other common stock. But unlike open-end funds, *all trading is done between investors in the open market*. The fund itself plays no role in either buy or sell transactions; once the shares are issued, the fund is out of the picture.

While open- and closed-end funds may appear to be much the same, major differences exist between them. To begin with, closed-end funds don't have to worry about stock redemptions or new money coming into the fund. Thus, they don't have to be concerned about keeping cash on hand to meet redemptions. Equally important, because closed-end funds don't have new money flowing in all the time, they don't have to worry about finding new investments for that money. Instead, they can concentrate on a set portfolio of securities and do the

StockThings/Shutterstock.com

best job they can in managing it. But this puts added pressures on the money managers because their in-vestment results are closely monitored and judged by the market. That is, the share prices of closed-end companies are determined not only by their NAVs, but also by general supply and demand conditions in the market. Depending on the market outlook and investor expectations, closed-end companies generally trade at a *discount* or *premium* to their NAVs.

13-1e ETFs

Combine some of the operating characteristics of an open-end fund with some of the trading characteristics of a closed-end fund, and you'll end up with something called an ETF. As defined above, an ETF is an investment company whose shares trade on a stock exchange. They have been around only since 1993, but ETFs are growing in popularity and offer a competitive alternative to comparable mutual funds in many cases. Most ETFs are structured as *index funds*, which are set up to match the performance of a certain market segment. They do this by owning all or a representative sample of the stocks (or bonds) in a targeted market segment or index. ETFs offer the professional money management of traditional mutual funds and the liquidity of an exchange traded stock. By 2016, there were about 1,700 ETFs managing $2.4 trillion in assets. About 4 percent (5.2 million) of U.S. households owned ETFs. And about 9 percent of households that own mutual funds also own ETFs.

Even though ETFs are like closed-end funds (they're traded on listed exchanges), *they are actually open-end mutual funds* whose number of shares outstanding can be increased or decreased in response to market demand. That is, ETFs can be bought or sold like any other stock, and *the ETF distributor can also create new shares or redeem old shares*. This is done to prevent the fund from trading at (much of) a premium

or discount to the underlying value of its holdings, thereby avoiding a major pitfall of closed-end funds.

These funds cover a wide array of domestic and international stock indexes and submarkets, as well as just about any type of U.S. Treasury, corporate, or municipal bond index. The biggest and oldest ETFs (dating back to 1993) are based on the S&P 500 and are known as *Spiders* (SPDRs). In addition, there are *Qubes* (based on the NASDAQ 100), *Diamonds* (based on the DJIA), and ETFs based on dozens of international markets (from Australia and Canada to Germany, Japan, and the United Kingdom). Just about every major U.S. index, in fact, has its own ETF, along with a lot of minor indexes covering specialized market segments. The NAVs of ETFs are set at a fraction of the underlying index value at any given time. For example, when the S&P 500 index was at 2,143.57 in October 2016. The ETF on that index traded at $214.14 (or about 1/10 of the index). Likewise, the ETF on the Dow is set at about 1/100 of the DJIA (so when the Dow was at 18,172.49 at this time, the ETF closed at $181.48.).

ETFs combine many advantages of closed-end funds with those of traditional (open-end) index funds. That is, like closed-end funds, ETFs can be bought and sold at *any time of the day*. You can place an order through your broker (and pay a standard commission just as you would with any other stock). In contrast, you *cannot* trade a traditional open-end fund on an intraday basis because all buy and sell orders for these funds are filled, at the closing prices, at the end of the trading day. What's more, because most ETFs are passively managed, they offer all the advantages of most index funds: low costs, low portfolio turnover, and low taxes. Yet because ETFs trade as securities, their prices can sometimes differ by a modest amount from their NAVs, which can dilute the cost advantage of ETFs over mutual funds. And whereas ETFs are traded for a fee using a broker, no-load mutual funds involve no trading costs. ETFs' tax liability is kept low because they rarely distribute any capital gains to shareholders.

Actively managed ETFs often have higher costs, portfolio turnover, and taxes than passively managed ETFs. As the name suggests, an actively managed ETF tries to outperform rather than to just track a given index. Leveraged ETFs seek to outperform a benchmark, which is usually achieved by using derivatives like options, futures, and swaps. If you're thinking that this can be extremely risky, you're right. Innovation continues in the ETF market to provide investors with more choices, so they can either moderate or enhance their risk exposure. Exhibit 13.2 lists some available ETF investments.

Exhibit 13.2

Examples of Available ETFs

The ETF market remains dominated by products that seek to track various domestic and international indexes. However, actively managed ETFs that focus on selecting and trading a dynamic mix of securities are growing. Below are representative examples of available ETFs.

Type of ETF	Ticker	Tracking Goal
U.S. Equity Indexes		
SPDR S&P 500 ETF	SPY	S&P 500 index.
PowerShares QQQ ETF	QQQ	NASDAQ-100 index.
SPDR Dow Jones Industrial Average ETF	DIA	Dow Jones Industrial Average index.
iShares Russell 2000 ETF	IWM	Russell 2000 index.
Vanguard Total Stock Market ETF	VTI	Overall stock market.
U.S. Equity Sector Indexes		
Energy Select Sector SPDR ETF*	XLE	Energy Select Sector Index.
Financial Select Sector SPDR ETF	XLF	Financial Select Sector Index.
Technology Select Sector SPDR ETF	XLK	Technology Select Sector Index.
U.S. Bond Market		
iShares Core U.S. Aggregate Bond ETF	AGG	Index of U.S. investment grade bond market.
Vanguard Short-Term Bond ETF	BSV	Market-weighted bond index with short-term, dollar-weighted average maturity.
iShares Core Core 10+ Year USD Bond ETF	ILTB	Index of U.S. dollar-denominated, investment-grade U.S. corporate and government bonds with maturities of at least 10 years.
International Markets		
MSCI EAFE ETF	EFA	MSCI European, Australasian, and Far Eastern "EAFE" index.
iShares MSCI Emerging Markets ETF	EEM	MSCI Emerging Markets Index.
Actively Managed Funds		**Goal**
PIMCO Enhanced Short Maturity Active ETF	MINT	Seeks greater income and total return than money market funds.
PowerShares Active U.S. Real Estate ETF	PSR	Selects securities in the FTSE NAREIT Equity REIT index.
iShares Enhanced U.S. Small-Cap ETF	IESM	Pursues long-term capital gains by investing in U.S. small-cap stocks.

*SPDRS are available on all of the S&P 500 sectors as well as on variously defined industries.

13-1f Choosing between ETFs and Mutual Funds

The preceding discussion identifies the relative advantages and disadvantages of mutual fund and ETF investing. Yet this begs the question of how you choose between ETFs and mutual funds. The answer depends on what you want to invest in and how sensitive you are to taxes and costs. Consider the following three criteria suggested by Morningstar:

▶ *Broad or narrow focus?* ETFs have been developed to accommodate investors pursuing narrow market segments. If you want to focus on a single market sector, industry, or geographic region, there's likely an ETF for you. Furthermore, there are far more ETFs that track single, foreign countries than mutual funds that do. The downside is that narrowly focused ETFs are not as well diversified as are many mutual funds. So consider mutual funds for broad index investing and ETFs for more narrow, targeted investing.

▶ *Tax management.* ETFs are set up to protect investors from capital gains taxes better than most mutual funds can. Most ETFs are index funds that trade less than the average actively managed mutual fund, which means that they should generate fewer taxable gains.

▶ *Costs.* ETFs have lower overhead expenses than most mutual funds because they don't have to manage customer accounts or staff call centers. This means that ETFs tend to have lower expense ratios than mutual funds. ETFs are often the most cost-effective choice for investors using discount brokers, for those investing a large, lump sum of money, and for those with a long-term horizon.

13-1g Some Important Cost Considerations

When you buy or sell shares in a *closed-end* investment company, or in an ETF for that matter, you pay a commission just as you would with any other type of listed or over-the-counter (OTC) common stock transaction. This isn't so with *open-end* funds, however. The cost of investing in an open-end mutual fund depends on the types of fees and load charges that the fund levies on its investors.

Load Funds Most open-end mutual funds are so-called load funds because they charge a commission *when the shares are purchased* (such charges are often referred to as *front-end loads*). Few funds today charge the maximum. Instead, many funds charge commissions of 2 or 3 percent—such funds are known as low-load mutual funds. The good news on front-end load funds is that there's normally no charge or commission to pay when you *sell* your shares! Occasionally, however, you'll run into funds that charge a commission—or a so-called *redemption fee*—when you sell your shares. Known as back-end load mutual funds, they may charge as much as 7 1/4 percent of the value of the shares sold, although back-end loads tend to decline over time and usually disappear altogether after five or six years.

No-Load Funds Some open-end investment companies charge you nothing at all to buy their funds. These are known as no-load mutual funds. Less than half of the funds sold today are true no-loads; all the rest charge some type of load or fee. Even funds that don't have front-end loads (and may be categorized as no-loads) can have back-end load charges—or something called a 12b-1 fee, which you'd pay as long as you hold your shares.

12b-1 Fees Also known as *hidden loads*, 12b-1 fees have been allowed by the Securities and Exchange Commission

(SEC) since 1980 and were originally designed to help no-load funds cover their distribution and marketing expenses. Not surprisingly, the popularity of these fees spread rapidly among fund distributors, so they're now used by most open-end mutual funds. The fees are assessed annually and can amount to as much as 1 percent of assets under management. In good markets and bad, they're paid right off the top—and that can take its toll. Consider, for instance, $10,000 in a fund that charges a 1 percent 12b-1 fee. That translates into an annual charge of *$100 a year*, which is certainly a significant amount of money.

yavuzunlu/Shutterstock.com

Management Fees The management fee is the cost that you incur to hire the professional money managers to run the fund's portfolio of investments. These fees are also assessed annually and usually range from less than 0.5 percent to as much as 3 or 4 percent of assets under management. All funds—whether they're load or no-load, open- or closed-end—have these fees. And like 12b-1 fees, they bear watching because high management fees will take their toll on performance. The size of the management fee is usually unrelated to the fund's performance. In addition to these management fees, some funds may charge an *annual maintenance fee* to help offset the costs of providing service to low-balance accounts.

Keeping Track of Fund Fees and Loads Fortunately, steps have been taken to bring fund fees and loads out into the open. For one thing, fund charges are more widely reported now than they were in the past. Most notably, today you can find detailed information about the types and amounts of fees and charges on just about any mutual fund by going to one of the dozens

---

load fund a fund that charges a fee at time of purchase

low-load mutual fund a fund that has a low purchase fee

back-end load mutual fund a commission charged for redeeming fund shares

no-load mutual fund a fund on which no transaction fees are charged

12b-1 fee an annual fee that's supposed to be used to offset the promotion and selling expenses

management fee a fee paid to the professional money managers who administer a mutual fund's portfolio

Exhibit 13.3

Mutual Fund Quotes

Open-end mutual funds are listed separately from other securities and have their own quotation system; an example is shown here in online quotes from *The Wall Street Journal*. Note that these securities are also quoted in dollars and cents, and that the quotes include not only the fund's NAV but also year-to-date (YTD) returns. Also included in the quotes is an indication of whether the fund charges redemption and/or 12b-1 fees.

Family/Fund	Symbol	NAV	Chg	YTD % Return	3-Year % Chg
American Century A					
CorePls *p*	ACCQX	11.00	−0.01	6.0	3.4
EmgMktA *t*	AEMMX	8.81	0.05	15.8	1.0
DiscGro	ADCVX	19.26	0.14	5.7	7.7
EqMktNtrl *p/r t*	ALIAX	10.88	−0.02	−0.8	0.4
Fidelity Advisor A					
FitRateA r	FFRAX	9.61	0.01	8.4	2.5
GroIncA *p*	FGIRX	25.75	0.09	8.6	6.8
IntCpApA *p*	FCPAX	15.51	0.01	2.6	3.5
MegaCapStock	FGTAX	16.49	0.07	7.0	7.3
RealEstA t	FHEAX	22.92	0.08	4.4	9.3
StrinA	FSTAX	12.11	−0.01	9.8	3.6

American Century Core Plus Fund; class A shares; a fund with both a 12b-1 fee (0.25%) and a front-end load (4.5%).

American Century Emerging Markets Fund, class A shares; a fund with both a 12b-1 fee (0.25%) and a front-end load (5.75%).

American Century Alternatives Equity Market Neutral Fund, class A shares; a fund with a 12b-1 fee (0.25%) and a front-end load fee (5.75%).

Fidelity Advisor International Capital Appreciation Fund; class A shares; a fund with both a 12b-1 fee (0.25%) and a front-end load fee (5.75%)

r—Redemption charge may apply.

p—Distribution costs apply, 12b-1.

t—Footnotes r and p apply.

Source: *The Wall Street Journal*, www.wsj.com/mdc/public/page/2_3048-usmfunds_A-usmfunds.html, data from October 24, 2016. NAV: net asset value. Chg: change in NAV from previous trading day. 3-Year % Change: trailing three-year annualized change.

of Internet sites that report on mutual funds, including **Quicken.com**, **Kiplinger.com**, **Morningstar.com**, and a host of others. Or you could use the mutual fund quotes that appear daily in (most) major newspapers and in *The Wall Street Journal*. For example, take a look at the online quotations in Exhibit 13.3; right after the (abbreviated) name of some funds, you'll find the letters *r*, *p*, or *t*. If you see an *r* after a fund's name, it means that the fund charges some type of redemption fee, or back-end load, when you sell your shares. The use of a *p* means that the fund levies a 12b-1 fee. Finally, a *t* indicates funds that charge redemption fees *and* 12b-1 fees. The quotations, of course, tell you only *what kinds of fees* are charged by the funds; they don't tell you *how much* is charged. What's more, these quotes *tell you nothing about the front-end loads*, if any, charged by the funds. You can access Internet (or other) sources to find out whether a particular fund charges a front-end load or to obtain specifics on any amounts charged.

Mutual funds are required by the SEC to *disclose fully* all their fees and expenses in a standardized, easy-to-understand format. Every fund prospectus must contain, right up front, a fairly detailed *fee table*, which breaks total fund fees into three parts. The first specifies all *shareholder transaction costs*. This section tells you what it's going to cost to buy and sell shares in the mutual fund. The next section lists all *annual operating expenses* of the fund. Showing these expenses as a percentage of average net assets, the fund must break out management fees, those elusive 12b-1 fees, and any other expenses. The third section gives the *total cost over time* of buying, selling, and owning the fund. This part of the table contains both transaction and operating expenses and shows what the total costs would be over hypothetical 1-, 3-, 5-, and 10-year holding periods.

13-1h Buying and Selling Funds

Buying and selling shares of closed-end investment companies or ETFs is no different from buying shares of

Behavioral Biases in Mutual Fund Investing

In theory, rational investors should pursue a simple investment strategy that involves well-diversified, low-expense mutual funds, accompanied by only minimal portfolio rebalancing. The time-tested advice is to choose index mutual funds with low fees and low portfolio turnover. In contrast, current research indicates that many individual investors exhibit the following puzzling behaviors:

- Investors tend to sell winners too quickly and hold losers too long.

- Investors often buy mutual funds with high fees in general and even pay high fees for index funds that passively hold the components of indexes like the S&P 500.

- Individual investors often chase funds with high past returns.

What does behavioral finance research have to say about the above biased behavior?

- **Disposition effect.** People dislike taking losses much more than they enjoy realizing gains. Consequently, they tend to hold assets that have lost value too long and tend to take gains too soon. In mutual fund investing, this bias may encourage some investors to overestimate their expected holding periods and mistakenly select high-expense (front-end load) funds, the effect of which declines with the expected holding period. This often leads to too-frequent trading.

- **Narrow framing.** It's possible that investors buy and sell mutual funds without adequately considering the effects of costs on their *total* portfolio. Similarly, if investors tend to view mutual funds as much safer than buying individual stocks, they may spend less time than they should evaluating mutual fund performance and costs.

- **Representativeness.** There is evidence that investors view recent performance as overly representative of a mutual fund's future performance (despite those warning statements we've probably all seen if we've read a prospectus). This could cause them to buy mutual funds inappropriately, just because of their past records. This bias may be partially explained by Morningstar's rating of funds based on past returns.

So what's the remedy for the above behavioral biases? The answer is clear: education! There is evidence that sophisticated investors are far less likely to fall into these behavioral traps. Sophisticated investors are better informed about key investment principles, understand these behavioral tendencies, are more experienced, and have higher incomes. They use mutual funds effectively, which means that they hold most funds for a long time, avoid high expense funds, and consequently enjoy relatively good performance. And based on what you now know, this could be you.

Source: Adapted from Warren Bailey, Alok Kumar, and David Ng, 2011, "Behavioral Biases of Mutual Fund Investors," *Journal of Financial Economics*, v. 102, pp.1–27.

---

common stock. The transactions are executed through brokers or dealers who handle the orders in the usual way. They're subject to the normal transaction costs and, because they're treated like any other listed or OTC stock, their shares can even be margined or sold short, as discussed in Chapter 11.

The situation is considerably different, however, with *open-end mutual funds*. Such funds can be bought through a discount or full-service broker, or directly from the mutual fund company itself. Most mutual funds allow you to open an account online, and once your account is open and the company has your initial deposit, you are ready to buy and sell shares. Selling shares in a fund is a do-it-yourself affair that simply requires using an online account or an 800 telephone number. When selling, it is wise to see whether your investment company offers the ability to switch funds. A common feature is the ability to go online (or pick up the phone) to move money from one fund to another—the only constraint is that the funds must be managed by the same "family" of funds. Most companies charge little or nothing for these shifts, although funds that offer free exchange privileges often limit the number of times you can switch each year.

13-2 TYPES OF FUNDS AND FUND SERVICES

LO3 Categorizing mutual funds and EFTs according to their investment policies and objectives is widely practiced in the investment industry. This is because it tends to reflect similarities not only in how the funds manage their money but also in their risk and return characteristics. Every fund has a particular stated investment objective, of which the most common are capital appreciation, income, tax-exempt income, preserving investment capital, or some combination thereof.

Some popular types of mutual funds include growth, aggressive growth, value, equity-income, balanced, growth-and-income, bond, money market, index, sector, socially responsible, international, and asset allocation funds. Let's now look at these funds to see what they are and what they have to offer investors. After that, we'll look at the kinds of investor services these funds offer.

13-2a Types of Funds

Growth Funds The objective of a *growth fund* is simple—capital appreciation. As a result, they invest primarily in common stocks with above-average growth potential. Because of the uncertainty concerning

---

Financial Planning Tips

HOW TO CHOOSE THE BEST MUTUAL FUNDS

Choosing the best mutual funds to achieve your financial objectives is mostly about doing your homework and focusing on a few key elements. Here are the steps and the main considerations:

- **Decide how much money you want to invest in mutual funds.** That depends on how much money you can afford to invest, how much money you need in the future, when you need it, and where your other money is invested. For example, are you hoping to fund a child's college education in 18 years, or are you investing for retirement?

- **Decide on your asset allocation.** This depends mostly on the length of time until you need the money and your risk tolerance. Let's say that you're investing for retirement. A reasonable starting point is the common rule of thumb that the percentage in bonds should equal your age, and the residual percentage should be in stocks. So if you're 25, it makes sense to have 25 percent of your money in bonds and 75 percent in stocks. You can fine-tune the percentages based on how comfortable you are with the risk implications of this rule-of-thumb allocation rule.

- **Diversify your investments over different types of mutual funds.** Research supports having some money invested in small-cap and value stocks as well as in both domestic and foreign stocks. For many people, the best choice in each fund category is a low-cost index fund, if available.

- **Put together a list of available mutual funds.** Compare each fund's historical performance with an appropriate benchmark. (Morningstar.com is a convenient source for such comparisons.) Then compare the expense ratios of each fund in the category that you are considering, which show how much the fund's returns are reduced by trading and operating expenses. Obviously, you would prefer the fund with the lowest expense ratio; over time, the higher net return will affect the amount of money in the fund significantly. Similarly, it's helpful to compare mutual funds' turnover ratios, which indicate the percentage of the assets held by the fund that were sold during the year. *Higher turnover ratios usually bring both higher expenses and higher taxes*, which depress net returns in the same way as higher expense ratios.

- **Avoid "dog" funds.** Many people just pick the fund with the best historical performance and figure that's the star. Doesn't that make sense—who wouldn't want to reach for the stars? However, that strategy is usually misguided. Although it's hard to identify the future stars, past performance does appear to be a reliable way of identifying the true losers. The worst funds often stay at the bottom of their category in terms of performance for years. And that can be measured using their returns, expense ratios, and turnover. So here's the best approach: *Don't search for the stars—just avoid the dogs!*

value funds are often viewed as a viable alternative for relatively conservative investors who are looking for the attractive returns that common stocks have to offer but want to keep share price volatility and investment risk in check.

Equity-Income Funds *Equity-income funds* emphasize current income, which they provide by investing primarily in high-yielding common stocks. Preserving capital is also a goal of these funds—as is increasing capital gains, although it's not their primary objective. These funds invest heavily in high-grade, common stocks, some convertible securities and preferred stocks, and occasionally even junk bonds. Because of their emphasis on dividends and current income, these funds tend to hold higher-quality securities that are subject to less price volatility than seen in the market as a whole. They're generally viewed as a fairly low-risk way of investing in stocks.

their future capital gains, growth funds are fairly risky. They're usually viewed as long-term investments that are most suitable for the aggressive investor who wants to build capital and has little interest in current income.

Aggressive Growth Funds *Aggressive growth funds* are highly speculative investments that seek large profits from capital gains. In many ways, they're really an extension of the growth fund concept. Many are fairly small with average assets under management of less than $300 million. They often buy stocks of small, unseasoned companies, stocks with relatively high price/earnings multiples, and stocks whose prices are highly volatile. All this is designed, of course, to yield big returns. However, aggressive growth funds are perhaps the most volatile of all the fund types.

Value Funds *Value funds* invest in stocks considered to be *undervalued* by the market. Consequently, the funds look for stocks that are fundamentally sound but have yet to be discovered and as such remain undervalued by the market. In stark contrast to growth funds, value funds look for stocks with relatively low price/earnings (P/E) ratios, high dividend yields, and moderate amounts of financial leverage. They prefer undiscovered companies that offer the potential for growth.

Value investing involves extensive evaluation of corporate financial statements and any other documents that will help fund managers *uncover value before the rest of the market does*—that's the key to getting low P/Es. And the approach seems to work: Even though value investing is generally regarded as being *less risky* than growth investing, the long-term returns to investors in value funds are quite competitive with those earned from growth or even aggressive growth funds. Thus,

Balanced Funds *Balanced funds* are so named because they tend to hold a balanced portfolio of both stocks and bonds, and they do so to generate a well-balanced return of current income and long-term capital gains. In many ways, they're like equity-income funds, except that balanced funds usually put much more into fixed-income securities: generally they keep 30 to 40 percent (and sometimes more) of their portfolios in bonds. The bonds are used primarily to provide current income, and stocks are selected mainly for their long-term growth potential. Balanced funds tend to confine their investing to high-grade securities and therefore are usually considered a relatively safe form of investing—one that can earn you a competitive rate of return without a lot of price volatility.

Life-cycle or *target-date funds* are balanced funds that automatically change the asset allocation from more to less equity exposure as an investor ages. Importantly, these funds should not all be considered the same because the rate at which the asset allocation becomes more conservative over time, the so-called "glide path," can vary greatly among funds.

Growth-and-Income Funds Like balanced funds, *growth-and-income funds* seek a balanced return made up of current income and long-term capital gains, but they put greater emphasis on growth of capital. Moreover, unlike balanced funds, growth-and-income funds put most of their money into equities. They tend to confine their investing to high-quality issues, so you can expect to find a lot of growth-oriented, blue-chip stocks in their portfolios along with a fair number of high-quality income stocks. These funds do involve a fair amount of risk if for no other reason than their emphasis on stocks and capital gains.

Bond Funds As their name implies, *bond funds* invest in various kinds of fixed-income securities. Income is their primary investment objective, although they don't ignore capital gains. There are three important advantages to buying shares in bond funds rather than investing directly in bonds. First, bond funds generally are more liquid. Second, they offer a cost-effective way of achieving a high degree of diversification in an otherwise expensive investment (most bonds carry minimum denominations of $1,000 to $5,000 or more in the United States). And third, bond funds automatically reinvest interest and other income, thereby allowing the investor to earn fully compounded rates of return.

Bond funds are considered to be fairly conservative, but they're not totally without risk because the prices of the bonds held in their portfolios will fluctuate with changing interest rates. In 2016, U.S. bond mutual funds had about $3.72 trillion under management, while bond ETFs had about $420.7 billion under management. Listed below are some of the different types of bond funds currently available in the market:

▶ **Government bond funds,** which invest in U.S. Treasury and agency securities.

▶ **Mortgage-backed bond funds,** which put their money into various types of mortgage-backed securities.

▶ **High-grade corporate bond funds,** which invest chiefly in high-grade securities rated triple-B or better.

▶ **High-yield corporate bond funds,** which are risky investments that buy *junk bonds* for the yields that they offer, which can be higher than standard bonds.

▶ **Convertible bond funds,** which invest in securities that can be converted or exchanged into common stocks.

▶ **Municipal bond funds,** which invest in tax-exempt securities.

▶ **Intermediate-term bond funds,** which invest in bonds with maturities of 7 to 10 years or less.

Money Market Mutual Funds Money market mutual funds invest in a widely diversified portfolio of short-term money market instruments. These funds are very popular with investors, and for good reason: They give investors with modest amounts of capital access to the higher-yielding end of the money market, where many instruments require minimum investments of $100,000 or more. Money market mutual funds in the United States hold about $2.72 *trillion* in assets.

There are several different kinds of money market mutual funds. **General-purpose money funds** essentially invest in any and all types of money market investments, from Treasury bills to corporate commercial paper and bank certificates of deposit. They invest their money wherever they can find attractive, short-term returns. Most money funds are of this type. The **tax-exempt money fund** limits its investments to tax-exempt municipal securities with very short (30- to 90-day) maturities. Because their income is free from federal income tax, they appeal predominantly to investors in high tax brackets. **Government securities money funds** eliminate any risk of default by confining their investments to Treasury bills (T-bills) and other short-term securities of the U.S. government or its agencies (such as the Government National Mortgage Association [GNMA]).

Money market funds are highly liquid investments that are low in risk because they're virtually immune to capital loss. However, the interest income that they produce will follow interest rate conditions, so the returns to shareholders are subject to the ups and downs of market interest rates.

Index Funds "If you can't beat 'em, join 'em." That's the idea behind the *index fund*, a type of fund that buys and holds a portfolio of stocks (or bonds) equivalent to those in a market index such as the S&P 500. An index fund that's trying to match the S&P 500, for example, would hold the same 500 stocks that are held in that index and in the same proportion. Rather than trying to beat the market, *index funds simply try to match the market*—that is, to match the performance of the index on which the fund is based. They do this through low-cost investment management. In many cases, the whole portfolio is run almost entirely by a computer that matches the fund's holdings with those of the targeted index.

Besides the S&P 500, a number of other market indexes are used, including the S&P MidCap 400, Russell 2000, and Wilshire 5000, as well as value stock indexes, growth stock indexes, international stock indexes, and even bond indexes. Index funds form a part of the overall mutual fund market, but they comprise the vast majority of ETFs.

general-purpose money fund a money fund that invests in virtually any type of short-term investment vehicle

tax-exempt money fund a money fund that limits its investments to short-term, tax-exempt municipal securities

government securities money fund a money fund that limits its investments to short-term securities of the U.S. government and its agencies

The investment approach of index funds is buy and hold. In fact, about the only time there's a change to the portfolio of an index fund is when the targeted market index alters its "market basket" of securities. A pleasant by-product of this buy-and-hold approach is that the funds have low portfolio turnover rates and therefore little in *realized* capital gains. As a result, aside from a modest amount of dividend income, these funds produce little taxable income from year to year, which leads many high-income investors to view them as a type of tax-sheltered investment. But these funds provide something else—they produce *highly competitive returns* for investors! It's tough to outperform the market consistently, so these don't even try. The net result is that, on average, index funds tend to produce better returns than do most other types of stock funds.

Sector Funds As the name implies, a *sector fund* restricts its investments to a particular sector of the market. These funds concentrate their investment holdings in the one or more industries that make up the targeted sector. For example, a *health care* sector fund confines its investments to those industries that make up this segment of the market: drug companies, hospital management firms, medical suppliers, and biotech concerns. The underlying investment objective of most sector funds is *capital gains*. The idea behind sector funds is that the really attractive returns come from small segments of the market. So, rather than diversifying a portfolio across wide segments of the market, put your money where the action is. Some popular sector funds invest in real estate (real estate investment trusts, or REITs), technology, financial services, natural resources, electronics, and telecommunications.

Socially Responsible Funds For some investors, the security selection process doesn't end with bottom lines, P/E ratios, and growth rates. Rather, it also includes the *active, explicit consideration of moral, ethical, and environmental issues*. The idea is that social concerns should play just as big a role in the investment decision as profits and other financial matters. **Socially responsible funds (SRFs)** consider only what they view as socially responsible companies for inclusion in their portfolios. If a company doesn't meet certain moral, ethical, or environmental tests, they simply won't consider buying the stock, no matter how good the bottom line looks. These funds generally abstain from investing in companies that derive revenues from tobacco, alcohol, or gambling; that are weapons contractors; or that operate nuclear power plants. They also tend to favor firms

wk1003mike/Shutterstock.com

that produce "responsible" products and services, have positive environmental records, and are socially responsive to the communities in which they operate. In the United States, at least $7 trillion is invested in strategies related to environmental, social, and corporate governance (ESG) causes.

International Funds In searching for higher returns and better diversification, American investors have shown increased interest in foreign securities. The mutual fund industry has responded with a wide array of **international funds**. Technically, the term *international fund* is used to describe a type of fund that *invests exclusively in foreign securities*, often confining the fund's activities to specific geographical regions (such as Mexico, Australia, Europe, or the Pacific Rim). In contrast, another class of international funds known as *global funds* invest not only in foreign securities *but also in U.S. companies*—usually multinational firms. As a rule, global funds provide more diversity and, with access to both foreign and domestic markets, can go wherever the action is.

Asset Allocation Funds The most important decision an investor can make is where to allocate his or her investment assets. This is known as *asset allocation*, and it involves deciding how you're going to divide your investments among different types of securities.

Because many individual investors have a tough time making asset allocation decisions, the mutual fund industry has created a product to do the job for them. Known as *asset allocation funds*, these funds spread investors' money across all different types of

socially responsible fund (SRF) a fund that invests only in companies meeting certain moral, ethical, and/or environmental criteria

international fund a mutual fund that does all or most of its investing in foreign securities markets. That is, whereas most mutual funds concentrate on one type of investment—whether it be stocks, bonds, or money market securities—asset allocation funds put money into all these markets. They're for people who want to hire fund managers not only to select individual securities for them, but also to make the strategic decision of how to allocate money among the various markets.

Here's how many asset allocation funds work. The money manager will establish a desired allocation mix, which might look something like this: 50 percent of the portfolio goes to U.S. stocks, 10 percent to foreign securities, 30 percent to bonds, and 10 percent to money market securities. Securities are then purchased for the fund in this proportion, and the overall portfolio maintains the desired mix. *As market conditions change over time, the asset allocation mix also changes.* Of course, there's no assurance that the money manager will make the right moves at the right time, but that's the idea behind these funds.

13-2b Services Offered by Mutual Funds

Ask most investors why they buy a particular mutual fund, and they'll probably tell you that the fund offers the kind of income and return they're looking for. Now, no one would question the importance of return in the investment decision, but there are other reasons for investing in mutual funds, not the least of which are the valuable services that they provide. Some of the most sought-after *mutual fund services* are automatic investment and reinvestment plans, regular income programs, conversion privileges, and retirement programs.

Automatic Investment Plans It takes money to make money, and for an investor that means being able to accumulate the capital to put into the market. Not to worry—most mutual funds provide a program that makes savings and capital accumulation as painless as possible. The **automatic investment plan** allows fund shareholders to funnel fixed amounts of money *from their paychecks or bank accounts* automatically into a mutual fund. It's much like a payroll deduction plan that treats savings a lot

automatic investment plan an automatic savings program that enables an investor to channel a set amount of money systematically into a given mutual fund

automatic reinvestment plan a plan that gives shareholders the option of electing to have dividends and capital gains distributions reinvested in additional fund shares

like insurance coverage—that is, just as insurance premiums are deducted automatically from your paycheck (or bank account), so too are investments to your mutual fund.

Just about every major fund group offers some kind of automatic investment plan. To enroll, you simply fill out a form authorizing the fund to transfer a set amount (usually it has to be a minimum of $25 to $100 per period) from your bank account or paycheck at regular intervals—typically monthly or quarterly. Once enrolled, you'll be buying shares in the funds of your choice every month or quarter (most funds deal in fractional shares). Of course, if it's a load fund, you'll still have to pay normal sales charges on your periodic investments.

Automatic Reinvestment Plans *Automatic reinvestment is one of the real draws of mutual funds,* and it's offered by just about every open-ended mutual fund. While automatic investment plans deal with money shareholders put into a fund, **automatic reinvestment plans** deal with the dividends and other distributions that the funds pay to their shareholders. Much like the dividend reinvestment plans we looked at with stocks, the automatic reinvestment plans of mutual funds enable you to keep all your capital fully employed. Through this service, dividend and capital gains income is *used to buy additional shares in the fund automatically,* which enables the investor to earn a fully compounded rate of return. Keep in mind, however, that even though you reinvest your dividends and capital gains, the Internal Revenue Service (IRS) still treats them as cash receipts and taxes them in the year that they're paid.

The important point is that, by plowing earnings (reinvested dividends and capital gains distributions) back into a fund, investors can put this money to work generating even more earnings. Indeed, the effects of these plans on total accumulated capital over the long haul can be substantial. Exhibit 13.4 shows the long-term impact of one such plan. (These are the actual performance numbers for a real mutual fund—Fidelity Contrafund, in this case.) In the illustration, we assume that the investor starts with $10,000 and, except for reinvesting dividends and capital gains distributions, *adds no new capital over time.* Even so, the initial investment of $10,000 grew to some $32,279 over the roughly 15-year period from 2001 to October 2016 (which, by the way, amounts to a compounded rate of return of about 7.7 percent). Clearly, so long as care is taken in selecting the fund, *attractive benefits can be derived from the systematic accumulation of capital offered by automatic reinvestment plans.*

Exhibit 13.4

Effects of Reinvesting Income

Reinvesting dividends and/or capital gains can have tremendous effects on your investment position. This graph shows the results of a hypothetical investor who initially invested $10,000 and reinvested all dividends and capital gains distributions in additional fund shares. No adjustment has been made for any fees or for income taxes payable by the shareholder, which would be appropriate provided that the fund was held in a tax-deferred account like an individual retirement account (IRA) or a 401(k) account. This example is for the Fidelity Contrafund (FCNTX).

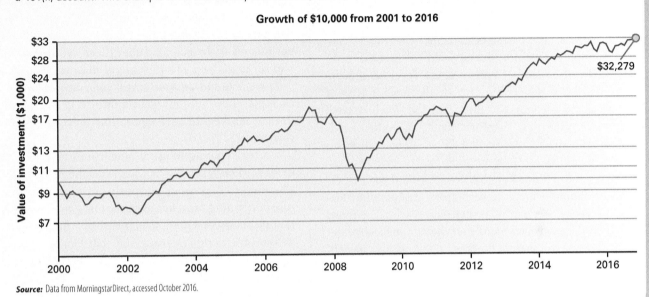

Growth of $10,000 from 2001 to 2016

$32,279

Source: Data from MorningstarDirect, accessed October 2016.

Regular Income Automatic reinvestment plans are great for the long-term investor, but how about the investor who's looking for a steady stream of income? Mutual funds also have a service to meet this need. It's called a **systematic withdrawal plan**, and it's offered by most open-ended funds. Once enrolled in one of these plans, you'll automatically receive a predetermined amount of money every month or quarter. Depending on how well the fund is doing, the annual return generated by the fund may actually be greater than the withdrawals, thus allowing the investor not only to receive regular income but also to enjoy an automatic accumulation of *additional* shares in the plan. On the other hand, if the fund isn't performing well the withdrawals could eventually deplete the original investment.

Conversion Privileges Sometimes investors find it necessary to switch out of one fund and into another; for example, their investment objectives may change or the investment environment itself may have changed. **Conversion (or exchange) privileges** conveniently and economically meet the needs of these investors. Investment companies that offer a number of different funds to the investing public—known as *fund families*—usually provide conversion privileges that enable shareholders to move easily from one fund to another; this can be done either online or by phone. The only limitation is that the investor must confine the switches to the same *family* of funds. For example, an investor can switch from a Fidelity growth fund to a Fidelity income fund, or to any other fund managed by Fidelity.

Conversion privileges are attractive because they permit investors to manage their holdings more aggressively by allowing them to move in and out of funds as the investment environment changes. There's one major drawback: although you never see the cash, the exchange of shares from one fund to another is regarded as a sale followed by the purchase of a new security. As a result, if any capital gains exist at the time of the exchange, the investor is liable for the taxes on that profit.

Retirement Plans Government legislation permits self-employed individuals to divert part of their income into self-directed *retirement*

systematic withdrawal plan a plan offered by mutual funds that allows shareholders to be paid specified amounts of money each period

conversion (or exchange) privilege a feature that allows investors to switch from one mutual fund to another within a family of funds

Lightspring/Shutterstock.com

plans. And all working Americans, whether they're self-employed or not, are allowed to establish individual retirement accounts—in the form of either a standard, tax-deductible IRA or the newest type of retirement account, the Roth IRA (all of which we'll look at in the next chapter). Today, all mutual funds provide a special service that allows individuals to set up tax-deferred retirement programs quickly and easily as either IRA or Keogh accounts—or, through their place of employment, to participate in a qualified, tax-sheltered retirement plan such as a 401(k). The funds set up the plans and handle all the administrative details so that the shareholders can take full advantage of available tax savings.

13-3 MAKING MUTUAL FUND AND ETF INVESTMENTS

LO4, LO5 Suppose you have money to invest and are trying to select the right place to put it. You obviously want to pick an investment that not only meets your idea of an acceptable risk, but also generates an attractive rate of return. The problem is that you have to choose from literally thousands of investments. Sound like a "mission impossible"? Well, that's what a typical investor is up against when trying to select a suitable mutual fund. But if you approach the problem systematically, it may not be so formidable. For, as we'll see, it is possible to whittle down the list of alternatives by matching your investment needs with the investment objectives of the funds.

13-3a The Selection Process

When it comes to mutual funds and ETFs, one question that every investor must answer is: Why invest in a mutual fund or an ETF to begin with?

> Mutual funds and ETFs provide far more diversification than most investors could ever achieve on their own.

Why not just go it alone (i.e., buy individual stocks and bonds directly)? For beginning investors, or investors with limited capital, the answer is simple— mutual funds and ETFs provide far more diversification than most investors could ever achieve on their own, plus investors get the help of professional money managers—and at a reasonable cost to boot.

The competitive returns offered by mutual funds and ETFs have to be a factor with many investors, but so do the services they provide. Many investors will use part of their capital to buy and sell individual securities on their own, and they'll use the rest *to buy mutual funds or ETFs that invest in areas they don't fully understand or aren't well informed about*. For example, they'll use mutual funds or ETFs to get into foreign markets or as a way to buy mortgage-backed securities.

After deciding to use mutual funds or ETFs, the investor then must decide which specific funds to buy. The selection process obviously plays an important role in defining the amount of success you'll have with mutual funds or ETFs. Given that you have an asset allocation strategy in place and that you're trying to select funds compatible with your targeted mix, the selection process begins with an assessment of your own investment needs. This sets the tone for your investment program. Many of these same principles also apply when choosing mutual funds and ETFs to include in a 401(k) retirement plan.

Objectives and Motives for Using Funds *The place to start is with your own investment objectives.* In other words, why do you want to invest in a mutual fund or an ETF, and what are you looking for in a fund? Obviously, an attractive rate of return would be desirable, but there's also the matter of ensuring a tolerable amount of risk exposure. More than likely, you'll discover that certain types of funds are more appealing to you than others.

Another important factor is the intended use of the mutual fund or ETF. That is, do you want to invest in mutual funds or ETFs as a way of *accumulating capital* over an extended time, to *speculate* with your money in the hopes of generating high rates of return, or to *conserve your capital* by investing in low-risk securities where preservation of capital is no less important than return on capital? Finally, there's the matter of the services provided. If you're particularly interested in some services, be sure to look for them in the funds that you select. Having assessed what you're looking for in a fund, now you can look at what the funds have to offer.

What Funds Have to Offer The ideal mutual fund or ETF has three characteristics:

1. achieve maximum capital growth when security prices rise;
2. provide complete protection against capital loss when prices decline, and
3. achieve high levels of current income at all times. Unfortunately, such funds don't exist.

Instead, just as each individual has a set of investment needs, each fund has its own *investment objective*, its own *manner or style of operation*, and its own *range of services*.

These three factors are useful in helping you assess investment alternatives. But where does the investor look for such information? One obvious place is the fund's *profile* (or its prospectus), where information on investment objectives, portfolio composition, management, and past performance can be obtained. In addition, there's a wealth of useful information in Morningstar's online (**http://morningstar.com**) and software-based products, *The Value Line Fund Advisor,* and *The Value Line ETF Survey* (these reports are similar to its stock reports, but they apply to both mutual funds and ETFs). These sources publish a wealth of operating and performance statistics in a convenient, easy-to-read format. Services are also available that provide background information and assessments on a wide variety of funds. And, of course, all sorts of performance statistics are available on the Internet. Exhibit 13.5 provides an example of the extensive information made available by Morningstar on a popular mutual fund, Fidelity Contrafund (ticker FCNTX).

Whittling Down the Alternatives At this point, fund selection becomes a process of elimination as you weigh your investment needs against the types of funds available. Many funds can be eliminated from consideration simply because they don't meet your needs. Some may be too risky; others may be unsuitable as a storehouse of value. Still others may have prohibitively high investment management fees. So, rather than trying to evaluate thousands of different funds, you can use a process of elimination to narrow the list down to two or three *types* of funds that best match your investment (and asset allocation) needs. From here, you can whittle the list down a bit more by introducing other constraints. For

Go to Smart Sites

Before investing in ETFs, visit Morningstar to learn more about index funds, get price quotes, and find the right ETF for your portfolio.

example, you may want to deal only in no-load or low-load funds, or you may be seeking certain fund services that are important to your investment goals.

Now we're ready to introduce the final (but certainly not the least important) element in the selection process: *the fund's investment performance*. Useful information includes (1) how the fund has performed over the past five to seven years; (2) the type of return (income vs. capital gains) after investment management fees it has generated in good markets as well as bad; (3) the level of dividend and capital gains distributions, which is an important indication not only of how much current income the fund distributes annually, but also of the fund's *tax efficiency* (funds with low dividends and low asset turnovers typically expose their shareholders to lower taxes and consequently have higher tax-efficiency ratings), and (4) the level of investment stability that the fund has enjoyed over time (or, put another way, the amount of volatility/risk in the fund's return). By evaluating such information, you can identify some of the more promising mutual funds—those that not only offer the investment objectives and services you seek, but also provide the best payoffs.

Stick with No-Load or Low-Load Mutual Funds There's a longstanding "debate" in the mutual fund industry regarding load funds and no-load funds. The question is, do load funds add enough value to overcome the

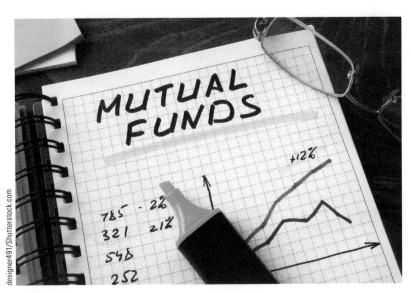

Exhibit 13.5

Release date 10-25-2016

Fidelity® Contrafund® Fund FCNTX

Morningstar Analyst Rating
🛡 Silver

NAV $	NAV Day Change %	Yield TTM %	Total Assets $ Bil	Status	Min. Inv.	Load	Expenses	Morningstar Rating™	Category	Investment Style
102.52	↑0.75 | 0.74	0.31	108.4	Open	$2,500	None	0.70%		Large Growth	▦ Large Growth

Growth of 10,000 10-24-2006 - 10-24-2016

- ■ Fidelity® Contrafund® Fund $22,224.86
- Large Growth $18,969.17
- S&P 500 TR USD $19,364.09

3 Year Average Morningstar Risk Measures

Risk vs. Category (1482) — Low
Return vs. Category (1482) — +Avg

Low Avg High

Investment Strategy

The investment seeks capital appreciation. The fund normally invests primarily in common stocks. It invests in securities of companies whose value the advisor believes is not fully recognized by the public. The fund invests in domestic and foreign issuers. It invests in either "growth" stocks or "value" stocks or both. The fund uses fundamental analysis of factors such as each issuer's financial condition and industry position, as well as market and economic conditions to select investments.

Pillars

Process	⊕	Positive
Performance	⊕	Positive
People	⊕	Positive
Parent	⊕	Positive
Price	⊕	Positive
Rating		🛡 Silver

Performance 10-24-2016

	YTD	1 Mo	1 Yr	3Yr Ann	5Yr Ann	10Yr Ann
Growth of 10,000	10,439	10,066	10,388	12,795	18,640	22,225
Fund	4.39	0.66	3.88	8.56	13.26	8.31
+/- S&P 500 TR USD	-2.72	1.13	-2.09	-0.80	-0.55	1.48
+/- Category	1.38	0.84	1.19	0.94	0.88	1.13
% Rank in Cat	28	12	32	37	32	23
# of Funds in Cat	1,596	1,629	1,576	1,431	1,238	890

* Currency is displayed in BASE

Style Map

⦿ Weighted Average of holdings

● 75% of fund's stock holdings

Giant / Large / Medium / Small / Micro

Deep Val / Core Val / Core / Core Grow / High Grow

Top Holdings 08-31-2016

	Weight %	Last Price	Day Chg %	52 Week Range
⊖ Facebook Inc A	6.12	132.31 BASE	-0.70 ↓	89.37 - 133.50
⊖ Berkshire Hathaway Inc A	4.83	— BASE	-0.18 ↓	186,900.00 - 226,490.00
⊖ Amazon.com Inc	3.87	834.70 BASE	-0.37 ↓	474.00 - 847.21
⊖ Alphabet Inc A	3.47	827.55 BASE	-0.96 ↓	672.66 - 838.50
⊖ Alphabet Inc C	3.07	806.28 BASE	-0.85 ↓	663.06 - 816.68
% Assets in Top 5 Holdings	21.35			

⊕ Increase   ⊖ Decrease   ☆ New to Portfolio

Asset Allocation

	% Net	% Short	% Long	Bench mark	Cat Avg
● Cash	0.64	0.03	0.67	0.00	2.10
● US Stock	90.82	0.00	90.82	99.96	92.34
● Non US Stock	7.40	0.00	7.40	0.04	5.45
● Bond	0.05	0.00	0.05	0.00	0.03
● Other	1.10	0.00	1.10	0.00	0.07

Top Sectors 08-31-2016

	Fund	3 Yr High	3 Yr Low	Cat Avg	
▦ Technology	30.86	30.86	23.03	26.61	■ Fund ▼ Cat Avg
▦ Consumer Cyclical	18.58	19.63	14.68	17.73	
▦ Financial Services	17.48	21.53	17.48	9.76	
▦ Healthcare	12.42	18.98	12.42	17.76	
▦ Industrials	6.47	8.25	6.47	10.17	

0 10 20 30 40

Management

	Start Date
William Danoff	09-17-1990

Dividend and Capital Gains Distributions

Distribution Date	Distribution NAV	Long-Term Capital Gain	Short-Term Captial Gain	Return of Capital	Dividend Income	Distribution Total
02-05-2016	88.14	0.6200	0.0000	0.0000	0.0100	0.6400
12-11-2015	97.64	4.0100	0.0000	0.0000	0.3100	4.3200
02-06-2015	97.92	0.9500	0.0000	0.0000	0.0000	0.9500
12-12-2014	96.19	5.9200	0.0000	0.0000	0.2500	6.1700
02-07-2014	94.21	0.9700	0.0000	0.0000	0.0000	0.9700

load fees? And if not, why pay the load charges? The evidence indicates that load fund returns generally aren't, on a risk-adjusted basis, any better than the returns from no-load funds. In fact, the funds with abnormally high loads and 12(b)-1 fees often produce returns that are far *less* than what you can get from no-loads after taking risk into account! That shouldn't be surprising, though, because big load charges and/or 12b-1 fees do nothing more than *reduce your invested capital*, thus reducing the amount of money you have working for you. In fact, the only way that a load fund can overcome this limitation is to *produce superior returns*—which is not easy to do, year in and year out. Granted, a handful of load funds have produced attractive returns over extended periods, but they're the exception rather than the rule.

Obviously, it's in your best interest to pay close attention to load charges (and other fees) whenever you're considering an investment in a mutual fund. In order to maximize returns, *you should seriously consider sticking to no-load funds, or low-loads* (funds with total load charges, including 12b-1 fees, of no more than 1 percent). At the very least, you should consider a more expensive load fund *only* if it has a much better performance record (and offers more return potential) than a less expensive fund.

13-3b Getting a Handle on Fund Performance

If you were to believe all the sales literature, you'd think there was no way you could go wrong by investing in mutual funds or ETFs. Just put your money into one of these funds and let the good times roll! Unfortunately, the hard facts of life are that *when it comes to investing, performance is never guaranteed*. And that applies just as much to mutual funds as it does to any other form of investing—perhaps even more so because, with mutual funds, the single variable driving a fund's market price and return behavior is the performance of its securities portfolio.

Measuring Fund Performance Any mutual fund (open- or closed-end) or any ETF has three potential sources of return: (1) dividend income, (2) capital gains distribution, and (3) change in the fund's share price. Depending on the type of fund, some will derive more income from one source than another. For example, we'd normally expect income-oriented funds to generate higher dividend income than capital gains–oriented funds do. Mutual funds regularly publish reports that recap investment performance. One such report is *The Summary of Income and Capital Changes*; an example of which is provided in Exhibit 13.6. Of interest to us in

this discussion is the top part of the report (from "Net asset value, beginning of period" through "Net asset value, end of period"—lines 1 to 10). This part shows the amount of dividend income and capital gains distributed to the shareholders, along with any change in NAV.

Dividend income (see line 7 of Exhibit 13.6) is the amount derived from the dividend and interest income earned on the security holdings of the mutual fund. When the fund receives dividends or interest payments, it passes these on to shareholders in the form of dividend payments. Because the mutual fund itself is tax exempt, any taxes due on dividend earnings are payable by the individual investor. For funds that are *not* held in tax-deferred accounts [examples include IRAs and 401(k)s], the amount of taxes due on dividends will depend on the source of such dividends. That is, *if these distributions are derived from dividends earned on the fund's common stock holdings, then they're subject to the preferential tax rate of 20 percent or less*. But if these distributions are

EXAMPLE: Calculating the Approximate Yield on a Mutual Fund A good way of measuring performance is to describe mutual fund returns based on the three major sources of return noted previously—dividends earned, capital gains distributions received, and change in share price. These payoffs can be converted to a convenient return figure by using the standard *approximate yield* formula that was introduced in Chapter 12. The calculations necessary for finding such a return measure can be shown using the 2016 figures from Exhibit 13.6. Referring to the exhibit, we can see that this hypothetical, no-load fund paid $0.55 per share in dividends and another $1.75 in capital gains distributions; also, its price (NAV) at the beginning of the year (i.e., at the end of 2016) of $24.47 rose to $29.14 by the end of the year (see lines 1 and 10, respectively). Putting this data into the familiar approximate yield formula, we see that the hypothetical mutual fund provided an annual rate of return of 26 percent.

$$\text{Approximate yield} = \frac{\text{Dividends and capital gains distributions} + \left[\dfrac{\text{Ending price} - \text{Beginning price}}{\text{Length of time period}}\right]}{\left[\dfrac{\text{Ending price} + \text{Beginning price}}{2}\right]}$$

$$= \frac{(\$0.55 + \$1.75) + \left[\dfrac{\$29.14 - \$24.47}{1}\right]}{\left[\dfrac{\$29.14 + \$24.47}{2}\right]}$$

$$= \frac{\$2.30 + \$4.67}{\$26.80} = \frac{\$6.97}{\$26.80} = 26.0 \text{ percent}$$

Exhibit 13.6

A Summary of Mutual Fund Income and Capital Changes

The return on a mutual fund is made up of (1) the (net) investment income the fund earns from dividends and interest and (2) the realized and unrealized capital gains the fund earns on its security transactions. Mutual funds provide such information to their shareholders in a standardized format (like the statement here) that highlights, among other things, the amount of income, expenses, and capital gains generated by the fund.

		2016	2015	2014
1.	**Net asset value, beginning of period:**	$ 24.47	$ 27.03	$ 24.26
2.	**Income from investment operations:**			
3.	Net investment income	$ 0.60	$ 0.66	$ 0.50
4.	Net gains on securities (realized and unrealized)	6.37	(1.74)	3.79
5.	Total from investment operations	6.97	(1.08)	4.29
6.	**Less distributions:**			
7.	Dividends from net investment income	($ 0.55)	($ 0.64)	($ 0.50)
8.	Distributions from realized gains	(1.75)	(.84)	(1.02)
9.	Total distributions	(2.30)	(1.48)	(1.52)
10.	**Net asset value, end of period:**	$ 29.14	$ 24.47	$ 27.03
11.	**Total return:**	28.48%	(4.00%)	17.68%
12.	**Ratios/supplemental data:**			
13.	Net assets, end of period ($000)	$307,951	$153,378	$108,904
14.	Ratio of expenses to average net assets	1.04%	0.85%	0.94%
15.	Ratio of net investment income to average net assets	1.47%	2.56%	2.39%
16.	Portfolio turnover rate*	85%	144%	74%

*Portfolio turnover rate measures the number of shares bought and sold by the fund against the total number of shares held in the fund's portfolio; a high turnover rate (e.g., exceeding 100%) would mean the fund has been doing a lot of trading.

derived from interest earnings on bonds, dividends from REITs, or dividends from most types of preferred stocks, then such dividends *do not qualify for preferential tax treatment* and instead are taxed as ordinary income (see Chapter 3 for details).

Capital gains distributions (see line 8) work on the same principle as dividends, except that they're derived from the *capital gains actually earned* by the fund. Note that these distributions apply only to *realized* capital gains—that is, where the securities holdings were actually sold and capital gains actually earned. *Unrealized* capital gains (or "paper profits") make up the third and final element in a mutual fund's return and represent the profit that shareholders would receive (and are entitled to) if the fund were to sell its holdings.

Evaluating ETF Performance ETFs and mutual funds are similar in that their prices depend on the value of the funds' underlying investments. Both have NAVs and depend on dividends and capital gains to generate returns. So let's focus on the aspects that are particularly important in ETF performance evaluation. As discussed previously, while there are some actively managed ETFs, the vast majority are designed to replicate an index. So now we'll consider the issues associated with evaluating the index-based form of ETF.

The primary reason for investing in an index-based ETF, of course, is to replicate the performance of the index. It follows that an important aspect of ETF performance is how well it tracks the performance of the underlying index. You can determine this by checking the so-called R-Squared (R^2) statistical measure, which shows how much of the variability in an ETF's total returns is explained by the variability in the total returns of the underlying index. The R^2 varies between 0 percent and a maximum of 100 percent. Obviously, the higher the R^2, the closer is the relationship between the ETF and the associated target index. It's also wise to check how the ETF's expense ratio compares with reasonable benchmarks.

Consider the example of the PowerShares QQQ ETF (QQQ). This ETF is designed to replicate the performance of the NASDAQ 100 index, which includes

CALCULATOR KEYSTROKES

You can just as easily find the *exact return* on this investment with a handheld financial calculator. Here's what you'd do: Using *annual compounding*, to find the return on this mutual fund for 2016, we use the same input data as given before. Namely, we start with a price at the beginning of the year of $24.47; add in total dividends and capital gains distributions of $2.30 a share (i.e., $0.55 + $1.75); and then, using a year-end price of $29.14, we enter the keystrokes shown below, where:

N = number of years you hold the fund

PV = the *initial* price of the fund (entered as a *negative number*)

PMT = *total* amount of dividends and capital gains distributions received

FV = the *ending* price of the fund

Note that our computed return (of 28.48 percent) is exactly the same as the "Total Return" shown on line 11 of Exhibit 13.6—that's because this is basically the same procedure that the mutual funds must use to report their return performance. The approximate yield measure (26 percent) may be close to the actual return, but clearly it's not close enough for fund-reporting purposes.

CALCULATOR

Inputs	Functions
1	N
−24.47	PV
2.30	PMT
29.14	FV
	CPT
	I/Y
Solution	
28.48	

See Appendix E for details.

the 100 largest domestic and international nonfinancial firms trading on the NASDAQ stock exchange. In October 2016, Morningstar reported that the R^2 of the QQQ ETF relative to the closely related, best-fitting Morningstar large-growth index over the last three years was 93.24 percent. This is a very tight fit. And Morningstar indicated that the net expense ratio for the QQQ ETF was only 0.20 percent, while the investment style category average was 0.37 percent, which is higher than the QQQ ETF. Thus, an investor wanting exposure to the large, nonfinancial, technology, growth stocks that characterize the NASDAQ 100 and Morningstar's related index could rest assured that the QQQ ETF replicates the performance of those indices well, with relatively low expenses.

What About Future Performance? There's no question that approximate yield and return on investment are simple yet highly effective measures that capture all the important elements of mutual fund and ETF returns. Looking at past performance is one thing, but what about the future? Ideally, we'd want to evaluate the same three elements of return over the future much as we did for the past. The trouble is, when it comes to the future performance of a mutual fund or an ETF, it's difficult—if not impossible—to get a handle on what the *future* holds for dividends, capital gains, and NAV. The reason is that a mutual fund's or an ETF's future investment performance is directly linked to the future makeup of its securities portfolio, which is impossible to predict.

> **YOU CAN DO IT NOW: How to Choose the Best ETF for You** Do ETFs sound right for you but you're not sure how to find the best ETF? Check out the ETF Selector provided on the Seeking Alpha site: **http://seekingalpha.com/page/etf-finder**. It provides a list of ETFs by asset class, explains how to use them, and provides links to articles that discuss key investor issues. You can **do it now**.

So where do you look for insight into the future? The key factors apply to the evaluation of both mutual funds and ETFs. First, carefully consider the *future direction of the market as a whole*. This is important because the behavior of a well-diversified mutual fund or ETF tends to reflect the general tone of the market. Thus, if the consensus forecast is that the market is going to be generally drifting up, that should bode well for the investment performance of mutual funds and ETFs. Second, take a hard look at the past performance of the fund itself in light of its risk and investment management fees. It's a good way to see how successful the fund's investment managers have been. The success of a mutual fund or an ETF rests largely *on the investment skills of the fund managers*. So, when investing in a fund, look for consistently good performance in up as well as down markets, as well as over extended periods (of five to seven years or more). Most importantly, check to see whether the same key people are still running the fund. Although past success is certainly no guarantee of future performance, a strong, consistent team of money managers can have a significant bearing on the level of fund returns. Put another way: When you buy a mutual fund or an ETF, you're buying a formula (investment policy + money management team), which has worked in the past, in the expectation that it will work again in the future.

13-4 INVESTING IN REAL ESTATE

LO6 For many years, investing in real estate was quite lucrative. Real estate, it seemed, was one of the few investment vehicles that just couldn't go wrong. When the economy is growing and inflation is relatively high, as it was in the 1970s and early 1980s, real estate prices are also strong. In the early 1990s, however, the market weakened and prices started to level off. That didn't last long, though, as real estate values began to climb again in the latter part of the 1990s. One example of this behavior was housing prices, which rose rapidly—indeed, shot almost straight up—from 2001 through 2006. But then, from a market peak in 2006, housing prices fell almost as quickly as they had risen, with the average price of a home plummeting nearly 33 percent by early 2011, which was the bottom. Prices had fallen by more than they had during the Great Depression. Housing prices recovered significantly from 2012 to 2016. While still below 2006 peak levels in 2016, housing prices were expected to rise at an average rate of 3 to 4 percent in the near term.

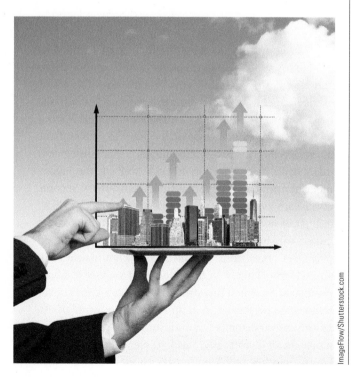

ImageFlow/Shutterstock.com

Real estate includes everything from homes and raw land to different types of income-producing properties such as warehouses, commercial and retail space, office and apartment buildings, and condominiums. Investments in real estate can take several forms. For example, investors can buy land or property directly, or they may prefer to invest in various types of real estate securities, such as real estate mutual funds (discussed earlier in this chapter), REITs, mortgages, stocks of real-estate-related companies, or real estate limited partnerships.

Adding real estate to your investment portfolio *provides greater diversification than does holding just stocks or bonds*. That's because *real estate typically doesn't move in tandem with stocks or bonds*. Before deciding to buy real estate for your portfolio, however, it's essential for you to evaluate such issues as the outlook for the national economy, interest rate levels, supply and demand for space, and regional considerations.

13-4a Some Basic Considerations

The attractiveness of a real estate investment depends on the expected cash flows over the planned holding period and the riskiness of those cash flows. The expected cash flows are determined by rent, depreciation, and taxes—and, of course, the all-important expected future sales price. The return on a real estate investment is determined by the relationship between the expected future cash flows relative to the initial investment, which is typically reduced by using a significant amount of borrowed funds. The value of the investment is assessed in light of the returns available on alternative investments of comparable risk (such as stocks, bonds, and mutual funds). Far more than with most other types of investments, financial leverage (borrowing) is a key determinant of real estate investment returns. We'll now briefly describe the basic factors affecting the value of real estate investments, including after-tax cash flows, appreciation in value, and the use of leverage.

Cash Flow and Taxes The after-tax *cash flows* on a real estate investment depend on the revenues generated by the property, on any operating expenses, and on depreciation and taxes. Real estate typically provides large depreciation write-offs that tend to lower the taxable income of certain (*qualified*) investors. Depreciation gives the property owner an allowance for the decline in the physical condition of real estate over time. Although it's a expense that's deductible for tax purposes, it involves no actual cash outflow. Depreciation can result in lower taxes. For this reason, it's viewed as a *tax shelter*.

For tax purposes, real estate is considered a *passive* investment. Therefore, the amount of expenses, *including depreciation*, that can be written off is generally limited to the amount of income generated by this and any other passive investments owned by the investor. For example, if you owned apartments that generated $25,000 a year in rental income, and if you had mortgage interest and other operating expenses of $20,000 annually, then you might be able to write off up to $5,000 in depreciation ($25,000 income minus $20,000 other expenses). However, if your *adjusted gross income (AGI)* is less than $100,000 a year, then you might be able to write off even more depreciation—specifically, as much as $25,000 in losses on *rented real estate* can be used to offset the ordinary income of people who "actively participate" in the rental activity of the buildings *and* whose AGI is less than $100,000. In this example, if you had $90,000 in adjusted gross income and $15,000 in depreciation expense, $5,000 of it could be written off as before against the remaining $5,000 of net rental income. The other $10,000 could be charged directly against your ordinary income, thereby reducing your taxable income and your taxes. Because of its effect on taxes, *depreciation is an important component of real estate investments.*

Appreciation in Value An investment evaluation of a proposed piece of real estate should include not only the recurring cash flows from the property, but also expected changes in property values. In most cases, such appreciation has a much greater impact on rate of return than does the ongoing net annual cash flow from the property. Hence, if the market price of the real estate is expected to increase by $100,000, then that price appreciation should be treated as capital gains and included as part of the return from the investment (minus, of course, the capital gains taxes paid).

Use of Leverage A big attraction for real estate investing is the high degree of financial leverage that it permits. Leverage involves using borrowed money to magnify returns. Because real estate is a tangible asset, investors can borrow as much as 75 percent to 90 percent of its cost. As a result, if the profit rate on the investment is greater than the cost of borrowing, then the return on a leveraged investment will be *proportionally greater* than the return generated from an unleveraged investment.

13-4b Speculating in Raw Land

One approach to investing in real estate that's popular with many investors is to *speculate in raw land*. In this

approach, *which is often viewed as highly risky*, investors seek to generate high rates of return by investing in property that they *hope* will undergo dramatic increases in value. The key to such speculation is to isolate areas of potential population growth and/or real estate demand (ideally, before anyone else does) and purchase property in these areas in anticipation of their eventual development.

13-4c Investing in Income Property

One of the most popular forms of real estate investing is the purchase of **income-producing property**, including both commercial and residential properties. Real estate income-producing properties offer both attractive returns and tax advantages for investors. The purchased real estate is leased to tenants to generate income from rent. And although the primary purpose of investing in income property is to produce an attractive annual cash flow, certain types of strategically located income properties also offer attractive opportunities for appreciation in value. Before buying income property, be sure you know what you're getting into. The owner of income property is responsible for leasing the units and maintaining the property.

Calculating the value of income-producing property requires estimating the annual net operating income (NOI), *which equals gross*

> Real estate income-producing properties offer both attractive returns and tax advantages for investors.

income-producing property real estate purchased for leasing or renting to tenants in order to generate ongoing monthly/annual income in the form of rent receipts rental income (less an allowance for vacancies and bad debts) minus all operating expenses, such as property (but not income) taxes, insurance, maintenance, and so on. Once you have a property's NOI, you can apply a *cap rate* (the expected annual rate of return on the property) to arrive at an estimated value for the property. A typical cap rate for income property is around 9 or 10 percent.

> **EXAMPLE: Calculating the Value of Income-Producing Property** You're thinking about buying an office building generating an estimated $50,000 per year in NOI. With a 9 percent cap rate, that property would have an estimated value of $555,556 = $50,000/0.09.

Commercial Properties Commercial income properties consists of everything from office buildings, industrial space, and warehouses to retail space and hotels. The risks and returns on commercial real estate investments are tied to business conditions and location. The value of commercial property, especially retail businesses, is enhanced by a location in a high-traffic area. Because commercial properties call for professional management and involve significant expenses, investing in this category of income property is generally the domain of more seasoned real estate investors.

Residential Properties First-time investors often choose income-producing *residential properties* such as homes, apartments, and smaller, multifamily buildings. This category of income property is available in various sizes, prices, and types ranging from single-family homes, duplexes, and triplexes, to large apartment buildings. Aside from the considerations of purchase and financing costs, major factors influencing the profitability of these investments are the occupancy rates—the percentage of available space rented over the year—and maintenance and management costs. Other factors to consider are the neighborhood where the units are located, local regulations regarding tenants, and supply and demand trends for the type of property.

Nerthuz/Shutterstock.com

> **real estate investment trust (REIT)** an investment company that accumulates money by selling shares to investors in order to invest it in various forms of real estate including mortgages; similar to a mutual fund, but REITs invest only in specific types of real estate or real estate–related products

⊙ Go to Smart Sites

Need investing ideas for which ETFs to add to your portfolio? Read the Blog at iShare's site, or follow them on Twitter: @iShares.

13-4d Other Ways to Invest in Real Estate

Another way to own real estate is by purchasing specialized securities. For example, you can buy shares in a *real estate mutual fund* (discussed earlier in this chapter). Or you can buy stock in *publicly traded real estate–related companies*. These include residential homebuilders, construction companies, mortgage lenders, home improvement retailers, and real estate brokerage firms. Let's now look at two of these investment vehicles: *real estate investment trusts (REITs)* and *real estate limited partnerships* (LPs; otherwise known as *limited liability companies*, or *LLCs*).

Real Estate Investment Trusts Arguably the best way for most individuals to invest in real estate is through a **real estate investment trust (REIT)**, which is a type of closed-end investment company that invests money in various types of real estate and real estate mortgages. REITs are like mutual funds in that they sell shares of stock to the investing public and use the proceeds, along with borrowed funds, to invest in a portfolio of real estate investments. The investor therefore owns part of the real estate portfolio held by the REIT.

REITs appeal to investors because they offer the benefits of real estate ownership without the headaches of property management. REITs are popular with investors because they have relatively low correlations with other market sectors, such as common stocks and bonds. In addition, they provide attractive dividend yields—well above the yields on common stocks. And they produce competitive returns. In fact, the average annual return on equity REITs over the last 20 years or so was about 11 percent, compared with about 10 percent for the S&P 500. The performance of REITs over this period is significantly influenced by the real estate losses resulting from the financial crisis of 2007–2009. REITs can be particularly attractive investments during periods of high inflation.

Like any investment fund, each REIT has certain, stated investment objectives that should be considered carefully before acquiring shares. There are three basic types of REITs:

► **Equity REITs.** They own and operate income-producing real estate such as office buildings and hotels.

► **Mortgage REITs.** These make both construction and mortgage loans to real estate investors.

► **Hybrid REITs.** They invest in both income-producing properties and mortgage loans.

Equity REITs produce both attractive current yields and the potential to earn excellent capital gains as their properties appreciate in value. In contrast, mortgage REITs tend to be more income oriented. They emphasize the high current yields they generate by investing in debt. Listed equity REITs hold least $1 trillion in U.S. real estate assets and constitute about 90 percent of the listed REIT market. Most of the rest of the market involves mortgage REITs.

The income earned by a REIT isn't taxed, but *the income distributed to owners is designated and taxed as ordinary income.* Although dividends on common stocks normally are taxed at preferential rates (of 15 or 20 percent or less), this is not the case with REITs, whose cash dividends are treated as ordinary income and taxed accordingly.

Real Estate Limited Partnerships or Limited Liability Companies Special-purpose syndicates organized to invest in real estate are another type of real estate investment. These can be structured as limited partnerships (LPs) or limited liability companies (LLCs). With LPs, the managers assume the role of *general partner*. This means their liability is unlimited and that the other investors are *limited partners* who are legally liable only for the amount of their initial investment. In recent years, the LLC has become a more popular way to form these entities. Rather than general and limited partners, the LLC has a managing member and other members—none of whom have any liability. Investors buy *units* in an LP or LLC; a unit represents an ownership position that is similar to a share of stock. Real estate LPs and LLCs are highly illiquid and are felt to be far riskier investments than REITs. They tend to appeal to affluent investors who can afford the typical cost of $100,000 per unit or more.

FINANCIAL IMPACT OF PERSONAL CHOICES

Bianca Finds a Simple Retirement Investment Plan

Bianca Costa, 27 years old, wants to get her retirement investing portfolio up and running. But she has a demanding job and little time to manage a portfolio closely. In doing some research, she read a short (16-page) booklet by William J. Bernstein, "If You Can" (**www.etf.com /docs/IfYouCan.pdf**). Bernstein argues that by age 25 it's important to invest at least 15 percent of your income annually in a 401(k), an IRA, or a taxable account (or all three) in just three mutual funds or ETFs:

• U.S. total stock market index fund
• International total stock market fund
• U.S. total bond market index fund

These funds will earn different rates of return over time, so once a year it makes sense to rebalance the amount in each account so they're equal. Bernstein convincingly argues that following this simple investment plan will beat most professional investors and would likely provide enough savings for Bianca to retire comfortably.

Bianca was convinced and estimated that keeping the plan in place would take no more than one or

Ismagilov/Shutterstock.com

two hours a year. So she invested equal amounts in the following ETFs:

• Vanguard Total International Stock ETF (VXUS)
• Vanguard Total Stock Market ETF (VXUS)
• Vanguard Total Bond Market ETF (BND)

Bianca will invest 15 percent of her income each year in these ETFs and rebalance them annually. Her research and simple, systematic approach will no doubt serve her well.

PLANNING OVER A LIFETIME

Investing in Mutual Funds, ETFs, and Real Estate

Here are some key considerations for investment planning in each stage of the life cycle.

PRE-FAMILY INDEPENDENCE: 20s

» Determine your major investment goals and how much money needs to be invested each month to achieve them.

» Determine your asset allocation among stocks, bonds, real estate, and cash based on your time horizon and attitude toward risk. Choose mutual funds and ETFs accordingly.

» Match your investments in any employer-sponsored 401(k) retirement plan with your overall asset allocation plan.

» Consider investing in mutual funds and ETFs under a traditional IRA, a Roth IRA, or both.

FAMILY FORMATION/CAREER DEVELOPMENT: 30–45

» Revise investments in mutual funds, ETFs, and real estate to focus more on retirement and funding children's education, if applicable.

» Review your asset allocation and rebalance it to be more consistent with your goals.

» Gradually increase the amount invested in any employer-sponsored 401(k) retirement plan and re-evaluate how it relates to your asset allocation plan.

» Consider increasing your contribution to traditional IRA, a Roth IRA, or both.

PRE-RETIREMENT: 45–65

» Revise your investment plan in light of recent developments.

» Review your asset allocation and rebalance investments among mutual funds, ETFs, and real estate if it is inconsistent with your goals.

» Continue to gradually increase the amount you invest in any employer-sponsored 401(k) retirement plan and re-evaluate how it relates to your asset allocation plan.

» Consider increasing your contribution to traditional and/or Roth IRAs using mutual funds and ETFs.

RETIREMENT: 65 AND BEYOND

» Revise your investment plan to lean more toward debt and cash instruments than to stocks in your mutual funds and ETFs.

» Review your asset allocation, and rebalance it if it is inconsistent with your goals.

» Integrate investment asset allocation strategy with estate planning.

» Plan carefully for mandatory withdrawals from tax-sheltered accounts and associated tax consequences.

STUDY TOOLS 13

LOCATED AT BACK OF THE TEXTBOOK
☐ Chapter Review Card

LOCATED AT WWW.CENGAGEBRAIN.COM
☐ Review Key Term flashcards and create your own cards.
☐ Track your knowledge and understanding of key concepts in personal finance.

☐ Complete practice and graded quizzes to prepare for tests.
☐ Complete interactive content at PFIN6 Online.
☐ View the chapter highlight boxes at PFIN6 Online.

©viphotos/Shutterstock140785408

Financial Planning Exercises

LO1, 2   **1. Choosing between a mutual fund and an ETF.** Maria Coffey is considering whether she should invest some extra money in a mutual fund or an ETF. Explain the key factors that should influence her decision.

LO2   **2. Estimating cost of mutual fund investments.** Using the mutual fund quotes in Exhibit 13.3, and assuming that you can buy these funds at their quoted NAVs, how much would you have to pay to buy each of the following funds?

    a.   AEMMX

    b.   ADCVX

    c.   FCPAX

    d.   FSFAX

According to the quotes, which of these four funds have 12b-1 fees? Which have redemption fees? Are any of them no-loads? Which fund has the highest year-to-date return? Which has the lowest?

LO2, 3   **3. Building a mutual fund portfolio.** Imagine that you've just inherited $40,000 from a rich uncle. Now you're faced with the problem of deciding how to spend it. You could make a down payment on a condo—or better yet, on that BMW that you've always wanted. Or you could spend your windfall more profitably by building a mutual fund portfolio. Let's say that, after a lot of soul-searching, you decide to build a mutual fund portfolio. Your task is to develop a $40,000 mutual fund portfolio. Use actual funds and actual quoted prices, invest as much of the $40,000 as you possibly can, and be specific! Briefly describe the portfolio that you end up with, including the investment objectives that you're trying to achieve.

LO2, 3   **4. Comparing ETF with SPDR.** Describe an ETF and explain how it combines the characteristics of open- and closed-end funds. In the Vanguard family of funds, which would most closely resemble a "Spider" (SPDR)? In what respects are the Vanguard fund (that you selected) and SPDRs the same? How are they different? If you could invest in only one of them, which would it be? Explain.

LO4   **5. Comparing risks of different mutual fund types.** For *each pair* of funds listed below, select the fund that would be the *least* risky and briefly explain your answer.

    a.   Growth versus growth-and-income

    b.   Equity-income versus high-grade corporate bonds

    c.   Intermediate-term bonds versus high-yield municipals

    d.   International versus balanced

LO4, 5   **6. Evaluating ETF performance.** Do an online search for information on the PowerShares QQQ ETF. Discuss what information you need to evaluate the performance of the ETF, and use what you find to evaluate the QQQ ETF. What kind of investor should invest in this ETF?

LO5   **7. Calculating approximate yield on mutual fund.** About a year ago, Gus Stanton bought some shares in the Anvil Fund. He bought the fund at $24.50 a share, and it now trades at $26.00. Last year, the fund paid dividends of 40 cents a share and had capital gains distributions of $1.83 a share. Using the approximate yield formula, what rate of return did Gus earn on his investment? Repeat the calculation using a financial calculator. Would he have made a 20 percent rate of return if the stock had risen to $30 a share?

LO5   **8. Calculating mutual fund approximate rate of return.** A year ago, the Stellar Fund was being quoted at an NAV of $21.50 and an offer price of $23.35; today, it's being quoted at $23.04 (NAV) and $25.04 (offer). Use the approximate yield formula or a financial calculator to find the rate of return on this load fund; it was purchased a year ago, and its dividends and capital gains distributions over the year totaled $1.05 a share. (*Hint:* As an investor, you buy fund shares at the offer price and sell at the NAV.)

LO6   **9. Investing in residential income-producing property.** Hope Sheppard is thinking about investing in residential income-producing property that she can purchase for $200,000. Hope can either pay cash for the full amount of the property or put up $50,000 of her own money and borrow the remaining $150,000 at 8 percent interest. The property is expected to generate $30,000 per year after all expenses but *before* interest and income taxes. Assume that Hope is in the 28 percent tax bracket. Calculate her annual profit and return on investment assuming that she (a) pays the full $200,000 from her own funds or (b) borrows $150,000 at 8 percent. Then discuss the effect, if any, of leverage on her rate of return. (*Hint:* Earnings Before Interest & Taxes *minus* Interest Expenses (if any) *equals* Earnings Before Taxes *minus* Income Taxes (at 28 percent) *equals* Profit After Taxes.)

LO6 10. **Different ways to invest in real estate.** Assume you've just inherited $100,000 and wish to use all or part of it to make a real estate investment.

a. Would you invest directly in real estate, or indirectly through something like a REIT? Explain.

b. Assuming that you decided to invest directly, would you invest in income-producing property or speculative property? Why? Describe the key characteristics of the types of income-producing or speculative property you would seek.

c. What financial and nonfinancial goals would you establish before beginning the search for suitable property?

d. If you decide to invest in real estate indirectly, which type(s) of securities would you buy, and why?

PFIN
ONLINE

STUDY YOUR WAY
WITH STUDYBITS!

WEAK

FAIR

STRONG

UNASSIGNED

Rate and Organize StudyBits

Collect What's Important

Create Flashcards From Your StudyBits

Track/Monitor Your Progress

85%

CORRECT

INCORRECT

INCORRECT

INCORRECT

Personalize Your Quizzes

Access PFIN6 ONLINE at www.cengagebrain.com

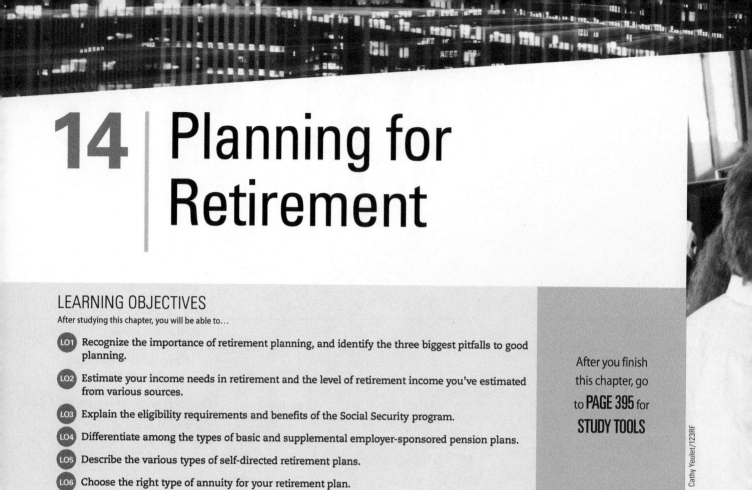

14 | Planning for Retirement

LEARNING OBJECTIVES

After studying this chapter, you will be able to...

LO1 Recognize the importance of retirement planning, and identify the three biggest pitfalls to good planning.

LO2 Estimate your income needs in retirement and the level of retirement income you've estimated from various sources.

LO3 Explain the eligibility requirements and benefits of the Social Security program.

LO4 Differentiate among the types of basic and supplemental employer-sponsored pension plans.

LO5 Describe the various types of self-directed retirement plans.

LO6 Choose the right type of annuity for your retirement plan.

After you finish this chapter, go to **PAGE 395** for **STUDY TOOLS**

Cathy Yeulet/123RF

How Will This Affect Me? While almost everyone understands that planning for retirement is important, far too few people actually implement a comprehensive plan, much less set aside enough savings to fund their retirement adequately. This chapter discusses the importance of retirement planning and encourages action by identifying the major pitfalls you must overcome. In order to make the process more concrete and accessible, the steps for estimating your retirement income needs and the income your investments will support are explained. Eligibility requirements to receive Social Security benefits and their amounts are detailed, as are the key aspects of supplemental employer-sponsored pension plans and the potential benefits of self-directed retirement programs like traditional and Roth individual retirement accounts (IRAs). In addition, the usefulness of various annuity products in retirement planning is evaluated. After reading this chapter, you should understand how to develop and implement a financial plan that will help you achieve your long-term retirement objectives.

14-1 AN OVERVIEW OF RETIREMENT PLANNING

LO1, LO2 Retiring is easy. What's difficult is retiring in style, and that's where retirement planning comes into play! But to enjoy a comfortable retirement, you must *start now*—for one of the biggest mistakes people make in retirement planning is waiting too long to begin. Accumulating adequate retirement funds is a daunting task that takes careful planning and disciplined execution over a lifetime. Like budgets, taxes, and investments, retirement planning is vital to your financial well-being and is a critical link in your personal financial plans.

14-1a Role of Retirement Planning in Personal Financial Planning

The financial planning process would be incomplete without retirement planning. Certainly no financial goal is more important than achieving a comfortable standard of living in retirement. In many respects, retirement planning captures the essence of financial planning. It is forward-looking, affects both your current and future standard of living, and can be highly rewarding and contribute significantly to your net worth.

The first step in retirement planning is to set *retirement goals* for yourself. Take some time to describe the things you want to do in retirement, the standard of living you hope to maintain, the level of income you'd like to receive, and any special retirement goals you may have (like buying a retirement home in Florida). Such goals are important because *they give direction to your retirement planning*. Of course, like all goals, they're subject to change over time as the situations and conditions in your life change.

Once you know what you want out of retirement, the next step is to establish the *size of the nest egg* that you're going to need to achieve your retirement goals. And while you're at it, you'll

> Certainly no financial goal is more important than achieving a comfortable standard of living in retirement.

also want to formulate an *investment program* that'll enable you to build up that required nest egg. This usually involves (1) creating a systematic savings plan in which you put away a certain amount of money each year and (2) identifying the specific investments that will best meet your retirement needs.

Investments and investment planning are the vehicles for building up your retirement funds. They're the active, ongoing part of retirement planning in which you invest and manage the funds you've set aside for retirement. It's no coincidence that a major portion of most individual investor portfolios is devoted to building up a pool of funds for retirement. Tax planning is also important because a major objective of sound retirement planning is to legitimately shield as much income as possible from taxes and, in so doing, maximize the accumulation of retirement funds.

14-1b The Three Biggest Pitfalls to Sound Retirement Planning

Human nature being what it is, people often have unrealistic expectations concerning the amount of money they want to build up for retirement. Having a nest egg of $4 or $5 million would be great, but it's beyond the reach of most people. Besides, you don't need that much to live comfortably in retirement. So set a more realistic goal. But when you set that goal, remember: it's not going to happen by itself. You'll have to do something to bring it about. And this is precisely where things start to fall apart. Why? Because when it comes to retirement planning, many people tend to make three big mistakes:

▶ Starting too late.

▶ Putting away too little.

▶ Investing too conservatively.

Many people in their 20s, or even 30s, find it hard to put money away for retirement. Most often that's because they have other, more pressing financial concerns—such as buying a house, paying off a student loan, or paying for child care. The net result is that they *put off retirement planning until later in life*—in many cases, until they're in their late 30s or 40s. Unfortunately, the longer people put it off, the less they're going to have in retirement. Or they won't to be able to retire as early as they'd hoped. Even worse, once people start a retirement program, *they tend to put away too little.* Although this may also be due to pressing financial needs, all too often it boils down to lifestyle choices. They'd rather spend today than save for tomorrow.

On top of all this, many *people tend to be far too conservative* in the way they invest their retirement money. They often place way too much of their retirement money into low-yielding, fixed-income securities such as CDs and Treasury notes. Although you should *never speculate* with something as important as your retirement plan, there's no need to avoid risk totally. There's nothing wrong with following an investment program that involves a reasonable amount of risk, provided that it results in a correspondingly higher level of expected return. Being overly cautious can be costly in the long run. Indeed, a low rate of return can have an enormous impact on the long-term accumulation of capital and, in many cases, may mean the difference between just getting by or enjoying a comfortable retirement.

Compounding the Errors All three of these pitfalls become even more important when we consider *compound interest*. That's because *compounding essentially magnifies the impact of these mistakes.* As an illustration, consider the first variable—starting too late. If you were to start a retirement program at age 35 and put away $2,000 a year, it would grow to almost $160,000 by the time you're 65 if invested at an average rate of return of 6 percent. Not a bad deal. But look at what you end up with if you start this investment program just 10 years earlier, at age 25: that same $2,000 a year will grow to over $309,000 by the time you're 65. Think of it—for another $20,000 ($2,000 a year for an extra 10 years), you can nearly double the terminal value of your investment! Of course, it's not the extra $20,000 that's doubling your money; rather, it's *compound interest* that's doing most of the work.

The same holds true for the rate of return that you earn on the investments in your retirement account. Take the second situation just described—starting a retirement program at age 25. Earning 6 percent generates a retirement nest egg of over $309,000. Increase that rate of return to 8 percent and your retirement nest egg will be worth just over $518,000! *You're still putting in the same amount of money,* but because your money is working harder, you end up with a much bigger nest egg. Of course, when you seek higher returns, that generally means you also have to take on more risks. But not everyone can tolerate higher levels of risk. And if that applies to you, then simply stay away from the higher-risk investments. Instead, stick to safer, lower-yielding securities and find some other way to build up your nest egg. For instance, contribute more each year to your plan or extend the length of your investment period. The only other option—and not a particularly appealing one—is to accept the possibility that you won't be able to build up as big a nest egg as you hoped and therefore will have to accept a lower standard of living in retirement.

14-1c Estimating Income Needs

Retirement planning would be much simpler if we lived in a static economy. But obviously we don't, so you'll have to live with the fact that both your personal budget and the general state of the economy will change over time. This makes accurate forecasting of retirement needs difficult at best. Even so, you'll have to live with the fact that it's a necessary task, and you can handle it in one of two ways. One strategy is to plan for retirement over *a series of short-run time frames*. A good way to do this is to state your retirement income objectives as a percentage of your present earnings. A common starting point is to project that your retirement income will need to be about 70 to 80 percent of your pre-retirement income due to reduced expenses in retirement. Then, every three to five years, you can revise and update your plan.

Alternatively, you can follow *a long-term approach* in which you formulate the level of income that you'd like to receive in retirement, along with the amount of funds that you must amass to achieve that desired standard of living. Rather than addressing the problem in a series of short-run plans, this approach goes 30 or 40 years into the future—to the time when you'll retire—in determining how much saving and investing you must do today in order to achieve your long-run retirement goals. Of course, if conditions or expectations should change dramatically in the future, then it may be necessary to make corresponding alterations to your long-run retirement goals and strategies.

Determining Future Retirement Needs To illustrate how future retirement needs and income requirements can be formulated, let's consider the case of Martin and Liv Moyer. In their mid-30s, they have two children and an annual income of about $80,000 before taxes. Even though it's still some 30 years away, Martin and Liv recognize it's now time to seriously consider if they'll be able to pursue the kind of retirement lifestyle that appeals to them. Worksheet 14.1 provides the basic steps to follow in determining retirement needs. It shows how the Moyers have estimated their retirement income and determined the amount of investment assets they must accumulate to meet their retirement objectives.

Martin and Liv began by determining what their *household expenditures* will likely be in retirement. A simple way to derive an estimate of expected household expenditures is to base it on the current level of such expenses. Assume that the Moyers' annual household expenditures (*excluding savings*) currently run about $56,000 a year (this information can be readily obtained by referring to their most recent income and expenditures statement). After making some obvious adjustments for the different lifestyle they'll have in retirement—for example, their children will no longer be living at home, their home will be paid for, and so on—the Moyers estimate that they should be able to achieve the standard of living they'd like in retirement at an annual level of household expenses equal to about 70 percent of the current amount. Thus, *based on today's dollars*, their estimated household expenditures in retirement will be $56,000 × 0.70 = $39,200. (This process is summarized in steps A through D in Worksheet 14.1.)

Estimating Retirement Income The next question is: Where will the Moyers get the money to meet their projected household expenses of $39,200 a year? They've addressed this problem by estimating what their *income* will be in retirement—again *based on today's dollars*. Their two basic sources of retirement income are Social Security and employer-sponsored pension plans. They estimate that they'll receive about $24,000 a year from Social Security and another $9,000 from their employer pension plans, for a total projected annual income of $33,000. When comparing this figure to their projected household expenditures, it's clear that the Moyers will be facing an annual shortfall of $6,200 (see steps E through I in Worksheet 14.1). This is the amount of additional retirement income they must come up with; otherwise, they'll have to reduce their standard of living they hope to enjoy in retirement.

At this point, we need to introduce the *inflation factor* to our projections in order to restate the annual shortfall of $6,200 in terms of retirement dollars. Here we assume that both income and expenditures will undergo approximately the same average annual rate of inflation, which will cause the shortfall to grow by that rate over time. In essence, 30 years from now, the annual shortfall is going to be a lot more than $6,200. How large this number becomes will, of course, depend on what happens to inflation. Assume that the Moyers expect inflation over the next 30 years to average 5 percent. While that's a bit on the high side by today's standards, the Moyers are concerned that the large federal deficit will cause inflation to rise. Using the

simez78/Shutterstock.com

A worksheet like this one will help you define your income requirements in retirement, the size of your retirement nest egg, and the amount you must save annually to achieve your retirement goals.

PROJECTING RETIREMENT INCOME AND INVESTMENT NEEDS

Name(s) _Martin and Liv Moyer_   Date _8/31/2017_

I. Estimated Household Expenditures in Retirement:

A. Approximate number of years to retirement   _30_

B. Current level of annual household expenditures, excluding savings $ _56,000_

C. Estimated household expenses in retirement as a *percent* of current *expenses*   _70 %_

D. Estimated annual household expenditures in retirement (B × C) $ _39,200_

II. Estimated Income in Retirement:

E. Social Security, annual income $ _24,000_

F. Company/employer pension plans, annual amounts $ _9,000_

G. Other sources, annual amounts $ _0_

H. Total annual income (E + F + G) $ _33,000_

I. Additional required income, or annual shortfall (D − H) $ _6,200_

III. Inflation Factor:

J. Expected average annual rate of inflation over the period to retirement   _5 %_

K. Inflation factor (in Appendix A):   Based on _30_ years to retirement (A) and an expected average annual rate of inflation (J) of _5 %_   _4.322_

L. Size of inflation-adjusted annual shortfall (I × K) $ _26,796_

IV. Funding the Shortfall:

M. Anticipated return on assets held *after* retirement   _6 %_

N. Amount of retirement funds required—size of nest egg (L ÷ M) $ _446,600_

O. Expected rate of return on investments *prior* to retirement   _8 %_

P. Compound interest factor (in Appendix B): Based on _30_ years to retirement (A) and an expected rate of return on investments of _8 %_   _113.283_

Q. Annual savings required to fund retirement nest egg (N ÷ P) $ _3,942_

Note: Parts I and II are prepared in terms of current (today's) dollars. Parts III and IV can be computed with a calculator that has a time value function.

---

compound value table from Appendix A, we find that the *inflation factor* for 5 percent and 30 years is 4.322; multiplying this inflation factor by the annual shortfall of $6,200 gives the Moyers an idea of what that figure will be by the time they retire: $6,200 × 4.322 = $26,796 (see steps J to L in Worksheet 14.1). Thus, based on their projections, the shortfall should amount to about $26,796 a year when they retire 30 years from now. *This is the annual shortfall they'll have to cover using their own supplemental retirement program.*

Funding the Shortfall The final two steps in the Moyers' estimation process are to determine (1) *how big the retirement nest egg must be* to cover the projected annual income shortfall and (2) *how much to save each year* to accumulate the required amount by the time they retire. To find out how much money they need to accumulate by retirement, they must estimate the rate of return they think they'll be able to earn on their investments *after* they retire. This will tell them how big their nest egg will have to be by retirement

EXAMPLE: Effect of Inflation on Future Retirement Needs Faith expects to retire in 35 years. She's been told that it's reasonable to expect a long-term inflation rate of 4 percent. Faith wants to have annual income of $80,000 in today's dollars. How much will she need in 35 years to have that much?

Using the future value interest factor in Appendix A for 4 percent and 35 years, Faith will need $80,000 × 3.946 = $315,680. While a daunting number, it's good Faith is planning for her retirement so carefully!

return: $26,796/0.06 = $446,600 (see steps M and N). Such a nest egg will yield $26,796 a year: $446,600 × 0.06 = $26,796. So long as the capital ($446,600) remains untouched, it will generate the same amount of annual income for as long as the Moyers live and can eventually become a part of their estate. Alternatively, some or all of the capital could be spent to offset the effects of future inflation on the value of the expected annual shortfall during retirement.

Now that the Moyers know how big their nest egg must be, the final question is: How are they going to accumulate such an amount by the time they retire? For most

CALCULATOR

Inputs	Functions
30	N
5.0	I/Y
−6,200	PV
	CPT
	FV
	Solution
	26,796.04

See Appendix E for details.

in order to eliminate the expected annual inflation-adjusted shortfall of $26,796.

Let's assume that lower risk is desired during retirement and that the associated expected rate of return is consequently 6 percent. Thus, the Moyers must accumulate $446,600 by retirement. This figure is found by *capitalizing* the estimated shortfall of $26,796 at an 6 percent rate of

BEHAVIOR MATTERS

Behavioral Biases in Retirement Planning

Theory argues that the rational investor forecasts retirement needs by considering expected future lifetime earnings, investment returns, tax rates, family and health situation, and expected longevity. However, research indicates that most people save too little, make questionable investment decisions, and tend to spend their accumulated assets too quickly in retirement. Surveys indicate that people are not particularly good at planning and saving for retirement. About 40 percent of people have not calculated how much they need to retire, 30 percent haven't saved a significant amount, and only 20 percent feel confident they can live comfortably in retirement.

There are some behavioral biases that explain this disturbing lack of preparation for retirement. Recognizing them is more than half of the battle:

- **Self-control.** Most people *intend* to save and plan, but they do not get around to doing so. Commitment approaches like "pay yourself first" and automatic 401(k) deductions are helpful ways to encourage saving and planning follow-through.

- **Choice overload.** Faced with complex retirement investment choices, many people just give up and choose a default or even decide not to participate in

an employer-offered plan. Making the decision to ask for help can make all the difference.

- **Inertia in managing retirement investments.** Many people tend to "anchor" on their *initial* retirement account investment mix and don't revise it enough over their lives. Recognizing this tendency and scheduling periodic investment reviews with an advisor can limit any resulting damage to your retirement accounts.

- **Representativeness and availability biases.** People tend to view recent investment returns as overly representative of returns in general and consequently are inclined to overweight them in their decision making. For example, just because a mutual fund was a top performer last year does not mean that it will be next year. Similarly, many people tend to rely on the most readily available information in making investment decisions. Just because data are easy to get does not mean they are sufficient to the task.

- **Overconfidence.** Many retirement investors are overconfident in their choices and consequently do not diversify their investments enough.

Source: Adapted from Olivia S. Mitchell and Stephen P. Utkus, "How Behavior Can Inform Retirement Plan Design," *Journal of Applied Corporate Finance*, Winter 2006, pp. 82–94.

Go to Smart Sites

CALCULATOR KEYSTROKES

As you might have suspected, the last few steps in the worksheet can easily be done on a financial calculator. For example, consider Part III, *the inflation-adjusted annual shortfall*. With the calculator in the *annual mode*, you can determine how big the current annual shortfall of $6,200 will grow to in 30 years (given an average annual inflation rate of 5 percent) by using these keystrokes, where:

N = number of *years* to retirement

I/Y = *expected* annual rate of inflation

PV = additional required annual income (line I in Worksheet 14.1), entered as a *negative number*

Enter CPT (FV) and you should end up with an answer (FV) that is close to $26,796 (see step L in Worksheet 14.1); in this case, it's $26,796.04.

Now take a look at Part IV, *funding the shortfall* (step Q in Worksheet 14.1). Again, with the calculator in the *annual mode*, to find the amount that must be put away annually to fund a $446,600 retirement nest egg in 30 years (given an expected return of 8 percent), use the keystrokes shown here, where:

N = number of *years* over which the retirement nest egg is to be accumulated

I/Y = *expected* annual return on invested capital

FV = the size of the targeted nest egg, entered as a *negative number*

Enter CPT (PMT) and a value of 3,942.33 should appear in the display, indicating the amount you must put away annually to reach a target of $446,600 in 30 years.

people, that means setting up a *systematic savings plan* and putting away a certain amount *each* year.

To find out how much must be saved each year to achieve a targeted sum in the future, we can use the table

of annuity factors in Appendix B. The appropriate interest factor depends on of the rate of return one can or expects to generate and the length of the investment period. In the Moyers' case, there are 30 years to go until retirement, meaning that the length of their investment period is 30 years. Suppose that they believe they can earn a 8 percent average rate of return on their investments over this 30-year period. From Appendix B, we see that the 8 percent, 30-year interest factor is 113.283. Because the Moyers must accumulate $446,600 by the time they retire, *the amount they'll have to save each year* (over the next 30 years) can be found by *dividing* the amount they need to accumulate by the appropriate interest factor; that is, $446,600/113.283 = $3,942 (see steps O to Q in Worksheet 14.1).

The Moyers now know what they must do to achieve the kind of retirement they want: *Put away $3,942 a year and invest it at an average annual rate of 8 percent over the next 30 years*. If they can do that, then they'll have their $446,600 retirement nest egg in 30 years. How they actually invest their money so as to achieve the desired 8 percent rate of return will, of course, depend on the investments and strategies they use. All the worksheet tells them is how much money they'll need, not how they will get there; it's at this point that investment management enters the picture.

CALCULATOR

Inputs	Functions
30	N
8.0	I/Y
−446,600	FV
	CPT
	PMT
Solution	
3,942.33	

See Appendix E for Details.

14-1d Sources of Retirement Income

As seen in Exhibit 14.1, the principal sources of income for retired people are Social Security, earnings from income-producing assets (such as savings, stocks, and bonds), earnings generated from full- or part-time jobs, and pension plans. The largest single source of income was Social Security, which represented about 38 percent of total retiree income. In recent years, earned income has come to account for a growing amount of total retirement income, as more and more people continue to work in retirement as a way to supplement their other sources of income. Keep in mind that these are percentage *sources* of retirement income and not dollar amounts. The *amount*

Exhibit 14.1

Sources of Income for the Average Retiree

Social Security is the single largest source of income for the average U.S. retiree. This source alone is larger than the amount the average retiree receives from pension plans and personal wealth/investment assets *combined*.

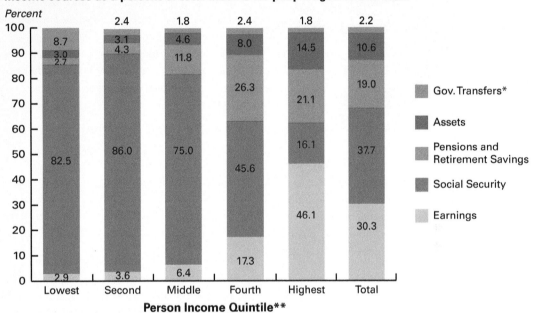

Income sources as a percent of total income for people aged 65 and older

Note: Numbers do not sum to 100 percent because other cash income, such as family financial assistance, is not shown.

*Government cash transfers include unemployment compensation, workers' compensation, veterans' benefits, Supplemental Security Income (SSI), Temporary Assistance for Needy Families (TANF), and education assistance.

**Income quintiles are based on personal total income. Quintile limits are as follows: $10,080, $16,043, $24,274 and $43,259.

Source: Adapted from Ke Bin Wu, "Sources of Income for Older Americans, 2012," AARP Public Policy Institute, Figure 1, p. 3, www.aarp.org/money/low-income-assistance/info-12-2013/sources-of-income-for-older-americans-2012-AARP-ppi-econ-sec.html, accessed October 2016.

of income retired individuals will receive, of course, will vary from amounts that are barely above the poverty line to six-figure incomes. Obviously, the more that individuals make before they retire, the more that they'll receive in Social Security benefits (up to a point) and from company-sponsored pension plans—and, very likely, the greater the amount of income-producing assets that they'll hold.

14-2 SOCIAL SECURITY

LO3 The Social Security Act of 1935 was landmark legislation. It created a basic retirement program for working Americans at all income levels, and it established several other social programs, all administered under the auspices of the *Old Age, Survivor's,*

Disability, and Health Insurance (OASDHI) program. Some of the other services include supplementary security income (SSI), Medicare, unemployment insurance, public assistance, welfare services, and provision for black lung benefits. In this section, we give primary attention to the old age and survivor's portions of the act because they bear directly on retirement planning. We discussed the disability and health/Medicare benefits of Social Security in Chapter 9.

14-2a Coverage

Social Security coverage today extends to nearly all gainfully employed workers. Only two major classes of employees are exempt from *mandatory* participation in the Social Security system: (1) federal *civilian* employees who were hired before 1984 and are covered under

JohnKwan/Shutterstock.com

by the *self-employed* was about $14,694 ($118,500 × 0.124). While the Social Security rate is paid up to taxable maximum, the Medicare rate is paid on all earnings. Further, individuals with earned income in excess of $200,000 ($250,00 for married couples filing jointly) pay an addition 0.9 percent in Medicare taxes. Importantly, this tax is not matched by the employer. It is paid only by the employee or self-employed individual. Thus, once the Social Security wage base is passed, employees become subject to a Medicare tax rate of 1.45 percent *on all earnings* over $118,500, whereas the added earnings of the self-employed are taxed at the rate of 2.9 percent. And, as noted, higher earners must also pay an additional 0.9 percent.

14-2c Social Security Retirement Benefits

Basic Social Security benefits that are important to retired people and their dependents include (1) retirement benefits and (2) survivor's benefits. Both programs provide extended benefits to covered workers and their spouses.

Retirement Benefits Workers who are fully covered (i.e., who have worked the required 40 quarters) may receive retirement benefits for life once they reach full retirement age. For anyone born in 1960 or later, the Social Security Administration defines "full retirement age" as age 67. (If you were born before 1960, your full retirement age is between 65 and 67; it can be determined at **www.ssa.gov**. Here, we'll use 67 as the full retirement age.) Workers who elect to retire early—at age 62—will receive reduced benefits, currently 70 percent to 80 percent of the full amount (again, depending on when they were born). If the retiree has a spouse age 67 or older, the spouse may be entitled to benefits equal to one-half of the amount received by the retired worker.

For retirement planning purposes, it seems reasonable to expect Social Security currently to provide the average retired wage earner (who is married) with perhaps 40 percent to 60 percent of the wages that he or she was earning in the year before retirement. However, the old age and disability trust funds supporting Social Security benefits are projected to be unable to pay full benefits by 2034! So benefits could be even less than this estimate. Clearly, by itself, Social Security is *insufficient to enable a worker and spouse to maintain their preretirement standard of living!*

In two-income families, both the husband and wife may be eligible for full Social Security benefits. When they retire, they can choose to receive their benefits in one of two ways: each can (1) take the full benefits to which each is entitled from his or her account or (2) take the husband and wife benefits of the higher-paid spouse.

the Civil Service Retirement System, and (2) employees of state and local governments who have chosen not to be covered (although most of these employees are covered through *voluntary participation* in Social Security). Certain marginal employment positions, such as full-time college students working for a university, are also exempt.

To obtain Social Security benefits, an application must be filed with the Social Security Administration, which then determines the applicant's eligibility for benefits based on whether he or she has had enough quarters (three-month periods) of participation in the system. To qualify for full retirement benefits, workers must be employed in a job covered by Social Security for at least 40 quarters, or 10 years. These quarters need not be consecutive. The surviving spouse and dependent children of a *deceased worker* are also eligible for monthly benefits if the worker was fully covered at the time of death.

14-2b Social Security Payroll Taxes

The cash benefits provided by Social Security are derived from the payroll (FICA) taxes paid by covered employees and their employers. The tax rate in 2016 was 6.2 percent for Social Security and 1.45 percent for Medicare, or a total of 7.65 percent. Self-employed people are also covered by Social Security. In 2016, they had to pay a Social Security rate of 12.4 percent and a Medicare rate of 2.9 percent for a total of 15.3 percent.

Whether the individual is an employee or self-employed, the indicated tax rate stays in effect only until the employee reaches a maximum *wage base*, which usually increases each year. For 2016, basic Social Security taxes were paid on the first $118,500 of wages earned or self-employed income. Thus, the maximum Social Security tax paid by an employee in 2016 was about $7,347 ($118,500 × 0.062) and

If each takes his or her own full share, there are no spousal benefits. In many cases, the spousal benefit may be higher than that of the spouse's own account. If this is the case, the spouse may retire at 62 and take benefits under his or her own account. Then when the other spouse retires at 67, he or she may switch to the spousal benefit.

Survivor's Benefits If a covered worker dies, the spouse can receive survivor's benefits from Social Security. These benefits include a small lump-sum payment of several hundred dollars, followed by monthly benefit checks. To be eligible for monthly payments, the surviving spouse generally must be at least 60 years of age or have a dependent and unmarried child of the deceased worker in his or her care. (To qualify for *full* benefits, the surviving spouse must be at least 67 years of age; reduced benefits are payable between ages 60 and 67.) If the children of a deceased worker reach age 16 before the spouse reaches age 60, the monthly benefits cease and do not resume until the spouse turns 60.

Gino Santa Maria/Shutterstock.com

14-2d How Much Are Monthly Social Security Benefits?

The amount of Social Security benefits to which an eligible person is entitled is set by law and determined using a fairly complex formula. But you don't need to worry about doing the math yourself; the Social Security Administration has a computerized service that does the benefits estimating for you. Indeed, the government is required by law to provide all covered workers with a *Social Security Statement*. You can request a statement by going to the Social Security Administration Internet site: **www.ssa.gov**. This statement lists the year-by-year Social Security earnings you've been credited with and shows (in today's dollars) what benefits you can expect under three scenarios: (1) if you retire at age 62 and receive 70 percent to 80 percent of the full benefit, (2) the full benefit at age 65 to 67, and (3) the increased benefit that's available if you delay retirement until age 70. The statement also estimates what your children and surviving spouse would get if you die and how much you'd receive monthly if you became disabled.

Range of Benefits Using information provided by the Social Security Administration, Exhibit 14.2 shows the *current average level of benefits* paid in 2016. The benefits shown here are for retired workers, spouses, and children. Bear in mind that these amounts will be adjusted upward each year with subsequent increases in the cost of living.

Note that Social Security *may be reduced* if the recipient is *under age 67 and still gainfully employed*—perhaps

---

Exhibit 14.2

Average Monthly Social Security Benefits Paid in 2016

The Social Security benefits listed here are averages that include a variety of ages at which beneficiaries retired. With the passage of time, the beneficiary will receive correspondingly higher benefits as the cost of living goes up. However, these average benefits dramatize that you should not rely on such benefits too heavily in your retirement planning.

Type of Beneficiary	Average Monthly Benefit
Retired worker	$1,340
Retired couple	$2,210
Disabled worker	$1,166
Disabled worker with a spouse and child	$1,984
Widow or widower	$1,285
Young widow or widower with two children	$2,647

Source: "Understanding the Benefits," SSA Publication No. 05-10024, ICN 454930, https://www.ssa.gov/pubs/EN-05-10024.pdf#page%031&zoom%03auto,0,576, accessed October 2016.

in a part-time job. In particular, given that full retirement age is now 67, retirees aged 62 through 66 are subject to an earnings test that effectively limits the amount of income they can earn before they start losing some (or all) of their Social Security benefits. In 2016, that limit was $15,720 per year. The rule states that if you're a Social Security recipient aged 62 through 66, you will lose $1 in benefits for every $2 you earn above the earnings test amount. So if you earned, say, $18,000 a year at a part-time job, you'd lose $1,140 in annual Social Security benefits—that is, $18,000 − $15,720 = $2,280, which is divided in two to yield $1,140. *Once you reach "full retirement age," the earnings test no longer applies, so you can earn any amount without penalty.*

In contrast to earned income, there never have been any limits on the so-called unearned income derived from such sources as interest, dividends, rents, or profits on securities transactions—a retiree can receive an unlimited amount of such income with no reduction in benefits.

> **YOU CAN DO IT NOW:** Get a Rough Estimate of Your Future Social Security Benefits It's easy to get a rough estimate of your future Social Security benefits. While the Quick Calculator doesn't access your actual earnings history, it does provide a useful rough estimate: **http://www.ssa.gov/oact/quickcalc/**. Remember that this estimate does not consider that future Social Security benefits could be reduced somewhat. Get an estimate of your benefits for planning purposes - you can **do it now.**

Taxes on Benefits Even though Social Security "contributions" are made in after-tax dollars, you may actually have to pay taxes (again) on at least some of your Social Security benefits. Specifically, in 2016, *Social Security retirement benefits are subject to federal income taxes if the beneficiary's annual income exceeds one of the following base amounts:* $25,000 for a single taxpayer, $32,000 for married taxpayers filing jointly, and zero for married taxpayers filing separately. In determining the amount of income that must be counted, the taxpayer starts with his or her *adjusted gross income (AGI)* as defined by current tax law (see Chapter 3) and then adds all nontaxable interest income (such as income from municipal bonds) plus a stipulated portion

Employee Retirement Income Security Act of 1974 (ERISA) a law enacted to ensure that workers eligible for pensions actually receive such benefits; also permits uncovered workers to establish individual tax-sheltered retirement plans

of the Social Security benefits received. For single taxpayers, if the resulting amount is between $25,000 and $34,000, 50 percent of Social Security benefits are taxable. If income exceeds $34,000, 85 percent of Social Security benefits are subject to income tax for a single taxpayer. If the combined income of married taxpayers filing joint returns is between $32,000 and $44,000, then 50 percent of the Social Security benefits are taxable; the percentage of benefits taxed increases to 85 percent when their combined income exceeds $44,000.

14-3 PENSION PLANS AND RETIREMENT PROGRAMS

LO4, LO5 Accompanying the expansion of the Social Security system has been a corresponding growth in employer-sponsored pension and retirement plans. In 1940, when the Social Security program was in its infancy, fewer than 25 percent of the workforce had the benefit of an employer-sponsored plan. Today, around 65 percent of all wage earners and salaried workers (in both the private and public sectors) are covered by some type of employer-sponsored retirement or profit-sharing plan.

In 1948, the National Labor Relations Board (NLRB) ruled that pensions and other types of insurance programs are legitimate subjects for collective bargaining. In response, many employers established new pension plans or liberalized the provisions of existing ones to meet or anticipate union demands. Qualified pension plans (discussed later in this section) allow firms to deduct for tax purposes their contributions to employee retirement programs. Even better, employees can exclude these contributions from their taxable income and can thus build up their own retirement funds on a tax-deferred basis.

Government red tape, however, has taken a toll on pension plans. In particular, the **Employee Retirement Income Security Act of 1974** (sometimes referred to as **ERISA** or the *Pension Reform Act*), which was established to protect employees participating in private employer retirement plans, has actually led to a reduction in the number of new retirement plans started among firms, especially the smaller ones. Indeed, the percentage of workers covered by company-sponsored plans has fallen dramatically since the late 1970s. It's estimated that today, *in the private sector, less than 20 percent of all full-time workers are covered by company-financed plans*—even worse, only about one-third (or less) of the part-time labor force is covered. In contrast, *there has been a significant increase in defined contribution forms of retirement* *plans* (discussed later in this chapter). In addition to ERISA, the widespread availability of Keogh plans, Roth, traditional, and SEP IRAs, and other programs have lessened the urgency for small firms (and bigger ones as well) to offer their own company-financed pension plans.

14-3a Employer-Sponsored Programs: Basic Plans

Employers can sponsor two types of retirement programs—*basic plans*, in which employees automatically participate after a certain period of employment, and *supplemental plans*, which are mostly voluntary programs that enable employees to increase the amount of funds being set aside for retirement.

Participation Requirements The vast majority of pension plans require that employees meet certain criteria before becoming eligible for participation. Most common are requirements relating to years of service, minimum age, level of earnings, and employment classification. Years of service and minimum age requirements are often incorporated into retirement plans in the belief that a much higher labor turnover rate applies to both newly hired and younger employees. Therefore, to reduce the administrative costs of the plans, employees in these categories are often excluded—at least initially—from participation. Once these (or any other) participation requirements are met, the employee automatically becomes eligible to participate in the program.

Importantly, not everyone who participates in a pension plan will earn *the right to receive retirement benefits*. Pension plans impose certain criteria that must be met before the employee can obtain a nonforfeitable right to a pension, known as **vested rights**. As the law now stands, *full vesting* rights are required after three to six years of employment. More specifically, companies must now choose between two vesting schedules. One, the so-called *cliff vesting*, requires full vesting after no more than three years of service—but you obtain no vesting privileges until then. Once vested, you're entitled to everything that's been paid in so far (your contributions *plus* your employer's) and everything that will be contributed in the future. Under the alternate procedure, the so-called *graded schedule*, vesting takes place gradually over the first six years of employment. At the minimum, after two years, you'd have a nonforfeiture right to at least 20 percent of the benefits, with an additional 20 percent each year thereafter until you're 100 percent vested after six years.

What happens if you quit your job and move to another employer? If you're not vested, you normally have no choice but to take out your money. But if you are vested, you can usually do one of two things: either take your money out or leave it in your current employer's retirement program. However, because of inflation, the value of the benefit for a worker who leaves the firm long before retirement age is typically very small. Consequently, the employee might be better off simply withdrawing his or her own contributions (which always vest immediately) and terminating participation in the plan at the same time he or she leaves the employer. Of course, any worker who leaves the firm before accumulating the required years of service would be entitled only to a return of his or her own contributions to the plan (plus nominal investment earnings).

Keep in mind that, whenever you terminate employment, it's important to *resist the urge to spend the money you have built up in your retirement account! Over time, that can have a devastating effect on your ability to accumulate retirement capital. Instead, when you take money out of one retirement account, roll it over into another one.*

> When you take money out of one retirement account, roll it over into another one.

What's Your Contribution? Whether you, as an employee, must make payments toward your own pension depends on the type of plan you're in. If you belong to a **noncontributory pension plan**, the employer pays the total cost of the benefits—you don't

vested rights employees' nonforfeitable rights to receive benefits in a pension plan based on their own and their employer's contributions

noncontributory pension plan a pension plan in which the employer pays the total cost of the benefits

Andrey_Popov/Shutterstock.com

have to pay a thing. Under a **contributory pension plan**, the employer and the employee share the cost. Today, the trend is toward contributory plans. In addition, nearly all plans for employees of federal, state, and local governments require a contribution from the employee. In contributory plans, the employee's share of the costs is often between 3 percent and 10 percent of annual wages and is typically paid through a payroll deduction. Probably the most common arrangement is for the employer to match the employee's contribution—the employee puts up half the annual contribution and the employer puts up the other half.

Defined Contributions or Defined Benefits The two most commonly used methods to compute benefits at retirement are the defined contribution plan and the defined benefit plan. A **defined contribution plan** specifies the amount of contribution that both the employer and employee must make. At retirement, the worker is awarded whatever level of monthly benefits those contributions will purchase.

Although such factors as age, income level, and the amount of contributions made to the plan have a great deal to do with the amount of monthly benefits received at retirement, probably no variable is more important than the level of *investment performance* generated on the contributed funds. A defined contribution plan promises nothing at retirement except the returns the fund managers have been able to obtain. The only thing that's defined is the amount of the contributions the employee and/or employer make. The benefits at retirement depend totally on investment results.

Under a **defined benefit plan**, the formula for computing benefits, not contributions, is stipulated in the plan provisions. These benefits are paid out regardless of how well (or poorly) the retirement funds are invested. If investment performance falls short, the employer must make up the difference in order to fund the benefits agreed to in the plan. This type of plan allows employees to calculate before retirement how much their monthly retirement income will be. Often the number of

> The employee is being forced to assume more responsibility for ensuring the desired level of postretirement income.

Employee Benefits

garagestock/Shutterstock.com

years of service and amount of earnings are prime factors in the formula. For example, workers might be paid 2.5 percent of their final 3-year average annual salary for each year of service. Thus, the *annual* benefit to an employee whose final 3-year average annual salary was $85,000 and who was with the company for 20 years would be $42,500 (2.5 percent × $85,000 × 20 years).

Many defined benefit plans also increase retirement benefits periodically to help retirees keep up with the cost of living. In periods of high inflation, these increases are essential to maintain retirees' standards of living. While the number of *people* covered by such plans continues to rise, especially in the ranks of government employees, the number of (private-sector) defined benefit *plans* in existence has steadily declined. In fact, there are now *more assets* held in defined contribution plans than there are in traditional (defined benefit) pension plans. And it's very likely that this shift to defined contribution plans will only accelerate in the coming years.

Regardless of the method used to calculate benefits, the employee's basic concern should be with the percentage of final take-home pay that the plan is likely to produce at retirement. A pension is usually thought to be good if, when combined with Social Security, it will result in a monthly income equal to about 70 percent to 80 percent of preretirement net earnings. To reach this goal, however, today's employees must take some responsibility because *there's a growing trend for companies to switch from defined benefit plans to defined contribution programs.* Companies don't like the idea of being faced with uncertain future pension liabilities. Now, more and more of them are avoiding these problems altogether by changing to defined contribution plans. As a result, *the employee is being forced to assume more responsibility for ensuring the desired level of postretirement income.*

This means that where you end up in retirement will depend, more than ever, on what *you've* done, rather than on what your employers have done. *Very likely, you're the one who is going to control not only how much goes into the company's retirement programs, but also where it goes.*

Qualified Pension Plans The Internal Revenue Code permits a corporate employer making contributions to a **qualified pension plan** to deduct its contributions to the plan from taxable income. While these contributions are a significant part of total compensation, the employees on whose behalf the contributions are made don't have to include these payments as part of their taxable income until the benefits are actually received. Further, in contributory plans, *employees can also shelter their contributions from taxes.* In other words, such contributions aren't counted as part of taxable income in the year that they're made; hence they act to reduce the amount of taxable income reported to the Internal Revenue Service (IRS) and therefore lead to lower taxes for the employee. Still another tax advantage of these plans is that any and all investment income is allowed to accumulate tax free; as a result, investment capital can build up more quickly.

14-3b Employer-Sponsored Programs: Supplemental Plans

In addition to basic retirement programs, many employers offer supplemental plans. These plans are often *voluntary* and enable employees not only to increase the amount of funds being held for retirement but also to enjoy attractive tax benefits. There are three types of supplemental plans: profit-sharing, thrift and savings, and salary reduction plans.

Profit-Sharing Plans Profit-sharing plans enable employees to participate in the earnings of their employer. A **profit-sharing plan** may be

> **qualified pension plan** a pension plan that meets specified criteria established by the Internal Revenue Code
>
> **profit-sharing plan** an arrangement in which the employees of a firm participate in the company's earnings

qualified under IRS rules and become eligible for essentially the same tax treatment as other types of pension plans. The major argument supporting the use of profit-sharing plans is that they encourage employees to work harder because the employees benefit when the firm prospers. Also, in years when the firm has no profit, the firm is not required to contribute to a profit-sharing plan. Contributions to these plans are invested in different types of fixed-interest products, stocks and bonds, and, in many cases, securities issued by the employing firm itself. Employees who receive the firm's securities may actually benefit twice. When profits are good, larger contributions are made to the profit-sharing plan, and the price of the shares already owned is likely to increase as well.

Some big companies offer *voluntary profit-sharing plans* that invest heavily (almost exclusively) in their own stock. It's common in many of these cases for long-term career employees to accumulate several hundred thousand dollars worth of the company's stock. And we're not talking just about highly paid corporate executives here; rather, these are just average employees who had the discipline to divert a portion of their salary consistently to the company's profit-sharing plan. However, *there is a real and significant downside to this practice*: If the company should hit hard times, then not only could you face salary cuts (or even worse, the loss of your job) but the value of your profit-sharing account will likely tumble as well. Just look at what happened to employees in the technology sector during the 2000–2002 bear market and to the broad population during the financial crisis of 2008–2009.

Thrift and Savings Plans

Thrift and savings plans were established to supplement pension and other fringe benefits. Most plans require the employer to make contributions to the savings plan in an amount equal to a set proportion of the amount contributed by the employee. For example, an employer might match an employee's contributions at the rate of 50 cents on the dollar up to, say, 6 percent of salary. These contributions are then deposited with a trustee, who invests the money in various types of securities, including stocks and bonds of the employing firm.

With IRS-qualified thrift and savings plans, the *employer's* contributions and earnings on the savings aren't included in the *employee's* taxable income until he or she withdraws the money. Unfortunately, this attractive tax feature doesn't extend to the *employee's contributions*, so any money put into one of these savings plans is still considered part of the employee's taxable income and subject to regular income taxes. An employee who has the option should seriously consider participating in a thrift plan. The returns are usually pretty favorable, especially when you factor in the employer's contributions.

jeff Metzger/Shutterstock.com

Go to Smart Sites

Is the future of Social Security secure? The nonpartisan Congressional Budget Office has forecasts under various policies.

Salary Reduction Plans Another type of supplemental retirement program—and certainly the most popular, judging by employee response—is the **salary reduction plan**, or the **401(k) plan** as it's more commonly known. Our discussion here centers on 401(k) plans, but similar programs are available for employees of public, nonprofit organizations, including public schools, colleges, hospitals, and state and local governments. Known as *403(b) plans* or *457 plans*, they offer many of the same features and tax shelter provisions as 401(k) plans.

More and more companies are cutting back on their contributions to traditional (defined benefit) retirement plans. They're turning instead to 401(k) plans, a type of defined contribution plan. A 401(k) plan gives employees the option to divert part of their salary to a company-sponsored, tax-sheltered investment account. In this way, the earnings diverted to the plan accumulate tax free. Taxes must be paid eventually, but not until the employee starts drawing down the account at retirement. In 2016, an individual employee could put as much as $18,000 into a tax-deferred 401(k) plan. (Contribution limits for 403(b) and 457 plans are the same as those for 401(k) plans.) And for those over 50 years old, there is

thrift and savings plans a plan to supplement pension and other fringe benefits; the firm contributes an amount equal to a set proportion of the employee's contribution

salary reduction or 401(k) plan an agreement by which part of a covered employee's pay is withheld and invested; taxes on the contributions and the account earnings are deferred until the funds are withdrawn

A few basic ideas on managing your 401(k) account can take you a long way:

- **A reasonable asset allocation is more important than choosing the "right" specific funds for your 401(k) account money.** Research shows that over 90 percent of your investment performance will be determined by how much you allocate to cash, bonds, and equity funds. So less than 10 percent of performance is determined by choosing the right funds and by trying to time the market (which is never a good idea anyway). Remember the conventional wisdom as a starting place: Put 100−your age as the percentage in equities, and the residual in bonds and cash. For example, if you're 30, start out with a plan to put 70 percent in equities and 30 percent in bonds and cash. Then adjust the mix to match your risk tolerance.

- **Invest enough in your 401(k) account.** Invest at least up to your company's matching amount, if you can possibly afford it. For example, if your company matches the first 6 percent of your annual contribution, then you should contribute at least that much or you're just throwing away money. A reasonable overall goal is to contribute at least 15 percent of your annual income to retirement investment accounts, which include 401(k)s, IRAs, and other investment vehicles.

- **Invest in your 401(k) consistently regardless of its performance.** Some investors panic when their 401(k) accounts lose money and *reduce or even stop* making contributions in an effort to protect themselves from further losses. This is the opposite of what you should do. When you're losing money, it's time to grit your teeth and contribute more to your account, not less! This is because you've got to make up for your losses. If you stop or reduce your contributions, you'll be even less likely to achieve your retirement goal. And keep in mind that when investment values fall, you're buying more shares at lower prices (a principle known as "dollar-cost averaging"). In the long term, this should contribute positively to performance.

---

a "catch-up" provision of $6,000 that allows them to contribute up to $24,000 in 2016.

According to Fidelity Investments, one of the largest 401(k) providers, the average 401(k) balance was around $91,800 in 2016. And the average balance was about $251,600 for employees having participated in a 401(k) for at least 10 years. Yet these averages are for those who participate in 401(k) programs. According to the National Institute on Retirement Security, more than 45 percent of households do not own any significant retirement account assets. When all households are considered, the median retirement account balance was a mere $3,000 and only $12,000 for those near retirement. Thus, up to 92 percent of households do not meet conservative retirement savings targets for their age and income levels! Thus, a retirement savings crisis is here and growing.

EXAMPLE: How Tax-Deferred Plans Work Nadia is under 50 years old, with taxable income of $75,000 in 2016. She would like to contribute the maximum allowable mount—$18,000—to the 401(k) plan where she works. Doing so reduces her taxable income to $57,000 and, assuming she's in the 25 percent tax bracket, lowers her federal tax bill by some $4,500 ($18,000 × 0.25). Such tax savings will offset a good portion—25 percent—of her contribution to the 401(k) savings plan. In effect, she'll add $18,000 to her retirement program with only $13,500 of her own money; the rest will come from the IRS via a reduced tax bill. What's more, all the *earnings* on her investment account will accumulate tax free as well. The downside is if Nadia needs the money before she is 59½. In that case, she will have to pay the tax on any withdrawals *plus* a 10 percent penalty to the IRS.

These plans are generally viewed as attractive *tax shelters* that offer not only substantial tax savings, but also a way to save for retirement. As long as you can afford to put the money aside, *you should seriously consider joining a 401(k)/403(b)/457 plan if one is offered at your place of employment.* This is especially true when one considers the matching features offered by many of these plans. Most companies that offer 401(k) plans have some type of matching contributions program, often putting up 50 cents (or more) for every dollar contributed by the employee. Such matching plans give both tax and savings incentives to individuals and clearly enhance the appeal of 401(k) plans.

Another kind of 401(k) plan is being offered by a growing number of firms. This retirement savings option, the so-called *Roth 401(k)*, is just like a traditional 401(k) except for one important difference: *All contributions to Roth 401(k) plans are made in after-tax dollars.* That means there are no tax savings to be derived from the annual employee contributions. If you earn, say, $75,000 a year and want to put $18,000 into your Roth 401(k), you'll end up paying taxes on the full $75,000. That's the bad news; now the good news. Because all contributions are made in after-tax dollars, *there are no taxes to be paid on plan withdrawals (in other words, they're tax free)*, provided you're at least 59½ and have held the account for five years or more.

Like traditional 401(k) plans, Roth 401(k)s also have a contribution cap of $18,000 (in 2016, for those under 50). And that limit applies to *total contributions to both types of 401(k) plans combined*, so you can't put $18,000 into a traditional 401(k) plan and then put another $18,000 into a Roth 401(k). You can also have employer matches with the Roth plans, although technically those matches will accumulate in a separate account that will be taxed as ordinary income at withdrawal. Essentially, *employer* contributions represent tax-free income to employees, so they'll pay taxes on that income (and on any account earnings) when the funds are withdrawn—as is done with a traditional 401(k).

Both Roth and traditional 401(k) plans typically offer their participants various investment options, including equity and fixed-income mutual funds, company stock, and a variety of interest-bearing vehicles such as bank CDs. Indeed, the typical 401(k) has about 10 choices, and some plans have as many as 20, or even more. Today, the trend is toward giving plan participants more options and providing seminars and other educational tools to help employees make informed retirement plan decisions.

14-3c Evaluating Employer-Sponsored Pension Plans

When participating in a company-sponsored pension plan, you're entitled to certain benefits in return for meeting certain conditions of membership—which may or may not include making contributions to the plan. Whether your participation is limited to the firm's basic plan or includes one or more of the supplemental programs, *it's vital that you take the time to acquaint*

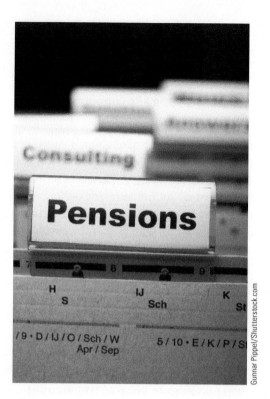

Gunnar Pippel/Shutterstock.com

yourself with the various benefits and provisions of these plans. And be sure to familiarize yourself not only with the basic plans, but also with any (voluntary) supplemental plans that you may be eligible to join.

How should you evaluate these plans? Most experts agree that you can get a pretty good handle on essential plan provisions and retirement benefits by taking a close look at the following features:

▶ **Eligibility requirements.** Precisely what are they?

▶ **Defined benefits or contributions.** Which one is defined? If it's the benefits, exactly what formula is used to define them? Pay particular attention to how Social Security benefits are treated in the formula. If it's a defined contribution program, do you have any control over how the money is invested? If so, what are your options?

▶ **Vesting procedures.** Does the company use a cliff or graded procedure?

▶ **Contributory or noncontributory.** If the plan is contributory, how much comes from you and how much from the company? If it's noncontributory, what is the company's contribution as a percentage of your salary?

▶ **Retirement age.** What's the normal retirement age, and what provisions are there for *early retirement*?

▶ **Portability.** Are the pension benefits *portable*—that is, can you take them with you if you change jobs?

▶ **Voluntary supplemental programs.** How much of your salary can you put into one or more of these plans, and what—if anything—is matched by the company?

Finding answers to these questions will help you determine where you stand and what improvements are needed to be made in your retirement plans. As part of this evaluation process, try to determine, as best as you can, *what your benefits are likely to be at retirement*. Before you start cranking out the numbers, check with the people who handle employee benefits at your workplace; they'll usually give you the help you need. Then, using a procedure similar to that followed in Worksheet 14.1, you can estimate what portion of your retirement needs will be met from your company's basic pension plan. If there's a shortfall—*and it's likely there will be*—it will indicate the extent to which you need to participate in some type of company-sponsored supplemental program, such as a 401(k) plan, or (alternatively) how much you'll need to rely on your own savings and investments to reach the standard of living you're looking for in retirement.

14-3d Self-Directed Retirement Programs

In addition to participating in company-sponsored retirement programs, individuals can set up their own tax-sheltered retirement plans. There are two basic types of self-directed retirement programs: *Keogh* and *SEP plans*, which are for self-employed individuals, and *individual retirement accounts (IRAs)*, which can be set up by almost anyone.

Keogh and SEP Plans **Keogh plans** were introduced in 1962 as part of the Self-Employed Individuals Retirement Act, or simply the Keogh Act. Keogh plans allow self-employed individuals to set up tax-deferred retirement plans for themselves and their employees. Like contributions to 401(k) plans, payments to Keogh accounts may be taken as deductions from taxable income. As a result, they reduce the tax bills of self-employed individuals. The maximum contribution to this tax-deferred retirement plan in 2016 is $53,000 or 25 percent of earned income for sole proprietors (20 percent for unincorporated businesses), whichever is less.

Any individual who is self-employed, either full- or part-time, is eligible to set up a Keogh account. These accounts can also be used by individuals who hold full-time jobs and moonlight part-time—for instance, the accountant who does tax returns on a freelance basis at night and on weekends. And note that even though he has a Keogh account, this individual is still eligible to receive full retirement benefits from his full-time job and to have his own IRA. (SEP plans are just like Keogh plans except that they're aimed at small business owners, particularly those with no employees, who want a plan that's simple and easy to administer. Except for some administrative details, they have the same features and limitations as standard Keogh accounts.)

Keogh accounts can be opened at banks, mutual funds, and other financial institutions. Annual contributions must be made at the time the respective tax return is filed or usually by April 15 of the following calendar year (e.g., you have until the filing due date of April 15, 2017, to contribute to your Keogh for 2016). Although a designated financial institution acts as custodian of all the funds held in a Keogh account, *actual investments held in the account are directed completely by the individual contributor*. These are self-directed retirement programs; the *individual* decides which investments to buy and sell.

Income earned from the investments must be reinvested in the account. This income also accrues tax free. All Keogh contributions and investment earnings must remain in the account until the individual turns 59½ unless he or she becomes seriously ill or disabled; early withdrawals for any other reason are subject to 10 percent tax penalties. However, the individual is not *required* to start withdrawing the funds at age 59½; the funds can stay in the account (and continue earning tax-free income) until the individual is 70½. Then the individual *must* begin withdrawing funds from the account—unless he or she continues to be gainfully employed past the age of 70½. Of course, once an individual starts withdrawing funds (upon or after turning 59½), all such withdrawals are treated as ordinary income and are subject to normal income taxes.

Individual Retirement Accounts (IRAs) Some people mistakenly believe that an IRA is a specialized type of investment. It's not. An **individual retirement account (IRA)**, is virtually the same as any other investment account you open with a bank, stockbroker, or mutual fund *except* that it's clearly designated as an IRA. That is, you complete a form that designates the account as an IRA and makes the institution its trustee. That's all there is to it. Any

Keogh plan an account to which self-employed persons may make specified payments that may be deducted from taxable income; earnings also accrue on a tax-deferred basis

individual retirement account (IRA) a retirement plan, open to any working American, to which a person may contribute a specified amount each year

YOU CAN DO IT NOW: Calculating the Benefits of a Traditional IRA If you want to estimate the potential value of a traditional IRA at retirement, try the calculator at http://www.bankrate.com/calculators /retirement/traditional-ira-plan-calculator.aspx. You can **do it now.**

gainfully employed person (and spouse) can have an IRA account, although the type of accounts that a person can have and the tax status of those accounts depend on several variables. All IRAs, however, have one thing in common: they're designed to encourage retirement savings for individuals. Today, an individual has three IRA types to choose from, as follows:

► **Traditional (deductible) IRAs,** which can be opened by anyone without a retirement plan at his or her place of employment, *regardless of income level*, or by couples filing jointly who—even if they are covered by retirement plans at their places of employment—have adjusted gross incomes of less than $98,000 (or single tax payers with AGIs of less than $61,000). In 2016, individuals under the age of 50 who qualify may make tax-deductible contributions of up to $5,500 a year to their accounts (an equal tax-deductible amount can be contributed by a nonworking spouse). All account earnings grow tax free until withdrawn, when ordinary tax rates apply (though a 10 percent penalty normally applies to withdrawals made before age 59½).

► **Nondeductible (after-tax) IRA,** which is open to anyone regardless of their income level or whether they're covered by a retirement plan at their workplace. In 2016, contributions of up to $5,500 a year can be made to this account, but they're *made with after-tax dollars* (i.e., the contributions are not tax deductible). However, *the earnings do accrue tax free and are not subject to tax until they are withdrawn* after the individual reaches age 59½ (funds withdrawn before age 59½ may be subject to the 10 percent penalty).

► **Roth IRAs** are a lot like Roth 401(k)s, which were discussed earlier. They can be opened by couples filing jointly with adjusted gross incomes in 2016 of up to $193,000 (singles up to $131,000), whether or not they have other retirement or pension plans. But the best part of the Roth IRA is its tax features—although the annual contributions of up to $6,500 a person in 2016 are made with nondeductible/after-tax dollars, all earnings in the account grow tax free. And *all withdrawals*

from the account are also tax free provided that the account has been open for at least five years and the individual is past the age of 59½. In other words, so long as these conditions are met, you won't have to pay taxes on any withdrawals you make from your Roth IRA!

EXAMPLE: Measuring the Benefits of a Roth IRA Roth IRAs provide no tax deduction for contributions. But all future earnings are sheltered from taxes under current law. So how much would you save over simply investing in a fully taxed fund if you're 25 years old and invested $5,500 a year at 6 percent until retirement at age 66?

Assuming you're in the 25 percent marginal tax bracket and you invested the money at the beginning of each year, you would have $962,228 in a Roth IRA and $648,586 in an unsheltered account at retirement. So the tax shelter afforded by the Roth IRA would be worth a whopping $313,642 more than the otherwise comparable but fully taxable account!

It is possible to convert a traditional IRA to a Roth IRA. If you convert, you will have to pay taxes on any earnings and pretax contributions. So why would you want to do that? It may make sense to convert if you expect your tax rate to remain the same or go up after retirement. Thus, converting to a Roth IRA could allow you to pay a lower amount of taxes on your IRA investments in the long run. However, it's important to be able to pay the taxes using money that doesn't come out of your IRA account. If you make a withdrawal from a traditional IRA account before age 59½, you generally owe a 10 percent penalty on that amount. And you would give up the opportunity for tax-free Roth IRA compounding on that amount—permanently. It usually makes less sense to convert a traditional IRA to a Roth IRA the older you are. This is because the older you are, the less time you have to make up for what you paid in taxes on the conversion. However, it can still be wise for an older person to convert a traditional to a Roth IRA for estate tax planning purposes. Conversions can be complicated, and it's best to consult a tax advisor. However, you can get a good idea of whether conversion looks like a reasonable move using an online conversion calculator like that offered by Fidelity (**http://personal.fidelity.com/misc/widgets/IRA_Evaluator/IRA_EVAL.html**).

Regardless of the type and notwithstanding the conditions just described, penalty-free withdrawals are generally allowed from an IRA so long as the funds are being used for first-time home purchases (up to $10,000), qualifying educational costs, certain major medical expenses, or other qualified emergencies. Also, with both the traditional/deductible and nondeductible IRAs, you must start making withdrawals from your account once you reach age 70½—although *this requirement does not apply to Roth IRAs*.

Self-Directed Accounts and Their Investment Vehicles IRAs are like Keogh and SEP plans; they're *self-directed accounts*, which means that you are free to make almost any kind of investment decision you want. An individual can be conservative or aggressive in choosing securities for an IRA (or Keogh), though conventional wisdom favors funding your IRA (and Keogh) with *income-producing assets*. While such assets tend to be lower in risk, income is also typically taxed at a higher rate than capital gains. This would also suggest that if you're looking for capital gains, it's best to do so *outside* your retirement account. This doesn't mean, however, that it would be totally inappropriate to place a good-quality growth stock or mutual fund in a Keogh or IRA. In fact, many advisors contend that growth investments should always have a place in your retirement account because of their often impressive performance and ability to protect against inflation. Such investments may pay off handsomely because they appreciate totally free of taxes. And in the end, *it's how much you have in your retirement account that matters, not how your earnings were made along the way*.

No matter what type of investment vehicle you use, keep in mind that once you place money in an IRA, it's meant to stay there for the long haul. Like most tax-sheltered retirement programs, there are restrictions on when you can withdraw the funds from an IRA. And

when you move your IRA account to a new firm (this is known as a *rollover*), the transfer will be subject to a *20 percent withholding tax* if the proceeds from the transfer are paid to you directly. The rule is very clear on this: if you take possession of the funds (even for just a few days), you'll be hit with the withholding tax. So, the best way to handle IRA rollovers is to *arrange for the transfer of funds from one investment trustee to another*.

So, should you contribute to an IRA or not? Obviously, as long as you qualify for either a traditional IRA or a Roth IRA, you should seriously consider making the maximum payments allowable. There are no special record-keeping requirements or forms to file, and the IRA is an excellent vehicle for sheltering income from taxes. Probably the biggest decision you'll have to make is which IRA is right for you—the traditional or the Roth?

14-4 ANNUITIES

LO6 An annuity is just the opposite of life insurance. As pointed out in Chapter 8, life insurance is the systematic accumulation of an estate that is used for protection against financial loss resulting from premature death. In contrast, an **annuity** is the systematic *liquidation* of an estate in such a way that it provides protection against the economic difficulties that could result from outliving personal financial resources. The period during which premiums are paid toward the purchase of an annuity is called the **accumulation period**; correspondingly, the period during which annuity payments are made is called the **distribution period**.

Under a pure life annuity contract, a life insurance company will guarantee regular monthly payments to an individual for as long as he or she lives. These benefits are composed of three parts: principal, interest, and survivorship benefits. The *principal* consists of the premium amounts paid in by the *annuitant* (person buying the annuity) during the accumulation period. *Interest* is the amount earned on these funds between the time they're paid and distributed. The interest earnings on an annuity accrue (i.e., accumulate) tax free—but note that, whereas the earnings in an annuity accumulate on a tax-sheltered basis, the amounts paid into an annuity are all made with *after-tax dollars* (i.e., no special tax treatment is given to the capital contributions). The portion of

annuity an investment product created by life insurance companies that provides a series of payments over time

accumulation period the period during which premiums are paid for the purchase of an annuity

distribution period the period during which annuity payments are made to an annuitant

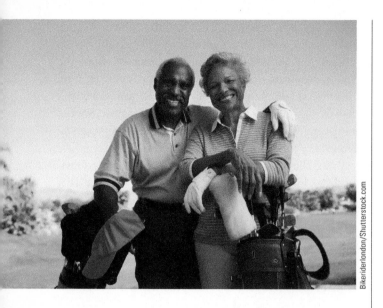
Bikerider london/Shutterstock.com

the principal and interest that has not been returned to the annuitant before death is the **survivorship benefit**. These funds are available to those members of the annuity group who survive in each subsequent period.

14-4a Classification of Annuities

As seen in Exhibit 14.3, annuities may be classified according to several key characteristics, including payment of premiums, payment method, disposition of proceeds, inception date of benefits, and method used in calculating benefits.

Single Premium or Installments There are two ways to pay the premiums when you purchase an annuity contract: you can make one large (lump-sum) payment up front, or pay the premium in installments. The **single premium annuity contract** usually requires a *minimum investment* of anywhere from $2,500 to $10,000, with $5,000 the most common figure. These annuities have become popular primarily because of their attractive tax features. They're often purchased just before retirement as a way

survivorship benefit on an annuity, the portion of premiums and interest that has not been returned to the annuitant before his or her death

single premium annuity contract an annuity contract purchased with a lump-sum payment

immediate annuity an annuity in which the annuitant begins receiving monthly benefits immediately

installment premium annuity contracts an annuity contract purchased through periodic payments made over time

deferred annuity an annuity in which benefit payments are postponed for a certain number of years

life annuity with no refund (pure life) an option under which an annuitant receives a specified amount of income for life, regardless of the length of the distribution period

guaranteed-minimum annuity (life annuity with refund) an annuity that provides a guaranteed minimum distribution of benefits

of creating a future stream of income. In these circumstances, the individual normally purchases an **immediate annuity**, in which case the stream of monthly benefits begins immediately—the first check arrives a month or so after purchase.

Although most *group* annuity policies are funded with single premiums, many *individuals* still buy annuities by paying for them in installments. With these **installment premium annuity contracts**, the set payments, which can start as low as $100, are made at regular intervals (monthly, quarterly, or annually) over an extended period of time. Sometimes these annuities are set up with a fairly large initial payment (of perhaps several thousand dollars) followed by a series of much smaller installment payments (of, say, $250 a quarter). This approach would be used to purchase a **deferred annuity**, a type of contract in which cash benefits are deferred for several years (note that single premiums can also be used to purchase deferred annuities). A big advantage of *installment premium deferred annuities* is that your savings can build up over time *free of taxes*. With no taxes to pay, you have more money working for you and can build up a bigger retirement nest egg. You'll have to pay taxes on your earnings eventually, of course, but not until you start receiving benefit payments from your annuity.

Disposition of Proceeds All annuities are based on the concept of "pay now, receive later," so they allow individuals to prepare for future cash needs, such as planning for retirement, while obtaining significant tax benefits. When the annuity is distributed, you can take a lump-sum payment or, as is more often the case, you can *annuitize* the distribution by systematically parceling out the money into regular payments over a defined or open-ended period. Because most people choose to annuitize their proceeds (which is how an annuity is intended to be used), let's look at the most common annuity disbursement options:

▶ **Life annuity with no refund (pure life).** The annuitant receives a specified amount of income for life, whether the disbursement period turns out to be 1 year or 50 years. The estate or family receives no refunds when the annuitant dies. This results in the largest monthly payments of any of the distribution methods.

▶ **Guaranteed-minimum annuity (life annuity with refund).** In this type of contract, the benefits (future cash flows) aren't limited to the annuitant only and may extend to named beneficiaries.

Exhibit 14.3

Types of Annuity Contracts

Annuity contracts vary according to how you pay for the annuity, how the proceeds are disbursed, how earnings accrue, and when you receive the benefits.

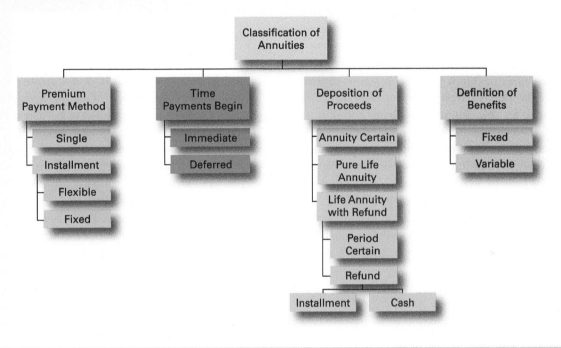

With a **life annuity, period certain**, the annuitant gets a guaranteed monthly income for life with the added provision that the insurance company will pay the monthly benefits for a minimum number of years (5 or 10, for example). If the annuitant dies soon after the distribution begins, then his or her beneficiaries receive the monthly benefits for the balance of the "period certain." With a **refund annuity**, if the annuitant dies, then the designated beneficiary receives monthly payments (or a lump-sum cash refund) until the total purchase price of the annuity has been refunded.

▶ **Annuity certain.** This type of annuity pays a set amount of monthly income for a specified number of years, thereby filling a need for monthly income that will expire after a certain length of time. An annuitant selecting a 10-year annuity certain receives payments for 10 years, regardless of whether he or she lives for 2 or 20 more years.

Fixed versus Variable Annuity When you put your money into an annuity, the premium is invested on your behalf by the insurance company, much as a mutual fund invests the money you put into it. From the time you pay the first (or only) annuity premium until it's paid back to you as a lump sum or as an annuitized monthly benefit, you'll earn a rate of return on your investment. How that rate of return is figured determines whether you own a fixed or variable annuity. In a **fixed-rate annuity**, the insurance company safeguards your principal and agrees to pay a guaranteed minimum rate of interest over the life of the contract. These are conservative, low-risk annuity products that essentially promise to return *the original investment plus interest* when the money is paid out to the annuitant (or any designated

life annuity, period certain a type of guaranteed-minimum annuity that guarantees the annuitant a stated amount of monthly income for life; the insurer agrees to pay for a minimum number of years

refund annuity a guaranteed-minimum annuity that, on the annuitant's death, makes monthly payments to the beneficiary until the total price of the annuity is refunded

annuity certain an annuity that provides a specified monthly income for a stated number of years without consideration of any life contingency

fixed-rate annuity an annuity in which the insurance company agrees to pay a guaranteed rate of interest on your money beneficiaries). Unlike bond mutual funds, fixed annuities don't fluctuate in value when interest rates rise or fall; so your principal is always secure.

Imagine an investment structured to let you move between stocks, bonds, and money funds and, at the same time, accumulate profits tax free. That, in a nutshell, is a variable annuity. With a **variable annuity**, the amount that's ultimately paid out to the annuitant varies with the investment results obtained by the insurance company—*nothing is guaranteed, not even the principal!* When you buy a variable annuity, *you decide* where your money will be invested based on your investment objectives and tolerance for risk. You can usually choose from stocks, bonds, money market securities, real estate, alternative investments, or some combination thereof. As an annuity holder, you can stay put with a single investment for the long haul. Or, as with most variable annuities, you can more aggressively play the market by switching from one fund to another. Obviously, when the market goes up, investors in variable annuities do well; but when the market falters, the returns on these policies will likewise be reduced.

 ## Go to Smart Sites

For tips on investing and saving strategies for retirement, Investopedia's retirement section has answers.

14-4b Sources of Annuities

Annuities are administered by life insurance companies, so it's no surprise that they're also the leading sellers of these financial products. Annuities can also be purchased from stock brokers, mutual fund organizations, banks, and financial planners. When you buy an annuity, the cost will vary with the annuitant's age at issue, the annuitant's age when payments begin, the method used to distribute benefits, the number of lives covered, and the annuitant's gender.

There can be substantial differences among the premiums charged by different companies. These differences confirm the need to shop around before making an annuity purchase. The cost to females is higher than the cost to males across all benefit levels because of the lower mortality rates among women.

variable annuity an annuity in which the monthly income provided by the policy varies as a function of the insurer's actual investment experience

YOU CAN DO IT NOW: What Do Annuities Cost? Want to get a sense of what an annuity costs? Representative quotes based on state, age, and gender can be found at https://www.nylaarp.com/Annuities/Income-Example. You can **do it now.**

As with mutual funds, there are some annual fees that you should be aware of. In particular, be prepared to pay insurance fees of 1 percent or more—in addition to the annual management fees of perhaps 1 percent to 2 percent paid on variable annuities. That's a total of 2 percent to 3 percent or more taken right off the top, year after year. There is also a *contract charge* (or maintenance fee) that's deducted annually to cover various contract-related expenses; these fees usually run from about $30 to $60 per year. Obviously, these fees can drag down returns and reduce the advantage of tax-deferred income. Finally, most annuities charge hefty *penalties for early withdrawal*. This means that, in order to get out of a poorly performing annuity, you'll have to forfeit a chunk of your money.

14-4c Investment and Income Properties of Annuities

A major attribute of most types of annuities is that they're a source of income that can't be outlived. Although individuals might be able to create a similar arrangement by simply living off the interest or dividends from their investments, they'd find it difficult to liquidate their principal systematically so that the last payment would coincide closely (or exactly) with their death. Another advantage is that the income earned in an annuity is allowed to accumulate tax free, so it's a form of *tax-sheltered investment*. Actually, the income from an annuity is *tax deferred*, meaning that taxes on the earnings will have to be paid when the annuity is liquidated. And importantly, even though part of the annuity's return is from capital gains and part is from dividends, all of the return is taxed as ordinary income.

Shelter from taxes is an attractive investment attribute, but there's a hitch. You may be faced with a big tax penalty if you close out or withdraw money from an annuity before it's time. Specifically, the IRS treats annuity withdrawals like IRA withdrawals: except in cases of serious illness, *anyone who takes money out before reaching age 59½ will incur a 10 percent penalty*. All of which only reinforces the notion that *an annuity should*

Financial Planning Tips

DOES AN ANNUITY MAKE SENSE FOR YOU?

Most of us don't have a traditional defined benefit pension and have to manage with a 401(k) plan along with careful investing to fund our retirement. But we still long for the steady income that defined benefit plans provide. Annuities are designed to provide a monthly income for the rest of your life. You enter into an agreement with an insurer that provides that benefit for a predefined time period after you pay in advance for this service. Annuities are designed to assure that you do not outlive your money.

So when does it make sense to buy an annuity? If you have guaranteed income from several different sources, you may not need an annuity. However, if you don't have a traditional pension plan and want the security of a fixed monthly payment in retirement, you may want to consider using some of your savings to purchase an annuity. Here is some more specific guidance.

A *deferred annuity* is worth considering when:

- You are making the maximum contribution to your employer-sponsored retirement plan and to your IRA (or if you're not eligible for an IRA).
- You don't expect to need the annuity funds until you are at least 59½ years old.
- You have an emergency fund that covers at least six months of living expenses.

An *immediate annuity* may be a good choice when:

- You want to convert part of your retirement savings into income now.
- You are in good health and expect to live at least another 20 years.
- You have sufficient assets to cover large expenses like medical bills.

Source: Adapted, in part, from Phil Taylor, "Do You Need an Annuity?" http://money.usnews.com/money/blogs/On-Retirement/2012/01/06/do-you-need-an-annuity, accessed October 2016.

---

always be considered a long-term investment. Assume that it's a part of your retirement program (after all, that's the way the IRS looks at it) and that you're getting in for the long haul.

From an investment perspective, the returns generated from an annuity can be, in some cases, a bit disappointing. For instance, as we discussed earlier, the returns on *variable annuities* are tied to returns in the money and capital markets. Even so, they're still no better than what you can get from other investment vehicles—indeed, they're often lower, in part because of higher annuity fees. Keep in mind that these differential returns aren't due to tax features because, in both cases, returns are measured on a before-tax basis. But *returns from annuities are tax sheltered*, so that makes those lower returns a lot more attractive.

If you're considering a variable annuity, go over it much as you would a traditional mutual fund. Look for superior past performance, proven management talent/track record, and the availability of attractive investment alternatives that you can switch in and out of. And *pay particular attention to an annuity's total expense rate.*

These products have a reputation of being heavily loaded with fees and charges, but it's possible to find annuities with both above-average performance and relatively low fee structures. That's the combination you're looking for.

One final point: If you're seriously considering buying an annuity, be sure to read the contract carefully and see what the guaranteed rates are, how long the initial rate applies, and if there's a bailout provision. (A *bailout provision* allows you to withdraw your money, free of any surrender fees, if the rate of return on your annuity falls below a specified minimum level. Of course, even if you exercise a bailout provision, you may still have to face a tax penalty for early withdrawal—unless you transfer the funds to another annuity through what's known as a *1035 exchange.*) Just as important, because *the annuity is only as good as the insurance company that stands behind it*, check to see how the company is rated by Best's, Standard & Poor's, or Moody's. It's important to make sure that the insurance company itself is financially sound before buying one of its annuity products. See Chapter 8 for more discussion on these insurance ratings and how they work.

PLANNING OVER A LIFETIME

Retirement Planning

Here are some key considerations for retirement planning in each stage of the life cycle.

PRE-FAMILY INDEPENDENCE: 20s

» Estimate how much you will need to retire comfortably while taking inflation into account.

» Determine your asset allocation among stocks, bonds, real estate, and cash based on your time horizon and attitude toward risk. Most people are comfortable taking more risk earlier in life.

» Match your investments in any employer-sponsored 401(k) retirement plan with your overall asset allocation plan.

» Start setting aside money for investment outside your employer's retirement plan. Consider investing in mutual funds and exchange-traded funds (ETFs) under a traditional IRA, a Roth IRA, or both.

FAMILY FORMATION/CAREER DEVELOPMENT: 30–45

» Aim to invest between 10 percent and 15 percent of your income for retirement. The more you invest early on, the better off you'll be at retirement.

» Review your asset allocation and rebalance it to be more consistent with your goals. Most people are more comfortable reducing the risk of their investments a bit.

» Gradually increase the amount invested in any employer-sponsored 401(k) retirement plan and re-evaluate how it relates to your asset allocation plan.

» Consider increasing your contribution to traditional IRA, a Roth IRA, or both.

PRE-RETIREMENT: 45–65

» Revise your retirement plan in light of recent developments. Try to save even more.

» Review your asset allocation and rebalance investments within and beyond your employer's retirement plan. Most people reduce the risk of their investments.

» Continue to increase the amount you invest in any employer-sponsored 401(k) retirement plan gradually, and re-evaluate it periodically to see how it fits into your asset allocation plan.

» Consider increasing your contribution to traditional and Roth IRAs using mutual funds and exchange traded funds (ETFs). Consider purchasing an annuity to supplement retirement income.

RETIREMENT: 65 AND BEYOND

» Revise your retirement plan to weight your investments more toward debt and liquid instruments than stocks.

» Compare your spending rate to your assets and reassess how long your spending rate can be maintained. Consider how the current income produced by your portfolio relates to your day-to-day spending needs.

» Integrate your investment asset allocation strategy with estate planning. Keep in mind that the equity in your home can be borrowed against if needed.

» Plan for mandatory withdrawals from tax-sheltered accounts and the associated tax consequences.

Joel and Dean's Different Approaches to a Traditional IRA

Joel Mullen and Dean Nixon, both 30 years old, are good friends who work together at a management consulting firm. They both take advantage of their firm's 401(k) plan. But they differ in how they set aside money in a traditional IRA. Joel has just started setting aside $5,500 a year in an IRA that he expects to earn 5 percent per year until he plans to retire at age 66. In contrast, while Dean also expects to retire at age 66, he believes it's too early in his career to bother investing in an IRA because it won't have that much impact in the long-term. He consequently plans to wait five years before following Joel's example.

At age 66 the pre-tax value of Joel's IRA should be about $553,455 while the value of Dean's account should be about $408,644. Joel invested $27,000 more than Dean but ended up with $144,811 more in his IRA account! That's because the IRA sheltered the earnings on Joel's investments from taxes, and he also

Monkey Business Images/Shutterstock.com

benefited handsomely from the compounding of returns on his money. There's a moral here: Invest early and often, and consider the impact of taxes on your investments.

STUDY TOOLS 14

LOCATED AT BACK OF THE TEXTBOOK
☐ Chapter Review Card

LOCATED AT WWW.CENGAGEBRAIN.COM
☐ Review Key Term flashcards and create your own cards.
☐ Track your knowledge and understanding of key concepts in personal finance.

☐ Complete practice and graded quizzes to prepare for tests.
☐ Complete interactive content at PFIN6 Online.
☐ View the chapter highlight boxes at PFIN6 Online.

©viphotos/Shutterstock140785408

Financial Planning Exercises

LO1 1. **Retirement planning pitfalls.** Explain the three most common pitfalls in retirement planning.

LO2 2. **Calculating amount available at retirement.** Jocelyn Booker, a 25-year-old personal loan officer at Second National Bank, understands the importance of starting early when it comes to saving for retirement. She has committed $3,000 per year for her retirement fund and assumes that she'll retire at age 65.

   a. How much will Jocelyn have accumulated when she turns 65 if she invests in equities and earns 8 percent on average?

   b. Jocelyn is urging her friend, Tyler Hinton, to start his plan right away, too, because he's 35. What would his nest egg amount to if he invested in the same manner as Jocelyn and he, too, retires at age 65? Comment on your findings.

LO2 3. **Calculating annual investment to meet retirement goal.** *Use Worksheet 14.1* to help Derek and Sally Archer who'd like to retire while they're still relatively young—in about 20 years. Both have promising careers, and both make good money. As a result, they're willing to put aside whatever is necessary to achieve a comfortable lifestyle in retirement. Their current level of household expenditures (excluding savings) is around $75,000 a year, and they expect to spend *even more* in retirement; they think they'll need about 125 percent of that amount. (*Note:* 125 percent equals a multiplier factor of 1.25.) They estimate that their Social Security benefits will amount to $20,000 a year in today's dollars and that they'll receive another $35,000 annually from their company pension plans. Derek and Sally feel that future inflation will amount to about 3 percent a year, and they think they'll be able to earn about 6 percent on their investments before retirement and about 4 percent afterward. Use Worksheet 14.1 to find out how big the Archers' investment nest egg will have to be and how much they'll have to save annually to accumulate the needed amount within the next 20 years.

LO3 4. **Average Social Security benefits and taxes.** *Use Exhibit 14.2* to estimate the average Social Security benefits for a retired couple. Assume that one spouse has a part-time job that pays $24,000 a year, and that this person also receives another $47,000 a year from a company pension. Based on current policies, would this couple be liable for any tax on their Social Security income?

LO3, 4 5. **Retirement planning.** At what age would you like to retire? Describe the type of lifestyle you envision—where you want to live, whether you want to work part-time, and so on. Discuss the steps you think you should take to realize this goal.

LO4 6. **Comparing retirement plans.** Alexa Rollins has just graduated from college and is considering job offers from two companies. Although the salary and insurance benefits are similar, the retirement programs are not. One firm offers a 401(k) plan that matches employee contributions with 25 cents for every dollar contributed by the employee, up to a $10,000 limit. The other has a contributory plan that allows employees to contribute up to 10 percent of their annual salary through payroll deduction and matches it dollar for dollar; this plan vests fully after five years. Because Alexa is unfamiliar with these plans, she turns to you for help. Explain the features of each plan so that Alexa can make an informed decision.

LO4 7. **After-tax cost of 401(k) contribution.** Ramon Flores is an operations manager for a large manufacturer. He earned $68,500 in 2016 and plans to contribute the maximum allowed to the firm's 401(k) plan. Assuming that Ramon is in the 25 percent tax bracket, calculate his taxable income and the amount of his tax savings. How much did it actually cost Ramon on an after-tax basis to make this retirement plan contribution?

LO4, 5 8. **Deciding between traditional and Roth IRAs.** Nate Galloway is in his early 30s and is thinking about opening an IRA. He can't decide whether to open a traditional/deductible IRA or a Roth IRA, so he turns to you for help.

   a. To support your explanation, you decide to *run some comparative numbers on the two types of accounts;* for starters, use a 25-year period to show Nate what contributions of $5,000 per year will amount to (after 25 years) if he can earn, say, 10 percent on his money. Will the type of account he opens have any impact on this amount? Explain.

Financial Planning Exercises

b. Assuming that Nate is in the 15 percent tax bracket (and will remain there for the next 25 years), determine the annual and total (over 25 years) tax savings he'll enjoy from the $5,500-a-year contributions to his IRA. Contrast the (annual and total) tax savings he'd generate from a traditional IRA with those from a Roth IRA.

c. Now, fast-forward 25 years. Given the size of Nate's account in 25 years (as computed in part a), assume that he takes it all out in one lump sum. If he's now in the 40 percent tax bracket, how much will he have, *after taxes*, with a traditional IRA as compared with a Roth IRA? How do the taxes computed here compare with those computed in part b? Comment on your findings.

d. Based on the numbers you have computed as well as any other factors, what kind of IRA would you recommend to Nate? Explain. Would knowing that maximum contributions are scheduled to increase to $7,000 per year make any difference in your analysis? Explain.

LO5 9. **Deciding whether to convert a traditional IRA to a Roth IRA.** Explain the circumstances in which it make sense to convert a traditional IRA to a Roth IRA.

LO6 10. **Comparing variable annuities and mutual funds.** Explain how buying a variable annuity is much like investing in a mutual fund. Do you, as a buyer, have any control over the amount of investment risk to which you're exposed in a variable annuity contract? Explain.

LO6 11. **Fixed vs. variable annuities.** What are the main differences between fixed and variable annuities? Which type is more appropriate for someone who is 60 years old and close to retirement?

15 | Preserving Your Estate

LEARNING OBJECTIVES

After studying this chapter, you will be able to...

LO1 Describe the role of estate planning in personal financial planning, and identify the seven steps involved in the process.

LO2 Recognize the importance of preparing a will and other documents to protect you and your estate.

LO3 Explain how trusts are used in estate planning.

LO4 Determine whether a gift will be taxable, and use planned gifts to reduce estate taxes.

LO5 Calculate federal taxes due on an estate.

LO6 Use effective estate planning techniques to minimize estate taxes.

After you finish this chapter, go to **PAGE 422** for **STUDY TOOLS**

Sally Anscombe/Getty Images

How Will This Affect Me? No, you can't take it with you. But there's a next best thing: A carefully designed estate plan will allow your loved ones and family to keep as much of your accumulated wealth as possible. This chapter explains the role and importance of estate planning and the need for a will. It discusses the use and design of living wills, advance medical directives, and trusts. It also explains how federal estate taxes are calculated. After reading this chapter you should understand the key elements in handling and preserving your estate for your loved ones.

15-1 PRINCIPLES OF ESTATE PLANNING

LO1 In the previous chapters, we have discussed how to build your wealth. Like it or not, no one lives forever. And you really cannot take it with you. So what happens to your wealth when you die? It will be transferred either to your beneficiaries—your family, friends, charities, and those you love—or, unless you do estate planning, to the government through either transfer taxes or the process of escheat.

Estate planning is the process of developing a plan to administer and distribute your assets, in a manner consistent with your wishes and the needs of your survivors, while minimizing taxes. It includes plans to manage your affairs if you become disabled and a statement of your personal wishes for medical care should you become unable to clearly state them.

A key focus of estate planning is to eliminate or minimize taxes and thereby maximize the amount of your estate that ultimately passes to your heirs and beneficiaries. Estate planning also includes steps to ensure that your estate is properly administered if you are unable to manage your assets because of illness or other incapacity. The plans you make are a form of insurance to protect your assets when you are not able to take care of them. These plans include directions about your medical care, whom to rely on for financial or legal advice, and other special instructions you want to give to your family when you are unable to do so personally.

If an individual fails to plan, then state and federal laws will control the disposition of that person's assets at death and determine who bears the burden of expenses and taxes, which may be higher because of the lack of planning. People who wish to plan their estates must systematically uncover problems in several important areas and solve them. Exhibit 15.1 lists the major types of problems and their associated causes or indicators.

Frequently, one of the major goals of estate planning is to minimize the amount of transfer taxes that your

> One of the major goals of estate planning is to minimize the amount of transfer taxes that your estate must pay.

estate must pay. Three kinds of taxes are of particular concern:

▶ Transfer taxes on gifts, referred to as the "gift tax"

▶ Transfer taxes on your estate, referred to as the "estate tax"

▶ Income taxes to be paid by your beneficiaries because of the property that they receive from your estate

Some have said that transfer taxes are elective. In other words, you elect to pay these taxes when you do no planning to avoid them. With planning and the discipline to follow through on the plan, most people will incur no transfer taxes and will minimize the related income taxes. Thus, you decide whether your property is transferred to the government or to your loved ones.

estate planning the process of developing a plan to administer and distribute your assets, in a manner consistent with your wishes and the needs of your survivors, while minimizing taxes

Exhibit 15.1

Potential Estate Planning Problems and Major Causes or Indicators

Careful estate planning can prevent many problems that arise when settling an estate. The first step toward preventing problems is an awareness and understanding of their major causes and indicators.

Problems	Major Causes or Indicators
Excessive transfer costs	Taxes and estate administrative expenses higher than necessary.
Lack of liquidity	Insufficient cash; not enough assets that are quickly and inexpensively convertible to cash within a short period of time to meet tax demands and other costs.
Improper disposition of assets	Beneficiaries receive the wrong asset, or the proper asset in the wrong manner or at the wrong time.
Inadequate income at retirement	Capital insufficient or not readily convertible to income-producing status.
Inadequate income, if disabled	High medical costs; capital insufficient or not readily convertible to income-producing status; difficulty in reducing living standards.
Inadequate income for family at estate owner's death	Any of the above causes.
Insufficient capital	Excessive taxes, inflation, improper investment planning.
Special problems	A family member with a serious illness or physical or emotional problem; children of a prior marriage; beneficiaries who have extraordinary medical or financial needs; beneficiaries who can't agree on how to handle various estate matters, business problems, or opportunities.

15-1a Who Needs Estate Planning?

Estate planning should be part of your financial plan, whether you're married or single and have five children or none. For example, married couples who own many assets jointly and have designated beneficiaries for them need to name an executor to administer the estate, specify a guardian for children, clarify how estate taxes will be paid, and direct the distribution of property that doesn't go directly to a joint owner. Unmarried partners and single persons also need estate planning, particularly if they own a home or other assets they want to leave to a partner, a specific individual, or to a charity. Estate planning involves both *people planning* and *asset planning*.

People Planning *People planning* means anticipating the psychological and financial needs of those you love and providing adequate resources to ensure continuation of their way of life. It involves keeping Mother's cameo brooch in the family or preserving the business that Granddad started 75 years ago. People planning is especially important for individuals with children who are minors; children who are exceptionally artistic or intellectually gifted; children or other dependents who are emotionally, mentally, or

physically disabled; and spouses who can't or don't want to handle money, securities, or a business.

Go to Smart Sites

What should you do first when someone close to you dies? The National Institutes of Health (NIH) has a publication to help you through difficult end-of-life issues. A highlight box in each chapter of PFIN Online includes "Smart Sites," a list of resources and sites that offer additional information on topics in the PFIN text.

How many of us are fully prepared to handle hundreds of thousands of dollars? Clearly, minor children can't legally handle large sums of money or deal directly with real estate or securities. Think of the burden that we place on others when we expect people who can't—or don't want to—handle such large sums of money or securities to do so. Engaging in people planning demonstrates a high degree of caring. People planning also involves talking about estate planning with your loved ones.

Asset Planning Because you care about the people in your life, you need to plan who

Overcoming Aversion to Ambiguity in Estate Planning

While many people recognize the need for an estate plan, they often have too little understanding of the process. Thus, too few of us take action at the right time. Why? Estate planning forces us to face our own mortality, which is hard to do. All too often, therefore, it takes a dramatic and serious health change to push the average American to plan for the worst. Consider how to overcome the *aversion to ambiguity* behavioral barrier so you can establish a timely and effective estate plan.

Estate planning can appear ambiguous to those who do not understand it. And most people dislike this ambiguity but fail to confront it. Two conflicting thoughts create this perceived ambiguity. First, we acknowledge that estate planning is important both for the planner and for the planner's family. Second, we often focus on living long and productive lives—a practice that is wrongly taken to imply that there is no hurry to start the estate planning process. The resulting conflicted feelings draw into question the importance of estate planning. Many, consequently, are paralyzed and do no planning.

So how do we move beyond the aversion to ambiguity and get the estate planning process going? We have to admit that life is too short and that we need to plan for the inevitable. After admitting this, the aversion to ambiguity barrier can be overcome by becoming more familiar with the basics of estate planning. This chapter should go a long way in addressing that issue. In summary, we must face our mortality, familiarize ourselves with the estate planning process, and decisively contact a professional to get the process moving forward.

Source: Adapted from Justin A. Reckers and Robert A. Simon, "Resolving the Aversion to Estate Planning," April 21, 2011, www.morningstar.com/advisor/t/42987539/resolving-the-aversion-to-estate-planning.htm, accessed October 2016.

will receive your assets upon your death or incapacity. Under the 2015 transfer tax law, estates of less than $5,430,000 will not be subject to taxes on their transfer either by gift or by estate. For a married couple, that number is doubled to $10,860,000. So it is not just about taxes. Your estate plan should match your assets with the people you wish to receive them. When an estate involves a closely held business, planning is essential to stabilize and maximize value not only during the owner's lifetime, but also upon the owner's death or disability. Likewise, estate planning is essential to avoid the special problems that occur when an estate owner holds title to property in more than one state. How you own your property (i.e., who is on the deed or title for the property) will affect your ability to plan for its transfer. The nature of the asset—whether it is cash, real property, cars, collectibles, stocks, or bonds—will also affect your ability to match your assets with the people you want to have them. Careful planning is needed to make sure that your assets will go to the desired beneficiaries.

15-1b Why Does an Estate Break Up?

Quite often, when people die, their estates die with them—not because they've done anything wrong, but because they haven't done anything. There are numerous forces that, if unchecked, tend to shrink an estate, reduce the usefulness of its assets, and frustrate the objectives of the person who built it. These include death-related costs, inflation, lack of liquidity, improper use of vehicles of transfer, and disabilities.

▶ **Death-related costs.** When someone dies, their estate incurs some death-related costs. For example, medical bills for a final illness and funeral expenses are good examples of *first-level death-related costs*. *Second-level death-related costs* consist of fees for attorneys, appraisers, and accountants, along with probate expenses—so-called administrative costs, federal estate taxes, and state death taxes. Most people also die with some current bills unpaid, outstanding long-term obligations (such as mortgages, business loans, and installment contracts), and unpaid income taxes and property taxes.

▶ **Inflation.** Failure to reappraise and rearrange an estate plan to counter the effects of inflation can impair the ability of assets—personal property and investments—to provide steady and adequate levels of financial security for your survivors.

▶ **Lack of liquidity.** Insufficient cash to cover death costs and other estate obligations has always been a

rusty426/Shutterstock.com

major factor in estate impairment. Sale of the choicest parcel of farmland or a business that's been in the family for generations, for instance, often has undesirable financial and psychological effects on the heirs.

▶ **Improper use of vehicles of transfer.** Improper use of vehicles of transfer may pass property to unintended beneficiaries or to the proper beneficiaries in an improper manner or at an incorrect time. For example, spendthrift spouses or minors may be left large sums of money outright in the form of life insurance, through joint ownership of a savings account, or as the beneficiaries of an employee fringe benefit plan.

▶ **Disabilities.** The prolonged and expensive disability of a family wage earner that results in loss of income is often called a *living death*. This financial situation is further complicated by inadequate management of currently owned assets. These circumstances can not only threaten a family's financial security, but can also quickly diminish the value of the estate.

15-1c What Is Your Estate?

Your **probate estate** consists of the real and personal property you own in your own name that can be transferred at death according to the terms of a will or, if you have no valid will, under *intestate* laws. The probate estate is distinct from the **gross estate**, which includes all the property owned by the decedent—both probate and nonprobate— that might be subject to federal estate taxes at your

probate estate the real and personal property owned by a person that can be transferred at death by will

gross estate all property owned by the decedent that might be subject to federal estate taxes upon a person's death

death. Life insurance owned by a life insurance trust, jointly held property with rights of survivorship, and property passing under certain employee benefit plans are common examples of nonprobate assets that might be subject to federal (and state) estate taxes.

Your gross estate includes all property that you *own* at the time of your death. Suppose, for example, you give your daughter cash that she uses to purchase a life insurance policy on your life. Later, upon your death, the proceeds from that policy are not in your gross estate because you do not own the policy. Similarly, proceeds from Social Security received by a surviving spouse were never yours, and so are not part of your gross estate. Property that you have previously given to others is not part of your gross estate, either. In short, planning what property you will continue to own until your death is an essential part of estate planning.

15-1d The Estate Planning Process

The estate planning process consists of seven important steps, as summarized in Exhibit 15.2. First, you must assess your family situation, evaluate its strengths and weaknesses, and set estate planning goals. Here is where you focus on "people planning" in setting up your goals. Next, gather comprehensive and accurate data on all aspects of the family. Then, you should take inventory and determine the ownership and value of your estate. Next, you must designate beneficiaries of your estate's assets, estimate estate transfer costs, and formulate and implement your plan. The final step is ongoing: review your estate plan periodically— at least every three to five years—and revise it as circumstances dictate. The Bonus Exhibit, "Data Needed for Estate Planning," summarizes the data that professionals require to prepare detailed estate plans. (Visit PFIN6 Online. Log in at **www.cengagebrain.com**.)

The objective of estate plans, of course, is to maximize the usefulness of people's assets during their lives

Exhibit 15.2

Steps in the Estate Planning Process

The estate planning process consists of seven important steps, listed here in the order they would be performed.

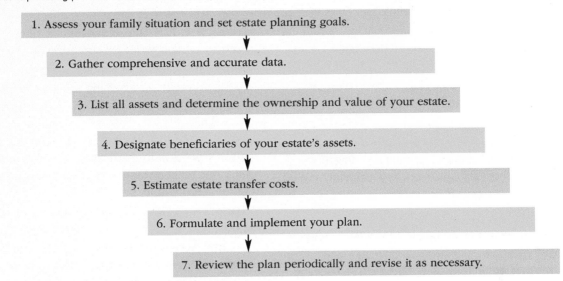

1. Assess your family situation and set estate planning goals.
2. Gather comprehensive and accurate data.
3. List all assets and determine the ownership and value of your estate.
4. Designate beneficiaries of your estate's assets.
5. Estimate estate transfer costs.
6. Formulate and implement your plan.
7. Review the plan periodically and revise it as necessary.

and to achieve their personal objectives after their deaths. As the needs, desires, and circumstances of the parties involved change, you must modify your estate plan. Key events that should trigger an estate plan review include the death or disability of a spouse or other family member, moving to another state, changing jobs, getting married or divorced, having children, acquiring new assets, and substantial changes in income, health, or living standards. Because of the general complexity of the laws relating to estate transfer, obtaining professional assistance from an attorney, accountant, and/or financial planner is often necessary to develop an effective estate plan.

15-2 THY WILL BE DONE...

LO2 A **will** is a written, legally enforceable expression or declaration of a person's wishes concerning the disposition of his or her property upon death. Unfortunately, the majority of Americans do not have valid wills. The importance of a valid will is apparent when you consider what happens when someone dies without one.

15-2a Absence of a Valid Will: Intestacy

Suppose that Jacob Gardner died without a valid will, a situation called **intestacy**. State intestacy laws "draw the will that the decedent failed to make" in order to determine the disposition of the probate property of those who have died intestate. Generally, under these statutes, the decedent's spouse is favored, followed by the children and then other offspring. If the spouse and children or other offspring (e.g., grandchildren or great-grandchildren) survive, they will divide the estate and other relatives will receive nothing. If no spouse, children, or other offspring survive, the deceased's parents, brothers, and sisters will receive a share of the estate.

After paying debts and taxes and deducting state-defined family exemptions, that individual's separately owned property would be distributed as shown. When property goes to the state due to the absence of any heirs, the property is said to *escheat* to the state. The Bonus Exhibit, "Distribution of a Typical Intestate Estate," gives an example of how a typical intestate estate is distributed. (View this exhibit at PFIN 6 Online. Log in at **www.cengagebrain.com**.)

In addition to not controlling the disposition of his or her property, a person who dies intestate also forfeits the privilege of naming a personal representative to guide the disposition of the estate, naming a guardian for persons and property,

will a written and legally enforceable document expressing how a person's property should be distributed upon his or her death

intestacy the situation that exists when a person dies without a valid will

Two out of three people don't have a will! Consider the following common excuses, and why they don't hold up.

- **I'm too young to need a will.** There's a chance you won't live as long as you hope. Without a will, your heirs will have to figure it all out. Youth is no excuse—you need a will at all ages.

- **My family knows what to do with my assets.** That may be true, but without a will the state decides who gets what. For example, even if you want your spouse to inherit all of your assets, your children will still be given a piece of your estate.

- **I don't have enough assets to need a will.** It's not just how much you have, it's who gets whatever you own.

- **My mother would take care of the kids.** Perhaps she would, but what if your mother-in-law also decides

she wants the kids? If there is no will, then a judge will decide who gets your children.

- **Writing a will is too expensive.** It doesn't cost much to write a will. Many state bar associations make available forms for a simple will.

- **My partner will get all of my assets.** A partner to whom you're not legally married may not get anything. While property and investments would likely go to your spouse or civil partner, without a will personal possessions might not go where you you want. And what if you and your partner both die at the same time without a will?

- **I have no kids and I'm single, so there is no one to protect.** Single or married, if you have no will then the state will leave everything to your relatives. And if you have no relatives, the state gets it all. A will can assure that your friends and chosen charities get something.

and specifying which beneficiaries would bear certain tax burdens. All of this is work is done for a fee that is set by the court. Estate planning and a valid will may also minimize the amount of estate shrinkage brought by fees and transfer taxes. Clearly, it's important to have a valid will—regardless of the estate size.

15-2b Preparing the Will

A will allows a person, called a **testator**, to direct the disposition of property at his or her death. The testator can change or revoke a will at any time; on the death of the testator, the will becomes operative.

Will preparation (or drafting) varies in difficulty and cost, depending on individual circumstances. In some cases, a two-page will costing $150 may be adequate; in others, a complex document costing $1,500 or more may be

necessary. A will must effectively accomplish the objectives specified for distributing assets, while also taking into consideration income, gift, and estate tax laws. Will preparation also requires a knowledge of corporate, trust, real estate, and securities laws.

Maxx-Studio/Shutterstock.com

A properly prepared will should meet these three important requirements:

▶ Provide a plan for distributing the testator's assets according to his or her wishes, the beneficiaries' needs, and federal and state dispositive and tax laws

▶ Consider the changes in family circumstances that might occur after its execution

▶ Be concise and complete in describing the testator's desires

Will drafting, no matter how modest the estate size, should not be attempted by a layperson. The complexity and interrelationships of tax, property, domestic relations, and other laws make the homemade will a potentially dangerous document. Few things may turn out to be more disastrous in the long run than a do-it-yourself will.

> Few things may turn out to be more disastrous in the long run than a do-it-yourself will.

YOU CAN DO IT NOW: Importance of Naming Alternative Beneficiaries When you name beneficiaries on financial accounts or in your will, it's important to name alternate (contingent) beneficiaries as well. This will make clear what happens if your first-choice beneficiary doesn't outlive you. See **http://www.nolo.com/legal-encyclopedia/why-naming-alternate-beneficiaries-your-will-is-so-important.html** for some useful tips on naming beneficiaries and related key issues. You can **do it now.**

15-2c Common Features of the Will

There's no absolute format that must be followed when preparing a will, but most wills contain similar distinct sections. Exhibit 15.3, which presents the will of Damian Michael Spencer, includes generalized examples of each of these clauses. Refer to the exhibit as you read these descriptions of the clauses:

▶ **Introductory clause.** An introductory clause, or preamble, normally states the testator's name and residence; this determines the county that will have legal jurisdiction and be considered the testator's domicile for tax purposes. The evocation statement nullifies old and forgotten wills and *codicils*—legally binding modifications of an existing will.

▶ **Direction of payments.** This clause directs the estate to make certain payments of expenses. As a general

rule, however, the rights of creditors are protected by law, so this clause might be left out of a professionally drafted will.

▶ **Disposition of property.** Damian's will has three examples of clauses dealing with disposition of property:

1. *Disposition of personal effects*: A testator may also make a separate detailed and specific list of personal property and carefully identify each item, and to whom it is given, as an informal guide to help the executor divide the property. (This list generally should not appear in the will itself because it's likely to be changed frequently.)

2. *Giving money to a specifically named party*: Be sure to use the correct legal title of a charity.

3. *Distribution of residual assets after specific gifts have been made*: Bequests to close relatives (as defined in the statute) who die before the testator will go to the relative's heirs unless the will directs otherwise. Bequests to nonrelatives who predecease the testator will go to the other residual beneficiaries.

▶ **Appointment clause.** Appointment clauses name the *executors* (the decedent's personal representatives who administer the estate), guardians for minor children, and trustees and their successors.

▶ **Tax clause.** In the absence of a specified provision in the will, the *apportionment statutes* of the testator's state will allocate the burden of taxes among the beneficiaries. The result may be an inappropriate and unintended reduction of certain beneficiaries' shares or adverse estate tax effects. Because the spouse's share and the portion going to a charity are deducted from the gross estate before arriving at the taxable estate, neither is charged with taxes.

▶ **Simultaneous death clause.** This clause describes what happens in the event of simultaneous death. Other types of clauses are similarly designed to avoid double probate of the same assets—duplication of administrative and probate costs. Such clauses require that the survivor live for a certain period, such as 30 or 60 days, to be a beneficiary under the will.

▶ **Execution and attestation clause.** Every will should be in writing and signed by the testator at its end as a precaution against fraud. Many attorneys suggest that the testator

testator the person who makes a will that provides for the disposition of property at his or her death

Exhibit 15.3

A Representative Will for Damian Michael Spencer

Damian Michael Spencer's will illustrates the eight distinct sections of most wills.

The Last Will and Testament of Damian Michael Spencer

Section 1 — Introductory Clause

I, Damian Michael Spencer, of the city of Chicago, state of Illinois, do, hereby make my last will and revoke all wills and codicils made prior to this will.

Section 2 — Direction of Payments

Article 1: Payment of Debts and Expenses

I direct payment out of my estate of all just debts and the expenses of my last illness and funeral.

Section 3 — Disposition of Property

Article 2: Disposition of Property

I give and bequeath to my wife, Sophia Jane Spencer, all my jewelry, automobiles, books, and photography equipment, as well as all other articles of personal and household use.

I give to the Chicago Historical Society the sum of $100,000.

All the rest, residue, and remainder of my estate, real and personal, wherever located, I give in equal one-half shares to my children, Griffin Wesley and Mila Frances, their heirs and assigns forever.

Section 4 — Appointment Clause

Article 3: Nomination of Executor and Guardian

I hereby nominate as the Executor of this Will my beloved wife, Sophia Jane Spencer, but if she is unable or unwilling to serve then I nominate my brother, Felix Lucas Spencer, In the event both persons named predecease me, or shall cease or fail to act, then I nominate as Executor in the place of said persons, the Midwestern Trust Bank of Chicago, Illinois.

If my wife does not survive me, I appoint my brother, Felix Lucas Spencer, Guardian of the person and property of my son, Griffin Wesley, during his minority.

Section 5 — Tax Clause

Article 4: Payment of Taxes

I direct that there shall be paid out of my residuary estate (from that portion which does not qualify for the marital deduction) all estate, inheritance, and similar taxes imposed by a government in respect to property includable in my estate for tax purposes, whether the property passes under this will or otherwise.

Section 6 — Simultaneous Death Clause

Article 5: Simultaneous Death

If my wife and I shall die under such circumstances that there is not sufficient evidence to determine the order of our deaths, then it shall be presumed that she survived me. My estate shall be administered and distributed in all respects in accordance with such assumption.

Section 7 — Execution and Attestation Clause

In witness thereof, I have affixed my signature to this, my last will and testament, which consists of five (5) pages, each of which I have initialed, this 15th day of September 2017.

Damian Michael Spencer
_____

Section 8 — Witness Clause

Signed, sealed, and published by Damian Michael Spencer, the testator, as his last will, in the presence of us, who, at his request, and in the presence of each other, all being present at the same time, have written our names as witnesses.

(Note: Normally the witness signatures and addresses would follow this clause.)

---

also initial each page after the last line or sign in a corner of each page.

▶ **Witness clause.** The final clause helps affirm that the will in question is really that of the deceased. All states require two witnesses to the testator's signing of the will. Most states require witnesses to sign in the presence of one another after they witness the signing by the testator. Their addresses should be noted on the will. If the testator is unable to sign his or her name for any reason, most states allow the testator to make a mark and to have another person (properly witnessed) sign for him or her.

15-2d Requirements of a Valid Will

To be valid, a will must be the product of a person with a sound mind, there must have been no *undue influence* (influence that would remove the testator's freedom of choice), the will itself must have been properly executed, and its execution must be free from fraud. More specifically, the following conditions must be met for the will to be valid:

▶ **Mental capacity.** You must be of "sound mind" to make a valid will. Generally, mental capacity is presumed. Setting aside a will requires clear and convincing proof of mental incapacity, and the burden of proof is on the person contesting the will.

▶ **Freedom of choice.** When you prepare and execute your will, you must not be under the undue influence of another person. Threats, misrepresentations, inordinate flattery, or physical or mental coercion employed to destroy the testator's freedom of choice are all types of undue influence.

▶ **Proper execution.** To be considered properly executed, a will must meet the requirements of the state's wills act or its equivalent. It must also be demonstrable that it is, in fact, the will of the testator. Most states have statutes that spell out who may make a will (generally any person of sound mind, age 18 or older, but 14 in Georgia and 16 in Louisiana), the form and execution the will must have (most states require a will to be in writing and to be signed by the testator at the logical end), and requirements for witnesses. Generally, a beneficiary should not serve as a witness.

15-2e Changing or Revoking the Will: Codicils

Because a will is inoperative until the testator's death, the testator (only) can change it at any time, as long as he or she has the mental capacity. In fact, periodic revisions should occur, especially upon these events:

▶ His or her (or the beneficiaries') health or financial circumstances change significantly.

▶ Births, deaths, marriages, or divorces alter the operative circumstances.

▶ The testator moves to a state other than where the will was executed.

▶ An executor, trustee, or guardian can no longer serve.

▶ Substantial changes occur in the tax law.

Changing the Will A **codicil** is a simple, often single-page, document that provides a convenient legal means

Photographee.eu/Shutterstock.com

of making minor changes in a will. It reaffirms all the existing provisions in the will except the one to be changed, and it should be executed and witnessed in the same formal manner as a will.

When a will requires substantial changes, a new will is usually preferable to a codicil. In addition, if a gift in the original will is removed, it may be best to make a new will and destroy the old will in order to avoid offending the omitted beneficiary. Sometimes, however, the prior will should not be destroyed even after the new will has been made and signed. If the new will fails for some reason (because of the testator's mental incapacity, for example), then the prior will may qualify. Also, a prior will could help prove a "continuity of testamentary purpose"—in other words, that the latest will (which may have provided a substantial gift to charity) continued an earlier intent and wasn't an afterthought or the result of an unduly influenced mind.

Revoking the Will A will may be revoked either by the testator or automatically by the law. A testator can revoke a will in one of four ways:

1. Making a later will that expressly revokes prior wills.

2. Making a codicil that expressly revokes all wills before the one being modified.

3. Making a later will that is inconsistent with a former will.

4. Physically mutilating, burning, tearing, or defacing the will with the intention of revoking it.

The law automatically modifies a will under certain circumstances, which vary from state to state but generally deal with divorce, marriage, birth or adoption, and murder. In many states, if a testator becomes divorced after making a will, all

> **codicil** a document that legally modifies a will without revoking it

provisions in the will relating to the spouse become ineffective. If a testator marries after making a will, the spouse receives that portion of the estate that would have been received had the testator died without a valid will. If a testator did not provide for a child born or adopted after the will was made (unless it appears that such lack of provision was intentional), the child receives that share of the estate not passing to the testator's spouse that would have been given to him or her had the deceased not had a will. Finally, almost all states have some type of slayer's statute that forbids a person who commits murder from acquiring property as the result of the crime.

15-2f Safeguarding the Will

In most cases, you should keep your original will in a safe-deposit box, with copies in a safe and accessible place at home and with the attorney who drafted it. Worksheet 15.1 contains an executor's checklist of documents and information that should be kept in a safe-deposit box. If each

---

WORKSHEET 15.1 **A CHECKLIST OF ITEMS TO KEEP IN A SAFE-DEPOSIT BOX**

This checklist itemizes the various documents and information that the executor may need to carry out the terms of the will effectively. These items should be kept in a safe-deposit box.

CHECKLIST FOR EXECUTORS

Name (Testator) _____ Date _____

_____ 1. Marriage certificates (including prior marriages)
_____ 2. Will and trust agreements
_____ 3. Life insurance policies or certificates
_____ 4. Social Security number
_____ 5. Military discharge papers
_____ 6. Bonds, stocks, and securities
_____ 7. Real estate deeds
_____ 8. Business agreements
_____ 9. Automobile titles and insurance policies
_____ 10. Property insurance policies
_____ 11. Tax information
_____ 12. Letter of last instructions

List all checking and savings account numbers, bank addresses, and locations of safe-deposit boxes:

_____ _____ _____

_____ _____ _____

List names, addresses, and phone numbers of property and life insurance agents:

_____ _____ _____

_____ _____ _____

List names, addresses, and phone numbers of attorney and accountant:

_____ _____ _____

_____ _____ _____

List names, addresses, and phone numbers of (current or last) employer. State retirement date, if applicable. Include employee benefits booklets:

_____ _____ _____

_____ _____ _____

List all debts owed to *and* by you, including names and account numbers:

_____ _____ _____

_____ _____ _____

List the names, addresses, telephone numbers, and birth dates of your children and other beneficiaries (including charities):

_____ _____ _____

_____ _____ _____

Sources: Based on Stephan R. Leimberg, Stephen N. Kandell, Ralph Gano Miller, Morey S. Rosenbloom, and Timothy C. Polacek, The Tools & Techniques of Estate Planning, 14th ed. (Upper Saddle River, NJ: Prentice Hall, 2006); Metropolitan Life Insurance Company, Executor's Checklist, www.metlife.com/assets /cao/mmi/life-advice/finances/taking-legal-action/executors-check-list.pdf, accessed October 2016.

spouse has a separate safe-deposit box, then the couple may want to keep their wills in each other's boxes. Some states provide for *lodging* of the will, a mechanism for filing and safekeeping it in the office of the probate court (also called *orphan's* or *surrogate's court*), which satisfies the need to safeguard the will.

15-2g Letter of Last Instructions

A **letter of last instructions** is the best way to communicate to others your thoughts and instructions that aren't appropriate to include in a will. It's typically an informal memorandum separate from the will. (The letter of last instructions should contain no bequests because it has no legal standing.) It's best to make several copies of the letter, keeping one at home and the others with the estate's executor or attorney, who can deliver it to beneficiaries at the appropriate time.

A letter of last instructions might provide directions regarding such items as:

▶ Location of the will and other documents

▶ Funeral and burial instructions (often a will is not opened until after the funeral)

▶ Suggestions or recommendations as to the continuation, sale, or liquidation of a business

▶ Personal matters that the testator might prefer not be made public in the will, such as statements (e.g., comments about a spendthrift spouse or a reckless son) that might sound unkind or inconsiderate but would be valuable to the executor

▶ Recommended legal and accounting services

▶ An explanation of the actions taken in the will, which may help avoid litigation (for instance, "I left only $5,000 to my son, Cole, because …" or "I made no provisions for my oldest daughter, Vivian because …")

▶ Suggestions on how to divide the personal property

15-2h Administration of an Estate

When people die, they usually own property and owe debts and may be owed money by other persons. The **probate process**, similar to that used in liquidating a business, is often required to settle an estate. A local court generally supervises the probate process through the *decedent's personal representative*—either an **executor** named in the decedent's will or, if the decedent died without a valid will, through a court-appointed **administrator**. The executor or administrator becomes the decedent's legal representative, taking care of such matters as collecting bank accounts and money owed the decedent, paying off debts, creating clear title to make real estate marketable, and distributing what's left to those entitled to it by will or the state's intestate laws. Clearly, an executor should not only be familiar with the testator's affairs but also be able to effectively handle the responsibilities of being an executor.

15-2i Other Important Estate Planning Documents

Several other documents that are useful in protecting your family and you include a durable power of attorney for financial matters, a living will, a durable power of attorney for health care, and an ethical will.

Power of Attorney A **durable power of attorney for financial matters** allows you to name the person (perhaps a spouse or other relative) that you want to take over your financial affairs in the event of a serious illness. Because this simple document transfers enormous power to your designated appointee, it is important to name a qualified, trustworthy person. To make it durable—that is, effective even when you are incapacitated—the document must explicitly state that your agent's authority to act on your behalf will continue during your incapacity. It is also a good idea to clear your power of attorney with all brokerage firms and mutual funds where you have accounts.

Living Will Suppose a person falls into a coma with little or no hope of recovery. Without a *living will* or *durable power of attorney for health care* to guide them, his family could face difficult decisions regarding his medical care. These documents specify the medical care a person wants to receive, or *not* receive, if he or she becomes seriously ill and is unable to give informed consent. The **living will** states, precisely, the desired treatments and the degree to which they are to be continued. The document must specifically state your wishes; otherwise, it might be put aside because it is too vague.

letter of last instructions an informal memorandum that is separate from a will and contains suggestions or recommendations for carrying out a decedent's wishes

probate process the court-supervised disposition of a decedent's estate

executor the personal representative of an estate designated in the decedent's will

administrator the personal representative of the estate appointed by the court if the decedent died intestate

durable power of attorney for financial matters a legal document that authorizes another person to take over someone's financial affairs and act on his or her behalf

living will a document that precisely states the treatments a person wants if he or she becomes terminally ill

John T Takai/Shutterstock.com

Estate Planning
- Wills
- Power of Attorney
- Advanced Healthcare Directive
- Trusts
- Probate

durable power of attorney for health care a written power of attorney authorizing an individual to make health care decisions on behalf of the principal when the principal is unable to make such decisions. Also called *advanced directive for health care*

ethical will a personal statement left for family, friends, and community that shares your values, blessings, life's lessons, and hopes and dreams for the future. Also called *legacy letter*

right of survivorship the right of surviving joint owners of property to receive title to the deceased joint owner's interest in the property

joint tenancy a type of ownership by two or more parties, with the survivor(s) continuing to hold all such property upon the death of one or more of the owners

tenancy by the entirety a form of ownership by husband and wife, recognized in certain states, in which property automatically passes to the surviving spouse

tenancy in common a form of co-ownership under which there *is no right of survivorship* and each co-owner can leave his or her share to whomever he or she desires

Durable Power of Attorney for Health Care

Many experts recommend a **durable power of attorney for health care**, often called an *advanced directive for health care*, instead of a living will. The durable power of attorney for health care authorizes an individual (your *agent*) to make health care decisions for you if you're unable to do so either temporarily or permanently. Unlike a living will, it applies in any case where you cannot communicate your wishes, not just when you're terminally ill. You should spend some time specifying the scope of the power and instructions for medical treatment. Then review your thinking with your family and the person you designate as your agent. These documents, held by your designated agent and your doctor, should

make it easier for your family to deal with these difficult issues.

Ethical Wills Many people today also prepare an **ethical will**, sometimes called *legacy letter*. They are informal documents that are usually added to formal wills and read at the same time. An ethical will is not a legal document and consequently does not distribute your material wealth. An ethical will offers a way to share your morals, life experiences, family stories and history, and more with future generations. Ethical wills may be in the form of handwritten letters or essays, computer files, videos, or other electronic media. It's a good idea to have your lawyer review your ethical will because its interpretation could lead to a challenge of your formal will.

15-2j What About Joint Ownership?

The two forms of joint ownership—*joint tenancy* or *tenants by the entirety*—share the following characteristics:

▶ Under the **right of survivorship**, the interest of a decedent passes directly to the surviving joint tenant(s)—that is, to the other joint owner(s)—by operation of the law and is free from the claims of the decedent's creditors, heirs, or personal representatives.

▶ A **joint tenancy** may consist of any number of persons, who don't have to be related. A **tenancy by the entirety** can exist only between husband and wife.

▶ In *joint tenancy*, each joint tenant can unilaterally sever the tenancy, whereas a *tenancy by the entirety* can be severed only by mutual agreement, divorce, or conveyance by both spouses to a third party.

▶ The co-owners must have equal interests.

Joint tenancy, the more common form of joint ownership, offers a sense of family security, quick and easy transfer to the spouse at death, exemption of jointly owned property from the claims of the deceased's creditors, and avoidance of delays and publicity in the estate settlement process. The key disadvantage of joint tenancy is the inability to control jointly owned property by a will, so that the first joint owner to die cannot control the property's disposition and management on his or her death.

EXAMPLE: Disadvantage of Joint Tenancy with the Right of Survivorship A father who has two unmarried children—a daughter with whom he has a good relationship, and an estranged son—purchases property and places it in his own and his daughter's name as joint tenants. The father has a will that leaves everything he has to his daughter and specifically disinherits his son. The daughter has no estate planning documents. While traveling together, the father is killed in a car accident and the daughter is severely injured. She never fully recovers and dies two months later. At her death, intestate, her estate will likely pass to her brother. Had her father held the property in his name only, he could have stipulated in his will a longer survivorship requirement (say, six months) with a provision that, in the event his daughter did not survive that period, there would be an alternative disposition (e.g., to a charity).

You should also be familiar with two other forms of ownership: *tenancy in common* and *community property*.

Tenancy in Common Under a **tenancy in common**, there is *no right of survivorship*, and each co-owner can leave his or her share to whomever he or she desires. Thus, the decedent owner's will controls the disposition of the decedent's partial interest in the asset. Unlike joint tenancy, where all interests must be equal, tenancy in common interests can be unequal; hence, a property owned by three co-owners could be apportioned such that their respective shares are 50 percent, 30 percent, and 20 percent of the property.

Community Property **Community property**, a form of marital ownership found primarily in Southwestern states, is all property acquired by the effort of either or both spouses during marriage while they reside in a community property state. For example, wages and commissions earned and property acquired by either spouse while living in a community property state are automatically owned equally by both spouses, even if only one was directly involved in acquiring the additional wealth. Property acquired before marriage or by gift or inheritance can be maintained as the acquiring spouse's separate property. Each spouse can leave his or her half of the community property to whomever he or she chooses, so there's *no right of survivorship* inherent in this form of ownership.

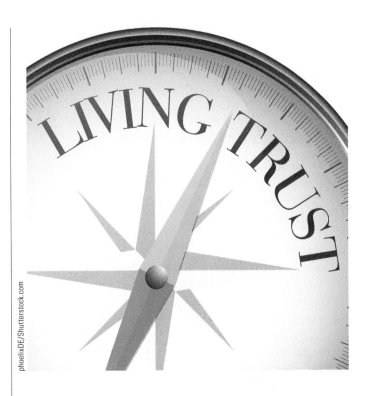

phoenixDE/Shutterstock.com

15-3 TRUSTS

LO3 Trusts facilitate the transfer of property and the income from that property to another party. A **trust** is a legal relationship created when one party, the **grantor** (also called the *settlor*, *trustor*, or *creator*), transfers property to a second party, the **trustee** (an organization or individual), for the benefit of third parties, the **beneficiaries**, who may or may not include the grantor. The property placed in the trust is called *trust principal* or *res* (pronounced "race"). The trustee holds the legal title to the property in the trust and must use the property and any income that it produces solely for the benefit of trust beneficiaries as specified by the grantor.

A trust may be *living* (funded during the grantor's life) or *testamentary* (created in a will and funded by the

> **community property** all marital property co-owned equally by both spouses while living in a community property state
>
> **trust** a legal relationship created when one party transfers property to a second party for the benefit of third parties
>
> **grantor** a person who creates a trust and whose property is transferred into it. Also called *settlor, trustor,* or *creator*
>
> **trustee** an organization or individual selected by a *grantor* to manage and conserve property placed in trust for the benefit of the *beneficiaries*
>
> **beneficiaries** those who receive benefits—property or income—from a trust or from the estate of a decedent. A grantor can be a beneficiary of his own trust

probate process). It may be *revocable* or *irrevocable*. The grantor can regain property placed into a revocable trust and alter or amend the terms of the trust. The grantor cannot recover property placed into an irrevocable trust during its term.

15-3a Why Use a Trust?

Trusts are designed for various purposes. The most common motives are to attain income and estate tax savings and to manage and conserve property over a long period.

Income and Estate Tax Savings Under certain circumstances, a grantor who is a high-bracket taxpayer can shift the burden of paying taxes on the income produced by securities, real estate, and other investments to a trust itself or to its beneficiary, both of whom are typically subject to lower income tax rates than the grantor. Impressive *estate tax* savings are possible because the appreciation in the value of property placed into such a trust can be entirely removed from the grantor's estate and possibly benefit several generations of family members without incurring adverse federal estate tax consequences.

Managing and Conserving Property The trustee assumes the responsibility for managing and conserving the property on behalf of the beneficiaries. Management by the trustee is sometimes held in reserve in case a healthy and vigorous individual is unexpectedly incapacitated and becomes unable or unwilling to manage his or her assets.

15-3b Selecting a Trustee

Five qualities are essential in a trustee. He or she must:

1. Possess sound business knowledge and judgment.
2. Have an intimate knowledge of the beneficiary's needs and financial situation.
3. Be skilled in investment and trust management.
4. Be available to beneficiaries (specifically, the trustee should be young enough to survive the trust term).
5. Be able to make decisions impartially.

A corporate trustee, such as a trust company or bank that has been authorized to perform trust duties, may be best able to meet these requirements. On the other hand,

---

Financial Planning Tips

REASONS TO SET UP A TRUST

Consider the key reasons for using trusts.

- **Avoid probate.** A trust may be used to avoid the probate process, which can cost as much as 5 percent of the value of an estate. However, the costs of setting up a trust should be compared with the expected cost of probate. It's important to keep in mind that a probated will is a public document and trusts offer greater privacy.

- **Protection in old age and disability.** You can set up a trust, name yourself as beneficiary, and then name yourself and another person as trustees. If you become gravely ill or mentally incapacitated, the other trustee can manage your assets and distribute them as you direct in the trust arrangement.

- **Provide for minors and young adults.** You can use a trust to leave assets to minors and young adults. The trustee will manage the trust until the beneficiary reaches the age that you designate is old enough to handle the assets responsibly.

- **Avoid estate taxes.** You can set up a trust to transfer assets to an irrevocable trust to avoid estate taxes. These assets are not included in your gross estate. However, it's important that the grantor trust is not also a beneficiary or there will be limits on distributions to shield from taxation. The possibility of gift taxes must be considered. And planning must recognize that if a grantor transfers a life insurance policy to an irrevocable trust within three years before the grantor's death, the policy may well be included in the estate.

- **Reduce income taxes.** Certain types of trusts may be used to transfer income to heirs in a lower income tax bracket, which can reduce overall taxes.

- **Benefit charity.** You can transfer assets to a trust, receive income from the trust, and distribute the assets to a charity upon death. Thus, trusts may be used to provide income and estate tax benefits to support your favorite charity.

Exhibit 15.4

Seven Popular Trusts

Trusts shift assets (and thus appreciation) out of one's estate while retaining some say in the future use of the assets. The drawback is that trusts can be cumbersome and expensive to arrange and administer. Here are brief descriptions of seven popular trusts:

- **Credit shelter trust.** The most common tax-saving trust for estate planning; couples with combined assets worth more than the applicable exclusion amount (AEA) can gain full use of each partner's exclusion by having that amount placed in a bypass trust—that is, one that bypasses the surviving spouse's taxable estate. It's called a *credit shelter trust* because, when one spouse dies, the trust receives assets from the decedent's estate equal in value to the estate AEA. So if the first death occurred in the year 2015, then the trust would be funded with assets worth exactly $5,430,000. This trust does not qualify for the marital deduction, but no tax is due because the tentative tax is equal to the available *unified credit*. The surviving spouse is usually given the right to all the trust income and, in an emergency, even has access to the principal. When the surviving spouse dies, the credit shelter trust is not included in his or her estate regardless of the trust's value, so it avoids having to pay a tax at both deaths. With the addition of the "portability" provision (discussed in this chapter), the need and usefulness of the credit shelter trust is less.

- **Qualified terminable interest property (QTIP) trust.** Usually set up in addition to a *credit shelter trust* to ensure that money stays in the family; it receives some or all of the estate assets over the applicable exclusion amount ($5,430,000 in 2015). Assets left outright to a spouse who remarries could be claimed by the new spouse. The survivor receives all income from the property until death, when the assets go to the persons chosen by the first spouse to die. Estate taxes on QTIP trust assets can be delayed until the second spouse dies. It is also useful for couples with children from prior marriages because the QTIP property can be distributed to the children of the grantor spouse only after the death of the surviving spouse; hence, the survivor benefits from the trust's income, and the deceased spouse's children are assured that they will receive the remainder of the QTIP trust eventually.

- **Special needs trust.** An irrevocable trust established for the benefit of a person with disabilities. It is designed to provide extra help and life enrichment without reducing state and federal government help to the beneficiary.

- **Minor's section 2503(c) trust.** Set up for a minor, often to receive tax-free gifts; however, assets must be distributed to the minor when he or she turns 21.

- **Crummey trust.** Named after the first person to successfully use this trust structure, this is used to make tax-free gifts up to the annual exclusion amounts to children; unlike a *minor's section 2503(c) trust*, these funds need not be distributed before age 21. However, the beneficiary can withdraw the funds placed into the trust for a limited time (e.g., for up to 30 days), after which the right to make a withdrawal ceases.

- **Charitable lead (or income) trust.** Pays some or all of its income to a charity for a period of time, after which the property is distributed to noncharitable beneficiaries; the grantor receives an immediate income tax deduction based on expected future payout to charity. If the grantor's children are the so-called remaindermen of the trust, then the value of the gift for gift or estate tax purposes is greatly reduced because their possession and enjoyment of the trust assets is delayed until the charitable interest terminates.

- **Charitable remainder trust.** Similar to a *charitable lead trust*, except that income goes to taxable beneficiaries (e.g., the grantor or the grantor's children) and the principal goes to a charity when the trust ends; the grantor gets an immediate income tax deduction based upon the value of the remainder interest that is promised to the charity.

---

a corporate trustee may charge high fees or be overly conservative in investments, be impersonal, or lack familiarity with and understanding of family problems and needs. Often a compromise involves appointing one or more individuals and a corporate trustee as co-trustees.

15-3c Common Types and Characteristics of Trusts

Although there are various types of trusts, the most common ones are the *living trust*, the *testamentary trust*, and the *irrevocable life insurance trust*, each of which is described in the following sections. Exhibit 15.4 describes seven other popular trusts.

Living Trusts A **living (inter vivos) trust** is one created and funded during the grantor's lifetime. It can be either revocable or irrevocable and can last for a limited period or continue long after the grantor's death.

Revocable Living Trust The grantor reserves the right to revoke the trust and regain trust property in a **revocable living trust**. For federal income tax purposes, grantors of these trusts are treated as owners of the property in the trust, and are therefore taxed on any income produced by the trust.

Revocable living trusts have three basic advantages:

1. Management continuity and income flow are ensured even

> **living (inter vivos) trust** a trust created and funded during the grantor's lifetime
>
> **revocable living trust** a trust in which the grantor reserves the right to revoke the trust and regain trust property. The grantor can serve as the initial trustee

after the grantor's death. No probate is necessary because the trust continues to operate after the death of the grantor just as it did while he or she was alive.

2. The trustee assumes the burdens of investment decisions and management responsibility. For example, an individual may want to control investment decisions and management policy as long as he or she is alive and healthy but sets up a trust to provide backup help in case he or she becomes unable or unwilling to continue managing the assets.

3. The details of the estate plan and the value of assets placed into the trust do not become public knowledge, as they would during the probate process.

The principal disadvantages of these trusts include the fees charged by the trustee for managing the property placed into the trust and the legal fees charged for drafting the trust instruments.

Irrevocable Living Trust Grantors who establish an **irrevocable living trust** relinquish title to the property that they place in it and give up the right to revoke or terminate the trust. Such trusts have all the advantages of revocable trusts plus the potential for reducing taxes. Disadvantages of such a trust relate to the fees charged by trustees for managing assets placed into it, possible gift taxes on assets placed into it, and the grantor's forfeiture of the right to alter the terms of the trust as circumstances change.

Living Trusts and Pour-Over Wills A will can be written so that it "pours over" designated assets into a previously established revocable or irrevocable living trust. The trust may also be named the beneficiary of the grantor's insurance policies. The **pour-over will** generally contains a provision passing the estate—after debts, expenses,

taxes, and specific bequests—to an existing living trust, ensuring that property left out of the living trust will make its way into the trust (i.e., "pour over" into it). Such an arrangement provides for easily coordinated and well-administered management of estate assets.

Testamentary Trust A trust created by a decedent's will is called a **testamentary trust**. Such a trust comes into existence only after the will is probated and a court order directs the executor to transfer the property to the trustee in order to fund the trust. The revocable living trust and the testamentary trust can have pretty much the same terms and long-range functions—for example, providing for asset management for the trustor's family long after the trustor has died. Indeed, the two main differences are: (1) only the living trust provides for management when and if the trustor becomes incapacitated; and (2) the living trust is funded by transfers to the trustee by assignment or deed during the trustor's life, whereas the funding mechanism for the testamentary trust is a court order distributing the property to the trustee at the end of the probate process.

Irrevocable Life Insurance Trust A wealthy individual might want to establish an **irrevocable life insurance trust** in which the major asset of the trust is life insurance on the grantor's life. To avoid having the proceeds of the policy included in the grantor's estate, the independent trustee usually acquires the policy on the life of the wealthy person and names the trustee as the beneficiary. The terms of the trust enable the trustee to use the proceeds to pay the grantor's estate taxes, to take care of the grantor's spouse and children, and probably eventually to distribute the remainder of the proceeds to the children or other beneficiaries as specified in the trust document.

15-4 FEDERAL UNIFIED TRANSFER TAXES

LO4 The **federal unified transfer tax** is a tax on the right to transfer property from one individual to another. The tax affects two types of transfers: transfer by gift, referred to as the **gift tax**; and transfers through the estate, referred to as the **estate tax**. The tax base for both transfers is the fair market value of the property that is transferred. The amount that can pass tax-free, called the **applicable exclusion amount (AEA)**, is $5,430,000 in 2015. In addition, taxable gifts are reduced by an annual exclusion of $14,000 (in 2015) per donee. This

---

irrevocable living trust a trust in which the grantor gives up the right to revoke or terminate the trust

pour-over will a provision in a will that provides for the passing of the estate—after debts, expenses, taxes, and specific bequests—to an existing living trust

testamentary trust a trust created by a decedent's will and funded through the probate process

irrevocable life insurance trust an irrevocable trust in which the major asset is life insurance on the grantor's life

federal unified transfer tax a tax on the right to transfer property from one individual to another

gift tax a tax levied on the value of certain gifts made during the giver's lifetime

estate tax a tax levied on the value of property transferred at the owner's death

applicable exclusion amount (AEA) credit given to each person that can be applied to the amount of federal estate tax owed by that person at death. In 2015, the AEA was $5,430,000 per spouse

Exhibit 15.5

Federal Unified Transfer Tax Rates

This *unified rate schedule* defines the amount of federal gift and estate taxes that estates of various sizes would have to pay; it incorporates the rates passed in the *American Taxpayer Relief Act of 2012*, signed into law on January 2, 2013. Estates and gifts under the exclusion amount pay no federal tax. The estate exclusion amount increased annually from $2,000,000 in 2006 to $5,430,000 in 2015. (see Exhibit 15.6). From 2009 to 2015, the top tax rates decreased from 45 percent to 40 percent.

| Taxable Estate Value | | Tentative Tax | | |
More Than	But Not More Than	Base Amount	+ Percent	On Excess Over
$ 0	$ 10,000	$ 0		
10,000	20,000	1,800	20%	$ 10,000
20,000	40,000	3,800	22	20,000
40,000	60,000	8,200	24	40,000
60,000	80,000	13,000	26	60,000
80,000	100,000	18,200	28	80,000
100,000	150,000	23,800	30	100,000
150,000	250,000	38,800	32	150,000
250,000	500,000	70,800	34	250,000
500,000	750,000	155,800	37	500,000
750,000	1,000,000	248,300	39	750,000
1,000,000		345,800	40	1,000,000

Source: Internal Revenue Code, Section 2001.

is adjusted by inflation, if present, each year. Thus, combined transfers of $5,430,000 plus the annual gift tax exclusion are not subject to the federal transfer tax. If the taxpayer is married, then the two married taxpayers each have an AEA of $5,430,000, or a total of $10,860,000, before any tax applies. The tax rate for gifts and estates is specified by the **unified rate schedule** (see the graduated table of rates in Exhibit 15.5). Also, when the first spouse dies, if the executor so elects on the estate tax return, then any unused applicable exclusion amount will carry over to the other spouse. This is referred to as the *portability* of the unified transfer tax credit.

Ninell/Shutterstock.com

The applicable exclusion amount is high enough to remove transfer taxes from the concerns of estate planning for the middle-income taxpayer. For the upper-income taxpayer, however, the transfer tax is a major concern. For example, if a couple has a taxable estate of $20,000,000, then the transfer tax due is $3,656,000. That is a significant concern. The remainder of this section addresses these issues.

15-4a Gifts and Taxes

The transfer tax applies to the fair market value of property transferred to a donee *less* the amount of compensation given to the donor. To determine the taxable gift, this amount is reduced by the annual exclusion ($14,000 in 2015). The annual exclusion applies to each donee who is given gifts. Thus, if the taxpayer gave three people $10,000 each, none of the transfers would be subject to the gift tax because the annual exclusion reduces each taxable gift to $0. The one requirement is that the transfer be a gift of *present interest*,

unified rate schedule a graduated table of rates applied to all taxable transfers; used for *both* federal gift and estate tax purposes

Exhibit 15.6

Unified Credits and Applicable Exclusion Amounts for Estates and Gifts

On January 2, 2013, the American Taxpayer Relief Act of 2012 was signed into law. The major features of the Act were to make the estate tax rate 40 percent, to make the annual adjustment to the applicable exclusion amount permanent, and to make the portability of the unified transfer tax credit permanent. This table shows the recent history of the unified credits and applicable exclusion amounts.

Year	Unified Tax Credit—Estates	Applicable Exclusion Amount—Estates	Unified Tax Credit—Gifts	Applicable Exclusion Amount—Gifts
2006	$780,800	$2,000,000	$345,800	$1,000,000
2007	$780,800	$2,000,000	$345,800	$1,000,000
2008	$780,800	$2,000,000	$345,800	$1,000,000
2009	$1,455,800	$3,500,000	$345,800	$1,000,000
2010	Estate tax repealed for 2010		$330,800	$1,000,000
2011	$1,730,800	$5,000,000	$1,730,800	$5,000,000
2012	$1,772,800	$5,120,000	$1,772,800	$5,120,000
2013	$2,045,800	$5,250,000	$2,045,800	$5,250,000
2014	$2,081,800	$5,340,000	$2,081,800	$5,340,000
2015	$2,117,800	$5,430,000	$2,117,800	$5,430,000

Source: Internal Revenue Service.

not of a future interest. A typical example of the latter is the transfer of money to a trust with the provision that the trust's beneficiary must be 30 before withdrawing funds from the trust. This beneficiary has only a future interest, not a present interest.

There are two major exceptions to the present interest rule. Transfers to a minor trust—that is, a trust that holds the property until the minor is 21—qualify for the annual exclusions. A second exception is the Crummey provision, which provides for withdrawal rights to the beneficiary for a specified period (e.g., 30 days). If the beneficiary does not ask for a withdrawal in that time period, the property must remain in the trust until it can be distributed according to the trust terms. Thus, with the Crummey withdrawal rights, transfers to the trust are considered a present interest and will qualify for the annual exclusion to the extent of the withdrawal right.

An essential first step to estate planning is making annual gifts to your potential heirs. Giving gifts reduce the taxable estate in two ways. First, any future appreciation of the gifted property is excluded from the estate because the decedent does not own the property on the date of death. Second, if the gift is so large that taxes are due, the money used to pay the tax is also removed from the estate. (There is an exception for gift taxes paid within three years of death.)

Another consideration when making gifts is their impact on the income taxes of the donee. If the gifted property is to be sold by the donee for a gain, it should be noted that property received by gift has a tax basis equal to its basis in the hands of the donor (i.e., a carryover basis). Property that is inherited has a basis equal to the fair market value at the date of death. For example, assume that a taxpayer owns a beach house that was purchased for $100,000 in 1990 and now has a value of $600,000. If the beach house is gifted, the basis to the donee will be $100,000; if passed through the estate, its basis to the heir will be $600,000. So long as the property is not sold or depreciated, the basis really does not matter. However, if it is sold, then there is a difference in income tax of $100,000 (20 percent capital gains rate multiplied by the difference in basis or $500,000) between receiving the property by gift rather than through the estate.

15-4b Is It Taxable?

Not everything that's transferred by an individual is subject to a gift tax. **Annual exclusions**, **gift splitting**,

annual exclusions under the federal gift tax law, the amount that can be given each year without being subject to gift tax—for example, $14,000. This amount is indexed for inflation

gift splitting a method of reducing gift taxes; a gift given by one spouse, with the consent of the other spouse, can be treated as if each had been given one-half of it charitable deductions, and marital deductions are all means of reducing the total amount for tax purposes.

▶ **Annual exclusions:** The gift tax law allows a person to give gifts up to a specified annual amount per calendar year—$14,000 in 2015—to any number of recipients. For example, a person could give gifts of $14,000 each to 30 individuals, for a total of $420,000, without using up any of the recipient's AEA (and, of course, without paying any gift tax). Furthermore, the ability to give tax-free gifts of $14,000 renews annually. This annual exclusion applies only for gifts given with "no strings attached" and generally only if the recipient is given a "present interest" in the gift, as discussed previously.

▶ **Marital deduction.** Transfers between spouses, either by gift or through the estate, are generally not subject to tax because of the marital deduction. The marital deduction is the fair market value of property transferred between a married couple minus the annual exclusion. The one potential issue is that the receiving spouse must have a terminable interest in the property. This means that, upon her (or his, the second to die) death, the property must be in her estate and subject to tax—although it may not be taxed because of the transfer tax credit or other deductions.

▶ **Gift splitting.** Recall that donors may make gifts up to the annual exclusion ($14,000 in 2015) with no tax impact. Thus, a husband and wife may give a total of $28,000 to a single donee and incur no tax. Sometimes it is convenient for only one of the spouses to transfer property to a single donee. If the amount is over the annual exclusion, it may be taxable. In such cases, the donor's spouse may elect to split the donation of a gift. Thus, two annual exclusions apply and each spouse's unified transfer tax credit will apply to the transfer. Because this election by the spouse must be reported, gift tax returns must be filed.

▶ **Charitable contributions.** Many estate plans include a provision for charitable contributions. Transfers to charities are not subject to tax because of the deduction for charitable contributions. Once the decision has been made to make charitable contributions, the issue becomes whether to give now (during life) or later (at death) through bequests from the estate. There are many advantages to giving now rather than later. A lifetime gift results in an income tax deduction (a tax savings of 39.6 percent at the top 2015 rate). In addition, such gifts are removed from the estate

and so there is an estate tax saving (40 percent top 2015 rate). Finally, a lifetime gift allows the donor to observe the effect of the gift on the charitable organization and to receive psychic income in the form of gratitude or other recognition. Another consideration is the need of funds for living. Obviously, you cannot give so much of your wealth to charity that you no longer have enough to live on. You must provide for yourself and your family before charity. However, most large estates are able and desire to give charitable gifts.

15-4c Reasons for Making Lifetime Gifts

Gift giving is the number one component of an estate plan. The reasons for its importance are listed here:

▶ **Gift tax annual exclusion.** As noted earlier, gifts up to the annual exclusion ($14,000 in 2015) may be transferred with no tax impact.

▶ **Gift tax exclusion escapes estate tax.** Property that qualifies for the annual exclusion is not taxable and thus is free from gift and estate taxes. Regardless of a gift's size—and even if it's made within three years of the donor's death—it's typically not treated as part of the donor's estate.

▶ **Impact of marital deduction.** The transfer tax marital deduction allows one spouse to give the other spouse an unlimited amount of property entirely transfer tax free without reducing the donor-spouse's annual exclusion amount.

▶ **Charitable contributions** given during life provide an income tax deduction and remove property from the estate.

▶ If **property is expected to appreciate in value**, transferring now, before that appreciation is realized, will reduce the amount of transfer tax assessed on the property.

> **EXAMPLE: Excluding Appreciated Value from an Estate** Suppose Luis gives his son, Andres, a gift of stock worth $35,000 in 2015. When Luis dies two years later, the stock is worth $60,000. The amount subject to transfer taxes in 2015 will be $21,000 ($35,000 − $14,000)—the adjusted taxable gift amount. None of the subsequent appreciation is subject to the gift or estate tax.

▶ The joy of seeing others enjoy your wealth creates psychic income that will brighten your days.

CALCULATING ESTATE TAXES

LO5 Federal estate taxes are levied on the transfer of property at death, so one goal of effective estate planning is to minimize the amount of estate taxes paid. The tax is based on the value of the property that the deceased transfers (or is deemed to transfer) to others. The phrase "is deemed to transfer" is important because the estate tax applies not only to transfers that a deceased actually makes at death, but also to certain transfers made during the person's lifetime—called *lifetime gifts*. For example, if the owner-insured gives away his or her life insurance policy within three years of his or her death, the proceeds will be included in the insured's gross estate.

"So much for the will! Now, before you start celebrating, I suggest you think about inheritance taxes, because, according to my calculations, you will be left with . . . ."

EXAMPLE: Use of Life Insurance in an Estate In 2015, two years before his death, Jasper gave his son, Gavin, a $1 million term insurance policy on Jasper's life. At the time of the gift, Jasper was in good health, and the value of the term insurance policy for gift tax purposes was clearly less than the $14,000 annual exclusion amount. Therefore, Jasper did not have to file a gift tax return. But because Jasper died within three years of gifting the life insurance policy, the $1 million payout is included in his gross estate for estate tax purposes. Had Jasper outlived the transfer by more than three years, the proceeds would not have been included in his gross estate.

15-5a Computing Federal Estate Tax

The computation of federal estate taxes involves six steps:

1. Determine the *gross estate*, the fair market value of all property in which the decedent had an interest and that is required to be included in the estate.

2. Find the *adjusted gross estate* by subtracting from the gross estate any allowable funeral and administrative expenses, debts, and other expenses incurred during administration.

3. Calculate the *taxable estate* by subtracting any allowable marital deduction or charitable deduction from the adjusted gross estate.

4. Compute the *estate tax base*. After determining the value of the taxable estate, any "adjusted taxable gifts" (i.e., gifts above the annual exclusion) made after 1976 are added to the taxable estate. The unified tax rate schedule, shown in Exhibit 15.5, is used to determine a *tentative tax* on the estate tax base.

5. After finding the tentative tax, subtract both the gift taxes the decedent paid (computed at the current tax rate, which could be lower than the rate when the tax was paid) on the adjusted taxable gifts and the **unified tax credit** ($2,117,800 in 2015). The result is the total death taxes.

6. Determine the *federal estate tax due*. Some estates will qualify for additional credits, which are fairly rare but when available result in a dollar-for-dollar reduction of the tax. After reducing the total death taxes by any eligible credits, the federal estate tax due is payable by the decedent's executor, generally within nine months of the decedent's death.

unified tax credit the credit that can be applied against the tentative tax on the estate tax base

This worksheet is useful in determining federal estate tax due. Note that taxes are payable at the marginal tax rate applicable to the estate tax base (line 7), which is the amount that exists before the tax-free exclusion is factored in by application of the unified credit.

COMPUTING FEDERAL ESTATE TAX DUE

Name _Cooper Bennett_   **Date** _9/5/2015_

Line	Computation	Item	Amount	Total Amount
1		*Gross estate*		$ 7,850,000
2	Subtract sum of:	(a) Funeral expenses	$ 6,800	
		(b) Administrative expenses	75,000	
		(c) Debts	125,000	
		(d) Other expenses	0	
		Total		(206,800)
3	Result:	*Adjusted gross estate*		$ 7,643,200
4	Subtract sum of:	(a) Marital deduction	0	
		(b) Charitable deduction	180,000	
		Total		(180,000)
5	Result:	*Taxable estate*		$ 7,463,200
6	Add:	*Adjusted taxable gifts (post-1976)*		$ 0
7	Result:	*Estate tax base*		$ 7,463,200
8	Compute:	*Tentative tax on estate tax base*[a]		$ 2,931,080
9	Subtract sum of:	(a) Gift tax payable on post-1976 gifts	$ 0	
		(b) Unified tax credit[b]	$ 2,117,800	
		Total		($ 2,117,800)
10	Result:	*Total estate taxes*		813,280
11	Subtract:	Other credits		($ 0)
12	Result:	*Federal estate tax due*		$ 813,280

[a]Use Exhibit 15.5 to calculate the tentative tax.

[b]Use Exhibit 15.6 to determine the appropriate unified credit.

[c]Note that the tax amount shown on line 7 is a significant number because most states use the same estate tax base that is used for the federal tax.

You can use Worksheet 15.2 to estimate federal estate taxes. The worksheet depicts the computations for a hypothetical situation involving a death in 2015, when the $5,430,000 estate AEA applies. Note that the AEA is not subtracted from the gross estate. The worksheet is useful in following the flow of dollars from the gross estate to the federal estate tax due. The worksheet factors the unified credit for the year 2015 into the calculation at line 9b. The $2,117,800 shown on that line is equal to the tentative tax on an estate tax base of $5,430,000, the AEA. Note that if the taxpayer is a surviving spouse, and his wife elected the portability provision, then the amount of uniform transfer tax credit is $4,235,600 less the credit used by his wife, the first-to-die spouse. If the tentative tax shown on line 8 is less than the unified credit available for the decedent's year of death, then no federal estate tax is due.

15-6 ESTATE PLANNING TECHNIQUES

LO6 Estate planning is the process of developing a plan to administer and distribute your estate after your death, in a manner consistent with your wishes and the needs of your survivors, while minimizing taxes. The primary taxes to consider are the income tax, the gift tax, and the estate tax. In developing a plan to distribute your estate, these three taxes must be taken into account. As noted earlier, in 2015 the applicable exemption amount is $5,430,000, with a portability feature that allows the surviving spouse to use the unified transfer tax credit not used by the deceased spouse. For a married couple, then, there is no transfer tax until $10,860,000 is transferred. In this section we discuss common estate planning techniques.

> One of the uses of trusts is to split income among family members and thereby reduce total income tax paid.

15-6a Gift Giving Program

With the annual exclusion of $14,000 and the ability to split gifts, a married couple may transfer $28,000 per year per donee. Giving gifts reduces the transfer tax and gives added joy to the donor. When selecting the property to give, the impact on income tax must be considered. Recall that the basis of gifted property is generally the cost of the property to the donor and that the basis of inherited property is the fair market value reported on the estate tax return. So if the property is expected to be sold, then there will be a higher gain for income tax purposes if the property is gifted (though only at the capital gains tax rate, at 20 percent in 2015 for taxpayers in the 39.6 percent bracket) than if the property is transferred at death through the estate. If the transfer will result in transfer taxes being paid, then the 40 percent transfer tax that applies to the entire value of the property transferred will probably be greater than the associated income tax that applies only to the gain from the property. In this case, it would be better to gift the property early, when the value is relatively low, even though the donee will have to pay tax on the gain when the property is sold.

zimmytws/Shutterstock.com

Charity

15-6b Use of the Unified Transfer Tax Credit

Prior to 2011, the unified transfer tax (UTT) credit was unique to the individual. Thus, if an individual did not use it, he or she would lose it. Beginning in 2011, Congress added portability to the credit, which allows the surviving spouse to use the unused deceased spouse's UTT credit. Prior to the portability rule, estates used a credit shelter trust (discussed in Exhibit 15.4) to achieve the same results.

15-6c Charitable Contributions

If the taxpayer desires to make charitable contributions, the question to answer is whether the contribution should be made now (during life) or later (at death). If made now, the taxpayer gets an income tax deduction and the property is out of the estate. The added benefit of the income tax savings tips the charitable contribution timing question in favor of giving during life. Of course, if the funds are needed to support the taxpayer, then no contribution should be made until death. Transfers to charity at death are appropriate in such cases.

15-6d Life Insurance Trust

Many estates have life insurance as one of their major assets. The primary purpose of life insurance is to replace lost income upon the death of the insured or to provide cash to pay a transfer tax at death and other end of life expenses. To minimize the transfer tax when that is the purpose of the insurance, the taxpayer may transfer the insurance to a life insurance trust in order to get the proceeds out of the estate. The transfer of the policy to the trust must be at least three years before death or it is ignored, in which case the life insurance benefits are included in the taxable estate.

15-6e Trusts

One of the many uses of trusts is to split income among family members and thereby reduce total income tax paid. However, the trust

PLANNING OVER A LIFETIME

Estate Planning

Here are some key considerations for estate planning in each stage of the life cycle.

PRE-FAMILY INDEPENDENCE: 20s

▸ While it might seem unnecessary when you're getting started, a will should be made.

▸ A living will is a good idea, as is a durable power of attorney for health care. Make them available to your family and physicians.

FAMILY FORMATION/CAREER DEVELOPMENT: 30–45

▸ Update your will as your circumstances change. Specify who will care for your children if you and your spouse die prematurely.

▸ Make sure your will is available to family members.

▸ Prepare a durable power of attorney for financial matters.

PRE-RETIREMENT: 45–65

▸ Start estate planning and consider trust arrangements for children.

▸ Revise your will as your children become adults and finish school.

▸ Review and revise as needed your durable power of attorney for financial matters and health care at least every few years.

RETIREMENT: 65 AND BEYOND

▸ Establish a well-thought-out estate plan. Update your will to be as specific as possible about the distribution of all property, especially personal property.

▸ Consider explaining to your children what they will inherit and your rationale.

▸ Make sure that a comprehensive list of your financial accounts is available to your spouse and family.

▸ You and your spouse should make and fund your funeral arrangements to spare your family this burden.

income tax rates are extremely compressed: in 2015, the top rate of 39.6 percent applies to income over $12,300. The trust income tax may be avoided by transferring income property to the beneficiaries. If the beneficiary is a minor, however, such income may be taxed at his or her parents' tax rate.

15-6f Valuation Issues

The tax base for the transfer tax is fair market value. When the estate includes closely held stocks, real estate, or large blocks of listed securities, there are discounts that apply to valuation of the property. The following are the most used discounts:

▶ **Minority interest.** If the ownership of a closely held company is less than 50 percent of the stock, then it is a minority interest. Discounts of 25 to 30 percent are common. Thus, if the stock is considered to have a value of $100 per share, a 30 percent minority interest discount will reduce the fair market value for inclusion in the taxable estate to $70 per share.

▶ **Marketability discount.** If a large amount of real estate is for sale in one market or area, the value will be reduced solely because of marketability factors. These discounts range from 10 to 30 percent.

▶ **Blockage discounts.** If a large block of stock of a listed company is sold, the market will react to reduce the price of the stock. For a publicly held company, 1 percent of the stock is a large enough block to reduce the value. So if that amount of stock is in the gross estate, then the value subject to the tax will be reduced by the blockage discount. Discounts of 5 to 15 percent are common.

15-6g Future of Estate Taxes

Congress is always discussing changes to the income and transfer tax. Currently, there are proposed laws to eliminate the estate tax but keep the gift tax. The gift tax is seen as necessary to prevent splitting the income among the family in order to minimize the family's income tax. There are proposals to reduce the AEA amount from the 2015 amount of $5,430,000 to $3,500,000. It is not known if any of these proposals will actually be enacted. Thus, when planning an estate, focus on flexibility so you can react when or if the law is changed. Obviously, the tax impact of your estate plan needs to reviewed annually to ensure the outcome is as you planned.

The transfer tax is a major concern to married taxpayers with wealth over $10,680,000, but much less so for less wealthy taxpayers. However, estate planning is a concern to all, and the general issues discussed in this chapter apply to all estates, large and small.

The Unintended Effects of Adam's Beneficiary Designations

Adam Russell died suddenly in 2015. He had amassed a significant estate and had an attorney write a will that would distribute his assets among his wife, Sarah, and two grown daughters, Jade and Eva, as he directed. Apart from his will, he had heard that it made sense to name beneficiaries on his investment accounts so that those assets would go directly to his family and bypass the sometimes long and costly probate process. Adam had been previously married to Tessa Russell, who survived him.

Adam named his wife, Sarah, as the beneficiary to most of his investment accounts and designated one account to his daughter, Jade, and one account to his daughter, Eva. He intended for his daughters to get equal amounts. While trying to be careful, Adam forgot that he hadn't changed the beneficiary on one investment account from Tessa, his prior wife, to his current wife, Sarah. That account was worth $50,000 at his death.

So what was the effect of Adam's beneficiary designations? His wife Sarah received most of the investment accounts as he had intended. However, the $50,000 account that had not been updated to name Sarah as the beneficiary went to Adam's prior wife, Tessa, which is not what he intended.

It seemed fair to Adam to designate one investment account to each of his daughters because the accounts had the same initial values. However, the accounts had grown to different values by the time of his death. Jade's account had grown to $100,000 while Eva's account had grown to $200,000. Adam had intended that his daughters receive equal amounts but they did not. Adam could have achieved his objective by naming *both* of his daughters as beneficiaries on *both* of the accounts. And had Adam reviewed his beneficiary designations at least once a year, he may well have discovered that he'd forgotten to make an important change.

robertlamphoto/Shutterstock.com

STUDY TOOLS 15

LOCATED AT BACK OF THE TEXTBOOK
☐ Chapter Review Card

LOCATED AT WWW.CENGAGEBRAIN.COM
☐ Review Key Term flashcards and create your own cards.
☐ Track your knowledge and understanding of key concepts in personal finance.

☐ Complete practice and graded quizzes to prepare for tests.
☐ Complete interactive content at PFIN6 Online.
☐ View the chapter highlight boxes at PFIN6 Online.

Financial Planning Exercises

LO1 1. **Estate planning objectives.** Generate a list of estate planning objectives that apply to your personal family situation. Be sure to consider the size of your potential estate as well as people planning and asset planning. Estate planning is not just about taxes.

LO2 2. **Importance of writing a will.** Cal and Elise Sanders are in their mid-30s and have two children, ages 8 and 5. They have combined annual income of $95,000 and own a house in joint tenancy with a market value of $310,000, on which they have a mortgage of $250,000. Cal has $100,000 in group term life insurance and an individual universal life policy for $150,000. However, the Sanders haven't prepared their wills. Cal plans to do one soon, but they think that Elise doesn't need one because the house is jointly owned. Explain why it's important for both Cal and Elise to draft wills as soon as possible.

LO2 3. **Qualifications of estate executor.** Your best friend has asked you to be executor of his estate. What qualifications do you need, and would you accept the responsibility?

LO2 4. **Will and last letter preparation.** Prepare a basic will for yourself, using the guidelines presented in the text; also prepare your brief letter of last instructions. Note that it is wisest to use an attorney to finalize a will.

LO2 5. **Topics in an ethical will.** State the topics you would cover in your ethical will. Would you consider recording it digitally?

LO2, 3, 5 6. **Trusts in estate planning.** Peter Myers, 48, and Margot Powell, 44, were married five years ago. They have children from their prior marriages, two children for Peter and one child for Margot. The couple's estate is valued at $1.4 million, including a house valued at $475,000, a vacation home in the mountains, investments, antique furniture that has been in Margot's family for many years, and jewelry belonging to Peter's first wife. Discuss how they could use trusts as part of their estate planning, and suggest some other ideas for them to consider when preparing their wills and related documents.

LO4, 5 7. **Calculation of estate taxes.** Use Worksheet 15.2. When Amos Jenkins died in 2015, he left an estate valued at $5,850,000. His trust directed distribution as follows: $20,000 to the local hospital, $160,000 to his alma mater, and the remainder to his three adult children. Death-related costs were $6,800 for funeral expenses, $40,000 paid to attorneys, $5,000 paid to accountants, and $30,000 paid to the trustee of his living trust. In addition, there were debts of $125,000. Use Exhibits 15.5 and 15.6 to calculate the federal estate tax due on Amos' estate.

LO4, 5 8. **Lifetime gifting strategy.** Regina Morales has accumulated substantial wealth and plans to gift some of her wealth to her son Eduardo. She is considering two assets: a beach house, which cost $150,000 twenty years ago and now has a fair market value of $500,000; and shares in three mutual funds, which cost her $400,000 five years ago and now have a fair market value of $500,000. Prepare a memo advising Regina which property to give to Eduardo. In your memo, consider two scenarios: one where Eduardo sells the property and one where he does not.

LO4, 5 9. **Calculating federal transfer tax on estate.** Jonah Foster died in 2015, leaving an estate of $23 million. Jonah's wife, Elizabeth, died in 2010. In 2009, Jonah gave his son Isaac, property that resulted in a taxable gift of $3 million and upon which Jonah paid $885,000 in transfer taxes. Jonah had made no other taxable gifts during his life. His will provided a charitable bequest of $1 million to his church. Determine the federal transfer tax on Jonah's estate.

LO6 10. **Recent estate tax developments and the need for estate planning.** Summarize important recent legislation affecting estate taxes, and briefly describe the impact on estate planning. Explain why getting rid of the estate tax doesn't eliminate the need for estate planning.

APPENDIX A

Table of Future Value Factors

Instructions: To use this table, find the future value factor that corresponds to both a given time period (year) and an interest rate. For example, if you want the future value factor for 6 years and 10%, move across from year 6 and down from 10% to the point at which the row and column intersect: 1.772. Other illustrations: for 3 years and 15%, the proper future value factor is 1.521; for 30 years and 8%, it is 10.063.

INTEREST RATE

Period	1%	2%	3%	4%	5%	6%	7%	8%	9%	10%	11%	12%	13%	14%	15%	16%	17%	18%	19%	20%	25%	30%
1	1.010	1.020	1.030	1.040	1.050	1.060	1.070	1.080	1.090	1.100	1.110	1.120	1.130	1.140	1.150	1.160	1.170	1.180	1.190	1.200	1.250	1.300
2	1.020	1.040	1.061	1.082	1.103	1.124	1.145	1.166	1.188	1.210	1.232	1.254	1.277	1.300	1.323	1.346	1.369	1.392	1.416	1.440	1.563	1.690
3	1.030	1.061	1.093	1.125	1.158	1.191	1.225	1.260	1.295	1.331	1.368	1.405	1.443	1.482	1.521	1.561	1.602	1.643	1.685	1.728	1.953	2.197
4	1.041	1.082	1.126	1.170	1.216	1.262	1.311	1.360	1.412	1.464	1.518	1.574	1.630	1.689	1.749	1.811	1.874	1.939	2.005	2.074	2.441	2.856
5	1.051	1.104	1.159	1.217	1.276	1.338	1.403	1.469	1.539	1.611	1.685	1.762	1.842	1.925	2.011	2.100	2.192	2.288	2.386	2.488	3.052	3.713
6	1.062	1.126	1.194	1.265	1.340	1.419	1.501	1.587	1.677	1.772	1.870	1.974	2.082	2.195	2.313	2.436	2.565	2.700	2.840	2.986	3.815	4.827
7	1.072	1.149	1.230	1.316	1.407	1.504	1.606	1.714	1.828	1.949	2.076	2.211	2.353	2.502	2.660	2.826	3.001	3.185	3.379	3.583	4.768	6.275
8	1.083	1.172	1.267	1.369	1.477	1.594	1.718	1.851	1.993	2.144	2.305	2.476	2.658	2.853	3.059	3.278	3.511	3.759	4.021	4.300	5.960	8.157
9	1.094	1.195	1.305	1.423	1.551	1.689	1.838	1.999	2.172	2.358	2.558	2.773	3.004	3.252	3.518	3.803	4.108	4.435	4.785	5.160	7.451	10.604
10	1.105	1.219	1.344	1.480	1.629	1.791	1.967	2.159	2.367	2.594	2.839	3.106	3.395	3.707	4.046	4.411	4.807	5.234	5.695	6.192	9.313	13.786
11	1.116	1.243	1.384	1.539	1.710	1.898	2.105	2.332	2.580	2.853	3.152	3.479	3.836	4.226	4.652	5.117	5.624	6.176	6.777	7.430	11.642	17.922
12	1.127	1.268	1.426	1.601	1.796	2.012	2.252	2.518	2.813	3.138	3.498	3.896	4.335	4.818	5.350	5.936	6.580	7.288	8.064	8.916	14.552	23.298
13	1.138	1.294	1.469	1.665	1.886	2.133	2.410	2.720	3.066	3.452	3.883	4.363	4.898	5.492	6.153	6.886	7.699	8.599	9.596	10.699	18.190	30.288
14	1.149	1.319	1.513	1.732	1.980	2.261	2.579	2.937	3.342	3.797	4.310	4.887	5.535	6.261	7.076	7.988	9.007	10.147	11.420	12.839	22.737	39.374
15	1.161	1.346	1.558	1.801	2.079	2.397	2.759	3.172	3.642	4.177	4.785	5.474	6.254	7.138	8.137	9.266	10.539	11.974	13.590	15.407	28.422	51.186
16	1.173	1.373	1.605	1.873	2.183	2.540	2.952	3.426	3.970	4.595	5.311	6.130	7.067	8.137	9.358	10.748	12.330	14.129	16.172	18.488	35.527	66.542
17	1.184	1.400	1.653	1.948	2.292	2.693	3.159	3.700	4.328	5.054	5.895	6.866	7.986	9.276	10.761	12.468	14.426	16.672	19.244	22.186	44.409	86.504
18	1.196	1.428	1.702	2.026	2.407	2.854	3.380	3.996	4.717	5.560	6.544	7.690	9.024	10.575	12.375	14.463	16.879	19.673	22.901	26.623	55.511	112.455
19	1.208	1.457	1.754	2.107	2.527	3.026	3.617	4.316	5.142	6.116	7.263	8.613	10.197	12.056	14.232	16.777	19.748	23.214	27.252	31.948	69.389	146.192
20	1.220	1.486	1.806	2.191	2.653	3.207	3.870	4.661	5.604	6.727	8.062	9.646	11.523	13.743	16.367	19.461	23.106	27.393	32.429	38.338	86.736	190.050
21	1.232	1.516	1.860	2.279	2.786	3.400	4.141	5.034	6.109	7.400	8.949	10.804	13.021	15.668	18.822	22.574	27.034	32.324	38.591	46.005	108.420	247.065
22	1.245	1.546	1.916	2.370	2.925	3.604	4.430	5.437	6.659	8.140	9.934	12.100	14.714	17.861	21.645	26.186	31.629	38.142	45.923	55.206	135.525	321.184
23	1.257	1.577	1.974	2.465	3.072	3.820	4.741	5.871	7.258	8.954	11.026	13.552	16.627	20.362	24.891	30.376	37.006	45.008	54.649	66.247	169.407	417.539
24	1.270	1.608	2.033	2.563	3.225	4.049	5.072	6.341	7.911	9.850	12.239	15.179	18.788	23.212	28.625	35.236	43.297	53.109	65.032	79.497	211.758	542.801
25	1.282	1.641	2.094	2.666	3.386	4.292	5.427	6.848	8.623	10.835	13.585	17.000	21.231	26.462	32.919	40.874	50.658	62.669	77.388	95.396	264.698	705.641
26	1.295	1.673	2.157	2.772	3.556	4.549	5.807	7.396	9.399	11.918	15.080	19.040	23.991	30.167	37.857	47.414	59.270	73.949	92.092	114.475	330.872	917.333
27	1.308	1.707	2.221	2.883	3.733	4.822	6.214	7.988	10.245	13.110	16.739	21.325	27.109	34.390	43.535	55.000	69.345	87.260	109.589	137.371	413.590	1,192.533
28	1.321	1.741	2.288	2.999	3.920	5.112	6.649	8.627	11.167	14.421	18.580	23.884	30.633	39.204	50.066	63.800	81.134	102.967	130.411	164.845	516.988	1,550.293
29	1.335	1.776	2.357	3.119	4.116	5.418	7.114	9.317	12.172	15.863	20.624	26.750	34.616	44.693	57.575	74.009	94.927	121.501	155.189	197.814	646.235	2,015.381
30	1.348	1.811	2.427	3.243	4.322	5.743	7.612	10.063	13.268	17.449	22.892	29.960	39.116	50.950	66.212	85.850	111.065	143.371	184.675	237.376	807.794	2,619.996
35	1.417	2.000	2.814	3.946	5.516	7.686	10.677	14.785	20.414	28.102	38.575	52.800	72.069	98.100	133.176	180.314	243.503	327.997	440.701	590.668	2,465.190	9,727.860
40	1.489	2.208	3.262	4.801	7.040	10.286	14.974	21.725	31.409	45.259	65.001	93.051	132.782	188.884	267.864	378.721	533.869	750.378	1,051.668	1,469.772	7,523.164	36,118.865

Note: All factors are rounded to the nearest 1/1000 in order to agree with values used in the text.

APPENDIX B

Table of Future Value Annuity Factors

Instructions: To use this table, find the future value of annuity factor that corresponds to both a given time period (year) and an interest rate. For example, if you want the future value of annuity factor for 6 years and 10%, move across from year 6 and down from 10% to the point at which the row and column intersect: 7.716. Other illustrations: for 3 years and 15%, the proper future value of annuity factor is 3.473; for 30 years and 6%, it is 79.058.

INTEREST RATE

Period	1%	2%	3%	4%	5%	6%	7%	8%	9%	10%	11%	12%	13%	14%	15%	16%	17%	18%	19%	20%	25%	30%
1	1.000	1.000	1.000	1.000	1.000	1.000	1.000	1.000	1.000	1.000	1.000	1.000	1.000	1.000	1.000	1.000	1.000	1.000	1.000	1.000	1.000	1.000
2	2.010	2.020	2.030	2.040	2.050	2.060	2.070	2.080	2.090	2.100	2.110	2.120	2.130	2.140	2.150	2.160	2.170	2.180	2.190	2.200	2.250	2.300
3	3.030	3.060	3.091	3.122	3.153	3.184	3.215	3.246	3.278	3.310	3.342	3.374	3.407	3.440	3.473	3.506	3.539	3.572	3.606	3.640	3.813	3.990
4	4.060	4.122	4.184	4.246	4.310	4.375	4.440	4.506	4.573	4.641	4.710	4.779	4.850	4.921	4.993	5.066	5.141	5.215	5.291	5.368	5.766	6.187
5	5.101	5.204	5.309	5.416	5.526	5.637	5.751	5.867	5.985	6.105	6.228	6.353	6.480	6.610	6.742	6.877	7.014	7.154	7.297	7.442	8.207	9.043
6	6.152	6.308	6.468	6.633	6.802	6.975	7.153	7.336	7.523	7.716	7.913	8.115	8.323	8.536	8.754	8.977	9.207	9.442	9.683	9.930	11.259	12.756
7	7.214	7.434	7.662	7.898	8.142	8.394	8.654	8.923	9.200	9.487	9.783	10.089	10.405	10.730	11.067	11.414	11.772	12.142	12.523	12.916	15.073	17.583
8	8.286	8.583	8.892	9.214	9.549	9.897	10.260	10.637	11.028	11.436	11.859	12.300	12.757	13.233	13.727	14.240	14.773	15.327	15.902	16.499	19.842	23.858
9	9.369	9.755	10.159	10.583	11.027	11.491	11.978	12.488	13.021	13.579	14.164	14.776	15.416	16.085	16.786	17.519	18.285	19.086	19.923	20.799	25.802	32.015
10	10.462	10.950	11.464	12.006	12.578	13.181	13.816	14.487	15.193	15.937	16.722	17.549	18.420	19.337	20.304	21.321	22.393	23.521	24.709	25.959	33.253	42.619
11	11.567	12.169	12.808	13.486	14.207	14.972	15.784	16.645	17.560	18.531	19.561	20.655	21.814	23.045	24.349	25.733	27.200	28.755	30.404	32.150	42.566	56.405
12	12.683	13.412	14.192	15.026	15.917	16.870	17.888	18.977	20.141	21.384	22.713	24.133	25.650	27.271	29.002	30.850	32.824	34.931	37.180	39.581	54.208	74.327
13	13.809	14.680	15.618	16.627	17.713	18.882	20.141	21.495	22.953	24.523	26.212	28.029	29.985	32.089	34.352	36.786	39.404	42.219	45.244	48.497	68.760	97.625
14	14.947	15.974	17.086	18.292	19.599	21.015	22.550	24.215	26.019	27.975	30.095	32.393	34.883	37.581	40.505	43.672	47.103	50.818	54.841	59.196	86.949	127.913
15	16.097	17.293	18.599	20.024	21.579	23.276	25.129	27.152	29.361	31.772	34.405	37.280	40.417	43.842	47.580	51.660	56.110	60.965	66.261	72.035	109.687	167.286
16	17.258	18.639	20.157	21.825	23.657	25.673	27.888	30.324	33.003	35.950	39.190	42.753	46.672	50.980	55.717	60.925	66.649	72.939	79.850	87.442	138.109	218.472
17	18.430	20.012	21.762	23.698	25.840	28.213	30.840	33.750	36.974	40.545	44.501	48.884	53.739	59.118	65.075	71.673	78.979	87.068	96.022	105.931	173.636	285.01
18	19.615	21.412	23.414	25.645	28.132	30.906	33.999	37.450	41.301	45.599	50.396	55.750	61.725	68.394	75.836	84.141	93.406	103.74	115.27	128.117	218.045	371.52
19	20.811	22.841	25.117	27.671	30.539	33.760	37.379	41.446	46.018	51.159	56.939	63.440	70.749	78.969	88.212	98.603	110.28	123.41	138.17	154.740	273.556	483.97
20	22.019	24.297	26.870	29.778	33.066	36.786	40.995	45.762	51.160	57.275	64.203	72.052	80.947	91.025	102.444	115.380	130.033	146.628	165.418	186.688	342.945	630.165
21	23.239	25.783	28.676	31.969	35.719	39.993	44.865	50.423	56.765	64.002	72.265	81.699	92.470	104.768	118.810	134.841	153.139	174.021	197.847	225.026	429.681	820.215
22	24.472	27.299	30.537	34.248	38.505	43.392	49.006	55.457	62.873	71.403	81.214	92.503	105.491	120.436	137.632	157.415	180.172	206.345	236.438	271.031	538.101	1,067.280
23	25.716	28.845	32.453	36.618	41.430	46.996	53.436	60.893	69.532	79.543	91.148	104.603	120.205	138.297	159.276	183.601	211.801	244.487	282.362	326.237	673.626	1,388.464
24	26.973	30.422	34.426	39.083	44.502	50.816	58.177	66.765	76.790	88.497	102.174	118.155	136.831	158.659	184.168	213.978	248.808	289.494	337.010	392.484	843.033	1,806.003
25	28.243	32.030	36.459	41.646	47.727	54.865	63.249	73.106	84.701	98.347	114.413	133.334	155.620	181.871	212.793	249.214	292.105	342.603	402.042	471.981	1,054.791	2,348.803
26	29.526	33.671	38.553	44.312	51.113	59.156	68.676	79.954	93.324	109.182	127.999	150.334	176.850	208.333	245.712	290.088	342.763	405.272	479.431	567.377	1,319.489	3,054.444
27	30.821	35.344	40.710	47.084	54.669	63.706	74.484	87.351	102.723	121.100	143.079	169.374	200.841	238.499	283.569	337.502	402.032	479.221	571.522	681.853	1,650.361	3,971.778
28	32.129	37.051	42.931	49.968	58.403	68.528	80.698	95.339	112.968	134.210	159.817	190.699	227.950	272.889	327.104	392.503	471.378	566.481	681.112	819.223	2,063.952	5,164.311
29	33.450	38.792	45.219	52.966	62.323	73.640	87.347	103.966	124.135	148.631	178.397	214.583	258.583	312.094	377.170	456.303	552.512	669.447	811.523	984.068	2,580.939	6,714.604
30	34.785	40.568	47.575	56.085	66.439	79.058	94.461	113.283	136.308	164.494	199.021	241.333	293.199	356.787	434.745	530.312	647.439	790.948	966.712	1,181.882	3,227.174	8,729.985
35	41.660	49.994	60.462	73.652	90.320	111.435	138.237	172.317	215.711	271.024	341.590	431.663	546.681	693.573	881.170	1,120.713	1,426.491	1,816.652	2,314.214	2,948.341	9,856.761	32,422.868
40	48.886	60.402	75.401	95.026	120.800	154.762	199.635	259.057	337.882	442.593	581.826	767.091	1,013.704	1,342.025	1,779.090	2,360.757	3,134.522	4,163.213	5,529.829	7,343.858	30,088.655	120,392.883

Note: All factors are rounded to the nearest 1/1000 in order to agree with values used in the text.

APPENDIX C

Table of Present Value Factors

Instructions: To use this table, find the present value factor that corresponds to both a given time period (year) and an interest rate. For example, if you want the present value factor for 25 years and 7%, move across from year 25 and down from 7% to the point at which the row and column intersect: .184. Other illustrations: for 3 years and 15%, the proper present value factor is .658; for 30 years and 8%, it is .099.

INTEREST RATE

Period	1%	2%	3%	4%	5%	6%	7%	8%	9%	10%	11%	12%	13%	14%	15%	16%	17%	18%	19%	20%	25%	30%
1	0.990	0.980	0.971	0.962	0.952	0.943	0.935	0.926	0.917	0.909	0.901	0.893	0.885	0.877	0.870	0.862	0.855	0.847	0.840	0.833	0.800	0.769
2	0.980	0.961	0.943	0.925	0.907	0.890	0.873	0.857	0.842	0.826	0.812	0.797	0.783	0.769	0.756	0.743	0.731	0.718	0.706	0.694	0.640	0.592
3	0.971	0.942	0.915	0.889	0.864	0.840	0.816	0.794	0.772	0.751	0.731	0.712	0.693	0.675	0.658	0.641	0.624	0.609	0.593	0.579	0.512	0.455
4	0.961	0.924	0.888	0.855	0.823	0.792	0.763	0.735	0.708	0.683	0.659	0.636	0.613	0.592	0.572	0.552	0.534	0.516	0.499	0.482	0.410	0.350
5	0.951	0.906	0.863	0.822	0.784	0.747	0.713	0.681	0.650	0.621	0.593	0.567	0.543	0.519	0.497	0.476	0.456	0.437	0.419	0.402	0.328	0.269
6	0.942	0.888	0.837	0.790	0.746	0.705	0.666	0.630	0.596	0.564	0.535	0.507	0.480	0.456	0.432	0.410	0.390	0.370	0.352	0.335	0.262	0.207
7	0.933	0.871	0.813	0.760	0.711	0.665	0.623	0.583	0.547	0.513	0.482	0.452	0.425	0.400	0.376	0.354	0.333	0.314	0.296	0.279	0.210	0.159
8	0.923	0.853	0.789	0.731	0.677	0.627	0.582	0.540	0.502	0.467	0.434	0.404	0.376	0.351	0.327	0.305	0.285	0.266	0.249	0.233	0.168	0.123
9	0.914	0.837	0.766	0.703	0.645	0.592	0.544	0.500	0.460	0.424	0.391	0.361	0.333	0.308	0.284	0.263	0.243	0.225	0.209	0.194	0.134	0.094
10	0.905	0.820	0.744	0.676	0.614	0.558	0.508	0.463	0.422	0.386	0.352	0.322	0.295	0.270	0.247	0.227	0.208	0.191	0.176	0.162	0.107	0.073
11	0.896	0.804	0.722	0.650	0.585	0.527	0.475	0.429	0.388	0.350	0.317	0.287	0.261	0.237	0.215	0.195	0.178	0.162	0.148	0.135	0.086	0.056
12	0.887	0.788	0.701	0.625	0.557	0.497	0.444	0.397	0.356	0.319	0.286	0.257	0.231	0.208	0.187	0.168	0.152	0.137	0.124	0.112	0.069	0.043
13	0.879	0.773	0.681	0.601	0.530	0.469	0.415	0.368	0.326	0.290	0.258	0.229	0.204	0.182	0.163	0.145	0.130	0.116	0.104	0.093	0.055	0.033
14	0.870	0.758	0.661	0.577	0.505	0.442	0.388	0.340	0.299	0.263	0.232	0.205	0.181	0.160	0.141	0.125	0.111	0.099	0.088	0.078	0.044	0.025
15	0.861	0.743	0.642	0.555	0.481	0.417	0.362	0.315	0.275	0.239	0.209	0.183	0.160	0.140	0.123	0.108	0.095	0.084	0.074	0.065	0.035	0.020
16	0.853	0.728	0.623	0.534	0.458	0.394	0.339	0.292	0.252	0.218	0.188	0.163	0.141	0.123	0.107	0.093	0.081	0.071	0.062	0.054	0.028	0.015
17	0.844	0.714	0.605	0.513	0.436	0.371	0.317	0.270	0.231	0.198	0.170	0.146	0.125	0.108	0.093	0.080	0.069	0.060	0.052	0.045	0.023	0.012
18	0.836	0.700	0.587	0.494	0.416	0.350	0.296	0.250	0.212	0.180	0.153	0.130	0.111	0.095	0.081	0.069	0.059	0.051	0.044	0.038	0.018	0.009
19	0.828	0.686	0.570	0.475	0.396	0.331	0.277	0.232	0.194	0.164	0.138	0.116	0.098	0.083	0.070	0.060	0.051	0.043	0.037	0.031	0.014	0.007
20	0.820	0.673	0.554	0.456	0.377	0.312	0.258	0.215	0.178	0.149	0.124	0.104	0.087	0.073	0.061	0.051	0.043	0.037	0.031	0.026	0.012	0.005
21	0.811	0.660	0.538	0.439	0.359	0.294	0.242	0.199	0.164	0.135	0.112	0.093	0.077	0.064	0.053	0.044	0.037	0.031	0.026	0.022	0.009	0.004
22	0.803	0.647	0.522	0.422	0.342	0.278	0.226	0.184	0.150	0.123	0.101	0.083	0.068	0.056	0.046	0.038	0.032	0.026	0.022	0.018	0.007	0.003
23	0.795	0.634	0.507	0.406	0.326	0.262	0.211	0.170	0.138	0.112	0.091	0.074	0.060	0.049	0.040	0.033	0.027	0.022	0.018	0.015	0.006	0.002
24	0.788	0.622	0.492	0.390	0.310	0.247	0.197	0.158	0.126	0.102	0.082	0.066	0.053	0.043	0.035	0.028	0.023	0.019	0.015	0.013	0.005	0.002
25	0.780	0.610	0.478	0.375	0.295	0.233	0.184	0.146	0.116	0.092	0.074	0.059	0.047	0.038	0.030	0.024	0.020	0.016	0.013	0.010	0.004	0.001
26	0.772	0.598	0.464	0.361	0.281	0.220	0.172	0.135	0.106	0.084	0.066	0.053	0.042	0.033	0.026	0.021	0.017	0.014	0.011	0.009	0.003	0.001
27	0.764	0.586	0.450	0.347	0.268	0.207	0.161	0.125	0.098	0.076	0.060	0.047	0.037	0.029	0.023	0.018	0.014	0.011	0.009	0.007	0.002	0.001
28	0.757	0.574	0.437	0.333	0.255	0.196	0.150	0.116	0.090	0.069	0.054	0.042	0.033	0.026	0.020	0.016	0.012	0.010	0.008	0.006	0.002	0.001
29	0.749	0.563	0.424	0.321	0.243	0.185	0.141	0.107	0.082	0.063	0.048	0.037	0.029	0.022	0.017	0.014	0.011	0.008	0.006	0.005	0.002	*
30	0.742	0.552	0.412	0.308	0.231	0.174	0.131	0.099	0.075	0.057	0.044	0.033	0.026	0.020	0.015	0.012	0.009	0.007	0.005	0.004	0.001	*
35	0.706	0.500	0.355	0.253	0.181	0.130	0.094	0.068	0.049	0.036	0.026	0.019	0.014	0.010	0.008	0.006	0.004	0.003	0.002	0.002	*	*
40	0.672	0.453	0.307	0.208	0.142	0.097	0.067	0.046	0.032	0.022	0.015	0.011	0.008	0.005	0.004	0.003	0.002	0.001	0.001	0.001	*	*

*present value factor is zero to three decimal places.

Note: All factors are rounded to the nearest 1/1000 in order to agree with values used in the text.

APPENDIX D

Table of Present Value Annuity Factors

Instructions: To use this table, find the present value of annuity factor that corresponds to both a given time period (year) and an interest rate. For example, if you want the present value of annuity factor for 30 years and 7%, move across from year 30 and down from 7% to the point at which the row and column intersect: 12.409. Other illustrations: for 3 years and 15%, the proper present value of annuity factor is 2.283; for 30 years and 8%, it is 11.258.

INTEREST RATE

Period	1%	2%	3%	4%	5%	6%	7%	8%	9%	10%	11%	12%	13%	14%	15%	16%	17%	18%	19%	20%	25%	30%
1	0.990	0.980	0.971	0.962	0.952	0.943	0.935	0.926	0.917	0.909	0.901	0.893	0.885	0.877	0.870	0.862	0.855	0.847	0.840	0.833	0.800	0.769
2	1.970	1.942	1.913	1.886	1.859	1.833	1.808	1.783	1.759	1.736	1.713	1.690	1.668	1.647	1.626	1.605	1.585	1.566	1.547	1.528	1.440	1.361
3	2.941	2.884	2.829	2.775	2.723	2.673	2.624	2.577	2.531	2.487	2.444	2.402	2.361	2.322	2.283	2.246	2.210	2.174	2.140	2.106	1.952	1.816
4	3.902	3.808	3.717	3.630	3.546	3.465	3.387	3.312	3.240	3.170	3.102	3.037	2.974	2.914	2.855	2.798	2.743	2.690	2.639	2.589	2.362	2.166
5	4.853	4.713	4.580	4.452	4.329	4.212	4.100	3.993	3.890	3.791	3.696	3.605	3.517	3.433	3.352	3.274	3.199	3.127	3.058	2.991	2.689	2.436
6	5.795	5.601	5.417	5.242	5.076	4.917	4.767	4.623	4.486	4.355	4.231	4.111	3.998	3.889	3.784	3.685	3.589	3.498	3.410	3.326	2.951	2.643
7	6.728	6.472	6.230	6.002	5.786	5.582	5.389	5.206	5.033	4.868	4.712	4.564	4.423	4.288	4.160	4.039	3.922	3.812	3.706	3.605	3.161	2.802
8	7.652	7.325	7.020	6.733	6.463	6.210	5.971	5.747	5.535	5.335	5.146	4.968	4.799	4.639	4.487	4.344	4.207	4.078	3.954	3.837	3.329	2.925
9	8.566	8.162	7.786	7.435	7.108	6.802	6.515	6.247	5.995	5.759	5.537	5.328	5.132	4.946	4.772	4.607	4.451	4.303	4.163	4.031	3.463	3.019
10	9.471	8.983	8.530	8.111	7.722	7.360	7.024	6.710	6.418	6.145	5.889	5.650	5.426	5.216	5.019	4.833	4.659	4.494	4.339	4.192	3.571	3.092
11	10.368	9.787	9.253	8.760	8.306	7.887	7.499	7.139	6.805	6.495	6.207	5.938	5.687	5.453	5.234	5.029	4.836	4.656	4.486	4.327	3.656	3.147
12	11.255	10.575	9.954	9.385	8.863	8.384	7.943	7.536	7.161	6.814	6.492	6.194	5.918	5.660	5.421	5.197	4.988	4.793	4.611	4.439	3.725	3.190
13	12.134	11.348	10.635	9.986	9.394	8.853	8.358	7.904	7.487	7.103	6.750	6.424	6.122	5.842	5.583	5.342	5.118	4.910	4.715	4.533	3.780	3.223
14	13.004	12.106	11.296	10.563	9.899	9.295	8.745	8.244	7.786	7.367	6.982	6.628	6.302	6.002	5.724	5.468	5.229	5.008	4.802	4.611	3.824	3.249
15	13.865	12.849	11.938	11.118	10.380	9.712	9.108	8.559	8.061	7.606	7.191	6.811	6.462	6.142	5.847	5.575	5.324	5.092	4.876	4.675	3.859	3.268
16	14.718	13.578	12.561	11.652	10.838	10.106	9.447	8.851	8.313	7.824	7.379	6.974	6.604	6.265	5.954	5.668	5.405	5.162	4.938	4.730	3.887	3.283
17	15.562	14.292	13.166	12.166	11.274	10.477	9.763	9.122	8.544	8.022	7.549	7.120	6.729	6.373	6.047	5.749	5.475	5.222	4.990	4.775	3.910	3.295
18	16.398	14.992	13.754	12.659	11.690	10.828	10.059	9.372	8.756	8.201	7.702	7.250	6.840	6.467	6.128	5.818	5.534	5.273	5.033	4.812	3.928	3.304
19	17.226	15.678	14.324	13.134	12.085	11.158	10.336	9.604	8.950	8.365	7.839	7.366	6.938	6.550	6.198	5.877	5.584	5.316	5.070	4.843	3.942	3.311
20	18.046	16.351	14.877	13.590	12.462	11.470	10.594	9.818	9.129	8.514	7.963	7.469	7.025	6.623	6.259	5.929	5.628	5.353	5.101	4.870	3.954	3.316
21	18.857	17.011	15.415	14.029	12.821	11.764	10.836	10.017	9.292	8.649	8.075	7.562	7.102	6.687	6.312	5.973	5.665	5.384	5.127	4.891	3.963	3.320
22	19.660	17.658	15.937	14.451	13.163	12.042	11.061	10.201	9.442	8.772	8.176	7.645	7.170	6.743	6.359	6.011	5.696	5.410	5.149	4.909	3.970	3.323
23	20.456	18.292	16.444	14.857	13.489	12.303	11.272	10.371	9.580	8.883	8.266	7.718	7.230	6.792	6.399	6.044	5.723	5.432	5.167	4.925	3.976	3.325
24	21.243	18.914	16.936	15.247	13.799	12.550	11.469	10.529	9.707	8.985	8.348	7.784	7.283	6.835	6.434	6.073	5.746	5.451	5.182	4.937	3.981	3.327
25	22.023	19.523	17.413	15.622	14.094	12.783	11.654	10.675	9.823	9.077	8.422	7.843	7.330	6.873	6.464	6.097	5.766	5.467	5.195	4.948	3.985	3.329
26	22.795	20.121	17.877	15.983	14.375	13.003	11.826	10.810	9.929	9.161	8.488	7.896	7.372	6.906	6.491	6.118	5.783	5.480	5.206	4.956	3.988	3.330
27	23.560	20.707	18.327	16.330	14.643	13.211	11.987	10.935	10.027	9.237	8.548	7.943	7.409	6.935	6.514	6.136	5.798	5.492	5.215	4.964	3.990	3.331
28	24.316	21.281	18.764	16.663	14.898	13.406	12.137	11.051	10.116	9.307	8.602	7.984	7.441	6.961	6.534	6.152	5.810	5.502	5.223	4.970	3.992	3.331
29	25.066	21.844	19.188	16.984	15.141	13.591	12.278	11.158	10.198	9.370	8.650	8.022	7.470	6.983	6.551	6.166	5.820	5.510	5.229	4.975	3.994	3.332
30	25.808	22.396	19.600	17.292	15.372	13.765	12.409	11.258	10.274	9.427	8.694	8.055	7.496	7.003	6.566	6.177	5.829	5.517	5.235	4.979	3.995	3.332
35	29.409	24.999	21.487	18.665	16.374	14.498	12.948	11.655	10.567	9.644	8.855	8.176	7.586	7.070	6.617	6.215	5.858	5.539	5.251	4.992	3.998	3.333
40	32.835	27.355	23.115	19.793	17.159	15.046	13.332	11.925	10.757	9.779	8.951	8.244	7.634	7.105	6.642	6.233	5.871	5.548	5.258	4.997	3.999	3.333

Note: All factors are rounded to the nearest 1/1000 in order to agree with values used in the text.

APPENDIX E

Using a Financial Calculator

Important Financial Keys on the Typical Financial Calculator

The important financial keys on a typical financial calculator are depicted and defined below. On some calculators, the keys may be labeled using lowercase characters for "N" and "I". Also, "I/Y" may be used in place of the "I" key.

CPT Compute key; used to initiate financial calculation once all values are input

N Number of periods

I Interest rate per period

PV Present value

PMT Amount of payment; used only for annuities

FV Future value

The handheld financial calculator makes it easy to calculate time value. Once you have mastered the time value of money concepts using tables, we suggest you use such a calculator. For one thing, it becomes cumbersome to use tables when calculating anything other than annual compounding. For another, calculators rather than tables are used almost exclusively in the business of personal financial planning.

However, you don't want to become overly dependent on calculators because you may not be able to recognize a nonsensical answer in the event that you accidentally push the wrong button. The important calculator keys are shown and labeled above. Before using your calculator to make the financial computations described in this text, be aware of the following points:

1. The keystrokes on some of the more sophisticated and expensive calculators are menu-driven: after you select the appropriate routine, the calculator prompts you to input each value; a compute key (CPT) is not needed to obtain a solution.

2. Many calculators allow the user to set the number of payments per year. Most of these calculators are preset for monthly payments, or 12 payments per year. Because we work primarily with *annual* payments—one payment per year—it is important to make sure that your calculator is set for one payment per year. Although most calculators are preset to recognize that all payments occur at the end of the period, it is also important to make sure your calculator is actually in that so-called END mode. Consult the reference guide that accompanies your calculator for instructions on these settings.

3. To avoid including previous data in current calculations, always clear all registers of your calculator before inputting values and making a new computation.

4. The known values can be punched into the calculator in any order; the order specified here and in the text simply reflects the authors' personal preference.

CALCULATOR

Inputs	Functions
5000	PV
6	N
5	I
	CPT
	FV
	Solution
	6,700.48

See Appendix E for details.

CALCULATOR

Inputs	Functions
6	N
5	I
38300	FV
	CPT
	PMT
	Solution
	5,630.77

See Appendix E for details.

CALCULATOR KEYSTROKES

Let's go back to the future value calculation on page 46, where we are trying to calculate the future value of $5,000 at the end of 6 years if invested at 5%. Here are the steps for solving the problem with a calculator:

1. Punch in 5000 and press PV.

2. Punch in 6 and press N.

3. Punch in 5 and press I.

4. To calculate the future value, press CPT and then FV. The future value of 6,700.48 should appear on the calculator display.

On many calculators, this value will be preceded by a minus sign, which is a way of distinguishing between cash inflows and cash outflows. For our purposes, this sign can be ignored.

To calculate the yearly savings (the amount of an annuity), let's continue with the example on page 47. For this example, the interest rate is 5%, the number of periods is 6, and the future value is $38,300. Your task is to solve the equation for the annuity. The steps using the calculator are:

1. Punch in 6 and press N.

2. Punch in 5 and press I.

3. Punch in 38300 and press FV.

4. To calculate the yearly payment or annuity, press CPT and then PMT.

The annuity of 5,630.77 should appear on the calculator display. Again, a negative sign can be ignored.

A similar procedure is used to find present value of a future sum or an annuity, except you would first input the FV or PMT before pressing CPT and then PV to calculate the desired result. To find the equal annual future withdrawals from an initial deposit, the PV would be input first; you solve for the PMT by pressing CPT and then PMT.

INDEX

future value, 45–47, 103–104
future value annuity factor, 46

G

GAAP (generally accepted accounting principles), 31
gatekeeper provisions, 242
GDP (gross domestic product), 21
GEICO, 271
General Electric Credit Corporation (GECC), 177
general obligation bonds, 330
generally accepted accounting principles (GAAP), 31
general-purpose money funds, 352
geographic factors, 23–24
gift giving program, 420
gift splitting, 416–417
gift tax, 414. *See also* unified transfer tax (UTT)
gift tax annual exclusion, 417
gift tax exclusion escapes estate tax, 417
gifts and taxes, 415–417
Ginnie Mae (Government National Mortgage Association), 329, 352
GIO (guaranteed insurability option), 248–249
goal dates, 10–12
gold, 317
good-student discount, 269
good-till-canceled (GTC) order, 293
Google Finance, 299
government, in planning environment, 20
government bond funds, 352
government health insurance plans, 229–232
Government National Mortgage Association (Ginnie Mae), 329, 352
government securities money funds, 352
grace period, 151, 164, 217–218
graded schedule, 381
graduated repayment schedule, 174
graduated-payment mortgages, 138
grantor, 411
gross domestic product (GDP), 21
gross earnings, 58
gross estate, 402, 418
gross income, 59–61, 68
group disability policy benefits, 245
group health insurance, 226–229, 240
group HMO, 228
group life insurance, 211–212
growing-equity mortgages, 138
growth funds, 350–351
growth stocks, 320
growth-and-income funds, 351–352

GTC (good-till-canceled) order, 293
guaranteed illustrations, 220
guaranteed insurability option (GIO), 248–249
guaranteed purchase option, 218–219
guaranteed renewability, 243, 247
guaranteed-minimum annuity, 390–391

H

H&R Block, 72, 77
The Hartford, 271
head of household, 57
health care sector fun, 353
health insurance
    available coverage and resources, 233–234
    behavioral biases, 235
    checklist, 237
    choosing a plan, 234–236
    decisions concerning, 232–236
    definition of, 197
    disability income insurance, 244–249
    government plans, 229–232
    health care cost risk, 232
    importance of, 225–226
    long-term care insurance, 241–244
    medical expense coverage and policy provisions, 236–241
    personal choices, impact of, 249
    planning over a lifetime, 248
    premiums, 226
    private plans, 226–229
    student health care under the ACA, 228
    types of compared, 227
    types of plans, 226–232
health insurance expenses, 62
Health Insurance Portability and Accountability Act (HIPAA), 240
health maintenance organizations (HMO), 227–228
health reimbursement account (HRA), 233
health savings account (HSA), 233
hidden loads, 347
high coupon bonds, 334
high income taxpayers, issues for, 72–73
higher education tuition costs, 61
high-grade corporate bond funds, 352
high-risk securities, 321
high-tech stocks, 296
high-yield corporate bond funds, 352
HIPAA (Health Insurance Portability and Accountability Act), 240
HMO (health maintenance organizations), 227–228
home equity credit line, 156–157, 186–187

home office deduction, 74
home remodeling projects, 133
home sale costs, 62
home-buying process, 131–134
home-buying strategies, 134
homeowner's fee, 121
homeowner's insurance
    costs, factors affecting, 258–259
    coverage, 260–261
    guide to, 257
    introduction to, 257–258
    limitations on payment, 261–263
    lowering premiums, 262
    as part of cost of ownership, 128–129
    perils covered, 258
    personal property floater, 259–260
    premiums, 263
    property covered, 259
    renter's insurance, 260
HomePath Mortgage Financing, 125
HomePath Renovation Mortgage Financing, 125
hospital income policies, 238
hospitalization, 236
hospitalization insurance policy, 236
household expenditures, 373
housing bubble, 118, 120, 362
housing decisions
    affordability, 124–131
    affordability analysis, 130–131
    financing the transaction, 135–141
    home-buying process, 131–134
    homeownership, benefits of, 124–125
    homeownership, costs of, 125–130
    housing prices and recent financial crisis, 118, 120
    impact of personal choices, 141
    planning over a lifetime, 140
    renting vs. buying, 121–124
    timing of buying first home, 131
    types of housing to meet needs, 120–124
housing prices, 118, 120
HRA (health reimbursement account), 233
HSA (health savings account), 233
Hurricane Katrina, 254
hybrid cars, 113
hybrid REITs, 365
hybrid securities, 282, 330

I

I savings bonds, 106–107
Icarra, 299
ICE (Intercontinental Exchange Group), 285
identity theft, 166

"If You Can" (Bernstein), 365
immediate annuity, 390, 393
inadequate income, 400
income
    age and education, effects on, 23
    example of, 38
    forecasting, 41
    on the income and expense statement, 35
    median annual wages for college-educated majors, 25
income and expense statement
    cash surplus or deficit, 37
    definition of, 30
    example of, 36, 38
    expenses, 35–37
    income, 35
    preparation of, 37–38
    ratios analysis, 40
income needs, estimating, 373–376
income shifting, 78
income stocks, 321
income taxes, 56–57, 399
income-contingent repayment plan, 174
income-producing property, 363–364
indemnity, 239
indemnity (fee-for-service) plans, 227
independent agents, 271
independent insurance brokers, 202
independent used car lots, 113
index funds, 345, 352–353
index rate, 136
individual practice association (IPA), 228
individual retirement accounts (IRAs), 16, 61, 79, 356, 387–389, 395
industrial life insurance, 212
industry data, 296
Industry Surveys, 296, 298
inflation, 21–22, 401
inflation factor, 373–375
inflation hedge, 124–125
inflation protection, 244
inflation-adjusted annual shortfall, 376
inforce reprojection, 220
informed investor, becoming, 294–296
initial principal, 189
injured persons, 265–266
insolvency, 33
installment loans
    as a consumer credit workhorse, 186–187
    finance charges, monthly payments, and the APR, 187–191
    overview of, 172–173
    vs. paying cash, 190, 191–192
installment payments, 112
installment premium annuity contracts, 390

U

UCR (usual, customary, and reasonable) charges, 227
unbundling, 209
underinsured motorist coverage, 266–267
underwriting, 198, 202–204, 283
underwriting syndicate, 283–284
undue influence, 407
unified rate schedule, 415
unified transfer tax credit, 418, 420
unified transfer tax (UTT), 414–417, 420
uninsured motorist coverage, 263, 266–267
uninsured motorist limit, 266
universal life insurance, 202, 209–211, 213
unrealized capital gains, 359
unscheduled personal property floater, 260
unsecured bonds, 328
unsecured personal credit lines, 155–156
U.S. Savings bond, 77, 78, 86, 105–106, 107
U.S. T-bond, 315
U.S. Treasury bill (T-bill), 86, 105, 315, 329
U.S. Veterans Administration, 138–139, 329
USA Today, 295
USAA, 271
used car salesperson strategy, 114
usual, customary, and reasonable (UCR) charges, 227
utility, 8
UTT (unified transfer tax), 414–417, 420

V

VA loan guarantees, 139–140
valuation issues, 421
value funds, 351
Value Line, 296
Value Line ETF Survey, 357
Value Line Fund Advisor, 357
Value Line Investment Survey, 298, 324
Vanguard Group, 286, 299
Vanguard Total Bond Market ETF, 326
Vanguard Total Stock Market ETF, 326
VantageScore, 160
variable annuity, 391–392, 393
variable expenses, 35
variable life insurance, 211, 213
vehicle, business use of, 74
vehicles of transfer, 402
vested rights, 381, 386
viatical settlements, 219
Visa, 92, 93, 150
volatile markets, 317
voluntary profit-sharing plans, 384–386
volunteer expenses, 62
voting rights, 316–317

W

W-4 form, 58
wage base, 378
Wage Earner Plan, 167
waiting period, 243, 247
waiver of co-insurance, 241
waiver of premium, 249
waiver-of-premium benefit, 218
walk-away lease, 117
Wall Street Journal, 278, 295, 296, 332, 348
wealth, 5–6
wedding planning, 9
Weiss, 215
whole life insurance, 202, 206–209, 213

wills
  codicils, 407
  common excuses for not writing, 404
  common features of, 405–406
  definition of, 403
  example of, 406
  intestacy, 403–404
  letter of last instructions, 409
  preparing, 404–405
  requirements of, 407
  revoking, 407–408
  safeguarding, 408–409
Wilshire 500, 352
witness clause, 406
workers' compensation insurance, 231

Y

Yahoo! Finance, 296, 299
year-to-date returns, 348
yield to maturity, 334–336

Z

Zacks Investment Research, 299
0 percent APR, 179

BUILD YOUR COURSE EXPERIENCE WITH PFIN⁶

PFIN provides print and online resources to help you enhance your course experience and assess your students!

The cards at the end of the instructors' edition provide a convenient reference to help you make the most of the PFIN resources. By chapter, you'll find:

List of Learning Objectives

What's new in this edition

Suggestions for additional resources

If you'd like to see the review cards that appear in the Student Edition, you can access the PDFs of the Student Review Cards online.

There are great resources available online, including the STUDENT VIEW of PFIN Online. To access:

1. Go to the Instructors Resource Center at www.cengage.com/login. Enter your user name and password. If you do not have an account, you can request one from customer service or your local consultant.

2. Add PFIN⁶ to your dashboard. Be sure to select PFIN Online as one of your resources.

3. On your Dashboard, you will see three resources associated with PFIN:

- Cengage Learning Testing by Cognero is a flexible, online system that allows you to author, edit, and manage test bank content in order to create and deliver tests versions in an instant, and deliver tests from your learning management system.

- Instructors Companion Website: Includes downloads of standard supplements like PowerPoint, as well as testing content that's been formatted for upload to a Learning Management System.

- PFIN Online: FULLY MOBILE Students access the complete textbook narrative, additional interactive media, the unique functionality of StudyBit, and YOUR assignments anytime, anywhere. Note that you will need to create a course to review the content of PFIN Online, though your students have the option to join your course or select self-study mode to work on their own.

PFIN ONLINE KEY FEATURES

- Assignment calendar to direct students to:
  - Chapter content (readings & video)
  - Assessments from the test bank
  - Documents
  - Your own links
- Gradebook captures student's progress on your assignments, and allows you to edit individual student assessment options
- Concept Tracker delivers data on how students are grasping concepts
- Manage Docs houses all instructor supplements and other resources in one place.

- FULL textbook narrative with integrated media
- Consistent navigation with print chapter
- Quick access to major topics for each chapter

Highlight boxes promote exploration
- Smart Sites
- Fact or Fiction
- Fun personal quizzing

Here's a list of other key resources that can aid you in your course:

Classroom	Powerpoint presentations for each chapter of PFIN
Inline Figures	Interactive figures from the text and matching activities help students test their understanding of the reading, and help them prep for the text.
Instructor Manual	Additional discussions, concepts and questions for classroom or online exploration
Excel Spreadsheets	Students can use our spreadsheets and templates to plan their own financial future.

PFIN also offers assistance to help get you and your students up and going. In addition to the first time user tips built right into the product, visit **http://services.cengage.com/dcs/4ltr-press/** for quick start handouts, PowerPoint, and "how to" videos.

LEARNING OBJECTIVES

LO1 Identify the benefits of using personal financial planning techniques to manage your finances.

LO2 Describe the personal financial planning process and define your goals.

LO3 Explain the life cycle of financial plans, their role in achieving your financial goals, how to deal with special planning concerns, and the use of professional financial planners.

LO4 Examine the economic environment's influence on personal financial planning.

LO5 Evaluate the impact of age, education, and geographic location on personal income.

LO6 Understand the importance of career choices and their relationship to personal financial planning.

You can access PFIN6 Online in the instructor's resource center at **www.cengage.com/login**. You will need to build a course to access the product. Note that your students can access the course you build with a course key, or can use the product on their own if they prefer.

NEW TO THIS EDITION

- **All figures, exhibits, and data updated**
- **New feature: "You Can Do It Now"**

CHAPTER PREP

CHAPTER EXHIBITS AND WORKSHEETS

Exhibit 1.1 Organizational Planning Model

Exhibit 1.2 The Average American, Financially Speaking

Exhibit 1.3 The Six-Step Financial Planning Process

Exhibit 1.4 The Personal Financial Planning Life Cycle

Exhibit 1.5 How a $1,000 Investment Grows over Time

Exhibit 1.6 The Financial Planning Environment

Exhibit 1.7 The Business Cycle

Exhibit 1.8 How Age and Education Affect Annual Income

Exhibit 1.9 Median Annual Wages for College-Educated Majors (Ages 25–59)

Worksheet 1.1 Summary of Personal Financial Goals

ADDITIONAL RESOURCES

PPT—The Highlights

Organization Planning Model

Six-Step Financial Planning Model

Plans to Achieve Your Financial Goals

What Determines Your Personal Income?

The following videos and exercises are available within PFIN 6 Online:

Kiplinger Videos

"Kip Tips" videos offer quick money management and investing advice.

▶ "Building Wealth the Old-Fashioned Way"

▶ "Healthy Habits that Save You Money"

▶ "3 Biggest Urban Myths of Personal Finance"

Critical Thinking Cases

Assign students the online cases about personal financial planning and finding a new job. Answers to Critical Thinking Questions are supplied for instructors only in the *Instructor's Manual*.

WHAT'S INSIDE

This chapter offers an introduction to the life cycle of financial planning and the impact that such factors as economic environment, age, geographic location, personal income, and career choice have on personal finances.

BEYOND THE CLASS

A selection of materials is in the Instructor's Manual, Cognero Test Banks, and PowerPoints.

LEARNING OBJECTIVES

LO1 Understand the relationship between financial plans and statements.

LO2 Prepare a personal balance sheet.

LO3 Generate a personal income and expense statement.

LO4 Develop a good record-keeping system and use ratios to evaluate personal financial statements.

LO5 Construct a cash budget and use it to monitor and control spending.

LO6 Apply time value of money concepts to put a monetary value on financial goals.

You can access PFIN6 Online in the instructor's resource center at **www.cengage.com/login**. You will need to build a course to access the product. Note that your students can access the course you build with a course key, or can use the product on their own if they prefer.

NEW TO THIS EDITION

- All data, figures and exhibits updated
- New feature box: "You Can Do It Now"

CHAPTER EXHIBITS AND WORKSHEETS

ADDITIONAL RESOURCES

PPT—The Highlights

Net Worth: Measure Your Financial Worth

Income and Expense Statement

Preparing the Income and Expense Statements

Using Your Personal Financial Statements

Using Budgets

Time Value of Money

The following videos and exercises are available within PFIN 6 Online:

Kiplinger Video

"Kip Tips" videos offer quick money management and investing advice.

▶ "Better Living Through Budgeting"

Applying Personal Finance

Assign students to read the exercise on assessing their financial condition. This exercise guides them to create their own balance sheet of income and expenses and challenges them to assess whether they like where they are and what they can do to change their financial condition.

Critical Thinking Cases

Answers to Critical Thinking Questions are supplied for instructors only in the *Instructor's Manual*.

WHAT'S INSIDE

Understanding income statements, creating personal balance sheets, income and expense statements, developing budgets to monitor spending, and learning the time value of money.

BEYOND THE CLASS

A selection of materials is in the Instructor's Manual, Cognero Test Banks, and PowerPoints.

LEARNING OBJECTIVES

LO1 Discuss the basic principles of income taxes and determine your filing status.

LO2 Describe the sources of gross income and adjustments to income, differentiate between standard and itemized deductions and exemptions, and calculate taxable income.

LO3 Prepare a basic tax return using the appropriate tax forms and rate schedules.

LO4 Explain who needs to pay estimated taxes, when to file or amend your return, and how to handle an audit.

LO5 Know where to get help with your taxes and how software can make tax return preparation easier.

LO6 Implement an effective tax planning strategy.

You can access PFIN6 Online in the instructor's resource center at **www.cengage.com/login**. You will need to build a course to access the product. Note that your students can access the course you build with a course key, or can use the product on their own if they prefer.

NEW TO THIS EDITION

- All figures, exhibits, worksheets, and data updated
- New section 3-3e, Issues for High Income Taxpayers
- New feature box: "You Can Do It Now"
- Several new end-of-chapter problems

CHAPTER EXHIBITS AND WORKSHEETS

Exhibit 3.1 Calculating Your Taxable Income and Total Tax Liability Owed

Exhibit 3.2 Capital Gains Tax Categories as of 2015

Exhibit 3.3 Sample Tax Rate Schedules

Exhibit 3.4 Taxable Income and the Amount of Income Taxes Due (2015)

Worksheet 3.1 2015 Tax Return (Form 1040EZ) for Mateo Castillo

Worksheet 3.2 2015 Tax Return (Form 1040) for the Burns Family

WHAT'S INSIDE

The basic principles of income taxes, how to prepare a basic tax return, where to get help with your taxes, and how to implement an effective tax-planning strategy.

BEYOND THE CLASS

A selection of materials is in the Instructor's Manual, Cognero Test Banks, and PowerPoints.

PPT—The Highlights

Progressive Tax Structure

Economics of Income Taxes

Three Kinds of Income

Calculating Your Taxes

Tax Credits versus Tax Deductions

Effective Tax Planning

The following videos and exercises are available within PFIN 6 Online:

Kiplinger Videos

"Kip Tips" videos offer quick money management and investing advice.

▶ "Get Next Year's Tax Refund Now"

▶ "Biggest IRS Tax Audit Red Flags"

▶ "Tax Tip: Is it Deductible?"

Applying Personal Finance

Assign students to read the exercise on tax relief. This exercise will help the students learn about any tax shelters currently allowed by law.

Critical Thinking Cases

Answers to Critical Thinking Questions are supplied for instructors only in the *Instructor's Manual*.

LEARNING OBJECTIVES

LO1 Understand the role of cash management in the personal financial planning process.

LO2 Describe today's financial services marketplace, both depository and nondepository financial institutions.

LO3 Select the checking, savings, electronic banking, and other bank services that meet your needs.

LO4 Open and use a checking account.

LO5 Calculate the interest earned on your money using compound interest and future value techniques.

LO6 Develop a cash management strategy that incorporates a variety of savings plans.

You can access PFIN6 Online in the instructor's resource center at **www.cengage.com/login**. You will need to build a course to access the product. Note that your students can access the course you build with a course key, or can use the product on their own if they prefer.

NEW TO THIS EDITION

- All data, figures, and exhibits updated
- New feature box: "You Can Do It Now"

CHAPTER EXHIBITS AND WORKSHEETS

Exhibit 4.1 Representative Rates of Return

Exhibit 4.2 Depository Financial Institutions

Exhibit 4.3 Federal Deposit Insurance Programs

Exhibit 4.4 Checking Accounts Comparison Chart

Exhibit 4.5 A Bank Statement

Exhibit 4.6 The Magic of Compounding

Worksheet 4.1 An Account Reconciliation Form: John Webb's May 2017 Statement

PPT—The Highlights

Examples of Liquid Assets

Today's Financial Services Marketplace

Types of Financial Institutions

How Safe Is Your Money?

Opening and Using a Checking Account

Establishing a Savings Program

The Magic of Compounding

The following videos and exercises are available within PFIN 6 Online:

Kiplinger Videos

"Kip Tips" videos offer quick money management and investing advice.

Videos

▶ "Worst Ways to Waste Your Money"

▶ "3 Things Not to Keep in Your Wallet"

▶ "Worst Buys at Drugstores"

Applying Personal Finance

Assign students to read the exercise on managing their cash. This exercise will help the students evaluate their cash management needs and the various financial services available, allowing them to select the one best suited for their needs.

Critical Thinking Cases

Answers to Critical Thinking Questions are supplied for instructors only in the *Instructor's Manual*.

WHAT'S INSIDE

Understanding cash management, using a checking account, calculating interest, and developing savings strategies.

BEYOND THE CLASS

A selection of materials is in the Instructor's Manual, Cognero Test Banks, and PowerPoints.

LEARNING OBJECTIVES

LO1 Design a plan to research and select a new or used automobile.

LO2 Decide whether to buy or lease a car.

LO3 Identify housing alternatives, assess the rental option, and perform a rent-or-buy analysis.

LO4 Evaluate the benefits and costs of homeownership and estimate how much you can afford to pay for a home.

LO5 Describe the home-buying process.

LO6 Choose mortgage financing that meets your needs.

You can access PFIN6 Online in the instructor's resource center at **www.cengage.com/login**. You will need to build a course to access the product. Note that your students can access the course you build with a course key, or can use the product on their own if they prefer.

NEW TO THIS EDITION

- All data, exhibits, and figures updated
- New feature box: "You Can Do It Now"
- Updated Financial Planning Tips box

CHAPTER EXHIBITS AND WORKSHEETS

Exhibit 5.1 Key Steps in Buying a New Car

Exhibit 5.2 Finding the Best Car for You

Exhibit 5.3 Relative Attractiveness of Renting versus Buying a House

Exhibit 5.4 Closing Costs: The Hidden Costs of Buying a Home

Exhibit 5.5 Typical Principal and Interest Payment Patterns on a Mortgage Loan

Exhibit 5.6 A Table of Monthly Mortgage Payments (Monthly Payments Necessary to Repay a $10,000 Loan)

Exhibit 5.7 Effective Home-Buying Strategies

Worksheet 5.1 Comparing Eleanor Clark's Automobile Lease versus Purchase Costs

Worksheet 5.2 Rent-or-Buy Cost Comparison

Worksheet 5.3 Home Affordability Analysis for the James and Cora Wright Family

Worksheet 5.4 Mortgage Refinancing Analysis for the Sanchez Family

WHAT'S INSIDE

Deciding whether to lease or buy an automobile, identifying housing alternatives, evaluating the benefits and costs of purchasing a home, and choosing appropriate mortgage financing.

BEYOND THE CLASS

A selection of materials is in the Instructor's Manual, Cognero Test Banks, and PowerPoints.

ADDITIONAL RESOURCES

PPT—The Highlights

Buying an Automobile

Lease Versus Purchase Analysis

Meeting Housing Needs: Buy or Rent?

Cost of Home Ownership

Closing Costs—The Hidden Costs of Buying a Home

Real Estate Short Sales

Types of Mortgage Loans

The following videos and exercises are available within PFIN 6 Online:

Kiplinger Videos

"Kip Tips" videos offer quick money management and investing advice. Ask your students to answer the corresponding questions.

▶ "Renting vs Owning a Home?"

▶ "Deducting Mortgage Points on your Tax Return"

▶ "Best Deal on Used Cars"

▶ "Buying a Car versus Leasing a Car"

1. What is the major determinate of whether you should buy or lease a car?

2. What do the leasing terms "money factor" and "residual value" mean?

Applying Personal Finance

Assign students to read the exercise on the housing market. For this exercise, the students will gather information on their local housing markets by reading recent issues of area newspapers and then describing the market for purchased and rental homes.

Critical Thinking Cases

Answers to Critical Thinking Questions are supplied for instructors only in the *Instructor's Manual*.

LEARNING OBJECTIVES

LO1 Describe the reasons for using consumer credit and identify its benefits and problems.

LO2 Develop a plan to establish a strong credit history.

LO3 Distinguish among the different forms of open account credit.

LO4 Apply for, obtain, and manage open forms of credit.

LO5 Choose the right credit cards and recognize their advantages and disadvantages.

LO6 Avoid credit problems, protect yourself against credit card fraud, and understand the personal bankruptcy process.

You can access PFIN6 Online in the instructor's resource center at **www.cengage.com/login**. You will need to build a course to access the product. Note that your students can access the course you build with a course key, or can use the product on their own if they prefer.

NEW TO THIS EDITION

- **Updated figures, exhibits and data**
- **New feature box, "You Can Do It Now"**

CHAPTER EXHIBITS AND WORKSHEETS

Exhibit 6.1 Minimum Payments Mean Maximum Years

Exhibit 6.2 An Example of a Credit Bureau Report

Exhibit 6.3 Finding the Average Daily Balance and Finance Charge

Exhibit 6.4 A Bank Credit Card Monthly Statement

Exhibit 6.5 Average Interest Rates for Different Types of Credit Cards

Worksheet 6.1 Evaluating Your Credit

PPT—The Highlights

The Basic Concepts of Credit

Establishing Credit

How Much Credit Can You Stand?

Computing Finance Charges

Avoiding Credit Problems

The following videos and exercises are available within PFIN 6 Online

Kiplinger Videos

"Kip Tips" videos offer quick money management and investing advice.

▶ "3 Reasons You Can't get Out of Debt"

▶ "Understand Your Credit Score"

1. List several measures you can take to ensure your credit score doesn't decline.

▶ "Getting a Grip on Student Loan Debt"

Applying Personal Finance

Assign students to read the exercise on credit. This exercise asks the student to obtain a copy of his or her credit report and examine it for any inaccuracies. Should the student need to improve his or her credit, what steps should be taken?

Critical Thinking Cases

Answers to Critical Thinking Questions are supplied for instructors only in the *Instructor's Manual*.

WHAT'S INSIDE

Deciding whether to lease or buy an automobile, identifying housing alternatives, evaluating the benefits and costs of purchasing a home, and choosing an appropriate mortgage financing.

BEYOND THE CLASS

A selection of materials is in the Instructor's Manual, Cognero Test Banks, and PowerPoints.

LEARNING OBJECTIVES

LO1 Know when to use consumer loans and be able to differentiate between the major types.

LO2 Identify the various sources of consumer loans.

LO3 Choose the best loans by comparing finance charges, maturity, collateral, and other loan terms.

LO4 Describe the features of, and calculate the finance charges on, single-payment loans.

LO5 Evaluate the benefits of an installment loan.

LO6 Determine the costs of installment loans and analyze whether it is better to pay cash or to take out a loan.

You can access PFIN6 Online in the instructor's resource center at **www.cengage.com/login**. You will need to build a course to access the product. Note that your students can access the course you build with a course key, or can use the product on their own if they prefer.

NEW TO THIS EDITION

- **All figures, data, and exhibits updated**
- **New feature box: "You Can Do It Now"**

CHAPTER EXHIBITS AND WORKSHEETS

ADDITIONAL RESOURCES

PPT—The Highlights

Different Types of Loans

Student Loans

Consumer Loans

Managing Your Credit

Finance Charges and the APR

The following videos and exercises are available within PFIN 6 Online:

Applying Personal Finance

Assign students to read the exercise on making new car payments. This exercise will help the students learn about how loan payments are determined and the obligation they take on as a borrower.

Kiplinger Videos

"Kip Tips" offer quick money management and investing advice.

▶ "How To Fix Errors in a Credit Report"

Critical Thinking Cases

Answers to Critical Thinking Questions are supplied for instructors only in the *Instructor's Manual*.

WHAT'S INSIDE

Know when to use consumer loans, and identify various sources. How to calculate the finance charges of single-payment loans and determine the costs of installment loans.

BEYOND THE CLASS

A selection of materials is in the Instructor's Manual, Cognero Test Banks, and PowerPoints.

LEARNING OBJECTIVES

LO1 Explain the concept of risk and the basics of insurance underwriting.

LO2 Discuss the primary reasons for life insurance and identify those who need coverage.

LO3 Calculate how much life insurance you need.

LO4 Distinguish among the various types of life insurance policies and describe their advantages and disadvantages.

LO5 Choose the best life insurance policy for your needs at the lowest cost.

LO6 Become familiar with the key features of life insurance policies.

You can access PFIN6 Online in the instructor's resource center at **www.cengage.com/login**. You will need to build a course to access the product. Note that your students can access the course you build with a course key, or can use the product on their own if they prefer.

NEW TO THIS EDITION

- All data, figures, and exhibits updated
- New feature box: "You Can Do It Now"

CHAPTER EXHIBITS AND WORKSHEETS

Exhibit 8.1 How Much Life Insurance Do You Need?

Exhibit 8.2 Representative Annual Renewable Term Life Insurance Premiums: $100,000 Policy, Preferred Nonsmoker Rates

Exhibit 8.3 Representative Level Premium Term Life Rates: $100,000 Preferred Nonsmoker Policy

Exhibit 8.4 Illustration of the Cash Value and Pure Death Protection in a Whole Life Policy

Exhibit 8.5 Representative Whole Life Insurance Annual Premiums: $100,000 Policy, Preferred Nonsmoker Rates

Exhibit 8.6 Representative Universal Life Insurance Annual Outlays: $100,000 Policy, Preferred Nonsmoker Rates

Exhibit 8.7 Representative Variable Life Insurance Values: $100,000 Policy, Preferred Nonsmoker, Male, Age 45

Exhibit 8.8 Major Advantages and Disadvantages of the Most Popular Types of Life Insurance

Worksheet 8.1 Determining the Reed Family's Need for Life Insurance

PPT—The Highlights

The Concept of Risk

Underwriting Basics

Benefits of Life Insurance

How Much Insurance Do You Need?

Types of Whole Life Policies

The following video and exercises are available within PFIN 6 Online:

Kiplinger Videos

"Kip Tips" videos offer quick money management and investing advice.

▶ "5 Things to Know About Life Insurance"

1. What basic calculations do you need to make to estimate how much life insurance you need?

2. Why would a stay-at-home parent require life insurance in addition to the employed parent?

Applying Personal Finance

Assign students to read the exercise on insuring their lives. This exercise will help the students determine current and future life insurance needs.

Critical Thinking Cases

Answers to Critical Thinking Questions are supplied for instructors only in the *Instructor's Manual*.

WHAT'S INSIDE

The concept of risk, the basics of underwriting, how to calculate the amount of insurance one needs, and how to become familiar with life insurance policies.

BEYOND THE CLASS

A selection of materials is in the Instructor's Manual, Cognero Test Banks, and PowerPoints.

LEARNING OBJECTIVES

LO1 Discuss why having adequate health insurance is important, and identify the factors contributing to the growing cost of health insurance.

LO2 Differentiate among the major types of health insurance plans, and identify major private and public health insurance providers and their programs.

LO3 Analyze your own health insurance needs and explain how to shop for appropriate coverage.

LO4 Explain the basic types of medical expenses covered by the policy provisions of health insurance plans.

LO5 Assess the need for and features of long-term-care insurance.

LO6 Discuss the features of disability income insurance and how to determine your need for it.

You can access PFIN6 Online in the instructor's resource center at **www.cengage.com/login**. You will need to build a course to access the product. Note that your students can access the course you build with a course key, or can use the product on their own if they prefer.

NEW TO THIS EDITION

- All data, figures, and exhibits updated
- New feature box: "You Can Do It Now"

CHAPTER EXHIBITS AND WORKSHEETS

Exhibit 9.1 Average Annual Worker and Employer Contributions to Premiums and Total Premiums for family Coverage, 1999–2015

Exhibit 9.2 How the Most Common Types of Health Plans Compare

Exhibit 9.3 Typical Provisions in Long-Term-Care Insurance Policies

Exhibit 9.4 Representative Disability Income Insurance Premium Costs

Worksheet 9.1 Health Insurance Checklist

Worksheet 9.2 Estimating Disability Income Insurance Needs

ADDITIONAL RESOURCES

PPT—The Highlights

Importance of Health Insurance

Traditional Indemnity Plans

Types of Managed Care Plans

Components of Medicare

Workers' Compensation Insurance

Long-Term-Care Insurance

The following videos and exercises are available within PFIN 6 Online:

Kiplinger Videos

"Kip Tips" videos offer quick money management and investing advice

▶ "Healthy Habits that Save You Money"

▶ "Paying for Alzheimer's"

Applying Personal Finance

Assign students to read the exercise on insuring their health. This exercise will help the students examine their health insurance needs and determine the appropriate coverage for them.

Critical Thinking Cases

Answers to Critical Thinking Questions are supplied for instructors only in the *Instructor's Manual.*

WHAT'S INSIDE

The importance of health insurance and the types of medical expenses covered, how to analyze health insurance needs, and the features of disability income insurance.

BEYOND THE CLASS

A selection of materials is in the Instructor's Manual, Cognero Test Banks, and PowerPoints.

LEARNING OBJECTIVES

LO1 Discuss the importance and basic principles of property insurance, including types of exposure, indemnity, and co-insurance.

LO2 Identify the types of coverage provided by homeowner's insurance.

LO3 Select the right homeowner's insurance policy for your needs.

LO4 Analyze the coverage in a personal automobile policy (PAP) and choose the most cost-effective policy.

LO5 Describe other types of property and liability insurance.

LO6 Choose a property and liability insurance agent and company, and settle claims.

You can access PFIN6 Online in the instructor's resource center at **www.cengage.com/login**. You will need to build a course to access the product. Note that your students can access the course you build with a course key, or can use the product on their own if they prefer.

NEW TO THIS EDITION

- All data, figures and exhibits updated
- New feature box: "You Can Do It Now"

CHAPTER EXHIBITS AND WORKSHEETS

Exhibit 10.1 A Personal Property Inventory Form

Exhibit 10.2 A Guide to Homeowner's Policies

Exhibit 10.3 Calculating Replacement Cost

Exhibit 10.4 The Four Parts of a Personal Automobile Policy (PAP)

Exhibit 10.5 Preventing Your Car from Being Stolen

ADDITIONAL RESOURCES

PPT—The Highlights

Principle of Indemnity

Factors Affecting Home Insurance Costs

Persons and Locations Covered

Types of Automobile Insurance Coverage

No-Fault Automobile Insurance

Property and Liability Insurance Agents

The following videos and exercises are available within PFIN 6 Online:

Kiplinger Videos

"Kip Tips" videos offer quick money management and investing advice.

▶ "Surprising Things Covered by Insurance"

▶ "Insurance Policies You Can Live Without"

Applying Personal Finance

Assign students to read the exercise on insuring property. This exercise will help the students determine property insurance needs.

Critical Thinking Cases

Answers to Critical Thinking Questions are supplied for instructors only in the *Instructor's Manual*.

WHAT'S INSIDE

The importance of property insurance and coverage, how to analyze and choose cost-effective policies, and other types of liability and property insurance.

BEYOND THE CLASS

A selection of materials is in the Instructor's Manual, Cognero Test Banks, and PowerPoints.

LEARNING OBJECTIVES

LO1 Discuss the role that investing plays in the personal financial planning process and identify several different investment objectives.

LO2 Distinguish between primary and secondary markets as well as between broker and dealer markets.

LO3 Explain the process of buying and selling securities and recognize the different types of orders.

LO4 Develop an appreciation of how various forms of investment information can lead to better investing skills and returns.

LO5 Gain a basic understanding of the impact of the Internet on the field of investments.

LO6 Describe an investment portfolio and how you'd go about developing, monitoring, and managing a portfolio of securities.

You can access PFIN6 Online in the instructor's resource center at **www.cengage.com/login**. You will need to build a course to access the product. Note that your students can access the course you build with a course key, or can use the product on their own if they prefer.

NEW TO THIS EDITION

- **All data, figures, and exhibits updated**
- **New feature box: "You Can Do It Now"**

CHAPTER EXHIBITS AND WORKSHEETS

WHAT'S INSIDE

Investments in the financial planning process, broker and dealer markets, buying and sealing securities, and developing a securities portfolio.

BEYOND THE CLASS

A selection of materials is in the Instructor's Manual, Cognero Test Banks, and PowerPoints.

ADDITIONAL RESOURCES

PPT—The Highlights

Objectives and Rewards of Investing

How Do I Get Started?

Different Ways to Invest

Securities Markets

Broker and Dealer Markets

Bull Market or Bear?

Making Transactions in the Securities Markets

Executing Trades

Types of Orders

The following videos and exercises are available within PFIN 6 Online.

Kiplinger Videos

"Kip Tips" videos offer quick money management and investing advice.

Videos:

▶ "The Time Value of Money"

▶ "Worst Mistakes Investors Make"

▶ "Seven Simple Rules of Investing"

▶ "3 Better Investments than Powerball"

▶ "Best Online Brokers"

▶ "Deadly Sins of Investing"

Applying Personal Finance

Assign students to read the exercise on researching your investments. This exercise will help students learn about the annual stockholders' report of a company they've selected.

Critical Thinking Cases

Answers to Critical Thinking Questions are supplied for instructors only in the *Instructor's Manual*.

LEARNING OBJECTIVES

LO1 Describe the various types of risks to which investors are exposed, as well as the sources of return.

LO2 Know how to search for an acceptable investment on the basis of risk, total return, and yield.

LO3 Discuss the merits of investing in common stock and be able to distinguish among the different types of stocks.

LO4 Become familiar with the various measures of performance and how to use them in placing a value on stocks.

LO5 Describe the basic issue characteristics of bonds as well as how these securities are used as investment vehicles.

LO6 Distinguish between the different types of bonds, gain an understanding of how bond prices behave, and know how to compute different measures of yield.

You can access PFIN6 Online in the instructor's resource center at **www.cengage.com/login**. You will need to build a course to access the product. Note that your students can access the course you build with a course key, or can use the product on their own if they prefer.

NEW TO THIS EDITION

- All data, exhibits, and figures updated
- New feature box: "You Can Do It Now"
- New feature: *How Do Stock and Bond Market Returns Compare This Year?*
- Updated list of junk bonds

12

CHAPTER EXHIBITS AND WORKSHEETS

Exhibit 12.1 Three Elements of Return for a 4 Percent, 20-Year Bond

Exhibit 12.2 The Risk–Return Relationship

Exhibit 12.3 Performance of Dow Jones Industrial Average and NASDAQ Composite, 2006 through 2016

Exhibit 12.4 Cash or Reinvested Dividends

Exhibit 12.5 Comparative Performance of Stocks and Bonds: 1996 to 2016

Exhibit 12.6 Moody's and Standard & Poor's Bond Ratings

Exhibit 12.7 Price Behavior of a Bond with a 4 Percent Coupon

ADDITIONAL RESOURCES

PPT—The Highlights

The Risks of Investing

Returns From Investing

The Risk-Return Trade-Off

Investing in Common Stock

Key Measures of Performance

Types of Common Stock

Bond Issue Characteristics

Bond Prices and Yields

The following videos and exercises are available within PFIN 6 Online:

Kiplinger Videos

"Kip Tips" videos offer quick money management and investing advice.

▶ "How to Survive a Stock Market Correction"

▶ "The Surprising Secret About Stock Splits"

Applying Personal Finance

Assign students to read the "What's Your Type?" exercise. This exercise will help students examine the returns on various types of common stock.

Critical Thinking Cases

Answers to Critical Thinking Questions are supplied for instructors only in the *Instructor's Manual*.

WHAT'S INSIDE

Types of investor risk, the merits of investing in common stock, issue characteristics of bonds, and the different types of bonds.

BEYOND THE CLASS

A selection of materials is in the Instructor's Manual, Cognero Test Banks, and PowerPoints.

LEARNING OBJECTIVES

LO1 Describe the basic features and operating characteristics of mutual funds and exchange traded funds.

LO2 Differentiate between open- and closed-end mutual funds, as well as exchange traded funds, and discuss the various types of fund loads and charges.

LO3 Discuss the types of funds available to investors and the different kinds of investor services offered by mutual funds and exchange traded funds.

LO4 Gain an understanding of the variables that should be considered when selecting funds for investment purposes.

LO5 Identify the sources of return and calculate the rate of return earned on an investment in a mutual fund, as well as evaluate the performance of an exchange traded fund.

LO6 Understand the role that real estate plays in a diversified investment portfolio along with the basics of investing in real estate, either directly or indirectly.

You can access PFIN6 Online in the instructor's resource center at **www.cengage.com/login**. You will need to build a course to access the product. Note that your students can access the course you build with a course key, or can use the product on their own if they prefer.

NEW TO THIS EDITION

- All exhibits, data, and figures updated
- New feature box: "You Can Do It Now"

CHAPTER EXHIBITS AND WORKSHEETS

Exhibit 13.1 Basic Mutual Fund Structure

Exhibit 13.2 Examples of Available ETFs

Exhibit 13.3 Mutual Fund Quotes

Exhibit 13.4 Effects of Reinvesting Income

Exhibit 13.6 A Summary of Mutual Fund Income and Capital Changes

ADDITIONAL RESOURCES

PPT—The Highlights

The Mutual Fund Concept

Why Invest in Mutual Funds

Open-End versus Closed-End

Exchange-Traded Funds (ETFs)

Services Offered by Mutual Funds

Investing in Income Property

The following videos and exercises are available within PFIN 6 Online:

Kiplinger Videos

"Kip Tips" videos offer quick money management and investing advice.

▶ "3 Things to Know About 401Ks"

▶ "Why You Need to Open a Roth IRA"

▶ "ETFs vs Traditional Mutual Funds?"

Applying Personal Finance

Assign students to read the exercise on mutual funds. This exercise will help students learn about the types of mutual funds and how to pick based on investment needs.

Critical Thinking Cases

Answers to Critical Thinking Questions are supplied for instructors only in the *Instructor's Manual*.

WHAT'S INSIDE

Mutual funds, open- and closed-ended funds, funds available to investors, ETFs, sources of return, and how to calculate the rate of return earned on an investment in a mutual fund.

BEYOND THE CLASS

A selection of materials is in the Instructor's Manual, Cognero Test Banks, and PowerPoints.

CHAPTER **PREP**

LEARNING OBJECTIVES

LO1 Recognize the importance of retirement planning, and identify the three biggest pitfalls to good planning.

LO2 Estimate your income needs in retirement and the level of retirement income you've estimated from various sources.

LO3 Explain the eligibility requirements and benefits of the Social Security program.

LO4 Differentiate among the types of basic and supplemental employer-sponsored pension plans.

LO5 Describe the various types of self-directed retirement plans.

LO6 Choose the right type of annuity for your retirement plan.

You can access PFIN6 Online in the instructor's resource center at **www.cengage.com/login**. You will need to build a course to access the product. Note that your students can access the course you build with a course key, or can use the product on their own if they prefer.

NEW TO THIS EDITION

- All figures, exhibits, and data updated
- New featere box: "You Can Do It Now"
- New feature: Measuring the Benefits of a Roth IRA

CHAPTER EXHIBITS AND WORKSHEETS

Exhibit 14.1 Sources of Income for the Average Retiree

Exhibit 14.2 Average Monthly Social Security Benefits Paid in 2016

Exhibit 14.3 Types of Annuity Contracts

Worksheet 14.1 Estimating Future Retirement Needs

WHAT'S INSIDE

Retirement planning, estimating income needs for retirement, types of employer-sponsored pension plans, and self-directed retirement plans.

BEYOND THE CLASS

A selection of materials is in the Instructor's Manual, Cognero Test Banks, and PowerPoints.

PPT—The Highlights

Three Biggest Pitfalls in Retirement Planning

Social Security Retirement Benefits

Employer-Sponsored Programs

Self-Directed Retirement Programs

Fixed versus Variable Annuity

The following videos and exercises are available within PFIN 6 Online:

Kiplinger Videos

"Kip Tips" videos offer quick money management and investing advice.

▶ "How to Retire When You Want"

▶ "How Earnings Affect Social Security Checks"

▶ "Good Reasons to Work Past Retirement Age"

▶ "Least Tax-Friendly States for Retirement"

▶ "Know Your Retirement Number"

Applying Personal Finance

Assign students to read the exercise on planning an ideal retirement plan. This exercise will help students learn about the retirement program that would best meet their needs.

Critical Thinking Cases

Answers to Critical Thinking Questions are supplied for instructors only in the *Instructor's Manual.*

LEARNING OBJECTIVES

LO1 Describe the role of estate planning in personal financial planning, and identify the seven steps involved in the process.

LO2 Recognize the importance of preparing a will and other documents to protect you and your estate.

LO3 Explain how trusts are used in estate planning.

LO4 Determine whether a gift will be taxable, and use planned gifts to reduce estate taxes.

LO5 Calculate federal taxes due on an estate.

LO6 Use effective estate planning techniques to minimize estate taxes.

You can access PFIN6 Online in the instructor's resource center at **www.cengage.com/login**. You will need to build a course to access the product. Note that your students can access the course you build with a course key, or can use the product on their own if they prefer.

NEW TO THIS EDITION

- New feature box: "You Can Do It Now"
- All data, figures, and exhibits updated
- New content on "Estate Planning Conversations"

CHAPTER EXHIBITS AND WORKSHEETS

Exhibit 15.1 Potential Estate Planning Problems and Major Causes or Indicators

Exhibit 15.2 Steps in the Estate Planning Process

Exhibit 15.3 A Representative Will for Damian Michael Spencer

Exhibit 15.4 Seven Popular Trusts

Exhibit 15.5 Federal Unified Transfer Tax Rates

Exhibit 15.6 Unified Credits and Applicable Exclusion Amounts for Estates and Gifts

Worksheet 15.1 A Checklist of Items to Keep in a Safe-Deposit Box

Worksheet 15.2 Computing Federal Estate Tax Due

ADDITIONAL RESOURCES

PPT—The Highlights

Who Needs Estate Planning?

What Is Your Estate?

The Estate Planning Process

Changing or Revoking a Will: Codicils

Joint Ownership

Types of Trusts

Reasons for Making Lifetime Gifts

The following videos and exercises are available within PFIN 6 Online:

Kiplinger Videos

"Kip Tips" videos offer quick money management and investing advice.

▶ "Why You Need a Will"

▶ "Death and Taxes on Capital Gains"

Applying Personal Finance

Assign students to read the exercise on preparing a will. This exercise will help students learn what their will should contain and how it can be changed based on future circumstances.

Critical Thinking Cases

Answers to Critical Thinking Questions are supplied for instructors only in the *Instructor's Manual*.

WHAT'S INSIDE

The role of estate planing, preparing a will, trusts, calculating federal taxes on an estate, and estate planning techniques.

BEYOND THE CLASS

A selection of materials is in the Instructor's Manual, Cognero Test Banks, and PowerPoints.